The Collected Courses of the Academy of European Law
Series Editors: Professor Philip Alston,
New York University School of Law;
Professor Gráinne de Búrca, *European*
University Institute, Florence; and
Professor Bruno de Witte,
European University Institute,
Florence
Assistant Editor: Barbara Ciomei, *European University*
Institute, Florence

VOLUME XII/3
Human Rights in Criminal Proceedings

The Collected Courses of the Academy of European Law
Edited by Professor Philip Alston, Professor Gráinne de Búrca,
and Professor Bruno de Witte

This series brings together the collected courses of the
Academy of European Law in Florence. The Academy's mission is to
produce scholarly analyses which are at the cutting edge of the two
fields in which it works: European Union law and human rights law.
A 'general course' is given each year in each field, by a
distinguished scholar and/or practitioner, who either examines the
field as a whole through a particular thematic, conceptual or
philosophical lens, or who looks at a particular theme in the context
of the overall body of law in the field. The Academy also publishes
each year a volume of collected essays with a specific theme in each
of the two fields.

Human Rights in Criminal Proceedings

STEFAN TRECHSEL

with the assistance of
Sarah J. Summers

Academy of European Law
European University Institute

OXFORD
UNIVERSITY PRESS

OXFORD
UNIVERSITY PRESS

Great Clarendon Street, Oxford OX2 6DP

Oxford University Press is a department of the University of Oxford.
It furthers the University's objective of excellence in research, scholarship,
and education by publishing worldwide in

Oxford New York

Auckland Cape Town Dar es Salaam Hong Kong Karachi
Kuala Lumpur Madrid Melbourne Mexico City Nairobi
New Delhi Shanghai Taipei Toronto

With offices in

Argentina Austria Brazil Chile Czech Republic France Greece
Guatemala Hungary Italy Japan Poland Portugal Singapore
South Korea Switzerland Thailand Turkey Ukraine Vietnam

Oxford is a registered trade mark of Oxford University Press
in the UK and in certain other countries

Published in the United States
by Oxford University Press Inc., New York

© S. Trechsel, 2005

The moral rights of the author have been asserted

Crown copyright material is reproduced under Class Licence
Number C01P0000148 with the permission of HMSO
and the Queen's Printer for Scotland

Database right Oxford University Press (maker)

First published 2005

British Library Cataloguing in Publication Data

Data available

Library of Congress Cataloging-in-Publication Data

Trechsel, Stefan.
Human rights in criminal proceedings / Stefan Trechsel.
p. cm. — (Collected courses of the Academy of European Law)
Includes bibliographical references and index.
ISBN 0-19-829936-2 (hardcover : alk. paper) 1. Due process of law—European Union
countries. 2. Fair trial—European Union countries. 3. Criminal procedure—European
Union countries. I. Title. II. Series.
KJE9485.T74 2005
345.24′056—dc22

2004030368

Typeset by Newgen Imaging Systems (P) Ltd., Chennai, India
Printed in Great Britain
on acid-free paper by
Antony Rowe Ltd., Chippenham, Wiltshire

ISBN 0–19–829936–2

3 5 7 9 10 8 6 4 2

To the memory of the European Commission of Human Rights

Acknowledgements

This book has taken several years to write, years during which quite a number of people have assisted me in various ways, by collecting material, by assisting in technical matters, by discussing issues, by correcting my language, and not the least by their encouragement. First of all, my gratitude goes to Philip Alston for his irresistible friendly pressure and encouragement. Then I would like to thank the members of my staff at Zurich University Law School: Rechtsanwältin Dr iur. Regula Schlauri, lic. iur. Kerstin Ziltner, lic. iur. Bruno Stoeckli, lic. iur. Juerg Keim, Fürsprecher Sararard Arquint, and Jacqueline Bollmann. Tahnissa Means at SLU was a great help in correcting the text. For their patience and support I have to thank OUP, and in particular Dr Gwen Booth. The book was finalized at the Hotel Monteconero near Ancona, and I have to thank Patrizia, Sabrina, and Sara for their assistance and for letting me monopolize the hotel's Internet access. And the most valuable help by far was that of Sarah J. Summers, LL B, who has not only done the linguistic corrections of which I needed much more than I, in my vanity, had anticipated but who also contributed her knowledge of the Scottish, and the common law, who was a critical observer, and a devoted, even enthusiastic, help. Finally, for encouragement and patience, I want to thank my wife Franca whom, for many months, I have reduced to a functional widow, but who nevertheless gave her unwavering and continual support to this project. Thank you also to all those I have not mentioned!

S. Trechsel

Summary Table of Contents

Contents

Part Two—The General Fair Trial Guarantees

Chapter 3. The Right to an Independent and Impartial Tribunal

Chapter 4. The General Right to a Fair Trial

Chapter 10. The Right to Defend Oneself and to Have the Assistance of Counsel

Part Four—Measures of Coercion

**Chapter 17. Liberty and Security of Person:
The Rules on Imprisonment**

Chapter 20. Other Fundamental Rights Affected by Criminal Proceedings

Tables of Cases

I. JUDGMENTS AND DECISIONS OF THE EUROPEAN COURT OF HUMAN RIGHTS

II. DECISIONS OF THE EUROPEAN COMMISSION
OF HUMAN RIGHTS—ALPHABETICAL

III. DECISIONS OF THE EUROPEAN COMMISSION OF HUMAN RIGHTS—NUMERICAL

Tables of Cases

IV. ARTICLE 31 REPORTS OF THE EUROPEAN COMMISSION ON HUMAN RIGHTS—ALPHABETICAL

V. DECISIONS AND VIEWS OF THE HUMAN RIGHTS COMMITTEE UNDER ARTICLE 28 OF THE INTERNATIONAL COVENANT ON CIVIL AND POLITICAL RIGHTS (ICCPR)

VI. JUDGMENTS OF THE INTER-AMERICAN COURT
OF HUMAN RIGHTS

VII. DECISIONS OF THE INTER-AMERICAN COMMISSION ON HUMAN RIGHTS

MISCELLANEOUS

List of Abbreviations

ACHR	American Convention on Human Rights
ACtHR	American Court of Human Rights
AJIL	American Journal of International Law
AJP	Aktuelle Juristische Praxis
Am. Bar Found. Res. J.	American Bar Foundation Research Journal
APC	Austrian Penal Code
AS	Austrian Schillings
ASA	Archiv für schweizerisches Abgaberecht
BGBL	Bundesgesetzblatt (Germany)
BGE	Entscheidungen des Schweizerischen Bundesgerichts
BJM	Basler Juristische Mitteilungen
Cal. L.R.	Californian Law Review
CDE	Cahiers de droit européen
CETS	Council of Europe Treaty Series
CHF	Swiss Francs
CLF	Criminal Law Forum
CLJ	Cambridge Law Journal
Court	European Court of Human Rights
Crim LR	Criminal Law Review
CD	Collection of Decisions of the European Commission of Human Rights
dec.	decision
DePaul L. Rev.	DePaul Law Review
Digest	Digest of Strasbourg Case-Law relating to the European Convention on Human Rights
DR	Decisions and Reports of the European Commission of Human Rights
Duke J. Comp. & Int'l L.	Duke Journal of Comparative and International Law
ECHR	Convention for the Protection of Human Rights and Fundamental Freedoms (European Convention on Human Rights)
ECtHR	European Court of Human Rights
ECommHR	European Commission of Human Rights

ECJ	European Court of Justice
edn.	edition
eds.	editors
EHRLR	European Human Rights Law Review
EHRR	European Human Rights Reports
EJIL	European Journal of International Law
ELRev	European Law Review
ELRevHR	European Law Review—Human Rights Survey
EMRK	Europäisches Menschenrechtskonvention
ETS	European Treaty Series
EU	European Union
EuGRZ	Europäische Grundrechte Zeitschrift
FCPC	French Code of Criminal Procedure
GA	Goltdammer's Archiv für Strafrecht
GBP	Pounds Sterling
GC	Grand Chamber of the European Court of Human Rights
GPC	German Penal Code
Harv. Hum. Rts. J.	Harvard Human Rights Journal
HRC	Human Rights Committee (UN)
HRLJ	Human Rights Law Journal
HRR	Human Rights Review
IACommHR	Inter-American Commission on Human Rights
IACtHR	Inter-American Court of Human Rights
ICCPR	International Covenant on Civil and Political Rights
ICLQ	International and Comparative Law Quarterly
ICTR	International Criminal Tribunal for Rwanda
ICTY	International Criminal Tribunal for the former Yugoslavia
IRPL	International Review of Penal Law
IsLR	Israel Law Review
JCP	Jurisclasseur périodique, la Semaine juridique (édition générale)
JR	Juristische Rundschau
JT	Journal des Tribunaux (Brussels)

KB	King's Bench Law Reports
LSR	Law and Society Review
Mich. L.R.	Michigan Law Review
MLR	Modern Law Review
NJB	Nederlands Juristenblad
NJW	Neue Juristische Wochenschrift
NJIL	Nordic Journal of International Law
NQHR	Netherlands Quarterly of Human Rights
ÖIM-Newsletter	Das Österreichische Institut für Menschenrechte Newsletter
RDH	Revue des Droits de l'homme
RGD	Revue générale de droit
Rev. dr. pénal criminol.	Revue de droit pénal et de criminologie
Rev. Sc. Crim.	Revue de science criminelle et de droit pénal comparé
Rev. trim. dr. h.	Revue Trimestrielle dees Droits de l'homme
RGDP	Revue générale de droit processuel
RIDP	Revue internationale de droit pénal
RIDU	Rivista internazionale dei diritti dell'uomo
scil.	scilicet, that is to say
SJZ	Schweizerische Juristenzeitung
SLT	Scots Law Times
SR	Systematische Sammlung des Bundesrechts (Switzerland)
UK	United Kingdom
UN	United Nations
US	United States of America
Vol.	volume
Web JCLI	Web Journal of Current Legal Issues
wistra	Zeitschrift für Wirtschafts- und Steuerstrafrecht
Y b	Yearbook of the European Convention on Human Rights
ZBl	Schweizerisches Zentralblatt für Staats- und Verwaltungsrecht

ZfV	Zeitschrift für Verwaltung
ZRP	Zeitschrift für Rechtspolitik
ZSR	Zeitschrift für Schweizerisches Recht
ZStrR	Schweizerische Zeitschrift für Strafrecht
ZStW	Zeitschrift für die gesamte Strafrechtswissenschaft

Part One

Introduction

Chapter 1

About this Book

In tutte le parti del mondo, là dove si comincia col negare le libertà fondamentali dell'Uomo, e l'uguaglianza fra gli uomini, si va verso il sistema concentrazionario, ed è questa una strada su cui è difficile fermarsi.

Primo Levi[1]

I. THE SUBJECT

This book deals with, as its title promises, human rights in criminal proceedings, that is to say, the various ways in which the regional and universal laws of fundamental rights and freedoms restrict the power of Contracting States, by requiring them to establish the prerequisites for the application of retributive sanctions against persons suspected of having acted against the law.

A. Definitions

The subject obviously comprises and confronts two distinct elements, and it might be useful to begin by defining what is meant by those terms. The purpose of these definitions is to serve the pragmatic goal of explaining what I am dealing with; they are thus not concerned with the abstract scientific ambition of saying, once and for all, what 'human rights' and 'criminal proceedings' are (i.e. until the next author publishes the next 'once and for all' definition). Anyhow, it is difficult in this area to keep ontological and normative aspects clearly separated.

1. 'Human Rights'

The term 'human rights' is used here in a positivistic sense to denote the rights guaranteed in international treaties, more precisely, the International Covenant on Civil and Political Rights (ICCPR) with its aspiration to universal application,

---

[1] *Se questo è un uomo, La tregua* (1989) 338. ('[I]n every part of the world, wherever you begin by denying the fundamentals of liberties of mankind, and equality among people, you move towards the concentration camp system, and it is a road on which it is difficult to halt'; trans. from the English edition, Levi (1987) 390–1.)

the European Convention for the Protection of Human Rights and Fundamental Freedoms, mostly referred to as the European Convention on Human Rights (ECHR), and the American Convention on Human Rights (ACHR), also known as 'the Pact of San José, Costa Rica'.

This is admittedly a very narrow view. There is a plethora of other international texts dealing with human rights.[2] They deal with single problems such as discrimination or with a specific group of individuals who are thought of as particularly vulnerable, such as children or persons deprived of their liberty. The law of war as codified, in particular, in the Geneva Conventions protects human rights, at least in Article 3, which is common to all four treaties.

Apart from the treaties, there are countless declarations, resolutions, and recommendations, beginning with the Universal Declaration on Human Rights (UDHR) of 10 December 1948, a date commemorated worldwide as Human Rights Day. Moreover there are many documents prepared by international and national non-governmental organizations, many of which, such as Amnesty International or the International Helsinki Federation, enjoy high prestige. Even associations dedicated to certain branches of the law, such as the International Association for Penal Law, also known as *Association Internationale de Droit Pénal* (AIDP), deal with human rights. The same is true for professional organizations. A publication entitled *Essential Texts on Human Rights for the Police: A Compilation of International Instruments*[3] lists no fewer than thirty-nine texts, ranging from the UDHR to the Guidelines on the Role of Prosecutors, Adopted by the Eighth United Nations Congress on the Prevention of Crime and the Treatment of Offenders, Havana, 27 August–7 September 1990.

All of these texts certainly have their merits; however, I want to stress that this is a book about the *law*. The title could be more precisely stated as *Human-Rights Law Relevant to Criminal Proceedings*, but this would be bulky and inelegant. I am gladly going to resist the temptation to embark on (another) definition of 'law'. What I mean is this: I conceive law mainly as a living set of norms which develops through its application, and more particularly through its application by the courts. 'Human rights' in the context of this book refers primarily to the rapidly growing body of case-law on a number of crucial Articles of the three instruments which are examined here. This is also the explanation for the fact that the African Charter has not been taken into account.

It is common knowledge that the mere existence of a normative text does not necessarily have a considerable impact on what actually happens. Most communist countries had a wonderful record as far as their ratification of human-rights instruments were concerned, while the reality bore no resemblance to the theoretical explanations. This book concerns human rights which are actually applied under the control of judicial or quasi-judicial bodies. This is also linked

---

[2] Cf. Trechsel (2000) (in English) and (1998) (in German).
[3] Crawshaw and Holmström (2001).

to my perspective as a human-rights lawyer which I shall comment upon in due course.

2. *Criminal Proceedings*

The term 'criminal proceedings' is understood here as encompassing all the activities of state agencies, from the police to the constitutional or supreme courts, which take as a point of departure the suspicion that an offence has been committed. These activities proceed through various stages, i.e. inquiry, investigation, charge, indictment, judgment, and appeal. The essence of criminal proceedings is rather well defined, although there is great variety in the manner and means of its implementation, involving the organization of the authorities and the distribution of tasks between different branches, the organization of the trial and the various cumulative or alternative possibilities of appeal. It is often stated that there are two models of criminal procedure, an accusatorial one, associated with the Anglo-Saxon common law, which features two distinct sides and a judge as a neutral arbiter, and the continental system shaped along an inquisitorial model, where the judge has a more active, somewhat paternalistic, role to play. The current development of criminal-procedure law goes rather in the direction of a certain convergence, in which the principle of adversariality has a dominant role to play. The newly instituted International Criminal Court (ICC) is the result of efforts to reach a compromise which is acceptable throughout the whole world.

3. *Limitations, Exclusions*

It is not possible to define a subject simply by giving a positive description; it is also essential to state what is not covered. Of course, the omissions are practically unlimited. I shall only mention a few points, although I am quite aware of the fact that there are many others which could be mentioned. It must be admitted quite frankly that there are aspects and issues which could have been included but which are missing simply because of practical reasons, mainly limitations in time, and the need to stop at some point. Perfectionism will never be satisfied.

(a) The Procedures for the Implementation of Human Rights

The approach to human rights, which concentrates on rights which are actually interpreted in a judicial way and implemented by domestic jurisdictions, perhaps even incorporated into the domestic law, must be linked to the mechanisms of implementation of the respective instruments. The reader might therefore expect that they be described and discussed here. However, anything other than the most rudimentary introductions to this subject would have required another fifty or hundred pages. It would also have necessitated a discussion of the exhaustion of domestic remedies which differs from one state to the next, and for a discussion of the status of human-rights law on the domestic level. I have therefore decided to exclude this field—the reader is referred to the abundant literature which already exists.

(b) The International Criminal Court(s)

This book does not deal with international criminal law. It will not comment, in any way, on the rules of procedure for international criminal law according to the Rome Statute. This is partly due to the fact that these rules were certainly drafted with the intention of carefully respecting the body of human-rights law, but this does not make them a *source* of that law. The case-law of the International Criminal Tribunals for Rwanda and Yugoslavia (ICTR and ICTY) is scrutinized with great interest by scholars. I also expect the ICC to be equally scrupulous in respecting international human-rights standards and this book may be of modest assistance in that endeavour.

(c) Criminal Proceedings against Children and Juveniles

Article 40 of the Convention on the Rights of the Child contains, as it were, rules parallel to those set out in Article 14 of the ICCPR, and the corresponding Articles in the Conventions, for proceedings involving children accused of committing crimes. Many countries also have special rules and even special legislation to deal with this matter. That subject is both important and interesting. A very difficult question concerns the coordination of the 'liberal' human rights applying to adults and the 'social', welfare-oriented attitude directed towards young persons.

Some aspects which have turned up in the case-law will be addressed here in their context, for example, the position of the judge.[4] However, there is no special chapter on the subject—I will leave this matter to the specialists.

(d) Domestic Case-law

A full analysis of human rights in criminal proceedings would have to include domestic case-law.[5] The national courts contribute to the development of that body of law and it is primarily their task to apply the international treaties. Again, a comprehensive and comparative study extended that far was not possible in view of the enormous quantity of material that would have had to be studied.

B. The Importance of the Subject

Is it possible to find an author who doubts the importance of his or her subject? Would anyone undertake the burden of writing a book of several hundred pages unless he or she were convinced of the importance of the subject? On a personal

---

[4] Cf. *Nortier* v. *Netherlands*.
[5] For a thorough analysis of the effect of the European Convention in domestic law, see Drzemczewski (1983).

note, I would not pretend that each one of my publications really deals with a very important subject. However, I have no hesitation in reaffirming my belief in the importance of the subject addressed in this book—I do not think that this importance can be doubted.

There is, first of all, a quantitative argument. A very large part of the international case-law on human rights is related to the administration of criminal justice. Leaving aside, as far as the Strasbourg case-law is concerned, the issue of the length of civil proceedings, it is the most important subject. The criminal-justice system in every country in the world is under stress, in many cases institutions are overburdened with work. One could hardly say that this is a remote or irrelevant subject.

The importance of human rights in criminal proceedings hardly needs any comment or explanation. Criminal proceedings are an area where vital interests of society and of the individual suspect collide. An individual's reputation, financial position, personal liberty, even life—not only in those countries where capital punishment still exists, but also where life-long prison sentences are imposed—is at stake. Society, on the other hand, has a considerable interest in order, peaceful coexistence, security, physical integrity, and the safety of potential victims. The situation may be complicated by the victim claiming a right to participate in the proceedings.

Much depends, when one approaches the problem of balancing these interests, on the image one has in mind as a point of departure. It could, for example, be that of hardened criminals, members of a criminal organization, who will attempt every trick they can think of to avoid conviction, including the killing of witnesses. Or it could be a man walking home at night from a bar who steps near a body lying in the street; he touches it and feels blood; he realizes that he has stepped in a pool of what might be blood; in panic he runs home, but is seen by a passer-by and identified, which leads to his being suspected of murder. The balancing must lead to acceptable results for both eventualities.

The two sides to the conflict, the individual and society, are obviously equipped with unequal power. Not only is the accused opposed by a well-organized and equipped adversary, he or she is also faced with the representatives of a strong moral superiority. Every accused person is presumed innocent. This is what the human-rights law says. Generally, however, the police, the prosecutor, and—much more importantly and dangerously—the media, and consequently 'the people', hold the suspect guilty. The crime calls for vengeance, even though enlightened and well-intended persons will deny this and justify the operation of the criminal law with the aim of reforming the criminal.

The state's efforts to employ efficient crime-control measures, and to limit the financial (and temporal) costs of criminal proceedings, are perfectly legitimate. The fear of crime is at least understandable. In the face of these realities, human rights must work their way against the current, upstream. Although it ought to be the other way round, in practice, when we speak with law-enforcement officers and 'ordinary people', we have to justify our commitment to the rights of the accused. We shall fail, if we do so with an excess of enthusiasm, forgetting the pain of the victim and the apprehension of the public. We will also fail if we are not consistent.

For this reason it is particularly important that the place of human rights in criminal proceedings be well defined, and consistently, pragmatically, and moderately applied. To the extent that this endeavour succeeds, a certain convergence of interests can be said to appear. In a democratic state based on the rule of law the administration of criminal justice is not just oriented towards achieving as many convictions as possible and imposing severe sentences. It also has the responsibility of ensuring that justice be done. I am convinced that procedural justice is at least of the same importance as outcome-related justice.[6]

At present there is another argument which enhances the importance of the subject of human rights in criminal proceedings, the so-called 'war on terrorism'. It cannot be denied that the present times are characterized by a recurrence of violence, a wave which is clearly much bigger than that witnessed in Europe, particularly in Germany and Italy, in the 1970s ('*anni di piomo*': lead years) which originated in the actions of the Red Army Faction ('*Rote Armee Fraktion*' (RAF)) and the Red Brigades (*brigate rosse*). There is a tendency to overreact to attacks like that on the World Trade Center in New York. The President of the United States has provided an unfortunate example not only by waging war on Iraq but also by locking up hundreds of men in Guantanamo and openly denying them even the most elementary human rights. Torture, inhuman, and degrading treatment were used by a state which used to boast leadership in the areas of democracy, the rule of law, and human rights.

In the face of such a devastating experience it is important to assert not only the moral superiority of human rights, but also their functional aspect. One cannot expect respect from persons and groups of persons to whom one denies human rights. In the long run, one cannot dominate nations, let alone religious groups, by sheer force, even with the assistance of sophisticated technology.

Of course, these considerations go far beyond criminal proceedings. Yet, these proceedings are an area in which, as I said, the rights of the individual and the interests of the state are in direct contact. It is here that the state must demonstrate its allegiance to higher values, and its readiness to use power with self-restraint. This book is about the details of such restrictions.

II. THE PERSPECTIVES

There are many different ways to approach our subject. It may therefore be justified and improve the understanding of the book if the author indicates his

---

[6] Trechsel (1997).

own perspectives which cannot be entirely separated from his background. This does not mean that the book is written from a strictly personal viewpoint. It does aspire to present solutions which are objectively correct or at least defendable. Yet, it would be naive to assume that such an unfettered objectivity can be fully achieved. In order not to let these considerations appear too personal, I shall refer to the author in the third person.

A. The Geographical Perspective

The intention was to present the international human-rights law without giving preference to one of the three 'jurisdictions', the universal one of the ICCPR, the American one, or the European one. Yet, it will be noted that the European viewpoint clearly prevails. In fact, there are several reasons for this.

For one, the author is European, Swiss to be precise. Furthermore, and this is of greater practical importance, the author served for almost a quarter of a century on the European Commission of Human Rights to the memory of which the book is dedicated. Familiarity with the European case-law has certainly left its traces. Yet, the main thrust is on the case-law of the Court which, as far as judgments of the former Court are concerned, has been influenced by the Commission, but is now moving on its own track. While the Court still refers to decisions of the Commission on admissibility, the value of that old case-law as precedent is, by and large, fading.

The preponderant role of the European law in this book cannot, however, be explained (or excused?) simply by reference to the author's background. It is an objective fact that the case-law of the European institutions exceeds that of the comparable bodies on the United Nations and American level by far. There are now more than 4,300 judgments of the Court and over 10,000 accessible decisions on admissibility. Many judgments have gained worldwide attention and are also referred to as authority by the Human Rights Committee (HRC) and the Inter-American Court of Human Rights. Furthermore, this case-law is easily accessible on the Internet.

While, naturally, quite a number of references to international and American case-law will be found in the book, the author cannot and indeed does not hide its generally European background.

B. The Legal Perspective

The author believes that it is also important to take his legal background into account in two particular respects.

First, the author is trained in criminal law and the law of criminal procedure. These are the matters he has taught throughout his professional life and also practised as a public prosecutor and, occasionally, as a defence lawyer. This is in contrast to the fact that human-rights law is primarily regarded as the province of specialists in international and in constitutional law. It is not for the author to qualify this fact.

Second, the author is trained in the 'continental' legal tradition, in criminal-procedural law that is close to the inquisitorial model. Hopefully, the book is not biased because of this. The author was lucky to find an assistant from Scotland, Sarah Summers, LL B, whose assistance was also of inestimable value in that she filled the lacunae in the author's knowledge of the common law.

C. The 'Political' Perspective

One may wonder what the justification is for speaking of a 'political' perspective in the context of a legal publication. It is the author's firm conviction that a clean and rigid separation of law and politics is not possible. Whether it is recognized or not, every legal decision has a political element. The science of jurisprudence has developed methods of interpretation which will apply and which, at least to some extent, may claim general recognition, although it may not be easy to transfer them to a system of case-law. Yet, even by strictly following the rules of methodology, the lawyer will typically reach a point where a value judgment must be made. Reasons can, up to a certain point, be given for a decision, but it cannot be explained entirely by logical deduction. The value judgment is necessarily, at least to some extent, an emanation of the person who makes it. This person will have made basic choices, be they 'progressive', 'conservative', 'liberal', or 'socialist', with an infinite variety of combinations. This choice will contribute to the judgment that will be made.

In the area of human rights, a number of different basic approaches can typically be distinguished.

There is the approach of the human-rights activist. This is the attitude often embraced by NGOs and it exists in many forms. At one extreme, activists display an attitude which approaches human rights as being intrinsically good, comparable to honey or money—the more, the better. It is an attitude characterized by an enthusiasm which must be credited for securing many important developments, particularly the promotion of new instruments for the protection of human rights. It is, however, not necessarily the approach needed for the interpretation of existing human-rights law, particularly in the area of criminal proceedings and in a jurisprudential context, because it tends to overstate the interests of the individual *vis-à-vis* those of society.

At the other extreme, as it were, is the 'government lawyer' whose tendency will be to defend the status quo, tradition, public order, and safety, and other similarly conservative values. He or she will display an attitude which seeks to save particularities of the national legal order, the slow steadiness of the evolution of the law, the subsidiarity of the international control.

The author has mainly practised human-rights law in a judicial setting, even though the Commission, with its multiple functions of deciding on admissibility (the negative decisions being final), of establishing the facts, sometimes in lengthy and complicated investigations, particularly in interstate cases such as *Ireland* v. *United Kingdom* or *Cyprus* v. *Turkey*, of drafting a report which reads like a judgment but which will never be the final decision, and of appearing before the Court in the function of *amicus curiae*, falls to be regarded as a quasi-judicial organ. As a consequence, his attitude lies between the two approaches described.

The answers proposed here are intended as practicable solutions which strike a fair balance between the interests of the individual and those of society. To the reader who tends towards human-rights activism this attitude will bring disappointment—the author does not always argue for a maximum of rights for the defence. But 'government lawyers' will, it is hoped, also be disappointed, because the author believes in reform and places strong emphasis on procedural justice, whereas the value of safety, to which governments tend to adhere and which is also cherished by the public at large, tends to favour outcome-related justice and the effectiveness of crime control.

D. The 'Scientific' Perspective

The author, being a professor, is also moved by the ambition of presenting a work of legal science. This ambition is, however, modest. It would have, from a scientific perspective, been preferable to produce a book with twice as many pages and footnotes. It would have been desirable to take into account every publication ever produced on the subject, discussing every opinion held by other academics. Alas, this was not possible.

It must be admitted that many, certainly very valuable, books and articles have not, or have only inadequately, been considered and discussed—the author apologizes in advance to neglected colleagues. In other words, this work is a compromise between a thorough legal analysis and a handbook for practitioners. To give a practical example, the information on the origins of guarantees has mainly been taken from David Weissbrodt's valuable book, complemented by examples found in Manfred Nowak's equally valuable commentary. The author does not claim to have presented, in these short paragraphs, the fruit of his own research.

It is, of course, not for the author to say whether there are certain redeeming values here, although, of course, he hopes that the reader will find some. Wondering what they might be, what comes to mind is this: here is a continental European lawyer, addressing readers in English. Maybe there can be a certain interest in, as it were, building a bridge across the Channel and the ocean. Looking at the admirable work of English-speaking colleagues, what might be considered as a distinguishing feature is the effort of the author at increased systematic order, an approach which is definitely influenced by German legal science, particularly in the field of criminal law.[7]

---

[7] For a fascinating effort to introduce the structural thought of the German doctrine to American readers, see Fletcher (2000).

III. THE STRUCTURE OF THE BOOK

The structure of this book is simple—I have followed the human-rights instruments which are structurally very similar. The road goes from the general to the specific, beginning with a discussion of the scope of application of the procedural guarantees and the right to an independent and impartial tribunal established by law, an element which is also of some relevance outwith the context of the guarantee of a fair trial. This is followed by an analysis of this guarantee, the general guarantees, and the specific rights of the defence. A relatively voluminous fourth part addresses fundamental rights relating to measures of coercion such as detention on remand and wire-tapping.

Chapter 2

The Scope of Application of the Right to a Fair Trial in Criminal Matters

I. INTRODUCTION

A. The Texts

> In the determination of any criminal charge against him . . . everyone . . .
>
> ICCPR, Art. 14 § 1

> In the determination . . . of any criminal charge against him, everyone . . .
>
> ECHR, Art. 6 § 1

> Every person . . . in the substantiation of any accusation of a criminal nature made against him . . .
>
> ACHR, Art. 8 § 1

Essentially the texts of the Covenant and the European Convention are identical on this matter. As is often the case, those responsible for drafting the American Convention have chosen to depart from the wording used in the other texts. There is, in my view, no difference in meaning between the terms 'substantiation' and 'determination' or between a 'criminal charge' and an 'accusation of a criminal nature'.

B. Three Aspects Concerning the Scope of the Provision

The terms which fall to be interpreted are 'criminal' on the one hand, and 'charge' or 'accusation' on the other. The nature of the terms 'everyone' or 'every person' will be discussed particularly in the context of the position of the victim in criminal proceedings.

Despite there being a clear distinction between the terms 'criminal' and 'charge', the Court does not distinguish them clearly and applies the criteria for 'criminal' when the issue is in fact whether or not a person is 'charged'.[1] Moreover, special rules have been developed with regard to the right to be presumed innocent, a right not necessarily connected to the guarantee of a fair trial.[2]

---

[1] Cf. *Phillips* v. *United Kingdom*, § 30.   [2] See further Chapter 7 below.

II. THE NOTION OF 'CRIMINAL'

A. General Observations

An examination of the cases in which a violation of Article 6 of the ECHR has been found reveals two distinct types of case. First, there are the ordinary cases: criminal proceedings where something went wrong as a result of inadequate legislation, neglect, arbitrariness, or some other reason. The other group concerns cases where, from the domestic point of view, nothing went wrong. Here, the violation is due to the fact that a certain issue was not regarded by the national courts as falling into the category of a 'criminal' case. This category is predominantly made up of proceedings that were regarded as administrative because they concerned disciplinary matters, petty offences, or misbehaviour of an administrative character, such as in connection with taxes. The explanation for the finding of a violation in such cases lies in the fact that the domestic legislator and/or authorities did not even attempt to comply with the requirements of Article 6 because they assumed that the guarantee did not apply in the first place.

It is therefore not surprising that the question of what constitutes a 'criminal' case has attracted, at least under the judicial mechanism of implementation in Europe, considerable interest. By contrast, the question has hardly been discussed under the Covenant,[3] there is no discussion as far as the reporting system is concerned,[4] nor has there been a decision on the term 'criminal'—a fact which is indeed, as McGoldrick notes, 'surprising'.[5] At any rate, even in the field of 'civil proceedings' the Human Rights Committee (HRC) is strongly influenced by the European case-law.[6] The 'Strasbourg-centric' focus of this chapter cannot therefore be described as 'local chauvinism' but is rather dictated by necessity.

B. The Autonomous Notion of the Term 'Criminal Charge'

At the outset, it would seem that two different answers might be given to the question as to what is meant by a 'criminal charge'. One possibility would be to refer to the domestic law at issue, another would be to attempt to create a new and general definition for the purposes of applying the Convention. The importance of the distinction should not to be overrated. It should be possible to create an autonomous notion which would not overrule traditional categories or deeply interfere with the traditions of domestic law. The vast majority of decisions concern cases which are classed as criminal in both the domestic and the European human-rights law. As a rule, criminal law covers theft, murder, rape, and all the other traditional offences, including more 'modern' ones such

---

[3] Nowak (1993) Art. 14 N 13.
[4] The contrary view of McGoldrick (1994) N 10.4 concerns only the 'civil' scope.
[5] Ibid.   [6] McGoldrick (1994) N 10.25.

as drug trafficking and money laundering—in other words those crimes which are usually set out in a penal code.[7] Difficulties only arise in those areas which lie on the edges of the criminal law.

Of course, the easier road would be to follow national law. While this may not be without problems, because even within the legal system concerned there may be a dispute as to whether a specific matter is 'penal' or 'criminal' in character or not, these difficulties do not appear to be particularly substantial. The Court has, for a number of good reasons, opted for the second alternative, that of establishing an autonomous notion. It embarked on this route early on in its jurisprudence, in *Neumeister*, when it examined the notion of 'charge' without, however, discussing the meaning any further.[8]

The leading case in relation to the definition of 'criminal' is *Engel and others* v. *Netherlands*. The Court had to determine whether military disciplinary proceedings were of a 'criminal' character within the meaning of Article 6—both the Government and the Commission had held that they were not. The Court, on the other hand, said this:

The Convention without any doubt allows the States, in the performance of their function as guardians of the public interest to maintain or establish a distinction between criminal law and disciplinary law, and to draw the dividing line, but only subject to certain conditions. The Convention leaves the States free to designate as a criminal offence an act or omission not constituting the normal exercise of one of the rights that it protects... Such a choice, which has the effect of rendering applicable Articles 6 and 7, in principle escapes supervision by the Court.

The converse choice, for its part, is subject to stricter rules. If the contracting States were able at their discretion to classify an offence as disciplinary instead of criminal, or to prosecute the author of a 'mixed' offence on the disciplinary rather than on the criminal plane, the operation of the fundamental clauses of Articles 6 and 7 would be subordinated to their sovereign will. A latitude extending thus far might lead to results incompatible with the purpose and object of the Convention. The Court therefore has jurisdiction, under Article 6... to satisfy itself that the disciplinary does not improperly encroach upon the criminal.[9]

Thus, the Court will not accept any 'tricks' a domestic legislator could be tempted to try in order to avoid the application of Article 6. It also aims—without saying so expressly in this judgment—to achieve the uniform application of the Convention in Europe. In fact, if states were free themselves to determine what matters were to be regarded as criminal, the scope of the

---

[7] This can be referred to as the nucleus of criminal law, the '*Kernstrafrecht*'; cf. Grabenwarter (1997) 90 with further references.   [8] *Neumeister* v. *Austria*, § 18.

[9] *Engel and others* v. *Netherlands*, § 81. The passage has been repeated many times; see e.g. *Campbell and Fell* v. *United Kingdom*; *Öztürk* v. *Germany*, § 49; *Vastberga Taxi Aktiebolag and Vulic* v. *Sweden*, § 78; *Ezeh and Connors* v. *United Kingdom (GC)*, §§ 83, 100; *Kremzow* v. *Austria* Application 16417/90; *Demel* v. *Austria* Application 30993/96; *Lee* v. *United Kingdom* Application 53429/99.

protection offered by Article 6 would differ substantially from one country to the other. This would hardly be compatible with a European Convention which aims to form the nucleus of a European constitution. To this extent the approach of the Court undoubtedly merits full approval. In fact, in the interpretation of the Convention the Strasbourg authorities have succeeded in creating an impressive number of autonomous notions—other examples include 'family' and 'home'.[10]

C. The Three Criteria First Established in *Engel*

In *Engel* the Court identified three criteria which must be applied in order to decide whether a charge has a 'criminal' character or not:

> ... it is first necessary to know whether the provision(s) defining the offence charged belong, according to the legal system of the respondent State, to criminal law, disciplinary law or both concurrently. This however provides no more than a starting point. The indications so afforded have only a formal and relative value and must be examined in the light of the common denominator of the respective legislation of the various Contracting States.
>
> The very nature of the offence is a factor of greater import. When a serviceman finds himself accused of an act or omission allegedly contravening a legal rule governing the operation of the armed forces, the State may in principle employ against him disciplinary law rather than criminal law ...
>
> However, supervision by the Court does not stop there. Such supervision would generally prove to be illusory if it did not also take into consideration the degree of severity of the penalty that the person concerned risks incurring. In a society subscribing to the rule of law, there belong to the 'criminal' sphere deprivations of liberty liable to be imposed as a punishment, except those which by their nature, duration or manner of execution cannot be appreciably detrimental. The seriousness of what is at stake, the traditions of the Contracting States and the importance attached by the Convention to respect for the physical liberty of the person all require that this should be so ...[11]

Twenty years later, and after many confirmations of this basic ruling, the formulation has been considerably simplified:

> The Court reiterates that the concept of 'criminal charge' within the meaning of Article 6 is an autonomous one. In earlier case-law the Court has established that there are three criteria to be taken into account when it is being decided whether a person was 'charged with a criminal offence' for the purposes of Article 6. These are the classification of the offence under national law, the nature of the offence and the nature and degree of severity of the penalty that the person concerned risked incurring ...[12]

---

[10] Cf. Harris, O'Boyle, and Warbrick (1995) 303.
[11] *Engel and others* v. *Netherlands*, § 82; the formula turns up again e.g. in *Campbell and Fell* v. *United Kingdom*, §§ 68, 69; *Ezeh and Connors* v. *United Kingdom (GC)*, § 82.
[12] *AP, MP and TP* v. *Switzerland*, § 39; *EL, RL and JO-L* v. *Switzerland*, § 44; see also *Kulpakko* v. *Finland* Application 25761/94.

The Court has consistently applied this tripartite test[13]—the only exception, which comes to mind, is the judgment in *Bendenoun* v. *France*[14] where tax surcharges (*'majorations d'impôt'*) were at issue. The Government had argued that in domestic law the sanction was considered as a 'tax penalty' and not a 'criminal penalty'. The offence was characterized as 'deceitfulness' (*'manoeuvres frauduleuses'*) rather than 'evasion' (*'soustraction frauduleuse'*). In relation to the sanction the Government stressed that it was only pecuniary in nature, that it was proportionate to the amount of taxes evaded, and that it did not have all the same consequences as a 'real' criminal sanction. It was not, for instance, entered in the criminal record.

The Court first stressed that nothing prevented the Contracting States from empowering administrative authorities to impose penalties for tax evasion 'as long as the taxpayer can bring any such decision affecting him before a court that affords the safeguards' of Article 6. It then indicated that it 'does not underestimate the importance of several of the points raised by the Government', but rebutted them by way of four arguments:

First, as to the character of the offence, the Court stressed that it covered all citizens in their capacity as taxpayers, not a group with a special status.

Second, as to the scope of the sanction, it served the aims of punishment and deterrence rather than compensation for damages.

Third, the sanctions were 'imposed under a general rule whose purpose is both deterrent and punitive'.

Fourth, the sums at issue were considerable—amounting to almost a million French francs—and Mr Bendenoun could have gone to prison if he had failed to pay.

The Court then evaluated each of the various aspects, and found that although none of them were decisive, 'taken together and cumulatively they made the "charge" in issue a "criminal" one within the meaning of Article 6 § 1'.

This departure from the earlier jurisprudence was, according to an important Austrian study written by Grabenwarter, the subject of considerable scholarly controversy.[15] However, I have not found any traces of that digression in later case-law. While Grabenwarter believes that the Court continued to apply a more general approach, I fail to detect any significant development.[16] In *Putz* v. *Austria*,[17] to give one example, the Court referred very summarily to 'the three alternative criteria laid down in its case-law' (and did not, of course, refer to *Bendenoun!*). Closer analysis reveals, furthermore, that the differences are indeed minimal—in *Bendenoun* the Court distinguished between the scope that lay

---

[13] Kuijer (2004) 126 et seq. separates the kind of punishment from the severity of the penalty and arrives at four criteria; this is possible but not very helpful because there is a strong link between the two which makes it difficult to separate them. For a very careful analysis, see Feteris (1993) 252 et seq.   [14] *Bendenoun* v. *France*, §§ 45 et seq.
[15] Grabenwarter (1997) 104 with references in n. 305.   [16] Ibid., 105.
[17] *Putz* v. *Austria*, § 31.

behind the sanction at issue on the one hand and the general scope of the legislation on the other. There is no explanation as to why this was necessary.

In its effort to adapt its case-law to the case under consideration, the Court stressed that in *Engel* it had in mind the military context, whereas *Campbell and Fell* and *Ezeh and Connors* were adapted to cover prison discipline. In the latter case the Court even embarked on a superficial discussion of what is necessary to maintain prison discipline, saying that the most effective means was not necessarily that of adding additional days of imprisonment to the punishment.[18] It did so because the parties had raised the issue, but it is hard to justify this discussion in the present case. In my view it is unconceivable that a state would 'need' to apply a sanction which would fall to be regarded as 'criminal' within the meaning of Article 6, without also securing the appropriate procedural guarantees.

Before discussing the question of whether these aspects are really three alternatives, it is necessary to carry out a closer examination of each of them.

D. The Substance of the Three Criteria

1. The Classification of the Offence under National Law

The first criterion, the classification of the offence under national law, is not especially remarkable. In fact, it will be difficult for a government to argue that a particular offence lacks the 'criminal' character if it is set out in the penal code. The Court itself stressed that 'this factor is of relative weight and serves only as a starting point'.[19] In fact, it is not a factor at all—the Court has never attached any weight to it. The problem only arises in cases where the behaviour in question is not classified as 'criminal', such as when, as in *Öztürk* for example, it has been the object of decriminalization.[20] Nevertheless, the Court found it appropriate to show some understanding for the German legislation and stressed that 'no absolute partition separates German criminal law from the law on "regulatory offences"'.[21]

Sanctions imposed for fiscal offences, such as incomplete declaration of revenues, also belong to the criminal sphere.[22]

On the other hand, in an application brought by Mr Kremzow, the Commission stressed that the domestic law made a clear distinction between disciplinary and criminal aspects, and it was decisive that disciplinary proceedings were at issue.[23]

---

[18] *Ezeh and Connors* v. *United Kingdom* (*GC*), §§ 88, 89.
[19] *Benham* v. *United Kingdom*, § 55; *Weber* v. *Switzerland*, § 31; *Campbell* v. *United Kingdom*, § 71; *Ravnsborg* v. *Sweden*, § 47; *Demicoli* v. *Malta*, § 33; *Tyler* v. *United Kingdom* Application 21283/93.   [20] *Öztürk* v. *Germany*, § 47.
[21] Ibid., § 51.
[22] *Bendenoun* v. *France*; *Vastberga Taxi Aktiebolag and Vulic* v. *Sweden*; *Hozee* v. *Netherlands*; *JB* v. *Switzerland*; *Janosevic* v. *Sweden*; *Hennig* v. *Austria*.
[23] *Kremzow* v. *Austria* Application 16417/90.

2. The Nature of the Offence

While it is a rather tautological observation, it must be said that the offence is 'criminal' if its nature is 'criminal'. There does not appear, however, to be any definition in the case-law. Some indications can be derived, indirectly, from the efforts of the Court to define disciplinary offences. A provisional and anticipatory definition leads to the conclusion that a charge is 'criminal' in nature if it concerns a norm which is basically addressed to everyone rather than to a restricted group of persons and if the sanction imposed pursues, in the first place, a retributive goal.[24] The most discussed issue is the 'opting out-aspect'; the presumption speaks in favour of the application of Article 6. Therefore, petty offences, particularly where they have been 'decriminalized' (which, in my personal opinion, often does not go far beyond attaching a new label to the old norm), continue to belong to the criminal law.[25]

(a) Not to be Confused with the Nature of Proceedings

The second criterion is the genuine one which affirms the autonomy of the term 'criminal' charge—it concerns the nature of the offence. Unfortunately, the Court seems to have lost track in this respect in the *Benham* judgment because instead of referring to the character of the offence it referred to the *character of the proceedings*.[26] With due respect, this is somewhat problematic because it confounds the answer with the question: the very issue is whether proceedings in the sense of Article 6 are required; the reason why the application has been brought lies in the fact that, according to the applicant, the national proceedings did not satisfy the requirements of that guarantee. The Court referred to *Ravnsborg* where it had said: 'Regard must be had to the realities of the procedure in question in order to determine whether there has been a "charge" within the meaning of Article 6 of the Convention'.[27] However, that is not identical to what was said in *Engel*.[28]

(b) General Considerations

How, then, does the Court find out whether the characteristics of a specific form of misbehaviour make it criminal or not? It has recourse to comparative law, to what is customary among the Contracting States.[29] Howard Yourow, in a thorough study on the doctrine of the margin of appreciation, found this to be a generally accepted method of the Court, perhaps the essential one.[30]

---

[24] I am fully aware of how risky a proposition this is in view of the fact that many authors reject retribution as a legitimate purpose of the criminal law.

[25] This was argued at length in *Öztürk* v. *Germany* and confirmed in *Lutz* v. *Germany; Gradinger* v. *Austria; Schmautzer* v. *Austria; Pfarrmeier* v. *Austria; Pramstaller* v. *Austria; Umlauft* v. *Austria; Kadubec* v. *Slovakia;* and *Lauko* v. *Slovakia.* See also *Michael Horst* v. *Austria* Application 25809/94; *Peter Hauser* v. *Austria* Application 26808/95.   [26] *Benham* v. *United Kingdom,* § 56.

[27] *Ravnsborg* v. *Sweden,* § 47.   [28] *Engel and others* v. *Netherlands,* § 84.

[29] Grabenwarter (1997) 91 et seq. with further references; for an explicit example, see *Putz* v. *Austria,* § 33.   [30] Yourow (1996) 195.

Does the Court look at the offence which has been actually or allegedly committed by the person concerned, or does it look rather at the body of regulations which form the basis of the sanction at issue? The second hypothesis is the correct one—the essential element is, as Grabenwarter points out, the *character of the legal rule* applied.[31]

(c) The Nature of Disciplinary Charges

The first category, and the one which gave rise to the *Engel* case, is that of disciplinary proceedings. In that first judgment, the Court did not attempt to define what the characteristics of disciplinary proceedings are. What it said was this: 'When a serviceman finds himself accused of an act or omission allegedly contravening a legal rule governing the operation of the armed forces, the State may in principle employ against him disciplinary law rather than criminal law'.[32]

The typical characteristics of a disciplinary offence are defined more precisely only much later. In my view the first analysis was conducted in the *Weber* case. In its report the Commission said:

... the Commission observes that the objective of the disputed provision [sc. Article 185 of the Vaud Code of Criminal Procedure prohibiting the parties from disclosing the secret of the investigation] is to guarantee that criminal investigations follow a normal course. Unlike Article 293 of the Swiss Criminal Code, which covers everyone, even those people who take no part in the investigation proceedings, Article 185 ... only covers the parties, their counsel, the employees of their counsel, expert witnesses and witnesses. This provision therefore covers a particular group of individuals whose common characteristic is that they are involved in the investigation proceedings and subject to a special discipline because of this. It is closely linked to the working of the investigation proceedings and does not affect the general interests of society.[33]

The Court followed this approach although it reached a different conclusion: 'Disciplinary sanctions are generally designed to ensure that the members of particular groups comply with the specific rules governing their conduct'.[34] Furthermore, the Court stated (without giving, however, any references) that 'in the great majority of Contracting States disclosure of information about an investigation still pending constitutes an act incompatible with such rules and punishable under a variety of provisions'. It added, again without any references, that as the parties only took part in the proceedings as people subject to the jurisdiction of the courts, they did not come within the disciplinary sphere of

---

[31] Grabenwarter (1997) 91.   [32] *Engel and others* v. *Netherlands*, § 82.

[33] *Weber* v. *Switzerland*, Report of the Commission, § 103. See also: *Eggs* v. *Switzerland* Application 10313/83, where the Commission found that the offence 'infringes a legal rule governing the internal operation of the armed forces; it does not, in the particular sector of the armed forces, affect the general interests of society normally protected by criminal law'; *Borrelli* v. *Switzerland* Application 17571/90: 'the duties amounted to a typical aspect of the internal operation of the military'.

[34] *Weber* v. *Switzerland*, § 33; see also *Sjöstörm* v. *Sweden* Application 19853/92.

the judicial system. As however the legislation at issue was potentially applicable to the whole population both the offence defined by it and the sanction attached to it fell to be regarded as 'criminal'.

In my view, this difference is not decisive. In order for a penalty to be characterized as 'disciplinary', it is essential that the rule cover a limited number of persons belonging to an identifiable group and that it is imposed in order to sanction behaviour against the internal order of that group. Further examples are prisons and court hearings.[35]

The Court itself has recognized this in a different context: 'Rules enabling a court to sanction disorderly conduct in proceedings before it are a common feature of the legal systems of most of the Contracting States . . . Measures ordered by courts under such rules are more akin to the exercise of disciplinary powers than to the imposition of a punishment for commission of a criminal offence'.[36]

(d) Offences of a 'Mixed Character'

It is not rare to find offences which have both disciplinary aspects and elements of a criminal nature. The question as to which character was to be regarded as dominant arose in the case of *Campbell and Fell*.[37] The conduct at issue was an assault on a prison officer. The Court stated that ' . . . it has to be borne in mind that misconduct by a prisoner may take different forms; certain acts are clearly no more than a question of internal discipline, whereas others cannot be seen in the same light. Firstly, some matters may be more serious than others; in fact, the Rules grade offences . . . Secondly, the illegality of some acts may not turn on the fact that they were committed in prison: certain conducts which constitute an offence under the Rules may also amount to an offence under the criminal law . . . '.[38]

I fully agree with this view. In fact, it is often the case that offences committed by persons subject to a regime of discipline, such as members of the armed forces or civil servants, or prisoners, are subject to two kinds of sanctions: criminal and disciplinary. It is also correct that these two types of sanctions should be determined in different sets of proceedings. At any rate, if there is only one set of proceedings, it must be criminal; a person cannot lose the protection of Article 6 because there is also, in addition to the criminal aspect, a disciplinary element involved.

---

[35] For further details on the Commission's case-law, see Frowein and Peukert (1996) Art. 6 N 36 and n. 105. For prisons, see *Campbell and Fell* v. *United Kingdom*, § 80. One might also think of schools, hospitals, or homes for the elderly.

[36] *Putz* v. *Austria*, § 33; *Ravnsborg* v. *Sweden*, § 34; in these cases the applicant was also a party to proceedings but the Court, as shall be shown, thought that disciplinary sanctions were necessary to react to disorderly conduct in proceedings—it is interesting to note that the misbehaviour sanctioned had not been committed in open court but in writing!

[37] *Campbell and Fell* v. *United Kingdom*; a 'mixed offence' was also in issue in *Ezeh and Connors* v. *United Kingdom (GC)*, § 104 (assault on a probation officer).

[38] Ibid., § 71; see also *Borrelli* v. *Switzerland* Application 17571/90.

3. The Nature and Degree of Severity of the Sanction Incurred

The third criterion seemed, for quite some time, to be the decisive one.[39] This is particularly logical in view of the approach which was initially taken by the Court in the *Engel* case: the Convention must be interpreted in such a way as to exclude any possibility of abuse by allowing the authorities to have recourse to disciplinary proceedings in order to inflict severe sanctions on someone without the necessity of respecting the procedural guarantees of Article 6.[40]

The sanction incurred has a decisive importance in the sense that there is no criminal charge unless the possibility of a conviction and sentence exists. This is not the case where a defendant is found to be unfit to plead—such a finding puts an end to criminal proceedings, even though, afterwards, a grand jury may establish whether the 'ex-accused' had actually committed the alleged acts. Such findings may lead to the decision on preventive measures, such as for example, confinement to a mental hospital.[41] This is perfectly in line with my own conception of the essence of a criminal charge. It means that the committal of a person lacking criminal responsibility to a mental hospital does not necessarily have to follow the guarantees of Article 6, although the strong procedural guarantees of Article 5 § 4 continue to apply.

(a) Deprivation of Liberty

The starting point in *Engel* was the consideration of the sanctions involving a deprivation of, or (further) restrictions on, liberty; deprivation of liberty as a rule leads to the offence having to be classified as criminal, said the Court, unless 'by their nature, duration or manner of execution [it] cannot be appreciably detrimental'.[42] In the actual case, two days' strict arrest was too little to be 'criminal'; three or four months' committal to a disciplinary unit, on the other hand, sufficed.[43] In *Eggs* and *Borrelli*, five days of strict arrest were not considered to be so severe as to give the case a 'criminal' character.[44] For Stavros 'it was policy rather than purely legal considerations that led the European Court to recognize the criminal character of the offences in *Engel*'.[45]

In *Campbell and Fell* the sanction was primarily the loss of remission, i.e. the time normally deducted from the sentence for good behaviour. The nature of this remission had already been discussed by the Commission in 1977 in the case of *Lazlo Kiss* when it was not regarded as deprivation of liberty.[46] In that case

---

[39]   This opinion is shared by Soyer and de Salvia (1995) 225. For Velu and Ergec (1990) N 445 the second criterion is more important in the case-law of the Court.

[40]   This is also stressed by Stavros (1993) 15.

[41]   *William Samuel Kerr* v. *United Kingdom* Application 63356/00; *Pierre Harrison Antoine* v. *United Kingdom* Application 62960/00.   [42]   *Engel and others* v. *Netherlands*, § 82.

[43]   Ibid., § 85.

[44]   *Eggs* v. *Switzerland* Application 10313/83 (1978); *Borrelli* v. *Switzerland* Application 17571/90.   [45]   Stavros (1993) 15.

[46]   *Lazlo Kiss* v. *United Kingdom* Application 6224/73.

80 days were imposed, 180 were at stake. In *Campbell and Fell*—where the period amounted to 570 days—the Commission and later the Court found the sentence incurred and actually imposed severe enough to make it 'criminal' and call for the application of Article 6.[47] In *Ezeh* the Court recognized 'that awards of additional days by the governor constitute fresh deprivations of liberty imposed for punitive reasons after a finding of culpability . . . Accordingly, given the deprivations of liberty, liable to be and actually imposed on the present applicants, there is a presumption that the charges against them were criminal'.[48] This presumption was not set aside, as the maximum sentence incurred was forty-two days.

A number of judges dissented.[49] They were all impressed by a report by Lord Woolf who had stated that the sanction 'did not increase a prisoner's sentence as a matter of domestic law'. However, this is not decisive—it suffices that the prisoner punished will actually spend additional days in prison. It is to be hoped that the Court will stick with this persuasive decision.

The way in which the Court determines the relevant quantum of the penalty is particularly interesting and will be addressed below. There is no deprivation of liberty in cases where only the regime of detention is concerned, such as when, for example, a prisoner is punished by segregation or solitary confinement.[50] If such a measure is taken for security purposes, one is even further away from a criminal sanction.[51]

A consideration of the case-law thus leads to the conclusion that the question as to whether a sanction of deprivation of liberty is a safe criterion to distinguish a criminal from a disciplinary sanction cannot be answered apodictically; there is however a strong presumption that it is.

(b) Pecuniary Sanctions

Pecuniary sanctions such as fines may also bring an offence within the sphere of the 'criminal'. However, it is very difficult to extract clear guidelines in this area from the Court's case-law. In *Weber* v. *Switzerland* the maximum fine was 500 Swiss francs—the Court found that '[w]hat was at stake was thus sufficiently important'.[52] In *Ravnsborg* the sum was 1,000 Swedish kronor (approximately 250 Swiss francs), convertible into imprisonment of no less than fourteen days and no more than three months.[53] Three such fines had been imposed, but that was not sufficiently important.[54] In *Putz* the fines incurred amounted to 5,000, 7,500, and 10,000 Austrian schillings, i.e. more than 2,000 Swiss francs. Yet, the Court did not find that this was in itself enough to make the offence

---

[47] *Campbell and Fell* v. *United Kingdom*, § 72; see also *Delazarus* v. *United Kingdom* Application 17525/90.   [48] *Ezeh and Connors* v. *United Kingdom (GC)*, §§ 125, 126.
[49] Judge Pellonpää, joined by Judges Wildhaber, Palm and Caflisch, and Judges Zupančič and Maruste.
[50] *Roelofs* v. *Netherlands* Application 19435/92; *D* v. *Germany* Application 11703/85.
[51] *Roelofs* v. *Netherlands* Application 19435/92.   [52] *Weber* v. *Switzerland*, § 34.
[53] *Ravnsborg* v. *Sweden*, § 24.   [54] Ibid., § 35.

'criminal'.[55] The same result was reached in *Garyfallou AEBE* where the applicant company was fined 500,000 drachmas (about 2,500 euros) and had risked a fine of three times that sum.[56] In *Öztürk* the Court actually declared the criterion as being of little importance: 'There is nothing to suggest that the criminal offence referred to in the Convention necessarily implies a certain degree of seriousness'.[57]

In connection with the discussion of the amount of the fines the Court also referred to two collateral issues: the question whether the fine can be commuted to deprivation of liberty (and if so, for how many days) and whether it is entered into some kind of police or other register.[58] The significance of these criteria is not however immediately apparent. In *Ravnsborg*, the fine was convertible to imprisonment for up to three months, but only following a hearing before the District Court—Article 6 was not applied. In *Öztürk* the deprivation of liberty only became possible as a method of enforcement but Article 6 did apply. In the same case, the fact that fines were not entered in the judicial criminal record but solely, in certain circumstances, on the central traffic register, did not eliminate the criminal character.[59]

Grabenwarter tries to explain why it would not be practicable to have a precise limit beyond which a fine becomes so important that it can no longer be regarded as disciplinary.[60] His explanations are compelling but not entirely convincing in the sense that they could not free the Court from giving some general indication as to the criteria to be applied. It is not enough to say that the decision is to be taken on a case-by-case basis, having regard to what is 'at stake' in the particular circumstances.[61] The amount could, for example, be related to the average monthly income or the actual income of the defendant.

In *Pierre-Bloch* one part of the penalty consisted of the obligation to pay a sum of money, equal to that unlawfully spent on an election campaign, to the Treasury. The Court concluded that 'apart from the fact that the amount

---

[55] *Putz* v. *Austria*, § 37; see also *C and EF* v. *Austria* Application 20517/92, where the fine amounted to 20,000 Austrian schillings which was not enough for the Commission to make the offence criminal; for other examples of the case-law of the Commission, see also Grabenwarter (1997) 97 n. 280; again the Court refers to 'a common feature of the legal systems of most of the Contracting States' without giving any reference; in *Vastberga Taxi Aktiebolag and Vulic* v. *Sweden*, § 80 the amount of actual and potential tax surcharges was so high that it left no room for doubt as to their severity.　　　　　　　　　　　　　[56] *Garyfallou AEBE* v. *Greece*, § 34.

[57] *Öztürk* v. *Germany*, § 53. See also *Schmautzer* v. *Austria*, where the applicant had omitted to use his safety belt and was fined 200 schilling which could be commuted to fourteen hours of detention—the Court noted that the offence was 'criminal' under domestic law and also referred to this potential deprivation of liberty; ibid., § 28. Stavros (1993) 26 criticizes the *Öztürk* judgment because of the 'generality of the pronouncement' that 'renders the task of identifying a viable criterion, on the basis of which to distinguish administrative from criminal wrong, almost impossible'. The answer to this criticism must be that there is no category of 'administrative' sanction other than disciplinary ones—in fact, the case-law does not even come near to giving any such example. See also Esser (2002) 64 et seq.

[58] Cf. e.g. *Ravnsborg* v. *Sweden*, § 35; *Putz* v. *Austria*, § 37.　　　　　[59] *Öztürk* v. *Germany*, § 52.

[60] Grabenwarter (1997) 97 et seq.

[61] See also the criticism of van Dijk and van Hoof (1998) 415 et seq.

payable is neither determined according to a fixed scale nor set in advance, several features differentiate this obligation to pay from criminal fines in the strict sense: no entry is made in the criminal record, the rule that consecutive sentences are not imposed in respect of multiple offences does not apply, and imprisonment is not available to sanction failure to pay. In view of its nature, the obligation to pay the Treasury a sum equal to the amount of the excess cannot be construed as a fine'.[62] Not all of these arguments are pertinent. For instance, fines in the field of income taxes are not set in advance either and may not be entered in the criminal record. In general the judgment is unconvincing.

(c) Other Sanctions

The sanctions which are nowadays applicable in the event of a breach of the criminal law are not limited to a period of detention or fines. Alternative sanctions include community service and the withdrawal of rights, such as the right to drive a car. The question then arises as to the severity of such sanctions.

The Court had to consider this problem in the case of *Malige* v. *France* which did not concern the confiscation of the licence itself but the deduction of points which could eventually, on accumulation of a certain number, lead to the withdrawal of the licence. It was an automatic consequence of the conviction and a rather severe punishment: 'It is indisputable that the right to drive a motor vehicle is very useful in everyday life and for carrying on an occupation'. The Court concluded rightly that Article 6 applied.[63]

A different sanction consisting in the withdrawal of a right was at issue in the *Pierre-Bloch* v. *France* case mentioned above. In addition to the obligation to pay a sum to the Treasury, the applicant was also disqualified by the constitutional court from standing for election for a period of one year:

The purpose of that penalty is to compel candidates to respect the maximum limit. The penalty is thus directly one of the measures designed to ensure the proper conduct of parliamentary elections, so that, by virtue of its purpose, it lies outside the 'criminal' sphere. Admittedly, as the applicant pointed out, disqualification from standing for election is also one of the forms of deprivation of civic rights provided in French criminal law. Nevertheless, in that instance the penalty is 'ancillary' or 'additional' to certain penalties imposed by the criminal courts . . . ; its criminal nature derives in that instance from the 'principal' penalty to which it attaches.[64]

The Court also stressed the fact that the sanction was limited to a period of one year. While this result is quite acceptable, the reasoning is not convincing. There may be other rules to ensure that elections are properly conducted, such as the prohibition of bribes. No one would doubt their criminal character. The decisive aspect is that the sanction is aimed at candidates, a limited number of persons, and is also directly linked to this quality. In fact, it comes close to a

---

[62] *Pierre-Bloch* v. *France*, § 58.   [63] *Malige* v. *France*, §§ 37–8.
[64] *Pierre-Bloch* v. *France*, § 56.

disciplinary measure.[65] The same can be said for the withdrawal of a licence to serve alcoholic beverages for non-compliance with the regulations attached to it.[66] Here the sanction was probably much more vital to the interests of the persons concerned.

(d) Actual, Probable, or Possible Severity of the Sanction?

Is it the actual sentence which is decisive, or the maximum sentence provided for in the rules? The Court has given a clear answer: 'the final outcome of the appeal cannot diminish the importance of what was initially at stake'.[67] The severity is 'determined by reference to the maximum potential penalty for which the relevant law provides'.[68] That the sanction eventually imposed cannot be the decisive element is certainly quite correct. It would not make sense to have the decision on whether certain qualified proceedings were called for depend upon the result of such proceedings.[69] It is therefore difficult to understand why, in *Campbell and Fell*, the Court nevertheless stressed that the maximum sanction had in fact been imposed.[70]

The Court also proceeds in this way when examining whether the interests of justice, in the light of the seriousness of what is at stake, warrant the granting of legal aid.[71] I believe that in those cases the relevant question is the sentence which could reasonably be expected rather than what was theoretically possible, particularly in a legal system which sets wide limits between minimum and maximum punishment.[72] However, here we are faced with another matter. The difference is that the question of legal aid must be decided on the specific facts of each case whereas the decision as to whether a certain sanction is a disciplinary one depends on the set of rules under which it is provided for. I therefore agree that the maximum penalty at stake is the relevant element, as far as severity of the sanction is concerned, in the determination of whether a disciplinary offence falls to be classified as criminal or not.

4. The Scope of the Sanction

The Court does not limit itself to taking into account the quantity of the penalty incurred but also refers to its scope. In cases where it comes to the conclusion that Article 6 ought to apply, it has stressed that the sanction serves a punitive purpose and one of deterrence.[73] It is interesting to note that this

---

[65] In the Commission the vote had been a close nine to eight, in the Court it was seven to two.
[66] *Tre Traktörer Aktiebolag* v. *Sweden*, § 46.
[67] *Campbell and Fell* v. *United Kingdom*, § 72.
[68] *Ezeh and Connors* v. *United Kingdom* (*GC*), § 120, referring to *Campbell and Fell* v. *United Kingdom*, § 72; *Weber* v. *Switzerland*, § 34; *Demicoli* v. *Malta*, § 34; *Benham* v. *United Kingdom*, § 56; and *Garyfallou AEBE* v. *Greece*, §§ 33, 34.
[69] The Court made such a mistake in *Schiesser* v. *Switzerland*. See further Chapter 19 below.
[70] *Campbell and Fell* v. *United Kingdom*, § 38.   [71] *Quaranta* v. *Switzerland*.
[72] This is the case e.g. for Swiss law, where a typical time frame for theft is from three days' imprisonment to five years.   [73] *Öztürk* v. *Germany*, § 53; *Bendenoun* v. *France*, § 67.

element is not usually referred to in order to qualify the severity of the sanction, the consequences it may entail for the person concerned, but it is used as a criterion to qualify the character of the offence itself. In *Ravnsborg*, the Court stated in relation to the nature of the offence that:

Rules enabling a court to sanction disorderly conduct in proceedings before it are a common feature of legal systems of the Contracting States. Such rules and sanctions derive from the indispensable power of a court to ensure the proper and orderly functioning of its own proceedings. Measures ordered by courts under such rules are more akin to the exercise of disciplinary powers than to the imposition of a punishment for commission of a criminal offence. It is, of course, open to States to bring what are considered to be more serious examples of disorderly conduct within the sphere of criminal law, but that has not been shown to be the case in the present instance as regards the fines imposed upon the applicant.[74]

However, the criterion of the punitive and deterrent character of the sanction is of little value. The scope of punishment has been the subject of discussions amongst philosophers, lawyers, and others at least since Plato put in the fourth century BC some crucial reflections on this topic into the mouth of Protagoras, the great sophist. For Stavros, at least, the scope of the violated rule is 'a distinguishing feature', but it 'cannot justify in itself the lack of protection for a series of disciplinary proceedings'.[75] Typically, criminal sanctions are also regarded as having educational or rehabilitative elements. Disciplinary sanctions also have a punitive character and serve as a deterrent, whether this is expressly stated or not.[76] The Court has now recognized the weakness of this argument: 'It does not find persuasive the Government's argument distinguishing between the punishment and deterrent aims of the offences in question, these objectives not being mutually exclusive and being recognised as characteristic features of criminal penalties'.[77]

5. The Relationship Between the Different Criteria

After having examined the different criteria which the Court applies in order to determine whether a specific sanction is of a 'criminal' character or not, the question arises as to the relationship between these criteria—must they be fulfilled cumulatively or is it enough that one is fulfilled? The Court has said that they are alternatives, which means that Article 6 applies if any one of them

[74] *Ravnsborg* v. *Sweden*, § 34; see also *JM* v. *Switzerland* Application 21083/92.
[75] Stavros (1993) 24.
[76] The punitive character may be an important criterion, however, to distinguish 'penalties' from purely preventive or coercive measures; on the autonomous notion of 'penalty' in connection with Art. 7, see *Welch* v. *United Kingdom*, where a retrospective confiscation order was at issue; in default of the payment the applicant was liable to serve two years in prison—the Court found a violation.
[77] *Ezeh and Connors* v. *United Kingdom (GC)*, § 105, referring to *Öztürk* v. *Germany*, §§ 53, 102.

is fulfilled.[78] The Court is not, however, quite consistent in this respect. In *Campbell and Fell*[79] it remained hesitant after examining the second point and looked to the third in order to make a general assessment: 'The Court considers that [the first two] factors, whilst not of themselves sufficient to lead to the conclusion that the offences with which the applicant was charged have to be regarded as "criminal" for Convention purposes, do give them a certain colouring which does not entirely coincide with that of a purely disciplinary matter'. Later, in *Ezeh* it only spoke of the second and third criteria as being alternatives.[80]

In *Bendenoun*, for example, it 'weighted the various aspects of the case', i.e. looked at the factors as a whole rather than at one or the other in isolation— but nevertheless stated *expressis verbis* that 'these criteria are not cumulative but alternative'.[81] Again, this is correct. If under one criterion a matter has a 'criminal' character, it is hard to imagine how that could be 'undone' by any other element.

E. Disciplinary Matters as 'Civil Rights and Obligations'

Before closing this discussion, it may be justified to comment on a technique employed by the Court in order to apply Article 6 of the ECHR to proceedings which are disciplinary but not 'criminal' in character and have such importance for the person concerned that they call for qualified judicial protection.

If we look at domestic law we find a number of types of disciplinary offences. Some of them have been dealt with in the case-law set out above, i.e. in the area of the armed forces,[82] the civil service,[83] prisons[84] or in the context of persons participating in court proceedings.[85] The issue of school discipline has also come up in the Court's case-law but in an entirely different context.[86] Others concern members of liberal professions such as medical doctors,[87] accountants, architects,

---

[78] e.g. *Ravnsborg* v. *Sweden*, § 30: 'the three alternative criteria laid down in [the Court's] case-law'; *Öztürk* v. *Germany*, § 54; *Lutz* v. *Germany*, § 54; *Bendenoun* v. *France*, § 61; in *Weber* v. *Switzerland*, § 33 et seq., however, the Court stated that the offence was 'criminal' in nature but nevertheless examined the third criterion.   [79] *Campbell and Fell*, § 71.
[80] *Ezeh and Connors* v. *United Kingdom (GC)*, § 86.   [81] *Bendenoun* v. *France*, § 61.
[82] *Engel and others* v. *Netherlands*; see also *Eggs* v. *Switzerland* Application 10313/83; *Borrelli* v. *Switzerland* Application 17571/90; *Sutter* v. *Switzerland*.
[83] *C* v. *United Kingdom* Application 11882/85; *Kremzow* v. *Austria* Application 16417/90; *Schatzmayr* v. *Austria* Application 32052/96. See also Application 26601/95; *Imam and other* v. *Greece* Application 29764/96; *Agko* v. *Greece* Application 31117/96; and *Dimitriadis* v. *Greece* Application 13877/88; *Leiningen-Westerburg* v. *Austria* Application 26601/95; *Jakobsson* v. *Sweden* Application 10878/84.   [84] *Campbell and Fell* v. *United Kingdom*.
[85] *Ravnsborg* v. *Sweden*; *Putz* v. *Austria*; cf. *Weber* v. *Switzerland*.
[86] Namely in connection with Art. 2 of Protocol No. 1, the right for parents to have their children educated in accordance with their own philosophical convictions, and Arts. 3 and 8 in connection with corporal punishment; see *Campbell and Cosans* v. *United Kingdom*; *Costello-Roberts* v. *United Kingdom*.
[87] e.g. *Wickramsinghe* v. *United Kingdom* Application 31503/96, decision of 9 Dec. 1997, unreported; and *Demmer* v. *Austria* Application 19130/91, decision of 28 Feb. 1994, unreported.

or lawyers.[88] They are bound, as a rule, by codes of professional ethics and sanctions may include reprimands, fines, suspension of the right to exercise the profession, or even withdrawal of the licence to practise. Usually special boards exist on which representatives of the profession sit together with lawyers to hear cases. There is no doubt that these are matters of a non-criminal nature.

Yet, the Court has nevertheless found ways and means to apply at least paragraph 1 of Article 6 to these proceedings. In *König*[89] it found that the determination of whether a medical doctor had behaved in violation of the code of conduct and whether he or she was to be suspended constituted a dispute as to his or her civil rights and obligations because they could lead to a prohibition, even though possibly limited in time, for the doctor to enter into private-law contracts with patients to whom he or she would extend their services. If, however, such disciplinary proceedings concerned, for example, a policeman who is found to have acted against the code of ethics and is dismissed, this does not concern civil rights and obligations nor an accusation in criminal matters, therefore, Article 6 does not apply.[90]

I must confess that I am not quite happy with this development and I find it difficult to approve. The inequality between members of liberal professions and public officials (*Beamte*) can, on the basis of the present Convention, only be eliminated by putting both categories on the same level. However, this is hard to reconcile with the case-law insofar as it does not regard disputes relating to the employment of public officials (*Beamte*) as concerning civil rights and obligations—nor is dismissal a sanction of a criminal character. Grabenwarter would, on the other hand, regard dismissal as a pecuniary sanction because it leads to a loss of salary.[91] I find this equally unsatisfactory because it would necessitate abandoning the concept of disciplinary sanctions entirely. On the other hand Grabenwarter rightly censures the Commission for regarding the sanction actually imposed as decisive rather than that which was at stake.[92]

F. Critical Appraisal of the Case-law of the Court

This discussion of the case-law on the characteristics of a 'criminal' charge has shown that the case-law itself does not excel in clarity and simplicity.[93] There are

---

[88] *Sjöström* v. *Sweden* Application 19853/92, decision of 12 Oct. 1994.

[89] *König* v. *Germany*. Cf. also *Gautrin and others* v. *France; Le Compte* v. *Belgium;* and *Albert* v. *Belgium.*

[90] *Otelo Saraiva de Carvalho* v. *Portugal* Application 9208/80 (1981) 26 DR 262, concerning an officer of the army transferred to the reserve.   [91] Grabenwarter (1997) 101.

[92] *Demmer* v. *Austria* Application 19130/91, decision of 28 Feb. 1994, unreported; *Bendenoun* v. *France; K* v. *Austria.*

[93] The criteria developed by the Court are also criticized by Frowein and Peukert (1996) Art. 6 N 50: they do not allow a clear distinction of the notion 'criminal'. Stavros (1993) 35 et seq. states that '[a] perusal of the reasoning of the relevant decisions reveals that policy, rather than legal considerations, usually determine what constitutes a "criminal charge" '. Furthermore, in his opinion, 'the protection afforded appears fragmented, often inconsistent and, one may say, incomplete'. For

numerous criteria and sub-criteria, but the relationship between these criteria is not obvious and there are a number of contradictions. The Court generally sticks to the three criteria although the first, admittedly, only provides a starting point. The second, the character of the offence, is the central point—this character is manifested not only by the nature of the misbehaviour and the norms which are infringed, but also in the type of sanctions which are incurred. In evaluating these elements the Court uses as a guideline the practice followed in the Contracting States. The third criterion, the gravity of the sanction, must be examined whenever the first two criteria do not permit a conclusion to be drawn.

The case-law could benefit from simplification. The first criterion ought to be dropped—at most it can be referred to in order to determine whether there are serious doubts (cf. the 'serious dispute' in civil cases) as to whether there exists a 'criminal' charge.

The second criterion ought to be the essential one. It would probably be preferable to take more clearly the 'criminal' charge as the rule and to define the exceptions. Such an exception prevails where the person concerned failed to observe a rule which applies to a limited number of persons who are subject to particularly strict control of the ethics of their behaviour by organs of the state: armed forces and civil servants, prison inmates, participants in court hearings, pupils at public schools, the liberal professions. The sanction must also be provided for in special legislation covering the specific profession or special situation. Deprivation or relatively strict restrictions on personal liberty will only be regarded as a typically disciplinary sanction in those situations where, at the outset, the liberty is restricted, such as in prisons and similar institutions, and in the army. I would also regard school detention—for example, for the afternoon—as being typically disciplinary. I am not aware of any case in which an offence other than one of a disciplinary nature was considered to fall outside the scope of Article 6. This is hardly an accident—I see no reason to extend the exception.

The *gravity* of the sanction ought to be dropped as a criterion with one exception: if it becomes obvious that the disciplinary label is designed to mask a criminal sanction. States enjoy a certain margin of appreciation when deciding whether and how to intervene in the case of a certain type of misbehaviour, with disciplinary means, with criminal law means, or with both. If an offence is disciplinary in character, the gravity of the sanction ought to change the character only if it appears downright arbitrary. The only example in the case-law which I would regard as falling under this category is *Campbell and Fell*. Here, where close to 600 days of remission were lost, it would have been possible to prosecute the applicants for the offence of 'assault occasioning actual bodily

him a more flexible approach appears desirable so that the 'entire range of administrative proceedings where penalties or quasi-penalties are imposed' is covered.

harm'. The authorities may find it easier to prosecute such an offence on the disciplinary level. If this is done, we are faced with an abuse and the autonomous notion of 'criminal' will apply.

III. THE NOTION OF 'CHARGE'

A. General Observations

The term 'criminal' denotes the type of dispute to which, together with those concerning 'civil rights and obligations', Articles 6 of the ECHR, 14 of the ICCPR, or 8 of the ACHR apply. Many decisions are taken, however, in the course of criminal proceedings and it is not necessary that each of them satisfy the requirements of that guarantee. On the other hand, the rights are definitely not limited to the trial hearing itself, although this is the central event in the process. There are two main issues which must be addressed. *First*, the limitations in time: when does the application of Article 6 of the ECHR, on which I shall concentrate for the reasons set out at the beginning of this chapter, begin, and when does it end; *second*, a distinction must be made between those parts of the proceedings to which it applies, and the other parts to which it does not.

The matter would be easy if clear-cut answers could be given. During the initial phase of the application of the Convention there was a dispute as to whether it applied to pre-trial proceedings or not.[94] This, though, is the wrong question; it is not possible to give a 'yes or no' answer. It is not difficult to identify more than a dozen different rights in Article 14 of the ICCPR and the corresponding guarantees in the other two treaties. The right to a public hearing clearly applies exclusively to the trial and to hearings on appeal. It is similarly clear that the right to be heard within a reasonable time is not restricted to the trial. The right to be informed of the accusation arises before the trial, the right to appeal proceedings afterwards. Finally, the Court regularly recalls that the fairness of proceedings falls to be assessed through an assessment of the proceedings as a whole.

Unfortunately, the Court does not seem to have realized, so far, that there is quite a difference between the question whether a person is charged or not and the question whether certain proceedings qualify as 'criminal'. It persistently uses the three-part criteria of the *Engel* judgment although, when one gets to ask whether a certain decision belongs to the determination of a (criminal) *charge*, this already presupposes a finding that one is within 'the criminal sphere'. This became particularly clear in *Phillips*.

---

[94] A positive answer was given by e.g. Poncet (1970) 418, 426, 434, 440; Poncet (1977) 31, 34, 132; Schubarth (1973) 263; and Schubarth (1975). For the opposite view, see e.g. H. Schultz's review of M. Schubarth, *Die Rechte des Beschuldigten im Untersuchungsverfahren, ZStrR* 91 (1975) 438, and H. Schultz's review of Hauser, *Kurzlehrbuch des schweizerischen Strafprozessrechts, ZStrR* 95 (1978) 452.

Mr Stephen Phillips had been convicted of drug offences. Following the conviction, a Customs and Excise-appointed drug financial investigation officer examined his financial situation in order to determine which of his assets were to be confiscated. The law contained a presumption which meant that the assets which he had acquired over the last six years were regarded as being the proceeds of the drug-trafficking offence, unless he could prove that in fact they were of 'innocent' origin. Mr Phillips declined to participate in those proceedings and eventually £91,400 was confiscated.

The Court first examined whether Article 6 § 2 applied and came to a negative result.[95] Then it determined that Article 6 § 1 did apply,[96] but held that there had been no violation.[97]

This example demonstrates the complexity of the issue; in fact most issues related to the interpretation of the notion 'charge' cannot usefully be dealt with, and are not dealt with here, in a general way but must be looked at in the context of the specific Article 6 guarantee at issue.

B. The Term 'Charge' as an Autonomous Notion

It is important that the term 'charge', as is the case in relation to the term 'criminal', be given an autonomous definition. Here it is necessary to recall again the issue of pre-trial proceedings. There is a clear possibility that states could postpone access to a lawyer, to the file, or perhaps even to the free assistance of an interpreter by organizing their criminal proceedings in such a way as to ensure that the formal 'charge' occurs at a very late point in the proceedings, i.e. at the close of the investigation. This could lead to a considerable reduction in the effectiveness of the guarantee. The Court has also repeated on many occasions that an autonomous notion is what it had in mind in the early judgments when it referred to 'the charge, as this word is understood within the meaning of the Convention'.[98] In *Deweer* the Court even made reference to 'the term "charge" which is very wide in scope'.[99]

C. Procedural Steps to which Article 6 Applies

Article 6 applies to all procedural steps which are directly relevant to the decision as to the guilt or innocence of the accused. This is expressed particularly clearly in the French text which speaks of the '*bien-fondé*' of the criminal charge. It begins with the police inquiry[100] and continues until the exhaustion of all domestic appeals, including those to the constitutional court.[101] The proceedings

---

[95] *Phillips* v. *United Kingdom*, §§ 28–35.   [96] Ibid., §§ 37–9.   [97] Ibid., §§ 40–7.
[98] *Neumeister* v. *Austria*, § 18. See also e.g. *Wemhoff* v. *Germany*, § 19; *Ringeisen* v. *Austria*, § 110; *Engel and others* v. *Netherlands*, § 81; *Deweer* v. *Belgium*, § 42; *Serves* v. *France*, § 42; *Hammern* v. *Norway* § 41.   [99] *Deweer* v. *Belgium*, § 42.
[100] See further Chapter 6, pp. 137 et seq below.
[101] *Gast and Popp* v. *Germany*, § 64; *Krcmár* v. *Czech Republic*, § 36; *Süssmann* v. *Germany*, § 39.

on the merits include those which are limited to the issue of the determination of the sentence.[102]

There is also an exception to the rule that Article 6 ceases to apply once a judgment becomes final. It concerns the execution of the judgment. The question arose in a rather extraordinary case, *Assanidze* v. *Georgia*. The applicant was still detained three years after his release had been ordered by a court. The Court rightly noted that: 'If the State administrative authorities could refuse or fail to comply with a judgment acquitting a defendant, or even delay in doing so, the Article 6 guarantees the defendant previously enjoyed during the judicial phase of the proceedings would become partly illusory'.[103]

D. Procedural Steps to which Article 6 Does Not Apply

1. Habeas Corpus Proceedings

There are a number of procedural steps to which Article 6 does not apply. The first issue arose in *Neumeister* v. *Austria*, where the Court said very clearly that it did not apply to habeas corpus proceedings. This finding is still valid and there are no indications of the Court changing its approach. However, the reasoning of the Court appears now to be partly outdated. Some members of the Commission had suggested that Article 6 might apply as 'civil rights and obligations' were at issue. To this the Court rightly answered 'that remedies relating to detention on remand undoubtedly belong to the realm of criminal law and that the text of the provision invoked expressly limits the requirement of a fair hearing to the determination . . . of any criminal charge, to which notion the remedies in question are obviously unrelated'. This confirms that the decisive element is the direct link to the decision on the guilt of the accused.

The Court, however, made the additional observation: 'Besides, Article 6 (1) does not merely require that the hearing should be fair, but also that it should be public. It is therefore impossible to maintain that the first requirement is applicable to the examination of requests for release without admitting the same to be true of the second. Publicity in such matters is not however in the interest of accused persons as it is generally understood.' This is indicative of an 'all or nothing' approach. Yet, while the Court adheres to the doctrine that the proceedings must be examined 'as a whole', it is clear that the public-hearing requirement is of limited application. Article 6 § 3(c) was applied to pre-trial proceedings and interpreted as including the right to communication between counsel and accused in private.[104] The idea that such communication ought to be 'public' is ridiculous. On the other hand, it is not obvious that habeas corpus proceedings should not be held in public. Even if one accepts that publicity would be undesirable, contrary to what was said by the Court, it is not

---

[102] Cf. e.g. *Phillips* v. *United Kingdom*, §§ 34, 39; *Malige* v. *France*.
[103] *Assanidze* v. *Georgia*, § 183.   [104] See e.g. *Can* v. *Austria*.

'impossible' to apply the basic rules of fairness contained in Article 6 but to exclude publicity—this is what happens in practice.[105]

2. Confiscation Orders

One case, mentioned above, concerned a confiscation order which was linked to a statutory presumption according to which '[i]n determining whether and to what extent the defendant has benefited from drug trafficking, section 4(2) and (3) of the 1994 [Drugs Trafficking] Act require the court to assume that any property appearing to have been held by the defendant at any time since his conviction or during the period of six years before the date on which the criminal proceedings were commenced was received as a payment or reward in connection with drug trafficking, and that any expenditure incurred by him during the same period was paid for out of the proceeds of drug trafficking'.[106]

To a large extent this case did not raise any new issues. The relevant precedent is *Raimondo* v. *Italy* which concerned the seizure and confiscation of assets belonging to a person suspected of being involved in organized crime. The relevant Italian law also contained a similar presumption.[107] In *Phillips*, however, the Court embarked upon a complicated and rather unhelpful examination of the applicability of Article 6 § 2. It decided that it was not applicable as there was no 'new charge'.[108] It then seemed to accept the severity of the sanction but added: 'However, the purpose of this procedure was not the conviction or acquittal of the applicant for any other drug-related offence'.[109] Furthermore, there was no entry in the register. And then the text is full of surprises, because the Court went on to confirm that the proceedings to assess the sum to be confiscated were 'analogous to the determination by a court of the amount of a fine or the length of a period of imprisonment to be imposed on a properly convicted offender'.[110]

The reader, aware of the uncontested fact that Article 6 also applies to the sentencing process, expects the Court to affirm the application of the provision. The Court, however, came to the opposite conclusion: 'Once an accused has properly been proved guilty of that offence, Article 6 § 2 can have no application in relation to allegations made about the accused's character and conduct as part of the sentencing process, unless such accusations are of such a nature and degree as to amount to the bringing of a new "charge" within the autonomous Convention meaning'.[111]

I disapprove of this finding in two respects. First, as far as the theoretical aspect goes, I do not agree that, in view of the impressive development of the case-law, it is still possible to rely on *Engel* as an authority on Article 6 § 2. The

---

[105] See further Chapter 18 below. [106] *Phillips* v. *United Kingdom*, § 21.
[107] *Raimondo* v. *Italy*, § 18. [108] *Phillips* v. *United Kingdom*, § 32. [109] Ibid., § 34.
[110] Ibid. [111] Ibid., § 35, referring to *Engel and others* v. *Netherlands*, § 90.

guarantee has been given a wide interpretation, rather wider than that of the right to a fair trial. How is it possible today to affirm that the presumption of innocence does not apply in the context of fixing the sentence while it applies in proceedings on compensation and costs? I cannot accept the idea that it does not apply at all, although I do accept that it is possible to discuss whether there was a violation in this case.

This is the second point on which I disagree—in my view Article 6 § 2 did not only apply but was also violated. It should be noted that the statute at issue covers the entire financial situation of the person convicted over the last six years. In the present case this goes back several years before the applicant committed the acts of which he was convicted. He had not been previously found guilty of any other drugs offences. Thus, the proceedings implicitly but unmistakably presumed that Mr Phillips had committed drug offences besides and before those for which he was tried, which were never the object of any proceedings. In my view this constitutes a clear violation of Article 6 § 2.

Another application which was declared inadmissible shows a rather restrictive attitude towards the presumption of innocence. The applicant was suspected of having driven a car without a driver's licence, an offence which he had earlier been convicted of. The sanctions imposed on him, before the judgment became final, included, *inter alia*, the confiscation and sale of his car. The Court, in examining whether this was compatible with Article 6 § 2, looked at the reasoning of the domestic court. There it was said 'that the suspicion against the applicant had not been dissipated at the trial'.[112] While the Court's finding is, at the very least, doubtful, it is nevertheless satisfying to note that the guarantee was applied without any discussion.

3. Immediate Confiscation of a Driving Licence

It is not uncommon for legal provisions to provide for the immediate confiscation of a driving licence following serious traffic offences which raise doubts as to whether a driver ought to be allowed on the street, for example, in accidents which had lethal consequences or which were caused by a driver under the influence of alcohol or other drugs. This was the case in *Escoubet*. The Court came to the conclusion that there was no criminal charge as the confiscation was ordered before any proceedings were started.[113] Its purpose under domestic law was 'to take a dangerous driver off the roads for a specific period of time'.[114] It was merely a precautionary measure, not linked to any finding of guilt.[115] Finally, it was also limited in time to fifteen days. Article 6 therefore did not apply.

---

[112] *Schmelzer* v. *Germany* Application 45176/99, decision of 12 Dec. 2000, unreported.
[113] *Escoubet* v. *Belgium*, § 35.   [114] Ibid., § 33.   [115] Ibid., § 37.

4. Proceedings in Relation to a Retrial

The aim of criminal proceedings is a final and definite judgment. This occurs after all remedies have been exhausted or withdrawn or when the time limit to file an appeal has expired. Once a judgment is final, there is no room for further proceedings under Article 6,[116] for instance there is no presumption of innocence any more. However, once the right to a retrial has been granted, all the guarantees of Article 6 apply to this new trial.

5. Extradition Proceedings

If a state requests the extradition of a person from another state, this presupposes that that person has been charged with a criminal offence. Still, extradition proceedings are not covered by Article 6 because the person concerned is not charged under the jurisdiction of the requested state.[117]

6. Proceedings for Challenging the Impartiality of a Judge

Preliminary proceedings which concern the question of whether a judge can be regarded as independent and impartial in a specific case do not determine the merits of that case and Article 6 therefore does not apply.[118]

IV. RIGHTS OF THE VICTIM

A. The Starting Point

The relevant texts indicate quite clearly the person who shall benefit from the procedural guarantees in criminal proceedings, namely, everyone: '[i]n the determination of any criminal charge against him' (ICCPR, Art. 14 §§ 1 and 3; ECHR, Art. 6 § 1); '[e]veryone charged with a criminal offence' (ICCPR, Art. 14 § 2; ECHR Art. 6 §§ 2 and 3); '[e]very person . . . in the substantiation of any accusation of a criminal nature made against him' (IACHR, Art. 8 § 1); '[e]very person accused of a criminal offence' (IACHR, Art. 8 § 2); 'the accused' (IACHR, Art. 8 § 2(a), (b), (d), (e)); 'the defence' (IACHR, Art. 8 § 3 (f)). The drafters seem to have had no doubt: the only persons involved in criminal proceedings who are entitled to protection are those who are accused of an offence. Accordingly, for a long time all applications by the victim were rejected

---

[116] *X* v. *Austria* Application 864/60 (1962) 9 CD 17 at 21; *X* v. *Austria* Application 1237/6 (1962) 5 Yb 96 at 102; *X* v. *Austria* Application 7761/77 (1978) 14 DR 171 at 173; *AB* v. *Germany* 11863/85, decision of 4 May 1987, unreported; *Fischer* v. *Austria* 27569/02, decision of 6 May 2003, unreported; *Wehrlé and Lauber* v. *Germany* 11360/03, 12 June 2003; and countless others.
[117] See e.g. *Mamatkulov and Abdurasulovic* v. *Turkey*, § 80.
[118] *Schreiber and Boetsch* v. *France*, decision on admissibility of 11 Dec. 2003, unreported; the case concerned civil proceedings.

as being inadmissible *ratione personae.*[119] This principle has been repeatedly confirmed in the European case-law: the Convention does not 'confer any rights . . . to "private revenge" '.[120]

B. Inconsistencies

This unilateral approach is not entirely consistent with some aspects of the case-law and the general attitude, in current thinking, *vis-à-vis* the victim.

First, the Court has recognized that the Convention not only obliges states to refrain from actively violating fundamental rights, but also requires them to take positive steps for protective action. It found support for this view in the wording of Article 1 according to which the parties 'shall secure' the rights set out in the Convention to everyone under their jurisdiction.[121] One of the leading cases in this field was brought by a father and his mentally handicapped daughter, who had been sexually assaulted by a person who did not belong to the staff of the institution where she was cared for.[122] It turned out that there was a lacuna in the Dutch criminal code—the perpetrator of the deed could not be punished. The Court concluded that this constituted a violation of the right to respect for her private life under Article 8. In relation to the position of a victim in criminal proceedings this means that the victim may have a right under the Convention that the offender is prosecuted and punished if guilty. At the same time, the same victim is, however, deprived of any procedural right. This raises an issue under Article 13, the right to an effective remedy to which everyone who has an arguable claim that he is a victim of a violation of a Convention right is entitled.

Second, an application is admissible only after prior exhaustion of domestic remedies (ECHR, Art. 34 § 1). The remedies to be exhausted must be effective, they can be of any kind, civil, administrative, or criminal.[123] As a result, an individual may be required, under the Convention, to pursue criminal proceedings, but at the same time lacking any procedural rights in those same proceedings.

Third, the Court has recognized the value of criminal prosecution for the protection of human rights in its case-law on Articles 2 and 3. It interprets the Convention as containing an obligation on states to engage upon an effective investigation and, as the case may be, criminal prosecution whenever a person

---

[119] See e.g. Vogler (1986) Art. 6 N 240 with further references.

[120] *Perez* v. *France*, § 70. See also *Helmers* v. *Sweden*, § 27; *Tolstoy Miloslavsky* v. *United Kingdom*, § 58; *Windsor* v. *United Kingdom* Application 13081/87, 14 Dec. 1998, unreported; *German Buitrago Montes and Jorge Perez Lopez* v. *United Kingdom* Application 18077/91, 2 Dec. 1992, unreported, where the question was dealt with under Art. 13.

[121] *Ireland* v. *United Kingdom*, § 239. See also Alkema (1988); Villiger (1991); Fleiner-Gerster (1983). [122] *X and Y* v. *Netherlands*.

[123] Etienne Picard (1985) 591 at 596; Frowein and Peukert (1996) Art. 26 N 23; Harris, O'Boyle and Warbrick (1995) 608–9; van Dijk and van Hoof (1998) 140, etc.

has died under suspicious circumstances or a *prima facie* case of ill-treatment at the hands of persons acting for the authorities has been made—these are the procedural aspects of the guarantees.[124] Yet, there is no right under Article 6 to pursue this guarantee in criminal proceedings against the perpetrator(s).

Fourth, a general trend in criminal policy has to some extent shifted the focus of the attention from the criminal to the victim. This can be observed in the science of criminology which, from its origins in the early nineteenth century, examined criminals and the influence of environmental factors on the development of criminality. Since World War II, under the label of victimology, the victim has become a subject of interest and research.[125] In some countries special legislation for the protection of victims of crime has been passed.[126]

In view of these developments, the fact that international instruments for the protection of human rights should leave the victim without any rights in proceedings against the suspected criminal is not only highly unsatisfactory but also rather antiquated. Political bodies have become aware of this. The Committee of Ministers of the Council of Europe has adopted a number of Recommendations on the subject. R(83)7 calls for legal aid for victims; R(85)11 recommends a number of rights, including the right to be informed of the date and place of the hearing and of the outcome of the proceedings; R(87)21 invites Member States to ensure that victims receive assistance during the criminal process and Rec(2000) 19 says that victims ought to be able to challenge decisions not to prosecute.[127]

There is no way round the fact that the specific rights of the defence do not benefit victims. The question is, then, to what extent victims can invoke procedural guarantees in the context of a determination concerning 'civil rights and obligations' or a 'suit at law' or 'rights and obligations of a civil, labor, fiscal or any other nature'.[128] The references indicate that this problem is not specific to the European Convention.

C. The Case-law Prior to *Perez* v. *France*

The chain of cases dealing with the question under consideration starts with *Moreira de Azevedo*. The applicant had availed himself of the possibility of taking part in the criminal proceedings as '*assistente*' against his brother-in-law who had shot him in the head. As he had not presented a claim for damages at the same time, the Commission had come to the conclusion that there had been

---

[124] See e.g. Sudre (2003) 232; Reed and Murdoch (2001) 4.27, 4.28; Grabenwarter (2003) § 20 N 14, 15; Starmer (1999) N 5.28/29.

[125] Kaiser (1996) § 47 N 3; Killias (2002); Kunz (2001) § 26 N 24.

[126] e.g. for Germany: *Opferschutzgesetz* of 18 Dec. 1986, BGBl I 2496; Switzerland: *Bundesgesetz über die Hilfe an Opfer von Straftaten* of 4 Oct. 1991, SR 312.5; Italy: *Norme a favore delle vittime del terrorismo e della criminalità organizzata, Legge 20 ottobre 1990*, n. 302.

[127] Quoted from *Perez* v. *France*, §§ 26–9.

[128] Texts quoted from ECHR, Art. 6 § 1; ICCPR, Art. 14 § 1; and ACHR, Art. 8 § 1.

no '*contestation*' regarding civil rights and obligations.[129] The Court, however, recalled that 'the right to a fair trial holds so prominent a place in a democratic society that there can be no justification for interpreting Article 6 para. 1 of the Convention restrictively' and that the term '*contestation*' had no equivalent in the English text. It also referred to a judgment of the Portuguese Supreme Court according to which 'to intervene as an *assistente* is equivalent to filing a claim for compensation in civil proceedings'. In fact, once criminal proceedings were under way it was possible to bring (separate) civil proceedings 'only where no action ha[d] been taken in the criminal proceedings for six months or more'.[130]

This legal particularity is also an element of French law. It is usually expressed by the sentence '*le pénal tient le civil en état*' (civil proceedings must await the outcome of criminal proceedings).[131] Therefore, a private party to criminal proceedings claiming damages could rely on Article 6 § 1.[132]

Surprisingly, the Court departed from these precedents, which had enabled the victim to benefit from Article 6, in *Hamer* where the applicant had not presented a claim for damages in the criminal proceedings but was nevertheless required to await their outcome before she could bring proceedings in the civil court. The critical argument was that the result of the criminal proceedings in this case was not decisive for the civil claim.[133]

In the next case, *Aït-Mouhoub*, Article 6 was again found to apply because the applicant had claimed damages even though he had not quantified his loss. The Court also found that the outcome of the criminal proceedings was decisive for his prospects in the criminal proceedings.[134] The latter point, if compared to *Hamer*, is not entirely convincing because the Court only referred to the fact that a conviction of the defendant would have allowed Mr Aït-Mouhoub to obtain compensation in the following civil proceedings. The same could have been said for Ms Hamer. Finally, the case of *Maini* was very similar to *Aït-Mouhoub* except that here the criminal proceedings had ended with a decision of 'no case to answer' ('*non-lieu*') and had thus extinguished the victim's prospects of success in further civil proceedings.[135]

Summing up, two conditions have to be met for a victim to be able to invoke Article 6 as a participant in criminal proceedings: he or she has to claim damages, even though the *quantum* must not necessarily be specified; and the criminal proceedings must have led to, or been aimed at, a result which could be regarded as decisive for the plaintiff's prospects of actually obtaining damages.[136] In view of *Hamer* the second point could be regarded as somewhat confused.

---

[129] *Moreira de Azevedo* v. *Portugal*, §§ 66, 67.
[130] Article 30 of the code of criminal procedure in force at the time in Portugal.
[131] Article 4 § 2 of the French code of criminal procedure; see *Perez* v. *France*, § 60.
[132] *Tomasi* v. *France*, § 212; the Court arrived at same result using more traditional reasoning in *Acquaviva* v. *France*, §§ 46, 47.   [133] *Hamer* v. *France*, §§ 77, 78.
[134] *Aït-Mouhoub* v. *France*, §§ 44, 45.   [135] *Maini* v. *France*, §§ 27–30.
[136] See also *Perez* v. *France*, § 54.

D. The Judgment in *Perez* v. *France*

In a rare display of self-criticism, the Court seized the opportunity offered by the *Perez* case to find in its prior case-law a tendency 'to over-complicate'. It conceded that its approach to cases where the criminal proceedings were still pending was particularly difficult, and promised 'to end the uncertainty'.[137]

As a first step[138] it stressed that it must also take into account the domestic law and it analysed the French law which offers the victim an option between civil and criminal proceedings. A victim who, as a civil party, claims damages in criminal proceedings is automatically recognized as a plaintiff within the meaning of Article 6. In other words, in comparison with the prior case-law it is not necessary any more to establish separately that the criminal proceedings are 'decisive' for the civil action.

Under French law it is also possible for the victim to participate in criminal proceedings as *'partie civile'* without claiming damages. The Court did not regard this as causing particular problems. Leaving aside its tendencies towards judicial self-restraint, it found that in fact all victims taking part in civil proceedings are entitled to claim compensation, even at a late stage in the proceedings. In fact, according to the Court who contradicted the Government, 'French law does not necessarily create a dichotomy between "civil-party proceedings" and a "civil claim"; the former is in reality only a type of the latter'.[139]

Returning to the line of argument used in *Moreira de Azevedo*, the Court also dispensed with the requirement of an actual claim for damages as a prerequisite for a *'contestation'*; 'by acquiring the status of civil parties, victims demonstrate the importance they attach not only to the criminal conviction of the offender but also to securing financial reparation for the damage sustained'.[140] Even 'where criminal proceedings are determinative only of a criminal charge', the Court continued, it is not impossible to regard them as civil proceedings for the victim, provided the civil component remains closely connected with the criminal one, whatever this means. Up to this point, one may have expected an actual turn in the case-law, and a conclusion that whenever victims take part in criminal proceedings they will enjoy the protection of Article 6 § 1.

However, the Court apparently did not find the courage to go that far. Article 6 is not to apply, it added, if the victim pursues 'purely punitive purposes'. At the very least, his or her intervention 'must be indissociable from the victim's exercise of a right to bring civil proceedings in domestic law, even if only to secure symbolic reparation or to protect a civil right such as the right to a "good reputation"'. Somewhat cryptically it added that 'the waiver of such a right must be established, where appropriate, in an unequivocal manner'.[141]

The Court believed that it had thus taken account of the victims' interests in a satisfactory way. It recalled that the Convention gives somewhat extended rights

[137] *Perez* v. *France* §§ 55, 56.   [138] Ibid., §§ 58 et seq.   [139] Ibid., § 63.
[140] Ibid., § 64.   [141] Ibid., § 70.

to the defence but that 'does not mean that the Court can ignore the plight of victims and downgrade their rights'.[142]

E. A Critical Appraisal

The effort of the Court to strengthen the position of the victim in criminal proceedings certainly merits approval, in particular as it also purported to simplify the law. Still, the judgment in *Perez* also leaves a number of questions open and stops short of offering a real solution to the problem.

A *first* question relates to the narrow connection which the Court establishes between its new doctrine and the domestic law. According to its own approach, this judgment is only applicable in France. Was the promise to simplify the case-law fulfilled in view of the fact that apparently a new examination must be undertaken for each of the other forty plus legal systems to which the Convention applies? Would it not have been possible—and certainly preferable—to establish autonomous rules to be applied uniformly throughout the Council of Europe? After all, the Recommendations of the Committee of Ministers to which the Court refers have this aspiration.

Second, one may wonder what the reference to a waiver in paragraph 70 means. Does it hide some sort of presumption? Would this mean that Article 6 applies unless the victim who takes part in the criminal proceedings has, in an unequivocal manner, waived the right to financial compensation? Such an approach would certainly be a long way from what is practically happening in the courts.

The Court also stated that the Convention gives no right to an '*actio popularis*'; but what is the link of the rights of the victims to *actio popularis*? There is no suggestion that persons not individually affected by a crime should be given any rights to act as a party in criminal proceedings.

Finally, the Court, in my view, overestimated the economic interests of people. It seemed to doubt that a victim would reasonably take part in criminal proceedings without having financial compensation in mind. This is particularly surprising if one takes into account the Court's own practice in connection with the right to compensation under Article 41. In that context it often concludes that the finding of a violation constitutes sufficient satisfaction. In analogy, the conviction of the suspect will often, or at least sometimes, constitute an important satisfaction to the victim. The Court also seemed fully to disregard the fact that typically damages awarded to a victim remain symbolic because the convict is devoid of any financial means. Should this empty, virtual, unreal claim make all the difference?

I find the distinction proposed by the Court rather formalistic. Victims of crime have a legitimate interest—and the Court seems to accept this—to take

---

[142] Ibid., § 72.

---

part in proceedings against a suspect. Whether they do so for financial or moral motives should make no difference. There is, in my view, no convincing reason not to recognize the interest in having the perpetrator of a crime convicted as a 'civil right' within the meaning of Article 6 of the Convention. I stress that this proposal concerns conviction and consciously excludes sentencing. In my view, and contrary to what appears to be the rule in the United States, I regard sentencing as the sole province of the state. Here the states are free to decide whether vindictive aspirations of the victim ought or ought not to be allowed to be heard and taken into account.[143]

It must also be kept in mind, however, that 'only' the rights under Article 6 § 1 are at issue, not the specific rights of paragraphs 2 and 3 which must clearly be reserved for the accused even though they may also be referred to in civil proceedings in the interpretation of the term 'fair'.[144] In particular the presumption of innocence cannot, of course, benefit both parties. From the outset the victim will have to accept the fact that any remaining doubt in establishing the facts will benefit the accused.[145] However, the rights to be assisted by an interpreter and counsel might apply.

I am not, however, proposing an absolute right of the victim to *initiate* criminal proceedings as a form of 'right of access to court'. To the extent that there is a possibility immediately to initiate civil proceedings for damages, the victim cannot complain of a refusal by the public prosecutor to institute criminal proceedings provided that it is financial compensation the victim is after. I therefore agree with the Court's finding in *Assenov*.[146]

---

[143] The Commission declared inadmissible an application which claimed the right to participate in the sentencing of a mother whose daughter had been murdered; *McCourt* v. *United Kingdom* Application 20433/92 (1993) 15 EHRR 110; the application was dealt with under Art. 8.

[144] *Albert and Le Compte* v. *Belgium*, § 39; *Dombo Beheer* v. *Netherlands*, § 32.

[145] See further Chapter 7 below.   [146] *Assenov* v. *Bulgaria*, §§ 108–12.

Part Two

The General Fair Trial Guarantees

Chapter 3

The Right to an Independent and Impartial Tribunal

I. INTRODUCTION

A. The Texts

...everyone shall be entitled to a...hearing by a competent, independent and impartial tribunal established by law...

ICCPR, Art. 14 § 1

...everyone is entitled to a...hearing...by an independent and impartial tribunal established by law.

ECHR, Art. 6 § 1

Every person has the right to a hearing...by a competent, independent, and impartial tribunal, previously established by law

ACHR, Art. 8 § 1

These texts show a great similarity. The essential elements are common to all and are set out in the same terms: 'tribunal', 'independent', 'impartial', and 'established by law'. In addition, the ICCPR and the ACHR also require that the tribunal be 'competent', a requirement which, under the ECHR, can be interpreted as being included in the term 'established by law'.

B. The Origins of the Guarantee

The words 'independent and impartial tribunal' were used in the first draft of the UDHR which was written by René Cassin.[1] At one point the United Kingdom proposed a text which dropped the word 'independent', but Mr Cassin, charged with incorporating the amendments, reinserted it—without, it seems, any discussion.[2] In a later draft, also prepared by Mr Cassin, 'tribunal' is replaced by 'court', but in the final version the word 'tribunal' reappeared.[3]

---

[1] Weissbrodt (2001) 13.   [2] Ibid., 14, 15.   [3] Ibid., 17, 33.

In discussions on the drafting of the Covenant, an early version proposed by the United States in 1947 referred to a 'competent and impartial tribunal', but in the draft of the Working Group the word 'independent' turned up again and remained in the text.[4]

The words 'established by law' can be traced back to a proposal by the Chilean delegate, Mr Sages. He suggested that the tribunal must also be 'regular', i.e. 'pre-established'. Although this proposal was not adopted,[5] at the end of this fifth session of the Commission, the words 'established by law' were added after 'tribunal'.[6]

Finally, during the eighth session, Mr Jevremovic from Yugoslavia suggested adding the word 'competent'. Mr Cassin was opposed to this, but the Commission nevertheless decided to adopt the proposal.[7]

C. The Importance of the Right to an Independent and Impartial Tribunal

By far the most important guarantee enshrined in Article 6 is that to an independent and impartial tribunal established by law. It is probably also one of the most important guarantees of the whole Convention. In fact, there are two aspects to this guarantee. On the one hand it is an individual human right which ensures that disputes in which the individual is involved are decided by a neutral authority. On the other hand, however, it has also an institutional aspect of constitutional importance: it lays the foundation for what has been labelled, since Montesquieu, the third power in a state after the legislative and the executive. While the right to free elections under Article 3 of the First Protocol protects the foundations of democracy, the guarantee to an independent and impartial tribunal lays the foundations for the rule of law.[8]

It does not seem necessary to enter into a long argument in order to establish that without independent courts there can be no rule of law. One may even wonder whether the law itself can have any real existence in the absence of the judiciary. In fact, an examination of the development of Roman law, leads to the conclusion that the judges (in particular the *praetor*) contributed more to the development of the law than the legislature. Judge-made law is still an essential ingredient of the law in Anglo-Saxon countries and by no means unimportant on the European continent.[9]

The fact that the guarantee of an independent and impartial tribunal is the essential element in Article 6 of the ECHR is not just a theoretical concept. It can also be seen reflected in the case-law. In particular, it is always the first element to be examined in a case brought under Article 6. If it turns out that a

---

[4] Weissbrodt (2001), 45, 46.   [5] Ibid., 51, 52.   [6] Ibid., 54.
[7] Ibid., 64.   [8] For Kuijer (2004) 452 the guarantee belongs to the *ordre public*.
[9] *Kruslin* v. *France*, § 29; *Huvig* v. *France*, § 28.

tribunal does not conform to the requirements of Article 6, there will be no further examination of the proceedings—proceedings before a tribunal which does not satisfy the criteria of independence and impartiality can never be fair and there is thus no reason either to examine whether a hearing before such a tribunal was held in public or within reasonable time.[10]

The guarantee was originally and mainly conceived as a protection against special jurisdictions, in particular tribunals set up, sometimes even *ex post*, for the purpose of trying one or a series of cases with political overtones. The HRC referred to this in its General Comment: 'The Committee notes the existence, in many countries, of military or special courts which try civilians. This could present serious problems as far as the equitable, impartial and independent administration of justice is concerned. Quite often the reason for the establishment of such courts is to enable exceptional procedures to be applied which do not comply with normal standards of justice'.[11]

The HRC also insists that the right is absolute and not subject to any exceptions.[12]

D. The Definition of 'Tribunal'

While the Court has, on a number of occasions, attempted to define the term 'tribunal', which must of course be given an autonomous meaning, these definitions have not really become important factors in the case-law. In *Belilos*,[13] to give but one example, we read this: 'According to the Court's case-law, a "tribunal" is characterised in the substantive sense of the term by its judicial function, that is to say determining matters within its competence on the basis of rules of law and after proceedings conducted in a prescribed manner . . . It must also satisfy a series of further requirements—independence, in particular of the executive; impartiality; duration of its members' terms of office; guarantees afforded by its procedure—several of which appear in the text of Article 6 § 1 itself . . .'. It is thus quite obvious that the 'definition' is to some extent superfluous in that properties which, according to the text of

---

[10] See e.g. *Demicoli* v. *Malta*, § 43; *Findlay* v. *United Kingdom*, § 80; *Incal* v. *Turkey*, § 74; *Özertikoglu* v. *Turkey*, § 25; *Çiraklar* v. *Turkey*, §§ 44, 45 et seq. There are, unfortunately, also exceptions to this rule, e.g. *Coëme* v. *Belgium*, § 80 with a dissenting opinion of Judge Lorenzen joined by Judges Rozakis and Baka; an exception is permitted in relation to the length of proceedings. A very important exception is *Öcalan* v. *Turkey* where many other points are then dealt with in detail, not the least for didactical reasons, one may assume. There is also a strong argument for nevertheless addressing the issue of the excessive length of proceedings in the context of compensation under Art. 41.

[11] HRC, General Comment 13, Art. 14 (21st Session, 1984), Compilation of General Comments and General Recommendations Adopted by Human Rights Treaty Bodies, UN Doc. HRI/GEN/1/Rev. 1 at 14 (1994), § 4.   [12] *González del Río* v. *Peru*.

[13] *Belilos* v. *Switzerland*, § 64. See also *Ringeisen* v. *Austria*, § 95; *Sramek* v. *Austria*, § 36; *Benthem* v. *Netherlands*, § 40 et seq.; *Le Compte, Van Leuven and De Meyere* v. *Belgium*, § 55; *H* v. *Belgium*, § 50; *Demicoli* v. *Malta*, § 3; *Beaumartin* v. *France*, § 38.

Article 6 § 1 are attached to the term, are here referred to as elements of its definition.

The essential point is that the Court does not give much importance to the label which is attached to the institutions that function as a court.[14] It is also acceptable for the body concerned to serve a variety of non-judicial purposes.[15]

E. The References to a Judge, a Tribunal, or a Court in the Convention

While the present Chapter will limit itself to the notion of tribunal as used in Article 6 of the Convention, it may be useful to recall that similar references are found elsewhere in the Convention.[16] Article 2 § 1, the unfortunate and now obsolete acceptance of the death penalty, refers to a 'sentence of a court'. Paragraph 1(a) of Article 5 refers to 'the competent court'; the 'lawful order of a court' comes up in paragraph 1(b), while paragraph 1(c) mentions arrest or detention for 'the purpose of bringing him before the competent legal authority'. Furthermore, according to paragraph 3, a person arrested must be brought before a 'judge or other officer authorised by law to exercise judicial power', and paragraph 4 gives the right to have the lawfulness of an arrest decided by a court. Finally, Article 2 of Protocol No. 7 guarantees to everyone convicted of a criminal offence by a 'tribunal' the right to have his conviction or sentence reviewed by a higher 'tribunal'.

With one possible exception it can be assumed that the qualities of the court prescribed in Article 6 also apply to these Articles and paragraphs.[17]

The exception concerns Article 5 § 3. This is not the proper place to discuss that matter. It is sufficient to recall that in *Schiesser* the Court seemed to accept that at least the 'other officer' could be a magistrate offering a reduced quality of independence and impartiality.[18] As *Schiesser* was later overruled,[19] it may be

---

[14] To give but a few examples, in *Ringeisen* v. *Austria*, § 95, a body called 'Regional commission' qualified as 'tribunal'; in *H* v. *Belgium*, § 50, the council of the order (of the Bar) qualified. See also *Campbell and Fell* v. *United Kingdom*, § 76 ('Board of Visitors'); *Sramek* v. *Austria*, § 36 ('Regional Authority'); *Demicoli* v. *Malta*, § 40 (House of Representatives). However, in *Belilos* v. *Switzerland*, § 65, the Court held that some terms (in the particular case, 'administrative authority') 'provide an important indication as to the nature of the body in question'.

[15] *H* v. *Belgium*, § 50; this was already implicit in *Campbell and Fell* v. *United Kingdom*, §§ 33 and 81.   [16] A similar count for the Covenant and the ACHR is not called for here.

[17] *De Wilde, Ooms and Versyp* v. *Belgium*, § 78: 'In all these different cases it denotes bodies which exhibit not only common fundamental features, of which the most important is independence of the executive and of the parties to the case . . . but also the guarantees of judicial procedure'. The Court pointed out that the form of the procedure need not always be the same. In *Neumeister* v. *Austria*, § 24 the term 'court'—in Art. 5 § 4—is defined for the first time: 'This term implies only that the authority called upon to decide thereon must possess a judicial character, that is to say, be independent both of the executive and of the parties to the case . . .'. *De Wilde, Ooms and Versyp* and *Neumeister* are later quoted in many judgments which discuss the term 'court' in the context of Art. 6 § 1 (see e.g. *Le Compte, Van Leuven and De Meyere* v. *Belgium*, § 55; and *Ringeisen* v. *Germany*, § 95).   [18] *Schiesser* v. *Switzerland*, § 29.

[19] *Huber* v. *Switzerland*, § 42 et seq.

asserted that nowadays even this 'other officer' has to be independent and impartial.

On the other hand, the Convention also refers to authorities which are clearly not required to show the same characteristics as the court. These are, on the one hand, the 'national authority' before which everyone whose rights and freedoms are violated shall have an effective remedy under Article 13, and, on the other hand, the 'competent authority' which is to control decisions of expulsion under Article 1 of Protocol No. 7.

F. The Relationship Between the Requirements of 'Independence', 'Impartiality', and 'Established by Law'

Before discussing the case-law on the issue under consideration, it might be useful to examine the relationship between 'independence', 'impartiality', and 'established by law'. It is a matter which has been discussed in scholarly writing and opinions are by no way unanimous. Some authors, and I tend to agree with them, say that they overlap and can hardly be distinguished in a clear way.[20] Others stress that they are different notions which must be distinguished.[21]

According to the general approach taken by the Court in the interpretation of the Convention, the first issue to be examined is whether the tribunal was 'established by law'—if this requirement is not met, there is no purpose in continuing to examine any of the other elements.[22] However, the Court does not apply such rules with much rigour, particularly in the context of Article 6. In *Oberschlick*, for example, it does not stop to assess whether the Vienna Court of Appeal was composed in accordance with the law, in this case Article 489 § 3 of the Code of Criminal Procedure, according to which a judge who has previously dealt with the case may not sit on the merits, but went on to mingle this question with the substantive issue of impartiality.[23] In fact, it clearly amalgamated the two aspects.

As to independence and impartiality, it is of course possible to describe separately what is meant by these terms. 'Independence' means essentially the lack of subordination to any other organ of the state, in particular to the executive. It could be said that independence reflects the constitutional position of the judiciary. Still, independence must also exist as far as higher judicial bodies are concerned. It is certainly no problem if courts are expected to respect precedents of higher courts. However, it would not be compatible with independence

[20] See e.g. Danelius (1997) 151.

[21] Van Dijk and van Hoof (1998) 451; Veldt (1997) 60 recognizes, however, that the distinction is often very difficult and criticizes the Court for its inconsistent terminology.

[22] Cf. e.g. *Rotaru* v. *Romania*, § 62, with a separate opinion of Judge Lorenzen; *Pfeifer and Plankl* v. *Austria*, Report of the Commission (1990) in Series A, No. 227, p. 25, § 62.

[23] *Oberschlick* v. *Austria*, § 49 et seq.; the distinction is drawn more clearly in the report of the Commission on the same application, p. 47, § 99.

if a higher court were competent to give orders to a lower court as to how a specific case should be dealt with.

'Impartiality', on the other hand, relates to the specific case at issue and essentially it is this part of the guarantee which constitutes the protection of human rights: it means that the judge is not biased in favour of either party. He or she must be, as it were, free to float hither and thither between the positions of the parties and finally reach a decision at the place which, in correct application of the rules of jurisprudence, marks the just solution. It follows, that for the individual the essential feature is not the independence but the impartiality of the judge. In fact, if he or she is not independent, this means that the judge is not free to find the solution but is under some influence. I do not regard it as decisive that this influence, in the case of a lack of impartiality, stems from another state organ rather than one of the parties. If a judge is not independent, there is definitely a suspicion that he or she will not be impartial, but this is not necessarily so—it may be that in a specific case the dependence is irrelevant. If, however, a judge is partial, he or she is not fit to sit, and it is immaterial whether he or she is independent or not.

It appears that the European Court of Human Rights itself does not attach much importance to the distinction. In *Findlay* v. *United Kingdom*[24] it states: 'The concepts of independence and objective impartiality are closely linked and the Court will consider them together as they relate to the present case'.[25]

II. A TRIBUNAL ESTABLISHED BY LAW

Why must tribunals be established by law? Again we are led back to the essential function of the judiciary. It can only serve the rule of law if it is itself rooted in the law.[26] As the Commission put it in its report in *Zand* v. *Austria*: '[T]he judicial organisation in a democratic society must not depend on the discretion of the Executive, but should be regulated by law emanating from Parliament'.[27] It appears that here the term 'law' falls to be interpreted in a stricter way than elsewhere in the Convention. Normally, 'law' refers to any norm of general

[24] *Findlay* v. *United Kingdom*, § 73. This formulation is regularly quoted later on in the Court's case-law, verbatim or not; see e.g. *McGonnell* v. *United Kingdom*, § 48; *Incal* v. *Turkey*, § 65; *Çiraklar* v. *Turkey*, § 38 (in this decision the Court points out that '[i]n the instant case it is difficult to dissociate impartiality from independence').

[25] The distinction between independence and impartiality is also missing in most of the further decisions relating to *Incal* and *Çiraklar* (without any comment): *Sener* v. *Turkey*, §§ 56 et seq.; *Gerger* v. *Turkey*, §§ 60 et seq.; *Okçuoglu* v. *Turkey*, §§ 57 et seq.; *Karatas* v. *Turkey*, §§ 61 et seq.; *Sürek and Özdemir* v. *Turkey*, §§ 77 et seq.; *Sürek* v. *Turkey (Nos. 1–4)*, §§ 74 et seq., 52 et seq., 53 et seq., and 72 et seq. respectively; *Baskaya and Okçuoglu* v. *Turkey*, §§ 78 et seq. In all of these cases a military officer was as such a member of the court.

[26] For the definition of 'law', see further Chapters 9 and 17 below.

[27] *Zand* v. *Austria* Application 7360/76.

application, the Court does not usually examine whether it was passed by Parliament or whether it was adopted by the Government or any other body. I would not hesitate to go one step further and say that the legal foundations of the judiciary must be vested in the constitution. This is where the organization of the state is regulated. However, the Convention text does not go that far.

In *Amann*, to give but one example, the Court referred to and accepted as 'law' such texts as 'section 414 of the Federal Council's Directives of 16 March 1981 applicable to the Processing of Personal Data in the Federal Administration and Article 7 of the Federal Decree of 9 October 1992 on the Consultation of Documents of the Federal Public Prosecutor's Office'.[28]

To my knowledge, *Zand* was the first reference in the entire case-law on the Convention to the formal procedures regulating the creation of legislation. The issue was taken up by the Court more than twenty years later in *Coëme*: the purpose of the rule is 'to ensure "that the judicial organisation in a democratic society [does] not depend on the discretion of the Executive, but that it [is] regulated by law emanating from Parliament"'.[29]

Still, not every detail must be regulated by the law in the formal sense, i.e. Acts of Parliament—details may be set out in delegated legislation, for example, the determination of the number and circumscription of labour courts can be left to a ministerial decree.[30] However, these texts will have to satisfy the general requirements of precision and foreseeability.[31]

The question then arises, which elements must be covered by the legal rules 'establishing' a tribunal? Again the report in the case of *Zand* serves as a source. The Commission held that '... the term "a tribunal established by law" in Article 6 (1) envisages the whole organisational set-up of the courts, including not only the matters coming within the jurisdiction of a certain category of courts, but also the establishment of the individual courts and the determination of their local jurisdiction'.[32]

This should also, in my view, include the determination of its competence,[33] not only *ratione loci*,[34] but also *ratione materiae*, its composition, and the

---

[28] *Amann* v. *Switzerland*, § 78.   [29] *Coëme* v. *Belgium*, § 98.
[30] *Zand* v. *Austria* Application 7360/76.
[31] More recently in the context of secret surveillance, see *Rotaru* v. *Romania*, § 55; *Amann* v. *Switzerland*, § 56.   [32] *Zand* v. *Austria* Application 7360/76.
[33] See also e.g. Frowein and Peukert (1996) Art. 6 N 122; Velu and Ergec (1990) N 537.
[34] The Commission refused, however, to examine whether a particular tribunal was competent when the Court of Cassation had given an affirmative answer: 'The provision cited above does not ... confer on the Commission the right to verify whether, in a particular case, the courts have correctly applied the provisions of domestic law in force, since it is in the first place for the national authorities, notably the courts, to interpret and apply that law (see, *inter alia*, Eur. Court H.R., Eriksson judgment of 22 June 1989, Series A no. 156, p. 25, para. 62). In this case the Commission notes that the Court of Cassation, to which this problem was submitted, held that the trial judges had correctly applied the rules governing jurisdiction in force and that their decision on this question duly rehearsed their reasons. Moreover, there is nothing in the file which suggests that this

proceedings the tribunal is to follow.[35] In this respect, however, the case-law has so far brought no clarification. Stephanos Stavros therefore comes to the conclusion ' . . . that [according to the Strasbourg case-law] only absolute and unfettered discretion of the executive over the jurisdiction of the courts entails a serious threat to judicial independence'.[36]

An issue which has been subject to intense discussion in Germany is the composition of chambers and the distribution of cases to the various chambers of a court.[37] Even the slightest suspicion that certain cases are attributed to judges in view of a specific outcome must be avoided. *Daktaras* v. *Lithuania* is an example of an unacceptable situation—the case was dealt with in the light of impartiality but in my view it primarily denotes a lack of legal regulation. The applicant had been charged with blackmail, was convicted at first instance and then acquitted on appeal. The president of the court of first instance thought this acquittal to be wrong and approached the president of the criminal division of the supreme court and formally requested that the appeal judgment be quashed. The president did this and brought the case before a chamber which he had composed himself. The Court rightly observed that this president in fact acted in much the same way as a prosecutor and the applicant could not be expected to regard the chamber as an impartial tribunal.[38]

A different element of lawfulness was at issue in the interstate case of *Cyprus* v. *Turkey*. Amongst a large number of complaints the applicant government had also claimed that no independent and impartial tribunals established by law were at the disposal of the Greek minority still living in the North, particularly in the Karpas area. Both the Commission and the Court rejected this claim which had obvious political overtones. The ECtHR pragmatically stated:

The Court observes from the evidence submitted to the Commission . . . that there is a functioning court system in the 'TRNC' for the settlement of disputes relating to civil rights and obligations defined in 'domestic law' and which is available to the Greek-Cypriot population. As the Commission observed, the court system in its functioning and procedures reflects the judicial and common-law tradition of Cyprus (. . .). In its opinion, having regard to the fact that it is the 'TRNC domestic law' which defines the substance of those rights and obligations for the benefit of the population as a whole it must follow that the domestic courts, set up by the 'law' of the 'TRNC', are the fora for their enforcement. For the Court, and for the purposes of adjudicating on 'civil rights and obligations' the local courts can be considered to be 'established by law' with reference to the 'constitutional and legal basis' on which they operate.[39]

---

might not have been the case.' *TS and FS* v. *Italy* Application 13274/87. In *WK* v. *Switzerland* Application 15668/89, the applicant alleged that the Zurich police had wrongfully stopped him and made him submit to a blood test in the canton of Schwyz, but the Commission accepted the view of the Federal Tribunal that the police had not acted illegally.

[35] See also the concurring opinion of Judge Ryssdal in *H* v. *Belgium*, § 41.
[36] Stavros (1993) 134 et seq.   [37] Cf. *Gerichtsverfassungsgesetz* (GVG), § 21g.
[38] *Daktaras* v. *Lithuania*, §§ 33–8.   [39] *Cyprus* v. *Turkey*, § 237.

III. INDEPENDENCE

'Independence' means that a court shall not be subordinated to any other state organ. This is not to say that a lack of independence from non-state entities, such as, for example, a warlord in Afghanistan or Somalia, or from a generous sponsor such as Coca-Cola or Shell, could be tolerated. It would, however, be the responsibility of the state to intervene if that were the case. So far it does not appear that the international organs have had to deal with such a case.[40] In the first place, independence from the executive is required.[41] However, independence from the legislator may be equally important. It is rather obvious that the legislator, while providing the 'raw material' with which tribunals work, namely the law, and also making regulations organizing the judiciary, cannot itself assume judicial functions. This was first stressed by the Commission in the case of *Crociani and others* v. *Italy* which concerned criminal proceedings against active ministers of government. As the parliament had, however, only assumed functions of investigation and indictment, the guarantee of Article 6 was not violated.[42]

In the case *Demicoli* v. *Malta*, parliament had, however, assumed the role of a tribunal in the case against a defendant who was accused of having made libellous observations with regard to members of that same parliament. Here it was quite obvious that the parliament could not be regarded as an *impartial* tribunal.[43]

On the other hand, the question arose whether a member of parliament could at the same time sit as a judge. While the Court shied away from giving a clear and general answer, it examined, as usual, the facts of the case and found no elements which could have objectively justified doubts as to that judge's impartiality. Implicitly, however, the judgment gives a clear answer: the fact that an individual is an MP does not exclude his functioning as a judge.[44] It would certainly be different if the court in question were a constitutional court.

Notwithstanding the fact that impartiality and independence are difficult to distinguish, the Court has developed a number of requirements which must be fulfilled for a court to have this quality. They were originally drawn up in the judgment of *Le Compte, Van Leuven and De Meyere* v. *Belgium* as criteria for the definition of the term 'tribunal' itself.[45] Over the years it has taken the following formulation which is quoted here from *Incal* v. *Turkey*: 'The Court reiterates that in order to establish whether a tribunal can be considered "independent" for the

---

[40] Even very thorough studies like Kiener (2001) do not mention such a possibility.

[41] *Oló Bahamonde* v. *Equatorial Guinea*, § 9.4.

[42] *Crociani and others* v. *Italy* Applications 8603/79, 8722/79, 8723/79, and 8729/79.

[43] *Demicoli* v. *Malta*, §§ 40 et seq. While the Court simply accepted that in the specific case the legislature exercised a judicial function, the Commission had more clearly found that it could not really be regarded as a tribunal.   [44] *Pabla Ky* v. *Finland*, §§ 31 et seq.

[45] *Le Compte, Van Leuven and De Meyere* v. *Belgium*, § 55.

purposes of Art. 6 § 1 regard must be had, *inter alia*, to the manner of appointment of its members and their term of office, the existence of safeguards against outside pressures and the question whether it presents an appearance of independence'.[46] It follows that the Court relies on four criteria in order to establish whether a tribunal is independent: the manner in which the judges are appointed; the term of office of the judges; the existence of particular safeguards against any pressure from outside; and the question of appearance.[47]

These four criteria will be discussed in turn, and this will be followed by reference to some further important aspects.

A. The Manner of Appointment

There exists in Europe and around the world a great number of different and varied systems for appointing judges. It is therefore not surprising that the Court is very reluctant to criticize states in this area. It seems that the manner of appointment has never been considered to cause a problem under Article 6. In both *Lithgow*[48] and *Sramek*[49] the Court saw no problem in the fact that members of a 'tribunal' were appointed by the government.

This approach is not entirely satisfactory, at least not if it is looked at in isolation. There is a nice saying in German: '*Wes Brot ich ess, des Lied ich sing*' ('I sing the song of the person whose bread I eat'). If a government had an unfettered power to appoint (and [not] reappoint) judges after a relatively short term of office, they could hardly be regarded as independent.[50] They would, of course, have strong motives for deciding cases in a way which pleased the government in order to avoid losing their position. Even where additional controls are in place, an uneasy feeling remains. It is not satisfactory, for instance, that the President of the United States can influence the attitude of the Supreme Court by appointing justices who are close to his personal political views.

On the other hand, it would be illusory to imagine that judges and tribunals are totally removed from political life and from the political currents prevailing

---

[46] *Incal v. Turkey*, § 65. These criteria are also mentioned (sometimes by using the identical formulation) in *McGonnell v. United Kingdom*, § 48; *Çıraklar v. Turkey*, § 38; *Lauko v. Slovakia*, § 63; *Kadubec v. Slovakia*, § 56; *Findlay v. United Kingdom*, § 73; *Bryan v. United Kingdom*, § 37; *Langborger v. Sweden*, § 32. In *Campbell and Fell v. United Kingdom*, § 78 Judge Sir Vincent Evans dissented but did not give reasons why he thought the Board of Visitors was independent and impartial.

[47] The same approach is taken, with reference to the European case-law, by the Inter-American Commission of Human Rights; see e.g. *Garcia v. Peru*, Case 11.006, Report No. 1/95, Inter-Am.C.H.R., OEA/Ser.L/V/II.88 rev.1 Doc. 9 at 71 (1995).

[48] *Lithgow and others v. United Kingdom*, § 202. [49] *Sramek v. Austria*, § 38.

[50] The problem also concerns the ECtHR itself where some judges earn up to a hundred times the salary of their colleagues at home; it has now been decided in Protocol No. 14 to prolong the term of office to nine years and exclude re-election. The limitation of the term of office caused considerable problems in Scotland when the domestic court ruled in *Starrs v. Ruxton* 2000 SLT 42 that for this reason temporary sheriffs could not be considered as judges in the sense of Art. 6; see O'Neill (2000) and Tierney (2000).

in a specific society at a certain time. Within certain limits it is acceptable and perhaps even desirable that judges share the kind of values which predominate in society as a whole. However, there must be some limits: even though a judge cannot simply be viewed as '*la bouche de la loi*' he or she is still obliged to decide cases essentially in accordance with the law. This means, in particular, that the tribunal ought to keep in mind the universally accepted values of human rights in their day-to-day activity.

In my view the most appropriate method for appointing and promoting judges is by way of a judicial council (*conseil supérieur de la magistrature*) which makes proposals that are binding on the head of the state or the minister of justice.

B. The Term of Office

In a number of states it is considered mandatory that judges be nominated for life. In its judgments, the ECtHR has remained a long way behind such a requirement. It has accepted terms of five[51] and even three years.[52] It is slightly disappointing that the Court gave no reason at all for accepting a term of three years. In fact, this seems excessively low. Even the term of six years for the judges of the new Court has been criticized as being rather short.[53]

Security of tenure is, however, not enough. Other elements such as the salary of judges are also important. In fact, in order to be fully independent, it is essential that judges are paid at the very least a salary which allows them to maintain a certain standard of living. When two so-called 'eminent lawyers' prepared a report on the question of whether Georgia fulfilled the prerequisites for joining the Council of Europe, they had heard that it was common for members of the judiciary to accept bribes. Faced with this allegation, President Shevardnadze openly admitted that there were perhaps two or three judges in Georgia who were not corrupt. This was not surprising because their salary amounted to a mere twenty dollars a month which made it impossible to meet the basic costs of living.[54]

C. Safeguards Against Outside Pressure

The third criterion, that there be sufficient safeguards against undue pressure from outside, is rather vague. It is closely connected to tenure as it includes the restrictions on the possibilities of removing a judge.[55] One such safeguard may

---

[51] *Ettl and others* v. *Austria*, § 41; *Ringeisen* v. *Germany*, § 95; six years was the term in *Le Compte, Van Leuven and De Meyere* v. *Belgium*, § 57.   [52] *Sramek* v. *Austria*, § 37 referring to § 26.
[53] See e.g. Krüger (1997) 399.
[54] Council of Europe, Parliamentary Assembly, 'Report on the Conformity of the Legal Order of Georgia with Council of Europe Standards', submitted by Stefan Trechsel and Isi Foighel, 25 Sept. 1997, AS/Bur/Georgia (1997) 1, § 115.   [55] *Sramek* v. *Austria*, § 38.

consist of the fact that judges are legally trained. This has been mentioned in particular where proceedings have been accompanied by demonstrations in the street. The influence of the media on the impartiality of judges constitutes a very real danger to their independence and impartiality. Here a conflict may arise between the rights guaranteed by Article 6 and the freedom of the press guaranteed in Article 10. Where the right to be presumed innocent as protected by Article 6 § 2 is under threat, it is clear that Article 6 must prevail.[56] It is essential that the judiciary react strongly against any such violations which serve not only to violate the applicant's right immediately but also tend to undermine the independence and impartiality of a tribunal.[57]

D. The Appearance of Independence

As we shall see, with regard to impartiality the Court has stressed the importance of appearances. This cannot be avoided because it is not possible to read a judge's mind in order to find out whether he or she is biased or not. To adopt the same test with regard to independence, however, does not make much sense.

The independence of a court must be decided exclusively on the basis of objective criteria. If one looks at the case-law more closely, one will find that whenever the Court refers to 'appearances' in connection with independence, what is in fact at issue is not independence but impartiality.[58] An example is *Belilos* v. *Switzerland*.[59] Ms Belilos complained of having been sentenced to a fine by a police board. The judge of this police board was a lawyer from the police force. He was truly independent for his term of office (four years) but was free after his tenure to return to the police. In the words of the Court: 'The ordinary citizen will tend to see him as a member of the police force subordinate to his superiors and loyal to his colleagues. A situation of this kind may undermine the confidence which must be inspired by the courts in a democratic society'.[60] It seems evident to me that here the Court is referring to impartiality rather than independence.[61] In *Incal* the Court seemed to require that two distinct groups have confidence in the courts when it stated that: 'What is at stake is the confidence which the courts in a democratic society must inspire in the public and above all . . . in the accused'.[62] However, the point of view of the accused is not the decisive but the main argument in *Incal* and all further cases referring to it.[63]

---

[56] See e.g. *Allenet de Ribemont* v. *France*, § 38; *Petra Krause* v. *Switzerland* Application 7986/77.

[57] See e.g. *Nielsen* v. *Denmark* Application 343/57; *X* v. *Austria* Application 1476/62; *X* v. *Germany* Application 6062/73; *Ensslin, Baader and Raspe* v. *Germany* Applications 572/76, 7586/76, and 7587/76.

[58] *Sramek* v. *Austria*, § 42, with reference to *Campbell and Fell* v. *United Kingdom*, § 78 and *Piersack* v. *Belgium*, § 30.   [59] *Belilos* v. *Switzerland*, §§ 66 et seq.

[60] Ibid., § 67.   [61] In the same vein, see van Dijk and van Hoof (1998) 452.

[62] *Incal* v. *Turkey*, § 71.

[63] Ibid., § 72. See also *Çiraklar* v. *Turkey*, § 38 where the Court first spoke of the appearance of *independence* but then changed to impartiality in the next sentence.

To these four criteria of independence which are regularly mentioned by the Court two important elements must be added: the authority of the judgment and the autonomy of the tribunal. Finally, the situation of civil servants as members of a court will call for some additional observations.

E. Additional Aspects of Independence

1. The Authority of the Judgment

As indicated above, a tribunal can only be regarded as independent if its decisions are binding on other organs of the state. In *Benthem* v. *Netherlands* the applicant wanted to install a liquid gas station. While a tribunal was competent to give an opinion as to whether the permission should be granted, the final decision lay with the Crown. As the Crown could not possibly be regarded as a court, the right to an independent trial had been violated.[64]

The question of the independence of the court could also have been discussed in the case of *Brumărescu* v. *Romania*, where the Procurator-General had successfully asked the Supreme Court to quash a judgment which had acquired the force of law. The Court, however, preferred simply to find a violation of the right to access to court under Article 6.[65]

As far as criminal matters are concerned, decisions relating to the execution of sentence may, to some extent, be left to administrative organs. This applies, for example, to the question of whether a fine can be paid in instalments or whether a person should be released on probation.[66] In *Assanidze* v. *Georgia* there was held to be a violation as the authorities had not implemented a decision acquitting the applicant, who was thus still in detention three years after his acquittal.[67] The Court noted that: 'If the State administrative authorities could refuse or fail to comply with a judgment acquitting a defendant, or even delay in doing so, the Article 6 guarantees the defendant previously enjoyed during the judicial phase of the proceedings would become partly illusory'.

A particularly delicate problem arises with the institution of pardon. To grant pardon is considered to be the distinctive privilege of the Sovereign. As a particular act of clemency, the King, the President, or Parliament may spare the convicted person part or all of the execution of the sentence although, and this is very important, it may not annul the judgment. Pardon is an institution which lies in a grey zone, on the border of the law because usually the organ invested with the right to grant a pardon enjoys unfettered discretion. Still, if the right to

---

[64] *Benthem* v. *Netherlands*, §§ 37 et seq.　　　[65] *Brumărescu* v. *Romania*, § 65.

[66] See e.g. *X* v. *Germany* Application 2428/65; *X* v. *Germany* Application 4984/71; *X* v. *Switzerland* Application 7648/76.

[67] *Assanidze* v. *Georgia*, §§ 182–4; this case is highly remarkable in that for the first time in its history the Court did not limit itself to finding a violation and determining just satisfaction but even ordered that the applicant be released (§§ 202, 203).

grant pardons is practised in an arbitrary, or discriminatory, way the authority of the court will be affected. It is particularly important to stress that pardons should never be motivated by doubts about the merits of the judgment. It should not be regarded as an alternative to an appeal. The most dangerous abuse of the right to pardon occurs where those convicted of politically motivated crimes are pardoned because their deeds correspond to the aims of the ruler or the ruling party. Unfortunately, I see no way in which the Convention could protect against such abuses.

2. The Autonomy of the Tribunal

The right to an independent tribunal implies that the tribunal has full control over its decision and does not depend upon the binding opinions of any other state organ. It must be competent fully to examine both the facts and the law at issue.[68] Two cases decided by the Court illustrate this point.

The first is *Obermeier* v. *Austria* which concerned civil proceedings.[69] The Court had to decide whether the applicant, a disabled person, had been illegally dismissed from his job. According to Austrian legislation a special board which cannot be regarded as a tribunal determined this question in a manner which was binding upon the courts. This was not compatible with Article 6.

The second case is *Beaumartin* v. *France*.[70] Here the court was bound by an opinion of the ministry for foreign affairs which meant that there was also a violation.

In a way, the autonomy of the Belgian Court of Cassation was also at stake in the cases of *Delcourt, Borgers*, and *Vermeulen*.[71] The Belgian Government had argued that the *avocat général*'s presence during the deliberations of the Court of Cassation was necessary so as to safeguard the uniformity of the case-law. However, a 'tribunal' within the meaning of Article 6 does not only not need, but does not support, any such 'guardian'. It must determine the case with regard exclusively to the proceedings and to the arguments which were the object of adversarial proceedings before it.

---

[68] The right of access to court implies, of course, that the court is entirely free fully to (re-)examine the facts and the law; see e.g. *Albert and Le Compte* v. *Belgium*, § 29; *Belilos* v. *Switzerland*, § 70; *Terra Woningen BV* v. *Netherlands*, § 52.   [69] *Obermeier* v. *Austria*, §§ 69 et seq.

[70] *Beaumartin* v. *France*, § 34 et seq. The *Conseil d'Etat* was obliged, when faced with a problem of interpretation of international law, to consult the Minister of Foreign Affairs whose opinion was binding; the Court found that 'Only an institution that has full jurisdiction and satisfies a number of requirements, such as independence of the executive and also of the parties, merits the designation "tribunal" within the meaning of Article 6 para. 1'; ibid., § 38. For a similar case concerning the admission of a medical doctor, see *Chevrol* v. *France*.

[71] *Delcourt* v. *Belgium*, §§ 31 et seq.; *Borgers* v. *Belgium*, §§ 26 et seq.; *Vermeulen* v. *Belgium*; see also Andersen (2000) 1. These cases are also discussed under the aspect of equality of arms. In *Delcourt* no violation was found but the Court came to a different view in *Borgers*.

3. Civil Servants as Members of a Tribunal

It is rather obvious that administrative bodies cannot be regarded as independent. This was found, for example, in relation to the district offices in Slovakia[72] and the Czech Republic (Mladá Boleslav Land Office).[73]

A particularly delicate situation arises when members of a tribunal who are not professional judges are at the same time civil servants. In the *Sramek* case the Court followed the Commission and accepted that the Tyrolian Regional Authority could not be regarded as independent. It was composed, *inter alia*, of three civil servants of the *Land* government. In the present case, the *Land* government had 'acquired the status of a party when they appealed to the Regional Authority against the first-instance decision in Mrs. Sramek's favour'.[74] The transaction officer who had represented the government was the hierarchical superior of one of the officers who sat on the Regional Authority. The Court stressed that there was no evidence of this hierarchical officer having given any instructions to the member of the board but it found a violation in view of the appearances: 'Where, as in the present case, a tribunal's members include a person who is in a subordinate position, in terms of his duties and the organisation of his service, *vis-à-vis* one of the parties, litigants may entertain a legitimate doubt about that person's independence. Such a situation seriously affects the confidence which the courts must inspire in a democratic society'.[75]

The situation had been different in *Ringeisen*. Here, the Court found that with regard to 'a board with mixed membership comprising, under the presidency of a judge, civil servants and representatives of interested bodies, the complaint made against one member for the single reason that he sat as nominee of the Upper Austrian Chamber of Agriculture cannot be said to bear out a charge of bias'.[76] In *Campbell and Fell* the allegation was that frequent contact with prison officials cast doubts on the impartiality of members of the Board of Visitors, but the Court rejected this argument.[77]

The case of *Ettl* involved a similar situation as was at issue in *Sramek*.[78] Here, however, the Court—contrary to the Commission—found no violation because there was no similarly intense relationship between the 'civil servant judges' and the administration concerned. I do not find this judgment convincing. Independence from the executive is not guaranteed when civil servants who normally act in the interests of the administration suddenly find themselves in the role of impartial judges in a case where that same administration is one of the parties. In particular, if appearances matter, it is essential that any suspicion of dependency be avoided.

---

[72] *Lauko* v. *Slovakia; Kadubec* v. *Slovakia.*   [73] *Malhous* v. *Czech Republic.*
[74] *Sramek* v. *Austria*, § 41.   [75] Ibid., § 42.   [76] *Ringeisen* v. *Austria*, § 97.
[77] *Campbell and Fell* v. *United Kingdom*, § 81.   [78] *Ettl* v. *Austria*, §§ 38 et seq.

No problems arise, however, if civil servants of a different political entity are concerned, for example, officials of a provincial government in a federal trial or vice versa, as long as there is no immediate relationship between the administrations concerned. The fact that these civil servants may be particularly well informed about the subject matter concerned is, in my view, no justification. On the contrary, it may well be that their professional involvement has built up all kinds of views which could be what goes under the label of '*déformation professionnelle*'. As they are trained and sometimes even sworn in to defend the interests of the state, they may, as far as their personal attitudes are concerned, still be regarded as independent. However, a person appearing before such a body is in my view justified in doubting their impartiality.

4. Military Judges Sitting in an Ordinary Court

Many states have a parallel system of criminal justice for their armed forces. Military justice as such does not cause special problems as long as it is only competent for offences committed by military personnel, together with military personnel, or against military personnel or institutions. As long as there are clear criteria determining its competencies it is not in any way contrary to international human-rights instruments. The criteria must also be convincing—a special justification is required if civil persons are tried by military tribunals.[79]

It is quite a different matter if military persons are members of civil tribunals. This was the case with the Turkish State Security Courts. The Court considered this structure to be in conflict with Article 6 of the ECHR.[80] It recognized that those military judges enjoyed a certain independence when fulfilling their judicial duties. They sat as individuals and were not submitted to orders or instructions with regard to this function. On the other hand they were still servicemen and, *inter alia*, 'remain subject to military discipline and assessment reports are compiled on them'.[81] The same applied to other types of courts in Turkey.[82]

In *Incal* the government justified the presence of a military person on the security court with the expertise of the army in fighting terrorist crime. The Court replied that in the case at issue the accused was prosecuted for having distributed separatist leaflets which did not incite violence.[83] I do not find this argument persuasive; it is tailored too narrowly to the facts of the case. In *Çiraklar* a better formulation was used: 'It is understandable that a civilian—such as

---

[79] See e.g. HRC, *Safarmo Kurbanova on behalf of her son, Abduali Ismatovich Kurbanov v. Tajikistan*, § 7.6.

[80] *Incal v. Turkey; Çiriklar v. Turkey*, §§ 38 et seq.; *Sener v. Turkey*, §§ 56 et seq.; *Gerger v. Turkey*, §§ 60 et seq.; *Okçuoglu v. Turkey*, §§ 57 et seq.; *Karatas v. Turkey*, §§ 61 et seq.; *Sürek and Özdemir v. Turkey*, §§ 77 et seq.; *Sürek v. Turkey (Nos. 1–4)*, §§ 74 et seq., 52 et seq., 53 et seq., and 72 et seq. respectively; *Baskaya and Okçuoglu v. Turkey*, §§ 78 et seq.; and many more, up to *Aksac v. Turkey* of 15 July 2004. [81] *Incal v. Turkey*, § 68.

[82] See e.g. the Commission's report in *Mitap and Müftüoglu v. Turkey* which the Court followed in *Sahiner v. Turkey*, §§ 33 et seq.; *Alfatlı and Others v. Turkey*, § 46; and *Koç v. Turkey*, §§ 31 et seq.

[83] Ibid., § 72.

Mr Çiraklar—prosecuted in a National Security Court for offences regarded ipso facto as directed against Turkey's territorial or national integrity, the democratic order or national security . . . should be apprehensive about being tried by a bench of three judges which includes a regular army officer, who is a member of the Military Legal Service'.[84]

In *Öcalan* the military judge was replaced at the last minute because the constitution had since been amended. However, the Court concluded that 'the last-minute replacement of the military judge was not capable of curing the defect in the composition of the court'.[85]

IV. IMPARTIALITY

A. Definition

The term 'impartiality' describes a state of mind in which the subject is balanced in a perfect equilibrium between parties—it is synonymous with 'non-partisan' or 'neutral'. It is generally defined—quite logically—in negative terms as 'the absence of prejudice or bias'.[86] A good formulation has been coined by the HRC: '"Impartiality" of the court implies that judges must not harbour pre-conceptions about the matter put before them, and that they must not act in ways that promote the interests of one of the parties'.[87] The parties to the proceedings must be justified in having full confidence that the members of the tribunal will decide the case exclusively on the basis of their reasonable assessment of the evidence and the application of the law.[88] It would not be realistic to expect that judges and tribunals make no mistakes, but such mistakes must be *bona fide* rather than the result of preferences or prejudices, be it towards the parties or in relation to the subject matter with which the proceedings are concerned.

As 'impartiality' is best described negatively as the absence of bias, it seems appropriate to discuss it by addressing the situations most likely to cause, or to be regarded as causing, bias. First, however, it is important to present a distinction which the Court makes in this connection.

B. The Objective and the Subjective Approach

Since the very first judgments addressing the issue of the right to an independent and impartial tribunal[89] the Court has made a distinction between two different

---

[84] *Çiraklar* v. *Turkey*, § 39.   [85] *Öcalan* v. *Turkey*, § 118.
[86] *Piersack* v. *Belgium*, § 30.
[87] *Karttunen* v. *Finland*, § 7.2; in this case there was a violation because one of the judges was barred from sitting according to domestic law.
[88] This is expressed by Eberhard Schmidt (1967) 39 in a way which, unfortunately, cannot be translated literally into English: the parties must be in a situation which allows for '*das Gefühl einer unbedingten Geborgenheit im Recht*'—the confidence that they will enjoy the full protection of the law.
[89] *Piersack* v. *Belgium*, § 30; *De Cubber* v. *Belgium*, § 24.

aspects of impartiality which it has labelled as the 'subjective' and the 'objective' test. To quote a rather recent passage: 'As to the condition of "impartiality" within the meaning of that provision, there are two tests to be applied: the first consists in trying to determine the personal conviction of a particular judge in a given case and the second in ascertaining whether the judge offered guarantees sufficient to exclude any legitimate doubt in this respect'.[90]

This separation between two tests—in some judgments the Court speaks of 'approaches'[91]—is quite convincing although the labels are not. It would be preferable to distinguish between an 'objective' test—is the judge objectively biased?—and a 'subjective' test—does the judge *appear* to be biased in the eyes of the accused?[92]

The essential element is the one which the Court calls the subjective aspect: the requirement that the judge have an impartial state of mind. However, it is obviously practically impossible to determine whether or not this condition is fulfilled. It is even very doubtful whether it is possible in theory, particularly if one has regard to the psychoanalytical school of psychology. There can hardly be any doubt that no human being will be entirely without bias. Mostly, however, we are not aware of our hidden tendencies. Lawyers in particular have a tendency grossly to overestimate their own objectivity. In practice, a judge who is aware of his or her own tendency to be biased and is capable of sufficient self-criticism and self-control will be more neutral than a judge who is entirely unaware of his or her predispositions.

In view of this difficulty the so-called objective test asks whether the judge could be regarded as biased in the eyes of a reasonable person or an 'ordinary citizen'.[93] It is not sufficient, of course, that the applicant be apprehensive with regard to the impartiality of a tribunal; his individual feelings cannot be more decisive than the actual bias of the judge, because they cannot be proven either. There would also and primarily be a considerable danger of abuse if individuals could decide whether they want to accept a tribunal or not, particularly in civil proceedings where the plaintiff and the defendant are likely to disagree in every respect, to the extent that the confidence of one party can be enough to arouse the suspicion of the other party. The applicant must give reasons for his or her fears and the Court will say whether they are sufficient to justify them or not.

---

[90] *Incal* v. *Turkey*, § 65, where the Court also refers to *Gautrin and others* v. *France*, § 58; see also e.g. *Hauschildt* v. *Denmark*, § 46; *Thorgeir Thorgeirson* v. *Iceland*, § 49.

[91] *Piersack* v. *Belgium* and *De Cubber* v. *Belgium*.

[92] Cf. Trechsel (1984) 385 at 394; Kiener (2001) 60 criticizes the Court for not always being clear and consistent.

[93] *Belilos* v. *Switzerland*, § 67. In *Pullar* v. *United Kingdom*, § 39, the Court used the expression 'objective observer'. Veldt (1997) 59 is wrong when she states that this approach was abandoned. She criticizes it as being too broad; in my view it is an acceptable test: even the ancient Romans referred to the *bonus pater familias*. Where a judge has recourse to a reasonable person, in the sense of a reasonable person in the situation of the specific person concerned or, for that matter, of the 'man in the street' or the 'ordinary citizen', or, as Lord Bowen famously put it, the 'man on the Clapham omnibus', the judge will in fact ask what his or her own view or reaction would have been.

This is not only a practicable solution, it is also the correct one, because it gives proper weight to the situation of the applicant, and not only the applicant. Luhmann has quite rightly stressed the importance of the element of demonstration in the administration of law for the maintenance of general confidence in the state.[94] In fact it goes far beyond that very important principle, quoted first (although not very precisely) by the Court in *Delcourt*[95] and repeated many times since, set out by Lord Heward in *R.* v. *Sussex Justices, ex parte McCarthy*: 'it is not merely of some importance but it is of fundamental importance that justice should not only be done, but should manifestly and undoubtedly be seen to be done'.[96]

In this context the Court often says that 'appearances may be of a certain importance'.[97] I would not hesitate to go a step further and say that when the impartiality of a tribunal is assessed, appearances are not just the wrapping or the facade. They are themselves the issue. A judge who in fact is perfectly impartial but does not seem so, *is not impartial* for the purposes of Article 6 § 1; on the other hand, if a judge appears to be impartial but is in fact not so, he or she still *is impartial* for the purposes of these proceedings—at least as long as the bias is not known; once it is known, the appearance, of course, also disappears.

I cannot, therefore, agree with Veldt who believes that in *Delcourt* the Court limited the scope of the 'objective' test by warning against exaggerations.[98] What the Court said was this: '. . . these considerations may allow doubts to arise about the satisfactory nature of the system in dispute [namely that the Procureur Général assists in the deliberations of the Court of Cassation in Belgium]. They do not, however, amount to proof of a violation of the right to a fair hearing'.[99] With due respect, this approach is misguided. The ensuing case-law has abandoned entirely this idea that the appearances 'prove' the lack of impartiality of a tribunal—on the contrary, they are referred to as a substitute for such proof! It is interesting to recall in passing that the Court eventually reversed its substantive finding in *Borgers*, even if it made a weak attempt at distinguishing the facts in order to maintain an appearance of the continuity of the old case-law.[100]

C. Lack of Impartiality Because of Personal Bias

The Court will only on very exceptional occasions seriously consider a judge—the 'subjective test' can only apply to individuals, not to a collective organ—to be personally biased; in fact, it shows a general reluctance to address any blame to a specific individual.[101] Therefore the Court approaches the issue with a

---

[94] Luhmann (1975). See also Trechsel (1997).   [95] *Delcourt* v. *Belgium*, §§ 31, 35.
[96] *R.* v. *Sussex Justices, ex parte McCarthy* [1924]1 KB 256 at 259.
[97] See e.g. *Hauschildt* v. *Denmark*, § 48; *Thorgeir Thorgeirson* v. *Iceland*, § 51; *Incal* v. *Turkey*, § 71; *Pullar* v. *United Kingdom*, § 38.   [98] Veldt (1997) 58.
[99] *Delcourt* v. *Belgium*, § 31.   [100] *Borgers* v. *Belgium*, § 24.
[101] The Court even seems to feel a certain solidarity with national judges; this may explain the vote in *Barfod* v. *Denmark*, where a journalist had been sanctioned for having criticized a judge who

presumption that the judge is impartial—very strong evidence is required to convince it that this is not the case.[102]

The reluctance of the Court to admit that there was lack of impartiality under the subjective test was particularly striking in the case of *Remli*.[103] The applicant, a man of Algerian origin, was the accused in a jury trial. One of the jurors seems to have said, during a break, 'What's more, I'm a racist'. This was brought to the knowledge of the presiding judge by a written declaration by Mrs M. The presiding judge found that he could not take formal note of the event because it had not occurred in the court's presence. In view of such strong indications of bias which was not really in doubt, the Court could have been expected to say: 'Here we must assume that we are in an analogous situation to that of a (subjectively assessed) biased judge. A juror has stated that he holds racist opinions and the accused is of a different race. His words can only be interpreted as meaning that he is prejudiced against the accused'. Yet, the Court did not even refer to the subjective test. Instead, like the Commission, it found a violation of Article 6 on the basis that the court had failed properly to examine the allegations made in Mrs M.'s handwritten note: 'Article 6 § 1 of the Convention imposes an obligation on every national court to check whether, as constituted, it is an "impartial tribunal" within the meaning of that provision where, as in the instant case, this is disputed on a ground that does not immediately appear to be manifestly devoid of merit'.[104]

A somewhat similar and equally sensitive situation arose in *Gregory* v. *United Kingdom*. After a bit more than a hundred minutes of deliberations, a note was passed to the judge from the jury which read: 'JURY SHOWING RACIAL OVERTONES. 1 MEMBER TO BE EXCUSED'. The judge convened both counsel. Counsel for the defence did not press strongly for dismissal of the jury. Thereupon the judge addressed a 'firmly worded redirection' to the jury. The Court came to the conclusion that he had thereby done all that he could have been expected to do under the circumstances and referred also to the 'significant' (non) reaction of defence counsel.[105] Thus, it found there to have been no violation. In fact, it was not possible in this case to establish personal bias.

Nor was it possible in the similar case of *Sander*. Here, an applicant who was of Asian origin, was accused together with another Asian of conspiracy to defraud. After the weekend following the judge's summing up, a juror brought the following notice to the judge:

I have decided I cannot remain silent any longer. For some time during the trial I have been concerned that fellow jurors are not taking their duties seriously. At least two have

---

was also a civil servant—the Commission had found a violation of Art. 10 by fourteen votes to one; the Court found by six votes to one that there had been no violation.

[102] *Piersack* v. *Belgium*, § 30; *De Cubber* v. *Belgium*, § 25; *Le Compte, Van Leuven and De Meyere* v. *Belgium*, § 58; *Hauschildt* v. *Denmark*, § 47; *Thorgeir Thorgeirson* v. *Iceland*, § 50; *Castillo Algar* v. *Spain*, § 44.   [103] *Remli* v. *France*.

[104] Ibid., § 48.   [105] *Gregory* v. *United Kingdom*, § 46.

been making openly racist remarks and jokes and I fear are going to convict the defendants not on the evidence but because they are Asian. My concern is the defendants will not therefore receive a fair verdict. Please could you advise me what I can do in this situation.

The judge then admonished the jury, and the next day he was given a letter signed by all of them which said:

We, the undersigned members of the jury, wish to put on record to the Court our response to yesterday's note from a juror implying possible racial bias.

1. We utterly refute the allegation.
2. We are deeply offended by the allegation.
3. We assure the Court that we intend to reach a verdict solely according to the evidence and without racial bias.

In addition, the judge received a letter from a juror who admitted to having made jokes which could have been (mis)understood as betraying a racist attitude which he, however, strongly denied. The judge decided to proceed with the trial. The applicant was convicted, and the other accused was acquitted. The Court distinguished this case from *Gregory*. It attached little credibility to the letter affirming the absence of bias and concluded that the applicant could well have had misgivings about the impartiality of the jury; consequently it found that there had been a violation.

Judge Loucaides, in a separate opinion, added that in his view a lack of subjective impartiality ought also to have been found, a view with which I sympathize. Sir Nicholas Bratza, on the other hand, and joined by Judges Costa and Fuhrmann, dissented—the finding of a violation was unsurprisingly narrowly reached with four votes to three. In fact, looking at the case from a psychological perspective, the view of the majority is rather convincing. From a judicial point of view the argument that certain doubts can never be entirely eliminated is certainly defendable. The majority's conclusion was that 'the judge should have reacted in a more robust manner than merely seeking vague assurances that the jurors could set aside their prejudices and try the case solely on the evidence'.[106] This is indeed itself a rather vague finding—it betrays a certain insecurity on the part of the Court.

There are also strong indications of personal bias in the case of *Ferrantelli and Santangelo v. Italy*.[107] In fact, the applicants appeared before a judge who had previously tried a co-accused. That judgment contained several references to the applicants' involvement in the crime: they were described as 'co-perpetrators' and the judgment said that Mr Santangelo had been responsible for carrying out the murders.[108] However, as the applicants had not challenged the personal impartiality of the judge, the Court found a violation by applying the objective test.

[106] *Sander* v. *United Kingdom*, § 34.   [107] *Ferrantelli and Santangelo* v. *Italy*, § 57.
[108] Ibid., § 59.

Kingsley v. *United Kingdom* is a good example of a civil case involving judicial bias. The applicant had been a director of a casino enterprise. After a raid involving several installations the gaming board decided that he was not a fit and proper person to exercise that function. The applicant wanted to challenge this decision before an independent tribunal, but had to submit to the jurisdiction of a panel composed of members of the gaming board.[109]

The Court, finally, accepted the presence of personal bias, i.e. lack of subjective impartiality, for the first time in *Kyprianou* v. *Cyprus*. The applicant was a lawyer who had been interrupted during his cross-examination of a witness. He was angry and he argued with the judges. The judges were then offended and the applicant was sentenced, on the spot, to five days in prison. The Court found a lack of objective impartiality established simply by the fact that the judges punished someone for having offended them.[110] But it also accepted that some personal partiality had indeed developed. This became apparent through the 'intemperate reaction of the judges to the conduct of the applicant, given their haste to try him summarily for the criminal offence of contempt of court without availing themselves of other alternative, less drastic, measures such as an admonition, reporting the applicant to his professional body, refusing to hear the applicant unless he withdrew his statements, or asking him to leave the court room' and in the wording they used.[111]

D. Lack of Impartiality Under the Objective Test

The Court has on several occasions defined what it understands by the 'objective test'. The question is 'whether the judge offered guarantees sufficient to exclude any legitimate doubt in this respect'.[112] These appearances are relevant in a number of situations. In practice the most important one concerns cases where there has been some prior involvement of the judge in the same case. Only marginal reference is made to the particular closeness of the judge to one of the parties, or to procedural particularities which may cast doubts on the impartiality of the judge.

1. Lack of Impartiality Due to Prior Involvement of the Judge in the Same Case

(a) As a Prosecutor

The very first judgment in which the Court found a violation of the right to an independent and impartial tribunal was *Piersack* v. *Belgium*. The Brabant Assizes

---

[109] *Kingsley* v. *United Kingdom*: the case was brought before a Grand Chamber which, however, was only asked to re-examine the issue under Art. 41 of the Convention.

[110] *Kyprianou* v. *Cyprus*, § 34. The Court referred to the Latin aphorism '*nemo judex in causa sua*' and cited the Supreme Court of the United States in the case of *Offutt* v. *USA* 348 US 11, 75 S.Ct. 11 (in § 35). In a rather complicated case, *Korellis* v. *Cyprus*, where the applicant claimed that the court had been partial because of previous collateral proceedings, the Court found no violation.   [111] *Kyprianou* v. *Cyprus*, § 35.

[112] *Incal* v. *Turkey*, § 65.

Court had convicted the applicant of murder; it was presided over by Mr Van de Walle who had, before his promotion, acted as a senior deputy to the public prosecutor in the same case. The Court rightly stressed that it would be going too far if a member of the public prosecutor's office were barred for the rest of his or her life from ever acting as a judge; yet, in the case at issue Mr Van de Walle had been the superior of the prosecutors who tried the case in court and there were indications that he had actually played a certain part in the proceedings. Therefore the Assizes Court did not appear entirely impartial.[113]

This solution is not surprising—one of the important developments of criminal procedure after the inquisition was the separation of the duties of accusation and adjudication, which finds its expression in the creation of a separate office of public prosecutor ('*ministère public*'). Françoise Tulkens is quite right in recalling, in this context, the principle of separation of powers.[114] Whatever his personal attitude, as seen from the defendant's point of view the prosecuting authority is an inimical body, the antagonist, the enemy. It is objectively justified to assume that a person who has acted within that framework will have formed a critical, even negative attitude towards the suspect and will not be able, at a later stage of the same proceedings, to eliminate those feelings and become entirely neutral again.[115]

A particularly opaque accumulation of functions in military criminal proceedings was revealed in *Findlay* v. *United Kingdom*. Here, the central role lay in the hands of the convening officer. 'He decided which charges should be brought and which type of court martial was most appropriate. He convened the court martial and appointed its members and the prosecuting and defending officers'. In addition, the members of the court-martial were all his subordinates and he acted as the 'confirming officer'. It was rather obvious, under these circumstances, that the applicant could have misgivings about the impartiality of the court-martial.[116]

The Court has had to deal with a number of similar cases concerning other parts of the armed forces.[117] In 1996 the law was changed. In *Morris* a chamber of the Court acknowledged that most of the problems which had led to the finding of a violation in *Findlay* had been solved, in particular the dominant role of the convening officer. However, the judges still doubted whether the court-martial could be regarded as independent and impartial. 'There were not sufficient safeguards against the risk of outside pressures on the two members who, with the permanent president, made up the court-martial. The two officers

---

[113] *Piersack* v. *Belgium*, §§ 30, 31.   [114] Tulkens (1992) 41; see also Veldt (1997) 140.

[115] This was a decisive argument in *Borgers* v. *Belgium*, § 26.

[116] *Findlay* v. *United Kingdom*, §§ 74–80, confirmed in *Wilkinson and Allen* v. *United Kingdom*; *Coyne* v. *United Kingdom*; *Mills* v. *United Kingdom*; and *Thompson* v. *United Kingdom* with an interesting and somewhat puzzling discussion about the possibility of waiver.

[117] e.g. for the Air Force, *Cable and others* v. *United Kingdom*.

concerned—both captains—had not received any legal training, remained subject to military discipline and assessment reports and were not insulated from army influence by any legal provision'.[118] Further reservations were caused by the fact that a non-judicial 'reviewing authority' was competent to quash the judgment.

Finally, the Grand Chamber examined the issue in *Cooper* which concerned the Royal Air Force. While, in *Morris*,[119] the chamber had been unanimous in finding a violation, in *Cooper* the Grand Chamber, again unanimously, reached the opposite result. It noted that there was now a clear separation of functions. The Higher Authority transferred the case to the Prosecuting Authority which was alone competent to decide on whether the suspect was to stand trial before the court-martial.[120] The Court did not regard it as decisive that the military judges were not legally trained as they could benefit from instructions and the guidance of the Judge Advocate, they received a briefing note from the Court-Martial Administration Unit, and they could not be reported on in connection with their judicial function.[121] As to the Review Authority, the Grand Chamber pointed out that the ultimate decision would always lie with the Court-Martial Appeal Court.[122]

The Grand Chamber also examined the question as to whether the Navy's court-martial could be regarded as independent and impartial.[123] Here it came to a negative result. The essential point lay in the position of the Judge Advocate who was not a civilian and who, due to the reporting system, could not be regarded as being entirely independent.[124]

The case of *Werner* v. *Poland* illustrates a possible parallel in civil proceedings: a judge submitted to his own court a motion for the applicant to be dismissed as a liquidator in insolvency proceedings. Under these circumstances 'she could be regarded as giving objective grounds for believing that the court deciding on this motion lacked impartiality'[125] but the same result could also be achieved by looking at the subjective aspect.[126]

(b) As a Member of the Police

In the application of Mr Jón Kristinsson, the Icelandic system of summary proceedings was at issue. The deputy chief of police handled minor offences entirely on his own—he also fulfilled the role of a criminal judge. The Commission came to the conclusion that 'there were reasons to fear that [the person concerned], in his capacity as judge, did not offer sufficient guarantees of

[118] Judge Costa summing up in his separate opinion in *Cooper* v. *United Kingdom*.
[119] *Morris* v. *United Kingdom*, §§ 59–77.   [120] *Cooper* v. *United Kingdom (GC)*, § 112.
[121] Ibid., §§ 123–5; the Grand Chamber rightly pointed out that in the domain of civil proceedings it was not unusual to have judges without legal training.   [122] Ibid., § 131.
[123] *Grieves* v. *United Kingdom (GC)*; see also *Smith and Ford* v. *United Kingdom*, § 25; and *Moore and Gordon* v. *United Kingdom*, § 24; *GK* v. *United Kingdom; Le Petit* v. *United Kingdom*.
[124] *Grieves* v. *United Kingdom (GC)*, §§ 87–90.   [125] *Werner* v. *Poland*, § 44.
[126] Ibid., § 41.

impartiality';[127] the Government seem to have accepted this conclusion and the case was settled and struck off the list of cases by the Court.[128]

(c) As an Investigator

The second leading case regarding lack of impartiality due to the judge having a succession of functions in the same proceedings is *De Cubber*. In this case Mr Pilate had first acted as an investigating judge and later as a trial judge in the same case against the applicant. The Court came to the conclusion that this was not compatible with the objective requirement of impartiality. It based this finding on a number of considerations:

- the fact that, in Belgian law, the investigating judge belonged to the 'criminal investigation police' (*'officier de la police judiciaire'*) and acted under the general supervision of the *procureur général*;
- the secret, inquisitorial character of the preparatory investigation;
- the fact that Mr Pilate had ordered the arrest of the applicant and interrogated him many times during the investigation;
- the fact that Mr Pilate knew the file very well, which gave him an advantage over his fellow judges in the chamber which also meant a particularly strong influence on the outcome of the trial;
- the fact that in this situation Mr Pilate might also have a pre-formed opinion on the conduct of the applicant;
- the fact that the trial court might be called upon 'to review the lawfulness of measures taken or ordered by the investigating judge'; and
- the rule that Mr Pilate would have been barred from presiding over an assizes court because he had acted as an investigating judge in the same case, which betrayed a certain concern of the Belgian legislator for the question of impartiality—at least as far as the appearance of impartiality is concerned.[129]

This judgment merits full approval, although the reasoning is not entirely satisfactory. In particular, the fact that the Court invoked a multitude of arguments falls to be criticized. In my view, the reasoning might have been a lot less complicated. If one analyses the role of an investigating judge who acts in the manner of Mr Pilate, the image of a sleuth-hound comes to mind. The investigating judge is out to find the truth, a truth which the suspect typically tries to conceal. The suspect senses that the investigating judge is after him or her and tries, as it were, to escape. He may also find that the race is not quite fair. In fact, the investigator is equipped with a variety of coercive powers, the most far-reaching of which is that of having the accused locked up. In this situation, it is impossible to conceive that the suspect would regard the investigating judge as anything other than an adversary. This impression will not

---

[127] *Jón Kristinsson* v. *Iceland* Application 12170/86, report of 8 Mar. 1989, annexed to the judgment, p. 52, § 57.
[128] A friendly settlement was also reached in the analogous case of *Sverrisson* v. *Iceland* Application 13291/87.   [129] *De Cubber* v. *Belgium*, §§ 29 et seq.

simply vanish when the accused is confronted with the same person as a judge at the trial. It may be that, under domestic law, the investigating judge is regarded as an impartial officer and that the law requires him to investigate also into circumstances favourable to the defence.[130] However, such abstract concepts cannot eliminate the psychological realities which must be decisive in this context. For this reason it seems fair to say that an investigation authority will always present an appearance of bias and cannot, therefore, ever be regarded as a fully impartial judge. In substance, this has been confirmed in *Tierce and others* v. *San Marino*.[131]

This view was not only accepted by the Belgian *cour de cassation* which changed its case-law accordingly,[132] but also adopted by the Swiss Federal Tribunal which had, earlier on, accepted as legitimate the existence of cumulative functions:[133] it adopted the Court's approach as a reaction to the *De Cubber* judgment.[134]

The case of *Pfeifer and Plankl* v. *Austria* confirmed the judgment in *De Cubber*, although the case presents two elements which can serve to distinguish it from the earlier case. First, the domestic legislation did not allow for a former investigating judge to function as a trial judge. It was not necessary for the Court, therefore, to examine the activities which the persons concerned had carried out during the pre-trial proceedings, as the law itself expressed doubts about their impartiality. Here, 'the complaint of the lack of an "impartial" tribunal and of that of the lack of a tribunal "established by law" coincide[d] in substance'.[135] The same problem came up again in *Bulut* where counsel for the defence clearly waived the right to challenge the judge in question. Despite this the Court still examined the question of impartiality. As the judge's role in the investigation was limited to the questioning of two witnesses the Court determined—under the objective test—that there had not been a violation of the Convention.[136]

The issue arose again in the case of *Fey* v. *Austria*. The applicant was tried by the Zell am Ziller District Court with Ms Andrea Kohlegger as a single judge. Ms Kohlegger had also performed a number of acts of investigation, including the gathering of information by telephone and interrogating the victim. The Commission had come to the conclusion, by sixteen votes to three, that there had been a violation; the Court, by seven votes to two, reached the opposite result.[137]

---

[130] This is usually the case e.g. in Swiss criminal proceedings, which led to some criticism of the judgment referred to hereafter (BGE 112 Ia 290 ff.) by a federal judge; see Spühler (1990) 328.

[131] *Tierce and others* v. *San Marino*, §§ 78 et seq.

[132] See the judgments quoted by Veldt (1997) 81.   [133] BGE 104 Ia 271 ff., 275.

[134] BGE 112 Ia 297.

[135] *Pfeifer and Plankl* v. *Austria*, § 36. In fact, the real issue in that case was whether the applicant had validly waived his right to an independent and impartial tribunal established by law; the answer was that he had not because he had done so when being visited by the judge in his prison cell in the absence of his lawyer.   [136] *Bulut* v. *Austria*, §§ 29 et seq.

[137] *Fey* v. *Austria*, § 23.

The reasoning of the Court took up the approach in *De Cubber*—there is a detailed analysis of what the judge had actually done in her earlier function: 'What matters is the extent and nature of the pre-trial measures taken by the judge'.[138] Here, the Court took into account

- that there had already been a formal preliminary investigation;[139]
- that it was true that Ms Kohlegger had interrogated the victim in these proceedings, but that she had done so under a letter rogatory from the investigating judge who had indicated which questions were to be put;
- that it had not been for her to examine the merits of the case;
- that it did not appear from the file that she actually had done so;
- that at the time she questioned the victim, there was no prospect that she would at a later stage try the case;
- that, while she later 'undertook certain pre-trial measures', 'these measures were, in the Court's view of a preparatory character, being designed to complete the case-file before the hearing';
- that by setting the case down for trial, she did not betray a belief that the applicant was probably guilty—it could not be equated to a 'formal decision to commit an accused for trial', such a step was not provided for in the proceedings in issue;
- that the judge faced the applicant for the first time at the court's hearing and that, accordingly, 'it was only at that stage she was in a position to form an opinion as to the applicant's guilt'; and
- that the judge had acquitted the applicant on one of two counts.[140]

The Court then summed up: 'Thus, the extent and nature of the pre-trial measures taken by the District Judge are clearly distinguishable from those that were dealt with in the above-mentioned *De Cubber* judgment'.[141]

The judgment in *Fey* has been interpreted as modifying the case-law, and as representing a less strict approach to impartiality in cases where the judge had dealt with the case before in a different capacity.[142] In my view, the Court has not really altered its jurisprudence but has followed the method adopted in *De Cubber*. My criticism refers to the methodology used by the Court and not just to the result. Rather than formulating clear criteria which could serve as a guideline and make its case-law predictable, the judgment enumerates a rather large number of details regarding the proceedings in issue. Its reasoning has an anecdotal touch to it. Furthermore, some of the criteria are not convincing at all, such as the fact that the judge had acquitted the defendant on one count. The radical concentration of the Court on the facts to be decided in the specific case at issue seems to represent an almost phobic rejection of any general principle,

---

[138] Ibid., § 30.

[139] It must be noted that the investigation carried out by the judge in the present case was a special procedure which is not carried out by an investigating judge. Therefore, there was no question of any violation of domestic law as had been the case in *Pfeifer and Plankl*.

[140] *Fey* v. *Austria*, §§ 31–4.   [141] Ibid., § 35.

[142] Veldt (1997) 87; see also the dissenting opinion of Judge Spielmann.

and is not satisfactory in a field such as criminal procedure where reliable and foreseeable rules actually take on the function of safeguards in their own right. In proceeding in this way, the Court disregards its responsibility for developing the European law of human rights. It ought to aim to set clear limits rather than fiddling around with the details of each single application.

Finally, the case of *Nortier* v. *Netherlands* must be mentioned in this context, although its significance lies elsewhere.[143] The judge here was a juvenile judge (a somewhat equivocal translation of the Dutch '*Kinderrechter*') who had also acted as investigating judge in accordance with the law. The Court examined the details and found that the judge had made pre-trial decisions 'relating to detention on remand'. 'Apart from his decisions relating to the applicant's detention on remand, Juvenile Judge Meulenbroek made no other pre-trial decisions than the one allowing the application made by the prosecution for a psychiatric examination of the applicant, which was not contested by the latter. He made no other use of his powers as investigating judge' and thus there was no violation of Article 6 § 1.[144]

(d) As Member of a Body Responsible for Preparing the Indictment

In *Ben Yaacoub* v. *Belgium* the Court was presented with another case in which one person had preformed a succession of functions: the applicant had been convicted of robbery by the Dendermonde Criminal Court presided over by Judge De Neve. This judge had previously sat as a single judge of the *chambre du conseil*; he had not only confirmed the warrant of arrest against the applicant but had also extended the period of his detention and finally taken a decision committing him to trial. The Commission came to the conclusion that it was justifiable for the applicant to have had doubts as to Mr De Neve's impartiality. It laid considerable weight on the fact that the judge had at one point refused to allow the applicant's release because 'there was sufficient evidence of his guilt'.[145] Furthermore, when deciding on the committal, he had to assess whether there was 'substantial evidence' of the applicant's guilt, which was not that far away from saying that his guilt was proved.[146] The arguments of the Commission were apparently convincing—the *cour de cassation* adapted its case-law accordingly and the case was settled before the Court.[147]

[143] The Court avoided deciding a very difficult issue in this case: the application of Art. 6 to proceedings against minors. The rule that the same person should act as an investigating magistrate and as judge on the merits has the purpose of avoiding an approach to young delinquents which is too formalized and institutional. Elements of a psychological and pedagogical character are mixed with considerations of fair trial. The question whether such a distinction is acceptable remains open to doubt. In the judgments *T and V* v. *United Kingdom*, the applicability of Art. 6 was not in question because the children had been dealt with in accordance with the rules set up for adults which was seen as amounting to a violation of Art. 6.   [144] *Nortier* v. *Netherlands*, §§ 34, 37.

[145] *Ben Yaacoub* v. *Belgium* Application 9976/82, Report of the Commission, § 108.

[146] Ibid., § 109.

[147] See references in *Ben Yaacoub* v. *Belgium*, § 15 and in Veldt (1997) 115, n. 138.

In a similar case, *Saraivo de Carvalho* v. *Portugal*, which turned up some years later, the Court found no breach of Article 6. Here, the judge, Mr Salvado, had issued a *despacho de pronúncia* which constitutes a decision that a case be brought before the court to be tried. According to the Portuguese Constitutional Court, this decision 'was designed solely to verify the probability of guilt in order to avoid a trial where there was no prima facie evidence. It was thus a decision on the viability of the indictment and did not entail any prejudice on the part of the judge when the merits were being considered'.[148]

The Court followed its usual method and examined in detail the activities of the judge in his earlier function. In particular, it noted:

- that Mr Salvado had found no irregularity in the preliminary investigation nor 'any other impediment to a trial on the merits';
- that he had decided, with regard to four co-defendants, 'that the evidence was not sufficient to enable a reliable assessment to be made of the probability that' they were guilty;
- that he admitted the charges against the applicant and other co-defendants; and
- that he ordered the accused to be kept in detention.[149]

Furthermore, the Court took into consideration, *inter alia*:

- that the issues Mr Salvado had to deal with were 'not the same as those which are decisive for his final judgment';
- that a number of co-defendants were finally acquitted;
- that the applicant had not appealed against the *despacho de pronúncia*; and
- that the 'preliminary assessment of the available evidence [could not] be regarded as a formal finding of guilt'.[150]

Again, not all of these criteria are convincing. The first one could be reversed—perhaps another judge who had not been involved would have found irregularities. The one mentioned last seems to be the most objectionable one because it has a slightly polemical touch to it. In fact, in none of the cases where the Court had found that doubts as to impartiality were justified, had there been a formal finding of guilt. Neither had any of those other judges had to deal with the same issues which were decisive for the judgment.

This decision has been criticized by Laurent Sermet.[151] In my view it can hardly be reconciled with *Ben Yaacoub*, but one has to bear in mind that there we have only the report of the Commission, the Court did not pronounce on the merits. But it is remarkable that in *Bulut* the Court stressed the fact that the judge in question, Mr Schaumburger, was not 'responsible for . . . deciding whether the accused should be brought to trial', while here this decision was taken by the judge in question.[152] It is difficult not to view this jurisprudence as being somewhat inconsistent. This might well be the result of the Court's

---

[148] *Saraiva de Carvalho* v. *Portugal*, § 20.   [149] Ibid., § 36.   [150] Ibid., §§ 37 et seq.
[151] Sermet (1994) at 262: 'un nivellement par le bas'.   [152] *Bulut* v. *Austria*, § 34.

methodology which I have already criticized for focusing on details of the facts rather than delineating clear principles.

A violation was, however, found in *Castillo Algar* where two of the judges had previously taken part in a decision on an appeal of the applicant for dismissal of the case.[153]

(e) Having Taken One or More Decisions Regarding the Defendant's Detention

A number of cases dealt with by the Commission and the Court concern judges who had taken decisions regarding the defendant's pre-trial detention—of course they were always decisions ordering or prolonging the applicant's deprivation of liberty, not decisions allowing his or her release, whether on bail or otherwise. The first such case to come before the Court was *Hauschildt* v. *Denmark*. The court which had tried the applicant had taken a number of decisions rejecting his applications for release. The Commission considered that this did not affect the aspect of impartiality, but the Court, while agreeing in principle, came to the opposite conclusion. For once, the specific features of the case worked in favour of the applicant. The decisive element was a particularity of Danish law. According to section 762(2) of the Administration of Justice Act, the judge had to be satisfied that there was a 'particularly confirmed suspicion' against the accused, which was equivalent to 'a very high degree of clarity with regard to the question of guilt... Thus the difference between the issue the judge has to settle when applying this section and the issue he will have to settle when giving judgment at the trial becomes tenuous'.[154]

While this judgment is quite convincing, it is important to stress what it does *not* say: it does not say that there are reasons to doubt the impartiality of a judge if he or she has previously taken one or more decisions allowing or prolonging the applicant's detention on remand. In fact, it is quite natural that once a case has been referred to the trial court, it is this court which has responsibility for the defendant's position and that applications for release must be addressed to this court. Normally, the decision whether or not to grant such requests is determined not by the degree of suspicion hanging over the applicant, although some suspicion must, of course, persist, but by the continuing danger that the accused may abscond or meddle with the evidence.[155] These are issues clearly distinguishable from the question of the applicant's guilt.[156]

The case of *Sainte-Marie* v. *France* confirms this, although it presents certain particularities. Here, two judges of the criminal appeals division of the Pau court of appeal had previously sat on the indictment division ('*chambre d'accusation*') which had dismissed the applicant's application for release. This application

[153] *Castillo Algar* v. *Spain*, §§ 46 et seq.   [154] *Hauschildt* v. *Denmark*, § 52.

[155] See further Chapter 5, section I below.

[156] A case of this kind was *Mulders* v. *Netherlands* Application 23231/94 (1995), decision of 6 Apr. 1995, unreported, which the Commission declared inadmissible; see also *Callens* v. *Belgium* Application 1314/87.

concerned different proceedings, and therefore, the principle established in the *Ben Yaacoub* case did not apply. However, the Court scarcely relied at all on the distinction that the investigation had been parallel to the one now in issue. The main argument was that the indictment division's decision had been based on the applicant's own statements which were furthermore corroborated by uncontested physical evidence. The special features which had been decisive in *Hauschildt* were not at issue in this case.[157]

(f) As a Judge on the Merits
A number of cases concern situations where a judgment was quashed and then sent back to the same court for a second trial. *Diennet* v. *France* involved a disciplinary body, the National Council of the *ordre des médecins*. The Court, which found that there had been no violation of the Convention, essentially relied on the argument that the second judgment was based on the same facts as the first one which had been quashed on procedural grounds and there were no new factors.[158]

In *Thomann* v. *Switzerland* the applicant was first tried in his absence; upon request he was granted the right to a retrial before the same court. The Court did not see this as justifying fears regarding the impartiality of the judges concerned: 'They undertake a fresh consideration of the whole case; all the issues raised by the case remain open and this time are examined in adversarial proceedings with the benefit of the more comprehensive information that may be obtained from the appearance of the defendant in person'.[159] The Court also accepted an argument of a more practical nature: it would be unfair if a person who had first been tried *in absentia* were entitled to a retrial before a new court and the judiciary would be burdened too heavily if a different tribunal would have to start examining such cases from scratch.[160]

The Court did, however, find a violation in *De Haan* v. *Netherlands*, where the judge had, as a first step, decreed a 'penal order' against the defendant. After the latter opposed the imposition of this order, the same judge presided over the trial. The Court considered this case to be closer to *Oberschlick* than to *Thomann*. In *Oberschlick* the problem had been that the judge who presided over the proceedings before the Vienna Court of Appeal had already sat in the first set of proceedings.[161] Another two judges were in the same situation and they all ought to have stepped down under Austrian law.[162] The distinction between these three cases is not very convincing and it is not surprising that it has met with criticism,[163] with which I tend to agree. It is remarkable that the Court

---

[157] *Sainte-Marie* v. *France*, §§ 32 et seq.; see also *Rossi* v. *France* Application 11879/75.
[158] *Diennet* v. *France*, § 38.   [159] *Thomann* v. *Switzerland*, § 35.   [160] Ibid., § 36.
[161] *Oberschlick* v. *Austria*, §§ 48–51.
[162] It is slightly ironic, to say the least, that according to the Convention as revised by Protocol No. 11, Art. 27 § 3, the President of the Chamber and the national member sit for a second time if a case is referred to the Grand Chamber after the Chamber has passed judgment. This has often been criticized; see e.g. Zanghí (2000) 308 et seq.   [163] Veldt (1997) 131.

attached so much weight to the possibility of the error being healed on appeal,[164] because this had been expressly and correctly excluded in *De Cubber*.[165] There, the Court made a distinction between cases concerning 'Article 6 in its traditional and natural sphere of application' as opposed to instances where the proceedings were not *a priori* considered as concerning a 'criminal charge', but only as a result of the 'autonomous' interpretation of that term by the Court. This is a rather extraordinary, and as I see it unique, observation. Otherwise, and contrary to what the Commission had attempted in its report in *Engel and others* v. *Netherlands*, it is 'either/or'. Either Article 6 applies or it does not. Here, the Court seemed to suggest that there exists something which one might be tempted to call 'Article 6 light' for cases which are only 'artificially' considered as being 'criminal'.

It seems that in *De Haan* like in *Thomann* the judge had first formed an opinion provisionally, being quite aware of the fact that he might be called upon to re-examine it in ordinary proceedings or in the presence of the accused. 'Penal orders' are regularly and routinely used—indeed the purpose of such proceedings is to economize the scarce resources of the judiciary.[166]

(g) As a Member of the *Conseil d'Etat* which had Given an Opinion on the Regulations at Issue

With regard to the Luxembourg *Conseil d'Etat* the Court saw a problem of 'structural impartiality'. In *Procola* the *Conseil d'Etat* was called upon to decide whether a regulation was lawful.[167] However, it had already passed an advisory opinion on this issue in its function as an organ to control the constitutionality of legislation, and four of its five members had taken part in that previous decision. It is rather obvious that with regard to these members there were valid reasons to assume that they had already formed an opinion on the question they were called upon to decide.

A similar issue arose in the Netherlands with regard to the Administrative Jurisdiction Division of the Council of State. However, here the Court found that the issue before that jurisdiction could not be regarded as 'the same case' or 'the same decision'. Therefore, there was no violation.[168]

Finally, the case of *McGonnell* can be mentioned here. It concerned the role of the Bailiff of the Caribbean island of St Martin which belongs to the United Kingdom. In this case he was called upon to sit on a dispute concerning the planning of constructions—he had himself been associated with the adoption of the plan and could therefore not be regarded as impartial.[169]

---

[164] The judgment refers to *Albert and Le Compte* v. *Belgium*, § 29 and to *British-American Tobacco Company Ltd* v. *Netherlands*, § 78.   [165] *De Cubber* v. *Belgium*, §§ 32 et seq.
[166] Which is perfectly in line with the Convention; cf. *Deweer* v. *Belgium*. On the other hand, the Swiss Federal Tribunal had in a way anticipated *De Haan* and come to the conclusion that ordinary proceedings ought not to take place before the judge who had issued the 'penal order'; BGE 114 Ia 143. See also Haefliger and Schürmann (1999) 173.
[167] *Procola* v. *Luxembourg*, §§ 44 et seq.   [168] *Kleyn and others* v. *Netherlands*, §§ 200–2.
[169] *McGonnell* v. *United Kingdom*, §§ 52–7.

(h) In a Combination of Multiple Functions

In *Padovani* v. *Italy* the Court was faced with a system instituted to facilitate and speed up proceedings. The applicant had been found in possession of stolen goods and was arrested by the police. He was brought before the Bergamo *pretore*. In the first place this magistrate performed the functions required under Article 5 § 3: after hearing the arrestee he confirmed his arrest. He then acted as an investigating judge by interrogating two witnesses. He fixed a hearing on the merits before himself and thereby exercised the function of an authority of indictment. After a hearing which lasted for half an hour, in which the public prosecutor's office was represented by counsel, he convicted the applicant and sentenced him to a suspended sentence of one year's imprisonment.[170]

The Commission found a violation by sixteen votes to two, while the Court (a Chamber of nine judges) was unanimous in finding that there had been no violation of Article 6 § 1. Not surprisingly, it stated that there was no proof of any 'subjective bias' with the *pretore*. On the objective side the Court recognized that the fact that the *pretore* 'had before the trial questioned the applicant, taken measures restricting his liberty and summoned him to appear before him . . . could occasion misgivings on the part of the applicant'. However, it was of the opinion that these misgivings were not justified. The investigation consisted only of the questioning of three suspects, the magistrate could have carried out further measures. The arrest warrant was issued through reliance on *inter alia* the applicant's statements. The *pretore* applied a procedure, *giudizio direttissimo*, which was designed for dealing speedily with suspects caught *in flagrante*.

Neither the decision nor the justification can be described as persuasive. It is understandable that the Court respected the efforts of the Italian legislation to speed up proceedings, but here we find a stark contrast to the earlier case-law, in particular to the judgment in *De Cubber*. The reasoning is again somewhat anecdotal rather than systematic. There seems to be an underlying assumption that any court would have convicted the applicant; that he did not establish that he had suffered any disadvantage because of the succession of functions fulfilled by the *pretore* in his case. However, in relation to the impartiality of the tribunal, the important principle stressed by the Court in *Artico*[171] must also apply: in response to the Government's objection that there was no evidence of any prejudice caused by the absence of a defence counsel it replied that 'an interpretation that introduced this requirement into the sub-paragraph would deprive it in large measure of its substance'.[172] The Italian Constitutional Court, however, declared these proceedings before the *pretore* to be unconstitutional.[173]

---

[170] *Padovani* v. *Italy*, §§ 18, 28.
[171] *Artico* v. *Italy*, § 35; see also the rejection by the Commission of the objection of the Government in *Jón Kristinsson* v. *Iceland* Application 12170/86, report of 8 Mar. 1989, annexed to the judgment, §§ 33–9.   [172] See also the criticism of Veldt (1997) 143 et seq.
[173] Chiavario (1992) 78.

(i) Conclusion

While many of the judgments passed on the issue of prior involvement are quite convincing, doubts arise with regard to the *reasoning* of the Court. It follows the general tendency of looking carefully at the specific features of each case rather than delineating clear guidelines. This makes it difficult to predict how the Court is going to decide the next case. I would suggest that a violation of Article 6 should always be found when a national judge successively acts in a number of functions which are attributed to different institutions under domestic law. Whether this results under domestic law in the judgment being declared null and void or whether it is only considered as grounds for nullity, is not, in my view, decisive.

Conversely, the interpretation of the Convention cannot, of course, rely entirely on domestic law. The fact that domestic law attributes different functions to the same judge does not mean that no problems of prior involvement under the Convention arise. It may be that, as for example in *Fey* and in *Bulut*, domestic law allows for one person to have cumulative functions which are separated in other legal orders. In such cases the Court will not be able to avoid examining in some detail these different functions. However, in the end it ought to decide on the basis of solid and clear principles which enhance legal certainty and improve the foreseeability of further developments in the case-law.

2. Lack of Impartiality Due to an Affiliation to One of the Parties

The impartiality of a tribunal may be affected by the fact that its composition cannot be regarded as neutral in the eyes of a party. This was the case in two applications against Sweden. In *Langborger* the applicant was bound by a negotiation clause in his leasing contract. He opposed the obligation to submit to such negotiation which had been agreed by organizations representing the interests of landlords and tenants. As the tribunal which was to decide on his claims was composed, *inter alia*, of representatives of both of these organizations, the court could not be regarded as being impartial, because the representatives of the two organizations which had agreed on the negotiation clause were likely jointly to oppose the applicant's claim.[174]

In *Holm* the applicant was a person of conservative political orientation.[175] In a publication edited by Tidens förlag AB he was described as having affinities to and contacts with Nazi circles. He filed a suit for libel which was decided by a court comprising lay judges, which was dominated by representatives of the Social Democratic Party. In this situation he was justified in his apprehensions that the court would not be impartial.[176]

The case of *Pullar* v. *United Kingdom* provides an example of the operation of this principle in criminal proceedings.[177] The applicant, a member of the

---

[174] *Langborger* v. *Sweden*, § 35.
[176] *Holm* v. *Sweden*, §§ 31, 33.
[175] For a similar case, see *Gautrin and others* v. *France*.
[177] *Pullar* v. *United Kingdom*, §§ 34 et seq.

Tayside Regional Council, was accused of having offered to take care of an engineer's interest in the town in return for a bribe. The engineer, however, did not accept the offer. Proceedings for corruption were brought in which the engineer was the main witness. At the trial, it turned out that one of the jurors was one of the engineer's fifteen employees. The applicant feared that this juror would be inclined, at the outset, to believe his employer, who was the main witness, rather than the defendant. The Commission had concluded that there was a violation of the right to an impartial tribunal, but the Court came to the opposite conclusion. The reasoning of this judgment is rather surprising in that reference is made to the fact that the juror in question was, at any rate, only one out of fifteen jurors. If an accused appears before a collective tribunal, the right to impartiality certainly must apply to each and every one of the members of such a tribunal. No judge of the Strasbourg Court would sit on a case although he or she was biased and then explain that he or she was only one out of seven or nineteen!

The small size of Switzerland, where the judiciary is in the competence of the cantons not the confederation, means that lawyers frequently hold various positions. For instance, a practising attorney may also serve as a judge on an administrative court. In *Wettstein* the applicant complained of the fact that Judge R who sat on the court had, in other proceedings, represented the party opposing him. The Court accepted that this could objectively justify the applicant's apprehension that Judge R. might not be entirely impartial.[178]

3. Procedural Issues

Finally, an interesting question arose in *Thorgeirson* v. *Iceland*.[179] The applicant was a journalist who had brought forward serious accusations against the police. He complained *inter alia* of the fact that the public prosecutor had been absent during certain sittings in his trial. He alleged that due to this absence the judge was called upon to formulate in his head all the arguments for the accusation.

Despite the fact that the Court came to the conclusion, as the Commission had before, that there was no violation of Article 6, it indicated quite clearly that it agreed with the applicant's basic analysis. At any rate, this is the conclusion which, in my view must be drawn from the approach taken by the Court: it examined in detail what had happened during the sessions where the prosecutor had *not* been represented. It found that these sessions were of no importance and that the court could not have been called upon to perform any acts which otherwise would have been the task of the prosecution. It follows that, in order to give the appearance of impartiality, the court must hear both parties, the public prosecutor must certainly plead on the merits in order that there can be an adversarial dispute.[180]

---

[178] *Wettstein* v. *Switzerland*, §§ 45–9.   [179] *Thorgeir Thorgeirson* v. *Iceland*, § 52 et seq.
[180] A somewhat embarrassing case must be mentioned here. In *Higgins and others* v. *France* the applicants were involved in civil proceedings in Tahiti and complained to the *cour de cassation* in

V. CONCLUSION

One might expect the question of whether a court can be regarded as independent and impartial to be a rather straightforward one which does not raise any difficult problems. That this assumption is erroneous is demonstrated by the fact that an abundance of problems have arisen. While the basic principles of independence and impartiality are universally accepted, difficulties arise when small political entities attribute different functions to the same person[181] or when efforts are made to streamline criminal proceedings.[182] While the majority of these problems have found a satisfactory solution in the case-law of the ECtHR, there are several judgments which must be criticized. In particular, it is to be regretted that the Court is so reluctant to set clear and binding rules.[183]

Paris about the lack of impartiality of the Papeete court of appeal. The *cour de cassation* agreed and transferred two proceedings to the *cour d'appel* of Paris, but apparently forgot the third set, although there was nothing to distinguish it from the others.

[181] Cf. the issue in *Jón Kristinsson* v. *Iceland*.   [182] Cf. *Padovani* v. *Italy*.

[183] For a deeper discussion of the subject, see *inter alia*: Dourneau-Josette (2003); Gonzales (2004); Costa (2002); van Dijk (2000); Costa (2001); Papier (2001); Hamm (2001); Sendler (2001); Dumont (2000); Poncet (2000); Van Compernolle (2000a); Van Compernolle (2000b); Koering Joulin (1998); Addo (1998); Bonichot (1998); Martens (1996); Spielmann (1996); Danelius (1992); and Senese (1992).

Chapter 4

The General Right to a Fair Trial

I. INTRODUCTION

A. The Texts

... everyone shall be entitled to a fair ... hearing ...

ICCPR, Art. 14 § 1

'... everyone is entitled to a fair ... hearing ...

ECHR, Art. 6 § 1

Every person has the right to a hearing, with due guarantees ...

AHRC, Art. 8 § 1

There are only minimal differences between the Covenant and the Convention and none are particularly significant. It could be argued that the Convention is more direct—perhaps even more authoritative—but any differences are largely a matter of style. What is striking, however, is that the Inter-American Convention avoids the use of the term 'fair'. It is not outwith the bounds of possibility that this omission of the term was due to its perceived ties to the common law and to the United States. There is no reason to assume, however, that the provision was intended to have a substantively different meaning from its counterparts in the other texts.

The term 'fair' is also used in Article 10 of the UDHR, Article 67 § 1 of the Rome Statute of the ICC, Article 130 of the Geneva Convention relative to the Treatment of Prisoners of War, Article 47 of the European Union Charter of Fundamental Rights, and Article 19(e) of the Cairo Declaration on Human Rights in Islam; it does not figure in the African Charter on Human and Peoples' Rights, but the African Commission on Human Rights has adopted a Resolution on the Right to Recourse Procedure and Fair Trial.[1]

B. The Origins

The right to a fair trial was included in Article 10 of the very first draft of the UDHR. The term did not figure, however, in Article 11, in which the specific

---

[1] Quoted from Myjer, Hancock, and Cowdery (2003) 75 et seq.

safeguards for the defence in criminal proceedings are set out. It was added following a proposal from the Panamanian representative, Mr Amado, which was supported by Mr Cassin.[2] In fact, this addition was somewhat unnecessary as Article 10 referred expressly to both civil and criminal proceedings.

There seem to have been hardly any discussions as to the meaning of the term, although this should not be misunderstood as indicating that the provisions were entirely unambiguous. At one point, the Egyptian representative, Mr Ramada, was of the opinion that the term 'fair' also covered the impartiality of the tribunal.[3]

What can definitely be said is that the term stems from the common law. It has no real equivalent in other languages—for lack of a better term the French decided to use '*équitablement*'.[4] In German the word 'fair' has simply been adopted by the Council of Europe and the Swiss[5] and Austrian[6] translations. Germany took the expression '*in billiger Weise*', but Vogler agrees that this cannot be regarded as a precise translation of the term 'fair'.[7] '*Billig*', in everyday language, means 'cheap'; as a legal term it corresponds largely to 'equitable'. This, again, derives from the Latin '*aequitas*' which means justice for the individual case as opposed to justice in the sense of reliability and legal certainty. In Dutch the term used is '*eerlijk*', related to 'honest', while the Italian term '*equamente*' corresponds to the French version.

'Fairness' is often associated with sporting activities, it evokes values such as respect for the opponent and for the rules of the game, honesty, self-restraint, a readiness to fight for victory, but not for victory at all costs.

Both the word and the idea of due process stem from the Anglo-Saxon tradition and can be traced back to Magna Carta of 1215.[8] This is particularly so in the context of the *topos* 'equality of arms', as expressed in Articles 14 § 3(e) of the ICCPR and 6 § 3(d) of the ECHR—although not in Article 8 § 2(f) of the ACHR—and developed in the case-law. This was sometimes perceived critically as a foreign influence on the European continent.[9]

C. Importance and Purpose

The ECtHR often uses a standard phrase to stress the importance of the right to a fair trial: 'The right to a fair trial holds so prominent a place in a democratic society that there can be no justification for interpreting the guarantees of Article 6 § 1 of the Convention restrictively'.[10] This is frequently, though not

---

[2] Weissbrodt (2001) 18.   [3] Ibid., 55.
[4] Mr Ordonneau admitted difficulties with the translation; cf. ibid., 55.   [5] SR 0.101.
[6] BGBl. Nr. 210/1958.   [7] Vogler (1986) Art. 6 N 341 with reference to Radbruch in n. 5.
[8] Nowak (1993) Art. 14 N 1.
[9] e.g. Levi (1989) 228. For a comparative study of equality of arms in English, German, and Polish criminal-procedure law, see Małgorzata Wąsek-Wiaderek (2000) 43 et seq.
[10] *AB* v. *Slovakia*, § 54. See also e.g. *Moreira de Azevedo* v. *Portugal*, § 66; *Belziuk* v. *Poland*, § 37; *Perez* v. *France*, § 64; *Adolf* v. *Austria*, § 30; *Artico* v. *Italy*, § 33; *De Cubber* v. *Belgium*, § 30; *Delcourt* v. *Belgium*, § 25. When the majority in a case finds no violation, dissenting judges like to quote this

exclusively,[11] used in cases where the Court concludes that the right to a fair trial has been violated.[12] I doubt, however, whether this phraseology has more than a rhetorical significance. In dissenting opinions to the *Sutter* judgment, Judge Ganshof van der Meersch stated that the Convention rights generally ought not to be interpreted restrictively, while Judge Bernhardt, joined by Judges Bindschedler-Robert and Matscher declared that 'Article 6 para. 1 can and should be interpreted restrictively'.[13]

I do not find either position particularly convincing and neither can be said to facilitate the interpretation of the Convention. The acceptance of either will be impossible without some sort of qualification.[14] In *Wemhoff* the Court rejected a presumption in favour of the state: '[I]t is also necessary to seek the interpretation that is most appropriate in order to realise the aim and achieve the object of the treaty, not that which would restrict to the greatest possible degree the obligations undertaken by the Parties'.[15] This is again a sentence which fits well in cases where the Court opts for a wide interpretation of the Convention rights and meets with the same objection. Matters are more complicated, because it is not unheard of for different fundamental rights to conflict with each other. This is particularly obvious in cases where freedom of expression is relied upon to offset an interference with the right to respect for private life.[16] But it also occurs in the context of criminal proceedings which may also have to serve the function of protecting the rights of the victim.[17]

The Court is also correct to stress the importance of the principle although, in my view, it is more accurate to link its importance to the rule of law, rather than to the abstract notion of democracy.

The guarantee of a fair trial is 'only' a procedural guarantee, designed to secure 'procedural justice' rather than 'result-orientated justice', i.e. a decision or judgment based on the true facts and the correct application of the law.[18] In fact, the Strasbourg organs, in hundreds if not thousands of judgments and decisions, have stressed that they have no mandate to act as a court of fourth instance; it is not their task to ascertain whether the domestic law at issue, be it substantive or even procedural, has been correctly applied or whether the facts have been correctly established.[19] Although there are many reasons supporting this approach, two are particularly important. First, despite the fact that the Convention is a living

---

passage; see e.g. De Meyer in *Kraska* v. *Switzerland* or Loucaides in *CG* v. *United Kingdom*. An analogous formula is also used in connection with other rights, e.g. freedom of assembly; see *Djavit An* v. *Turkey*, § 56.

[11] e.g. *Adolf* v. *Austria*.   [12] Cf. the brilliant study by Olivier de Schutter (1992).
[13] *Sutter* v. *Switzerland*.   [14] Trechsel (1974) 143.
[15] *Wemhoff* v. *Germany*, § 8; see also *Delcourt* v. *Belgium*, § 25.
[16] *Von Hannover* v. *Germany*, § 56 et seq.   [17] See e.g. *X and Y* v. *Netherlands*.
[18] Trechsel (1997) 94; Trechsel (2000); the contrary view is held by Loucaides (2003) 27 at 30 et seq. For Reed and Murdoch (2001) N 5.53 the guarantee is of 'paramount importance'.
[19] See e.g. *Anderson* v. *United Kingdom* Application 44958/98; and *Johnson* v. *United Kingdom* Application 42246/98. The same approach is taken by the HRC; see McGoldrick (1994/2001) 417.

instrument, which has had a very important effect on the development of, *inter alia*, criminal-procedure law, the Court is restricted to something of a subsidiary role. The responsibility of implementing the Convention falls, in the first place, to the national authorities.[20] Second, on a more practical level, the Court would be unable to take on this function. It is not even equipped to carry out those tasks that have been assigned to it; it is in crisis and there is a risk that even its current functions will have to be seriously curtailed. It is entirely illusory to imagine that it could assume the role of a 'European Super-Court of Appeals'.

Notwithstanding such limitations, it can be said that the right to a fair trial is at the centre of both the rights of the defence, and the guarantee of the rule of law.[21] It has infiltrated, as Esser[22] rightly observes, the guarantees to personal liberty, particularly in the context of habeas corpus proceedings, and even fundamental liberties such as to the right to respect for the home,[23] and the right to life, which has been extended to include the right to an effective investigation in cases of sudden death in suspicious circumstances.[24]

There is a wealth of literature on the subject and it will not be possible, within the framework of the present study, to do justice to the many authors who have set out their ideas about the notion and the importance of the right to a fair trial. It is, at the very least, important to refer to Packer's theory of two basic models of criminal justice, crime control and due process. Despite the fact that this was written in 1968, it still provides a valid frame of reference.[25] Crime control emphasizes outcome justice, effectiveness, and speediness, while due process centres on the rights of the individual, the rights of defence, in short the concept of procedural justice. In reality most procedure laws try to find a balance between these two models. The nature of international human-rights law obviously means that it is closer to the due-process model. Nevertheless, it will try to avoid, on the one hand, excessive interference with domestic law and practice—the principle of subsidiarity—and, on the other, interventions that excessively hinder the effectiveness of the prosecution, which may also have an importance in the context of human rights, particularly in relation to victims of crime.

D. The Scope of the Right to a Fair Trial

The terms 'fair trial' and 'fair hearing' are characterized by considerable vagueness.[26] Harris, O'Boyle, and Warbrick refer to 'fair trial' as having an 'open-ended, residual quality'.[27] In fact, when the Convention came into force, it was

---

[20] See e.g. Reed and Murdoch (2001) N 3.80 et seq.

[21] *Golder* v. *United Kingdom*, 34; Sudre (2003) 299 et seq.   [22] Esser (2002) 401.

[23] Cf. *Miailhe* v. *France*.

[24] For a relatively recent example, see *Tahsin* v. *Turkey*, §§ 220 et seq.   [25] Packer (1968).

[26] Gomien, Harris, and Zwaak (1997) 187 call it 'nebulous'; Peters (2003) 127 holds that this leads to a broad margin of appreciation which is true only to a limited extent. Unfortunately, the case-law is also characterized by 'some lack of clarity'; see Reed and Murdoch (2001) N 5.54.

[27] Harris, O'Boyle, and Warbrick (1995) 202.

regarded as being so uncertain that it could not be applied by domestic courts.[28] This ambiguity is, however, a quality which it shares with other important legal terms such as 'due process' or even the principle of proportionality. The task of giving such terms a manageable shape with tangible contours falls to the judiciary, with the assistance of academic works.

To some extent, a part of this work was already done at the drafting stages. In each of the international instruments, the right to a fair trial has two components: a general one, with application in all relevant proceedings (civil, criminal and, in view of the case-law, administrative), and a specific one involving the rights of the defence in criminal proceedings. It is possible, in other words, to differentiate between the right to fair trial in the broader and in the narrower sense. This chapter concentrates on the narrower notion of fair trial. In fact, one can easily distinguish three circles covered by the term. This chapter is limited to the general guarantee set out in the first paragraph. The 'medium range' includes the rights of the defence set out in the same Article.[29] Finally, one can include the whole range of procedural guarantees, including those surrounding arrest and detention.[30]

In its standard formula for the definition of the right to a fair trial, the Court mentions two aspects: the principle of equality of arms and the right to adversarial proceedings.[31] These apply indistinctly in civil and criminal cases although the Court *did* in fact refer to a slight difference, which stems from the fact that there are specific detailed rights of the defence, which 'have a certain relevance outside the strict confines of criminal law'. It concluded that the 'the Contracting States have greater latitude when dealing with cases concerning civil rights and obligations than they have when dealing with criminal cases'.[32]

The two principles are not always clearly distinguished; in particular there are a number of judgments that rely on the equality of arms even though it is actually the adversarial character of the proceedings that is at issue. As the term 'equality of arms' indicates, this criterion is a comparative one. A comparison of the treatment of the opposing parties must be undertaken in order to ascertain whether the applicant has been disadvantaged. The notion of 'adversarial proceedings' presupposes adversaries and in a sense is more specific. It requires that the accused be informed of the case against him or her, in the sense of knowing all the evidence or arguments which the court could take into account when determining the charge and that he or she have the opportunity to challenge this evidence and contradict the arguments.

An examination of the case-law reveals that the notion of fair trial is interpreted as also including other elements, in particular the right to a reasoned decision.

---

[28] Trechsel (1974) 151 with references and criticism.
[29] Pradel (2002) N 338 distinguishes these two aspects.
[30] See also Wąsek-Wiaderek (2000) 16 on the various approaches taken by Polish authors.
[31] See e.g. *Belziuk* v. *Poland*, § 37; *Brandstetter* v. *Austria*, § 66; *Jasper* v. *United Kingdom*, § 51; *Rowe and Davis* v. *United Kingdom*, § 60; *IJL, GMR and AKP* v. *United Kingdom*, § 112; *PG and JH* v. *United Kingdom*, § 69; *GB* v. *France*, § 56.   [32] *Dombo Beheer* v. *Netherlands*, § 32.

The HRC seems to have a slightly wider view than that of the Strasbourg authorities. In *Morael* v. *France* it stated that the right to fair trial includes 'equality of arms, respect for the principle of adversary proceedings, preclusion of *ex officio reformatio in pejus*, and expeditious procedure'.[33]

Before looking at these issues in more detail it is necessary to give closer attention to the relationship between the general requirement of fairness and the specific rights of the defence.

E. The Relationship Between the General Rule and the Specific Rights: Evaluation of the Proceedings '*As a Whole*'

The texts of the relevant instruments are relatively clear. First a general rule is set out in the first paragraph of Article 14 of the ICCPR, Article 6 of the ECHR, and Article 8 of the ACHR. Then the specific rights of the defence are presented as 'minimum guarantees' (ICCPR, Art. 14 § 3; ACHR, Art. 8 § 2) or 'minimum rights' (ECHR, Art. 6 § 3).[34] This means that within the rather amorphous provision for the right to a fair trial, there are several more concrete, clear-cut guarantees.[35] If any of these guarantees are not respected, the trial cannot be viewed as having been fair—and any further discussion becomes superfluous. However, on the other hand, the fact that those rights have been respected does not yet guarantee that the trial was fair—there may be other aspects, which lead to a different result.[36]

The Court gave an impressive and, in my view, convincing example of this second approach in the *Barberà* case.[37] It took into account 'the belated transfer of the applicants from Barcelona to Madrid, the unexpected change in the court's membership immediately before the hearing opened, the brevity of the trial and, above all, the fact that very important pieces of evidence were not adequately adduced and discussed at the trial in the applicants' presence and under the watchful eye of the public' and concluded that, considered as a whole, the trial had not been fair.[38]

In cases where the conviction was partly[39] or wholly[40] based on unlawfully obtained evidence, the Court has, as a result of the combination of its limited competence and this holistic approach, come to the conclusion that there has

---

[33] *Yves Morael* v. *France*, § 210.

[34] The French text of the ICCPR and the IACHR says '*droit . . . au moins aux garanties suivantes*'; however, the ECHR reads '*droit notamment à*'. There is a slight difference: the text of the ECHR is somewhat softer, corresponding to '*inter alia*'. In case of doubt, the English text prevails.

[35] The Commission already said so in *Nielsen* v. *Denmark* Application 343/57. See also Wąsek-Wiaderek (2000) 22.

[36] *Nielsen* v. *Denmark* Application 343/57 and many later decisions and judgments. See also HRC, General Comment 13 § 5.

[37] The Commission had already introduced this approach; see e.g. *X* v. *Switzerland* Application 9000/80; *H* v. *United Kingdom* Application 10000/82.

[38] *Barberà, Messegué and Jabardo* v. *Spain*, § 89; see also *Miailhe* v. *France (No. 2)*, § 43.

[39] *Schenk* v. *Switzerland*; *Miailhe* v. *France.*   [40] *Khan* v. *United Kingdom.*

been no violation: 'It is not for the Court to substitute its view for that of the national courts which are primarily competent to determine the admissibility of evidence. It must nevertheless satisfy itself that the proceedings as a whole were fair, having regard to any possible irregularities before the case was brought before the courts of trial and appeal and checking that those courts had been able to remedy them if there were any'.[41] It is certainly possible to criticize this restrictive attitude, particularly in view of the Latin saying that *ex iniuria ius non oritur*.[42] On the other hand, the Court is certainly right in pointing out that appeal proceedings provide a way of rectifying errors made in earlier phases of the proceedings. It is, however, neither necessary nor helpful to invoke the argument of examining the proceedings 'as a whole' in order to recognize this.

Regrettably, the Court has held in a number of cases that although some of the minimum guarantees had not been complied with, an evaluation of the proceedings as a whole revealed that the trial had nevertheless been fair.[43] Thus, in *Asch* the defendant had not had the opportunity to cross-examine the main witness—yet, the Court decided that taken as a whole, the trial could not be characterized as having been unfair.[44] This was also the conclusion in *Stanford* where acoustic problems meant that the applicant, who was hard of hearing, was unable to follow the trial.[45]

These judgments are clearly unsatisfactory. In my view, the problem is related to the Court's reluctance to provide an exact meaning to the specific rights of the defence as set out in Article 6 § 3. Rather than interpreting the specific guarantees so as to give them a more precise definition, the Court seems to prefer to leave Article 6 in a cloud of ambiguity. This is perhaps most noticeable in relation to the Court's tendency not to examine whether a specific minimum guarantee has been respected or not, but to combine at the outset the specific guarantees with the general right to a fair trial and to deal with them together without proper distinction.[46] One even finds judgments where the Court states

---

[41] *Miailhe* v. *France (No. 2)*, § 43. See also in the same sense *Schenk* v. *Switzerland*, § 46; *Van Mechelen* v. *Netherlands*, § 50; *Doorson* v. *Netherlands*, § 67; *Teixeira de Castro* v. *Portugal*, § 34; *Khan* v. *United Kingdom*, § 34; *Vidal* v. *Belgium*, § 34; *Pisano* v. *Italy*, § 21; *Atlan* v. *United Kingdom*, § 39 ('proceedings in their entirety'); *H* v. *France*, § 61; *Delta* v. *France*, § 35; *Pélissier and Sassi* v. *France*, § 46; *APBP* v. *France*.

[42] Cf. the dissenting opinions of Judges Pettiti, Spielmann, De Meyer, and Carrillo Salcedo in the *Schenk* judgment; the members Trechsel and Vandenberghe in the Commission's report in *Schenk*; Loucaides in *Khan* v. *United Kingdom*.

[43] This case-law was also adopted by the Commission; see e.g. *Choudhary* v. *United Kingdom* Application 12509/86.   [44] *Asch* v. *Austria*; *Doorson* v. *Netherlands*; see Chapter 11.

[45] In *Stanford* v. *United Kingdom*, § 26 the applicant had not been able to follow the hearing because of acoustic problems—the Court blamed him for not having informed the trial court but also relied on the global appreciation of the proceedings.

[46] Cases which deal specifically and exclusively with a specific guarantee constitute the exception. In *Luedicke, Belkacem and Koç* v. *Germany* there was a violation of Art. 6 § 3(e); in *Can* v. *Austria* Application 9300/81, report of 12 July 1984, annexed to the judgment *Can* v. *Austria*, the Commission found a violation of Art. 6 § 3 (c). However, in *Goddi* v. *Italy*, § 28, the Court declared that it 'made an overall assessment' although it was a very clear case of a violation of the right to be assisted by counsel.

nonchalantly that it will examine the facts under paragraphs 1 and 3 of Article 6 without specifying which sub-paragraph of paragraph 3 it has in mind.[47]

It is thus of little surprise that this approach has drawn considerable criticism from commentators. Rzepka regards it as not only contrary to the letter but also the meaning of Article 6.[48] It also means that the Court neglects its task to develop the jurisprudence of the Convention in a clear way.[49]

This criticism is, to a large extent, justified. Yet, the reluctance of the Court to deal with problems relating to the admissibility of evidence is, as I have already indicated, not entirely without foundation. This issue is not only one of the most difficult issues in criminal-procedure law, but it is dealt with differently in different legal systems.[50] However, there ought, in my view, to be a clear limit where the evidence has been obtained in violation of the Convention.[51] Furthermore, there is no justification for the Court's policy of blurring the application of paragraphs 1 and 3 of Article 6. For the purposes of the present study, issues which are considered by the Court under Article 6 § 1 and under a specific guarantee contained in Article 6 § 3 will be addressed under the relevant specific guarantee. The reader is invited to consult certain issues under both headings, the distinction between 'lack of fairness by reason of a failure to disclose' or by a lack of 'adequate facilities for the preparation of the defence' is particularly difficult.

It is also essential to remember that the rights set out in paragraph 3 apply exclusively to the defence. This means that they do not, in principle, apply in civil proceedings. Nevertheless, the Court has interpreted 6 § 1 in such a way as to enable the application of some of the specific rights in civil proceedings. A good example is the *Airey* case where the Court convincingly extended the right to free legal assistance to civil cases where vital interests were at stake.[52] Rights which could be dealt with under Article 6 § 3(b) in criminal cases will be examined under the heading 'right to disclosure' in civil proceedings.[53]

The ambiguity in the Court's approach is particularly evident in the following passage from *Helle* v. *Finland*: 'The Court's task is to assess whether or not [the] proceedings taken as a whole were fair within the meaning of Article 6 § 1 having regard to all the relevant circumstances, including the nature of the dispute and the character of the proceedings in issue, the way in which the evidence was dealt with and whether the proceedings afforded the applicant an opportunity to state his case under conditions which did not place him at a substantial disadvantage *vis-à-vis* his [adversary]'.[54] This approach entirely neglects legal certainty in

[47] *Hadjianastassiou* v. *Greece*, § 31.
[48] Rzepka (2000) 104; other criticism is voiced by Esser (2002) 404; and Reed and Murdoch (2001) N 5.54.
[49] Esser (2002) 404, 860; Rzepka (2000) 103; Schroeder (2003) 293 at 295 and 297.
[50] Pradel (2002) N 342 et seq.; Fornito (2000); van den Wyngaert (1991) II, 775 et seq.
[51] Cf. *Khan* v. *United Kingdom*; see further Chapter 20 below.
[52] *Airey* v. *Ireland*: involving a separation in Ireland where divorce was not available.
[53] e.g. *McMichael* v. *United Kingdom*.   [54] *Helle* v. *Finland*, § 53.

favour of equity. Each judgment decided by the Court has two aspects: one concerns justice for the specific applicant, the other concerns the development of the Court's jurisprudence. Here, the latter is neglected to such a degree that the Court's methodology must be criticized.

The HRC has had to consider a number of cases where the proceedings had been so blatantly unfair, that no detailed examination was required.[55]

II. THE RIGHT TO ADVERSARIAL PROCEEDINGS

A. The Principle and its Meaning

The most fundamental aspect of 'fairness' in proceedings is the right to be heard ('*droit d'être entendu*', '*rechtliches Gehör*'). This means that no decision, which is not entirely and unconditionally in favour of an individual, may be taken unless the person concerned was previously given an opportunity to state his or her position on the issue. Of course, the right also implies that the courts have an obligation to take the submissions of the defence into account, an aspect which is an obvious condition for the effectiveness of adversarial proceedings. In *Quadrelli* the Italian court of cassation had omitted to take into account a memorandum presented by the defence; this constituted a violation of Article 6.[56] There was also held to be a violation in *Dulaurans* where the Court was bold enough to find that the argument on which the French *cour de cassation* had based its rejection of the applicant's appeal was blatantly wrong.[57]

The right to be heard has various aspects. On a utilitarian level it contributes to the quality of decision-making. The person concerned will often have information relevant to the matter and his or her views may be of interest and serve to influence the outcome of the proceedings. Moreover from the perspective of the rule of law, which is also tied to the principle of democracy, it is essential that those affected by a decision of the authorities be involved in the decision-making process. This facilitates the acceptance of a result. Finally, from a philosophical perspective, it promotes the notion that the individual is a subject rather than merely an object of the process. It would be an exaggeration to speak of a partnership, particularly in the context of criminal proceedings. It would in fact be quite unrealistic. Still, there is empirical evidence which shows

---

[55] See the views quoted by Nowak (1993) Art. 14 N 20, 21.

[56] *Quadrelli* v. *Italy*, § 34; contrary to Fribergh (2001) 192, I do not regard this as pertaining to the right to a reasoned judgment although there is a close link between the two aspects. See further section IV below.

[57] In *Dulaurans* v. *France*, the court had said that the applicant had raised a new complaint, whereas he had in fact relied on it before. Renucci (2002) N 142 finds this an '*approche extensive . . . surprenante et même critiquable*' because the Court addressed the merits of the domestic decision; still, he accepts that the Court's anxiousness to interpret the Convention in an effective way made this development inevitable.

that fairness is a major factor for the acceptance of the conviction and the sentence.[58]

In the Court's case-law, the right to adversarial proceedings is not always clearly separated from the principle of equality of arms;[59] however, I have found nothing to indicate that this inconsistency has had any influence on the outcome of the cases.

B. The Definition

According to the Court, '[t]he right to an adversarial trial means, in a criminal case, that both prosecution and defence must be given the opportunity to have knowledge of and comment on the observations filed and evidence adduced by the other party'.[60] This applies irrespective of whether the material filed by the other party concerns the establishment of the facts, legal argument on the merits, or submissions on procedural issues.[61]

One part of the definition is rather surprising. The Court said clearly that the right applies both to the prosecution and to the defence. I would respectfully point out that while this may, from a theoretical perspective, be true, it makes no sense in the context of the Convention. Only individuals can benefit from the protection of international human-rights instruments and the prosecution clearly falls outwith this remit. As a matter of fact, the prosecution will not always have the chance to reply to the defence, as the last word at the trial will normally belong to the accused.

C. The Characteristics of the Guarantee

The right to be heard can be classified as an absolute guarantee. For once, the Court has not only accepted this but has also expressed it in clear terms. Thus, it was not impressed by 'the Government's plea that the Attorney-General's observations merely requested that the case be dealt with under Article 285d of the Code of Criminal Procedure without giving any reasons'. It answered correctly by pointing out that it was 'a matter for the defence to assess whether

---

[58] Tyler (1990); Heinz (1985) 13 et seq.; Caspar (1978) 237 et seq.; Thibaul and Walker (1975); Caspar, Tyler, and Fisher (1988) 483 et seq.; Landis and Goodstein (1986) 675 et seq.

[59] See e.g. *Borgers* v. *Belgium*, § 27; *Foucher* v. *France*, § 36; *Reinhardt and Slimane-Kaïd* v. *France*, § 106; *Kuopila* v. *Finland*, § 38; *Lanz* v. *Austria*, §§ 57–63; *PG and JH* v. *United Kingdom*, § 73.

[60] *Laukkanen and Manninen* v. *Finland*, § 34. With occasional minor variations, see too e.g. *Kamasinski* v. *Austria*, § 102; *Brandstetter* v. *Austria*, § 67; *Rowe and Davis* v. *United Kingdom*, § 60; *Fitt* v. *United Kingdom*, § 44; *IJL, GMR and AKP* v. *United Kingdom*, § 112; *Göç* v. *Turkey*, § 34; *Meftah* v. *France*, § 51; *PG and JH* v. *United Kingdom*, § 67; *JJ* v. *Netherlands*, § 43; *Ernst and others* v. *Belgium*, § 60; *Duriez-Costes* v. *France*, § 32; *Skondrianos* v. *Greece*, § 29. For civil cases, see e.g. *Krcmár* v. *Czech Republic*, § 40; *Nideröst-Huber* v. *Switzerland*, § 24.

[61] This is stressed e.g. in *Kamasinski* v. *Austria*, § 102.

a submission deserves a reaction'.[62] This is irrespective of the emphasis that the Court placed on the document.[63]

It is true that in other judgments the Court stressed the importance of the material for the defence in a specific case.[64] However, this ought not to be read as reducing the force of the right to adversarial proceedings—if it has not been respected, it is inconceivable that the proceedings could nevertheless be regarded as fair. The Court even accepted that the authorities are under an obligation to assist the accused in taking cognizance of the prosection material:

As to the argument that the applicant could have consulted the case file at the Court of Cassation and obtained a copy of the Principal Public Prosecutor's opinion, the Court is of the view that this of itself is not a sufficient safeguard to ensure the applicant's right to an adversarial procedure. In its view, and as a matter of fairness, it was incumbent on the registry of the Court of Cassation to inform the applicant that the opinion had been filed and that he could, if he so wished, comment on it in writing. It appears to the Court that this requirement is not secured in domestic law. The Government have contended that the applicant's lawyer should have known that consultation of the case file was possible as a matter of practice. However, the Court considers that to require the applicant's lawyer to take the initiative and inform himself periodically on whether any new elements have been included in the case file would amount to imposing a disproportionate burden on him and would not necessarily have guaranteed a real opportunity to comment on the opinion since he was never made aware of the timetable for the processing of the appeal.[65]

D. The Case-law

The case-law regarding the right to adversarial proceedings is not particularly varied and is mainly dominated by two types of case. The first type concerns cases where the defence was not given an opportunity to reply properly to submissions of the public prosecutor's office, the other relates to the duty of the prosecution to disclose evidence.

1. Submissions of the Procurator General to Supreme Jurisdictions

The discussion of 'fairness' in the jurisprudence of the Strasbourg authorities started in a series of cases against Austria where a violation was alleged due to the fact that the procurator general was able to file a *'croquis'*, a draft judgment to the supreme court, to which the defence had no possibility to reply.[66] Analogous

---

[62] *Bulut* v. *Austria*, § 49; cf. also *Lobo Machado* v. *Portugal*, § 31; *Nideröst-Huber* v. *Switzerland*, § 29.
[63] *Kuopila* v. *Finland*, § 35.
[64] e.g. *Foucher* v. *France*, § 32. The same comment also applies to the Court's formula, 'regard being had to what was at stake for the applicant' e.g. in *JJ* v. *Netherlands*, § 43; and *Lobo Machado* v. *Portugal*, § 31.   [65] *Göç* v. *Turkey (GC)*, § 57.
[66] *Ofner and Hopfinger* v. *Austria* Application 524/59; *Patacki and Dunshirn* v. *Austria* Applications 596/59 and 789/60. See also, more recently, *Brandstetter* v. *Austria*, § 67; *Bulut* v. *Austria*, §§ 44–50; Wąsek-Wiaderek (2000) 24 et seq.

problems turned up in a number of different countries including France,[67] the Netherlands,[68] Turkey,[69] and Portugal.[70] A similar issue arose in Switzerland, where the Federal Tribunal received observations from the lower court which the appellant was unable to comment on,[71] and in Austria where the presiding judge of the supreme court called the chairman of the lower court to obtain information about the interpreter's services. He then used the information, without giving the defence a chance to comment on it, even though the complaint was directed against the activity of this very chairman.[72]

2. The Duty to Disclose Evidence

A specific aspect of the right to adversarial procedure concerns the authorities' duty to disclose evidence. This has been particularly relevant in a number of cases against the United Kingdom where it was alleged that the prosecution withheld evidence. It is also conceivable that a court may be under a certain 'duty to disclose' material.

(a) Material Withheld by the Prosecuting Authority

The right to adversarial proceedings, as defined by the Court, calls for disclosure of material submitted to the tribunal which has the responsibility for determining the conviction and the sentence. One problematic issue has concerned the tendency of the prosecution to withhold certain material, such as reports, recordings, statements, and information about witnesses. In order to deal with such cases, the Court has formulated a fundamental rule: 'The Court considers that it is a requirement of fairness under paragraph 1 of Article 6, indeed one which is recognised under English law, that the prosecution authorities disclose to the defence all material evidence for or against the accused and that the failure to do so in the present case gave rise to a defect in the trial proceedings'.[73]

Yet, this obligation is not unlimited—material may be withheld under certain circumstances: 'In any criminal proceedings there may be competing interests, such as national security or the need to protect witnesses at risk of reprisals or to keep secret police methods of investigation of crime, which must be weighed against the rights of the accused'; but 'only such measures restricting the rights of the defence which are strictly necessary are permissible', and sufficient measures

---

[67] *Voisine* v. *France*, § 31; *Reinhardt and Slimane-Kaïd* v. *France*, § 107; *Richen and Gaucher* v. *France*, § 39; *Meftah* v. *France*, § 51; *Menher* v. *France*, § 12; *Duriez-Costes* v. *France*, § 32; *Gaucher* v. *France*, § 15; *Adoud and Bosoni* v. *France*, §§ 20, 21. Renucci (2002) N 144 regards this case-law as severe and even rather unjust towards the *avocat général* but accepts that it is justified in view of the importance of appearances.   [68] *JJ* v. *Netherlands*, § 43.

[69] *Göç* v. *Turkey (GC)*, §§ 55–8.

[70] *Lobo Machado* v. *Portugal*, § 31 (regarding a dispute relating to social rights).

[71] *Nideröst-Huber* v. *Switzerland*.   [72] *Kamasinski* v. *Austria*, § 102.

[73] *Edwards* v. *United Kingdom*, § 36; see also, more or less verbatim, *Jasper* v. *United Kingdom*, § 51; *Rowe and Davis* v. *United Kingdom*, § 60; *Fitt* v. *United Kingdom*, § 44; *Dowsett* v. *United Kingdom*, § 41; *IJL, GMR and AKP* v. *United Kingdom*, § 112; *PG and JH* v. *United Kingdom*, § 67.

must be taken to counterbalance the restrictions if they cannot be avoided.[74] This is a general problem which comes up in several different contexts in the case-law.[75] The Court, however, will not examine whether the non-disclosure was strictly necessary—it will only review the domestic authorities' claim to have complied 'as far as possible' with the requirements of a fair trial.[76]

This is not a very strong statement. In particular, the words 'as far as possible' are somewhat vague, especially if read in conjunction with the refusal to ascertain whether the limitations were 'strictly necessary'. Yet, such judicial self-restraint on the part of the Court is realistic and must be accepted.

The cases decided by the Court fall into two categories. The first contains those cases where there was held to be no violation because the domestic authorities had carefully examined the conflicting interests involved. This was the case, for example, where the defence had the opportunity, to some extent, to comment on the issue; where the undisclosed material was not put to the jury; and where the trial judge assessed at all times the need for disclosure.[77] In another case the material was disclosed before the start of the appeal proceedings. The defence had the chance to discuss it fully and the Court of Appeal conducted such an intensive review of the issue that this served to correct the earlier shortcomings.[78]

In the second category of cases, the Court finds there to have been a violation. This has occurred, for instance, when the prosecution decided to withhold evidence from the judge. Such unilateral decision-making on the part of the prosecution is clearly incompatible with Article 6. The fact that the defence was informed at the beginning of the appeal proceedings did not remedy the defect, as the Court of Appeal did not actually hear the evidence.[79] In *Atlan* there was a suspicion that the case had involved entrapment; again the Court of Appeal could not remedy the situation—the trial judge should have been informed of this hidden evidence.[80] Owen has a refreshing comment on this: 'No doubt the prospect of having no choice but to quash a conviction and order a retrial whenever public interest immunity material emerges after conviction is an unpalatable one to both the prosecuting authorities and courts. But this seems an

---

[74] *Jasper* v. *United Kingdom*, § 52; the passage can also be found in the judgments just quoted.

[75] In particular with regard to 'facilities for the preparation of the defence' (Art. 6 § 3(b)), the control of contacts between accused and counsel (Art. 6 § 3(c)), and the right to interrogate witnesses (Art. 6 § 3(d)); see Chapters 9, 10 and 11. Owen (2001) 132 et seq. chose this heading to deal with Art. 6 § 3(b).

[76] *Jasper* v. *United Kingdom*, § 53 and the other judgments referred to above.

[77] *Jasper* v. *United Kingdom*, §§ 55–6; see also *Fitt* v. *United Kingdom*, §§ 47–9, *PG and JH* v. *United Kingdom*, §§ 70–3.

[78] *IJL, GMR and AKP* v. *United Kingdom*, §§ 114–18; the same result was found in *Edwards* v. *United Kingdom*. For criticism, see Esser (2002) 405 who rightly observes that the Court is much more meticulous in matters concerning personal liberty.

[79] *Rowe and Davis* v. *United Kingdom*, §§ 63–6; and *Dowsett* v. *United Kingdom*, §§ 44–51.

[80] *Atlan* v. *United Kingdom*, §§ 42–6; in *Edwards and Lewis* v. *United Kingdom*, §§ 50–9, the violation occurred also in the context of an alleged entrapment.

inevitable consequence of a procedure whose somewhat fragile integrity crucially depends on the role of the first instance judge in conducting a scrupulous and continuing review of the disclosure issue'.[81]

(b) Duty of the Court to Disclose

In exceptional circumstances, a court can also be under a duty to disclose information. This is the essence of the judgment in *Skondrianos*. In this case the applicant had filed an appeal with the Greek court of cassation. The prosecutor opposed this on the basis of one single reason and the accused had thus to concentrate his argument on this ground. The court then rejected the appeal on the basis of an entirely different argument. The applicant complained that he had never had a chance to put forward any reasons to rebut the arguments set out in the decision.

The Court stated that the applicant was only informed of the prosecutor's submissions and taken by surprise when the Court relied on an entirely different reason. Reading between the lines it is clear that the argument which the court relied on did not convince the Strasbourg Court—although, of course, it is not competent to comment on such matters and refrains from doing so. It somewhat abruptly concluded, at any rate, that the right to adversarial proceedings was not respected and that there had been a violation of Article 6 § 1.[82]

This goes a considerable way towards imposing an obligation on state authorities, including the judiciary, to respect the position of the defence and even to assist applicants by letting them know in advance where the court is aiming when it plans to reject an appeal. No doubt, this judgment constitutes an important step towards improving the effectiveness of the application of the right to a fair trial. It is regrettable that the Court refrained from exposing in an unequivocal way the evolutionary, if not downright explosive, potential of this development.

III. THE PRINCIPLE OF EQUALITY OF ARMS

A. The Principle

Although there is no express reference to the equality of arms in either Article 6 § 1 of the ECHR or Article 14 § 1 of the ICCPR,[83] it is nevertheless generally agreed that it is an essential element of a fair trial. This notion of equality evokes the general prohibition of discrimination as set out in Article 14 of the ECHR. The first sentence of Article 14 of the ICCPR sets out a general guarantee of

---

[81]   Owen (2001) 150–1.

[82]   '[L]a Cour estime que la procédure devant la chambre du conseil de la Cour de cassation a méconnu le principe du contradictoire': *Skondrianos v. Greece*, § 31.

[83]   A clear hint is, however, given in ECHR, Art. 6 § 3(d) and ICCPR, Art. 14 § 3(e) (there is no parallel in the ACHR).

equality before the courts and tribunals, while Article 8 § 2 of the ACHR introduces the rights of the defence with the words 'with full equality'. Some authors in fact link equality of arms to the general guarantee of non-discrimination, but, in my view, such a connection is incorrect.[84]

It is essential to keep in mind that a number of countries in the United Nations experienced years of colonial rule, and this may go some way to explain the particular emphasis in the UN on the fight against all forms of discrimination. In my view, the reference to 'equality' in the Covenant[85] and in the ACHR refers to this general aspect rather than to an aspect of fairness. Here, the issue is equality between the parties, not equality between sexes, persons of different national origin, or religion, etc.

The principle of equality and the prohibition of discrimination requires equal treatment for persons in essentially equal situations.[86] It would be discriminatory, for example, if Jews were allowed to submit an appeal, but Muslims were denied this opportunity. This is the kind of equality that the international and American instruments have in mind.[87] Equality of arms, however, relates to persons with essentially opposing interests.

The principle of equality of arms first appears, in substance, though the express term is not used, in the case-law of the Commission in a case concerning civil proceedings. A Polish applicant complained of the refusal to allow him to travel to Sweden where he wanted to plead his case in a family-law dispute.[88] The doctrine later appears in a series of cases in the criminal context involving proceedings in cassation.[89] The principle was later adopted by the Court[90] and also figures in the case-law of the HRC.[91]

Taken literally, this principle certainly can be applied in civil proceedings where two private parties confront each other before the neutral tribunal. Even here, full equality is not possible. One of the parties will have to have the last word—it cannot be given to both.[92] There will also normally be rules governing

---

[84]   e.g. Frowein and Peukert (1996) Art. 6 N 83; Grabenwarter (1997) 596.

[85]   Achermann, Caroni, and Kälin (1997) 184.

[86]   See e.g. *Fredin* v. *Sweden (No. 1)*, § 60: 'discrimination, that is treating differently, without an objective and reasonable justification, persons in "relevantly" similar situations'.

[87]   See e.g. Nowak (1993) Art. 14 N 5.

[88]   *Szwabowiez* v. *Sweden* Application No. 434/58; the primary issue was the right to be present at the hearing. See also e.g. *Günther Struppat* v. *Germany* Application 2804/66; *J and R Kaufman* v. *Belgium* Application 10938/84.

[89]   *Ofner and Hopfinger* v. *Austria* Application 524/59; *Patacki and Dunshirn* v. *Austria* Applications 596/59 and 789/60. For references to early publications on the equality of arms, see Trechsel (1979) 376–7, n. 161.

[90]   *Neumeister* v. *Austria*, The Law, § 22, where the Court said it did not apply to habeas corpus proceedings; this view was later overturned; see Chapter 18.

[91]   *Frank Robinson* v. *Jamaica*, § 10.4: the author was charged with murder; while the hearing had been postponed no less than seven times because the prosecution had not been able to present its main witness, postponement for the defence was refused when counsel had withdrawn.

[92]   This seems to have been one of the issues in *J and R Kaufman* v. *Belgium* Application 10938/84.

which party has to bear the risk of a failure to establish the facts—usually it will be the plaintiff. On the whole, however, it cannot be denied that the image reflects reality to an acceptable degree. A typical example is *Dombo Beheer* where one of the parties was permitted to call a witness who had participated in the contested negotiations, while the other was barred as he was himself the party.[93]

Full 'equality of arms' in criminal proceedings, however, is not a fitting image at all.[94] From the very beginning of the criminal process, the prosecution and the defence are in very different positions. The prosecution acts (at least in theory) without any 'personal' interest—its sole aim is to find the truth and to ensure that the law is applied correctly, i.e. to serve justice, while the accused only acts in his or her own personal interest and is not under any duty to serve justice.[95] While the prosecution is equipped with measures of coercion such as arrest warrants, wire-tapping, search and seizure, and has increasingly complex technology at its service, the accused has none of that at his or her disposal but is in possession, if he or she is guilty, of precise knowledge of the facts of the case. The burden of proof rests on the prosecution, and the accused can choose to remain passive and silent throughout the proceedings. Equality can only be conceived of, in this context, as a certain equivalence. One might recall fights of gladiators in ancient Rome where one was in armour and equipped with a sword, whilst the other was unprotected and equipped with a net and a trident.[96]

B. The Definition

The earliest definition of the principle can be found in *Dombo Beheer* where it was held that 'as regards litigation involving opposing private interests, "equality of arms" implies that each party must be afforded a reasonable opportunity to present his case—including his evidence—under conditions that do not place him at a substantial disadvantage *vis-à-vis* his opponent'.[97] The formula then turns up, almost word for word, in a criminal case: 'each party must be afforded a reasonable opportunity to present his case under conditions that do not place him at a disadvantage *vis-à-vis* his opponent'.[98] There are two differences, although there is little explanation for this. First, the reference to 'evidence' is missing. This could perhaps be due to the fact that, in criminal proceedings, the

---

[93] *Dombo Beheer* v. *Netherlands*. In *Acklin* v. *Switzerland* a similar difference was at issue, but the Court found no violation because the difference between a person giving evidence as a witness and a party relating facts was merely a formal one in view of the freedom left to the judge to appraise the evidence.

[94] See also Wąsek-Wiaderek (2000) 50; Müller (1976) N 24; Chiavario (2001) 195; van Dijk and van Hoof (1998) 430; Villiger (1999) N 476 is of the opinion that it applies to the hearing but not to the preliminary proceedings.   [95] See Chapter 13.

[96] Trechsel (1978) 558. See also Raymond (1970) 81 at 103; Velu and Ergec (1990) N 470; with regard to administrative proceedings, see Grabenwarter (1997) 597.

[97] *Dombo Beheer* v. *Netherlands*, § 33; in French the expression is '*net désavantage*'.

[98] *Bulut* v. *Austria*, § 47.

defence does not really have to present its evidence. Second, the adjective 'substantial' which accompanied 'disadvantage' has also been omitted.

Does this mean that in criminal cases no disadvantage of any kind is allowed, while in civil proceedings only partial equality is required? An examination of the different cases demonstrates that this restrictive element is included in almost all cases concerning civil proceedings.[99] It is missing in the majority of criminal cases, but the Court does not explain this difference and it can be assumed that it is of little significance.[100] In one case, the Court referred to another judgment where the word 'substantial' is included, but then proceeded to omit it from its own formulation.[101]

In connection with Article 6 § 3(d) the point is sometimes enhanced; the Court has called for '*full* equality of arms',[102] '*complète "égalité d'armes"*'.[103] This special wording does not seem to have any practical relevance.

C. Aspects of Equality

1. The Relativity of Equality

Equality has a very special role in the context of human rights. Its complexity cannot be discussed in depth in the present context.[104] It should be noted, however, that the guarantee of equality will in itself be of no assistance whatsoever in situations where a person is deprived of a right of which other individuals have also been deprived.

This observation has particular relevance in the context of the case-law on 'equality of arms', and it is this element which distinguishes this notion from the right to 'adversarial proceedings':[105] there can be no violation of the principle (the Court has not formulated a 'right' to equality of arms, but has used such terms as 'principle',[106] 'requirement'[107] or 'concept',[108] or says that 'there should be equality of arms'[109]) when both sides are denied something that might have been useful. Thus, in *Jasper* the applicant complained that the results of

---

[99] *Hentrich* v. *France*, § 56; *Niederöst-Huber* v. *Switzerland*, § 23; *Ankerl* v. *Switzerland*, § 38; *De Haes and Gijsels* v. *Belgium*, § 53; *Krcmár* v. *Czech Republic*, § 39; *Werner* v. *Austria*, § 63; *Morel* v. *France*, § 27; *Platakou* v. *Greece*, § 47; *Beer* v. *Austria* § 17; *FR* v. *Switzerland*, § 34; *Buchberger* v. *Austria*, § 50; *Fretté* v. *France*, § 47; *Komanicki* v. *Slovakia*, § 45; *Wierzbicki* v. *Poland*, § 39; *AB* v. *Slovakia*, § 55; *Yvon* v. *France*, § 31. The one exception is *Apeh Uldozotteinek Szovetsege* v. *Hungary*, § 39. The same rule with the same text is also to be found in administrative cases: *Immeubles Groupe Kosser* v. *France*, § 22; *Kress* v. *France*, § 72.

[100] *Foucher* v. *France*, § 23; *Kuopila* v. *Finland*, § 37; *Lanz* v. *Austria*, § 57; *Öcalan* v. *Turkey*, § 159; *Josef Fischer* v. *Austria*, § 18. Exceptions are *Coëme* v. *Belgium* § 162; *GB* v. *France*, § 58; *Ernst and others* v. *Belgium*, § 50.

[101] See e.g. *Lanz* v. *Austria*, § 57, a criminal case, which refers to *Dombo Beheer* v. *Netherlands*, § 33.

[102] *Engel and others* v. *Netherlands*, § 49; *Bönisch* v. *Austria*, § 32.   [103] *Pisano* v. *Italy*, § 21.

[104] For a more thorough analysis see e.g. Trechsel (2003) 119 et seq. with further references.

[105] Renucci (2002) N 144, however, regards the right to adversarial proceedings as implied in the principle of equality of arms.   [106] e.g. *Neumeister* v. *Austria*, § 22.

[107] *Dombo Beheer* v. *Netherlands*, § 33.   [108] *Solakov* v. *Macedonia*, § 57.

[109] *Edwards and Lewis* v. *United Kingdom*, § 52. See also *Nideröst-Huber* v. *Switzerland*, § 23.

a wire-tapping exercise had been withheld from the defence; the Court, however, noted that as 'both the prosecution and the defence were prohibited from adducing any evidence which might tend to suggest that calls had been intercepted by the State authorities, the principle of equality of arms was respected'.[110] The same reasoning was applied with regard to the right to be present at leave-to-appeal proceedings in the United Kingdom: there was no violation as neither the prosecution nor the defence were allowed to attend.[111]

2. *The Importance of the Presence of the Prosecution at the Hearing*

One might assume that there is even less of a problem when the defence is party to privileges which are not bestowed on the prosecution. This may be so in some cases, but one has to be careful. If, for example, the defence is represented at an oral hearing but the prosecution is not, a problem may arise as to the impartiality of the court as, instead of relying on the pleadings of the prosecutor, the judge will be forced to formulate the arguments her- or himself in favour of a conviction and/or sentence. This problem arose in the case of *Thorgeir Thorgeirson* v. *Iceland* and is discussed more fully in the context of the independence of the court.[112] This problem does not arise, of course, when both parties are absent.[113]

3. *The Abstract Value of Equality*

In a sense, equality of arms might also have an absolute aspect in that any inequality which is to the detriment of the defence will lead to a violation of the right to fair proceedings, irrespective of whether the defence can show that it suffered any prejudice. The Court seemed to say as much in *Lanz*: '[T]he principle of the equality of arms does not depend on further, quantifiable unfairness flowing from a procedural inequality'.[114]

However, other statements seem to cast doubt on this assumption. Thus, in *Kremzow* the Court stressed that 'the defence was not in any way prejudiced by the difference' which had been found to exist, therefore there was no violation.[115] In another case, there was indeed held to be a violation, and the Court explained

---

[110] *Jasper* v. *United Kingdom*, § 57. See also *Ekbatani* v. *Sweden*, § 30; *Nideröst-Huber* v. *Switzerland*, § 23; *Monnell and Morris* v. *United Kingdom*, § 62; *APBP* v. *France*, § 24; *Krcmár* v. *Czech Republic*, § 39.

[111] e.g. *X* v. *United Kingdom* Application 5871/72; *X* v. *United Kingdom* Application 7413/76; *EM* v. *Norway* Application 20087/92. This '*égalité par le bas*' has been criticized by Poncet (1977) 54 and Velu and Ergec (1990) N 471; the criticism is not justified to the extent that only the element of 'equality' is concerned, whereas the basic stock of rights remains untouched.

[112] See Chapter 3, section IV.D.3 above. In *Delcourt* v. *Belgium*, § 34, the Court also mentioned the absence of a prosecuting party, but only in so far as to say that this could not exclude a different unfair disadvantage.   [113] *Krčmár* v. *Czech Republic*, § 39.

[114] *Lanz* v. *Austria*, § 58; see also *Bulut* v. *Austria*, § 49.

[115] *Kremzow* v. *Austria*, § 75. Actually, this decision should not be criticized because the information only concerned the identity of the reporting judge which, at least in theory, cannot be of any importance for the course of the proceedings.

in great detail how the fact that the prosecution presented an important document at a very late stage had influenced the outcome of the proceedings.[116]

It would seem therefore that any departure from the maintenance of a strict policy of equality between the prosecution and the defence will *not* automatically mean that the trial was unfair; some sort of detrimental effect on the defence will have to be shown. This does not give cause for concern—after all, the very definition of the principle refers to the fact that the defence has suffered some type of 'disadvantage'.

D. The Case-law

Despite the popularity of the principle, only a relatively modest number of cases have been decided. Cases concerning witness evidence will be dealt with under Article 6 § 3(d) rather than here.[117] Other cases concerning proceedings at first instance have involved the right to adversarial proceedings, the right to defend oneself in person or with the assistance of counsel, and, finally, the right to 'adequate time and facilities'. Those cases concerning access to an appeal will not be examined here. Just two issues remain in the context of appeals, the presence of the prosecution during the deliberations of the court and the system whereby the prosecution passes a report or even a draft judgment to the court but not to the defence.

1. The Presence of a Prosecutor at the Deliberations of the Court

One of the very first cases brought before the Court concerned an aspect of the proceedings before the Belgian court of cassation. The applicant complained that a member of the *Procureur général*'s department had taken part in the deliberations of the court.[118] The Government argued successfully that this high judicial officer represented an institution created to preserve the uniformity of the case-law and had the function of an adviser to the Court. He could not therefore be regarded as an 'adversary' of the applicant. The Court admitted that it was possible that the procedure may appear somewhat dubious, but decided that it was essential to look beyond such appearances and was swayed by the fact that the procedure had had a long tradition.[119]

---

[116] *GB* v. *France*, §§ 64–70. Although the Court relied on equality of arms, it is in fact the adversarial character, and more precisely, the adequate time and facilities for the preparation of the defence which were at issue. See also *Solakov* v. *Former Yugoslav Republic of Macedonia*, § 62; and *Kuopila* v. *Finland*, § 35; *Ernst and others* v. *Belgium*, § 61.   [117] See Chapter 11.
[118] *Delcourt* v. *Belgium*.
[119] Ibid., § 31. The importance of appearances is often stressed in the context of the right to a fair trial; see e.g. *Lanz* v. *Austria*, § 57; *Slimane-Kaïd (No. 2)* v. *France*, § 20 with further references. Stavros (1993) 243 regards this as 'indicative of a new phase of maturity in the case-law, which stems from an increased realization that the administration of justice remains a futile exercise, if it cannot inspire confidence in the members of society'.

More than twenty years later the same issue arose again before the Court. The Commission, which by this time was differently composed, had declared the application admissible and had come to the conclusion that the representative of the *Procureur général*'s office was the only representative of the state appearing before the Court of Cassation and he was opposed to the applicant's appeal. The Court, of course also differently composed, referred to developments in its case-law and came to the same conclusion as the Commission.[120] This time it rejected the Government's attempts to justify the system:

> Further and above all, the inequality was increased even more by the avocat général's participation, in an advisory capacity, in the Court's deliberations. Assistance of this nature, given with total objectivity, may be of some use in drafting judgments, although this task falls in the first place to the Court of Cassation itself. It is however hard to see how such assistance can remain limited to stylistic considerations, which are in any case often indissociable from substantive matters, if it is in addition intended, as the Government also affirmed, to contribute towards maintaining the consistency of the case-law. Even if such assistance was so limited in the present case, it could reasonably be thought that the deliberations afforded the avocat général an additional opportunity to promote, without fear of contradiction by the applicant, his submissions to the effect that the appeal should be dismissed.[121]

The finding of a violation of the right to a fair trial is entirely convincing. A court which deliberates together with a representative of the prosecuting authority cannot be considered to be impartial, particularly from the perspective of the accused.[122] It is thus no surprise to find reference, in the description of the equality of arms in this context, to the importance of 'appearances'.[123] As with impartiality, the decisive element is 'whether the doubts raised by appearances can be held objectively justified'.[124]

The Court subsequently confirmed this approach in similar cases concerning Belgium, France, Portugal, and the Netherlands.[125]

2. Privileged Information for the Prosecution

It is necessary to distinguish three ways in which the defence can be disadvantaged through restrictions on its right to vital information. First, in relation to access to the file and to any documents added to the file during the trial; second, concerning access to any document which the prosecution, or any

---

[120] *Borgers* v. *Belgium*, §§ 24–8.   [121] Ibid., § 28.

[122] See Chapter 3, section IV above.

[123] *Borgers* v. *Belgium*, §§ 24 and 29; see also *Vermeulen* v. *Belgium*, § 34; *Bulut* v. *Austria*, § 47; *Lanz* v. *Austria*, § 57; *Slimane-Kaïd (No. 2)* v. *France*, § 20; *Öcalan* v. *Turkey*, § 159; *Kress* v. *France*, §§ 81, 82 (for the role of the *commissaire du gouvernement*).

[124] *Brandstetter* v. *Austria*, § 44, in the context of the impartiality of an expert witness.

[125] *Vermeulen* v. *Belgium*, § 34; *Fontaine and Bertin* v. *France*, §§ 64–6; *Slimane-Kaïd (No. 2)* v. *France*, § 20; *Kress* v. *France*, §§ 77 et seq.; *APBP* v. *France*, §§ 28, 29; *Lobo Machado* v. *Portugal*, §§ 32, 34. See also *JJ* v. *Netherlands*.

other party opposed to the defence, files with a view to influencing the court; and third in connection with drafts of the reporting member of the court communicated exclusively to the prosecution.

In my view, the first of these three groups is basically covered by the specific right as set out in Article 6 § 3(b) to time and facilities for the preparation of the defence, although the Court has also discussed these issues under the general 'umbrella' of the right to a fair trial under Article 6 § 1. The second group is *the* issue which falls to be considered under the heading of the 'right to adversarial proceedings'; while, in my view, the last one ought to be rightly regarded as relating to the 'equality of arms'.

It is thus the last aspect which will be considered here, though it is essential to note that the Court does not always follow a clear and consistent approach and often combines or mixes the equality of arms and the principle of adversarial proceedings.

(a) Failure to Inform the Appellant of the Date of the Hearing before the French *cour de cassation*

Only specially qualified lawyers are permitted to act in the French *Cour de Cassation* and the *Conseil d'Etat*. Despite this, individuals are allowed to file appeals either without the assistance of a lawyer, or with the aid of a lawyer not qualified to plead before the highest judicial bodies. If the individual chooses either of these options, however, he or she will not be informed either of the date of the hearing or of the deadline for filing reasons.

This issue first reached the Strasbourg organs in the case of *Melin*, involving an applicant who had formerly been a lawyer. He had filed an appeal which, some four-and-a-half months later, was dismissed on the basis that no grounds for the appeal had been filed. Mr Melin explained that he was prevented from formulating such grounds as the judgment, which he had wanted to appeal against, had not been served on him. The Commission unanimously found a violation of Article 6, but the Court took a different approach. It accepted the Government's argument that the applicant could have taken steps to obtain the judgment and could have received information from the registry of the court of cassation about the proposed date of the hearing. As he had voluntarily waived his right to be assisted by a qualified lawyer, he ought to have employed the necessary diligence himself.[126]

The next case alleging a similar violation led to a different result. The case could be distinguished from *Melin* in two respects: first, in this case the applicant had filed his grounds within a reasonable time (although this was still too late, as the court of cassation had already made its decision), and second, he was not a lawyer.[127] 'The Court emphasises that States must ensure that everyone charged with a criminal offence benefits from the safeguards provided by Article 6 para. 3.

---

[126] *Melin* v. *France*, §§ 24, 25.   [127] *Vacher* v. *France*, § 26.

Putting the onus on convicted appellants to find out when an allotted period of time starts to run or expires is not compatible with the "diligence" which the Contracting States must exercise to ensure that the rights guaranteed by Article 6 are enjoyed in an effective manner'.[128] This judgment was followed in subsequent cases.[129]

As the passage quoted above indicates, the judgments are based on a combined application of Article 6 §§ 1 and 3. As the prosecuting authority was, however, undoubtedly informed of the progress of the proceedings and the date of the hearing, there was also a violation of the equality of arms.

(b) Communication of the *Rapporteur*'s Draft to the Prosecution, but Not to the Defence

The French court of cassation had a rather special method for preparing its judgments, whereby a member of the court was designated as the *Rapporteur* responsible for the preparation of the deliberations and the judgment.[130] His or her job was to prepare, in advance, a report which then served as the basis for the discussions. What was rather unusual was that this draft was communicated to the advocate general, but not to the defence. The defence lawyers were later informed by a note of the essence of the report, but did not receive the detailed reasoning. The Court rightly found that this procedure was incompatible with the right to a fair trial—although here it is really the equality of arms which was at issue.[131]

IV. THE RIGHT TO A REASONED JUDGMENT

A. The Meaning and Function of the Right to a Reasoned Judgment

There is no reference in any of the instruments to an obligation on judicial authorities to give reasons for their decisions or judgments.[132] It may even seem strange that such a right should be discussed within the context of the guarantee of a fair trial as the reasoning of a judgment is only relevant after the conclusion of the trial. This argument of course loses its force if the fairness requirement is taken to apply not just to the trial but also to the proceedings as a whole. One reason put forward to support the requirement that a judgment be reasoned is that in order to be able to appeal, it is essential to know the reasons for the failure at the earlier instance. This justification breaks down however when applied to the requirement that the court of final instance should also give

---

[128] *Vacher* v. *France*, § 28.   [129] *Fretté* v. *France*, § 49.

[130] This method was used by the former Commission of Human Rights and is still used by the Court.

[131] *Reinhardt and Slimane-Kaïd* v. *France*, § 105. See also *MacGee* v. *France*, § 15; *Berger* v. *France*, §§ 42, 43; *Fontaine and Bertin* v. *France*, §§ 61–3; *Lilly* v. *France*, § 24; *Slimane-Kaïd (No. 2)* v. *France*, § 17; *Crochard and Six others* v. *France*, § 13; *Weil* v. *France*, §§ 26, 27; *Pascolini* v. *Italy*, § 23.

[132] See Trechsel (2001) 161; Spencer (2001) 173; Fribergh (2001) 187.

reasons. Nevertheless, the application of Article 6 does not end with the judgment—it has its effects even beyond that point.[133] It must serve the interests of justice, and it will be shown that the interests of justice cannot be achieved unless a decision is fully reasoned.

Any judicial decision, in fact. The obligation to give reasons is not limited to judgments. In *Bricmont*, for example, the Commission held that there was a violation because no reasons had been given for the refusal to grant the applicant's request that a witness be heard.[134]

1. Reasons of a Functional Orientation

As was just mentioned, a relatively obvious justification for the requirement that a reasoned judgment be produced involves the possibility of appeal.[135] In order to be able effectively to use the right to appeal,[136] prospective appellants must have the opportunity to study the reasons on which the original judgment was based, so as to be able to present their counter-arguments. In the words of the Court: 'The national courts must . . . indicate with sufficient clarity the grounds on which they based their decision. It is this, *inter alia*, which makes it possible for the accused to exercise usefully the rights of appeal available to him'.[137]

This does not mean that there is no need for a reasoned judgment in cases where there would be no further appeal. This opinion, which was held by the Swiss Federal Tribunal[138] and certain authors,[139] is rightly rejected by Haefliger and Schürmann.[140]

2. Reasons of Legal Theory

The need to give reasons for a legal decision is closely linked to the character of law and of legal science. It belongs to the arts rather than to the natural sciences. Whether an assertion in law is right or wrong cannot be ascertained by a method comparable to a scientific experiment. The only possibility to verify a hypothesis in law lies in the reasons given. They must be complete and logical. Without reasons, a decision cannot claim to have legal character, let alone to be correct. Thus, without reasoning it would not be possible to distinguish a correct judgment from an arbitrary one. In other words, a judgment which does not give reasons may not be, but certainly appears to

---

[133] *Assanidze* v. *Georgia*, §§ 181 et seq.

[134] *Bricmont* v. *Belgium*, Report of the Commission, §§ 151–3, relying on Art. 6 § 3(d).

[135] This seems to be the primary reason for Esser (2002) 745 et seq.; Gollwitzer (1992) Art. 6 N 73. In *PK* v. *Finland* the insufficient reasoning of the district court was the main issue even in the domestic proceedings.

[136] ECHR, Protocol No. 7, Art. 2; ICCPR, Art. 14 § 5; IACHR, Art. 8 § 2(f).

[137] *Hadjianastassiou* v. *Greece*, § 33.   [138] BGE 103 Ia 206.

[139] Peukert (1980) 267; Wildhaber (1979).   [140] Haefliger and Schürmann (1999) 189.

be arbitrary.[141] It may be interesting to note that in Italy the absence or lack of logic in the reasoning is a specific reason for an appeal in cassation.[142]

3. Reasons of Acceptability

A judgment will normally have an adverse result for one of the parties. In order to make such a result acceptable, it is necessary to give convincing reasons. Without reasoning, a judgment is not justifiable. This aspect was important in one case where a lawyer who had been disbarred sought to have his name restored to the roll. This was possible under certain conditions. The Court stressed 'the imprecise nature of the statutory concept of "exceptional circumstances"' and continued that 'this very lack of precision made it all the more necessary to give sufficient reasons for the two impugned decisions on the issue in question'.[143] In this case, no reasons had been given for rejecting the application.

4. Reasons of Transparency

The obligation to give reasons for a judgment can also be linked to the right to a public trial. It is not only the parties who must be convinced that the solution given by the court to their problem is the right one, or at least an acceptable one, but it is also important that the public be assured that the proceedings have been conducted fairly, that appropriate care has been given to determining the result, and that the outcome is not the result of improper motives.

5. The Right to a Reasoned Decision as an Aspect of the Right to be Heard

Finally, the right to receive a reasoned judgment can also be seen as being part of the right to be heard.[144] This is, from the perspective of an international body, a rather difficult aspect, because it is so closely connected to the determination of the case. The equality of arms and adversarial character of the proceedings both serve to enable a party to express its views as to fact and law, and to present those arguments which it believes necessary to convince the decision-making body to decide in its favour. This requirement, however, cannot guarantee the attention of the decision-making body. It is of course not possible to verify directly whether somebody has actually listened to or understood what has been said, or whether a document has been given the necessary attention. It is not

---

[141] Renucci (2002) N 143.

[142] ICCP, Art. 606 § 1(e): '*mancanza o manifesta illogicità della motivazione*'.

[143] *H* v. *Belgium*, § 53. Lack of precision also called for more detail in *Georgiades* v. *Greece*, § 43, where compensation for unlawful detention was refused with a mere reference to the applicant's own 'gross negligence' without specifying what this allegedly consisted of; or *Karakasis* v. *Greece*, § 27 where 'the domestic court did not invoke any reasons for precluding compensation'.

[144] See also Trechsel (2001) 165.

even easy to know whether a judge who closed his eyes had actually been sleeping or not.[145]

The Court has only had one occasion to examine this issue directly. In *Kraska* the applicant complained of a violation of Article 6 because a member of the chamber of the Federal Court which had examined his public-law appeal allegedly admitted that he had not examined the entire file, and in particular had not read all of the lengthy submissions of the applicant.

According to the Court, '[t]he effect of Article 6 para. 1 is, *inter alia*, to place the "tribunal" under a duty to conduct a proper examination of the submissions, arguments and evidence adduced by the parties, without prejudice to its assessment of whether they are relevant to its decision'.[146] The Court noted that the judge in question had taken part in the discussion and concluded: 'All things considered, there is no evidence to suggest that its members failed to examine the appeal with due care before taking their decision'.[147] It felt that this view had been confirmed by the fact that none of the judges had proposed that the examination of the case be postponed.

This judgment demonstrates the respect of the Court for their Swiss colleagues, which is understandable, yet puzzling in view of the fact that the judge in question had—rather stupidly, it must be added—openly admitted that he had not had the time to read all of the material submitted in the case. Leaving political correctness aside, it is perhaps not entirely wrong to assume that many, if not all, judges will have, at one time or another, taken part in a decision without having attentively read every sentence contained in the file—every judge also knows that large sections of the file will consist of repetitions of other parts of the file and will not contribute in any way to finding the correct result. This is a reality, however, which should remain 'unspoken'.

There is perhaps an element of irony in the fact that the Court made express reference to the importance of appearances: 'The Court has already stressed on numerous occasions the importance of appearances in the administration of justice, but it has at the same time made clear that the standpoint of the persons concerned is not in itself decisive. The misgivings of the individuals before the courts, for instance with regard to the fairness of the proceedings, must in addition be capable of being held to be objectively justified'.[148] The Court did not explain why the applicant's reservations were not justified although it, rather exceptionally, clearly criticized the judge in question.[149]

Returning to the point under consideration, the reasons given for a judgment play a significant role in demonstrating that the person concerned has actually

---

[145] This is alas not simply a hypothetical point, as is borne out by the facts in *Senn* v. *Switzerland* Application 17601/91, decision of 7 Apr. 1994, unreported.

[146] *Kraska* v. *Switzerland*, § 30; *Van der Hurk* v. *Netherlands*, § 59.

[147] *Kraska* v. *Switzerland*, § 32.   [148] Ibid.

[149] Ibid., § 33: 'Judge Y's comment is open to criticism'! Not the fact that he took part in the decision, but the fact that he had admitted to not having read the whole file. This leaves no room for doubt that we are faced with an element of hypocrisy here.

been heard. The rejection of arguments, in the absence of any reasoning, indicates either that the tribunal did not listen or that it took an arbitrary decision. This demonstrates that the element of fairness which is constituted by the right to a reasoned judgment comes close to the right to a correct judgment, which cannot, in my view, be regarded as a 'human right'.[150] The judgments in *Hiro Balani* v. *Spain* and *Ruiz Torija* v. *Spain* indeed seem to suggest that the Court very simply thinks that the judgment in question was wrong in substance, an impression which will be shared by anyone reading the judgment of the court. A similar situation arose in *Dulaurans* where the Court criticized the French *Cour de Cassation* for having erroneously rejected an appeal. Renucci sees that judgment as representing a particularly important development because it implied that 'Strasbourg' was prepared to examine whether domestic law had been correctly applied.[151] This is in line with the views expressed by Judge Loucaides.[152]

In my view, this is an exaggeration. The sheer volume of work which would arise were the Court to become a true court of fourth instance would prevent it from assuming this role. In fact, in *Dulaurans*, the Court did not examine the issue of lawfulness, but rather evaluated whether the decision was arbitrary, a distinction which is well known in countries like Germany, Austria, and Switzerland. A decision is arbitrary if it is not based on reason and as such amounts to an interference with the principles of justice.[153] This is confirmed by the subsequent judgments dealing with the *cour de cassation*.[154]

B. The Standards of the Reasoning

What are the criteria which ought to be used to decide whether the reasoning of a judgment is sufficient or not? Once again, the Court has been rather vague:

The extent to which this duty to give reasons applies may vary according to the nature of the decision. It is . . . necessary to take into account, inter alia, the diversity of the submissions that a litigant may bring before the courts and the differences existing in the Contracting States with regard to statutory provisions, customary rules, legal opinion and the presentation of judgments. That is why the question whether a court has failed to fulfil the obligation to state reasons, deriving from Article 6 of the Convention, can only be determined in the light of the circumstances of the case.[155]

---

[150] See, however, Loucaides (2003) 30 et seq.

[151] Renucci (2002) N 142 with further references.

[152] Loucaides (2003); Barreto (1999) 137 goes too far when he states that wrong reasoning equates to no reasoning, with reference to Application 15394/89, decision of 2 Oct. 1989, unreported. This would mean that the Court would be called upon to ascertain whether the reasoning is correct or not which would put it again in the position of a court of fourth instance.

[153] See e.g. Schefer (2001) 507 et seq.

[154] See e.g. *Annoni di Gussola and others* v. *France*; and *Mortier* v. *France* where the *Cour de Cassation* had struck appeals out of the list because the applicant had failed to comply with the impugned judgment of the court of appeal. Similar judgments can be found with regard to other countries, e.g. *Pérez de Rada Cavanilles* v. *Spain* and *Miragall Escolano* v. *Spain*, regarding the time limit for an appeal (Judge Pellonpää dissenting); *Yagtzilar and others* v. *Greece*.

[155] *Hiro Balani* v. *Spain*, § 27; *Ruiz Torija* v. *Spain*, § 29; *Helle* v. *Finland*, § 55. In simplified formulation, see also *Higgins and others* v. *France*, § 42; *Garcia Ruiz* v. *Spain*, § 26; and see the early

While there is nothing wrong with this formula as such, it provides little
assistance to the domestic judge or, for that matter, to the person challenging
the adequacy of the reasoning in the judgment.

Some additional clarity can be found in the judgments in which there was held
to be no violation, where it is sometimes stated that the guarantee 'cannot be
understood as requiring a detailed answer to every argument'.[156] On the contrary,
this suggests that reasons must be given in answer to every argument put forward
by the party which could be relevant for the decision; in other words, those
reasons 'which would, if accepted, be decisive for the outcome of the case'.[157] The
Court often stresses that it is not competent to take a stand on this question, but at
the same time it must at least find that the argument is not clearly unfounded.[158]

The reasoning must cover all important points, such as the evaluation of the
evidence and the establishment of the facts, the legal arguments, and also procedural issues.[159] It is legitimate for this to take the form of a summary—
a reference, for instance, to the Article on which the denial of the appeal is based,
may suffice, providing this is sufficiently clear.[160] However, with regard to the
establishment of the facts, it is more difficult to set clear standards.[161]

C. Limits to the Requirement that Reasons be Given

1. The Jury Trial

The jury trial imposes serious restrictions on the right to a reasoned judgment.
Here, rather than producing a reasoned decision, the jurors will come up with a
'verdict', a term derived from the Latin *'vere dictum'*, 'truly spoken'. This
explains why the right to a reasoned judgment is not part of the common-law
tradition.[162] The Swiss Federal Tribunal found this system incompatible with
federal law because it did not allow the Tribunal to verify whether federal law
had been correctly applied—at least a summary of the reasoning was
required.[163] Such reasoning can take the form of a series of questions formulated
by the presiding judge which are then answered by the jury. The questions (and,
at the same time, the reasoning) are also implied in the judge's summing up.[164]
Spencer rightly points out that the Court has not yet had the opportunity to
address this problem.[165]

decision of *Firestone Tire and Rubber Co, Firestone Tyre and Rubber Co Ltd, and International
Synthetic Rubber Co Ltd* v. *United Kingdom* Application 5460/72.

[156] *Van der Hurk* v. *Netherlands*, § 61; *Garcia Ruiz* v. *Spain*, § 26; *Helle* v. *Finland*, § 55. For
details, see Velu and Ergec (1990) N 478.   [157] Harris, O'Boyle, and Warbrick (1995) 215.
[158] This is stressed in *Hiro Balani* v. *Spain*, § 38; and *Ruiz Torija* v. *Spain*, § 30.
[159] As in *Higgins and others* v. *France*.   [160] *X* v. *Germany* Application 8769/79.
[161] It may be difficult to explain why the court believes one witness rather than another, but
basically the court cannot be freed from this task; cf. Frowein (2001) 215.
[162] Spencer (2001) 173, at 175.
[163] BGE 78 IV 134 (1952); Hauser and Schweri (2002) § 20 N 9.
[164] Stavros (1993) 258, who, in n. 813, points to precarious substitutes for the French system.
[165] Spencer (2001) 180; see also Chiavario (2001) 198.

2. Appeal Judgments

The nature of the appeals process is, of course, dependent on the structure of the specific procedural system and requires, for the purposes of this section, some clarification. A distinction must be made between two types of appeal: first, the 'ordinary appeal' (*'appel'*, *'Berufung'*) where a court of higher instance is called upon to re-examine the whole case as to both the facts and the law, and second, the appeal 'in cassation', or on points of law (*'recours en cassation'*, *'Nichtig-keitsbeschwerde'* [Austria, Switzerland], *'Revision'* [Germany]). The latter type of appeal only allows the appellant to complain about specific defects of the judgment, and relates mainly to procedural issues or to the way in which the law was interpreted and applied.[166]

Any decision made in response to an appeal 'in cassation' must always be accompanied by reasons. The court must indicate why the criticism of the previous judgment or proceedings is, or is not, justified when deciding whether or not to quash the judgment. The 'ordinary' appeal, however, may lead to a new judgment which is identical to the earlier one. In this case it is acceptable for the court of second instance to rely principally on the same reasoning and simply to refer to that judgment rather than repeat everything that has already been written there.[167] Unfortunately, the Court was not very clear on this point when it said that 'the notion of a fair procedure requires that a national court which has given sparse reasons for its decisions, whether by incorporating the reasons of a lower court or otherwise, did in fact address the essential issues which were submitted to its jurisdiction and did not merely endorse without further ado the findings reached by a lower court. This requirement is all the more important where a litigant has not been able to present his case orally in the domestic proceed-ings.'[168] This can only mean that while reliance on the reasoning of the previous instance is acceptable, the court of appeal must at least respond to any new arguments put forward by the applicant.

D. The Case-law

The jurisprudence relating the obligation to give reasons is not especially varied, and the vast majority of cases concern civil proceedings. The first case decided by the Court involved, however, criminal proceedings.

In *Hadjianastassiou* v. *Greece* the applicant invoked Article 6 §§ 1 and 3(b) and argued that he had been forced, in order to comply with a statutory time limit, to file his appeal on points of law before receiving the reasons for his

---

[166] An interesting historical examination of the appeals in cassation can be found in Merryman (1985) 39, 120, 121.

[167] See *X* v. *Germany* Application 1035/61; *Firestone Tire and Rubber Co, Firestone Tyre and Rubber Co Ltd, and International Synthetic Rubber Co Ltd* v. *United Kingdom* Application 5460/72.

[168] *Helle* v. *Finland*, § 60.

conviction.[169] Obviously, this was not compatible with the right to a fair trial. One violation of the Convention consisted of the fact that the lower court, the *judex a quo*, had failed to produce a reasoned judgment in time.

In *Van de Hurk* v. *Netherlands*, the applicant complained that the court had not discussed an alternative method for calculating the compensation he had claimed, a method he had suggested for the first time at the oral hearing. The Court found there to have been no violation as it could not find the decision of the tribunal to have been 'insufficiently reasoned'.

The Court also had to consider two cases against Spain, *Hirano Balani* and *Ruiz Torija*, which were decided on the same day, and which concerned civil proceedings before the supreme court. The court had ignored the applicants' arguments which, even in the reluctant evaluation of the Court, could have been decisive for the outcome of the proceedings. This constituted a violation of Article 6 § 1, and one cannot help but notice that the Court came close here to acting as a 'fourth instance'.[170]

Similarly, in *Higgins and others* v. *France* the court of cassation had apparently forgotten to address one of the applicants' complaints. In two cases it had accepted that the Papeetee court of appeal could not be regarded as having been impartial and transferred the proceedings to Paris. In relation to the third set of proceedings however, which appeared to be exactly the same, it did not do so. In the Court's opinion it was 'impossible to know whether the Court of Cassation simply neglected to make an order in respect of the third set of proceedings or whether it decided not to order transfer and, if so, why'.[171]

In *Pisano* v. *France* the complaint concerned insufficient reasoning in a decision not to call a witness proposed by the applicant. In this case the Court stressed the limits of its own competence in that area and added, quite convincingly, that the judgment itself, by evaluating the totality of the evidence, gave adequate reasons as to why the witness was not called.[172]

In *Garcia Ruiz* v. *Spain* the applicant was a trained lawyer who worked as a nurse but alleged that he had done legal work and claimed a fee. He lost because he could not establish that he had in fact provided those services. The Court found no violation: 'The factual and legal reasons for the first-instance decision dismissing his claim were set out at length. In the judgment at the appeal stage the Audiencia Provincial endorsed the statement of the facts and the legal reasoning set out in the judgment at first instance in so far as they did not conflict with its own findings. The applicant may not therefore validly argue that this

---

[169] The Commission had already held that Art. 6 called for reasons to be given by a court for its decisions in: *Firestone Tire and Rubber Co and others* v. *United Kingdom* Application 5460/72; *X* v. *Germany*, Application 1035/61; *Bricmont* v. *Belgium* Application 10857/84; *X* v. *Germany* Application 8769/79; *WR* v. *Belgium* Application 15957/90; particularly in cases where there is a possibility to appeal, *X* v. *Germany* Application 1035/61.   [170] Trechsel (2001) 165.
[171] *Higgins and others* v. *France*, § 43.   [172] *Pisano* v. *Italy*, § 24.

judgment lacked reasons, even though in the present case a more substantial statement of reasons might have been desirable.'[173]

Helle v. *Finland* concerned a complex labour dispute in a church setting—the Court saw no flaw in the reasoning of the contested decisions.[174]

V. OTHER ASPECTS OF FAIRNESS

A. *Nullum Judicium Sine Lege*

A rather extraordinary situation arose in the case of *Coëme* v. *Belgium* which concerned a criminal prosecution against a government minister. He had to stand trial before the full court of cassation which, by virtue of Article 103 of the Constitution, was the only jurisdiction competent to try a person holding that constitutional function. The basic rule had been established by the Constitution of 1831. Laws governing implementation had been passed for the purpose of dealing with single cases, but never as a definitive rule.

In the proceedings against the applicant, the procedure normally employed by the ordinary criminal courts was applied with certain modifications. The applicant complained that as the Court of Cassation had itself laid down rules of procedure, it had disregarded the separation of powers.

The Court acknowledged that the ordinary rules of criminal procedure were mainly applied, but 'only in so far as they were compatible "with the provisions governing the procedure in the Court of Cassation sitting as a full court"'.[175] Although the possibility of creating other rules was not actually used, it nevertheless created some uncertainty as to which rules would apply. This case prompted the Court to extend the scope of its case-law and to recognize a new element of lawfulness in criminal proceedings:

> The Court reiterates that the principle that the rules of criminal procedure must be laid down by law is a general principle of law. It stands side by side with the requirement that the rules of substantive criminal law must likewise be established by law and is enshrined in the maxim '*nullum judicium sine lege*'. It imposes certain specific requirements regarding the conduct of proceedings, with a view to guaranteeing a fair trial, which entails respect for equality of arms... The Court further observes that the primary purpose of procedural rules is to protect the defendant against any abuse of authority and it is therefore the defence which is the most likely to suffer from omissions and lack of clarity in such rules.[176]

Not surprisingly, it came to the conclusion that in this case the principle was not respected, a conclusion which merits approval. Less convincing was the Court's decision to base this conclusion on the need to respect the 'equality of arms'. It unconvincingly stated that 'the uncertainty caused by the lack of procedural

---

[173] *Garcia Ruiz* v. *Spain*, § 29. [174] *Helle* v. *Finland*, §§ 56 et seq.
[175] *Coëme* v. *Belgium*, § 101. [176] Ibid., § 102.

rules established beforehand placed the applicant at a considerable disadvantage *vis-à-vis* the prosecution',[177] but failed to explain why. Certainly it must be presumed, in the absence of any indication to the contrary, that the uncertainty affected both parties.

Particularly problematic is the fact that, in the passage reproduced, the Court seemed to draw a parallel between the fundamental rule of *nullum crimen sine lege* formulated by Feuerbach in the early nineteenth century but dating back to Magna Carta of 1215 and adopted in all human-rights instruments since the early American Constitutions and the *Déclaration des droits de l'homme et du citoyen* of 1789, laid down as a right which cannot be derogated from even in times of national crisis.[178]

In fact, *nullum judicium sine lege* cannot be put into the same category as *nullum crimen sine lege*. While it is agreed that the substantive criminal law only applies to conduct which occurs after its entry into force (except if the new law is less severe, i.e. *lex mitior*[179]) whenever procedural law is reformed there is a presumption that the new law is better and will be applied as soon as it comes into force. The individual will, at least to some extent, adapt his or her actions to the substantive law, for example, adapt his speed on motorways accordingly, but procedural law does not have a comparable function.

Instead of invoking the principle of equality of arms it would have been preferable to argue that the notion of fairness includes the requirement that there be legal rules governing the proceedings. Another possibility, which again would have been clearly preferable in my view, would have been to examine the issue in the context of the guarantee of a tribunal established by law. Jörg Paul Müller, writing in 1970, suggested that the notion of tribunal ought to be extended to cover the proceedings applied by such a body.[180] It would have been more convincing if the Court had said that the right to a tribunal established by law extended to the procedure applied by such tribunal, and that this too had to be set out in a legislative document.

B. Entrapment

Certain crimes which promise huge profits, such as drug trafficking, the production and distribution of counterfeit money, large-scale fraud, smuggling, 'slave trade for the purpose of prostitution', child pornography, and terrorist crimes are regularly committed within an organized network which will often go out of its way to conceal its existence and fight criminal prosecutions. Over the last decades, governments have become increasingly convinced that in order to combat such criminal activities, it is necessary *inter alia* to use clandestine methods such as using undercover agents to infiltrate organizations or pose as customers in illegal markets.

---

[177] Ibid., § 103. [178] ICCPR, Art. 4 § 2; ECHR, Art. 15 § 2; ACHR, Art. 27 § 2.
[179] This rule is incorporated in the third sentence of ACHR, Art. 9. [180] Müller (1970).

Several such cases have come before the international human-rights tribunals. One problem is that the agents are not, at least not openly, available as a witnesses as their identity must be kept concealed for their protection and to ensure that they can be further employed in the same field. These problems will be dealt with in the context of the right to call and question witnesses.[181] Another issue is whether the fact that an agent is sent out covertly to survey a person interferes with the right to respect for private life.[182] A third aspect which is relevant in the context of the right to a fair trial, concerns cases where undercover agents have actually instigated the commission of a crime in order to arrest the perpetrator.

One example of this is the case of *Teixeira de Castro* which originated because of the excessive zeal of two Portuguese policemen. One evening they set out to find the dealer who had sold drugs to a petty dealer. When their inquiries failed, they approached another person and asked him to find drugs for them. Through him they eventually found and approached the applicant. Mr Teixeira de Castro did not himself have any drugs but he finally succeeded, with the help of some other people, in finding some heroin. When he delivered it to the policemen, they told him that he was under arrest. He was later convicted and sentenced to six years' imprisonment.

The Court took the opportunity in this case to set out general guidelines for the use of undercover agents: 'The use of undercover agents must be restricted and safeguards put in place even in cases concerning the fight against drug trafficking. While the rise in organised crime undoubtedly requires that appropriate measures be taken, the right to a fair administration of justice nevertheless holds such a prominent place . . . that it cannot be sacrificed for the sake of expedience'.[183] One would, then, expect the Court to have examined whether, in the case at issue, the use of that method could have been justified at all. However, this question was not addressed in the judgment and it is rather unlikely that the Court will ever examine the legitimacy, or even the proportionality, of this method—at least not before it reassesses its opinion that secret surveillance does not constitute an interference with the right to respect for private life.

With regard to the specific case the Court stated first that the operation had neither been ordered nor supervised by a judge, an aspect which, in my view, was entirely irrelevant—if a person falls into a trap it is irrelevant who laid it. Then, however, it addressed the essential points: there had been no suspicion whatsoever that Mr Teixeira de Castro had been involved in drug trafficking, he had no criminal record, although this cannot be held to be decisive, and he was not in possession of any drugs. The Court also referred to the admissibility of evidence and noted that the applicant 'had been convicted mainly on the basis of the statements of the two police officers',[184] elements which were not connected to the point at issue. The relevant point was 'that the two police officers' actions went beyond those of undercover agents because they instigated the offence and

---

[181] See further Chapter 11 below.   [182] *Lüdi* v. *Switzerland*.
[183] *Teixeira de Castro* v. *Portugal*, § 36.   [184] Ibid., § 38.

there is nothing to suggest that without their intervention it would have been committed'.[185]

This case is in fact characterized by gross unfairness. The state provokes an offence and then punishes the author—a classical case of *agent provocateur* as they were used in dictatorships.[186] Yet, it is not obvious that this unfairness concerns the proceedings. Here, it was indeed a focus on the facts 'as a whole' which led to the finding of a violation. The proceedings themselves could not really be criticized, it was the entire operation which clearly started before Mr Teixeira de Castro could, by any standards, be regarded as being 'accused' of a criminal offence.

Entrapment was also the central problem in *Edwards and Lewis* v. *United Kingdom*, although in a slightly different context. The defence was of the opinion that the accused had been incited to commit the offence by undercover agents and had requested disclosure of all of the evidence relating to the operations which had led to their arrest. This was, however, denied. Under English law, entrapment was not a defence in substance, but the judge would have had the duty to stay the proceedings or to exclude the evidence.[187] It appeared that the material, which the trial judge was familiar with, included elements detrimental to the defence (in particular prior involvement in drugs offences) which it had had no chance to oppose. Therefore, the right to adversarial proceedings had been denied.[188]

Yet a different type of entrapment was at issue in *Khan*. The question was whether evidence which stemmed from a listening device which had been installed without any legal authority could be used by a court without violating the right to a fair trial. The Court held that this was indeed possible and mentioned, *inter alia*, that 'the admissions made by the applicant during the conversation with B. were made voluntarily, there being no entrapment and the applicant being under no inducement to make such admissions'.[189] One can deduce from this that had the accused been induced to make admissions by an undercover agent or through some other trick, this would have constituted entrapment and would have violated the right to a fair trial. Still, the assertion that there had been no entrapment is rather unconvincing. To record a conversation which the participants are entitled to consider as confidential is certainly the equivalent of setting a trap. The method is also hard to reconcile with the accused's right not to be compelled to incriminate him- or herself.

C. Compulsion to Accept a 'Settlement'

The organization and management of the criminal process is a rather onerous task. After the investigation phase, a decision must be taken as to whether or not

---

[185] Ibid., § 39.
[186] The only dissenting opinion was that of Judge Butkevich from the Ukraine. This might be explained by the fact that under the communist regime considerations of functionality usually had precedence over considerations of legality; cf. Bernhardt, Trechsel, Weitzel, and Ermacora (1994) 249 et seq.   [187] *Edwards and Lewis* v. *United Kingdom*, §§ 28, 50.
[188] Ibid., § 58.   [189] *Khan* v. *United Kingdom*, § 36.

to indict the suspect. This must then be followed by a public hearing, the public pronouncement of the judgment, possibly one or more appeals, and finally the enforcement of the sentence. This is justified in important cases or in cases where one or several of the points at issue are contested. However, the majority of cases are neither particularly serious nor the object of serious controversy. One way to deal with such cases is to process them by way of special, simplified proceedings. In the United States, plea-bargaining is used to avoid extremely onerous jury trials, while in Europe the use of summary judgments and penalty orders is widespread. Such alternative types of proceedings are recommended by the Committee of Ministers of the Council of Europe.[190]

The Court has also endorsed shortened proceedings of this kind as being compatible with the Convention, in that it correctly regarded the acceptance of such a settlement as a waiver. Waivers are common in relation to minor offences and they also benefit the person concerned. However, it will always be essential that it has been freely made, and this means that an accused must not be improperly compelled to submit to alternative procedures.[191]

In *Deweer*, an official of the Economic Inspectorate General was of the opinion that the applicant, a butcher, had sold meat at an excessive price. A transactional fine was imposed on Mr Deweer and at the same time he was threatened with closure of his business if he were to insist on opting for ordinary criminal proceedings. As closing the shop would have ruined the applicant, he agreed to pay the fine. This was held to be incompatible with the right to a fair trial.

D. Interference by a Non-judicial Authority

In the case-law concerning civil proceedings, we find cases where the state as a party to the proceedings intervened by way of legislation to avoid an undesired judgment. Indeed, this has been the subject of a number of complaints against Greece.[192] Obviously, this constitutes utter abuse of power, can in no way be reconciled with the rule of law, and is so blatantly unfair as to render further discussion unnecessary.

E. Miscellaneous Elements of Unfairness

1. Legal Certainty

In Romania the Procurator-General had the power to apply for a final judgment to be quashed—a power which was not subject to any time limit. This meant, according to the Court, 'that, by allowing the application lodged under that power, the Supreme Court of Justice set at naught an entire judicial process

---

[190] Recommendation of the Committee of Ministers concerning the simplification of criminal justice R (87) 18, adopted on 17 Sept. 1987.   [191] *Deweer* v. *Belgium*, § 49.
[192] *Stran Greek Refineries and Stratis Andreades* v. *Greece*; *Papageorgiou* v. *Greece*. See also *Zielinski and others* v. *France*.

which had ended in—to use the Supreme Court of Justice's words—a judicial decision that was "irreversible" and thus *res judicata*—and which had, moreover, been executed'.[193] It is interesting to note here that the Court introduced a new aspect into the notion of fair trial, namely that of legal certainty.

One may again wonder whether it is correct to deal with this in the context of the right to a 'fair trial'. I would have thought that it belongs to the issue of the right to an independent court, because a court cannot be considered to be independent if its final decisions do not bind all other state authorities.[194] At any rate, there can be no doubt that the principle, developed in connection with civil cases and equally valid for criminal proceedings,[195] constitutes an important aspect of the rule of law.[196]

However, legal certainty also has a much broader aspect. Renucci[197] finds it in the general definition of the term 'law' which was given by the Court in the *Sunday Times* judgment: 'Firstly, the law must be adequately accessible: the citizen must be able to have an indication that is adequate in the circumstances of the legal rules applicable to a given case. Secondly, a norm cannot be regarded as a "law" unless it is formulated with sufficient precision to enable the citizen to regulate his conduct: he must be able—if need be with appropriate advice—to foresee, to a degree that is reasonable in the circumstances, the consequences which a given action may entail'.[198]

We are thus faced with two aspects of legal certainty, a procedural one (a judgment acquires the force of law and cannot be quashed except under narrowly circumscribed conditions, for example, the discovery of new facts) and a substantial one (embodied for the field of criminal law in Article 7 of the ECHR, Article 15 of the ICCPR, and Article 9 of the ACHR).

2. Respect for Judgments

The same approach can be encountered in respect of the right to enforce the judgment. In a case against Georgia, which can only be described as scandalous, and a result of political disorder since overcome, a person who was acquitted and whose release had been ordered by the Supreme Court, was nevertheless kept imprisoned for over three years.

The Court dealt with the issue under Article 6 § 1. No further specification can be found in the text of the judgment. The Court argued here on the basis of sheer reasonableness:

. . . the guarantees afforded by Article 6 of the Convention would be illusory if a Contracting State's domestic legal or administrative system allowed a final, binding judicial decision to acquit to remain inoperative to the detriment of the person acquitted. It

---

[193] *Brumarescu* v. *Romania*, § 62; see also *Potop* v. *Romania* and *Popescu* v. *Romania*.
[194] Cf., *mutatis mutandis, Benthem* v. *Netherlands*, §§ 37 et seq.   [195] Esser (2002) 422.
[196] Sudre (2003) 332; Velu and Ergec (1990) N 466; Jennings (2001) 152.
[197] Renucci (2002) N 142, N 311.   [198] *Sunday Times* v. *United Kingdom*, § 49.

would be inconceivable that paragraph 1 of Article 6, taken together with paragraph 3, should require a Contracting State to take positive measures with regard to anyone accused of a criminal offence . . . and describe in detail procedural guarantees afforded to litigants—proceedings that are fair, public and expeditious—without at the same time protecting the implementation of a decision to acquit delivered at the end of those proceedings.[199]

The logic of this argument is impeccable. Still I do not regard this global approach as satisfactory. Again it is the independence of the tribunal which is at issue and it would have certainly been in the interests of legal certainty for the Court to have interpreted the Convention in this way.

3. Pro Memoria

Finally it should be noted that 'fairness' is, in particular, as far as criminal proceedings are concerned, exemplified by the specific rights of the defence as set out in Article 14 §§ 2–7 of the ICCPR, Article 6 §§ 2 and 3 of, and Articles 2–4 of Protocol No. 7 to, the ECHR, and in Article 8 §§ 2–5 of the ACHR.[200]

---

[199] *Assanidze* v. *Georgia*, § 181.
[200] For further decisions of the Commission regarding fairness, see Frowein and Peukert (1996) Art. 6 N 113.

Chapter 5

The Right to a Public Hearing

I. INTRODUCTION

A. The Texts

...In the determination of any criminal charge against him, or of his rights and obligations in a suit at law, everybody shall be entitled to a...public hearing...The press and the public may be excluded from all or part of a trial for reasons of morals, public order (*ordre public*) or national security in a democratic society, or when the interest of the private lives of the parties so requires, or to the extent strictly necessary in the opinion of the court in special circumstances where publicity would prejudice the interests of justice; but any judgement rendered in a criminal case...shall be made public except when the interests of juvenile persons otherwise requires or the proceedings concern matrimonial disputes or the guardianship of children.

ICCPR, Art. 14 § 1

In the determination of...any criminal charge against him, everyone is entitled to a...public hearing...Judgment shall be pronounced publicly but the press and public may be excluded from all or part of the trial in the interest of morals, public order or national security in a democratic society, where the interests of juveniles or the protection of the private life of the parties so require, or to the extent strictly necessary in the opinion of the court in special circumstances where publicity would prejudice the interests of justice.

ECHR, Art. 6 § 1

Criminal proceedings shall be public, except insofar as may be necessary to protect the interests of justice.

ACHR, Art. 8 § 5

A comparison of these texts reveals five significant differences.

First, the ACHR restricts the guarantee of a public hearing to criminal proceedings. The ICCPR and the ECHR expressly require that all disputes, to which the right to a fair trial applies, take place in public.

Second, both the ICCPR and the ECHR split the provision into two distinct guarantees by distinguishing between the public-hearing requirement and the requirement that the judgment be pronounced publicly. The ACHR places the right to a public hearing in a separate paragraph and sweepingly demands that the 'criminal proceedings' take place in public. This sentence cannot be interpreted literally. It certainly does not refer to the entire proceedings but only to the trial hearing.[1] Even here it is hard to imagine that there will be no exceptions, for instance in proceedings involving children (particularly in cases concerning sexual offences) or state secrets.

Third, while the ICCPR sets out three exceptions to the rule that the judgment be pronounced publicly, the ECHR is drafted in absolute terms. This proved rather unfortunate and forced the Commission and Court to interpret the provision *contra legem*.

Fourth, the ICCPR requires that judgments in criminal matters be 'made public', while the Convention states that '[j]udgment shall be pronounced publicly'. Again the absolute nature of the wording proved problematic and also led to an interpretation *contra legem*.

Fifth, and perhaps most importantly, at least from a theoretical perspective, there appears to be a fundamental difference between the text of the ACHR and the texts of the other two instruments. The ECHR and the ICCPR clearly describe the guarantee as an individual right of the accused in criminal proceedings (or as a party to non-criminal proceedings to which the right to a fair trial applies). Article 8 § 5 of the ACHR on the other hand is broader in that it enunciates a general principle rather than an individual right. This means that the guarantee could potentially be invoked by someone other than the accused, such as, for instance, a victim or a member of the press.[2] The American Court has not yet had the opportunity to address this issue. The cases which it has dealt with have all concerned very clear cases of proceedings held *in camera*.[3]

Other differences are of less importance. The ACHR only provides for an exception to the public-hearing requirement in cases where a closed hearing is in the interests of justice. This is not only rather broad, but also quite surprising when compared to the exceptions set out in the other instruments which predominantly provide for the exclusion of the public where this is in the interest of individuals involved.

Finally, the ECHR expressly refers to the interests of juveniles as one reason for excluding the public—although this aspect will normally be covered by 'the protection of the private life of the parties'. In fact it seems likely that in most situations it would be relatively easy to fit the protection of juveniles into one of the other categories—in particular, the interests-of-morals exception. In my view the express reference to juveniles must be understood as allowing for a lower

[1] Cf. for the European system, *Ernst and others* v. *Belgium*, § 67.
[2] See further section II.B below.
[3] *Duran and Ugarte Case* (against Peru), judgment of 16 Aug. 2000, Series C No. 68, §§ 141 et seq.; *Castillo Petruzzi et al Case* (against Peru), judgment of 30 May 1999, Series C No. 52, § 172. The Inter American Commission on Human Rights frequently refers to the jurisprudence of the ECtHR, see e.g. IACommHR Report No. 50/00, Case 11.298, *Reinaldo Figueredo Planchart* v. *Venezuela*, report of 13 Apr. 2000, §§ 132–6, referring to *Axen* v. *Germany*.

standard than in the case of adults—the restriction will be more easily regarded as being 'strictly necessary'.

B. The Origins of the Guarantee

The right to a public hearing was one of the original trial rights considered in the quest to draft an international instrument for the protection of human rights. It was the subject of lively discussions and at one point, late on in the drafting process, the Argentinean delegation questioned whether such a principle should be included, even in criminal cases.[4] The requirement that there be a public hearing in civil cases was heavily disputed although, as we have seen, only the ACHR opted to restrict the guarantee to criminal proceedings.

Unfortunately, the record of these discussions does not permit any firm conclusions to be drawn as to what the drafters actually had in mind when they introduced the right to a public trial in criminal matters into the international Bill of Human Rights. Typically, the discussions centred on exceptions to the principle.

The discussions concerning the text of the UDHR show that it was thought necessary that possible exceptions to the principle be covered by the general rule set out in Article 29 § 2, which is drafted in terms similar to the second paragraph of Articles 8–11 of the ECHR.[5] This was not an option for the Covenant, which does not have such a general rule covering exceptions.

Exceptions were proposed for 'cases of immorality' and for the purpose of protecting secret information.[6] In a drafting committee, the United Kingdom proposed to allow trials *in camera* in the interests of 'public security, morality, decency and the interest of juvenile offenders'.[7] Similar concerns were raised by the delegations from the Philippines and the USA. The Egyptian delegate, Mr Loutfi, was the first to suggest that at the very least 'the judgment must be made public',[8] and this proposal was later taken up by Ms Ciselet of Belgium. Israel had unsuccessfully proposed that it be deleted.[9]

C. The Purpose of the Guarantee of a Public Trial

1. The Case-law

The HRC addressed the purpose of the right to a public hearing in General Comment No. 13 § 6. It noted that it 'is an important safeguard in the interest

---

[4] Weissbrodt (2001) 69; Nowak (1993) Art. 14 N 23; this happened during the 16th Session— the argument was that in Latin America written proceedings were the norm. This is somewhat surprising in the light of the fact that earlier the Inter-American Juridical Committee had proposed a text which included the right to a public trial; Weissbrodt (2001) 16.

[5] Weissbrodt (2001) 16.

[6] e.g. by René Cassin, Weissbrodt (2001) 18; and Mr Pavlov (USSR), Weissbrodt (2001) 21.

[7] Weissbrodt (2001) 47. [8] Ibid., 52. [9] Nowak (1993) Art. 14 N 22, 29.

of the individual and of society at large'. This is not very precise, but it does highlight the fact that the guarantee affects two distinct interest groups: the parties to the proceedings and the public.

In a number of judgments the Court, generally using standard wording, has commented on the purpose of the guarantee. Its approach in relation to the obligation to pronounce the judgment publicly has been much less specific.

The Court generally begins by recalling that 'the holding of court hearings in public constitutes a fundamental principle enshrined in paragraph 1 of Article 6'.[10] This statement is rather banal and is practically tautological. It does not give any indication as to the meaning and purpose of the guarantee.

The Court will often continue by stating that '[t]his public character protects litigants against the administration of justice in secret with no public scrutiny'. Again, these comments are unhelpful and somewhat circular. It is quite obvious that the obligation to hold a trial in public protects against a trial in private. Still, the reference to 'public scrutiny' does give an indication of the purpose of the guarantee.

The Court goes on to explain: 'it is also one of the means whereby confidence in the courts can be maintained'. In other words, the opportunity to observe the working of the courts will instil in the population the conviction that the judiciary continues to function in the way they expect it to, and characterizes the old adage that justice must not only be done but must also be seen to be done.

Finally the Court often holds that: '[b]y rendering the administration of justice transparent, publicity contributes to the achievement of the aim of Article 6 § 1, namely a fair trial, the guarantee of which is one of the fundamental principles of any democratic society, within the meaning of the Convention'. It is not particularly clear, however, how public hearings support fairness. The wording clearly indicates that it is not a constituent element of fairness; it only 'contributes' to it. But there is nevertheless no indication of *how* this should happen. We must assume that the Court refers back to the possibility of public scrutiny and assumes that the possibility of public scrutiny will encourage courts to take particular care to respect the rules of fairness. At any rate, fairness and publicity are two distinct values—it is certainly possible for the Court to find

---

[10] *Pretto* v. *Italy*, § 21; *Sutter* v. *Switzerland*, § 26; *Diennet* v. *France*, § 33; *Szücz* v. *Austria*, § 42; *Guisset* v. *France*, § 72; *Werner* v. *Austria*, § 55; *Lamanna* v. *Austria*, § 30; *Ernst and others* v. *Belgium*, § 65; *Riepan* v. *Austria*, § 27; *Stefanelli* v. *San Marino*, § 19; among many others. The following quotations are from the same paragraphs. The Commission's reasoning in *Ekbatani* v. *Sweden*, § 28, was slightly more substantial. This was later summarized by the Court: 'the Commission observed that the accused's right to a public hearing was not only an additional guarantee that an endeavour would be made to establish the truth but also helped to ensure that he was satisfied that his case was being determined by a tribunal, the independence and impartiality of which he could verify. Furthermore, the Commission considered that this right followed from the object and purpose of Article 6 taken as a whole; in particular, the rights contained in sub-paragraphs (c) and (d) of paragraph 3 of Article 6', *Jan Åke Anderson* v. *Sweden*, § 24; *Fejde* v. *Sweden*, § 28. With slightly different wording, see also *Helmers* v. *Sweden*, § 33; *Tierce and others* v. *San Marino*, § 92; *Axen* v. *Germany*, § 25; *Sutter* v. *Switzerland*, § 26.

that both the public-hearing requirement and the requirement that the proceedings be adversarial have been violated.[11]

With disarming honesty the Court recognized in the *Engel* case the relatively low value of a public trial, observing that 'the applicants do not seem to have suffered on that account'.[12] Yet, while this may well be the case in many proceedings, the principle has an importance which goes beyond personal interests.

2. Weakness of the Court's View

As noted above, the reasoning used by the Court to justify the principle has little substantive content and is not particularly convincing.[13] First, experience shows that in practice most trials take place in the absence of the public—visitors are the exception not the rule.[14] Still, it is possible that even the potential appearance of members of the public may, in itself, have a salutary effect on the prosecution and the judiciary and encourage them to act appropriately. Even if the public is represented, however, the assumption that this will contribute to the fairness of the proceedings is somewhat naive. It is by no means certain that non-lawyers will be familiar with the rules of fair procedure. Indeed it is possible that they may not even desire that the trial be fair. Let us assume that the accused is suspected of involvement in a hideous terrorist crime or of having negligently caused an air crash[15]—it is not unlikely that the public will be very hostile towards the defence and react angrily if the defence is perceived to be advantaged by the need to respect the principle of fairness or if the accused is acquitted on the basis of so-called 'technical grounds'. In such a situation there is a clear danger that pressure could be exerted on the judge. It may then be necessary to *exclude* the public in order to safeguard the fairness of the proceedings.

3. Individual Right or Institutional Guarantee?

It is even doubtful whether it is correct to characterize the rule that trials have to be held in public as an individual right. One author sees its role exclusively in connection with the values of democracy and the rule of law.[16] Does a public hearing really serve the interests of an accused? It seems fair to assume that in

---

[11] *Göç* v. *Turkey (GC)*, § 46.

[12] *Engel and others* v. *Netherlands*, § 89. The Court referred to the fact that the sentence of one of the accused was reduced, a fact which lacks even the most tenuous of links with the right to a public hearing. The Court returned to the element of control of the impartiality of the court in *Tierce and others* v. *San Marino*, § 92; *Forcellini* v. *San Marino*, § 34; *De Biagi* v. *San Marino*, § 22.

[13] The following discussion is inspired by Bommer (2002) 671; see also Grabenwarter (1997) 473 et seq.   [14] Grabenwarter (1997) 472.

[15] This is not simply a theoretical example: a man who lost his whole family in an air crash is currently awaiting trial in Switzerland for stabbing to death the air-traffic controller who had been on duty at the time of the crash.   [16] Peters (2003) 121.

many cases it does not.[17] For many accused persons a public trial is likely to be a negative experience. Indeed, media interest and reporting may prove more detrimental to the accused than a fine or a suspended prison sentence.

Of course, there are applications in the Court's jurisprudence where it has been alleged that the right to a public hearing has been violated, but can it really be said that the applicants are seriously aggrieved because of the facts which they allege? It is legitimate to question the real aim of such applications, and I cannot help but think that the right to a public trial may often be a convenient vehicle used by the applicants to obtain a judgment that the Convention has been violated in the hope of ultimately improving the chances of a more favourable result. This is a strategy which although not corresponding to the essential aim pursued by the Convention, is nevertheless quite legitimate.

Interestingly, in *Neumeister*, the Court explicitly noted that those detained on remand have no interest in public proceedings, in order to strengthen its point that Article 6 did not apply to habeas corpus proceedings under Article 5 § 4.[18] The real reason for this is, however, that these proceedings do not concern the determination of a criminal charge.[19] The HRC also stressed that the public-hearing requirement only applies to the trial: it does not apply 'to pre-trial decisions made by prosecutors and public authorities'.[20] This is also the position in respect of the 'indictment chamber' ('*chambre d'accusation*', '*chambre du conseil*', '*Anklagekammer*', '*Raadkamer*'), a judicial body set up to decide whether there should be an indictment and to determine appeals against decisions taken by the public prosecutor's office or the investigating judge during the invest-igation phase.[21]

On the other hand, there may be a considerable public interest in being able to follow court proceedings. Such an interest may be particularly important in states which have recently embraced principles such as democracy and the rule of law. Here a significant role is often played by NGOs such as Amnesty Inter-national, the International Helsinki Federation for Human Rights, or the International Commission of Jurists who send observers to monitor trials and also use their observations to help improve the education of those involved in the criminal process and to assist in criminal-procedure reforms. As, however, the rights under Article 6 are conceived as individual rights, a representative of an NGO or a journalist who finds him- or herself excluded from the courtroom would not be able to complain of any violation of the right to a public hearing.[22] This is certainly quite unsatisfactory.

In my personal view, there is a way in which the Convention could be used to accommodate such an application. Third parties could invoke the right to obtain

---

[17] Haefliger and Schürmann (1999) 194.   [18] *Neumeister* v. *Austria*, § 23.
[19] See also Esser (2002) 708.   [20] *Joseph Kavanagh* v. *Ireland*.
[21] Velu and Ergec (1990) N 502.
[22] See also Gollwitzer (1992) Art. 6 N 91; Velu and Ergec (1990) N 510 cannot be correct if they affirm that the right also benefits the press and the public.

information as set out in Article 10. It is true that, as a basic rule, this Article only gives a right to receive information, which the holder is willing to impart.[23] Where, however, the Convention itself orders disclosure, as is the case with the right to a public hearing, it is hardly conceivable that a refusal would be accepted. The Commission followed this approach in *Guerra* where the applicants complained that the Government had failed to take steps to inform them about the hazard to the public of a 'high risk' factory.[24] As the Government was under an obligation imposed by domestic law to inform the public, the persons concerned had an entitlement to receive it.

In a case where a journalist was refused access to a sentencing hearing, the Commission accepted the approach in principle; the application was, however, declared inadmissible because the court could rely on the exceptions set out in Article 6.[25]

This was also the interpretation given to the First Amendment to the US Constitution by the Supreme Court. It held that the press has an autonomous right to be given access to court proceedings unless an overriding interest justified the exclusion of the public.[26]

It must be acknowledged that the public-hearing guarantee comprises two distinct aspects. On the one hand, it is set out in Article 6 as an individual right of the accused, of somewhat doubtful value. It might conceivably be in his or her interest to be tried in open court so that anybody, in particular friends and supporters, may follow the proceedings and have the chance to challenge any incorrectness on the part of the representatives of the state; but equally it may well add greatly to his or her distress and worsen an already difficult situation.

On the other hand, it constitutes an institutional guarantee, a way of ensuring that the administration of (criminal) justice is subject to public scrutiny and contributes to respect for the law and the persons involved—not just the accused but also witnesses, experts, and other persons appearing before the court. This latter function, however, is not effectively protected under Article 6, but only indirectly and partially through the application of the right to information.[27]

The somewhat precarious character of the guarantee to a public trial has definitely had a strong influence on the Court's case-law. There are clearly lower requirements for the validity of a waiver and in some cases the guarantee has quite simply been denied *contra legem* for reasons of expediency.[28]

---

[23] *Leander* v. *Sweden*, § 74; *Gaskin* v. *United Kingdom*, §§ 20, 21.
[24] *Guerra and others* v. *Italy*, §§ 41 et seq. The vote was taken by twenty-one votes to eight. The Court preferred to deal with the case under Article 8 as it had done in another 'ecological case', *López Ostra* v. *Spain*.
[25] *Atkinson, Crook, and the Independent* v. *United Kingdom* Application 13366/87.
[26] *Richmond Newspapers, Inc.* v. *Virginia*, 448 U.S. 555 (1980).
[27] See also the detailed analysis by Bommer (2002).
[28] See e.g. *Schuler-Zgraggen* v. *Switzerland*, § 58.

4. The Obligation to Pronounce the Judgment Publicly

In cases involving a failure to pronounce the judgment publicly, the Court sometimes mentions the purpose of the public trial.[29] It has never attempted to explain, however, why the public pronouncement of a judgment is of importance to an accused. In fact, an answer to this question is hard to find. There is undoubtedly a certain *public* interest. The vast majority of judgments will be of little interest to persons other than those directly involved, but it still ought to be possible for the public not only to observe the work of the courts but, also and perhaps even more importantly, to be able to find out the decision. However, no real value for an accused can be found in the public pronouncement of the judgment. He or she will certainly have to be served with the judgment—which, in principle, must include reasons.[30] It is doubtful, however, whether a public ceremony can really be seen as being in the interests of an individual accused. It is certainly desirable that the judgment be accessible to the public. Whether it will become widely known or not will depend on the general interest in the proceedings. From the standpoint of the accused the public pronouncement is hardly essential. He has the possibility of making it known to the public in many ways.

D. The Possibility of Waiving the Right to a Public Trial

As a general rule, the defence is entitled to waive its rights, although there are some exceptions.[31] The Commission was of the opinion that failure to ask for a hearing at first instance could not be regarded as a waiver.[32]

The public-hearing requirement is, if one keeps in mind the divergent interests served by the guarantee, a special one. In fact, as we are not dealing with a purely individual right, a waiver should not per se be valid unless one of the exceptions mentioned in the second sentence is invoked.[33] The Court has generally held that certain conditions must be fulfilled for the waiver to take effect: 'the waiver of a right guaranteed by the Convention—insofar as it is permissible—must be established in an unequivocal manner . . . Moreover, the Court agrees with the Commission that in the case of procedural rights a waiver, in order to be effective for Convention purposes, requires minimum guarantees commensurate to its importance'.[34]

With regard to the right to a public trial the Court has, however, accepted far less stringent prerequisites. Here, a waiver is possible 'whether expressly or

---

[29] e.g. in *Pretto v. Italy*, § 21; *Szücz v. Austria*, § 42; *Werner v. Austria*, § 55; *Lamanna v. Austria*, § 30; *Riepan v. Austria*, § 27.   [30] See Chapter 4, section IV above.
[31] For an exception, see *De Wilde, Ooms, and Versyp v. Belgium*, § 65. Judge Loucaides, in a somewhat exaggerated manner, rejects generally the idea of waiving human rights; Loucaides (2003) 48–9.   [32] *Adler v. Switzerland* Application 9486/81.
[33] Grabenwarter (1997) 511; Velu and Ergec (1990) N 511. No limitation is envisaged by Ovey and White (2002) 169.
[34] *Pfeifer and Plankl v. Austria*, § 37, referring to *Oberschlick v. Austria*, § 51.

tacitly';[35] in some cases the Court also requires the waiver to be made 'in an unequivocal manner',[36] although it is not entirely obvious how a waiver can be both unequivocal and tacit.

Occasionally the Court even goes one step further and assumes *a priori* a tacit waiver. In other words, it not only facilitates the opting out of a right but requires that the defence 'opt in'—this is, it must be admitted, a rather unusual way of dealing with fundamental rights. In *Håkansson and Sturesson* the Court found that although it was possible for the Göta Court of Appeal to hold a public hearing, this was not the usual procedure in cases such as that of the applicants. Therefore, 'the applicants could have been expected to ask for such a hearing if they had found it important that one be held'.[37] This approach has been the subject of criticism.[38]

It must be stressed that these cases all concern proceedings involving the determination of civil rights and obligations. It appears that the Court attaches greater weight to a public hearing in criminal proceedings, where there can be no presumption in favour of a waiver.

E. A Right to a Closed Hearing?

Finally, another aspect, linked to the possibility of waiving the right to a hearing, is whether the accused has the right to a non-public trial. Exceptionally, in its interpretation of the Convention, the Court has had to consider such negative, reverse arguments. One such situation concerned the issue of the closed shop where the question was whether the right to join an association encompassed the 'negative' right of *not* joining a union and still being entitled to retain one's job. This issue was discussed but not resolved in *Young, James, and Webster*.[39] The Commission came to an affirmative result in a case which concerned the refusal of a person to testify as a witness against his co-accused; it held that the right to freedom of expression had to be interpreted as also covering the right not to express an opinion or give information—although this had to be understood as being subject to the same possible exceptions as the 'positive' application of the right.[40]

---

[35] *Le Compte, van Leuven, and de Meyere* v. *Belgium*, § 59. In *Håkansson and Sturesson* v. *Sweden* Judge Walsh dissented—an opting-in system is not compatible with the text. See also Harris, O'Boyle, and Warbrick (1995) 220.

[36] *Albert and Le Compte* v. *Belgium*, § 35; *H* v. *Belgium*, § 54; *Håkansson and Sturesson* v. *Sweden*, § 66.

[37] *Håkansson and Sturesson* v. *Sweden*, § 67. In the same sense, see *Pauger* v. *Austria*, § 60; *Salomonsson* v. *Sweden*, § 35; *Döry* v. *Sweden*, § 38. There had been no waiver in *Werner* v. *Austria*, § 48, nor in *Göç* v. *Turkey (GC)*, § 48—in this case, however, there would have been no prospect of success. In *Malhous* v. *Czech Republic*, § 59, there was no link between the silence of the applicant and the absence of a public hearing because the court had examined the issue *ex officio*.

[38] Haefliger and Schürmann (1999) 194–5 think that the Court neglects the public-interest aspect of the guarantee. [39] *Young, James, and Webster* v. *United Kingdom*, § 52.

[40] *K* v. *Austria*, §§ 10 et seq. A friendly settlement was reached before the Court.

In my view, it would not be right to apply this principle to the right to a public hearing. For one, it must be borne in mind that the point at issue here is not a freedom, but a right. Moreover, this right can only be partly characterized as an individual right. It is something of a hybrid and the public interest in this guarantee is so strong as almost to outweigh that of the accused.[41] I therefore think that Article 6 § 1 of the ECHR, Article 14 § 1 of the ICCPR, and Article 8 § 5 of the ACHR cannot be interpreted as encompassing a right to be tried in private.[42] The Court's case-law supports this view insofar as it stresses that a waiver 'must not run counter to any important public interest'.[43] This is quite independent, of course, of the possibility of alternative types of proceedings. A public trial can be avoided where proceedings end by way of an agreement, such as following a plea bargain.[44]

A different approach may be taken when the accused are children. In *T and V* the Court even considered whether the fact that the trial had been publicly conducted amounted to treatment contrary to Article 3.[45]

II. THE SUBSTANCE OF THE RIGHT TO A PUBLIC HEARING

A. Immediate Publicity

The most obvious manifestation of the right to a public hearing is the oral hearing[46] and the assurance that the public will always be able to access the court. Any person should be able to enter the courtroom at anytime. The only general limitation is necessitated by the recognition of public-order considerations. It is of course legitimate to remove persons who disturb a hearing. It is moreover generally accepted that the court's deliberations take place in private.[47]

---

[41] Bommer (2002) 672.

[42] See also Grabenwarter (1997) 505–6; van Dijk and van Hoof (1998) 439. In *Campbell and Fell* v. *United Kingdom*, § 87, the Court said that 'ordinary criminal proceedings . . . take place in public, notwithstanding . . . the wishes of the accused'.

[43] *Pauger* v. *Austria*, § 58. See also *X, Y, and Z* v. *Switzerland* Application 7945/77; Gollwitzer (1992) Art. 6 N 100 and Frowein and Peukert (1996) Art. 6 N 121 suggest that a right to opt out of a public hearing can be based on the right to the protection of private life, but the decision referred to (*V* v. *Malta* Application 18280/90) does not support such a view. Still, it cannot be excluded *a priori* that, in the event of an acute conflict of interests, the Court might give precedence to the right to private life over the importance of the public trial. This is particularly probable with regard to the possibility of televised coverage of the trial; Grabenwarter (1997) 481.

[44] e.g. *Deweer* v. *Belgium*.

[45] *T* v. *United Kingdom*, § 75; *V* v. *United Kingdom*, § 77.

[46] *Lundevall* v. *Sweden*, § 34; Harris, O'Boyle, and Warbrick (1995) 218; Stavros (1993) 189. As a matter of course there is a violation of the right to a *public* hearing in cases where even the right to a *hearing* is wrongly denied. For a thorough discussion of the right to an *oral* hearing, see Grabenwarter (1997) 467 et seq.

[47] e.g. Grabenwarter (1997) 470. There are exotic exceptions to this rule in Switzerland; cf. Hauser and Schweri (2002) § 52 N 10.

The Commission rejected an application where it was alleged that the 'legal instruction' of the jury in Austria ought to have taken place in public; it accepted the argument that it formed part of the deliberations.[48]

Difficulties of a technical nature may arise, particularly if the hearing is held in a prison. In an earlier judgment the Court recognized that this 'would undoubtedly occasion difficulties of greater magnitude than those that arise in ordinary criminal proceedings'—if the proceedings were held outside the prison, the difficulties would involve the secure transportation of the prisoner.[49] In a much later case, other considerations led to a different result. The Court stressed that '[t]he public character of the proceedings assumes a particular importance in a case such as the present, where the defendant in the criminal proceedings is a prisoner, where the charges relate to the making of threats against prison officers and where the witnesses are officers of the prison in which the defendant is detained'.[50] The fact that the trial was held in a prison did not exclude the possibility of a public hearing, even if members of the public would have to undergo identity, and possibly also security, checks. However, the Court went on to comment on the importance of ensuring the effective application of the guarantee:

a trial complies with the requirement of publicity only if the public is able to obtain information about its date and place and if this place is easily accessible to the public. In many cases these conditions will be fulfilled by the simple fact that a hearing is held in a regular courtroom large enough to accommodate spectators. However, the Court observes that the holding of a trial outside a regular courtroom, in particular in a place like a prison, to which the general public in principle has no access, presents a serious obstacle to its public character. In such a case, the State is under an obligation to take compensatory measures in order to ensure that the public and the media are duly informed about the place of the hearing and are granted effective access.[51]

In the *Riepan* case these conditions were not met—the Court held that special measures ought to have been taken 'such as a separate announcement on the Regional Court's notice-board accompanied, if need be, by information about how to reach Garsten Prison, with a clear indication of the access conditions'.[52] In other words, in special cases the authorities must take active steps to ensure the effectiveness of the public-trial requirement. If the hearing is held aboard a ship, it must at least be open to the passengers and crew. Similarly, if there is a particularly strong public interest in a particular case, it will have to be transferred to a larger courtroom.

This is a new and welcome development—the Commission had earlier been of the opinion that there was no obligation on the authorities to inform the

[48] *Kremzow* v. *Austria* Application 12350/86.
[49] *Campbell and Fell* v. *United Kingdom*, § 87.   [50] *Riepan* v. *Austria*, § 27.
[51] Ibid., § 29. In the same sense see the HRC case, *Van Meurs* v. *Netherlands*, § 55 without a prison context; here, the courtroom was very small and eight of nine available seats were taken by officials.   [52] *Riepan* v. *Austria*, § 30.

public.[53] The ICCPR has been similarly interpreted. The HRC found a violation of Article 14 § 1 of the ICCPR in a case where the trial was held at a remote prison before 'faceless judges' ('*juezes sin rostro*')—they wore hoods for security reasons—and where the public were excluded.[54]

B. The Role of the Media

The media also have an important role in publicizing trials. As far as the press is concerned, no special problems arise. It is even possible, in specific cases, to admit members of the press, even though the general public has been excluded, where for instance this is required for the protection of morals.[55]

In some countries the taking of photographs in the courtroom is prohibited. This rule exists to protect both the privacy of the persons involved and the order of the proceedings, and is fully compatible with the fundamental right to a public hearing.[56]

Other aspects of media reporting, particularly the televised reporting of proceedings, have proven especially controversial. While it can be argued that this type of publicity is accurate in that 'everyone can see for him- or herself' what happens, this view is rather naive. The programme will be edited and devices such as close-ups will enable a focus on the participants and their reactions (perhaps without them even being aware of it) to an extent, which would go well beyond the observations of those present in court. Dramatic technique will determine whether to show the entire room, a group of persons, or a single face, and from which angle. In short, while the programme may give the impression of being objective and accurate, it may well transmit a highly personal view of the proceedings. The Court in Strasbourg, which itself held a hearing which was broadcast live, can be expected to have a less sceptical view. Yet, there has not yet been a judgment dealing with the issue. In my view the decision ought to be left with the domestic courts. There is no right of the accused to have the trial broadcast live or filmed for later broadcast—in other words, the exclusion of audio-visual media does not violate the right to a public trial.[57] Whether a broadcast against the will of an accused would constitute a violation of his or her private life, is a question which falls to be decided on a case-by-case basis.

C. The Substance of the Public Hearing

What must occur during the public hearing? As will be shown, it has a particular importance in those cases where evidence is heard. The Court has rightly and

---

[53] *S* v. *United Kingdom* Application 8512/79, a decision which Harris, O'Boyle, and Warbrick (1995) 218 approve of.   [54] *Victor Alfredo Polay Campos, husband of the author* v. *Perú*.
[55] Chiavario (2001) 201.   [56] Gollwitzer (1992) Art. 6 N 88; Strasser (1988) 613.
[57] See also Grabenwarter (2003) § 24 N 48; Grabenwarter (1997) 481.

clearly held that 'all the evidence should, in principle, be produced in the presence of the accused at a public hearing with a view to adversarial argument'.[58] This requirement which embodies the 'principle of immediacy' is thereby given a double function—it is both an element of the fairness of the proceedings and a prerequisite for the effective implementation of the right to a *public* trial.

III. LIMITATIONS AND EXCEPTIONS

A. Implied Limitations?

In *Campbell and Fell* the Court raised the question whether there were any implied limitations in the right to a public trial. Contrasting the issue with those which arose in the *Golder* case, it came to the conclusion that there were not, because the Convention expressly provided for a number of exceptions.[59] With regard to cases concerning the determination of civil rights and obligations, the Court has developed a doctrine which has, until now, not been applied in the context of criminal cases and which casts doubt on the theory that the public-hearing requirement applies equally to civil and criminal cases.[60] In *Schuler-Zgraggen* it noted that '[a]bove all, it does not appear that the dispute raised issues of public importance such as to make a hearing necessary. Since it was highly technical, it was better dealt with in writing than in oral argument; furthermore, its private, medical nature would no doubt have deterred the applicant from seeking to have the public present'.[61] However, this passage must be read in conjunction with the Court's assumption that there had been a tacit waiver.

On the other hand, we also find rather surprising statements such as that 'Article 6 does not always require a right to a public hearing'.[62] In *Göç* the Court examined at length whether the hearing could have had any meaningful purpose—the Convention does not set out any such requirement.[63] However, no less than eight judges dissented.[64] They were all of the opinion that an oral hearing was not necessary unless required by some public-interest issue. It appears that this problem has not yet been solved.

---

[58] e.g. *Barberà, Messengué, and Jabardo v. Spain*, § 78; *Imbrioscia v. Switzerland*. See Chapter 4, section II above.

[59] *Campbell and Fell v. United Kingdom*, § 90; the argument fails totally with regard to the public pronouncement of the judgment.   [60] *Albert and Le Compte v. Belgium*, § 30.

[61] *Schuler-Zgraggen v. Switzerland*, § 30. This approach was confirmed in *Zumtobel v. Austria*, § 23. In *Fischer v. Austria*, § 44, the issues were serious enough to warrant a hearing. See also the decision on (in)admissibility in *Lino Carlos Varela Assalino v. Portugal* Application 64336/01. For criticism of this case-law, see Esser (2002) 711.

[62] *Botten v. Norway*, § 39. It must be assumed that the statement refers only to appeal proceedings.   [63] *Göç v. Turkey (GC)*, § 51.

[64] Judges Wildhaber, Costa, Ress, Türmen, Bîrsan, Jungwiert, Maruste, and Ugrekhelidze.

In criminal proceedings, however, there must always be at least one public hearing before a court, which hears the evidence and decides on all the issues raised by the charge.[65]

B. The Limitations Set Out in the Text

All three texts provide for exceptions to the public-trial requirement. The ACHR simply refers to 'the interests of justice' and thereby leaves the national authorities a wide margin of appreciation. One might be tempted to take a literal approach and to view this provision as being more restrictive than those found in the other instruments. However, it can hardly be correct to interpret it as meaning, for instance, that the interests of the private lives of the parties would not justify the exclusion of the public.[66] In fact, even under the ECHR the margin of appreciation left to domestic authorities is broad.[67] It is remarkable that the exception does not state that the exclusion must be 'prescribed by law'.

The exceptions set out in the ECHR have hardly been discussed in the Strasbourg case-law.[68] The Court has only repeated in a few judgments that none of the exceptions applied—this was done *ex officio* as the grounds had not been invoked by the domestic courts. Reasons of public order and security were accepted in *Campbell and Fell*.[69] In *Diennet*, which concerned disciplinary proceedings against a medical doctor, it was not legitimate to apply this exception to cover the interests of the private lives of his patients because no such information would be disclosed. Here the Court found that an exception must be 'strictly required',[70] although, in fact, the public was automatically excluded.[71] Sometimes the Court just finds that there were 'no special features' justifying the absence of a public hearing.[72]

Although the text seems to indicate that the court must decide in each case whether or not the public ought to be excluded, the Court did not find a violation in a case where a general rule stated that matters involving family law were to be heard in private.[73] Two judges strongly disagreed with this approach.[74] It might be thought that, at the very least, all of the parties would have to agree that the proceedings should not be heard in public.

---

[65] In the same sense, see Esser (2002) 709.

[66] Haefliger and Schürmann (1999) 197 rightly criticize the fact that this is limited to the parties—witnesses and others appearing before the court may also have a strong legitimate interest in not having to divulge personal matters in public.   [67] Velu and Ergec (1990) N 509.

[68] For a more detailed discussion, see Gollwitzer (1992) Art. 6 N 96 et seq.; Grabenwarter (2003) § 24 N 49–54; Grabenwarter (1997) 481–504; Haefliger and Schürmann (1999) 196 et seq. On the margin of appreciation in this context, see Stavros (1993) 193.

[69] *Campbell and Fell* v. *United Kingdom*, § 89.

[70] This can hardly be understood as meaning more than the existence of a 'pressing social need'; cf. also Harris, O'Boyle, and Warbrick (1995) 219.   [71] *Diennet* v. *France*, § 34.

[72] *Botten* v. *Norway*, § 53.

[73] *B* and *P* v. *United Kingdom*; legislation generally excluding the public from proceedings regarding family matters exists also in France; see Charrier (2002) Art. 6 N 54.

[74] Judges Loukis Loucaides and Françoise Tulkens.

C. Appeal Proceedings

Quite a number of cases have involved the question of a public hearing in appeal proceedings. In all these cases the issue is linked to the right to a hearing as such, including the right to be heard in person. It is doubtful whether it is justified to make such a connection. Civil proceedings raise different questions[75] as compared to criminal proceedings but it is not clear to what extent the court takes this into account.[76] The right to a public hearing is also dealt with in the context of the right to defend oneself in person. Renucci rejects any restriction of the public-hearing requirement in appeal proceedings.[77]

In applying the ICCPR, the HRC initially made the sweeping statement that a public hearing was not required on appeal.[78] Later, it reversed this rule in cases where, on appeal, the court still had the responsibility for determining a criminal charge.[79] In essence, this can be said to correspond to the approach taken by the Strasbourg authorities.

D. Cases Where Violations Were Found

There have only been a few cases where the Court has come to the conclusion that the right to a public hearing had been violated. Generally the problem lies with antiquated or specialized legislation. San Marino has come in for particular criticism.[80] There are also, of course, cases, which, under domestic law, were considered not to fall under Article 6 at all.[81] The third group concerns cases where the right to a public hearing was wrongfully denied on appeal.[82]

IV. 'JUDGMENT SHALL BE PRONOUNCED PUBLICLY'

The most controversial issue in the context of the right to a public hearing is the requirement that the 'judgment shall be pronounced publicly'. Here, it can be said with conviction that the drafters of the ECHR made a mistake, a mistake which was avoided in the Covenant. It was drafted in more flexible terms, stating only that the judgment shall be 'made public' not that it must be 'pronounced publicly'. In addition it also provides for exceptions to the rule. According to the text of the ECHR, the judgment must in all cases be read out in public.

---

[75] Grabenwarter (1997) 512.
[76] See the criticism of Haefliger and Schürmann (1999) 192–3 who suggest that the issue of being heard in person and of the public trial be separated.   [77] Renucci (2002) 276.
[78] *RM* v. *Finland*.   [79] *Arvo O Karttunen* v. *Finland*; see also Chapter 10 II.
[80] See the cases of *Stefanelli, Tierce and others, Forcellini,* and *De Biagi* (all v. *San Marino*).
[81] *Le Compte, van Leuven, and de Meyere* v. *Belgium; Albert and Le Compte* v. *Belgium; Campbell and Fell* v. *United Kingdom; Diennet* v. *France; Guisset* v. *France; Weber* v. *Switzerland*.
[82] *Ekbatani* v. *Sweden; Botten* v. *Norway*.

When faced with this problem for the first time, the Court did not beat around the bush.[83] It noted that quite a number of states employed different mechanisms for making judgments public, for example, by depositing them in a court registry. It supposed, over-optimistically in my view, that the drafters could not have overlooked this; it admitted however in a slightly veiled formulation that the *travaux préparatoires* did not really support its view. Therefore, it found that the rule was complied with as long as the judgment was 'made public'.[84]

This interpretation *contra legem* has since been confirmed in a number of cases. In two child-custody cases, the Court even applied by analogy exceptions meant to apply to the publicity of the hearing itself, in order to prevent the protection from being undermined.[85] This possible danger has also been noted by scholars;[86] it will not be possible effectively to make an anonymous version of the judgment because those present will be informed about the issue. On the other hand, if it is possible to make an anonymous judgment, the publication will be without interest, as Sir Nicholas Bratza rightly observes.[87] Although the basic argument was confirmed, the Court found a violation in cases against Austria because the judgment was accessible only to persons who showed a legitimate interest and at the discretion of the court.[88] This is in contrast to the finding in *Sutter* where an analogous rule had been regarded as satisfactory— quite wrongly in my view.[89] Finally, in *Lamanna* the judgment on compensation for unlawful imprisonment was only delivered publicly six years after the decision, a fact which was justified by the need to wait for the acquittal to become final.[90]

One cannot help having mixed feelings about this issue. If it is accepted that this guarantee is of limited value as an individual right (after all, nothing prevents the accused from making the judgment public), the interpretation *contra legem* can be viewed as being acceptable. The respect for the various domestic traditions has hardly had any negative impact on the individual rights. Moreover, contrary to the aims of the EU in many areas, the human-rights instruments are not intended to impose general uniformity upon the contracting parties.

---

[83] Haefliger and Schürmann (1999) 199 speak of a 'somewhat daring' interpretation.

[84] *Axen* v. *Germany*, § 31; see also *Pretto* v. *Italy*, §§ 30–2; *Sutter* v. *Switzerland*, §§ 32–4 (all decided on the same day).

[85] *B and P* v. *United Kingdom*, §§ 45 et seq., Judge Loucaides dissented, joined by Judge Tulkens. In a later publication (Loucaides (2003)) he concluded that neither the majority nor the minority had been right and that '[i]t is an area possibly demanding modifications of the Convention'. I agree.   [86] Haefliger and Schürmann (1999) 198.

[87] Separate opinion of Sir Nicholas Bratza to the *B* v. *United Kingdom* and *P* v. *United Kingdom* judgment.

[88] *Szücz* v. *Austria*, §§ 44 et seq.; *Werner* v. *Austria*, §§ 57 et seq.; *Rushiti* v. *Austria*, § 22.

[89] In the same sense, see Esser (2002) 754; Merrills and Robertson (2001) 113.

[90] *Lamanna* v. *Austria*, § 33.

The HCR had to deal with a more extreme case where even the convicted person himself had not received a copy of the written judgment; it concluded that the latter had not been made public.[91]

Only the operative part of the judgment and a summary of the reasoning must be made public—the complete arguments can be produced later in writing.[92]

[91] *Louis Touron* v. *Uruguay.*
[92] *Crociani and others* v. *Italy* Applications 8608/79, 8722/79, 8723/79, 1729/79; Application 8880/80. Chiavario (2001) 206 seems to say that the public pronouncement of the operative part is sufficient; for Nowak (1993) Art. 14 N 31 the publication of a summary may be justified where the public was excluded from the hearing.

Chapter 6

The Right to be Tried Within a Reasonable Time

I. INTRODUCTION

A. The Texts

> In the determination of any criminal charge against him, everyone shall be entitled to the following minimum guarantees, in full equality: . . . To be tried without undue delay . . .
>
> ICCPR, Art. 14 § 3

> In the determination . . . of any criminal charge against him, everyone is entitled to a . . . hearing within a reasonable time . . .
>
> ECHR, Art. 6 § 1

> Every person has the right to a hearing . . . within a reasonable time . . .
>
> ACHR, Art. 8 § 1

The Covenant differs from the ACHR and the ECHR in two principal respects. First, read literally, the right to a speedy trial only applies to accused persons in criminal proceedings. The HRC acted quickly to remedy this situation, declaring simply that any undue delay was incompatible with the right to a fair trial.[1] In fact there is hardly any difference in the manner in which the guarantee is applied to civil and to criminal proceedings.[2] The Court occasionally, and sometimes without even acknowledging the fact, refers to its jurisprudence concerning the length of civil proceedings, even though the case at issue concerns criminal proceedings.[3]

While this difference is of considerable importance in terms of an evaluation of the instrument as a whole, it is of little relevance within the scope of this study. The second notable difference is that the Covenant requires that the proceedings

---

[1] *Casanovas* v. *France*.
[2] Although, contrary to what Nowak (1993) Art. 14 N 44 writes, they are not 'synonymous'.
[3] e.g. *Eckle* v. *Germany*, § 80, refers to *Koenig* v. *Germany* and at § 82 to *Buchholz* v. *Germany; Garyfallou AEBE* v. *Greece*, § 39, refers to *Phocas* v. *France; Pélissier and Sassi* v. *France*, § 74 refers to *Duclos* v. *France; Hennig* v. *Austria*, § 38, refers to *Spentzouris* v. *Greece*.

take place 'without undue delay' rather than 'within a reasonable time'. Despite this it will be shown that these terms actually have an identical meaning. The time used for the proceedings will be 'reasonable' as long as there has been no 'undue delay'.

B. The Origins of the Guarantee

The first draft of what was to become Article 14 of the ICCPR was introduced by the United States and was split into two distinct parts. Article 6 concerned the rights of the accused in criminal proceedings, while Article 27 regulated civil proceedings. It is rather ironic, in view of the current position, that the only reference to 'undue delay' was to be found in Article 27.[4] The guarantee was introduced into Article 14 following a proposal made by Mr Baror on behalf of the Israeli delegation.[5] Undue delay, he stated, 'almost invariably constituted a denial of justice'.[6]

C. The Purpose of the Guarantee

In one of its first judgments the Court clearly and convincingly set out the purpose of the right to be tried within a reasonable time: 'the precise aim of this provision in criminal matters is to ensure that accused persons do not have to lie under a charge for too long and that the charge is determined'.[7] Prolonged proceedings can put a considerable strain on accused persons and have the potential to exacerbate existing concerns such as uncertainty as to the future, fear of conviction, and the threat of a sanction of an unknown severity. This may go some way to explaining the frequency with which this right is invoked. The Court has determined almost 250[8] cases, and many more have been the subject of friendly settlements or have never reached the Court, either because the decision lacked jurisprudential interest and was left with the Committee of Ministers under Article 32 of the (old) ECHR,[9] or because they were declared inadmissible. One might also guess that in some cases this is the only way which promises some remedy—within the framework of negotiations on a friendly settlement it may be possible to obtain a reduction of sentence.[10]

---

[4] Weissbrodt (2001) 45.   [5] Nowak (1993) Art. 14 N 44.

[6] UN Doc. A/C.3/SR.961, para. 12 (19 Nov. 1959), quoted by Weissbrodt (2001) 72.

[7] *Wemhoff* v. *Germany*, The Law, § 18.

[8] This does not include cases concerning civil proceedings which are even more numerous. Peters (2003) 123 states that there have already been over 10,000 about prolonged proceedings against Italy since 1987. Up until 30 June 2001, some 60% of the judgments concerned the length of proceedings; see Reed and Murdoch (2001) N 5.91, n. 1. According to Grabenwarter (2003) § 24 N 44, this is the most frequently invoked guarantee before the ECtHR and the main cause for the backlog—the latter observation is open to doubt.

[9] Not all of these cases will be referred to here—references are to be understood merely as examples.   [10] See section V below.

On a more abstract level, it is quite clear that the right to be tried by a court can only be effectively enforced if a decision is reached within a reasonable time. The alternative would be postponement *ad calendas graecas*—a denial of justice.[11] The importance of the right to be tried within a reasonable time becomes even more evident if one keeps in mind that access to court is one of the fundamental elements of the rule of law.[12]

Yet it must be acknowledged that speedy proceedings are not always in the defendant's interests, particularly if he or she is not remanded in custody. The accused may have the chance to benefit, for example, from a statute of limitations which may encourage the defence to use delaying tactics. In one case the time element amounted to a question of life or death. Mr Chadee brought a communication before the HRC in which he alleged that the Attorney General of Trinidad and Tobago had complete control over the speed of appeal proceedings. Proceedings which lasted too long would prohibit the execution taking place; in his case the proceedings had been carried out with unusual speed. The HRC examined whether there had been a violation of the right to adequate time for the preparation of the defence but came to a negative result—thus, there had been no violation of the ICCPR.[13]

There is also a public interest in avoiding undue delay. The criminal-justice system is normally perceived as having broader aims than simply those of facilitating the reaching of a judgment. Other goals, such as the rehabilitation of the offender or the creation of restorative-justice initiatives, must also be acknowledged. Delay can also be seen as detrimental to such policy aims.[14] For the purposes of applications under the international human-rights instruments, however, such considerations are of little relevance.

Stavros suggests that the right to a speedy trial can also be viewed as a means of assisting the accused in mounting an effective defence—'the passage of time may result in the loss of exculpatory evidence'.[15] I do not find this rationale particularly convincing. The passage of time has the potential to have a similarly, or perhaps even more, detrimental effect on the prosecution case than on that of the defence. Moreover, the accused also has the chance to profit from *lex mitior*, as happened in *Kangaslouma*.[16]

D. Length of Proceedings and Length of Detention on Remand

The provisions concerning the length of proceedings have obvious parallels with those relating to the length of detention on remand. The latter are of course stricter, reflecting the more invasive nature of remand detention. Custodial detention pending trial is obviously a considerable burden and this is the reason

---

[11] Gollwitzer (1992) Art. 6 N 76.
[12] Charrier (2002) Art. 6 N 42; Chiavario (2001) 156.
[13] *Dole Chadee et al* v. *Trinidad and Tobago.*   [14] Peters (2003) 123.
[15] Stavros (1993) 77.   [16] *Kangasluoma* v. *Finland*, § 34.

for the additional guarantee set out in Article 9 § 3 of the ICCPR, Article 5 § 3 of the ECHR, and Article 7 § 3 of the ACHR.[17] In *Wemhoff*, the Court had found that the length of time spent on remand had not been excessive; logically, it had to follow that there had been no contravention of the less stringent obligation contained in Article 6 § 1 of the Convention.[18] This will not always be the case. Proceedings may last much longer than the duration of the detention on remand when the accused has been released or when the delays occurred during the appeal phase. This may occur, for example, because of the time taken to draft the written judgment; it is then possible that the Court will find a violation of Article 6 § 1 but not of Article 5 § 3.

E. The Points to be Discussed

The legal aspects of the right to be tried within a reasonable time are relatively simple. The main difficulties, particularly during the early stages of the implementation of the Convention, were the factual aspects of the cases considered. The Commission was often required to analyse, in detail, proceedings lasting several years in order to determine whether the delay could be justified.[19] Even in recent years there have still been a number of lengthy decisions,[20] but the Court has also found the courage to deal with this issue in a more concise way.[21]

Basically, there are three questions, which arise in the context of the right to be tried within a reasonable time: when does the period begin, when does it end, and what are the criteria used to distinguish proceedings of reasonable length from those involving undue delay? Furthermore, reference must be made to the possibility of the domestic authorities compensating the accused for the excessive length of the proceedings.

II. THE BEGINNING OF THE RELEVANT PERIOD

A. The 'Autonomous' Interpretation of the Term 'Charged'

According to the ICCPR and the ECHR, the right to a fair trial arises once a person has been 'charged' with a criminal offence. In domestic criminal-procedure law there will usually be an act which marks the bringing of a charge. It may consist of the official opening of a criminal investigation without the

---

[17] See e.g. *Stögmüller* v. *Austria*, p. 40, § 5; *Jablonski* v. *Poland*, § 104; *Punzelt* v. *Czech Republic*, § 98; the subject is dealt with in Chapter 19 below.   [18] *Wemhoff* v. *Germany*, The Law, § 20.

[19] Cf. e.g. *Haase* v. *Germany* Application 7412/76; *Bonnechaux* v. *Switzerland* Application 8224/78; *Pannetier* v. *Switzerland* Application 9299/81; *Schertenleib* v. *Switzerland* Application 8339/78; *Hätti* v. *Germany* Application 6181/73.

[20] e.g. *Szeloch* v. *Poland; Lavents* v. *Latvia; Kalashnikov* v. *Russia.*

[21] The first of these brief judgments seems to be *Messina* v. *Italy*. See also *Olstowski* v. *Poland; Vieziez* v. *France; Andrea Corsi* v. *Italy; Meilus* v. *Lithuania; Yankov* v. *Bulgaria;* and *Alfatle* v. *Turkey.*

term 'charge' being used. If the international bodies were to rely on the cate-
gorization made in domestic law, states would have the possibility to manipulate
the length of proceedings by ensuring that the formal 'charge' occurs at a late
stage in the proceedings, such as following the end of the investigation. This
could seriously undermine the purpose of the guarantee and prevent it from
being uniformly applied. The obvious solution to this problem, and the one
which has been adopted, is the development of an autonomous notion of the
term, enabling uniform application throughout the Member States.

B. The General Rule

The Court outlined, relatively early on in the development of its case-law, a
definition for the moment when 'the clock starts running'. Despite the fact that
this notion has remained unchanged over decades, the judgment betrays some
uncertainty. The Court argued that the 'charge' had to be the starting point, 'for
otherwise it would not be possible to determine the charge'. It then went on to
refer to the autonomous notion of the term: 'as this word is understood within
the meaning of the Convention'.[22] In *Eckle* the Court held that the relevant
moment may precede the trial and could be 'the date of arrest, the date when the
person concerned was officially notified that he would be prosecuted or the date
when preliminary investigations were opened'.[23] In this case the Court provided
the first definition of the term 'charge', stating that it 'may be defined as "the
official notification given to an individual by the competent authority of an
allegation that he has committed a criminal offence", a definition that also
corresponds to the test whether "the situation of the [suspect] has been substantially affected"'.[24] The reference to *Deweer* highlights the fact that this
definition was intended to mark not just the beginning of the 'reasonable time'
period, but also the point at which Article 6 starts to apply.

A rather recent judgment shows that the jurisprudence has hardly changed
at all:

The Court recalls that the period to be taken into account in the assessment of the length
of the proceedings starts from an official notification given to an individual by the
competent authority of an allegation that he has committed a criminal offence or from
some other act which carries the implication of such an allegation and which likewise
substantially affects the situation of the suspect . . . According to the Court's constant
case-law, a person has been found to be subject to a 'charge', inter alia, when a preliminary investigation has been opened in his case and, although not under arrest, the
applicant has officially learned of the investigation or has begun to be affected by it. In the

---

[22] *Neumeister* v. *Austria*, The Law, § 18.
[23] *Eckle* v. *Germany*, § 73 with further references. In *De Varga-Hirsch* v. *France* Application
9559/81, the Commission did not regard the *garde à vue* ('police arrest') as initiating the period—
this must be regarded as an error; see also the criticism voiced by Stavros (1993) 80.
[24] *Eckle* v. *Germany*, § 73, with reference to *Deweer* v. *Belgium*, § 46.

present case the Court finds that the applicant officially learned of the investigation at the time when he was interrogated by police for the first time, in December 1990.[25]

The relevant moment has also been held to have been marked by the first interrogation by the police,[26] and by a search.[27]

It is essential, however, that the applicant is the subject of the proceedings. In one case the investigation focused initially on a corporation, although it was later extended to cover the applicant who was suspected of being involved in the same offence. Even though the applicant had, during the initial investigations into the affairs of the company, been taken into custody and had had her home searched, the Court somewhat surprisingly considered that at this point in time she had not yet been 'charged' within the meaning of the Convention.[28]

There is also some uncertainty as to what constitutes an investigation which can 'substantially affect' a person when the criminal proceedings are preceded by an administrative inquiry. In *IJL, GMR, and AKP* v. *United Kingdom*, for instance, interviews conducted by Department of Trade and Industry-appointed inspectors were not regarded as marking the beginning of the proceedings,[29] while in *Bertin-Mouret* the period started when the applicant, who was suspected of illegally exporting a painting, was interrogated by customs officers.[30]

There is also a lack of clarity in relation to proceedings following an administrative fine. In *Hozee*, the Court said that 'the imposition of a fiscal penalty under section 21 of the General Act on State Taxes does not give rise to criminal proceedings in the absence of elements which would justify the intervention of the FIOD [the *Fiscale inlichtingen- en opsporingsdienst* ("Fiscal Intelligence and Investigation Department")]'.[31] In my view, the imposition of a penalty must always be regarded as a 'declaration of war' by the prosecuting authority against the defendant. In cases where the investigation is triggered by an 'objection', the time taken by the defendant to decide will, however, not be held against the government.[32] Yet, in *Garyfallou AEBE*, administrative proceedings aimed at challenging the legal basis of an administrative fine were, without any discussion, examined under Article 6 § 1 and found to be of excessive length.[33]

Another particularity can be found in the case of *GC* v. *Poland* where the Court did not use the date of the arrest, instead speculating that 'the "wanted" notice had inevitably to be issued at least several days before the applicant's

---

[25] *Kangasluoma* v. *Finland*, § 26, referring to *Corigliano* v. *Italy*, § 34; see also e.g. *Foti and others* v. *Italy*, § 52; *Bertin-Mourot* v. *France*, § 52; *IJL, GMR, and AKP* v. *United Kingdom*, § 131; *Jablonski* v. *Poland*, § 102; *Mitap and Müftüoğlu* v. *Turkey*, § 31; *Zana* v. *Turkey*, § 74; *Hozee* v. *Netherlands*, § 43; *Włoch* v. *Poland*, § 144; *Sari* v. *Turkey*, § 66; *Metzger* v. *Germany*, § 31; *Pantea* v. *Romania*, § 275.   [26] *Martins and García Alves* v. *Portugal*, § 20.

[27] *Diamantides* v. *Greece*, § 21; *Coëme* v. *Belgium*, § 133.

[28] *Reinhardt and Slimane-Kaïd* v. *France*, § 93; *Hozee* v. *Netherlands*, § 44.

[29] *IJL, GMR, and AKP* v. *United Kingdom*, § 131.   [30] *Bertin-Mourot* v. *France*, § 53.

[31] *Hozee* v. *Netherlands*, § 44.   [32] The same view is, in effect, held by Peters (2003) 124.

[33] *Garyfallou AEBE* v. *Greece*, §§ 40 et seq.

apprehension'.[34] The Court ought at least to have established whether the applicant had been aware of the notice.

C. Proceedings Commenced Before the Entry into Force of the Convention

A special problem arises when the Court has to assess the length of proceedings which had commenced before the responding state was bound by the Convention. A state cannot be held responsible for proceedings, or a part of the proceedings, which took place before the Convention had come into force. In such cases the starting date will be taken to be the date on which the Convention entered into force. The length of the proceedings prior to that day is not entirely irrelevant—the Court will take it into account. In other words, if a considerable amount of time has already been used, the authorities will have to make a particular effort in order to bring the proceedings to an end. The standard formula used by the Court is this: 'the Court can only consider the period of two years, five months and twenty-four days that elapsed between 22 January 1990, the date on which the declaration whereby Turkey recognised the Court's compulsory jurisdiction was deposited, and 16 July 1992. Nevertheless, it must take into account the fact that by the critical date the proceedings had already lasted more than two years'.[35]

III. THE END OF THE RELEVANT PERIOD

The period to be considered ends when the proceedings end. The text of Article 6 § 1 of the ECHR and of Article 8 § 1 of the ACHR[36] is misleading to the extent that they refer to 'a...hearing within a reasonable time'. The ECtHR made it clear in *Wemhoff* that the period to be considered lasts at least until there has been an acquittal or conviction, even if this is on appeal.[37] It is also possible to limit the complaint as to the excessive length of the proceedings to the appeal phase.[38] This is also the view of the HRC.[39] The judgment includes the final sentencing hearing,[40] but separate proceedings which serve to coordinate sentences pronounced by different judgments are not included.

[34] *GK* v. *Poland*, § 98.
[35] *Yağı and Sargın* v. *Turkey*, § 58; see also *Mitap and Müftüoglu* v. *Turkey*, § 31; *Zana* v. *Turkey*, §§ 74 and 82; *Majaric* v. *Slovenia*, § 31; *Trzaska* v. *Poland*, § 82; *Ivanczuk* v. *Poland*, § 72; *Szeloch* v. *Poland*, § 98; *Pietiläinen* v. *Finland*, § 29; *Kalashnikov* v. *Russia*, § 124; *Pantea* v. *Romania*, §§ 267, 277; *Panek* v. *Poland*, §§ 26, 27.
[36] No such problem arises under the ICCPR, Art. 14 § 2(c) which refers to the right 'to be tried without delay'.
[37] *Wemhoff* v. *Germany*, § 18; see also *Neumeister* v. *Austria*, § 19; *Eckle* v. *Germany*, § 77.
[38] *Portington* v. *Greece*, § 20.
[39] General Comment No. 13, § 10; *Drescher Caldas* v. *Uruguay*, §§ 12.2, 13.4, 14.
[40] *Eckle* v. *Germany*, § 77.

The judgment must become final; if, for example, it is quashed by a court of appeal and sent back for a retrial, the period continues to run.[41] Again, the decisive element is not the terminology used in domestic law. In Germany, for example, a judgment is considered to be final, despite the fact that an application has been filed with the Federal Constitutional Court which has the power to reverse the judgment if it violated the applicant's constitutional rights. The ECtHR has thus held that the time used by the Constitutional Court must be included in the period referred to in Article 6 § 1.[42]

Furthermore, the period does not stop running until the judgment has been served on the accused; a delay between the oral decision and delivery of the reasoned judgment may lead to a violation.[43]

It is possible to submit an application to the Strasbourg authorities before the conclusion of the proceedings.[44] It would be absurd if an accused were required to await the outcome of proceedings which have already lasted for too long, before lodging such an application.

IV. THE ASSESSMENT OF THE PERIOD

A. The General Rule

The easiest way to determine whether proceedings have been concluded within a reasonable time would be to fix a specific time limit. It is highly unlikely however that such a course of action would lead to acceptable results. In some cases the time allowed would be too short, in others too long. It is therefore essential that each case be assessed on its own merits.[45] General guidelines are difficult to detect.[46] For this reason, I do not regard it as useful to introduce here a list of the cases which have been decided, indicating the respective length of the proceedings.[47]

The Court generally uses a standard formula to define its approach to the assessment of the length of criminal proceedings. The most complete text is found in *Philis (No. 2)*: 'The Court reiterates at the outset that the reasonableness of the length of proceedings must be assessed in the light of the particular circumstances of the case and having regard to the criteria laid down in its case-law, in particular the complexity of the case and the conduct of the applicant and

---

[41] *IA* v. *France*, § 115; for the Covenant, see Nowak (1993) Art. 14 N 44.
[42] *Metzger* v. *Germany*, § 34; see also *Gast and Popp* v. *Germany*, § 65.
[43] Villiger (1999) N 453; *B* v. *Austria*.   [44] *Donsimoni* v. *France*, §§ 30, 31.
[45] See also Villiger (1999) N 448. There has still been some criticism that the Court proceeded in an overly systematic way (with regard to proceedings on bankruptcy); cf. Chiavario (2001) 206.
[46] Chiavario (2001) 211; Harris, O'Boyle, and Warbrick (1995) 229; Reed and Murdoch (2001) N 5.97. For an interesting although now rather outdated approach, see Stavros (1993) 99 et seq.
[47] In the same sense Stavros (1993) 106; for such lists, see De Salvia (1998) 179; Frowein and Peukert (1996) Art. 6 N 153, 154; Villiger (1999) N 463.

of the relevant authorities. It is necessary among other things to take account of the importance of what is at stake for the applicant in the litigation'.[48]

In this text, the reference to its own case-law does not have any substantive meaning. Four criteria can be distinguished: the conduct of the applicant, the complexity of the case, the importance of what is at stake for the applicant, and the conduct of the authorities. It is sometimes asserted that these factors are first examined separately, whereupon their cumulative effect is assessed.[49] In fact, the approach can be described more precisely. It must first be established whether the unreasonable duration of the proceedings can be attributed to the improper conduct of the defence. If this is the case, then there will be no violation. The complexity of the case, as will be explained later on, has no relevance beyond the rather obvious observation that more complicated cases will require more time than simple ones. The decisive element is the conduct of the authorities. In case of doubt, the specific importance of the case for the accused may call for special efforts to speed up the proceedings and thus strike the balance in favour or against the finding of a violation.

Although the Court never says so expressly, it appears that it differentiates according to whether, at first sight, the proceedings appear to have taken too long. In the first case that was decided, one senses a presumption that the duration was excessive. The Court then went on to examine whether the Government's arguments provided sufficient justification for the length.[50] If the overall duration does not *prima facie* appear excessive, it will examine whether the applicant can show periods of inactivity on the part of the authorities.[51] Another mechanism which can be used to simplify the examination of the case, is to point out obvious delays.[52]

B. The Conduct of the Applicant (and/or Counsel)

While the authorities are responsible for organizing and running the criminal proceedings, the attitude of the defence may influence the length. A cooperative approach on the part of the defence may serve to speed up the process; on the other hand, it is quite probable that complaints, recourses, motions, and other interventions may have exactly the opposite effect. It is important to keep in

---

[48] *Philis* v. *Greece (No. 2)*, § 35. See also, among very many others and as examples picked at random: *Eckle* v. *Germany*, § 80; *Corigliano* v. *Italy*, § 37; *Foti and others* v. *Italy*, § 56; *Kemmache* v. *France (Nos. 1 and 2)*, § 60; *Pélissier et Sassi* v. *France (GC)*, § 67; *Mitap and Müftüoglu* v. *Turkey*, § 32; *Zana* v. *Turkey*, § 75; *Portington* v. *Greece*, § 21; *IA* v. *France*, § 119; *Pietiläinen* v. *Finland*, § 41; *Kitov* v. *Bulgaria*, § 68; *Phocas* v. *France*, §71; *Frydlender* v. *France (GC)*, § 43; *Humen* v. *Poland (GC)*, § 60; *Panek* v. *Poland*, § 32; *Nemeth* v. *Hungary*, § 27; *Kangasluoma* v. *Finland*, § 29; *GK* v. *Poland*, § 99.   [49] Harris, O'Boyle, and Warbrick (1995) 223; Velu and Ergec (1990) N 521.
[50] e.g. *Eckle* v. *Germany*, §§ 80–93; *Kangasluoma* v. *Finland*, § 35.
[51] e.g. *Kadri* v. *France; Orlandi* v. *Italy; Ciacci* v. *Italy; Mangascia* v. *Italy*.
[52] See Grabenwarter (2003) § 24 N 46 for an example concerning civil proceedings.

mind that there is an inherent tension between the right to be tried within a reasonable time and the right to sufficient time to prepare the defence. Any time reasonably spent on such preparation could not possibly lead to a violation of the right to be tried within reasonable time.[53]

There are two possible ways in which an accused could be held responsible for delays. The most common one is through excessive use of procedural remedies, such as by repeatedly asking for hearings to be postponed. Delay which can be attributed to such requests will be attributed to the accused. Moreover, the conduct of the defence may be such as to cast doubt on the accused's interest in the speedy conclusion of the proceedings. In one case, the Court observed that the applicant had filed a large number of motions which were unfounded and did not, therefore, delay the proceedings. 'However', the Court observed, 'they do cast some doubt as to whether it was indeed the applicant's intention to have the proceedings concluded speedily'.[54] Stavros, describing the origins of that case-law in the Commission, speaks of an 'implicit waiver' of the right to a speedy trial and of a 'clean hands' approach.[55]

The Court is rightly very reluctant to impute responsibility for the length of proceedings to the accused, stressing that the defence has the *right* to use procedural remedies. As a rule, it is not for the authorities—national or international—to pass judgment on whether the defence's actions, which may have contributed to the length of the proceedings, were reasonable or not. Additionally, there is no obligation whatsoever on the accused to assist in the investigation, thus he or she must not be disadvantaged for exercising the right to remain silent.[56] Even the request that a hearing be postponed, providing that this is based on plausible grounds, cannot be held against the accused.[57] Examples of cases where responsibility for the delay was ascribed to the applicant, are rather rare.[58] The Court clearly applies a type of moral reasoning, so while an accused cannot be held responsible for an illness,[59] there is a basic duty to attend the proceedings, and if an accused absconds any resulting delay will be deemed to be his or her responsibility.[60] An accused also bears responsibility for delays

[53] There is also no violation when postponements have been agreed with the defendant; see *Kemmache* v. *France (Nos. 1 and 2)*, § 64.

[54] *Sałapa* v. *Poland*, § 88; *IA* v. *France*, § 121: 'a deliberate attempt by Mr I. A. to delay the investigation is evident from the file—one example being the fact that he waited to be informed that communication of the file to the public prosecutor was imminent before requesting, on 19 July 1995, a number of additional investigative measures'. [55] Stavros (1993) 98.

[56] See e.g. *Corigliano* v. *Italy*, §§ 41, 42; *Dobbertin* v. *France*, § 43; *Ledonne* v. *Italy*, § 25; *Saccomanno* v. *Italy*, § 24; *Dominiconi* v. *France*, § 37; *De Blasiis* v. *Italy*, § 23; *Barfuss* v. *Czech Republic*, § 83; *Yagci and Sargin* v. *Turkey*, § 66; *Richet* v. *France*, § 75; *Debbasch* v. *France*, § 41; and *Nemeth* v. *Hungary*, § 29. [57] *Portington* v. *Greece*, §§ 28, 29.

[58] Cf. *Ringeisen* v. *Austria*, § 110; *Eckle* v. *Germany*, § 82; *Mōtsnik* v. *Estonia*, § 42; *Punzelt* v. *Czech Republic*, § 94. [59] *Lavents* v. *Latvia*, § 101.

[60] *Girolami* v. *Italy*, § 15; *Gelli* v. *Italy*, § 38; *Sari* v. *Turkey and Denmark*, §§ 85, 86; *Bunkate* v. *Netherlands*, § 21; *Ventura* v. *Italy* Application 7438/76.

caused by hunger strikes,[61] and for a refusal to leave a cell,[62] unless he has a good reason.[63]

It is important, however, that the significance of this aspect is not over-estimated. While an accused cannot be 'blamed' for filing numerous appeals, this does not mean that the time used for processing the appeals can be held against the state. The essential question is not whether the accused is responsible for the delay, but whether the state can be held responsible. Therefore, while delay due to the bad health of the defendant cannot be held against him or her, neither does it engage the responsibility of the state.[64] In a case where the co-defendant caused delays by not appearing for the hearings, it was decisive that the state had taken reasonable steps to bring them to trial, thus the length of the proceedings did not lead to the finding of a violation.[65]

C. The Importance of the Proceedings for the Accused

The Court convincingly brings a subjective element into the assessment of the reasonableness of the length of criminal proceedings: the higher the stakes and more pressing the issue for the accused, the stronger the obligation on the authorities to act diligently to avoid any delay.

Examples of reasons which call for extra diligence are the death penalty,[66] the (old) age or ill health of the accused,[67] and the fact that the defendant is detained on remand pending the outcome of the proceedings.[68]

D. The Complexity of the Case

It is obvious that the time required for the proceedings will increase in proportion to the complexity of the case. With the exception of those cases which demonstrate obvious flaws in the operation of a justice system, cases brought before the Strasbourg authorities are generally characterized by a certain complexity. Economic crimes are especially prevalent, particularly where a large number of victims are involved and where complicated schemes were developed and utilized to defraud them. The complexity is generally highlighted by reference to the size of the file and to the number of the accused and/or witnesses involved.[69] But one will also find cases of political offences[70] or espionage.[71]

---

[61] *Jablonski* v. *Poland*, § 104.   [62] *Trzaska* v. *Poland*, § 89.

[63] In *Mellors* v. *United Kingdom* this was accepted because the applicant had been unlawfully refused permission to wear civilian clothes.   [64] See e.g. *Lavents* v. *Latvia*, § 101.

[65] *GK* v. *Poland*, § 102.

[66] *Portington* v. *Greece*, § 37; this example betrays the cynicism associated with this sanction—one could also argue that the risk of capital punishment could justify any delay as it amounts to saving or at least prolonging a human life.   [67] *Beljanski* v. *France*, § 40; *X* v. *France*, § 47.

[68] *Mõtsnik* v. *Estonia*, § 40; *Abdoellah* v. *Netherlands*, § 24.

[69] See e.g. *Neumeister* v. *Austria*; *Eckle* v. *Germany*; *Kemmache (Nos. 1 and 2)* v. *France*; *Hozee* v. *Netherlands*; *CP and others* v. *France*; *Lavents* v. *Latvia*; *Kangasluoma* v. *Finland*; and *GK* v. *Poland*.

[70] e.g. *Mitap and Müftüoglu* v. *Turkey*.   [71] e.g. *Dobbertin* v. *France*.

Typically, complications arise when offences have an international dimension and involve letters rogatory or extradition.[72] The Commission has also had to take into account the particular difficulties associated with the prosecution of crimes committed under the Nazi regime.[73]

Sometimes the applicant points to ways in which the proceedings could have been more efficiently conducted. It is difficult to detect a consistent pattern in the Court's response to such arguments. In *Neumeister*, for example, it considered that there was no obligation on the domestic authorities to sever the applicant's case from that of his co-accused and that moreover they were under an obligation to ensure the 'good administration of justice'.[74] In other words, speediness is not required at the expense of quality. On the other hand, in *Kemmache* the Court, like the Commission, felt that the proceedings against the applicant ought to have been separated from those against his co-accused,[75] whereas in *Boddaert* it found that the authorities had joined the proceedings in order to secure the good administration of justice which could not be criticized.[76] In *Eckle* where the 'enormous number of cases subjected to inquiry' was criticized, the Court was not satisfied that this was unavoidable even when taking into account the principle of obligatory prosecution of all criminal offences ('*Legalitätsprinzip*').[77]

Of course, the complexity must lie in the facts of the case. In *Dobbertin* the protracted proceedings were the result of a succession of legislative amendments which led to a repeated change of venue of the trial.[78] This was held to be entirely the state's responsibility.

If one looks more closely at the case-law, it seems that, contrary to first impressions, the complexity of the proceedings is not a criterion which permits an evaluation of whether the duration of criminal proceedings was excessive or not.[79] The early jurisprudence seems to have been influenced by the notion of complexity,[80] but the later case-law has not confirmed this approach. Violations have also been found in proceedings where the case denoted a certain or even a considerable complexity.[81]

The *only* decisive element is, in fact, the way in which the authorities dealt with the case. Whether the case is complex or not is in essence entirely irrelevant—a violation will only be found when there have been periods during the proceedings where no action was taken, although something could and should have been done.

---

[72] e.g. *Neumeister* v. *Austria*, § 21; *Sari* v. *Turkey and Denmark*.

[73] See Frowein and Peukert (1996) Art. 6 N 145 with references in n. 627.

[74] *Neumeister* v. *Austria*, § 21; see also *Cankoçak* v. *Turkey*, § 31, *Coëme* v. *Belgium*, § 139.

[75] *Kemmache* v. *France*, § 70.   [76] *Boddaert* v. *Belgium*, § 39; see also *PB* v. *France*, § 34.

[77] *Eckle* v. *Germany*, § 84.   [78] *Dobbertin* v. *France*, §§ 10 et seq.

[79] For a different view, see Stavros (1993) 93.

[80] See *Wemhoff* v. *Germany*; *Neumeister* v. *Austria*; *Stögmüller* v. *Austria*; *Matznetter* v. *Austria*; and *Ringeisen* v. *Austria*.

[81] e.g. *Eckle* v. *Germany*; *Schumacher* v. *Luxembourg*; *Gonzàles Doria Duràn de Quiroga* v. *Spain*; *Beladina* v. *France*; *Mouesca* v. *France*; *Panek* v. *Poland*; *Kangasluoma* v. *Finland*.

E. The Conduct of the Domestic Authorities

1. The Principle

The essential point, then, lies with the conduct of the domestic authorities.[82] The question is whether there were any unexplained delays or periods of inactivity.[83] Only in exceptional circumstances, and especially when they have not contributed to a considerable prolongation of the proceedings, will a case with such delays be regarded as acceptable—this happened in *Pretto v. Italy* which, however, concerned civil proceedings.[84] In one case the Court rather harshly criticized the authorities for having 'shown neither diligence nor rigour in the handling of the proceedings'.[85] Such delay will lead to the finding of a violation, even when it is not the only reason for the lengthy duration of the proceedings.[86]

The delay can occur in any phase of the process. During the preliminary investigation,[87] or the investigation[88] examples include the ordering of unnecessary investigative measures such as expert opinions,[89] or the failure to carry out a proper audit.[90] Ineffective organization of the trial hearing involving, for example, endless sessions devoted exclusively to the reading out of documents,[91] delay in the transfer of documents,[92] delay in the production of transcripts of the trial,[93] or delay in the drafting of the judgment,[94] will also violate the provision. Finally, issues have arisen in relation to delay at the appeal stage,[95] including delay in the drafting of the appeal judgment,[96] in relation to an appeal on cassation,[97] and in relation to proceedings before the constitutional court.[98] The length of the proceedings was also held to have been unacceptable in a case where a judge had to be replaced and seventy-one hearings repeated.[99]

---

[82] In the same sense, see Chiavario (2001) 214; Gollwitzer (1992) Art. 6 N 78.

[83] Of the cases where a violation was found in 2002, to give an example, this was the result in *Lavents v. Latvia; Pugliese v. Italy; Lisiak v. Poland; Pietiläinen v. Finland; Gil Leal Pereira v. Portugal; Ottomani v. France; Vieziez v. France; Kalashnikov v. Russia; Spinello v. Italy; Boldrin v. Italy; Andrea Corsi v. Italy; Pascazi v. Italy; Tumbarello and Titone v. Italy; Carbone v. Italy; Mucciacciaro v. Italy; Del Federico v. Italy; Casadei v. Italy; Falcone v. Italy; Barattelli v. Italy; Nuvoli v. Italy; Georgiadis v. Cyprus; Dede and others v. Turkey; Beljanski v. France; Uygur v. Turkey; Dinleten v. Turkey; Metinoglu v. Turkey; Saritaç v. Turkey; Zülal v. Turkey; Çilengir v. Turkey; Binbir v. Turkey; Maurer v. Austria*. There was held to be no violation in just two cases—this can be explained by the fact that routine cases, such as those where the proceedings are alleged to have taken too long, will only be declared admissible when it is probable that a violation will be found.   [84] *Pretto v. Italy*, § 37.

[85] *Šleževičius v. Lithuania*, 28.   [86] e.g. *Djaid v. France*, §§ 32, 33; *Panek v. Poland*, § 35.

[87] *Corigliano v. Italy*, §§ 49, 50.

[88] *Reinhardt and Slimane-Kaïd v. France*, § 100; *Pélissier and Sassi v. France*, § 73.

[89] *Szeloch v. Poland*, § 110.   [90] *Grauslys v. Lithuania*, § 61; *Girdauskas v. Lithuania*, § 27.

[91] e.g. *Yağcı and Sargın v. Turkey*, §§ 68, 69.

[92] *Abdoella v. Netherlands*, § 23; *Ilijko v. Bulgaria*, § 118.

[93] *HRC Larry James Pinkney v. Canada*, § 12.   [94] *B v. Austria*, § 52.

[95] *Portington v. Greece*, § 33.

[96] HRC, *Earl Pratt and Ivan Morgan v. Jamaica*, § 222; *Kelly v. Jamaica*, § 241.

[97] *Djaid v. France*, § 33; *Zana v. Turkey*, § 80.   [98] *Gast and Popp v. Germany*, §§ 75 et seq.

[99] See *Ivańczuk v. Poland*, § 78.

Domestic law will often set certain time limits; if these are not respected, it does not automatically mean that the length of the proceedings will be held to be excessive—the Court always makes an independent and comprehensive examination of the case. But the fact that such time limits have been disregarded may be an indication that the length of the proceedings was unreasonable.[100]

2. Ineffective Justifications

Governments regularly invoke reasons to justify delay—these are generally stereotypical and are often rejected by the Court which uses similarly stereo-typical reasoning. The most commonly used excuse is that the prosecuting authorities and/or judicial authorities were hindered by an excessive case-load. In answer to this, the Court regularly states that 'the Convention places the Contracting States under a duty to organise their legal systems so as to enable the courts to comply with the requirements of Article 6 § 1, including that of trial within a "reasonable time"; nonetheless, a temporary backlog of business does not involve liability on the part of the Contracting States provided that they take, with the requisite promptness, remedial action to deal with an exceptional situation of this kind'.[101]

The rare exception when the state had taken effective measures to cope with the increased case-load concerned civil proceedings.[102] This case, fortunately, has remained unique. In fact, it appears excessively moralistic to deny a violation of a fundamental right, even though the applicant's rights were violated, just because the state has taken steps to improve the situation in order to avoid future violations of the same kind. It should be recalled 'that the Convention is intended to guarantee not rights that are theoretical or illusory but rights that are practical and effective'.[103] A violation ought to be found if the proceedings against an accused have lasted longer than a reasonable time, irrespective of whether the state has taken steps to improve the situation. After all, the purpose of the international instruments charged with safeguarding human rights is to protect individuals, not to discipline governments and states. However, such steps are important in the proceedings implementing the judgment.

Other justifications for the length of proceedings, such as the illness of a judge[104] or the authorities' lack of experience with a new type of crime,[105] have also been rejected.

---

[100] A good example is *B* v. *Austria* where the Austrian Code of Criminal Procedure specified that the written judgment be delivered within fourteen days; in fact it took the judge thirty-three months to complete this task.

[101] *Baggetta* v. *Italy*, § 23. See also in the same sense e.g. *Eckle* v. *Germany*, § 92; *Milasi* v. *Italy*, § 18; *Abdoella* v. *Netherlands*, § 24; *Mansur* v. *Turkey*, § 68; *Pélissier and Sassi* v. *France*, § 74; *Ikonomitsios* v. *Greece*, § 21; *Şahiner* v. *Turkey*, § 29; *Arvelakis* v. *Greece*, § 26; *Henning* v. *Austria*, § 38; *Vocaturo* v. *Italy*, § 32; or *Spentsouris* v. *Greece*, § 27.

[102] *Buchholz* v. *Germany*, §§ 51, 61 and 63.   [103] *Artico* v. *Italy*, § 33, and many others.

[104] *Panek* v. *Poland*, §§ 30, 35—the Court did not even find it necessary to comment on this issue.   [105] *Eckle* v. *Germany*, § 85.

3. Effective Justifications

On the other hand, certain explanations have been accepted as justifying the
length of the proceedings. These have included delays caused by a lawyer's
strike[106] and by public unrest in the region where the proceedings were being
held.[107]

In relation to time spent awaiting the results of letters rogatory, a differentiation must be made between cases where the investigating authorities simply
wait for the results and where they take active steps to speed up or control this
procedure. The Court found a violation in one case where an investigating judge
simply waited for a period of two years without doing anything.[108] However
there was no violation in another case where the 'prosecution took measures to
expedite the proceedings, by repeatedly requesting the competent Polish
authorities to take appropriate steps to urge the United States authorities to
accelerate the process of gathering evidence'.[109]

V. COMPENSATION FOR THE EXCESSIVE LENGTH OF PROCEEDINGS

Domestic authorities have the opportunity to avoid liability under Article 6 by
compensating the affected person for the excessive length of proceedings. In order
to do this, two distinct elements are required. First, there must be some *recognition* of the fact that the length of the proceedings was unreasonable.[110] Second,
there must be an adequate *reduction of the sentence* and it must be clear that the
purpose of this sentence reduction is to compensate the person for the excessive
length of the proceedings.[111] Although there is no case-law to illustrate this, other
forms of compensation, for example, pecuniary, are not excluded. If both conditions are met, the applicant will no longer be able to claim to be a victim.[112]

In cases where the Court has found a violation of this provision, financial
compensation is generally awarded under Article 41. Prior to the entry into force
of Protocol No. 11, such awards were made by the Committee of Ministers
following a proposal from the Commission.

---

[106] *Ledonne v. Italy (No. 2)*, § 22; *Giannangeli v. Italy*, § 18; *Icolaro v. Italy*, § 25; *Tommaso Palumbo v. Italy*, § 19; *Arvelakis v. Greece*, § 25; *Tumbarello and Titone v. Italy*, § 27. It must be noted, however, that in all of these cases there was finally a finding of a violation because of delays which could not be justified by the strike!

[107] *Foti and others v. Italy*, § 61; *Milasi v. Italy*, § 19; here too there was nevertheless held to be a violation.   [108] *Ikanga v. France*, § 20.

[109] *Włoch v. Poland*, § 150.   [110] This was not the case in *Pietiläinen v. Finland*, § 44.

[111] In *Eckle v. Germany*, §§ 66, 87; this condition had not been met in *Beck v. Norway*, §§ 27, 28; or in *Hozee v. Netherlands*, § 54.

[112] This was initiated by the Commission in *Pannetier v. Switzerland* Application 9299/81; see also Stavros (1993) 90 et seq.

If one were to add up the sums thereby imposed on the Member States, particularly if damages for the excessive length of civil proceedings are included, one would come up with a figure of several million euros. Yet, ultimately, the international system for the protection of human rights can hardly be praised for its success in speeding up proceedings.[113] A comparison of the cases decided in 2002 and those determined in 2003, demonstrates that violations by Italy accounted for more than a third of the cases decided in 2002, while it does not feature at all in the cases decided in 2003. It seems that the former communist states now account for over a third of the violations of this provision. However, to date this remains the most important single issue in the case-law of the Court in connection with criminal proceedings where a violation is found.[114]

[113] See also Chiavario (2001) 207.
[114] For a further discussion of the subject, see Walsh (1990); Baauw (1998); Schroth (1990); Steinmann (1991); Rothenflüh (1983); Küng-Hofer (1984); Priebe (1983); Nancoz (1983); Driendl (1981); Berz (1982).

Part Three

The Specific Rights of the Defence

Chapter 7

The Right to be Presumed Innocent

I. INTRODUCTION

A. The Texts

Everyone charged with a criminal offence shall have the right to be presumed innocent until proved guilty according to law.

ICCPR, Art. 14 § 2

Everyone charged with a criminal offence shall be presumed innocent until proved guilty according to law.

ECHR, Art. 6 § 2

Every person accused of a criminal offense has the right to be presumed innocent so long as his guilt has not been proven according to law.

ACHR, Art. 8 § 2

The three texts vary in two principal respects, neither of which is of particular relevance.

The first distinction is literary in that there are slight differences in the wording. The European Convention, which is the oldest text, is the most succinct. The Covenant states additionally that a 'right' is guaranteed, although this seems somewhat superfluous.[1] The American version uses almost the same text as the Covenant but replaces 'until' with 'so long as . . . not'.

The second difference is structural. The ACHR places the presumption of innocence together with the specific rights of the accused rather than setting it out as a guarantee in its own right.

B. The Origins of the Guarantee

The presumption of innocence has a considerable history and forms part of the famous *Déclaration des droits de l'homme et du citoyen* of 28 August 1789.[2] It was

---

[1] It is true that in *Salabiaku* v. *France*, p. 28, § 5, Mr Tenekides, in a dissenting opinion, criticized the majority for not having recognized the presumption of innocence as a 'right'. However, this must be the result of a misunderstanding—there can be no doubt that the European institutions have always recognized and treated the presumption of innocence as a right.

[2] See www.justice.gouvfr/textfond/ddhc.htm.

also included in Article 11 § 1 of the first draft of the UDHR: 'Everyone charged with a penal offence has the right to be presumed innocent until proved guilty according to law in a public trial at which he has had all the guarantees necessary for his defence'. Here, the presumption is closely linked to the guarantee of a fair trial. The text of the ACHR comes closest to this elucidation of the right, although it goes into considerable detail as to the 'guarantees necessary for [the] defence'.

There were hardly any discussions during the drafting of the Covenant about the text. Two items are, however, worth mentioning.

First, in an earlier draft the guarantee was set out in a more general form. Rather than stating that the guarantee applied to 'Everyone charged with a criminal offence', it referred to 'any person'[3] or 'everyone'[4] or, as Mr Cassin put it, 'No one shall be held guilty . . . '.[5] The text was later changed as it was noted that the French text contained the word '*accusé*'. The English text was then simply adapted to mirror the French version.[6] No reason is given and it can be assumed that the drafters did not see any difference between the two versions. I regard this episode as being of interest and shall return to it shortly.

The second point concerns preparatory work for the Covenant. It had been proposed to introduce the words 'beyond reasonable doubt' to qualify the standard of proof required. However, the proposal was (rightly) rejected because it was felt that this was already implied by the words 'presumed innocent until proved guilty'.[7]

C. General Characteristics of the Guarantee and some Basic Definitions

While the right to be presumed innocent is a familiar term forming part of the layman's knowledge of the law, its wording causes some perplexity. The presumption applies, according to the text, to persons charged with, or accused of, a criminal offence. This seems to suggest that the person is presumed to have committed an offence. He or she is thus presumed to be guilty but at the same time has the right to be presumed innocent. We are faced with a *contradictio in adjecto*, a contradiction in terms. This calls for some explanation—the literal meaning cannot be the true sense of the guarantee. Actually, Article 5 § 1(c) indicates very clearly that it is not contrary to the Convention to suspect someone of having committed an offence. Such suspicion is also at the basis of extradition proceedings.[8]

There is, of course, no contradiction. 'Suspicion' simply means that someone might *perhaps* be guilty, not that he or she *definitely is* guilty. Yet, I find it useful to start this chapter with a discussion of some of the basic textual elements of the guarantee.

---

[3] Proposal of Mrs Roosevelt; see Weissbrodt (2001) 18.   [4] Ibid., 20.   [5] Ibid., 17.
[6] Ibid.   [7] Nowak (1993) Art. 14 N 35; Weissbrodt (2001) 56.
[8] *P, RH, and LL* v. *Austria* Application 15776/89. It is somewhat exaggerated to say that Art. 6 § 2 does not apply at all to extradition proceedings; *X* v. *Austria* Application 1918/63.

1. 'Charged with a Criminal Offence'

The expression 'charged with a criminal offence' is, as it were, the entrance to the rights of the defence. It is used in the general provision of paragraph 1 and in the introduction to paragraph 3 of the Covenant and the Convention—the rights contained in paragraphs 2 and 3 of Article 6 of the ECHR are combined in one paragraph in the ACHR.

The question arises whether it is justified to restrict the presumption to persons charged with a criminal offence. As we have just seen, the drafting history is rather tortuous in this respect. A number of drafts did not refer to the requirement that the provision apply in the context of a 'criminal charge'. It is of course clear that the presumption must relate to 'criminal' conduct. It cannot, for instance, be invoked in deportation proceedings.[9]

With regard to the 'charged' part of the term, the answer is, in my view, somewhat different; here the restriction is not justified. In fact, the presumption of innocence differs in character from the other procedural guarantees set out in international human-rights instruments.

The restriction of the application of the specific fair-trial rights to criminal proceedings, as opposed to civil, administrative, disciplinary, or other proceedings, is legitimate. These rights are intrinsically tied to the criminal context. The presumption of innocence is different. Why should a person who has been charged with an offence be presumed innocent, while another, who is not subject to a charge, be presumed guilty? This would be an absurd proposition.

One could be tempted to turn the argument around and ask if it is not the case that a person presumed guilty is automatically charged with a criminal offence. The first answer that comes to mind is that 'charged' is a technical term which presupposes some formal action by the competent authorities, be it the police, the public prosecutor's office, an investigating judge, or whoever else is endowed with the competence to 'charge' under domestic law. Yet, it has been shown that the term 'charged' is (and must be) interpreted as an autonomous notion by bodies charged with implementing international human-rights instruments.[10] So one could indeed argue that any expression by a public authority that a person is guilty of an offence, which he or she has not yet been convicted of, constitutes in reality a type of 'charge'. Yet, this is not the approach which has been taken by the Court.

Despite this, I believe that the restriction is redundant. Mrs Roosevelt and Mr Cassin were right; the guarantee should benefit 'everyone', irrespective of his or her involvement in criminal proceedings. The reference to the 'charge' can be explained by pointing out that persons against whom criminal proceedings are brought are particularly vulnerable as far as this presumption goes; they need protection against the eagerness of prosecutors who will tend to anticipate their own success and treat or present the suspect as guilty. *A fortiori*, however, the

---

[9] *X* v. *Austria* Application 1918/63.   [10] See Chapter 2.

presumption of innocence must benefit persons who are not (yet, or not any more) so charged. This problem will be discussed more thoroughly later on.

2. 'Presumed'

Article 6 § 2 refers to a 'presumption'. A presumption can imply several things. As a psychological term it refers to a state of mind. To prescribe a presumption means to order persons to think and to feel in a specific way. This, obviously, is not the appropriate definition of the term in the present context—thoughts and feelings cannot be regulated.

On a logical level it represents a hypothesis, a fictional position which represents the starting point for an experiment or other methodical examination, which will lead to its verification or falsification. This is not a convincing interpretation either. Criminal proceedings are governed and pursued not on the hypothesis that the defendant is innocent but rather, on the contrary, that he or she is, or rather may well be, guilty. This is precisely the meaning of the term 'suspicion', which forms the foundation of the criminal prosecution.

The presumption referred to in the legal instruments must be regarded as a guiding principle which exists in order to regulate the treatment of persons who have not yet been convicted. Such people must be dealt with in a way that is compatible with the possibility that they are innocent. Two types of behaviour *vis-à-vis* a suspect can be distinguished: factual and verbal. No measure may be taken, no restriction imposed which implies the guilt of the suspect. Further, declarations that a suspect is guilty of an offence are forbidden. Under certain circumstances, such as following an acquittal, not even a suspicion of guilt may be uttered.[11]

3. 'Innocent'

The term 'innocent' is not unequivocal either. Primarily it is a negative term and means 'free from guilt'.

As a matter of course the law cannot be concerned with biblical notions such as freedom from original sin. 'Innocent' within the meaning of the guarantee does not mean 'innocent' in the normal sense of the word. It means 'not guilty of the offence which the person is accused of (or charged with)' (or—after acquittal—was suspected).[12] Even this formula remains open to interpretation, particularly with regard to two important questions: Does the presumption refer to guilt in the technical sense given to the term in criminal law, i.e. *mens rea*, or does it only refer to the objective conduct? And, is the presumption limited to

---

[11] See e.g. *Asan Rushiti* v. *Austria*.

[12] See also Trechsel (1981) 318; the Italian Constitution, Art. 27, says '*L'imputato non è considerato colpevole sino alla condanna definitiva*' ('The accused is not considered guilty until he has been finally convicted'), a formulation which avoids the term 'innocence'.

behaviour that, in the circumstances of a specific case, is liable to be sanctioned by criminal punishment?

(a) *Nullum Crimen Sine Culpa?* The Issue of *Mens Rea*

The first point leads to a fundamental question: Does the state have the right to punish certain conduct without first determining the *mens rea* of the perpetrator? Is the entitlement not to be sanctioned for behaviour for which one cannot be held responsible a human right? The Court has not yet had to consider this issue, but the case-law suggests that the guarantee would not extend that far.

The first case to mention here should be regarded as something of an exception rather than a foundation stone in the jurisprudence. In *Silva Rocha* the applicant had been charged with a dangerous crime, but was acquitted for lack of criminal responsibility and was committed to a mental institution. The Court found that the committal order could be regarded as a 'conviction' and thus justified his detention for at least three years, irrespective of whether his mental state justified further confinement.[13] In my view, it would not be fair to interpret this judgment as taking a stand on whether the Convention protects the principle of *nulla poena sine culpa*, with which it would clearly not be compatible. In fact, the Court here allows retributive considerations to determine the minimum term of confinement of a person who is mentally ill—something which would be unacceptable from the perspective of an enlightened approach to criminal law.

The issue was addressed more directly in *Salabiaku* and the approach later confirmed in *Vastberga*: 'Contracting States may, in principle and under certain conditions, penalise a simple or objective fact as such, irrespective of whether it results from criminal intent or from negligence'.[14] Although the notion of guilt/ personal responsibility/*mens rea* is by no means identical to that of 'intent or negligence', it is fair to assume that the Court was referring to what is often referred to as 'strict liability'.[15]

Although it is certainly a fundamental principle of the criminal law that no one be punished for an offence if he or she could not have acted otherwise,[16] there are certain areas where exceptions seem to be widespread. The Court, at

---

[13] *Silva Rocha* v. *Portugal*, § 28; see also Chapter 18 below.

[14] *Salabiaku* v. *France*, § 27; *Vastberga Taxi Aktiebolag and Vulic* v. *Sweden*, § 112; see also *Janosevic* v. *Sweden*. [15] See also *Källender* v. *Sweden* Application 12693/87.

[16] I am referring to the persuasive definition of *mens rea* as adopted by the German *Bundesgerichtshof*, 2 BGHSt 200 (1952): '*Strafe setzt Schuld voraus. Schuld ist Vorwerfbarkeit. Mit dem Unwerturteil der Schuld wird dem Täter vorgeworfen, dass er sich nicht rechtmässig verhalten, dass er sich für das Unrecht entschieden hat, obwohl er sich rechtmässig verhalten, sich für das Recht hätte entscheiden können*'. ('Punishment presupposes guilt. Guilt means that somebody can be held responsible. If a person is determined to be guilty, this means that the person has decided to behave contrary to the law, even though he could also have acted in conformity with the law, could have decided to respect the law.'). See also Roxin (1998); Seiler (2003); Stratenwerth (1996) 254 et seq.

any rate, has stressed that '[s]uch offences may be found in the laws of the Contracting States'.[17] Regrettably, it does not give a single example. Such legislation exists in relation to the criminal liability of legal persons, particularly in the context of corporate crime where *'mens rea'* cannot be determined in the same way as it is used in relation to natural persons. Furthermore, although the *nullum crimen sine culpa* principle is generally accepted as a fundamental principle of the criminal law, there are instances where it is not fully satisfied. Indeed, one of the most significant goals of academics in the field of the criminal law is to reduce the gap between the ideal and the reality in this respect.

Although an idealistic approach to human rights might lead to criticism of the Court's approach, this is nevertheless a difficult issue. On the one hand, the punishment of persons who cannot be blamed for their acts or omissions must generally be regarded as entirely arbitrary and unacceptable. In very serious cases it might even amount to degrading or inhuman punishment. As a basic principle, the *nullum crimen sine culpa* rule ought to be regarded as embodying a fundamental human right; its violations should be regarded as contrary to the presumption of innocence.

However, at the same time this area requires considerable judicial self-restraint on the part of international bodies set up to implement the human-rights treaties. Borderline cases are usually the subject of lively dispute among academics. Dubious legislation may be the fruit of difficult political balancing, as is the case, for example, with regard to persons who have committed a crime after having become voluntarily intoxicated.[18] Another example is the notoriously contested issue as to whether and to what extent error as to the law ought to be relevant to criminal law.[19] Moreover, the issue of the punishment of legal persons must also be considered. An international body lacks both the experience and the legitimacy to tackle such delicate issues.

Finally, it must be recalled that the principle *nullum crimen sine culpa* is not universally accepted. While it is deeply rooted in German, Swiss, and Austrian law, it has less authority in, for example, France, Belgium, and Canada.[20] One important exception must however be mentioned, a situation where the rule *nulla poena sine culpa* must be respected: the case of vicarious liability, i.e. the situations where one person is made to suffer a penalty for an offence which was committed by another person—it will be dealt with shortly.[21]

---

[17] *Salabiaku* v. *France*, § 27; *Vastberga Taxi Aktiebolag and Vulic* v. *Sweden*, § 112; *Janosevic* v. *Sweden*.

[18] See e.g. GPC, § 323a, discussed by Cramer and Steinbert-Lieben in Schönke and Schröder (2001); CHPC, Art. 263, examined by Bommer in BJK StGB-II; W. Brandenberger, *Bemerkungen zu der Verübung einer Tat in selbstverschuldeter Yurechnungsunfähigkeit* (Bern: Stämpfli & Cie AG, 1970).

[19] Cf. Pradel (2002) N 237 with reference, *inter alia*, to the *Bailey* case (1800) Russ and Ry 1, 168 ER 651, where a sailor was punished for having violated a rule created while he was out at sea. He would not have been punished under Swiss law; cf. e.g. Trechsel and Noll (2004) § 29 A 2.

[20] Pradel (2002) N 305.   [21] See p. 171 below.

(b) 'Innocent' or 'Not Liable to be Punished'?

We have already seen that 'innocence' cannot be understood as meaning a general absence of *mens rea*, but must instead be understood in the sense of the 'absence of responsibility for a specific offence'. While there are of course exceptions, as a basic rule it includes the notion of guilt. A declaration that someone has caused the death of another person but cannot be held responsible for their acts or omissions would not, in my view, violate the presumption of innocence.[22] This does not mean that it would be absolutely irrelevant in the context of human-rights law. If such a comment were to be uttered by the judge in civil proceedings, it may well be an indication of bias.

What if a court declares that someone has acted in a way which could constitute an offence, but rules that the episode was too insignificant to be sanctioned by the criminal law? This was the case in *Adolf* v. *Austria*. The applicant had been involved in a dispute that culminated in an envelope containing a key being thrown across the room. It hit a woman causing a superficial abrasion to her hand. The applicant, who was later charged with causing actual bodily harm, denied having thrown the object. The proceedings were discontinued in accordance with APC, § 42 because of the minor character of the incident. In its reasoning the district court said: 'The investigation . . . [has] . . . shown that in the course of a quarrel the accused flew into a rage and threw an envelope containing a key in the direction of [the complainant] . . .'. The applicant appealed to the Supreme Court which stated that despite its wording the district court had only expressed a suspicion and not proclaimed the applicant guilty.

In Strasbourg the applicant claimed not only that his right to be presumed innocent had been violated by the declaration of the district court, but also alleged that the law itself was contrary to the Convention. In line with its consistent case-law, whereby the Court refuses to examine the laws of the Member States *in abstracto*, the Court refused this second argument. It did agree, however, with the Commission that the statement in question was incompatible with the presumption of innocence.[23] It rejected the Government's argument that the impugned wording did not figure in the operative part of the judgment but only in the reasoning. Instead it accepted the argument of the Commission's delegate, Mr Melchior, that 'the decision's reasoning forms a whole with and cannot be dissociated from the operative provisions'.[24] In the end it held that

---

[22] Neither does the statement that someone has acted thoughtlessly (*'à la légère'*): *M* v. *Switzerland* Application 11263/84.

[23] *Adolf* v. *Austria*, § 38; see also *W* v. *Austria* Application 12990/87, for an analogous case concerning juveniles.

[24] *Adolf* v. *Austria*, § 39. As a general proposition this statement cannot be left without comment. It is not at all true. On the contrary, there is a fundamental difference between the operative part of a judgment, i.e. the decision taken by a court or tribunal, and the reasons given for that decision. It is often the case that an appeal is only possible against the operative part; cf. Hauser and Schweri (2002) § 94 N 14; Roxin (1998) § 51 B II 1 (c). The fact that the Court accepts the proposition with regard to the presumption of innocence is another indication that we are not within the limits of the issue of 'fair trial' any more.

there was no violation, accepting the Government's argument that any short-comings in the decision of the district court, were healed on appeal by the judgment of the Supreme Court. The latter had declared 'that a decision taken in pursuance of section 42 of the Penal Code does not, because of its very character and whatever may be its wording, involve anything in the nature of a verdict of guilt'.[25]

I agree with the finding that there was no breach of Article 6 § 2, but do so on the basis of different reasoning. The role of the presumption of innocence as a fundamental right must remain attached, albeit perhaps tenuously, to the criminal law. It should not be regarded as a general protection against defamation. If a decision to terminate proceedings contains any reference to the fact that the accused has 'committed' adultery, which is no longer an offence in the respective legal order, that cannot be regarded as violating the presumption of innocence even though it may well constitute a negative value judgment. I find it decisive in *Adolf* that the applicant was only 'accused' of having thrown an envelope and causing a light abrasion, while, at the same time, the same court also found that the event was so minor as not even to warrant the consideration of the criminal-justice system. In my view it is not justified to regard such a situation as an interference with the right to be presumed innocent.[26]

The Court's answer is somewhat circular, something of a *petitio principii*: '[a]s regards the concept of a non-punishable act, it is clearly in line with the title and text of section 42 (*mangelnde Strafwürdigkeit, nicht strafbar*). Nevertheless, non-punishable or unpunished criminal offences do exist and Article 6 of the Convention does not distinguish between them and other criminal offences: it applies whenever a person is "charged" with a criminal offence'.[27] I would respectfully submit, however, that non-punishable offences and unpunished offences are two entirely different phenomena. Unpunished offences certainly remain offences, but 'non-punishable offences'? Is an offence not characterized by the very fact that it is a behaviour which is liable to be punished? The Court's affirmation is not supported by any reference or further argument. It is not convincing.

While the issue might appear insignificant, it is, in fact, of considerable importance. Criminal policy has been dominated since the 1960s by efforts devoted to 'decriminalization'. Increasing awareness of the undesirable side-effects of punishment, particularly in respect of prison sentences, has led, in some legal systems, to the removal of cases of minor importance from the criminal code and to their reclassification as petty offences.[28] Some legal systems have introduced legislation which allows proceedings to be terminated where the

---

[25] *Adolf* v. *Austria*, § 40.
[26] Similarly, the Commission declared inadmissible an application where the applicant had allegedly been treated as a deserter from the Indian army. The Commission held that as a certificate had been issued which the applicant could have appealed against, the presumption was not irrebuttable; see *C* v. *United Kingdom* Application 10427/83.   [27] *Adolf* v. *Austria*, § 33 in fine.
[28] An illustration of this development can be found in the case of *Öztürk* v. *Germany*.

conduct at issue and its consequences are not serious enough to warrant sanctioning by the state. In other jurisdictions the decision to prosecute lies within the discretion of the prosecutor. It should be clear that such decisions do not infringe the right to be presumed innocent.

4. 'Proved' Guilty

According to the texts the presumption of innocence is only rebutted after the suspect has been 'proved' guilty according to law. This requires some clarification. The text essentially refers to the classical proceedings in which the evidence is presented at trial and evaluated by the judge and/or the jury. Yet, nowadays the vast majority of proceedings do not culminate in such a hearing, which is seen to be a complicated, risky, and expensive process. Indeed, frequently proceedings end following a plea of guilty.

This is particularly so in the United States where plea-bargaining has replaced the jury trial in the vast majority of cases. The ACHR expressly regulates this procedure stating that '[a] confession of guilt by the accused shall be valid only if it is made without coercion of any kind'.[29] While there is no similar provision in either the ICCPR or the ECHR, both instruments undoubtedly implicitly contain and guarantee this principle. Guilty pleas are often entered because the accused fears conviction and extremely harsh punishment, or even possibly the death penalty. Certainly the degree of coercion varies across jurisdictions. To some extent the same phenomenon is also developing in other legal systems.[30] I shall not pursue this argument, because it needs deeper analysis than can be given in the context of this book.

It is difficult, however, to justify the protection of the presumption of innocence in the face of a confession. A plea of guilty will, under the common law, usually be accepted and have the same effect as a conviction. The same cannot be said for continental procedure. The confession is one piece of evidence amongst others and the court will carefully examine whether it is true, and whether it is corroborated by other proofs. This does not mean though that it is irrelevant in the context of the presumption of innocence.[31]

In *Lutz* the Court referred in passing to 'the applicant's statements' without recognizing that they cannot be interpreted as anything other than a confession.[32] In my opinion those statements serve to rebut the presumption of innocence.[33] To make a confession and then claim to have the right to be presumed innocent constitutes *venire contra factum (recte: dictum) proprium*. The Commission has followed this approach in a number of cases. In one of them, it declared the application inadmissible, even though the applicant had had his

---

[29] AHCR, Art. 8 § 3.   [30] For a comparative analysis, see e.g. Trüg (2003).
[31] *Contra* Wimmer (1968) 375.   [32] *Lutz* v. *Germany*, § 62.
[33] See also my dissenting opinion, joined by Mr Frowein, which is attached to the Commission's report, *Lutz* v. *Germany*, pp. 38 and 39; Trechsel (1981) 226.

suspended sentence revoked on the bases of newly committed crimes for which he had not yet been convicted but which he had admitted.[34]

5. *Proved Guilty 'According to Law'*

Only the establishment of the accused's guilt 'according to law' can rebut the presumption of innocence. This formula has led some authors to suggest that any unlawfulness in the proceedings regarding the presentation of evidence must automatically lead to a violation of the right to be presumed innocent.[35] The Commission refrained from following this approach in *Scheichelbauer*.[36] The Court subsequently gave a clear answer in *Schenk*, which concerned the use of unlawfully obtained evidence. The Court's response was somewhat laconic: 'In the Court's opinion, the record of the hearings of 9–13 August and the judgment of 13 August 1982 contain nothing to suggest that the Rolle Criminal Court treated Mr. Schenk as if he were guilty before it convicted him. The mere inclusion of the cassette in the evidence cannot suffice to support the applicant's allegation, with the result that there was no breach of the Convention here either'.[37]

While this reasoning certainly leaves a lot to be desired, the doctrine behind it is unavoidable. International bodies called upon to implement treaties for the protection of human rights may not adopt the position of a court of cassation, competent generally to control the lawfulness of domestic proceedings. They must limit themselves to assessing whether the internationally guaranteed fundamental rights have been respected. This gives rise to a certain dilemma when reference is made to the domestic legal order through such words as 'lawful' or 'according to law'. Here, the principle of subsidiarity calls for judicial self-restraint—the responsibility for determining whether domestic law has been correctly applied lies in the first instance with the national authorities. The international institutions limit their role to that of a safety net. Intervention is only permissible in cases where there has been a flagrant violation or entirely arbitrary interpretation of the law.

The requirement of proof according to law refers to the conclusion, to the operative part of the judgment, and not to every element taken into account by the court. In *Kremzow* the applicant alleged that in discussing his motives for the murder of a colleague the court had spoken of 'financial misdeeds' and thereby had found him guilty of fraud. The Court rejected this claim because the remark related only to the applicant's motive.[38]

---

[34] *Houswitschka* v. *Germany* Application 12380/86; *R* v. *Germany* Application 12669/87; and *S* v. *Germany* Application 15871/89.

[35] Poncet (1977) 84 et seq. I was of the same view; see Trechsel (1981) 24.

[36] *Scheichlbauer* v. *Austria* Application 2645/65. The evidence included a recording which had been unlawfully obtained.   [37] *Schenk* v. *Switzerland*, § 51.

[38] *Kremzow* v. *Austria*, §§ 76–7.

The presumption of innocence ends when a person has been finally convicted. It can be set aside by a decision allowing the reopening of the proceedings. In reopening proceedings, however, Article 6 does not apply at all.[39]

D. The Two Distinct Aspects of the Presumption of Innocence

The complex character of the presumption of innocence means that there can be no simple and single answer as to the purpose or purposes that it serves. Two fundamentally different aspects must be distinguished. The task is not facilitated by the fact that, so far, the Court has refused to acknowledge this duality of purposes.

The first approach was taken, for example, in *Deweer* where the applicant was put under considerable economic pressure to accept a 'friendly' settlement by agreeing to pay a fine. He had invoked, *inter alia*, paragraphs 2 and 3 of Article 6. In reaching its decision the Court noted that 'these two paragraphs represent specific applications of the general principle stated in paragraph 1 of the Article. The presumption of innocence embodied in paragraph 2 and the various rights . . . in paragraph 3 . . . are constituent elements, amongst others, of the notion of a fair trial in criminal proceedings'.[40] An even wider and somewhat weightier aim is promoted in *Salabiaku* where the Court stated that the presumption of innocence, as an element of fair trial, 'is intended to enshrine the fundamental principle of the rule of law'.[41]

This statement refers to what I call the 'outcome-related aspect' of the guarantee, which is closely linked to the outcome of the proceedings. The passages just quoted from the Court's case-law refer to this aspect of the presumption. The right to be presumed innocent can be regarded as being connected to the psychological climate in which proceedings ought to unfold and it requires that the prosecutor and the judge adopt a particular attitude. Even though, deep down in their hearts, they may be convinced of the accused's guilt, they must remain open to a change of opinion in view of the result of the evidence. They are prohibited from doing or saying anything, before the judgment has been delivered, which implies that the defendant has already been convicted.[42] The question as to the guilt or innocence of the accused, which is, after all, the essence of the proceedings, must remain open, even if the evidence against the accused appears to be overwhelming.[43] Finally, the accusation must

---

[39] *X* v. *Germany* Application 2136/64.

[40] *Deweer* v. *Belgium*, § 56 with reference to the Commission's report in *Nielsen* v. *Denmark* (1961) 5 YB 548–50. The formula, repeated verbatim or with just slight alterations, turns up regularly in later judgments, e.g. *Minelli* v. *Switzerland*, § 27; *Bernard* v. *France*, § 37; *Allenet de Ribemont* v. *France*, § 35; *Daktaras* v. *Lithuania*, § 41; *Marziano* v. *Italy*, § 28; *Böhmer* v. *Germany*, § 53; *Gökceli* v. *Turkey*, § 45; *Kyprianou* v. *Cyprus*, § 52. See also Nowak (1993) Art. 14 N 33.

[41] *Salabiaku* v. *France*, § 28.   [42] See *Austria* v. *Italy* Application 788/60.

[43] With an exception, of course, for those cases in which an accused has pleaded guilty.

be proved beyond reasonable doubt. The purpose of the guarantee is essentially to avoid unjustified convictions and to uphold the fairness of the trial.

This aspect of the guarantee is addressed primarily to the decision-maker responsible for deciding whether the accused is guilty or not. If the court finds in favour of the accused, there can be no violation of this aspect of the presumption of innocence.

The second aspect, which the guarantee attempts to protect, is closer to Article 8 than to Article 6 and can be referred to as the 'reputation-related' aspect. It is quite far removed from the issue of conviction/acquittal, but aims to protect the image of the person concerned as 'innocent', i.e. not guilty of a specific offence. In other words, it protects the good reputation of the suspect. This means, for example, that a person who has not been convicted in criminal proceedings must not be treated or referred to by persons acting for the state as guilty of an offence. In many judgments the introductory formula just cited is followed by the sentence: 'It [scil. the right to be presumed innocent] will be violated if a statement of a public official concerning a person charged with a criminal offence reflects an opinion that he is guilty before he has been proved so according to law'.[44] In earlier judgments, the words 'judicial decision' were used in place of 'public official'.[45] The case of *Allenet de Ribemont* led to a widening of the definition when such a statement was made on television by a high-ranking police officer. Here, the Court also added that 'it suffices, even in the absence of any formal finding, that there is some reasoning suggesting that the court or the official regards the accused as guilty'.[46]

It is clear that such cases are less concerned with the attitude of the judge than with the opinion of the general public; after a public statement has been made, as was the case in *Allenet de Ribemont*, nobody will believe any more that the person is innocent. The connection with judicial proceedings is thus somewhat loose— even if there is no subsequent trial, as was the case in *Allenet de Ribemont*, there can nevertheless be a violation.

E. The Relationship Between the Presumption of Innocence and Other Aspects of the Right to a Fair Trial

1. The Presumption of Innocence and the Impartiality of the Judge

The presumption of innocence is, insofar as it requires that the judge maintain an open mind, closely linked to the right to an impartial tribunal. It 'requires, *inter alia*, that when carrying out their duties, the members of a court should not start with the preconceived idea that the accused has committed the offence

---

[44] See e.g. *Daktaras* v. *Lithuania*, § 41; *Böhmer* v. *Germany*, § 54.

[45] See e.g. *Allenet de Ribemont* v. *France*, § 37; *Minelli* v. *Switzerland*, § 37; but also, probably due to an oversight, *Marziano* v. *Italy*, § 28.

[46] *Minelli* v. *Switzerland*, § 37; *Allenet de Ribemont* v. *France*, § 35; *Daktaras* v. *Lithuania*, § 41; *Böhmer* v. *Germany*, § 54; *Lavents* v. *Latvia*, § 126.

charged.'[47] It is, however, broader in that it also binds other authorities involved in the proceedings.[48]

It does not mean that the public prosecutor must be impartial, but it does require that he or she act in a way that does not betray his or her belief in the guilt of the suspect. The difference is perhaps somewhat sophisticated, if not downright artificial. The judge ought not even think that the applicant is guilty, at least he or she must not express such thoughts. Keeping in mind that an essential part of the job of the prosecutor is to plead in favour of conviction, the presumption must be more restrictively applied. The prosecuting authority may express the opinion that it considers the accused to be guilty. This, after all, is the hypothesis justifying the indictment. It must, however, keep in mind that, notwithstanding its opinion, the defendant may still be acquitted, and therefore should not be objectively regarded or *treated* as guilty.

2. The Presumption of Innocence and the Right to a Fair Trial

In a number of cases applicants have claimed a violation both of their right to a fair trial and of their right to be presumed innocent. In such cases, the Court will often begin by determining whether there has been a violation of Article 6 § 1. If Article 6 § 1 has been held to have been violated, the Court will generally not consider the Article 6 § 2 issue, holding instead that it is 'absorbed' by the earlier finding and that no further examination is necessary.[49] Exceptionally, it has also held—without further reasoning—that Article 6 § 2 had not been violated.[50]

3. The Presumption of Innocence and the Right to be Informed of the Charge

In a relatively early judgment the Court said that a natural consequence of the presumption of innocence was 'that it is for the prosecution to inform the accused of the case that will be made against him, so that he may prepare and present his defence accordingly'.[51] I find this rather far-fetched, although it is not unusual to find the principle used as a panacea for a whole number of other guarantees and some academic commentators even seem to regard it as the cornerstone of the right to a fair trial.[52]

I do not agree with this view. The principle is certainly very important and it is of great significance to the fairness of criminal proceedings that it is respected.

---

[47] *Barberà, Messegué and Jabardo* v. *Spain*, § 77; *Lavents* v. *Latvia*, § 125.

[48] *Lavents* v. *Latvia*, § 125.

[49] See e.g. *Deweer* v. *Belgium*, § 56; *Bönisch* v. *Austria*, § 37; *Delta* v. *France*, § 37; *Demicoli* v. *Malta*, § 34; *Funke* v. *France*, § 45; *IJL, GMR, and AKP* v. *United Kingdom*, § 142; *Coëme and others* v. *Belgium*, 104; *Büyükdag* v. *Turkey*, §§ 78, 79.

[50] *Hentrich* v. *France*, § 64; more substantial reasoning can be found in the Commission's report, § 84 et seq. The existence of a tax fraud is no prerequisite for the pre-emption, thus this measure does not amount to a finding of guilt.   [51] *Barberà, Messegué, and Jabardo* v. *Spain*, § 77.

[52] See e.g. Pradel (2002) N 300.

Still, the specific guarantees of the defence as set out in Article 14 § 3 of the ICCPR and Article 6 § 3 of the ECHR, and the equality of arms and the principle of adversarial proceedings must be regarded as elements which remain independently indispensable. One could perhaps see the presumption of innocence as regulating the atmosphere of the proceedings, whereas it is the specific rights which actually rule it.

4. The Presumption of Innocence and the Privilege against Self-incrimination

Even though the Convention does not contain a paragraph which directly corresponds to Article 14 § 3(g) of the ICCPR or Article 8 §§ 2(g) and 3 of the ACHR, it also protects the accused's right to remain silent and not to be improperly compelled to give evidence which would incriminate him- or herself. This guarantee is closely linked to the presumption of innocence and the Court has expressly confirmed this in a number of cases.[53] The right to silence will, however, be dealt with in Chapter 13 below.

5. The Presumption of Innocence in Civil Proceedings

Technically, the presumption of innocence applies only to a defendant in *criminal* proceedings. The concept is however not entirely foreign to civil proceedings, although there may be differences in its application. In civil proceedings it is generally the plaintiff who must prove that his claim exists. On the other hand, however, the rules of evidence may be different from those in criminal proceedings.[54]

F. The Specific Problems Arising with the Guarantee

The discussion focusing on the specific aspects of the presumption of innocence will be divided into two parts. First, I shall deal with the 'relative', 'outcome-related' aspect of the guarantee. This will include issues involving the burden of proof, which may arise either during criminal *proceedings* or in respect of *legislation*. Questions pertinent to the evaluation of evidence will also be examined.

The problems surrounding the application of the 'reputation-related' aspect of the guarantee are more complex. The Court uses various criteria in order to decide whether declarations, statements, or decisions which insinuate that a person is guilty or is still under suspicion, are compatible with the presumption of innocence. Such issues may arise in relation to statements made at an early stage in the proceedings, or, more commonly, statements made following the termination of proceedings or which have no particular relevance to any criminal proceedings at all.

---

[53] *Saunders* v. *United Kingdom*, § 68; *Heaney and McGuiness* v. *Ireland*, § 40; *Quinn* v. *Ireland*, § 40.
[54] See e.g. *Ringvold* v. *Norway*, a case to be discussed below.

II. THE 'OUTCOME-RELATED' ASPECTS
OF THE GUARANTEE

A. The Burden of Proof

Usually the issue of the presumption of innocence arises in cases where the facts are contested. However, this is not necessarily so, as the case of *Kyprianou* shows. The applicant, a lawyer, had been charged with contempt of court while representing a client in a murder case. The national court considered that: 'What has just been said by Mr Kyprianou and in particular the manner with which he speaks to the Court is considered by us as a contempt of court and Mr Kyprianou has two choices: either to insist on what he said and to give reasons why no sentence should be imposed on him or it is a matter for him to decide whether he should not insist. We give him this opportunity exceptionally. Article 44.1 (a) of the Courts of Justice Law applies fully'.[55] The applicant chose the first option and was sentenced to a term of imprisonment. In spite of the fact that the Court had already found that the tribunal had not been impartial it addressed the issue and found there also to have been a violation of the presumption of innocence.[56]

1. The Burden of Proof in the Proceedings

In criminal proceedings, the presumption of innocence means that the burden of proof lies on the prosecution. The prosecution must convince the court of the guilt of the accused; it is not for the latter to prove his or her innocence.[57] In other words, in the event that there is insufficient evidence, the accused must be acquitted.

This is not uncontested. Figueiredo Dias, for example, states that continental criminal-procedure law does not know the problem of *onus probationis*, because it is for the judge to establish the facts.[58] No such reservation is made by Pradel.[59] In my view, the distinction made by the Portuguese scholar is too theoretical.

This aspect is, however, of negligible importance in practice. It is highly unlikely that a court would state that the accused's conviction is based on the fact that he or she failed to prove his or her innocence.

A more detailed look at this issue highlights a number of problems, particularly in the area of justification and exculpation. Is it legitimate to require that a defendant prove a defence in order to be acquitted if the prosecution cannot prove the contrary beyond reasonable doubt? Is it compatible with the presumption of innocence that the accused be compelled to present the evidence as to his alleged insanity at the time of the offence? These are important and

---

[55] *Kyprianou* v. *Cyprus*, § 53.   [56] Ibid., § 56.
[57] HRC, General Comment 13, Article 14 (21st Session, 1974), Compilation of the General Comments and General Recommendations Adopted by Human Rights Treaty Bodies, UN Doc. HRI/GEN/1/Rev. 1 at 14 (1994), § 7.   [58] De Figueiredo Dias (1974).
[59] Pradel (2002) N 298; see also Hauser and Schweri (2002), § 23.

difficult issues; yet, until now there is little trace of them in the case-law of the international bodies charged with protecting the presumption of innocence. This is not particularly surprising. Indeed, considerable differences exist in the treatment of these issues in different jurisdictions. Regard must be had to the difficulty in proving the non-existence of a fact. It is quite acceptable that the law requires at least a *prima facie* case for the facts invoked to justify or excuse an otherwise criminal behaviour.[60] Further, it is not for an international body set up to implement conventions on fundamental rights to impose specific standards in such a delicate area.

Still, the Commission has held that the obligation on the defence to bring evidence as to mental illness was not contrary to Article 6 § 2.[61]

2. Reversal of the Burden of Proof by Legislation

(a) Legal Presumptions to the Detriment of the Accused

(i) Salabiaku and Similar Judgments Presumptions are prevalent in the legislation of most legal systems.[62] A distinction must be made between *praesumptiones legis* on the one hand, and *praesumptiones legis et de lege* on the other. While the former can always be disproved, the latter are irrebuttable. It is remarkable to note that even the legislator can violate the presumption of innocence.[63] *Praesumptiones legis et de lege* which detrimentally affect the accused are incompatible with the presumption of innocence.[64] There are no examples in the case-law of such presumptions. There have, however, been cases that have concerned legislation, which enabled the drawing of conclusions from certain facts in the form of presumptions.

The leading cases dealt with by the Court in Strasbourg are *Salabiaku* and *Pham Hoang*. In *Salabiaku* the applicant, a national of Zaire, went to the airport to pick up a parcel. He claimed that he had expected the parcel to contain samples of African food. Despite having been warned by an Air Zaire employee, he picked up a padlocked trunk which had no name or address on it, and carried it away using the 'nothing to declare' exit. When customs officials stopped him and forced the lock of the trunk they found, underneath some foodstuffs, ten kilos of herbal and seed cannabis. Two days later a parcel addressed to Mr Salabiaku arrived in Brussels. It had been erroneously sent there instead of to Paris, which had been the intended destination.

---

[60] Starmer (1999) N 8.43 et seq.

[61] *H* v. *United Kingdom* Application 15023/89, regarding the so-called McNaghten Rules of 1843, 877 *LS Gaz* 31; Starmer (1999) 8.46.   [62] See e.g. Pradel (2002) N 306.

[63] Van Dijk and van Hoof (1998) 459; in the HRC Mr Tomuschat had also pointed to this possibility; he objected to very broadly defined crimes such as 'subversive association'; see McGoldrick (2001) 404.

[64] According to Harris, O'Boyle, and Warbrick (1995) 244 strict liability is compatible with the Convention—I do not agree with this proposition which is exaggerated and disregards the reference of the Court to the possibility to invoke *force majeure*.

The applicant was eventually given the benefit of doubt and acquitted of the charge of importing drugs; however, he was found guilty and fined for smuggling, a customs offence. The relevant law established a presumption according to which a person found in possession of undeclared goods is presumed guilty of smuggling. The only available defence was one of '*force majeure*', such as 'the absolute impossibility of knowing the contents of a package'.[65]

The Court began its judgment by setting out the general principle: 'Presumptions of fact or of law operate in every legal system. Clearly, the Convention does not prohibit such presumptions in principle. It does, however, require the Contracting States to remain within certain limits in this respect as regards criminal law'.[66] The Court then criticized the Commission for having suggested that the presumption was actually an element of the offence itself, which the domestic courts had correctly applied.[67] It pointed out that the fundamental guarantees of Article 6 could be undermined if the legislator were to be given *carte blanche*. 'Article 6 § 2 does not therefore regard presumptions of fact or of law provided for in the criminal law with indifference. It requires States to confine them within reasonable limits which take into account the importance of what is at stake and maintain the rights of the defence'.[68]

This is rather imprecise. In particular, it would be interesting to know what the Court meant by the term 'the importance of what is at stake'. Should presumptions be more easily admitted in cases of very serious crimes or, to the contrary, in cases of minor importance? Presumably they would be more acceptable in cases falling into the latter category. Some support for this interpretation can be derived from the fact that the offence, which Mr Salabiaku was convicted of, carried only a fine, even though the amount was quite substantial.[69]

The Court also seemed to attach considerable weight to the fact that the presumption was not entirely irrebuttable. Thus, the accused was not 'left entirely without a means of defence'.[70] This also meant that the courts had 'a genuine freedom of assessment in this area'. Moreover there were also some indications that Mr Salabiaku was not entirely innocent of the offence, particularly as he had shown no surprise when the drugs were unpacked. The Court also addressed the question as to whether there was an inherent contradiction between the acquittal for the drugs offence and the conviction for the customs offence. It decided that there was no incongruity, but I do not find the arguments very convincing. The Court repeated that the error of the applicant was not unavoidable. He failed personally to verify the contents of the trunk.[71]

---

[65] *Salabiaku* v. *France*, § 19.   [66] Ibid., § 28.

[67] Commission's report, *Salabiaku* v. *France*, p. 24 §§ 74–5.

[68] See also *Vastberga Taxi Aktiebolag and Vulic* v. *Sweden*, § 113.

[69] 100,000 French francs, i.e. roughly in the order of 15,000 euros; in case of non-payment, the fine would be commuted to a term of imprisonment.

[70] *Salabiaku* v. *France*, § 29; Esser (2002) 743 criticizes the very restricted possibility of rebutting the presumption; Starmer (1999) 8.47 supposes that such strict rules would not apply if the offence concerned the exercise of a Convention right.   [71] *Salabiaku* v. *France*, § 30.

The case of *Pham Hoang* was very similar. The applicant was arrested in his car, as two other persons carrying heroin, were about to climb in. The prosecution invoked Article 373 of the French customs code, which states: 'In any proceedings concerning a seizure of goods, the burden of proving that no offence has been committed shall be on the person whose goods have been seized'.[72] The applicant was convicted, but this provision was not cited. The Court found no violation of Article 6 § 2 because the evidence had been carefully assessed and there had been no automatic reliance on any presumption.[73]

More recently, the Court had to consider Swedish tax legislation. It confirmed the approach taken in *Salabiaku* and held that the sanction was not automatically applicable—exceptional circumstances could have allowed the court to apply grounds for remission even on an *ex officio* basis.[74] Here, the Court went further in explaining the justification of the presumption. It referred to the financial interests of the state and the need to rely on standardized rules for the imposition of sanctions. The regulation at issue and its application to the case were deemed to be confined within reasonable limits.[75]

The Commission has also had to deal with presumptions in connection with road-traffic offences. It has held that the imposition of criminal liability on a car owner whose car was found wrongly parked without his being able or willing to name the driver or to establish that the car had been used against his will did not violate Article 6.[76]

(ii) Assessment While the result of the judgment in *Salabiaku* is satisfactory, the reasoning used to reach the conclusion is rather less so. In essence, the Court seemed to be saying that although the custom-offences legislation contained a presumption of guilt the existence of the principle of *force majeure* meant that the defence still had the chance to prove its innocence. This is tantamount to admitting that there is a presumption of guilt, but holding that as it is rebuttable there is no violation of the right to be presumed innocent.

The Court's reasoning lacks an explanation for the justification of the presumption in the first place. The reason for this can be found in the circumstances of the specific case. Customs legislation requires persons who take possession of imported goods to make sure that the customs formalities have been complied with. In other words, they are under a specific obligation of carefulness. It is not reasonable to expect the customs' authorities to prove the 'negative fact' that the

---

[72] *Pham Hoang* v. *France*, § 21.

[73] Ibid., § 36, confirmed in three unreported decisions of 16 Jan. 1996 concerning dangerous dogs: *Bates, Foster,* and *Brock* (all v. *United Kingdom*). For criticism, see Esser (2002) 743.

[74] *Vastberga Taxi Aktiebolag and Vulic* v. *Sweden*, § 112; see also the similar case of *Janosevic* v. *Sweden*.   [75] *Vastberga Taxi Aktiebolag and Vulic* v. *Sweden*, § 116.

[76] *JP, KR, and GH* v. *Austria* Applications 15135/89, 15136/89, and 15137/89. Such rules also exist in other jurisdictions, e.g. France; see Charrier (2002) Art. 6 N 69. In *Duhs* v. *Sweden* Application 12995/87, the Commission denied a violation of Art. 6 § 2 although there was no possibility of rebuttal—it appears that the petty character of the offence was decisive. Charrier (2002) criticizes the decision as going back to the position in *Öztürk* v. *Germany*.

necessary care was not applied. On the other hand, going through the required formalities leaves traces which it is easy to produce in evidence. To take possession of imported goods without such proof is connected with a risk. Creating this risk is the offence—it is usually proved without difficulty. It is not unfair, then, to require the person concerned to show that in this specific case the formalities were complied with.

This is an approach which explains in a more substantial way the difference between smuggling and dealing with intoxicating drugs. Here we have no risky behaviour, no violation of a duty to carefulness. Therefore, it must be established *ab ovo*, as it were, that the accused knew he was carrying forbidden drugs, whereas, with the customs offence, it was of no importance whether the goods were objectionable or not, as long as a tribute was due. A somewhat similar situation may arise in the context of defamation. In order to ensure compatibility with freedom of expression, criminal law usually gives a person who has defamed someone by casting blame on his honour the opportunity to prove the truth of such allegations. Schubarth has raised the question whether this is compatible with the presumption of innocence.[77] The Commission gave an affirmative answer.[78] Indeed, it can hardly be doubted that to affirm facts casting a negative light on the honour of a person is a risky conduct. Again, it seems fair that a person engaging in such conduct be expected to prove the veracity of his or her assertion.[79]

(b) Criminal Liability for the Conduct of Others (Vicarious Liability)

'It is a fundamental rule of criminal law that criminal liability does not survive the person who has committed the criminal act'.[80] This sentence forms part of the judgment in a case brought against Switzerland. In this case a fine for tax evasion was imposed on the heirs of someone who had failed to declare part of his income. While a majority of the Commission concluded that the fine formed part of the inheritance and the obligation on the heirs to pay it did not violate the presumption of innocence,[81] the Court rightly came to the opposite conclusion. Referring to the presumption of innocence it found that '[i]nheritance of the guilt of the dead is not compatible with the standards of criminal justice in a society governed by the rule of law'.[82]

(c) Prosecution of Legal Persons

In recent years, the old adage '*societas delinquere non potest*' has lost much of its relevance. Increasingly corporations are being held criminally responsible in

---

[77] Schubarth (1984) Art. 173 N 63–5.
[78] *Lingens and Leitgeb* v. *Austria* Applications 8803/79 and 1112/81.
[79] See also de Figueiredo Dias (1974) 216; Trechsel (1981) 320 et seq. with further examples.
[80] *AP, MP, and TP* v. *Switzerland*, § 48; *EL, RL, and JO-L* v. *Switzerland*, § 53; these two judgments are entirely identical—henceforth only the former will be cited.
[81] *AP, MP, and TP* v. *Switzerland*, pp. 1495 and 1496, dissenting opinions, pp. 1500, 1501, 1502, and 1504.   [82] *AP, MP, and TP* v. *Switzerland*, § 48.

areas such as environmental protection, tax offences, money laundering, unfair competition, and consumer protection.[83] The actions of a legal person depend, of course, on natural persons, thus this issue has a certain similarity to vicarious liability.

Until now, international bodies called upon to implement human-rights law have not had to deal with the question. It is clearly established that legal persons are entitled to bring applications.[84] It is to be expected that the Strasbourg Court would also apply the presumption of innocence (as well as other elements of the right to a fair trial) *mutatis mutandis* to entities such as corporations. It is not possible to address such problems in the present context.

3. Problems Related to Sentencing

In a very early judgment, *Engel and others*, the Court had to consider an allegation that Article 6 § 2 had been violated by a reference made during sentencing to the applicants' previous conduct even though it had not given rise to a criminal prosecution, let alone a conviction. The Court's response was somewhat draconian: 'As its [Art. 6 § 2] wording shows, it deals only with the proof of guilt and not with the kind or level of punishment. It thus does not prevent the national judge, when deciding upon the penalty to impose on an accused . . . from having regard to factors relating to the individual's personality'.[85] The issue arose again in a different form in the case of *Albert and Le Compte*. Dr Albert had complained that his criminal record had been taken into account in determining his sentence. The Court rejected this claim.[86] The case-law goes back to an early decision of the Commission.[87] It is not satisfactory. This is especially problematic when a jury and other lay judges are involved who may become biased if told that the accused has committed an offence or several offences for which he was not convicted before, particularly if they are of the same kind as the offence at issue.

The reasoning in the *Engel* case, however, requires further comment. The development of the case-law shows quite clearly that the presumption of innocence continues to have effect after an acquittal or conviction. If, for example, previous criminal activities were held to constitute an aggravating circumstance, whether formally in the sense of recidivism or in some other way, the presumption of innocence would be violated if a court were to apply such a rule in the absence of prior convictions. Later on in the judgment the Court also restricted the scope of this rule stating that there is no problem 'unless they [scil. 'allegations made about an accused's personality as part of the sentencing

---

[83] e.g. Pradel (1999); Heine (1998); Schünemann (1998); Préfontaine (1998).

[84] See e.g. Abraham (2001) 578 at 585; Ovey and White (2002) 405; Grabenwarter (2003) § 13 N 8; Golsong (1970) 15.

[85] *Engel and others* v. *Netherlands*, § 90; see also *E* v. *Switzerland* Application 12117/86.

[86] *Albert and Le Compte* v. *Belgium*, § 40.   [87] *X* v. *Austria* Application 2742/66.

process'] are of such a nature and degree as to amount to the bringing of a new charge within the autonomous meaning of the Convention'.[88]

4. The Revocation of a Suspended Sentence

The introduction of suspended sentences constitutes one of the most important developments in twentieth-century sentencing law. The sentence (which is often custodial) is imposed following conviction, but is then deferred. A period of probation is fixed. If, during this period, the offender does not commit a new offence and fulfils any other conditions set out in the judgment, he or she will be free from further sanction. If, on the other hand, the offender commits a new offence or acts in a way which is contrary to the conditions, the suspension is revoked.

In Germany the revocation of the sentence is determined by the judge who passed the original sentence. There is no requirement in domestic law that any offence committed during the critical period be 'proven according to law' in order for the revocation to be justified. The Commission, faced with an application alleging that this practice was contrary to Article 6 § 2, declared it admissible—the case ended with a friendly settlement.[89] The Government had declared that it would draw the attention of the judicial authorities of the *Länder* to the need to respect the presumption of innocence in this respect. Although this seemed to indicate that it agreed with the provisional opinion of the Commission that the right had not been respected, the law, GPC, § 56f (1)(1), was not subsequently amended.

The issue arose again, this time before the Court, in *Böhmer*. In this case the Hamburg district court had even taken evidence to ascertain whether the applicant had committed an offence, not with a view to his conviction, but only to establish whether the suspended sentence should be revoked. The Court held this to constitute a violation of the presumption of innocence. It held that the case differed significantly from previous cases concerning the revocation of a suspended sentence which the Commission had declared inadmissible. These cases had involved issues such as whether there could be a violation despite the fact that the applicant had already confessed.[90]

It must be admitted that this case does not really belong to the 'outcome-related' aspect of the presumption of innocence as the aim of the proceedings was not to convict or acquit the defendant. Further, the judge responsible for determining the revocation will not necessarily be the same judge who was called upon

---

[88] *Böhmer* v. *Germany*, § 55; *Phillips* v. *the United Kingdom*, § 35.

[89] *X* v. *Germany* Application 12748/87. In other cases it considered that there was no violation because the applicant had not yet been finally convicted; *Houswitschka* v. *Germany* Application 12380/86; and *R* v. *Germany* Application 12669/87. The result is acceptable as the applicants had already confessed. See also Harris, O'Boyle, and Warbrick (1995) 244.

[90] *Böhmer* v. *Germany*, § 65, referring to decisions *Houswitschka* v. *Germany* Application 12380/86; *R* v. *Germany* Application 12669/87; and *S* v. *Germany* Application 15871/89 of 8 Oct. 1992.

to determine the original charge, and his or her task will be to decide on a related issue in proceedings to which Article 6 as such consequently does not apply.

B. The Evaluation of the Evidence

1. General Observations: The 'Fourth-instance' Issue

The requirement that where doubt remains as to an accused's guilt the accused must be acquitted, lies at the centre of the principle *in dubio pro reo*. It is particularly important at trial and on appeal, and becomes much less so in proceedings which concentrate on a plea of nullity. The decision as to whether an applicant is guilty or not is *the* decision which must be taken at the domestic level. If an international body were to intervene it would inevitably act as a 'fourth instance' and thus comment directly on the merits. It is generally accepted that this cannot be the scope of proceedings under the international covenants and conventions created to protect fundamental rights.[91]

A violation will only occur if it can be established from the judgment that the court convicted the accused despite lingering doubts as to his or her guilt. In one case the Reykjavik district court convicted a defendant on the basis that 'it cannot be seen from the facts of the case and the statements described in the . . . judgment . . . that she is more likely to be innocent than guilty'. This can hardly be reconciled with the obligation to give an accused the benefit of doubt. The case was settled, the Government paid some compensation.[92]

2. The Issue of Bias

(a) Judicial Bias

As I have already indicated above, a central element in the protection of the presumption of innocence lies in ensuring the impartiality of the judge. He or she 'should not start with the conviction or the assumption that the accused committed the act with which he is charged'.[93] I see no justification for making a difference in this respect between the protection of Article 6 § 1 and § 2. The link between the two guarantees was first made in *Austria* v. *Italy* where the Commission said that conviction was only possible 'on the basis of direct or indirect evidence sufficiently strong in the eyes of the law to establish guilt'.[94]

There have, however, been cases which were dealt with entirely in the light of Article 6 § 2. In *Lavents* the judge called upon to determine the charge, had declared to the press that she did not believe that the accused was innocent,

---

[91] For examples of typical 'fourth-instance' cases, see *D* v. *Switzerland* Application 11497/85; *O* v. *Switzerland* Application 11495/85; *Hersin* v. *France* Application 12528/86; *Beaudet-Barat* v. *France* Application 12418/86; and *KB* v. *Austria* Application 11170/84, all with relatively thorough reasoning.   [92] *Vilborg Yrsa Sigurðardóttir* v. *Iceland*, § 10.
[93] *X* v. *Germany* Application 4124/69.
[94] *Austria* v. *Italy* Application 788/60; Merrills and Robertson (2001) 114.

stating that the most he could hope for would be a partial acquittal. In another interview she suggested that he should prove his innocence.[95]

The Court was unmoved by the fact that she had made the statements in an interrogative form, because the right to be presumed innocent had to be interpreted in such a way as to ensure that it be a practical and effective guarantee.[96] There had thus been a clear violation.[97]

A difficult issue involving the use of previous convictions was decided by the Commission somewhat unconvincingly. The applicant complained that in proceedings concerning rape the jury had been informed of his previous convictions. The arguments used by the Commission to reject this application were purely pragmatic. It held that the practice existed in several countries.[98] Yet, the dangers of such information are well known and modern justice systems separate the sentencing hearing, where it is legitimate to take the record into account, from the proceedings on the determination of the charge.[99] In another case the fact that the accused was handcuffed during a hearing which was held outside the courthouse did not violate the presumption.[100] In a way, this creates the impression that the accused is dangerous and may lead to the (premature) conclusion, in the eyes of lay participants, that he or she must be guilty. However, if the authorities consider such security methods to be necessary, they will have to act in the least conspicuous way possible when bringing the accused into the courtroom and then take the handcuffs off.

(b) Bias of Other Participants in the Proceedings

(i) The Prosecuting Authority I have already indicated that the prosecution authority is bound to respect the presumption of innocence but need not be fully impartial. A violation of the presumption of innocence in its outcome-related aspect is therefore not to be expected. The requirement of fairness is not as such endangered by a partial prosecutor. One might be tempted to argue to the contrary. Adversarial proceedings however presuppose opponents, on one side the public prosecutor whose activity is based on a *de facto* presumption of guilt, and on the other, the defence.

(ii) The Expert Experts, on the other hand, have a special type of responsibility. Their role will necessarily depend to a certain extent on the procedural system within which they operate.[101] In Scotland and in England and Wales, experts are

---

[95] *Lavents* v. *Latvia*, § 124.   [96] Ibid., § 126.

[97] Other cases held to be inadmissible which raised the issue of virulent press campaigns in the context of the presumption of innocence include *Ensslin, Baader, and Raspe* v. *Germany* Applications 7572/76, 7586/76 and 7587/76; and *Ninn-Hansen* v. *Denmark*.

[98] *X* v. *Denmark* Application 2518/65; *X* v. *Austria* Application 2676/65. See also *X* v. *Germany* Application 5620/72.

[99] e.g. Roxin (1998) § 2 A II, § 42 G II; Wolffers (1999); Schmid (2004) N 4.3.1; Hauser and Schweri (2002) N 17.   [100] *X* v. *Austria* Application 2291/64.

[101] For a comparative examination of expert evidence in Europe, see Nijboer and Sprangers (2000).

normally appointed by the parties and cannot strictly speaking be expected to be impartial.

In other procedural systems, however, they are appointed by the court, and should therefore be regarded as its assistants. Their impartiality is of great importance. In *Bönisch*, the Court did not really contradict the Austrian Government's assertion 'that under Austrian law an "expert" was a neutral and impartial auxiliary of the Court'.[102] It doubted the impartiality of the expert, who, due to his prior functions, seemed to be 'more like a witness against the accused'.[103] This seems to imply that experts are also bound by the presumption of innocence.

The question arose again in *Bernard* v. *France* where the applicant had pleaded not guilty. One of the psychiatric reports concerning the applicant was riddled with language which portrayed him as a hardened criminal: 'Mr. Bernard is a gangster . . . The conduct of the operation shows . . . that it was very well planned [details given] and the work of an expert team [specifications given]. All Mr. Bernard's major offences (both past and present) fall into the category of organised crime . . . Mr. Bernard is not a casual offender, but a real professional', and so on.[104] The appeal court did not find a violation, because in presenting his evidence the expert had repeatedly mentioned that Mr Bernard had denied having committed the offences.[105] The court of cassation, in the somewhat laconic style for which it is well known, rejected the appeal 'holding that the comments referred to in that ground of appeal did not constitute a breach of the oath sworn by the experts to assist the court on their honour and according to their conscience'.[106] The Commission was split on the question of violation of Article 6 § 1—with the casting vote of the President it decided that there had been a violation and ruled that it was unnecessary to examine the complaint from the standpoint of Article 6 § 2.

The Court, however, went with the minority and concluded that there had been no violation of Article 6 §§ 1 or 2. It recalled that the expert 'logically had to start from the working hypothesis that the applicant had committed the crimes which had given rise to the prosecution'.[107] The conclusion is drafted in very sweeping terms: 'The file shows that the applicant's conviction was based on . . . evidence obtained during the investigation and discussed at the hearings . . . That being so, the Court cannot regard the statements in issue, which formed only one part of the evidence submitted to the jury, as contrary to the requirement of a fair trial and the presumption of innocence'.[108]

This case illustrates very clearly the difference between the outcome-related and the reputation-related aspects of the guarantee. The Court concentrated here on the former aspect. Without saying so very clearly, it examined whether the expert's opinion could have led to an unsafe conviction, and decided to the

---

[102] *Bönisch* v. *Austria*, § 30.   [103] Ibid., § 32.   [104] *Bernard* v. *France*, § 13.
[105] Ibid., § 16.   [106] Ibid., § 20.   [107] Ibid., § 38.   [108] Ibid., § 40.

contrary. If it had taken the other approach, however, it would have asked whether the statement of the expert 'reflected an opinion that [the applicant was] guilty before he ha[d] been proved guilty according to law'. It is worth noting that in setting out the general principles the Court omitted this sentence! The judgment is even more surprising if one keeps in mind that the Court considered the choice of words to be particularly important.[109]

It must be recalled in this context that experts are not public officials, so their statements cannot violate the Convention, as such. However, the Contracting States are, by virtue of Article 1, under an obligation to 'secure' the fundamental rights set out therein to every person under their jurisdiction. In this case the court ought to have reacted to the verbal excesses of the expert as the technical majority of the Commission suggested, by way of a jury direction.

(iii) Others What has been said with regard to experts must also apply to other persons participating in the proceedings, for example, witnesses and private plaintiffs. The state is not directly responsible for their conduct but the authorities must intervene whenever a person participating in the proceedings makes statements which are not compatible with the presumption of innocence. Some personal bias, however, does not yet fall under this category.

(c) The Media

Media publicity can have particularly dangerous consequences for the presumption of innocence. While it is certainly legitimate to inform the public about criminal proceedings, even sometimes during the preparatory stages, it is nevertheless essential that statements presenting the accused as guilty are avoided. It is essential that the judge makes it clear that he or she will not be influenced by a press campaign and gives a clear warning to jurors and other lay participants to that effect.[110] As the Convention only binds Member States, private media and those acting for them cannot immediately violate the presumption of innocence as set out in Article 6 § 2. However, the state, under Article 1 of the ECHR, has a duty to 'secure' individual rights and to intervene if they are threatened or violated by whomsoever.[111]

A case of this kind was dealt with by the HRC. There had been considerable pre-trial publicity which had presented the accused as a notorious drug baron. As the authorities had taken measures to counteract that publicity, it was decided that there had been no violation.[112]

---

[109] Cf. *Daktaras* v. *Lithuania*, § 41; *Böhmer* v. *Germany*, § 56.

[110] In *Kropf* v. *Germany* Application 14733/89, the Commission declared the application inadmissible because the applicant had been acquitted; it is obvious that it did not take into consideration the 'absolute' effect. The same can be said with regard to *X* v. *United Kingdom* Application 3860/68 where the appeal court had found that the evidence was so overwhelming that no jury could have come to a different verdict.

[111] Peters (2003) 133: '*indirekte Drittwirkung*'.

[112] *Dole Chadee and others* v. *Trinidad and Tobago*.

Authorities may inform the public in the course of proceedings but must make it clear that the suspect is not considered guilty.[113]

3. No Right of Access to Court in Order to Establish One's Innocence

The right to be presumed innocent does not include the right to establish one's innocence in a court. In other words, there is no right to oppose a decision to terminate the proceedings before any hearing on the merits.[114] This is quite logical—as everybody is presumed to be innocent there is no justification for access to court only to prove this fact.

III. THE 'REPUTATION-RELATED' ASPECTS OF THE GUARANTEE

A. Introduction

It may be useful to recall that the 'reputation-related aspect' of the presumption of innocence refers to situations in which the acts or a statements of a public authority imply that it believes a person to be guilty of an offence before that person has been convicted, even if the act or statement is not instrumental in the determination of the eventual judgment. In this sense the presumption of innocence is not really a procedural guarantee any more.[115]

I shall begin by presenting the case-law on the subject. It concerns declarations made during the pre-trial phase of the proceedings, the application of measures of coercion, decisions, and reasons given in the context of the termination of criminal proceedings other than by conviction and declarations made by public authorities which are not related directly to criminal proceedings.

Finally, I shall address the theoretical foundations on which this jurisprudence rests.

B. Statements During the Pre-trial Phase of the Proceedings

Generally, acts and declarations made in the course of criminal proceedings belong to the 'outcome-related' aspect of the presumption of innocence as they endanger the impartiality of the court's decision. However, there are some exceptions.

An example is provided by the case of *Daktaras* v. *Lithuania*. In this case the applicant had requested that the prosecutor discontinue the case against him on the basis that there was insufficient evidence to justify the prosecution.

---

[113] *X* v. *Netherlands* Application 8361/78.
[114] *Soltikov* v. *Germany* Application 2257/64; *X* v. *Netherlands* Application 8585/79. This was also at issue in *Marziano* v. *Italy*. See further *L* v. *Netherlands* Application 12241/86; and *Kayhan* v. *Germany* Application 11585/85.   [115] Sudre (2003) N 218.

The prosecutor rejected this request stating that it was 'ill-founded, as it has been established from the evidence collected in the course of the pre-trial investigation that the applicant is guilty of these crimes.'[116] He then went on to discuss in more detail the evidence, which 'proved' the different accusations.

The Court accepted that the presumption of innocence could be infringed by the prosecution, particularly 'where a prosecutor . . . performs a quasi-judicial function when ruling on the applicant's request to dismiss the charges.'[117] 'Nevertheless', it continued, 'whether a statement of a public official is in breach of the principle of the presumption of innocence must be determined in the context of the particular circumstances in which the impugned statement is made'.[118]

In *Daktaras* the assertion was made 'internally', in a procedural decision, not at a press conference. The prosecutor had used the term 'proved' to answer the accused's allegations that the facts were 'not proved'. The term was certainly 'unfortunate', but in the context it was used it did not amount to a violation of Article 6 § 2.[119]

This finding is convincing. The prosecution is expected to press for a guilty verdict, thus even if it expresses this opinion before the final pleadings, this is unlikely unduly to influence the verdict. On the other hand, this case again illustrates the difference between the two different aspects of the principle. Had the statement been addressed to the public, the result is likely to have been quite different, although not with regard to the proceedings themselves. It would have constituted an unjustified interference with the applicant's right to the protection of his reputation.[120]

C. Measures of Coercion, in Particular Detention on Remand

1. The Principle

In order to facilitate the gathering of evidence and to prevent the suspect jeopardizing the successful course of the proceedings, a variety of measures of coercion, which necessarily interfere with suspects' rights, are at the disposal of the investigating authorities. They include, *inter alia*, wire-tapping, surveillance, whether it be electronic or otherwise, the taking of samples of blood or saliva, search and seizure[121] and, most importantly, detention on remand. These measures are definitely compatible with the right to be presumed innocent.[122] They are based on the suspicion prescribed in Article 5 § 1(c) of the ECHR.[123]

---

[116] *Daktaras* v. *Lithuania*, § 13.   [117] Ibid., § 42.   [118] Ibid., § 43.
[119] Ibid., §§ 44–5.   [120] Cf. *Butkevicius* v. *Lithuania*.
[121] Seized property can also serve as a lien in favour of the government in event of an acquittal; *X* v. *Austria* Application 4338/69.
[122] This includes the obligation on someone suspected of driving under the influence of drink or drugs to submit to a blood test; see *X* v. *Netherlands* Application 8239/78.
[123] For the compatibility of the expression of suspicion in connection with the seizure of a book, see *Gökceli* v. *Turkey*.

2. The Limits

(a) General Aspects

Some of these measures[124] may become so intrusive that they must be viewed as anticipating the punishment.[125] This could even be the case with seizure, if it lasts for an excessive length of time and if the goods seized consequently lose their value.[126] The greatest dangers, however, arise in relation to detention on remand. For this reason such detention is subject to strict limits and must not last beyond a 'reasonable time'.[127] The details of this guarantee are discussed elsewhere.

This issue has also been discussed insofar as it relates to the presumption of innocence. The HRC discussed the matter in its comments on State Reports concerning Italy,[128] Ecuador,[129] Argentina,[130] Romania,[131] and Luxembourg.[132] The European Commission of Human Rights also had to consider a number of applications alleging violations of both Articles 5 § 3 and 6 § 2 which were based on the length of detention on remand.[133] The connection between these two principles is by no means tenuous. Research has shown that courts have a tendency to take the length of detention on remand into account in sentencing and tend to avoid sentences lower than the time already 'served' on remand.[134]

Thus provisional coercive measures may represent a type of repressive sanction, imposed even before the person concerned has been convicted.

When Article 6 § 2 is invoked together with Article 5 § 3, the latter has precedence as the *lex specialis*; if a violation is found due to excessive length of detention on remand, an examination of whether the presumption of innocence has been violated becomes unnecessary.[135]

A particularly difficult issue arose in a case against Sweden which concerned tax evasion, as the decision to impose tax surcharges was enforced before the court had even decided that they were in fact due. The Court stated that the Convention does not prohibit anticipatory enforcement measures and added that 'provisions allowing early enforcement of certain criminal penalties can be found in the laws of other Contracting States' (unfortunately it again fails to provide any examples).[136] Contrary to the supplementary tax itself, the

---

[124] Definitely not the taking of a blood sample; see *X* v. *Netherlands* Application 8239/78.

[125] *B* v. *Spain* Application 12476/86. See also *Ventura* v. *Italy* Application 7438/76.

[126] Cf. *Raimondo* v. *Italy*.   [127] ICCPR, Art. 9 § 3; EHCR, Art. 5 § 3; ACHR, Art. 7 § 5.

[128] Concluding Observations of the HRC: Italy, UN Doc. CCPR/C/79/Add.94 (1998).

[129] Concluding Observations of the HRC: Ecuador, UN Doc. CCPR/C/79/Add.92 (1998).

[130] Concluding Observations of the HRC: Argentina, A/40/50, §§ 144–65 (1965).

[131] Concluding Observations of the HRC: Romania, UN Doc. CCPR/C/79/Add.30 (1993).

[132] Concluding Observations of the HRC: Luxembourg, UN Doc. CCPR/C/79/Add.11 (1992).

[133] See e.g. *Bonnechaux* v. *Switzerland* Application 8224/78; and also *Hellegouarch* v. *France* Application 11994/86.   [134] Robert (1972) 128 et seq.

[135] *Erdem* v. *Germany*, § 49.

[136] *Vastberga Taxi Aktiebolag and Vulic* v. *Sweden*, § 118; see also the parallel case of *Janosevic* v. *Sweden*.

provisional enforcement cannot be justified by referring to fiscal interests. The Court went into considerable detail in describing the possibilities of redress in the event that the final judgment did not impose any supplementary tax, and finally held that the safeguards provided by Swedish law were sufficient.[137]

The wording of this judgment betrays a number of hesitations. In my view, the seizure of the taxpayer's assets could be justified in order to secure the payment of the supplementary tax. It is difficult to see, however, why an anticipatory execution of a penal sanction should be necessary and how it can be reconciled with the presumption of innocence.

(b) The Nature of Detention on Remand

The nature and conditions of the detention on remand must be compatible with the presumption of innocence. Here, the Covenant gives clear directions: 'Accused persons shall, save in exceptional circumstances, be segregated from convicted persons and shall be subject to separate treatment appropriate to their status as unconvicted persons'.[138] Depriving a person presumed innocent of his or her liberty does not allow for any restriction that goes beyond what is strictly necessary to achieve the aim pursued, which is mainly the prevention of flight, recidivism, and interference with the evidence. This means that detainees cannot be compelled to work, have the right to wear their own clothes, and may order their own food, at least in so far as this is compatible with prison order.

The Court however disregarded this principle in *Peers* where the applicant complained that although he was detained on remand, he was subject to the same regime as the convicted prisoners. The Court rather brusquely brushed this complaint aside, arguing that 'the Convention contains no Article providing for separate treatment for convicted and accused'.[139] There are two reasons why this reasoning is unsatisfactory.

First, the Court ought to be aware of the provisions of the Covenant. Protocol No. 7 was created to eliminate any differences in the protection offered by the Convention and the Covenant. Certain proposals were removed from the first draft because the right in question was regarded as being implicit in the Convention.[140] This creates a presumption that the Convention ought to be interpreted in such a way as to guarantee the same level of protection as is provided by the Covenant.

Second, the Court ought to have operated a more detailed examination of the facts and should not have simply contented itself with such a formalistic argument. The possibility that the normal prison regime contained features that were incompatible with the presumption of innocence cannot be excluded. In the same case, however, the Court found a violation of Article 3 due to the prison conditions; in comparison to other complaints the one concerning Article 6 § 2 may have been regarded as trivial from the outset. Yet, it would then have

---

[137] Ibid., §§ 119–21.   [138] ICCPR, Art. 10 § 2(a).   [139] *Peers* v. *Greece*, § 78.
[140] Trechsel (1988), 195 et seq. with further references.

been preferable if the Court had concluded that no separate issue arose under Article 6 § 2.

D. Violation of the Presumption of Innocence in Cases where the Proceedings have Ended in Some Way Other than by Conviction and Sentence

There are essentially two different ways of concluding proceedings other than by conviction. The first obviously entails an acquittal. The second category involves a variety of procedural decisions, such as the decision of the public prosecutor or other authority with similar powers, not to prosecute on the basis that the chances of a successful prosecution are too small. Another example would be when an obstacle, such as a statute of limitation or the death of the accused, hinders either the trial or the appeal. Finally, it is also possible that the prosecution close a case because even in the event of a conviction the sentence would be negligible.

It may be thought strange that decisions which, after all, favour the accused in releasing him or her from the attention of the criminal-justice authorities, lead to problems affecting the presumption of innocence. In fact, a variety of issues may arise.

In all of these cases some reasoning will be given by the deciding authority. It is possible that these reasons reflect negatively on the defendant's innocence;[141] the defendant may be refused compensation for detention on remand or the costs of his defence;[142] costs of the proceedings may be awarded against the defendant, possibly together with an obligation to pay the costs of the other side;[143] finally, there is the possibility that despite the acquittal the defendant will nevertheless be ordered to pay compensation to the victim.[144]

There is a considerable volume of case-law on these issues. An examination of the jurisprudence need not deal with every category separately, but a distinction must in any event be made between the cases involving an acquittal and the others. In fact, the Court makes a distinction on the basis of whether or not the authority has actually taken a final decision on the merits.

1. The Effect of an Acquittal on the Presumption of Innocence

Once an acquittal has become final, the person concerned is protected from new proceedings by virtue of Article 14 § 7 of the ICCPR, Article 4 of Protocol No. 7 to the ECHR, or Article 8 § 4 of the ACHR, from any official statement which insinuates that he or she is guilty, and from any such statement which says that he or she is still under suspicion, even if the reasoning of the

---

[141] *Marziano* v. *Italy; Asan Rushiti* v. *Austria,* §§ 15, 32.
[142] *Lutz* v. *Germany; Englert* v. *Germany; Nölkenbockhoff* v. *Germany; Sekanina* v. *Austria; Rushiti* v. *Austria; Lamanna* v. *Austria; Weixelbraun* v. *Austria; Vostic* v. *Austria; Demir* v. *Austria; Leutscher* v. *Netherlands; Baars* v. *Netherlands; Hammern* v. *Norway;* and *O* v. *Norway.*
[143] *Minelli* v. *Switzerland.*   [144] *Ringvold* v. *Norway; Y* v. *Norway.*

judgment—whether it be public or secret—reflects doubts as to the accused's innocence. This principle has been upheld by the Court in a number of cases.[145]

In one case national law made the clearing of suspicion a prerequisite for the payment of compensation, and placed the *onus probandi* on the person claiming compensation. The Court pointed out quite correctly that the only exception to this rule arises in cases where the proceedings are to be reopened—after such a decision the person concerned again becomes the subject of a 'charge'.[146]

In *Y* v. *Norway* the person, who had earlier been acquitted, was ordered to pay compensation to the victim; the decision was taken by the same court the day after the acquittal. The Court concluded that there had been a violation of the right to be presumed innocent, as the domestic court found it 'clearly probable that [the applicant] had committed the offences'.[147] 'The Court is mindful of the fact that the domestic courts took note that the applicant had been acquitted of the criminal charges. However, in seeking to protect the legitimate interests of the purported victim, the Court considers that the language employed by the High Court, upheld by the Supreme Court, overstepped the bounds of the civil forum, thereby casting doubt on the correctness of that acquittal.'[148]

It reached a different conclusion in *Ringvold*, which was decided on the same day as *Hammern*, and *O* and *Y* v. *Norway*. The starting point was the same: a man had been prosecuted for sexually abusing a minor and was eventually acquitted.

In *Ringvold*, the alleged victim had brought a claim for compensation for non-pecuniary damages which was rejected by the high court. The victim appealed to the Supreme Court against this decision. Further evidence was taken and the file of the criminal proceedings was joined to the file of these civil proceedings. The Supreme Court finally decided in favour of the victim. In explaining the judgment Mrs Justice Gjølstad recalled that the normal standard of proof in compensation proceedings was the balance of probabilities. In view of the particular impact that the judgment could have on the defendant, it had to be stricter in this case, although not as strict as the standard in criminal proceedings. Although the acquittal had been based on the verdict of a jury, the Supreme Court discussed the views of the high court in relation to some evidence. The high court did not share the same hesitations as the jury about the evidentiary value of a video recording.

The Court distinguished this case from the others and found there to have been no violation. It accepted that the proceedings for compensation did not concern the determination of a criminal charge. Its main concern was that if this were not so,

as rightly pointed out by the Government, Article 6 § 2 would give a criminal acquittal the undesirable effect of pre-empting the victim's possibilities of claiming compensation

---

[145] *Sekanina* v. *Austria*, § 30; *Rushiti* v. *Austria*, § 31. In the same sense, see also the judgments in *Lamanna, Weixelbraun, Vostic* and *Demir* (all v. *Austria*); *Hammern* v. *Norway*, §§ 47–8; in the same sense, *O* v. *Norway*.   [146] *Weixelbraun* v. *Austria*, § 29.

[147] *Y* v. *Norway*, § 44.   [148] Ibid., § 46.

under the civil law of tort, entailing an arbitrary and disproportionate limitation on his or her right of access to court under Article 6 § 1 of the Convention. This again could give an acquitted perpetrator, who would be deemed responsible according to the civil burden of proof, the undue advantage of avoiding any responsibility for his or her actions. Such an extensive interpretation would not be supported either by the wording of Article 6 § 2 or any common ground in the national legal systems within the Convention community. On the contrary, in a significant number of Contracting States, an acquittal does not preclude establishing civil liability in relation to the same facts.

Thus, the Court considers that, while the acquittal from criminal liability ought to be maintained in the compensation proceedings, it should not preclude the establishment of civil liability to pay compensation arising out of the same facts on the basis of a less strict burden of proof... If the national decision on compensation were to contain a statement imputing the criminal liability of the respondent party, this would raise an issue falling within the ambit of Article 6 § 2 of the Convention.[149]

The Court referred to the case-law of the Commission which had already stressed the distinction between criminal and other proceedings, and in particular the lower standard of proof in other proceedings, where the decisions did not 'determine whether a criminal offence had been committed'.[150]

The difference between the approach of the Court and that of the Commission lies in the respective reasoning. The Commission limited itself to saying that the dismissal (or establishment of civil liability) did not amount to a statement that the person concerned was guilty of a crime. The Court did not even reach this point. It concluded that Article 6 § 2 did not apply because there was a lack of a sufficient link between the criminal case and the compensation case. 'The Court reiterates that the outcome of the criminal proceedings was not decisive for the compensation issue'.[151] Therefore, the Court concluded that it was barred from examining on the merits the question as to whether there had been a violation of Article 6 § 2.

In a dissenting opinion Judge Costa held that in his opinion 'the civil wrong still has to be distinct from the criminal wrong and the acts regarded as wrongful and prejudicial in civil law must not be exactly the same as those of which the defendant was accused in the criminal proceedings. Otherwise, both the presumption of innocence and the finding that the person acquitted was not guilty would be deprived of any useful purpose if judgment were given against that person in civil proceedings, as it would be paradoxical to protect a mere presumption for as long as it had not been rebutted by a ruling and yet to disregard the proof which reinforced that presumption'. He rightly pointed out

---

[149] _Ringvold_ v. _Norway_, § 38.
[150] _MC_ v. _United Kingdom_ Application 11882/85: the applicant had been dismissed, _inter alia_, because of an incident in which he had been acquitted of a charge of theft. In _Rebasso_ v. _Austria_ Application 12007/86, the Commission had confirmed that civil liability could arise from the same facts as criminal conduct. In this case, however, the Court of Appeal's wording could not be regarded as violating the presumption of innocence. See also _X_ v. _Austria_ Application 9295/81.
[151] _Ringvold_ v. _Norway_, § 41.

that Mrs 'Justice Gjølstad found that the evidence satisfied the standard of proof, establishing that sexual abuse had occurred and that, on the balance of probabilities, it was clear that the applicant was the abuser'.

This opinion must be applauded. This is not to say that there cannot be civil proceedings for damages arising out of the same facts as those which led to the acquittal. But it must be possible to distinguish clearly the civil liability from the criminal responsibility for the criminal offence. I shall return to the Court's methodology shortly.

In addition, a further issue calls for comment. The applicant had complained that the Supreme Court, for the purposes of the civil proceedings, had made available the case file of the criminal case. The Court answered this point in passing. '[T]he fact that an act that may give rise to a civil compensation claim under the law of tort is also covered by the objective constitutive elements of a criminal offence could not, notwithstanding its gravity, provide a sufficient ground for regarding the person allegedly responsible for the act in the context of a tort case as being "charged with a criminal offence". Nor could the fact that evidence from the criminal trial is used to determine the civil law consequences of the act warrant such a characterisation.'[152]

This statement however hardly addresses the question which the applicant raised. The problem lies in the fact that in criminal proceedings the establishment of the facts benefits from the prosecution apparatus. Measures of coercion are possible which are not available to a party in civil proceedings. The Court did not bother to examine whether the evidence contained in the criminal file would have been available in civil proceedings. Yet, it would be quite unfair if someone who claims to be the victim of an offence could benefit from special privileges in pursuing her claim. The privilege is acceptable in cases where the defendant has actually been convicted, but not when he or she has been acquitted.

2. The Effect of a Procedural Termination of Criminal Proceedings on the Presumption of Innocence

The Court's jurisprudence on the presumption of innocence is particularly varied in the area of the closing of criminal proceedings for procedural reasons. Quite a number of distinctions can be made on the basis of different criteria.

A differentiation can be made on the basis of the issue which is alleged to have violated the presumption. Applicants have complained that the authorities expressed doubts as to their innocence,[153] that they were denied compensation for their procedural expenses or for detention on remand by reference to continuing suspicion,[154] and that they were ordered to pay for some procedural expenses and to compensate the plaintiffs for their procedural costs.[155]

---

[152] Ibid., § 38.   [153] *Marziano* v. *Italy.*
[154] *Lutz* v. *Germany; Englert* v. *Germany; Nölkenbockhoff* v. *Germany; Leutscher* v. *Netherlands; Baars* v. *Netherlands.*   [155] The applicant in *Minelli* v. *Switzerland* was ordered to do both.

Other distinctions can be made depending on whether the impugned statement mentioned suspicion or affirmed guilt,[156] or whether the decision was detailed or limited to evoking the probability of guilt. One could also distinguish on the basis of the reasons for terminating the proceedings: insufficient evidence to justify the bringing of an indictment,[157] a statute of limitation,[158] the death of the accused,[159] or the fact that any sentence in the eventuality of conviction would be negligible.[160] Finally, it is also possible that a differentiation is made on the basis of whether the termination occurred after the defendant had been found guilty at first instance.[161]

(a) Order to Pay Costs and Compensation to the Plaintiff

The first case in which the 'reputation-related' function of the presumption of innocence was upheld was *Minelli* v. *Switzerland*. The applicant, a journalist, had written an article accusing a business of having acted fraudulently, an accusation which resulted in him being charged with defamation. The proceedings were stayed to await parallel proceedings against another journalist in a different canton. By the time that the proceedings were able to be resumed, they had become time-barred. The applicant was nevertheless ordered to pay court costs and compensation to the plaintiff. This order was justified by reference to the fact that Mr Minelli 'would in all probability have been convicted of defamation if the present proceedings had not been terminated on account of limitation'—a conclusion reached after a discussion of the evidence.[162]

The Court dealt first with the question of whether Article 6 § 2 applied at all to the case. It then followed the Commission in accepting that the imposition of costs on an accused after a case has been 'discontinued, discharged or . . . terminated on account of limitation'[163] was not prohibited by the Convention. The principle that 'neither Article 6 § 2 nor any other provision of the Convention gives a person "charged with a criminal offence" a right to reimbursement of his costs where proceedings taken against him are discontinued'[164] is often referred to in subsequent cases.[165] The Court found, however, that by

---

[156] e.g. *Lutz* v. *Germany* and *Minelli* v. *Switzerland*.   [157] *Marziano* v. *Italy*.

[158] *Minelli* v. *Switzerland; Lutz* v. *Germany; Leutscher* v. *Netherlands; Baars* v. *Netherlands*.

[159] *Nölkenbockhoff* v. *Germany*.   [160] *Englert* v. *Germany*.

[161] *Lutz* v. *Germany* (only a regulatory fine was imposed on the applicant who lodged an objection, §§ 13 et seq.); *Englert* v. *Germany* (convicted at first instance; the judgment was quashed on appeal; afterwards the proceedings were terminated because the sentence would have been negligible); *Nölkenbockhoff* v. *Germany* (the applicant died during the appeal proceedings); *Leutscher* v. *Netherlands* (convicted at first instance, judgment quashed on appeal, time-barred when proceedings resumed).   [162] *Minelli* v. *Switzerland*.

[163] *Minelli* v. *Switzerland*, § 34.

[164] e.g. *Lutz* v. *Germany*, § 59. See also *P, RH, and LL* v. *Austria* Application 15776/89. It is obvious that Art. 3 of Protocol No. 7 to the ECHR, ICCPR, Art. 14 § 6, and ACHR, Art. 10 do not cover these cases.

[165] e.g. *Englert* v. *Germany*, § 36; *Nölkenbockhoff* v. *Germany*, § 36; *Masson and Van Zon* v. *Netherlands*, § 49; *Leutscher* v. *Netherlands*, § 29; *Baars* v. *Netherlands*, § 27. The claim that Art. 6 § 2 should grant the right to deduct costs for counsel for tax purposes after proceedings were discontinued is rather far-fetched; see *SM* v. *Austria* Application 11919/86.

stating that Mr Minelli would very probably have been convicted, the chamber had treated the offence as if it had been proved and that it was clear that Mr Minelli was guilty.[166] This was held to constitute a violation of Article 6 § 2.

(b) The Refusal of Compensation

The Court distinguished the situation in *Minelli* from cases where there had only been a refusal to pay compensation, stressing that the refusal of compensation did not 'amount to a penalty or a measure that can be equated with a penalty'.[167] In *Lutz* the same formulation is used as in *Minelli*—'the defendant would most probably have been convicted'.[168] However, the court did not go on to examine the evidence in detail. This led the Court to find that only a suspicion had been uttered, not a statement that the defendant (who had actually admitted the offence) was guilty.

In *Englert* the court had stated that 'in the light of the course of the trial so far, the circumstances rebutting the presumption of innocence are . . . so overwhelming that a conviction is clearly more likely than an acquittal'.[169] In *Nölkenbockhoff* the reasoning was that 'the defendant would almost certainly have been convicted or his conviction almost certainly have been upheld'.

In all three cases (*Lutz, Englert,* and *Nölkenbockhoff*) the Court found no violation.[170] The same conclusion was reached in *Leutscher*, where there had previously been a conviction *in absentia*, and where the court justified the refusal of compensation on the basis that 'neither the file of the criminal investigation nor that relating to the present request [gave] any cause to doubt that this conviction [had been] correct'.[171]

In *Baars*, the refusal to compensate the applicant was justified by 'circumstances, from which it follows that the applicant—if the prosecution department had not forfeited the right to prosecute by exceeding a reasonable time and [the prosecution] had not been declared inadmissible by the Regional Court for that reason—would in all likelihood (*met grote mate van waarschijnlijkheid*) have been convicted'.[172] Here, the Court *did* find a violation of Article 6 § 2 because the evidence had been discussed in some detail.

These decisions seem to follow a clear pattern. There will be a violation where the domestic court not only justifies its refusal of compensation on the basis that it was highly likely that the applicant is guilty but also discusses the evidence, in some detail, before reaching that conclusion. A further difference, which the judgments do not refer to, is the fact that a violation was found where there had

---

[166] *Minelli* v. *Switzerland*, § 38.

[167] *Lutz* v. *Germany*, § 63; *Englert* v. *Germany*, § 39; *Nölkenbockhoff* v. *Germany*, § 40; *Leutscher* v. *Netherlands*, § 29. The argument is not convincing—imposition of costs is ordered for reasons of equity, not as a penalty.   [168] *Lutz* v. *Germany*, § 16.

[169] *Englert* v. *Germany*, § 29.

[170] 'Surprisingly', according to Merrills and Robertson (2001) 116, and contrary to the Commission; Judge Cremona wrote a forceful dissenting opinion.

[171] *Leutscher* v. *Netherlands*, § 31.   [172] *Baars* v. *Netherlands*, § 17.

not been a conviction at first instance. This could hardly be a valid reason, and therefore it is not mentioned. In fact, theoretically (at least in the legal systems concerned, those of Austria and the Netherlands), the presumption of innocence is set aside as soon as the convicted person files an appeal ('*Berufung*', '*hooger Beroep*'). Yet, in practice, the authorities seem to find it difficult to act as if there had never been a conviction at first instance.

The Court now and then stresses the 'importance of the choice of words by public officials'.[173] It is regrettable that in the cases referred to this rule has not been applied.[174] The reasons given for the difference made between those cases where, as in *Minelli* and *Baars*, a violation was found, and the other ones, are not particularly convincing. It is certainly acceptable that compensation is denied— even if costs are awarded against a defendant, in cases where proceedings are terminated for procedural or technical reasons after a conviction at first instance. This should however be clearly set out in a rule, for example, 'if proceedings are terminated after a conviction at first instance and before a decision on appeal has been taken, the costs are to be borne by the accused'. This would avoid statements which are hard to reconcile with the presumption of innocence.

(c) The Affirmation of Continuing Suspicion
In one case, the applicant, who was accused of having sexually assaulted a child, complained that the proceedings against him were terminated leaving him no opportunity to prove his innocence. The judge responsible for the preliminary investigation ('*giudice per le indagini preliminari*') had used wording which stressed the persistence of strong suspicions against him, which in turn had led to a refusal by his ex-wife to let him see his daughter. The majority held that there had been no violation. Although the Court recalled the importance of the choice of words, it held that notwithstanding the wording of the order ('*malgré les termes employés dans l'ordonnance*') the decision had only expressed a 'state of suspicion'.[175]

In a convincing dissenting opinion Judge Rozakis pointed out that the wording clearly betrayed the conviction of the judge that the applicant was guilty. In ordinary words, what the decision expressed was this: 'I am convinced that the applicant is guilty; however, unfortunately, I doubt whether it will be possible to convince the court at the trial of this guilt due to the weakness of some elements of proof'. I agree with Judge Rozakis that this is not compatible with the presumption of innocence—there is a slightly cynical touch to the alternative view.

3. Statements Unrelated to Criminal Proceedings

So far there have been two cases where public officials have made statements outside criminal proceedings which have nevertheless been considered to raise

---

[173] *Daktaras* v. *Lithuania*, § 41; *Marziano* v. *Italy*, § 28; *Böhmer* v. *Germany*, § 56.
[174] Merrills and Robertson (2001) 117 also criticize these judgments.
[175] *Marziano* v. *Italy*, §§ 28, 30.

problems pertinent to the presumption of innocence. An episode of this kind made the front pages when President Nixon spoke of Manson as a murderer before he was convicted.[176]

The first case concerned the then Swiss minister of justice who, after the arrest of Ms Petra Krause (later convicted in Switzerland of being a terrorist linked to the Baader-Meinhof gang) referred to her as a criminal but added that she would have to stand trial. As there had been no formal declaration that she was guilty, the Commission declared the application inadmissible.[177]

Much later, Mr Allenet de Ribemont was arrested in France on suspicion of involvement in the murder of Mr Jean de Broglie. At a press conference, which was also attended by the Minister of the Interior, the Director of the Paris Criminal Investigation Department referred to the applicant as the 'instigator of the murder'.[178]

The Court held that the Convention 'must be interpreted in such a way as to guarantee rights which are practical and effective as opposed to theoretical and illusory' and that Article 6 § 2 was applicable because there existed a link with the criminal investigation which had started a few days earlier. It recognized that the presumption of innocence did not prevent the authorities from providing information about ongoing investigations, but held that this must be done in a way which is compatible with the presumption. In this case, a declaration of the applicant's guilt had quite clearly been made.[179]

Even a simple police report which states that a suspect is guilty can violate the right to be presumed innocent, even though there is ultimately no conviction and the name of the person concerned is struck off the police register.[180]

E. Assessment

The 'reputation-related' aspect has not received unanimous approval. Particularly harsh criticism has been voiced by Gollwitzer who has objected to a procedural guarantee being applied to non-procedural facts.[181] I do not agree with him and believe that, with some exceptions, the Court is right in maintaining the approach initiated by the Commission.

It would undoubtedly be preferable, however, if the Court could accept that what it is in fact doing is 'directly' applying a vision of Article 6 § 2 which is not tied to criminal proceedings in a way concordant with those defined by Article 6 § 1, namely, those concerned with 'the determination ... of any criminal charge'.

[176] Cf. e.g. *Time Magazine*, 17 Aug. 1970.
[177] *Petra Krause* v. *Switzerland* Application 7986/77.
[178] *Allenet de Ribemont* v. *France*, § 10.
[179] Ibid., §§ 35–41. See also *W* v. *Germany* Application 11526/85.
[180] *Babjak and others* v. *Slovakia*, decision of 30 Mar. 2004; the application was declared inadmissible for non-exhaustion of domestic remedies.
[181] Gollwitzer (1992) Art. 6 N 121 et seq.

In almost all the judgments concerning Article 6 § 2 it goes out of its way to demonstrate that Article 6 applies. In particular, with regard to the term 'criminal' it sets out the criteria developed in *Engel and others* and goes on to examine whether they are applicable in the case at issue. Since the decision in *Minelli*, however, most of those cases, while somehow linked to criminal proceedings, concern a person who is no longer 'charged' with a criminal offence.[182]

In the *Minelli* case the Court went so far as to suggest that when the Assize Court decided that the applicant would have to bear two-thirds of the court costs and pay compensation to the private plaintiffs, it 'still regarded the applicant as being "charged with a criminal offence", within the meaning of Article 6.'[183] This is not at all convincing, especially in view of the fact that a few sentences later the Court admitted 'that the limitation had extinguished the criminal action instituted against the applicant'. It has to be one or the other—the charge disappears as soon as the criminal proceedings come to an end.

In the case where fines for tax offences imposed on a deceased individual were transferred to his heirs,[184] the applicants had definitely never been charged. It is true that, referring to *Öztürk* v. *Germany*, the Court discussed the applicability of Article 6.[185] However, it was the deceased individual who had been subject to the charge, not the applicants. The fact that they were asked to pay the fine cannot possibly be regarded as a charge—there was never any examination of whether they were guilty of an offence or not.

The attitude changed in *Sekanina*. The Court referred to the Commission which had always taken the direct approach by stating 'that the presumption of innocence was obligatory not only for criminal courts ruling on the merits of a charge, but also for other authorities'.[186] However, while the Commission did not try to link the prerequisites for its application and the substance of Article 6 § 2, the Court made such an attempt. It stated that even after an acquittal, Austrian law linked the question of criminal responsibility to that of compensation 'to such a degree that the decision on the latter issue can be regarded as a consequence and, to some extent, the concomitant of the decision on the former'; the same court was competent in the matter and the decision not to pay compensation 'relied heavily on the evidence from the Assize Court's case file'.[187] Article 6 applies to persons 'charged with a criminal offence' which is of course the subject of autonomous interpretation.[188] However, it appears that in the context of Article 6 § 2 the Court gives it a different meaning than that utilized

---

[182] An exception can be made for the case of *Allenet de Ribemont* v. *France* where the applicant could be said in reality to have been 'charged' with instigating the murder of Mr de Broglie. An early decision of the Commission which used a narrower interpretation of the term 'charged', *X* v. *Germany* Application 4483/70, must be regarded as having been overruled.

[183] *Minelli* v. *Switzerland*, § 32.

[184] *AP, MP, and TP* v. *Switzerland* and *EL, RL, and JO-L* v. *Switzerland*.

[185] *AP, MP, and TP* v. *Switzerland*, §§ 39–43; *EL, RL, and JO-L* v. *Switzerland*, §§ 44–8.

[186] *Sekanina* v. *Austria*, § 21, with reference to *X* v. *Austria* Application 9295/81.

[187] *Sekanina* v. *Austria*, § 22.   [188] See further Chapter 2.

in the context of Article 6 § 1. This cannot be correct. It is in any case difficult
to see how the term 'charged' could be interpreted as also meaning 'not charged
any more'.

The extinction of the charge is particularly obvious in cases where the
applicant has been acquitted. In the four cases brought against Norway, the
Court finally accepted that the applicants could no longer be regarded as
'charged with a criminal offence'—the denial of a violation of Article 6 § 2 is
justified by considerations of mere expediency: it would not be fair if the victim
of a crime, due to the acquittal of the suspect, was precluded from a finding in
his favour in civil proceedings 'on the basis of a less strict burden of evidence'.[189]

In my view, the approach of the Commission is to be preferred. I held that the
right to be presumed innocent 'is not only a procedural guarantee in criminal
proceedings, but requires all State organs to refrain from statements on the guilt
of the accused before that guilt has been established by the competent Court'.[190]
It simply reads Article 6 § 2 as if the wording proposed by René Cassin or
Eleanor Roosevelt had been adopted.[191]

[189] *Hammern* v. *Norway*, § 41; *O* v. *Norway*, §40; *Ringvold* v. *Norway*, § 40; *Y* v. *Norway*, § 40.
[190] *P, RH, and LL* v. *Austria* Application 15776/89; in one case, the Commission hesitated on
this issue. In proceedings on a tax deduction of costs for counsel in proceedings which were
terminated because of the statute of limitation the administrative court had referred to the continuing suspicion; the Commission said that the person was not, at that moment, 'charged' with an
offence. However, the case was declared inadmissible because the finding had essentially been that
there had been no acquittal, which was quite correct; *SM* v. *Austria* Application 11919/86.
Occasionally, however, the Commission seemed to argue in a very narrow way, e.g. *AA* v. *Sweden*
Application 11531/85. This applies also to the Covenant, General Comment No. 13 § 7; Nowak
(1993) Art. 14 N 36; McGoldrick (1994) 405.
[191] For further discussion on this subject, see Chiavaro (2000) 189 et seq.; Farthouat (1998);
Auvret (1994); Lombois (1950).

Chapter 8

The Right to be Informed of the Accusation

I. INTRODUCTION

A. The Texts

[3. In the determination of any criminal charge against him, everyone shall be entitled to the following minimum guarantees, in full equality:]
(a) To be informed promptly and in detail in a language which he understands of the nature and cause of the charge against him;

ICCPR, Art. 14 § 3(a)

[3. Everyone charged with a criminal offence has the following minimum rights:]
(a) to be informed promptly, in a language which he understands and in detail, of the nature and cause of the accusation against him;

ECHR, Art. 6 § 3(a)

[2. . . . During the proceedings, every person is entitled, with full equality, to the following minimum guarantees:]
(b) prior notification in detail to the accused of the charges against him:

ACHR, Art. 8 § 2(b)

Article 6 § 3(a) guarantees every accused the right 'to be informed promptly, in a language which he understands and in detail, of the nature and cause of the accusation against him'. Article 14 § 3(a) of the ICCPR is almost identical—the order of the words differs without changing the sense, and instead of 'accusation' the term 'charge' is used. Finally, Article 8 § 2(b) of the American Convention uses a somewhat simplified formula: it guarantees the right to 'prior notification in detail to the accused of the charges against him.'

B. The Origins of the Guarantee

This guarantee originated in the *travaux préparatoires* of the ICCPR and was first proposed by Mr Ingles (Philippines) and incorporated into the text adopted at the end of the fifth session of the (UN) Commission on Human Rights in June 1949.[1]

The guarantee evokes that protected by Article 5 § 2 which dictates that information must be provided as to the reason for a person's arrest, including 'any charge against him'.[2] There is general agreement that the fair-trial guarantee requires more precise information.[3]

C. The Purpose of the Guarantee

The purpose of this clause seems clear: the right to defend oneself can only be exercised effectively, i.e. with a minimum of chances of success, if the accused knows what he or she is accused of.[4] Otherwise, a Kafkaesque situation arises.

Sufficient time is also needed to summon witnesses for the defence in the exercise of the right under Article 6 § 3(d).[5]

If one looks closely at the case-law, however, two different approaches can be found, a functional one and an abstract or absolutist one.

1. The Functional Approach

The functional approach to Article 6 § 3(a) is focused on the role of information for the preparation of the defence. It only covers such information as is necessary, or at least useful, for the accused's case.[6] From this perspective, Article 6 § 3(a) is practically superfluous. There can be no doubt that information is an essential 'facility' for the preparation of the defence. It is therefore entirely covered by sub-paragraph (b). The fact that it stands at the head of paragraph 3 can be explained by the fact that it is, chronologically, the first facility needed for the defence at the trial. It is certainly of particular importance, because the practical application of the functional approach means that there can be no violation of Article 6 § 3(a) unless it has been shown that the accused, due to missing, misleading, or otherwise insufficient information, was hampered in his or her defence.

2. The Absolutist Approach

The absolutist approach sees Article 6 § 3(a) as a guarantee which stands alone, independent of the other guarantees. A violation could be found even in the

---

[1] Weissbrodt (2001) 49; only the reference to 'detail' was still missing at that time.

[2] ICCPR, Art. 9 § 2, ECHR, Art. 5 § 2; different wording is used in Art. 7 § 4 of the ACHR. See further Chapter 18 below.

[3] Chiavario (2001) N 7.1; Harris, O'Boyle, and Warbrick (1995) 251; Merrills and Robertson (2001) 119; Nowak (1993) Art. 14 N 38; Ovey and White (2002) 181; Starmer (2001) N 7.44.

[4] Here lies the essential difference to the right to information upon arrest which serves the purpose of permitting the arrestee to challenge his or her deprivation of liberty, Harris, O'Boyle, and Warbrick (1995) 250.   [5] Weissbrodt (2001) 113.

[6] Frowein and Peukert (1996) Art. 6 N 175; Gollwitzer (1992) Art. 6 N 162; Stavros (1993) 171; Villiger (1999) N 496.

absence of evidence that better information would have increased the defence's possibilities of success. This approach introduces a humanitarian touch to the Convention. It takes into account the anxiety created by the introduction of criminal proceedings.

3. The Case-law

The case-law stemming from Article 6 § 3(a) of the ECHR clearly betrays a functional approach. This can be seen in two features of the reasoning.

First, the Court regularly comments on whether the alleged insufficiency of the information had a damaging effect on the defence. Thus, in *Sipavicius*, it said that the circumstances 'certainly impaired his ability to defend himself'.[7]

Second, the functional approach is also manifest in the Court's approach to examining the proceedings 'as a whole'. With regard to the issue of information the Court has accepted that shortcomings at first instance can be healed, or remedied at the appeal stage, provided that the court of appeal is competent to review the case in its entirety as to both fact and law and to pass a new judgment.[8] This contrasts, for example, with the ruling in *De Cubber*[9] which concerned the impartiality of a judge—even a full appeal could not remedy the deficiencies of the first-instance trial. One can infer from this difference that the Court regards a trial before a court which does not fulfil the requirements of Article 6 § 1 as null and void, whereas a trial where the defence was not correctly informed of the accusation still retains a certain value.

4. Assessment

I would not go so far as to state that the Court's interpretation of the Convention is wrong, but the absolute approach is clearly preferable.[10] The requirement of establishing particular difficulties for the defence due to shortcomings in the information puts the Court in an awkward role. It will assume, *ex hypothesi*, the position of a defence counsel and compare different strategies and lines of arguments. In envisaging alternatives it forms an opinion as to their validity. The Court is not equipped to do this, it simply lacks the necessary professional skill and experience.

More generally, an instrumentalization of the rights of the defence tends to make the task for applicants too difficult. This is clearly demonstrated in *Artico*.

---

[7] *Sipavicius* v. *Lithuania*, § 29. See also *Mattoccia* v. *Italy*, § 71: 'the defence was confronted with exceptional difficulties'; *Sadak* v. *Turkey*, § 55; and *Pélissier and Sassi* v. *France*, § 60: 'the defences would have been different'.

[8] *Dallos* v. *Hungary*, §§ 55, 56; *Lakatos* v. *Hungary*, decision of 20 Sept. 2001, unreported. See also *Sipavicius* v. *Lithuania*, § 33. In *T* v. *Austria*, § 31 the prerequisites were not fulfilled.

[9] *De Cubber* v. *Belgium*, § 33.

[10] In the same sense, see Stavros (1993) 172, who points out that the text does not require prejudice.

In this case, the applicant had been deprived of the assistance of counsel and the Italian Government argued that in order to violate Article 6 § 3(c) 'the lack of assistance must have actually prejudiced the person charged with a criminal offence'. The Court rightly replied 'that here the Government are asking for the impossible . . . Above all, there is nothing in Article 6 § 3(c) indicating that such proof is necessary . . . the existence of a violation is conceivable even in the absence of prejudice'.[11] In my view, this argument is equally applicable to Article 6 § 3(a).

The Court would therefore be justified in finding a violation whenever the obligation to inform the accused as to the charge had not been correctly fulfilled, irrespective of whether this had detrimentally affected the defence's case.

D. Two Aspects of the Guarantee

The right to be informed of the charge has two different aspects. The first and primary one concerns the right of the defence to receive the information immediately—or at least early enough in the course of the proceedings—of the allegations which they must meet. Seen from another angle, this corresponds to the maxim '*nemo iudex sine actore*'.

The second aspect is a logical consequence of the first—once the information has been communicated, the charge cannot be modified unless there is a new communication and a sufficient period of time to allow the defence to adapt to the new situation. This principle is also known as the 'principle of immutability'.[12] It is quite possible that under domestic law a court is not bound by the legal qualification given to the incriminated conduct by the public prosecutor, but this only shifts the duty to inform from the latter to the former—if any such change is being envisaged, the court must inform the defence and adjourn the hearing to allow them to adapt their defence to the new accusation.[13]

Examples relating to this latter aspect are to be found in the judgments of *Chichlian and Ekindjian* v. *France* (settled in Court), *Gea Catalàn* v. *Spain*, *Pélissier and Sassi* v. *France*, *Dallos* v. *Hungary*, *Sadak and others* v. *Turkey*, and *Sipavicius* v. *Lithuania*.

E. The Structure of the Guarantee

The structure of Article 6 § 3(a) is not complicated. It contains elements of substance and elements of form. With regard to the substantive requirement, the information must describe in detail the 'charge' or 'accusation', and more particularly its 'nature' and 'cause'. As to form, the text requires that the language be adapted to ensure that the accused can understand it and there is the element of time expressed by the word 'promptly', which turns out to be quite enigmatic.

---

[11] *Artico* v. *Italy*, § 35.
[12] See e.g. Hauser and Schweri (2002) § 50 N 8 et seq., § 82 N 13.
[13] *Pélissier and Sassi* v. *France*, § 50 and § 62.

II. ELEMENTS OF SUBSTANCE

A. The Term 'Charge'/'Accusation'

The Covenant and the ACHR require information on the 'charge', whereas the ECHR refers to the 'accusation'. Does this difference have any significance? In other words, does Article 6 § 3(c) apply to the indictment or also to the 'charge' in the narrow sense of the word? The formulation in the English text calls for a comparison with the respective duties to inform someone deprived of her or his liberty of any charge against them. Here, all three instruments use the term 'charge'.[14] It seems legitimate to assume in relation to the ECHR that the difference in terminology denotes a difference in meaning, although, in fairness, it must be admitted that the French text of the ECHR uses the same word, '*accusation*', throughout.

In my view, two phases of the proceedings must be distinguished. At an early stage, a criminal investigation is formally opened. Technically, in the Anglo-Saxon system of criminal procedure, this is expressed by the term 'charged'. The charge determines the direction and the aim of the investigation. At a later point in time, once the investigation or inquiry comes to a close, the question arises whether the suspicion against a person is sufficiently strong to justify court proceedings. This decision, in American criminal procedure, is entrusted to a grand jury.[15] The grand jury will decide upon an 'indictment'. This document sets the programe for the trial, it is the 'accusation' in a more formal understanding of the term.

This indictment, in my view, is the 'accusation' which the guarantee refers to, while 'any charge' in Article 9 § 2 of the ICCPR, Article 5 § 2 of the ECHR, and Article 7 § 2 of the ACHR refers to the 'charge' in the technical sense, the formulated suspicion which directs the investigation. It is not quite evident what line is followed by the Court.

1. The Case-law

The European case-law on this issue is not very clear. The first judgment in which Article 6 § 3(a) was held to have been violated was *Brozicek*.[16] The applicant, a German national living in Germany, had been arrested in Italy for having removed ornamental flags of a political party. When the police intervened there was a struggle in which an officer was wounded. Half a year after these events, the Public Prosecutor's Office opened an investigation and informed the applicant by letter in Italian of the prosecution. Mr Brozicek wrote back (in German) that he did not understand Italian and requested a translation

---

[14] ICCPR, Art. 9 § 2; ECHR, Art. 5 § 2; ACHR, Art. 7 § 4.

[15] In most American states the District Attorney can bring capital crimes directly before the court; Schmid (1993) 58. See e.g. *US* v. *Broce* 488 US 563 (1989).   [16] *Brozicek* v. *Italy*.

into German or 'one of the international official languages of the United Nations'. Two-and-a-half years later, the Public Prosecutor's Office sent another letter, again written in Italian, to the applicant. Like the first letter, it was labelled '*communicazione giudiziaria*' (judicial notification). The applicant was asked to provide an address in Italy where documents could be sent to. It was disputed whether this letter had ever reached Mr Brozicek. The trial was finally held *in absentia* and the applicant was convicted.

Quite obviously, this was not a fair trial and it would have been simple to find a violation of Article 6 § 1,[17] possibly in connection with the right to defend oneself under Article 6 § 3(c). However, the Commission and Court both found a violation of Article 6 § 3(a).

Both the judgment and the Commission's report under Article 31 contain a passage which could be read as giving an answer to the question we have set out to answer. In the judgment we read: 'The Court notes that this document constituted an "accusation" within the meaning of Article 6 (see the *Corigliano* judgment of 10 December 1982, Series A no. 57, p. 14, § 35)'.[18] The report states: 'The Commission considers . . . that "accusation" (or "charge") must be understood within the meaning of the Convention'.[19] This is another example of 'autonomous' interpretation. It means no more than that the domestic definition is not decisive, but it does not refer to a specific meaning of the term 'accusation'. In my view it cannot be read as implying that the two terms are synonymous.

It is furthermore helpful, in order to understand these sentences, to follow the reference and to recall that the *Corigliano* judgment dealt with the problem of length of proceedings. The Court had to determine the point in time at which the relevant period starts. It is the moment when the applicant is first 'substantially affected' by proceedings brought against him;[20] in both *Corigliano* and *Brozieck* the situation of 'being charged' began following delivery of the '*communicazione giudiziaria*'. The Court, in *Corigliano* quite rightly rejected the Government's argument that the period to be assessed only started with the bringing of formal 'charges' against the defendant, i.e. the moment at which he was indicted. Having regard to the time often taken by preliminary invest-igations, it would have been quite incompatible with the scope of the right to a 'speedy trial' to exclude that period during which the person concerned already suffers from the uncertainty about his or her fate, from the period which Article 6, by setting out the right to trial 'within a reasonable time', aims to keep as short as possible.

The issue in *Brozicek* bears no resemblance to that problem. Actually, there was no reason to determine the meaning of 'accusation' as the applicant had neither been informed of charges brought against him nor of any indictment.

---

[17] Cf. the separate opinion of Mr Nørgaard, ibid., p. 36, as well as *Colozza* v. *Italy* and *Rubinat* v. *Italy*. [18] Ibid., § 38.
[19] Ibid., § 70.   [20] *Corigliano* v. *Italy*, § 34.

The Strasbourg authorities emphasized that the applicant fell to be regarded as being under a 'criminal charge' within the meaning of Article 6 § 1. At any rate, *Brozicek* does not answer the question whether 'accusation' and 'charge' mean the same thing.

The Court seems to have answered this question in *Lutz*: 'The Court . . . proceeded on the basis that in using the terms "criminal charge" (*accusation en matière pénale*) and "charged with a criminal offence" (*accusé, accusé d'une infraction*) the three paragraphs of Article 6 referred to identical situations'.[21] However, the issue is again the applicability of Article 6 as such. The judgment does not exclude a differentiating approach to the two notions.

In sum, the case-law has not yet provided a clear answer to this question.

2. The Opinions of Legal Scholars

Legal scholars tend to regard the 'charge' rather than the 'indictment' as the object of the guarantee in Article 6 § 3(a), although none, of course, would deny that the information contained in the indictment is also a necessary requirement of a fair trial.

Van Dijk and van Hoof say that the information must be given 'as soon as it has been decided to institute criminal proceedings . . . However, the defence may be of great importance already in the phase preceding the ultimate decision as to whether or not to institute proceedings, and may affect this decision, so that it results from the rationale of paragraphs 3(a) and 3(b) that even before this formal decision the accused must be kept informed as fully as possible of the suspicion against him'.[22] This opinion is shared by Velu and Ergec.[23] Stavros[24] derives inspiration from the HRC which has held that the information must be given 'as soon as the charge is first made by a competent authority', i.e. 'when in the course of an investigation a court or an authority of the prosecution decides to take procedural steps against a person suspected of a crime or publicly names him as such'.[25] Of course, it must be recalled that the Covenant does not distinguish between 'charge' and 'accusation'.

Harris, O'Boyle, and Warbrick establish a strong link between Article 5 § 2 and Article 6 § 3(a).[26] In their view, the latter provision 'is reduced in importance for a suspect who is under arrest because of the reasons available to him by virtue of Article 5(2) and the fact that the difference in the detail required under the

---

[21] *Lutz* v. *Germany*, § 52. The Court referred to *Öztürk* v. *Germany*, §§ 50, 54. See also Soyer and de Salvia (1995) 269.

[22] Van Dijk and van Hoof (1998) 345 et seq. Jacot-Guillarmod (1993) 400 simply 'assumes' that Art. 6 (3)(a) 'applies to the preliminary investigation phase of the procedure (in French, "instruction préparatoire")'. In the same sense, see Esser (2002) 440; Gollwitzer (1992) Art. 6, N 163; Nowak (1993) Art. 14 N 39; Starmer (2001) N 7.43.

[23] Velu and Ergec (1990) N 581.   [24] Stavros (1993) 64.

[25] Para. 8 of its General Comment on Article 14.

[26] Harris, O'Boyle, and Warbrick (1995) 251.

two provisions is, as they have been interpreted, not great'. The authors conclude that '[s]uch a ruling leaves little room for the distinction that should exist between Articles 6(3)(a) and 5(2)' and suggest that the question of detail could be tackled more effectively under Article 6 § 3(b).[27]

Vogler[28] seems to follow a dynamic approach. He requires the communication to the accused not only of those decisions by which the criminal prosecution is opened or a formal charge is brought, but also of the decision to start preliminary police investigations, with reasons and as soon as possible. Apparently, Vogler has more in mind than the one-off conveyance of information on the nature and cause of the accusation, namely a continuous flow of information, consisting at least of notification of every decision by which the criminal proceedings are brought one step further. The same view is held by other authors writing in German.[29]

Charrier seems to take a different approach; according to him the information is usually provided with the communication of the indictment ('*acte d'accusation*').[30]

In essence, then, it may be said that legal writers tend to be rather vague about the substance which must be covered by the information but want it to be given as early in the course of the proceedings as possible. I fully approve of the tendency to make the Convention protection as effective as possible and agree that early involvement of the defence, by keeping it informed, is of paramount importance. Nevertheless, in my view Article 6 § 1(a) must be given a more specific meaning.

3. Assessment

My starting point in interpreting Article 6 § 3(a) is the rule of *effet utile*, i.e. it must be presumed that a specific clause in a statute or a treaty was adopted with the intention to give it some effect. If there is a choice between two ways of interpretation and one renders the clause redundant, the other must prevail.

According to Article 5 § 2, every person who is arrested must be informed promptly of the reasons for the arrest, including 'any charge against him'. To the extent that Article 6 § 3(a) is supposed to apply at the same time, it becomes redundant. There is no need for another duty to inform. On the other hand, if Article 6 § 3(a) were to be interpreted as giving a right to information at a very early stage of the proceedings, the repetition of the obligation, except for the reference to detail, with regard to those suspects who had been arrested would be incomprehensible. In that case, Article 5 § 2 would become entirely pointless.

Furthermore, it must be stressed that Article 6 § 3(a) requires information *in detail*. This means that the information must set out the accusation in a precise

---

[27] Ibid., 252.   [28] Vogler (1986) Art. 6 EMRK N 477.
[29] Frowein and Peukert (1996) Art. 6 N 175; Gollwitzer (1992) Art. 6 N 166; Zweifel (1992/93) 453 et seq.   [30] Charrier (2002) Art. 6 N 70.

and reliable way. At the beginning of an investigation this is not possible. It is the very purpose of the inquiry and investigation to gather sufficient information in order to be able to decide whether and for what offences a person is to be brought to trial. These details are known at the end of the investigation, at the point when the indictment is drafted. Only at this point in time are the details of the accusation known. Now, they have to be formally brought to the cognizance of the accused and counsel.

This does not necessarily imply that there is no right to information during earlier stages of the proceedings. But that right concerns the file, not the charge. The right of access to the file is one of the main 'facilities' mentioned in Article 6 § 3(b)—there is no need for a supplementary guarantee.

For these reasons the object of the information under Article 6 § 3(a) is the indictment.[31] Weissbrodt, commenting on the ICCPR, stresses that the information must also cover the place and time of the trial.[32] This is not necessarily what is covered by Article 6 § 3(a). It is information contained in the summons to the trial which may or may not be part of the indictment. On the European continent it is definitely not: it is the court which organizes the trial and the presiding judge who will issue the summons.

Notwithstanding my conviction that the information mentioned in Article 6 § 3(a) is that which is contained in the indictment, comprehensive information may of course already be provided at an earlier stage of the proceedings, for example, with the warrant of arrest.[33]

B. 'Nature and Cause' and 'Detail'

The accused must be informed in *detail of the nature and cause* of the accusation. Nature and cause refer to the facts and the legal qualification of the accusation against a person.[34] The language does not make this clear, but it is intrinsically obvious. It is equally obvious that the information must be clear and correct.[35]

Two important limitations of the right to be informed must be acknowledged. For one, there is a right to information, but not to a warning. To the extent that the '*Miranda* warning' is considered to be included in the right to a fair trial it cannot be based on Article 6 § 3(a) or the similar provision in the other instruments. On the other hand, the information does not have to stipulate on which evidence the accusation is based.[36] This may, however, be a requirement

---

[31] In *Kamasinski* v. *Austria*, §§ 79, 80, the Court referred expressly to the 'indictment'. For the same opinion, see Linke (1971) 402; cf. furthermore Esser (2002) 442; Stavros (1993) 174 et seq.

[32] Weissbrodt (2001) 113.

[33] As was the case in *Sacramati* v. *Italy* Application No. 23369/94.

[34] *Chichlian and Ekindjian* v. *France*, Report of the Commission, § 50, with reference to earlier decisions.   [35] Stavros (1993) 169 et seq.

[36] *Sacramenti* v. *Italy* Application 23369/94; *X* v. *Belgium* Application 7628/67. Harris, O'Boyle, and Warbrick (1995) 251; Jennings (2001) N 14.9; van Dijk and van Hoof (1998) 464.

of the right to the facilities which are necessary for the preparation of the defence and for the adversarial character of the proceedings.[37]

1. With Regard to the Facts

The incriminated conduct must be identified with precision: what is the accused alleged to have done, what was his conduct, when did the facts take place, where, possibly also with whom? An illustrative case is *Mattoccia* where the driver of a school bus was accused of having sexually abused a mentally handicapped girl. In this judgment the Court observed that 'the information contained in the accusation was characterised by vagueness as to essential details concerning time and place, was repeatedly contradicted and amended in the course of the trial, and . . . fairness required that the applicant should have been afforded greater opportunity and facilities to defend himself in a practical and effective manner, for example by calling witnesses to establish an alibi'. The Court therefore could not 'see how the evidence gathered at trial could be sufficient, given that the "cause" of the accusation had been changed at a stage . . . when the applicant could no longer react to it other than on appeal.'[38] This passage also illustrates the Court's tendency to take an 'integrated approach'—defects of information as required by Article 6 § 3(a) are combined with considerations taken from Article 6 § 3(b) and (d) as well as the general element of fairness.

It seems necessary, at this point, to express a warning. While, as a rule, particularly in cases concerning a single offence or a small number of offences, precise indications as to time and place can be given,[39] such expectations can become highly unrealistic in cases of criminal behaviour which extends over a certain amount of time. For instance, a father may be accused of having sexually abused his daughter over a period of several years, or a person could stand accused of drug dealing over months or years. In such a case many details will have been forgotten, whereas, on the other hand, the gist of the accusation may be entirely evident. In this case the reference to detail loses much of its relevance. The degree of precision required will also depend upon the domestic regulations in substantive and procedural law.

2. With Regard to the Law

The case-law presents more examples of insufficiencies in relation to information as to the legal requirement than in the factual field. Violations have been found in cases where the conviction did not correspond to the indictment. The first such case ended with a friendly settlement before the Court after the

---

[37] See e.g. *Fitt* v. *United Kingdom*, § 44; *Papageorgiu* v. *Greece*, § 36.
[38] *Mattoccia* v. *Italy*, §§ 70, 71.
[39] See also Esser (2002) 438, with a critical comment on *Steel* v. *United Kingdom*. For further examples, see Villiger (1999) 498.

Commission in its report had concluded that there had been a violation.[40] The Court rightly found a violation in *Pélissier and Sassi* where the applicants had been accused of criminal bankruptcy, but were convicted of aiding and abetting criminal bankruptcy.[41] The essential element was the finding that 'aiding and abetting did not constitute an element intrinsic to the initial accusation'.[42] In *Dallos*, 'aggravated embezzlement' had become 'fraud',[43] in *Sadak* 'treason against the integrity of the State' was changed to 'belonging to an armed organisation set up for the purpose of destroying the integrity of the State',[44] and in *Sipavicius* the accusation of 'abuse of office' was changed to 'official negligence'.[45] In these cases, however, no violation was found because there had been a full rehearing on appeal which had served to cure the defects of the first trial.

On the other hand, applications where the indictment mentioned an offence while the conviction was limited to attempting to commit an offence were rejected. The Commission correctly followed the domestic courts in finding that the two were in fact 'one single offence . . . committed in two different ways'.[46] This, however, only works one way. If someone is accused of attempting to commit an offence, a conviction for the completed offence would not be acceptable, because in that case the result and the nexus of causality have to be established which require additional evidence.

The domestic law of criminal procedure may provide for the possibility of an alternative accusation—for example, a person who was found in possession of stolen goods may be accused of either theft or receiving stolen goods. This is not contrary to the right to a fair trial as it does not impair the possibilities of the defence.[47]

Two applications raised issues which could also have been considered under the *nullum crimen sine lege* aspect, in that they alleged insufficient precision of the offence. One concerned 'mutiny',[48] the other 'breach of the peace'.[49] In the first case the Court just referred to the possibility that the applicants would have had to receive additional information at a hearing, in the second it did not address the issue. In another decision the Commission stressed that the accused could reasonably foresee that his conduct 'might be considered as being contrary to the Media Act'.[50] Such argument has no place in the context of Article 6 § 3(a).

Finally, in two cases against Spain the Commission and Court had differing views. In both cases the problem consisted of the fact that the indictment had

---

[40] *Chichlian and Ekindjian* v. *France* (report); the court of appeal had altered the legal classification.   [41] *Pélissier and Sassi* v. *France*, §§ 55–62.

[42] Ibid., § 61.   [43] *Dallos* v. *Hungary*, § 48.

[44] *Sadak and others* v. *Turkey*, §§ 51, 52.   [45] *Sipavicius* v. *Lithuania*, §§ 29, 30.

[46] *KL* v. *United Kingdom* Application 32715/06 and *Shahzad* v. *United Kingdom* Application 34225/96.   [47] Haefliger and Schürmann (1999) 220; Stavros (1993) 170.

[48] *Campbell and Fell* v. *United Kingdom*, § 96.

[49] *Steel and others* v. *United Kingdom*, § 84.

[50] *Nederlandse Omroepprogramma Stichting* v. *Netherlands* Application 15844/90.

not, at least not clearly, mentioned the aggravated form of the offence for which the applicant had been convicted.[51] The Court missed an opportunity to enhance the protection offered to the defence by Article 6 § 3(a) in these cases. Particularly in *Salvador Torres* the legal situation seems to have been far from clear, even though, *ex post*, it might appear less confusing.[52] In it the Supreme Court applied a qualification on its own initiative. It concluded that 'Mr de Salvador is a civil servant and that he took advantage of his position in order to commit the offence of which he was found guilty. Therefore ... the aggravating circumstance in Article 10 para. 10 must be applied'. The question was whether the defendant could have foreseen that the qualification would be applied despite the fact that it had neither been applied by the tribunal at first instance nor referred to by the public prosecutor's office.

Even assuming that a clerical error occurred in the drafting of the indictment, a sensible interpretation of Article 6 § 3(a) requires that it be strictly applied and that the defendant is not expected to do intelligent guesswork. The consequence of errors must be borne by those who commit them—it is not acceptable that the defendant pay for errors made by the prosecution.

C. A Right 'To Be Informed'

Article 6 § 3(a) grants a right 'to be informed'. If one reads these words in isolation, they can mean one of two things: first, that the accused is entitled to *have* the information—from whatever source; second, that the authorities are obliged to give the relevant information to the defendant—and one will add that this has to be done automatically. If one looks at the text of the disposition, it becomes obvious that it means the second alternative. This is expressed by the word 'promptly'. The case-law, however, does not adhere to this logical argument—it even suggests that the essential element of the guarantee lies in the first variant. The Court does not ask whether the authorities fulfilled their duty, but whether the defendant had the information necessary for her or his defence—or perhaps, even less satisfactorily, whether the accused could have obtained the relevant information.

In *Pélissier and Sassi*, this was finally denied, but the Court discussed the question whether the lawyer for the injured party had raised the alternative charge, aiding and abetting criminal bankruptcy, with sufficient clarity. It considered 'that the mere fact that the civil party's additional submissions were made available at the Court of Appeal's registry could not suffice, by itself, to satisfy the requirements of paragraph 3(a) of Article 6 of the Convention'.[53] By implication it can be assumed that the Court would have accepted as sufficient

---

[51] *Gea Catalàn* v. *Spain*. The applicant had been charged with the offence under paragraph 1 of Article 529 of the Criminal Code, but was convicted under paragraph 7—the Court, contrary to the Commission, considered that this discrepancy was due to a mere clerical error.

[52] *De Salvador Torres* v. *Spain*, §§ 8–12.   [53] *Pélissier and Sassi* v. *France*, § 55.

the information of the private party had it been served on the defence. This could only be accepted if, in the domestic law of criminal procedure, the private party had the right to correct or supplement the indictment.

In other cases, it was regarded as being sufficient that the accused had been interrogated on the subject. Thus, in *Kamasinski*, the Court found that the applicant 'had been questioned at length and in the presence of interpreters about the suspected offences, firstly by the police and then by the investigating judges... On this basis alone he must have been made aware in sufficient detail of the accusations levelled against him'.[54]

Generally, the accused is expected to take steps in order to learn about the indictment. In one case he was responsible for his ignorance because he had not made sure his letterbox would be emptied during his absence.[55] Mr Campbell refused to attend the hearing before the Board of Visitors where he could have obtained the information due.[56] In another case, the Commission expressed serious doubts as to whether the indictment was sufficiently detailed, but declared the application nevertheless inadmissible because the defence had in fact addressed the issue which was not clearly mentioned in the indictment.[57]

Again, we find a rather restrictive interpretation of Article 6 § 3(a). The guarantee is interpreted in a simply functional perspective—instead of insisting on a clear act of the authorities which informs the defendant in a reliable way of the accusations against him or her, the Court lets it suffice if the accused, with due diligence, had the possibility of acquiring the information necessary for his or her defence, or if a circumspective strategy of the defence had in any case covered the point which was missing in the information.

Still, the Court accepts that there are limitations to what can be expected from a defendant. Especially when an accused is abroad, the authorities must employ the necessary diligence in order to make sure he or she receives the information.[58] One also finds strong statements which tend to support our view: the duty to inform 'rests entirely on the prosecuting authority's shoulders and cannot be complied with passively by making information available without bringing it to the attention of the defence'.[59] This, in fact, appears to be the correct approach. It is also the approach taken by the UN Committee.[60]

---

[54] *Kamasinski* v. *Austria*, § 80. See also *Y* v. *Germany* Application 11777/85; *Kozlov* v. *Finland* Application 16832/90; *Kuibishev* v. *Bulgaria* Application 39271/98.

[55] *Hennings* v. *Germany.* See also *Salinga* v. *Germany* Application 22534/93.

[56] *Campbell and Fell* v. *United Kingdom*, § 96.

[57] *Rabenseifer* v. *Austria* Application 24154/94 and *Stoitchkov and Shindarov* v. *Bulgaria* Applications 24571/94 and 24572/94. For references to earlier case-law, see Trechsel (1979) 344, n. 19.

[58] See e.g. *T* v. *Italy*, §§ 28, 29; also *Colozza* v. *Italy* where the accused could not be found within the country due to a lack of diligence on the part of the authorities.

[59] *Mattoccia* v. *Italy*, § 65.   [60] *Mbenge* v. *Zaire*, p. 134.

III. ELEMENTS OF FORM

There are two requirements of form mentioned in Article 6 § 3(a): that the information must be 'in a language which [the accused] understands' and that it be given 'promptly'. First, however, we shall address the general question—is any form prescribed for the indictment? More specifically, must the information be given in writing?

A. Must the Information be Given in Writing?

As to the manner in which the accused must be informed, the Covenant and Convention texts are both silent. The case-law of the ECtHR seems to be contradictory. On the one hand, in stereotypical form it repeats that 'Article 6 § 3(a) does not impose any special formal requirement as to the manner in which the accused is to be informed of the nature and cause of the accusation against him'.[61]

On the other hand, in the same judgment, in the previous paragraph, we find the following statement: 'The provisions of paragraph 3(a) of Article 6 point to the need for special attention to be paid to the notification of the "accusation" to the defendant. Particulars of the offence play a crucial role in the criminal process, in that it is from the moment of their service that the suspect is formally put on written notice of the factual and legal basis of the charges against him.'[62] The reference to *written* notice had already appeared in *Kamasinski*.[63] In between these two judgments, the word 'written' was omitted in decisions on Article 6 § 3(a).[64] Was *this* a 'mere clerical error'? One would not expect anything of the kind in a judgment of the Court. One must therefore conclude that the Court itself is hesitating.

The two passages in *Kamasinski*, one speaking of 'written notice', the other one affirming that no formal requirements exist, are difficult to reconcile. Perhaps the reference to 'written notice' must be read as a factual reference to domestic law where, in fact, there had been a written indictment. But that had also been the case in *Pélissier and Sassi*. So why would the word be omitted there?

Again, in another judgment the Court seems to insist on at least some formality. 'To inform someone of a prosecution brought against him is, however, a legal act of such importance that it must be carried out in accordance with procedural and substantive requirements capable of guaranteeing the effective exercise of the accused's rights, as is moreover clear from Article 6 para. 3 (a) of the Convention'.[65]

---

[61] *Sipavicius* v. *Lithuania*, § 30; see also *Pélissier and Sassi* v. *France*, § 53; *Kamasinski* v. *Austria*, § 79. That no written information is required was also said in *Harward* v. *Norway* Application 14170/88; *Hayward* v. *Sweden* Application 14106/88; and *Mortensen* v. *Denmark* Application 24867/94.   [62] *Sipavicius* v. *Lithuania*, § 27.

[63] *Kamasinski* v. *Austria*, § 79.   [64] *Pélissier and Sassi* v. *France*, § 51.

[65] *T* v. *Italy*, § 28.

This case-law is particularly unsatisfactory—it gives the impression of a certain disorientation.[66] The Court shies away from setting clear guidelines and requirements. In my view it would be time to state clearly that every accused must be served with a written indictment containing the necessary information.[67] There might be room for exceptions—for example, the translation could be made orally—but the fundamental importance of such information requires the insistence on a formal document.

B. The Language

The information must be given 'in a language which [the accused] understands'. These words are, in my view, superfluous—actually, the ACHR does not have a parallel phrase. The very term 'information' implies the use of a language which the accused can understand. On the other hand, there is the fundamental right to the services of an interpreter for an accused who cannot understand or speak the language used in court.[68] Finally, the protection against discrimination on the basis of language could be invoked.[69] Some importance may lie in the negative aspect that it need not be his or her own language. This may have some importance in multilingual countries where tensions across the language barrier exist.

The first case in which the Court found a violation actually concerned this problem as Mr Brozicek (who was unable to understand Italian) was informed in Italian of the accusation against him. Although he drew attention to this problem, no translation was provided—as he was convicted in his absence and without having been properly summonsed nor ever heard on the charges, there was a clear violation of Article 6.[70]

In *Kamasinski* there was no formal translation, but the Court concluded from circumstantial elements that the applicant had been sufficiently informed.[71]

C. 'Promptly'

The information under Article 6 § 3(a), must be given 'promptly (*'dans le plus court délai'*). Here, again, the formulation found in the ACHR is, in my view, preferable. It speaks of 'prior notification'. The term 'promptly' causes problems because it means 'within a short lapse of time', which, in turn, raises the further question: after which event? This question leads us back to the issue discussed

---

[66] In *Nielsen* v. *Denmark* Application 343/57, the Commission had adopted a more formal stance; see Stavros (1993) 172 et seq.

[67] In the same direction, see Esser (2002), 438; for cases with a certain complexity, see Haefliger and Schürmann (1999) 220.   [68] See Chapter 12 below.

[69] ICCPR, Art. 2 § 1; ECHR, Art. 14; ACHR, Art. 1 § 1.

[70] The Court only concluded that there was a violation of Art. 6 § 3(a); *Brozicek* v. *Italy*, § 41. According to later practice it might well have added Art. 6 § 1 as well as Art. 6 § 3(b) and (c).

[71] *Kamasinski* v. *Austria*, § 80.

above. In my view the sub-paragraph refers to the indictment. Therefore, this document must be served on the defence as soon as it has been prepared. This is also the opinion expressed in a General Comment by the HRC.[72]

At any rate, if one looks at the purpose of the guarantee, the lapse of time between the drafting of the indictment, and its communication to the defence is of relatively little interest for the defence.[73] What is decisive is set out in sub-paragraph (b): sufficient time for the preparation of the defence. So, it is the time span between the communication of the indictment and the beginning of the trial, or between any change in the legal qualification of the conduct in issue and the final pleadings, which is decisive.

This is not exclusive of any other right to be informed of the course of the proceedings—such information forms part of the 'facilities' to which an accused is also entitled under sub-paragraph (b). In fact, the obviously close connection between the two guarantees is often referred to in the case-law[74] and in scholarly writing.[75] The pragmatic approach of the Court means that it neglects its task to clarify the meaning of the Convention in an effort to reach an acceptable solution in the specific case before it, and it prefers a vague reference to the proceedings as a whole and to fairness in general to the meticulous analysis of each guarantee which we attempt to give in this book.

[72] Compilation of General Comments and General Recommendations Adopted by Human Rights Treaty Bodies, UN Doc. HRI\GEN\1\Rev. 1 at 14 (1994).

[73] Esser (2002) 440 is critical of the fact that the Court accepted a 'delay' of ten hours in *Steel*, an opinion which it is difficult to follow.

[74] See e.g. *Albert and Le Compte* v. *Belgium*, § 41; *Mattoccia* v. *Italy*, § 71; *Pélissier and Sassi* v. *France*, §§ 54, 62, 63 etc.

[75] See for many others, Harris, O'Boyle, and Warbrick (1995) 252; Reed and Murdoch (2001) N 5.118; Stavros (1993) 186.

Chapter 9

Adequate Time and Facilities

I. INTRODUCTION

This chapter will begin with a few general observations on the character of Article 6 § 3(b) of the ECHR and its relative nature. This will be followed by an examination of the right to adequate time and adequate facilities to prepare the defence. The two limbs are not entirely unrelated: the more 'adequate' the facilities for the preparation of the defence are, the longer the defence will need to use them effectively.

A. The Texts

[3. In the determination of any criminal charge against him, everyone shall be entitled to the following minimum guarantees, in full equality:] . . .
  (b) to have adequate time and facilities for the preparation of his defence and to communicate with counsel of his own choosing;

ICCPR, Art. 14 § 3(b)

[3. Everyone charged with a criminal offence has the following minimum rights:] . . .
  (b) to have adequate time and facilities for the preparation of his defence;

ECHR, Art. 6 § 3(a)

[2. . . . During the proceedings, every person is entitled, with full equality, to the following minimum guarantees:] . . .
  (c) adequate time and means for the preparation of his defence

ACHR, Art. 8 § 2(b)

These texts are largely identical. The ACHR uses the term 'means' rather than 'facilities', but this cannot be interpreted as representing an intention to give the guarantee a different meaning. The Covenant adds a reference to the right to contact with counsel, which is certainly a valuable 'facility'. It shall be dealt with in the context of the right to counsel.

B. The Origins of the Guarantee

It is no coincidence that the texts of the right to adequate time and facilities in the ICCPR and the ECHR are identical. It was not part of the original draft of the ICCPR, but was included following a suggestion from the Secretary-General[1] and a British proposal based on the text of Article 6 § 3(b) of the ECHR.[2] The remainder of the provision was added on the basis of a proposal from the Israeli delegate, Mr Baror.[3]

C. The Purpose and Importance of the Guarantee

The right to adequate time and facilities for the preparation of the defence is located inconspicuously in Article 6 § 3(b) among the specific rights of a person charged with a criminal offence, between the right to be informed of the charge and the right to defend oneself or be assisted by counsel. Yet, if we look for an indication of what facilities are deemed to be necessary for the preparation of the defence, we find Article 6 § 3 full of possibilities: the right to be informed of the nature of the charge (sub-paragraph (a)),[4] the right to counsel (sub-paragraph (c)),[5] the right to summon and question witnesses (sub-paragraph (d)),[6] and the right to the services of an interpreter (sub-paragraph (e))[7] can all be regarded as 'facilities'. Furthermore, the right to adequate time for the preparation of the defence is in substance also guaranteed by sub-paragraph (a). Moreover, if one looks at Article 6 § 1 one can identify as an essential element of fairness the right to be heard and to have the opportunity to put one's arguments relating to both fact and law effectively before a tribunal. Again, this could be seen as a 'facility' for the preparation of the defence.[8] It is of no surprise therefore that this guarantee 'does not appear to have been clearly defined in the case-law'[9] and indeed it would be unrealistic to expect sharp definition here. Thus it would be understandable to conclude that Article 6 § 3(b) resembles an overarching right to a fair trial.

Still, in practice, the role of Article 6 § 3(b) is rather modest.[10] It would be more appropriate to regard it as a 'subsidiary', a general guarantee which will only be invoked to the extent that none of the other specific guarantees apply.

---

[1] Weissbrodt (2001) 62.   [2] Ibid., 66.   [3] Ibid., 72.

[4] See, in particular, *Pélissier and Sassi v. France*, § 54 at 63; *Mattoccia v. Italy*, § 60 et seq.; *Dallos v. Hungary*, § 47.

[5] See e.g. *Melin v. France*, § 21; *S v. United Kingdom* Application 12370/86, where the Commission found that the refusal of legal aid did not have a negative effect on the rights guaranteed by Art. 6 § 3(b).

[6] In *Mattoccia v. Italy*, § 71 the Court found a violation of Article 6 §§ 1 and 3(a) and (b), although one of the reasons was that the applicant had not been able to call witnesses!

[7] *Caresana v. United Kingdom* Application 31541/96; *Harvard v. Norway* (HRC).

[8] This aspect is dealt with by the Court in the context with the issue of 'adversarial procedure', e.g. *Foucher v. France*, § 34.   [9] Stavros (1993) 185; Corstens and Pradel (2002) N 357.

[10] Ovey and White (1996) 182; Sudre (2003) when dealing with the specific rights of the defence under Art. 6 § 3 does not even mention it; see pp. 261 et seq. The Court has so far found ten violations of Art. 6 § 3(b) (*Campbell and Fell v. United Kingdom; Hadjianastassiou v. Greece; Domenichini v. Italy; Vacher v. France; Pélissier and Sassi v. France; Mattoccia v. Italy; T v. Austria; Sadak and others v. Turkey; GB v. France; Lanz v. Austria*) and just one friendly settlement was reached (*Chichlian and Ekindjian v. France*).

There is, perhaps, one exception to this rule. While we are going to discuss the right of access to and free communication with counsel in the context of Article 6 § 3(c), this matter is often dealt with both in legal writing and in the Strasbourg case-law as a 'facility' within the meaning of sub-paragraph (b).[11] This may be explained, *inter alia*, by the fact that the ICCPR mentions the right 'to communicate with counsel of his own choosing' in Article 14 § 3(b) which otherwise corresponds to Article 6 § 3(b) of the ECHR. Most writers also stress the close relationship between sub-paragraphs (b) and (c).[12] However, the Court now seems to be altering its approach: in *Brennan* v. *United Kingdom* the matter was dealt with as part of the right to counsel.[13] One cannot help but assume that there is an element of chance in determining whether the matter will be discussed in the light of one Article or the other; much depends on which one the applicant chooses to invoke. This is another example of the lack of coherence in the Court's jurisprudence. There is even a third Convention guarantee which might be applied: in *Erdem* v. *Germany*, where a suspected PKK terrorist complained about interference with his correspondence with counsel, the issue was dealt with under Article 8.[14]

While, at first sight, this may look like a typically professorial discussion, it is not without practical importance. This stems from the fact that the guarantees of Article 6 § 3(b) and (c) differ in one fundamental respect. As we shall see, sub-paragraph (b) contains a 'relative guarantee'—i.e. the applicant must show some degree of prejudice. The right to be assisted by counsel, on the other hand, can be regarded as an absolute guarantee which makes it considerably easier to establish a violation.[15] It is interesting to note, however, that in *Domenichini* v. *Italy* the Court dealt with a problem of correspondence between accused and counsel exclusively under Article 6 § 3(b) without any reference to sub-paragraph (c), but also without any hint as to whether the interference might have caused difficulties for the defence.[16]

---

[11]   The leading case on this is *Can* v. *Austria*, report of 12 July 1984. See also *Campbell and Fell* v. *United Kingdom*, § 99. More recently, in *Domenichini* v. *Italy*, the Court found a violation of Art. 6 § 3(b) because a letter written by the applicant to counsel on the subject of his appeal had been intercepted by the authorities—the Commission had examined the case under paras. (b) and (c) and found a violation of 'Article 6 § 3'. See also *Lanz* v. *Austria*, where the Court examined the issues arising under 6 §§ 3(c) and 3(b) together. The Court will often examine an application under the general provision of Article 6 § 1 on the basis that the 'requirements of paragraph 3 of Article 6 constitute specific aspects of the right to a fair trial, guaranteed under paragraph 1'; *Hadjianastassiou* v. *Greece*, § 31; *Melin* v. *France*, § 21; *Bricmont* v. *Belgium*, §75. Again, in *Campbell and Fell* v. *United Kingdom*, the issue of unsupervised contact was considered under Art. 6 § 1.

[12]   Barreto (1999) N 9.2.2; Chiavario (2001) Art. 6 N 7.2: Danelius (1997) Ch. 7; van Dijk and van Hoof (1998) 465; Frowein and Peukert (1996) Art. 6 N 183; Gollwitzer (1992) Art 6 N 175, 177; Haefliger and Schürmann (1999) 223; Harris, O'Boyle, and Warbrick (1995) 254; Merrills and Robertson (2001) 122; Corstens and Pradel (2002) N 357; Villiger (1999) N 503; Vogler (1986) N 481 et seq.   [13]   *Brennan* v. *United Kingdom*.

[14]   *Erdem* v. *Germany*; this was convenient, because it made it easier for the Court to apply a test of proportionality.   [15]   See Chapter 10, section III below.

[16]   *Domenichini* v. *Italy*.

D. The Relative Character of the Guarantee

1. The General Relativity

The wording of Article 6 § 3(b) indicates quite clearly that this is a 'relative' guarantee. If an accused has been acquitted, there can be no violation.[17] When examining whether there has been a violation, the Court will be tempted to look at whether the applicant would also have been convicted if he or she had had been granted more time or facilities to prepare the defence, namely those facilities that the defence had requested. In other words, the applicant must show 'actual prejudice'.[18] This places an almost unbearable burden on the applicant. How could he or she, except in very rare circumstances, be able to bring evidence for such a hypothesis? There are no absolute standards dictating which facilities or how much time must be at the disposal of the defence—'no hard and fast rules'[19] should be expected.[20] The determination of whether there has been a violation will take place on a case-by-case basis: 'The manner in which Article 6 applies clearly depends upon the special features of the proceedings involved'.[21]

It is understandable that Harris, O'Boyle, and Warbrick use rather vague language on the issue of proving prejudice: 'actual prejudice might need to be shown'.[22] Stavros proposes a complex solution: 'The question which the Convention organs should ask themselves is whether one factor . . . could be reasonably expected to limit, in the circumstance of the case, the opportunity of the defence to present its case. Proof of specific prejudice should be required from the accused where the answer is negative'.[23]

The task is not made easier by the fact that there is a clear difference between the French and the English texts. The English version states that 'adequate' time and facilities are required, while the corresponding term in French text is '*nécessaire*'. If one looks at the official translations of the Convention, one will generally find terms which would perhaps best be translated into English by the word 'sufficient';[24] in French, '*suffisant*'.

In my view, there is also a difference in substance between the two versions. The French text uses the stricter term, which would narrow the scope of the guarantee: there would only be a violation if it were shown that without the time

---

[17] *X* v. *Austria* Application 2291/64; *S* v. *United Kingdom* Application 12370/86.

[18] Harris, O'Boyle, and Warbrick (1995) 253, 255, with reference to *X* v. *United Kingdom* Application 4042/69, and *Murphy* v. *United Kingdom* Application 4681/79.

[19] Starmer (2000) N 7.72; see also Stavros (1993) 178.

[20] Stavros (1993), however, comes to the conclusion that Art. 6 § 3(b) falls to be subdivided in two parts: advance knowledge of the prosecution's case and access to evidence favouring the defence are considered to be 'absolute' guarantees. While this approach merits support *de lege ferenda* and, perhaps, as a postulate for a more evolutive interpretation of the Convention, it cannot be said to reflect the current law.   [21] *Vacher* v. *France*, § 24.

[22] Harris, O'Boyle, and Warbrick (1995) 255.   [23] Stavros (1993) 186.

[24] e.g. German: '*ausreichend*'; Italian: '*necessarie*'; Spanish: '*adecuados*'; Ukrainian: '*гостатньо*'; Russian: '*гостаточньо*'.

and/or facility requested, the defence would not have had any prospect of success. If one were to follow the French text, the applicant would indeed have to show that he could not defend himself without the time and facilities requested, whereas the English text leaves room for a more flexible approach. It would be enough to show that the chances of the defence would have been much better, had the request been granted. The difference is a rather subtle one, but it is important, in my view, to give preference to the English version which provides for a more effective protection of the defence.[25]

The case of *Foucher* v. *France* is a useful example. The Court was confronted with the opinion of the French *Cour de Cassation* stating that 'the European Convention for the Protection of Human Rights and Fundamental Freedoms did not require that the case file be made available to the defendant himself . . .'.[26] It was sufficient that it was put at the disposal of his counsel. The Court answered by highlighting three important elements of fact: the applicant did not have counsel but had chosen to defend himself; there had been no preliminary investigation and, therefore, no issue of confidentiality of the investigation arose; and his conviction had been based on a warden's official report which was 'good evidence in the absence of proof to the contrary'. The Court, like the Commission, therefore considered that it was important for the applicant to have 'access to his case file and to obtain a copy of the documents it contained in order to be able to challenge the official report concerning him'.[27]

The result of this judgment—the finding of a breach of Article 6 § 1 taken together with Article 6 § 3[28]—is certainly correct. However, the reasoning calls for criticism. Let us leave aside, for the moment, the rule that access to the file can be restricted to counsel—we shall return to that issue. By mentioning the preliminary proceedings the Court implies that the confidentiality of the investigation might justify the denial of access to the file. In this general formulation, such a proposition is certainly unacceptable. The third point consists, if one considers its deeper meaning, of an evaluation of the evidence in the present criminal case by the Court. The Court found that what was in the file was important to the defence's case and therefore the latter should have had access to the file. On the other hand, the Court did not go so far as to examine the file in detail and to determine whether access to it would have led to a more favourable outcome for the applicant. In this respect the Court has not exhausted

---

[25] In a rather early case, the Commission showed a very restrictive approach. Admittedly, parts of the file had gone missing. The Commission not only guessed that the situation had also become more difficult for the prosecution, but suggested that 'the applicant failed to show that the evidence which had disappeared contained anything which was likely to undermine the correctness of the court's basic assumption and which would therefore have required the taking of even further evidence . . .', Application 8770/79.

[26] As quoted in *Foucher* v. *France*, § 32. Later, the *Cour de Cassation* adopted a more liberal attitude; ibid., § 37.   [27] Ibid., §§ 35 et seq.

[28] There is no reference here to one of the specific sub-paragraphs; obviously the Court wanted to avoid having to decide between sub-paras. (b) and (c). It is not improbable that the judges could not agree either.

all the possibilities which a narrow interpretation of Article 6 § 3(b) might open. The Commission, using the more restrictive approach, rejected an earlier application on the basis that the applicant had not shown that the scarcity of time available for the preparation of the hearing had actually constituted a handicap.[29] Stavros suggests that the applicant must make a *prima facie* case 'that the evidence held by the prosecution could be of some assistance for his defence'.[30] This, in my view, is too narrow. It is certainly not in line with the idea of equality of arms.[31]

In this case the Court's approach is to be preferred—it is clearly closer to the English text and sufficiently realistic in the sense that it does not seem extravagant to request that the defence prove that the time or facility refused was of some importance.

2. The Specific Relativity

It is obvious that apart from the general notion of relativity there is also a specific element. The amount of time and the type of facilities required in order to ensure compatibility with Article 6 § 3(b) will depend on the specific facts of each case.

An indication of the standards required can be drawn from the Court's jurisprudence. In one case, for example, an applicant claimed that the police had taken away documents that he had prepared for his defence. The application was declared inadmissible because there was no indication that the material was actually used against him.[32]

As we shall see, this relativity is particularly evident with regard to the time element. In each case the tasks faced by the defence and the amount and complexity of work will have to be examined.[33] The stage of the proceedings may also be of importance.[34] Moreover, there may be many different facilities which could assist the defence. One facility which will normally be required is access to the file. Details fall to be discussed in the context of both 'time' and 'facilities'.

There may also be a certain relativity linking the necessity of a particular facility to the chances of the outcome of the proceedings. This might be inferred from a decision of the Commission in a case where the applicant had complained of insufficient access to legal materials to prepare his appeal; the decision declaring the application inadmissible for being manifestly ill-founded may have been influenced by the fact that his counsel had considered there to be no chance of success.[35]

---

[29] *X* v. *Austria* Application 2370/64; this is criticized by Trechsel (1979) 356. See also Frowein and Peukert (1996) Art. 6 N 180. [30] Stavros (1993) 179.

[31] See Chapter 4, section III above.

[32] *François* v. *United Kingdom* Application 11058/84.

[33] See e.g. Frowein and Peukert (1996) Art. 6 N 180.

[34] *X* v. *Belgium* Application 7628/76. [35] *Ross* v. *United Kingdom* Application 11396/85.

3. The Diligence Required from the Defence

With regard to both time and facilities, a certain degree of diligence on the part of the defence is expected and indeed required. The defence can only complain of a violation of their rights if they did everything required by the domestic law to obtain the respective (extension of) time or facility.[36] In *Melin* v. *France*, the Court, by five votes to four, concluded that the applicant was to blame for the fact that he had not been able to present a memorandum.[37] The principle requiring some diligence merits approval. It resembles the requirement of exhaustion of domestic remedies and also corresponds to the subsidiary character of the Convention. Its application to the *Melin* case, however, must be criticized.[38]

Mr Melin complained that he was not served with the judgment that he had appealed against to the court of cassation, nor had he been informed of the date of the hearing. The Court, contrary to the Commission,[39] considered that the applicant, a lawyer, ought to have consulted the original judgment of the Court of Appeal of Versailles at the registry, repeated his request for a copy of the judgment, or made enquiries at the court of cassation's registry.[40]

In my view, the Court definitely put an excessive burden of diligence on Mr Melin. He had appealed to the court of cassation against a judgment, the reasons for which he had not been told, he had not been informed of the proceedings, in particular of the date of the hearing and the observations of the civil party.[41] It would seem clear, however, that in criminal proceedings such information must be given *ex officio*.

The Court showed more understanding in *Vacher* v. *France*, where the applicant was not a lawyer.[42] In this case it refers to the "'diligence" which the Contracting States must exercise to ensure that the rights guaranteed by Article 6 are enjoyed in an effective manner'.[43] It seems that the burden of diligence has shifted from the applicant to the respondent government and this is far more satisfactory. Like the indictment, the judgment against which an appeal is open must be served *ex officio* on the prospective appellant. In a way, this situation can even be compared to the communication of the details of the accusation which is

[36] *X* v. *United Kingdom* Application 8386/78; *Ross* v. *United Kingdom* Application 11396/85; Renucci (2002) N 123, p. 193. The same requirement applies under the ICCPR; see *Steadman* v. *Jamaica; Harward* v. *Norway; Junior Leslie* v. *Jamaica.*   [37] *Melin* v. *France*, § 25.
[38] For a critical comment regarding excessive demands of diligence made by the Commission in the *Jespers* v. *Belgium* case, see Stavros (1993) 180.
[39] The Commission decision had been unanimous.
[40] A very similar issue arose in *Zoon* v. *Netherlands*; the Court noted that the applicant had heard the operative part of the judgment at the hearing and could have looked at an abridged version of the reasoned judgment at the registry of the Regional Court of Rotterdam. This judgment merits the same criticism as *Melin.*
[41] Dissenting opinion of Judges Bernhard, Pekkanen, Baka, and Wildhaber.
[42] *Vacher* v. *France.*   [43] Ibid., § 28.

regulated in Article 6 § 3(a).[44] In *Vacher* the Court noted that '[p]utting the onus on convicted appellants to find out when an allotted period of time starts to run or expires is not compatible with the "diligence" which the Contracting States must exercise to ensure that the rights guaranteed by Article 6 are enjoyed in an effective manner'.[45] The Court also noted that the Code of Criminal Procedure had been amended in the meantime because so many appeals had been dismissed for want of grounds of appeal.

Unfortunately, as *Zoon* came some four years after *Vacher*, the improvement achieved there seems not to have really indicated a new attitude of the Court.

It amounts to *venire contra factum proprium* if the applicant complains of the absence of a facility he has himself made impossible. This was the case in *Bricmont* v. *Belgium*, where the applicant complained of the absence of an audit. The Court agreed that it would have been helpful to have one, but pointed out that 'the applicants themselves had alleged that most of the transactions had been carried out without any accessible banking records being made, through companies which observed a rule of secrecy. The Belgian courts could thus reasonably have believed that such an audit would not have served any useful purpose'.[46]

On the other hand, only such diligence which offers a reasonable prospect of success is required. In *Foucher* the Government argued that the applicant ought to have asked for the file; however, the Court of Cassation had said that the Convention did not require access to the file.[47] Therefore, the request would have been without any effect.

The duty to make use of all the possibilities under domestic law in order to obtain the facilities considered necessary for the defence is very close to the obligation to exhaust domestic remedies. In *Vilhunen* v. *Finland* this was in fact the reason why the application was declared inadmissible—the defence had neither questioned the alleged lack of facilities before the District Court nor requested an adjournment.[48]

II. THE RIGHT TO ADEQUATE TIME

A. The Purpose of the Guarantee

It may appear rather fatuous to examine the aim of the right to 'have adequate time . . . for the preparation of his defence', as the text itself mentions the purpose: to allow for the preparation of the defence and to prevent a 'hasty

---

[44] It is true that the Court noted that in Dutch law the appeal is not against the first-instance judgment but against the charge brought against the accused (§ 48); yet, this does not diminish the importance of that judgment as regards the elaboration of the grounds of appeal.

[45] *Vacher* v. *France*, § 28.   [46] *Bricmont* v. *Belgium*, §§ 90 et seq.

[47] *Foucher* v. *France*, § 32.   [48] *Vilhunen* v. *Finland* Application 30509/96.

trial'.[49] In most cases, this does not give any material for discussion. However, there are many different ways to use time. People with a keen interest in their work will often need much less time to complete a task than those who are bored by what they are supposed to do. Conversely, perfectionists will take much more time to accomplish their work than less scrupulous workers.

What we are dealing with here is, to a considerable extent, the amount of time to be allotted to lawyers. The exercise of this profession is characterized by considerable flexibility, especially as regards the preparation of the defence. While there are certainly a number of standard minimum acts to perform, such as studying the file, some lawyers will be well acquainted with the law; others will need time to freshen up their knowledge. Some will prepare pleadings in writing, others will plead from notes and, as a consequence, need less time for the preparation of their pleadings. The law cannot be individualized, however, to take account of such particularities. Adequacy must therefore be assessed on the basis of an average standard. This means that the guarantee must give a lawyer the amount of time which can reasonably be considered to be sufficient for the average lawyer. Thus, the guarantee also protects a lawyer from being put under excessive pressure. In other words, it would not be fair to assess the 'adequate time' entirely *in abstracto* on the assumption that counsel can devote all of his time, e.g. twelve hours a day, for the preparation of this specific defence.

B. The Relation of the Guarantee to the Other Rights of the Defence

1. The Relationship to Article 6 § 1, the Right to Trial 'Within a Reasonable Time'

A cursory glance at the Convention, immediately shows an apparent contradiction between Article 6 § 1, which guarantees the right to trial 'within a reasonable time', and Article 6 § 3(b) which grants 'adequate time' for the preparation of the defence. The general guarantee calls for speed, the specific one protects against speed. A number of authors have commented on this.[50] Of course, there is no contradiction between Articles 6 § § 1 and 3. The priority lies clearly with the *lex specialis* of Article 6 § 3(b). In the case-law concerning the length of proceedings, the exercise of the right to prepare the defence has never even been considered as a possible excuse for a violation.

2. The Relationship to the Principle of 'Equality of Arms'

Occasionally, 'equality of arms' is mentioned in connection with the right to adequate time for the preparation of the defence.[51] This can only mean that the same amount of time must be available to the defence and to the prosecution. It is obvious that such a comparison is devoid of any justification as far as the

---

[49] *Kröcher and Möller* v. *Switzerland* Application 8463/78.
[50] Harris, O'Boyle, and Warbrick (1995) 252 et seq.; Chiavario (2001) Art. 6 N 7.2.
[51] e.g. *U* v. *Luxemburg* Application 10142/82.

proceedings up to the judgment of first instance are concerned.[52] Equality is conceivable with regard to time limits for the filing of an appeal. Yet, even here some differences may be justified at this stage of the proceedings. It must be borne in mind that the public prosecutor's office may be a complex institution in which decisions on whether to appeal a judgment or not must be agreed upon by several officers. Furthermore, the public prosecutor may make his decision as to whether or not to appeal dependent upon whether the defendant files an appeal. When this was examined by the Commission it focused narrowly on the facts of the specific case—*inter alia* it noted that the prosecutor had only used part of the extra time provided for by law.[53] The latter argument is entirely without merit; as a rule, the defence will not suffer any notable disadvantage if the time limit for the prosecution is longer than its own.

As to 'facilities', the Commission was satisfied that equality of arms was secured in a case where evidence had been lost at the prosecution's office: it stressed that the missing elements could also have assisted their cause.[54]

3. The Relationship to Article 6 § 3(a)

The link between Article 6 §§ 3(b) and 3(a) is particularly strong.[55] Sub-paragraph (a) also refers to the time element—the earlier an accused is informed about the charge, the more time he has for the preparation of the defence. In fact, violations of Article 6 § 3(b) with regard to the time element were only found in cases where Article 6 § 3(a) applied as well. This was the case in *Pélissier and Sassi* v. *France* and, more recently, in *Sadak* v. *Turkey*. The relevant text in the judgments is identical—I shall discuss the issue referring to *Sadak*.

The applicants were former members of the DEP party. They complained, *inter alia*, of the fact that the charge against them was changed at the last court hearing. Initially they were charged with supporting separatism and being a threat to national integrity; immediately before pronouncing the judgment, the Security Court informed them of the new charge of belonging to an illegal armed organization.[56] According to the Court, the applicants were entitled to the time necessary to adapt their defence to the revised charge, which could in no way be regarded as identical to the original one.[57]

It seems rather far-fetched to apply Article 6 § 3(b) to this case because the applicants did not have any possibility and no time at all for the preparation of a

---

[52] In the same sense, see Gollwitzer (1992) Art. 6 N 183.

[53] *X* v. *Germany* Application 441/58. In *U* v. *Luxembourg* Application 10142/82, the Commission envisaged a violation 'if the inequality as regards time for entering an appeal was so shocking that of itself it could constitute a violation of the right of access to the courts, the principle of equality of arms or the right to have the same facilities for preparing one's defence'.

[54] Application 8770/79.

[55] *Pélissier and Sassi* v. *France*, § 54; *Sadak and others* v. *Turkey*, § 50; see also *Mattoccia* v. *Italy*.

[56] *Sadak and others* v. *Turkey*, § 44; Reed and Murdoch (2001) N 5 121; van Dijk and van Hoof (1998) 464.   [57] *Sadak and others* v. *Turkey*, § 57.

defence against the revised charge—the violation of Article 6 § 3(a) is manifest. The Court did, however, refer to Article 6 § 3(b) in its arguments. What happened in both cases furthermore constitutes a flagrant violation of the right to be heard, which is one of the most fundamental elements of the right to fair trial. Technically, the Court took a different approach from that of the Commission in *Chichlian and Ekindjian* v. *France*.[58] Although Article 6 § 3(b) had also been raised by the applicants and is mentioned under 'points at issue',[59] the Commission limited itself to an examination under Article 6 § 3(a) which it found to have been violated. In fact, each time there is a violation of Article 6 § 3(a), paragraph 3(b) is necessarily violated as well—a sheer matter of logic. On the other hand, there are many possibilities whereby there could be a violation of the latter guarantee without there being any problem with regard to the former.

4. The Relationship to Article 6 § 3(c)

The connection[60] between Article 6 § 3(b) and (c) is much less obvious. In fact, it is of a practical rather than jurisprudential character.[61]

If one looks at the case-law, one will find that problems that relate to the time element of Article 6 § 3(b) have arisen mainly in the context of legal assistance. Thus, in a very early application, the problem which led to limited time for the preparation of the defence was mainly caused by a rule applying to appeal proceedings which required that a new lawyer be appointed at each stage.[62] Many other cases have concerned a change of lawyers because of objective reasons[63] or because the applicant dismissed him shortly before the trial[64] or because of the belated appointment of legal aid counsel.[65] On the other hand, in *Goddi* v. *Italy*, where legal-aid counsel was only appointed at the beginning of the trial, sub-paragraph (b) was not even mentioned.[66]

C. What Constitutes 'Adequate Time'?

1. The Relevant Period

When examining the question of whether adequate time for the defence was granted, different criteria have to be taken into account. If one looks at the issue from some distance and with an effort to find answers of a general character, one

---

[58] *Chichlian and Ekindjian* v. *France*, Report of 29 Nov. 1989, Series A, 162-B, § 14 et seq. (the case was later settled and struck off the list by the Court).   [59] Ibid., § 47.

[60] Van Dijk and van Hoof (1998) 465.   [61] Cf. *Lanz* v. *Austria*.

[62] *Köplinger* v. *Austria* Application 1850/630.

[63] Such as problems with the lawyer's health; see *X* v. *Austria* Application 11255/84.

[64] Application 6404/73; *X* v. *Austria* Application 8251/78—in this case the Commission suspected the applicant of having speculated on receiving an adjournment, whereas the lawyer appointed on the first day of the trial had not asked for the opening to be postponed.

[65] *X and Y* v. *Austria* Application 7909/77; Frowein and Peukert (1996) Art. 6 N 180.

[66] However, *Goddi* v. *Italy* is mentioned in connection with this by Starmer (2000) N 7.75.

must first try to find out which period to look at. In cases concerning the length of the proceedings (Article 6 § 1) or the duration of detention on remand (Article 5 § 3), it is relatively easy to fix the points in time when the relevant period starts and ends.[67] However, with regard to the requirement of 'adequate time' to enable the preparation of the defence, this is not possible. When Harris, O'Boyle, and Warbrick say that the guarantee 'begins to run from the moment that a person is subject to a criminal charge',[68] they are right in the sense that it is not restricted to the trial or appeal stage; however, the 'charge' does not mark the beginning of a period in the way that it does under Article 6 § 1. In *Hadjianastassiou* v. *Greece* the applicant had five days to present his appeal. However, this time limit ran from the moment that the judgment was read out, even though the reasons had not been finally drafted. Therefore, the period referred to in Article 6 § 3(b) had not even begun at that time.[69]

The relativity of the term 'adequate' is dictated by the extent to which different approaches are required for different phases of the proceedings: 'The time necessary to prepare a defence must indeed be estimated on a different basis at the various stages of the proceedings'.[70] Also, there is not *one* period of time needed for the defence, but there will be a succession of such instances, in particular, but not exclusively, in the context of appeals. As we are dealing with the entire proceedings, it seems appropriate, to examine the whole process from the point at which the proceedings are concluded, i.e. in reverse order.

The last period in proceedings is the time needed for the preparation of the ultimate hearing on appeal.[71] Prior to this there is the period for the preparation of the appeal, at least in cases where reasons have to be given. In this case, 'time and facilities' appear as a whole. The preparation will generally have to be based on the text of the judgment against which the appeal is directed. Yet, it would not be correct to speak of simply one period of a certain number of days. The appeal can, to a certain degree, be prepared on the basis of the operative part of the judgment and the reasons given orally when judgment is pronounced. The least that can be said is that there will have to be some time permitted to enable the defence to take the fully reasoned written judgment into account.

If we go back to the first instance, some time must be allotted for the preparation of the trial hearing, but also for comments on the act of indictment to be made, if the procedural law allows for such comments to be filed. In *Padin Gestoso* v. *Spain*, the Court noted that the 'investigation of the case continued for several years, so that the applicant had sufficient time, after being served with the

---

[67] See Chapter 6, section II above and Chapter 19, section III below.
[68] Harris, O'Boyle, and Warbrick (1995) 253.   [69] *Hadjianastassiou* v. *Greece*, § 34.
[70] *Herbert Huber* v. *Austria* Application 5523/72; *X* v. *Belgium* Application 7628/76; *X and Y* v. *Austria* Application 7909/74; see also Frowein and Peukert (1996) Art. 6 N 179; Reed and Murdoch (2001) N 5 121, with reference to *X* v. *Belgium* Application 7628/76.
[71] In *X* v. *Germany* Application 441/58, the Commission stressed that contrary to the opinion of the German courts, including the Constitutional Court, Art. 6 § 3(b) also applied to appeal proceedings.

decision to charge him of 11 June 1990, for the preparation of his defence, which is the main purpose of Article 6 § 3(b) of the Convention'.[72] There is no requirement that an accused should have 'adequate' time to prepare habeas corpus proceedings, as it is for the detainee to determine when he wants to apply.

Furthermore, some preparation time must also be granted *after* certain occurrences. Generally it can be said that every time the situation changes in a relevant way, the defence must have an opportunity to react and have the necessary time to prepare its reaction. The most important example of this is a change in the charge,[73] but it could also be a new piece of evidence, for example, a new witness,[74] or, on the contrary, the disappearance of a witness. Whenever there is an opportunity for the defence to act in any way, some time must be at its disposal in order for it to prepare its response.

2. The Assessment of What is 'Adequate'

When determining whether the time allowed was 'adequate' for the preparation of the defence, one will tend to look at the case-law. What one finds, however, is a series of decisions in which periods of between one day and more than a year are at issue.[75] This makes it extremely difficult to draw any particularly useful conclusions or guidance from those decisions. For one, without exception, they all find that there was no violation. Only in cases where the defence was denied time to react to a change of the indictment, have the Strasbourg authorities found a violation of the right to adequate time.

It is true that the decisions refer to the number of pages or files to be studied, to the complexity of the case, to prior experience and familiarity with the case, but even with those indications the dominating impression one gains from reading them is that of an almost unconstrained vagueness. One issue is more specific: the relationship between the time at the disposal for the defence and rules of the domestic law. In one case, the Commission found no violation even

---

[72] *Padin Gestoso* v. *Spain* Application 39519/98.

[73] Cf. *Pélissier and Sassi* v. *France; Hadjianastassiou* v. *Greece; Sadak* v. *Turkey; Sipavicius* v. *Lithuania*.

[74] *X* v. *United Kingdom* Application 5327/71. See also *GB* v. *France*, where the applicant complained that the alteration of a witness's testimony during the trial was incompatible with Art. 6 § 3(b).

[75] A few examples: *Campbell and Fell* v. *United Kingdom*, § 98 (one day to study the file, five days to prepare the hearing); *S* v. *United Kingdom* Application 11821/85 (four days to study witness statements); Application 11255/84 (one week); *Perez Mahia* v. *Spain* Application 11022/84 (ten days); *Herbert Huber* v. *Austria* Application 5523/72 (two weeks to file an appeal); *Albert and Le Compte* v. *Belgium*, § 41 (fifteen days for the preparation of a disciplinary hearing); *X and Y* v. *Austria* Application 7909/74 (seventeen days [ten working days]); *Kremzow* v. *Austria*, § 45 (three weeks to study the Attorney General's position paper ['*croquis*']); *Ross* v. *United Kingdom* Application 11396/85 (twenty-nine days); *Hilden* v. *Finland* Application 32523/96 (thirty days); *Erdem* v. *Germany* Application 38321/97 (one month); *Svinarenkov* v. *Estonia* Application 42551/98 (five weeks plus the time between hearings); *Harward* v. *Norway* Application 14170/88 (more than one year).

though it expressly noted that the defence had had 'less than the "29 clear days" notice required by statute'.[76] This is difficult to accept. It is not directly contrary to the wording of Article 53,[77] but it is certainly difficult to reconcile with its spirit. If national law provides that the applicant must be afforded a certain amount of time, ought the Court not assume that any reduction of this time is contrary to Article 6 § 3(b)? Although such a conclusion is tempting, the approach merits approval. The Court is not set up to implement national legislation. The criteria it applies must be substantive, not formal, and it is not its task to watch over the correct application of domestic law.

3. Proposals

The following criteria are to be taken into account when examining the issue of adequate time:

- The complexity of the case in fact and in law, i.e. the amount of materials to be studied, files of the investigation on the one hand, textbooks, cases, and other legal materials on the other.[78]
- The degree of importance of the activity for which time is required; for example, if the defence wishes to consult files concerning previous convictions.[79]
- The importance of the step in the proceedings which is being prepared;[80] for example, more time will be needed to prepare the trial than to prepare the hearing of a witness.
- The degree to which the defence can be expected to have already had some knowledge of the matter at issue. This allows for less time the more the proceedings have progressed.[81]
- Normally, a lawyer should not be expected to work extra hours, although exceptions to this principle may be justified by the particularities of a specific case.
- When there is a change in lawyers, the full time needed for the new study of the case must be granted, unless there are grounds for an exception. (Such an exception might arise from the fact that the defendant dismisses counsel for non-compelling reasons including where he obviously aims at prolonging the proceedings.)

4. Accelerated Proceedings

Some authors address the question as to whether accelerated criminal proceedings are compatible with Article 6 § 3(b). Harris, O'Boyle, and Warbrick

---

[76] *Ross* v. *United Kingdom* Application 11396/85.

[77] 'Nothing in this Convention shall be construed as limiting or derogating from any of the human rights and fundamental freedoms which may be ensured under the laws of any High Contracting Party or under any other agreement to which it is a Party'.

[78] *S* v. *United Kingdom* Application 11821/85.

[79] Cf. e.g. *Samer* v. *Germany* Application 4319/69.   [80] Gollwitzer (1992) Art. 6 N 183.

[81] *Huber* v. *Austria* Application 5523/72; *Donnelly* v. *United Kingdom* Application 43694/98.

raise the question and leave it open.[82] Charrier, for example, thinks that with those proceedings there is a particular need to protect the rights of the defence—an argument which is not reasoned and not convincing.[83] Frowein and Peukert[84] do not see any problem as long as the defendant has the possibility of asking for ordinary proceedings, while Gollwitzer expects the court to refuse accelerated proceedings if the case presents a certain complexity.[85]

I fully agree with Frowein and Peukert. It is impossible to deal with low- and middle-range criminality without having resource to abbreviated and simplified proceedings. This is also in the interest of the accused who may save costs and time. However, as a sort of 'safety valve', there must be a possibility to ask for ordinary proceedings without any further reasons. There must also be enough time to decide whether to accept the simplified proceedings or not.

III. THE RIGHT TO ADEQUATE FACILITIES

A. Access to the File

1. General Observations

According to the Commission, 'facilities' within the meaning of Article 6 § 3(b) 'include the opportunity [for the accused] to acquaint himself, for the purposes of preparing his defence, with the results of investigations carried out throughout the proceedings'.[86] In practice this is by far the most important aspect of the 'facilities' for the defence.[87] It is, as indicated above, an aspect of the 'right to be heard'.[88] In order to answer the charges, the defence must not only be aware of the accusation,[89] but also have knowledge of the grounds on which the accusation is based.

Often this right is also described as an element of the 'equality of arms' principle. The Commission expressed this idea very clearly in *Jespers* v. *Belgium*:

As regards the interpretation of the terms 'facilities', the Commission notes firstly that in any criminal proceedings brought by a state authority, the prosecution has at its disposal, to back the accusation, facilities deriving from its powers of investigation supported by

---

[82] Harris, O'Boyle, and Warbrick (1995) 262.   [83] e.g. Charrier (2002) Art. 6 N 75.
[84] Frowein and Peukert (1996) Art. 6 N 186.   [85] Gollwitzer (1992) Art. 6 N 186.
[86] *Guy Jespers* v. *Belgium* Application 8404/78, § 56. See also *Foucher* v. *France*, § 27; *Jasper* v. *United Kingdom*, §§ 55–7; *Fitt* v. *United Kingdom*, §§ 46–50; *Rowe and Davies* v. *United Kingdom*, §§ 46–50. The earlier decision of the Commission in *X* v. *Austria* Application 7138/75 has definitely been overruled.
[87] Pradel and Corstens (2002) N 356 are of the somewhat unconvincing opinion that this right is attached to Art. 6 § 3 generally rather than to sub-para. (b).
[88] A typical example can be found in the case of *Serves* v. *France*, where a fine was imposed upon the applicant by the investigating judge for having refused to take the oath as a witness, without the applicant being heard on this issue; the Court, contrary to the Commission, considered that the fault had been remedied on appeal, with the result that there was no violation.
[89] This is covered by Art. 6 § 3(a).

judicial and police machinery with considerable technical resources and means of coercion... [i]t is... to establish... equality that the 'rights of the defence'... have been instituted. The Commission has already had occasion to point out[90] that the so-called 'equality of arms' principle could be based not only on Article 6, paragraph 1, but also on Article 6, paragraph 3, especially sub-paragraph (b).[91]

The defence ought to have the same information as the prosecuting authority.[92] To some degree, this is correct. However, a mere consideration of equality does not exhaust the right under Article 6 § 3(b); on the other hand, time and facilities may be adequate even if there remains a certain advantage for the prosecution.

The principle of equality has, in any case, not always been strictly upheld by the Strasbourg organs. In *Kremzow* v. *Austria*, for example, the alleged violation consisted of the fact that the '*croquis*' (the Attorney General's position paper) was only communicated to the defence three weeks before the hearing—of course, the prosecution authority was already very well acquainted with the document at that time. Nevertheless, the Court considered that, 'although the applicant may have been to some extent disadvantaged in the preparation of his defence, he nevertheless had "adequate time and facilities" to formulate his response to the "croquis"' and thus it did not bother about the obvious inequality.[93] Actually, it is rather obvious that the prosecuting authority will always have an advantage over the suspect,[94] with the exception of those parts of the investigation in which the defence assists. As a counter-weight, the defence enjoys the presumption of innocence.

In *Barberà, Messegué and Jabardo* the Court also attempted to establish a link between Article 6 § 3(b) and the right to be presumed innocent: 'It also follows [from Art. 6 § 2] that it is for the prosecution to inform the accused of the case that will be made against him, so that he may prepare and present his defence accordingly'.[95] However, this idea was not followed up later on—it is in fact not really convincing.

2. Four Aspects of Access to the File

I propose to examine four different aspects of the 'facility' that we are dealing with here: the right of access under the continental system; discovery under the Anglo-Saxon system; discovery of 'hidden material' under both systems; and investigation by the defence.

---

[90] Referring to *Ofner and Hopfinger* v. *Austria* Applications 524/59 and 617/59, § 46; *Patacki and Dunshirn* v. *Austria* Applications 596/59 and 789/60, § 36.

[91] *Guy Jespers* v. *Belgium* Application 8404/78, § 55. Equality of arms is also mentioned in connection with the right to access to the file in *Foucher* v. *France*, §§ 33 et seq.; *Lamy* v. *Belgium*, § 29.

[92] See also Haefliger and Schürmann (1999) 223; Harris, O'Boyle, and Warbrick (1995) 255; Merrills and Robertson (2001); Stavros (1993) 182. Reed and Murdoch (2001) N 5 121 seem to regard Art. 6 § 1(b) as the very source of the principle of equality of arms, as they refer to *Bulut* v. *Austria*, where no issue under Art. 6 § 3(b) had been raised.   [93] *Kremzow* v. *Austria*, § 50.

[94] On this point, see e.g. McConville (1991); McBarnet (1981).

[95] *Barberà, Messegué and Jabardo* v. *Spain*, § 77.

(a) Access to the file under the continental system

In the continental system with its inquisitorial preliminary phase, the investigation produces a file which will be an important element at the trial or 'main hearing' ('*Hauptverhandlung*' in the German terminology). We must keep in mind that that the hearing itself does not always, and not to the extent which is essential to the common-law system, follow the rule which is referred to as the 'principle of immediacy' ('*Unmittelbarkeitsprinzip*'). The principle means that all evidence must be produced live at the hearing. In some cases the reality is quite different. The verdict is not handed down by a jury but by professional judges, sometimes assisted by lay judges. The professional judge(s) at least will have studied the file, which ideally should have been prepared with great care during the investigation. It contains the transcripts of the interrogations of the defendant and witnesses by the police, the investigating authority, or the public prosecutor's office, expert opinions, pictures of the crime scene, maps and plans, reports on searches, and other documents as well as pieces of evidence such as *instrumenta sceleris*. The judges are familiar with all that material. The judgment will then be based on the contents of the file and the (repeated or complementary) evidence gathered during the hearing.

It is obvious that under this system advance knowledge of the file is of essential importance for the defence.

(b) Discovery under the common-law system

The situation is somewhat different under the common-law system. Normally or ideally[96]—the Diplock courts in Northern Ireland are a prominent exception—the verdict will be handed down by a jury exclusively on the basis of evidence presented 'live' at the hearing. No juror or judge will see any transcripts. The file prepared by the prosecuting authority—essentially the police—will not constitute a basis for the decision. It is merely the background which will serve as a 'programme' along which the prosecution will present the evidence.

As a consequence, contrary to the continental system, the prosecution file is not, as it were, 'on the table' of the tribunal. It is in the hands of the prosecuting authority. Nevertheless, the defence has a legitimate interest to know what to expect. They must have advance knowledge of the prosecutor's case in order to be able to oppose it effectively. However, as the file does not form an integral part of the hearing and is not in the possession of an independent and impartial authority, it seems more appropriate, in this case, to speak of 'discovery' rather than of 'access'.[97] The basic rule for proceedings in the English Crown Court is that the prosecution must disclose to the defence the evidence on which it intends to rely at the trial.[98] In *Atlan*, the Court found that 'Article 6 § 1 requires

---

[96] Although it should be noted that only about 1% of criminal cases in the United Kingdom result in a jury trial. In Scotland there are several different models of 'trial' including a summary procedure where often the case is heard by one professional judge who sits without a jury.
[97] For details, see e.g. Corker (1996).   [98] Ibid., 1–18 et seq.

in principle that the prosecution authorities should disclose to the defence all material evidence in their possession for or against the accused'.[99] The Court limited itself to examining the case under Article 6 § 1. It is true that the Commission in its early case-law took a rather restrictive view, when it said that Article 6 § 3(b) does 'not require that the prosecuting authorities should give an accused person notice of all the evidence which may be given during his trial'.[100] Today, such a finding is clearly outdated.

(c) Discovery of 'hidden material'

So far we have dealt with (timely) access to material used by the court or the prosecution at the trial. While this is essential, it is not in itself enough.

In fact, under both systems it will not be uncommon for the prosecution to be selective in deciding which material ought to figure in the file or be used at the trial. In the best case, the prosecution will only withhold material which is of no relevance at all for the case. The prosecution may 'legitimately keep a file containing personal notes and internal correspondence'.[101] Here, the Commission's view may even be a bit too restrictive.[102] The file might also contain material which, in the course of the investigation, turned out to be of no relevance at all to the proceedings, for example, interviews with persons first regarded as potential suspects, with persons who were first regarded as potential witnesses but turned out not to have made any pertinent observation, reports on fruitless searches, etc. Not to include such elements in the file may be called for in the interests of respect for private life[103] of the persons concerned and also for reasons of procedural economy.[104]

Yet, who should determine what material is relevant to the case? It may well be of considerable relevance to know that certain steps of the investigation were fruitless. This is convincingly highlighted by the case of *Edwards* v. *United Kingdom*. The applicant had not been informed that a witness who had stated that she would recognize her assailant failed to identify the applicant in a photograph, nor had he been told of the absence of fingerprints at the scene of the crime. The Court found no violation because the Court of Appeal had looked into the matter and come to the conclusion that the applicant would have been convicted anyway. Judges Pettiti and De Meyer, however, dissented.

If we look closely at the reasoning of the Court, we will find that two aspects of the argument must be distinguished. As far as the right to disclosure is concerned, the following passage is decisive: 'The Court considers that it is a requirement of fairness under paragraph 1 of Article 6, indeed one which is

[99] *Atlan* v. *United Kingdom*, § 40; see also *Rowe and Davis* v. *United Kingdom*, § 60.
[100] e.g. *X* v. *United Kingdom* Application 5282/71; for a description of these earlier developments, see Stavros (1993) 182 et seq.   [101] *Guy Jespers* v. *Belgium* Application 8404/78, § 59.
[102] For a critical appraisal, see also Stavros (1993) 179. The author seems to be surprised that the file in question was never opened by the Commission; however, the latter would not have accepted information which would have to be concealed from the applicant!   [103] ECHR, Art. 8.
[104] On this issue, see e.g. Krauss (1983) 49 et seq.

recognised under English law, that the prosecution authorities disclose to the defence all material evidence for or against the accused and that the failure to do so in the present case gave rise to a defect in the trial proceedings'.[105] It may be regretted that the Court has not been more specific, saying that full and unfettered access to the entire file prepared by the prosecuting authority forms part of the 'adequate facilities' of which Article 6 § 3(b) speaks.[106] In substance, however, it is difficult to read the passage in any other way than this: in the present case the minimum right to adequate facilities for the preparation of the defence has not been respected.

The reasons why the Court did not, in the end, find a violation of Article 6 lie elsewhere, namely in the unfortunate approach which consists of looking at the proceedings as a whole; the lack of diligence of the applicant on appeal; and the finding that 'defects of the original trial were remedied by the subsequent procedure before the Court of Appeal'. Field and Young consider that the case must be seen as an example of the differences between the adversarial and the inquisitorial model of criminal proceedings.[107] However, a number of judges voted with the majority although their 'procedural background' is clearly closer to the continental system.[108]

It is true that the Commission also found no violation in *Edwards*, but this was based on an argument which I find more solid: the applicant had in fact made a full confession.[109] This may still not be accepted as fully convincing. It could be argued that the confession was made on the basis of deception and therefore would have been inadmissible under continental law. However, no such allegation had been made.

The question remains open: who is to decide whether the file has been correctly constituted or whether parts were not included which should have been?[110]

In practice, there is hardly any control—the decision is taken by the investigating and/or prosecuting authority. However, even assuming that these authorities act in good faith, they cannot be trusted to make this important decision. As they pursue a legitimate interest, namely to obtain convictions for the authors of criminal acts, they will tend to have this purpose in mind whenever they take a decision. The defence is there to re-establish a fair balance, but it cannot fulfil this function to the extent that it ignores what its adversaries are doing.

Of course, it would be wholly unrealistic to leave this decision to the defence which is not even in theory bound to decide objectively. Nor is joint responsibility

[105] *Edwards* v. *United Kingdom*, § 36.
[106] With the exception, of course, of material which is not in any way of use for the decision of the case, in particular to the extent that it touches upon the private lives of persons not related to the case.   [107] Field and Young (1994) 264.
[108] Judges, Matscher, Russo, and Bigi.
[109] Report of 10 July 1991, attached to the judgment, § 53.
[110] On this issue, see also Trechsel (2002) 999.

conceivable. To the extent that personal information about persons not connected to the offence are concerned, there would not be any serious protection of their right to privacy.

The solution must therefore lie in vesting in a neutral authority the task of verifying whether the file is complete. Gollwitzer proposes to vest this power in the judge on the merits, which might, however, conflict with his or her impartiality.[111] In my view, it would be preferable to convey the task to the (president of the) *chambre d'accusation/Anklagekammer*, the jurisdiction charged with supervising the investigating and prosecuting authorities, where such an institution exists. An *ombudsman* would also be a possibility, or indeed the task could be conferred to a lawyers' association ('*le barreau*'). It should be possible to provide that the defence must, if it feels that there ought to be a neutral inspection of the prosecution's file, show that there are specific reasons for its distrust.

Denmark has an institution of this kind. A lawyer not otherwise involved can be appointed to protect the interests of the accused, for example, when there is an interference with that person's private life.[112]

(d) Investigation by the defence

Finally, it must also be possible for the defence to investigate. This is an obvious requirement following on from the principle of 'equality of arms'. It must be possible to interview persons who could be presented as witnesses, to look for documents and other material evidence and to call upon experts to prepare a report.

Of course, in this area the equality will be limited. In particular, the defence will not have any means of coercion. It will not, at least not under the continental system, have the possibility of formally interrogating persons as witnesses, of monitoring the correspondence—including by telephone or e-mail—of other persons, or of obtaining a search warrant, let alone an arrest warrant.

As a minimum, it must be possible for the defence to approach the prosecuting authority with a request for complementary inquiries, including the use of coercive measures. In case of refusal there must be a possibility to apply to a judicial body. The authorities may not reject such applications without solid reason, for example, when the evidence sought is irrelevant, when it is unlawful (operating a search at the premises of an embassy), when it is obviously superfluous, such as where the facts to be proven have already been established, or if the request constitutes an abuse of proceedings.[113] The difficulty arising in this context is that it may be difficult to assess whether the proposed evidence is relevant. This calls to some extent for an anticipated evaluation of the evidence. However, the request may only be refused if its irrelevance is obvious.

[111] Gollwitzer (1992) Art. 6 N 181.
[112] § 729 c stk. 5 and 784 retsplejeloven. (I owe this information to Professor Eva Smith of Copenhagen University.)
[113] Hauser and Schweri (2002) § 55 N 9; for a detailed analysis, see Pieth (1984).

There are various other obstacles which hinder the defence's ability to gather evidence. In countries following the continental system, where the gathering of evidence is regarded as a task for the authorities and the right to cross-examine at trial does not exist, any contact between the defence and a prospective witness is looked upon with suspicion. There is considerable fear of attempts to influence witnesses. Therefore, such contacts may be entirely prohibited. Another difficulty may arise with regard to international relations. In Switzerland, for example, there is an offence of carrying out activities that are matter for public authorities on Swiss territory for the benefit of a foreign state or organization.[114] As gathering evidence is considered to be to be the responsibility of the authorities, a foreign attorney questioning witnesses in Switzerland may commit that offence. However, informal conversations with the purpose of preparing an interrogation pursuant to formal proceedings for letters rogatory are permitted.[115]

3. The Modalities of Discovery and Access to the File

(a) The Object

I have already given some indication as to what the file, to which Article 6 § 3(b) gives a right of access, contains. The Commission gave the following advice: 'It matters little . . . by whom and when the investigation is carried out. In view of the diversity of legal systems existing in the states party to the Convention the Commission cannot restrict the scope of the term "facilities" to acts carried out during certain specified phases of the proceedings, e.g. the preliminary investigation . . . Any investigations [the Public Prosecutor's Department] causes to be carried out in connection with criminal proceedings and the findings thereof consequently form part of the "facilities" within the meaning of Article 6 paragraph 3(b) of the Convention'.[116] The Commission even went one step further when, in summing up, it stated that the Convention 'recognises the right of the accused to have at his disposal, for the purposes of exonerating himself or of obtaining a reduction in his sentence, all relevant elements that have been *or could be* collected by the competent authorities'.[117]

This goes clearly beyond the traditional contents of a file in that it includes 'facilities' which are not (yet) in existence but which the authorities are obliged to produce. The words 'could be' must, however, be read in conjunction with 'relevant'. It seems correct to interpret this passage as imposing a duty upon the prosecution to investigate in favour of the defence. Here, we are clearly faced with a view influenced by the inquisitorial model.[118]

However, the later case-law does not really confirm this attitude. On the contrary, as indicated above, the emphasis shifts to the diligence which must be

---

[114] SPC, Art. 271.   [115] Cf. BGE 114 IV 128.

[116] *Guy Jespers* v. *Belgium* Application 8404/78, § 56.   [117] Ibid., § 58 (emphasis added).

[118] Stavros (1993) 178 rightly sees this passage as confirmation that, here too, the state has an obligation to become active.

applied by the defence. In a number of cases, the Court has declined to find a violation as it would have been possible for the defence to take the necessary steps in order to present its evidence to the tribunal. In the same report in *Jespers*, the Commission found that it was for the defence to call as a witness a person whose statement had not been included in the file.[119]

Is it sufficient if the defence is given access to photocopies? It depends. As a rule it should be, because it is only the contents that counts. Exceptionally, however, it will be necessary to see and examine originals. If the proceedings concern a contested forgery, for instance, it may be necessary for the defence to have the possibility to submit the object to an expert.

Further, the 'file' may also contain other things besides documentary evidence. In *Bricmont* the applicant complained of the fact that he could not produce a gouache painted and dedicated to him by his adversary, the Count of Flanders. The Court found no violation but did not in any way indicate that this object was not, in principle, covered by the right under Article 6 § 3(d).[120]

Sometimes a difference is made between 'evidence favouring the case of the defence' and other evidence.[121] The right of access is considered to be particularly important with regard to the former. I do not regard this as a useful distinction. For one, it is hard to tell whether an element will or will not favour the defence. For instance, it may be favourable to know the identity of a witness whose deposition will be negative, but whose credibility is weak. On the other hand, it is exclusively a matter for the defence to decide whether it has an interest in any item of the file. It is true, however, that denial of full access will not normally lead as such to the finding of a violation of the Convention, because it must be shown that the material was at least of some use to the defence. This is a weakness inherent in the text of the Convention. The Court would have a way to strengthen its case-law if it were to adopt a maxim which it has applied when deciding whether a judge could be regarded as impartial: that 'appearances matter'.[122] It is in fact entirely unsatisfactory if it is only possible to ascertain after the conclusion of the proceedings whether or not the refusal of access to parts of the file was contrary to Article 6 § 3(b).

Another approach, which in my view is too narrow, is taken by Haefliger and Schürmann[123] who speak of 'evidence' ('*Beweismittel*') important for the defence. However, it may also be necessary to have access to material which cannot be used as evidence but might lead to evidence. On the other hand, they merit approval when they state that information which had not previously been seen by the defence may only be used as evidence if the defence had at least the opportunity to get acquainted with its essential contents.

---

[119] *Guy Jespers* v. *Belgium* Application 8404/78, § 64.

[120] *Bricmont* v. *Belgium*, §§ 92 et seq. See also *Donnelly* v. *United Kingdom* Application 43694/98 (inadmissible).   [121] e.g. Stavros (1993) 181 et seq.; Villiger (1999) N 502.

[122] See e.g. *Hauschildt* v. *Denmark*, § 48; *Thorgeir Thorgeirson* v. *Iceland*, § 51; *Incal* v. *Turkey*, § 71; *Pullar* v. *United Kingdom*, § 38.   [123] Haefliger and Schürmann (1999) 225.

(b) Who has Access to the File?

A question which has been dealt with in several cases concerns the beneficiary of the right. Is it sufficient if access is only granted either to the accused or to counsel?

This question was already answered by the Commission in 1960, when it said that 'the rights guaranteed by Article 6, paragraph (3) are both those of the accused and of the defence in general; . . . a defending counsel, whether the legal representative of the accused or simply a person acting on his behalf, is entitled *mutatis mutandis* to the rights mentioned in the said paragraph (3) since these rights are intended to ensure the proper defence of the accused; as a consequence, . . . in order to determine whether the right to have adequate time and facilities for the preparation of the defence has been respected, account must be taken of the general situation of the defence and not only of the situation of the accused'.[124]

The Court first dealt with this issue in *Kamasinski* v. *Austria*. It concluded that the lawyer 'was afforded adequate access to the court files, including the possibility of making copies thereof, and adequate facilities for consulting his client'.[125] The system of granting access only to the lawyer was not regarded as incompatible with Article 6 § 3(b). In fact, the main complaint was directed against counsel rather than against the authorities. In *Kremzow* v. *Austria*, however, the Court made a more sweeping statement: 'Restriction of the right to inspect the court file to an accused's lawyer is not incompatible with the rights of the defence under Article 6'.[126] *Foucher* v. *France* is quite consistent with this—here, a violation was found, because the applicant himself was not given access to the file, but contrary to the cases mentioned previously he had not retained counsel.[127]

This case-law is primarily acceptable to the extent that counsel is allowed to make copies which may be shown to the defendant. As a matter of principle, however, it must be stressed that both the accused himself and counsel must enjoy access. It is necessary for counsel, because of his professional expertise, to be able to assess the relevance of the material for the proceedings. On the other hand, only the accused has first-hand knowledge of what happened at the time he is alleged to have committed the offence with which he is charged. Only he will be in a position to say, for example, whether the deposition of a witness is plausible or not. As a rule it will be sufficient for him to look at photocopies. However, in exceptional cases, it will also be necessary to see an original document.

In Denmark, counsel is not allowed to hand over the file to the accused without permission of the police. This is to prevent abuse. However, it is possible

---

[124] *Ofner* v. *Austria* Application 524/59; the facts of this case betray an extremely bureaucratic attitude of the Austrian authorities—Ofner was prevented from taking notes, which was justified on the basis of insufficient staffing, an explanation which would not be regarded as acceptable today.
[125] *Kamasinski* v. *Austria*, § 52. See also *X* v. *United Kingdom* Application 4042/69; *Harward* v. *Norway* Application 14170/88.   [126] *Kremzow* v. *Austria*, § 52.
[127] *Foucher* v. *France*, § 35; confirmed in *Kitov* v. *Denmark* Application 29759/96.

to let the defendant consult the file at the lawyer's office.[128] Presumably, the lawyer is allowed to show the file to a defendant detained on remand. While such a rule may constitute a certain difficulty for the defence, it is still compatible with Article 6 § 3(b). In *Kitov* v. *Denmark*, the applicant also had retained counsel in the Netherlands; he complained of the fact that the file was not sent there. The Court, rather vaguely, found that a fair balance had been struck 'between, on the one hand, the purpose of preventing misuse of the case file and, on the other, a proper defence for the applicant'.[129] In my view, a restriction with regard to sending the original file to a foreign country is quite acceptable.

In its early phase, the Commission was also faced, in *Köplinger* v. *Austria*,[130] with a case where the defendant was prohibited from bringing his manuscripts and his annotated documents with him when he was taken to meet counsel. It simply stated that the applicant was 'not prevented from preparing his appeal'.[131] This can hardly be justified—the Commission asked the wrong question. The question was not whether the applicant was *prevented* from preparing his appeal, but whether he had adequate facilities. In particular, there is not the slightest substantial reason for this petty restriction. It is true that while the Convention gives a right to adequate facilities, it does not expressly prohibit interferences that are not 'necessary in a democratic society'.[132] It must have been difficult for the applicant to show that he was actually hampered in his defence, but to ask for such proof would be quite unreasonable.

Stavros warns that the approach which regards the accused and counsel as one unit may be illusory in cases of legal-aid counsel; he suggests that there must be some mechanism to ensure that the latter acts effectively.[133] This certainly merits approval. At the same time, it is also necessary to recall the independence of the Bar. While the defendant must have the possibility to complain about the inactivity or inadequacy of legal-aid counsel,[134] any supervision by state authorities over the activity of a defence lawyer is unacceptable.

(c) When does the Right of Access Arise?

At which point in the course of the proceedings must access to the file be granted? In *Bonzi* the Commission asked: 'Does Article 6 § 3(b), which protects the accused against a hasty trial in which he does not have access to all the documents in the case in the same conditions as the prosecution, apply to the

---

[128] Section 745(1) of the Danish Administration of Justice Act.
[129] *Kitov* v. *Denmark* Application 29759/96.
[130] *Köplinger* v. *Austria* Application 1850/93.
[131] For Mr Balta, dissenting, the applicant had encountered obstacles in the preparation of his defence which, in itself, constituted a violation of the Convention.
[132] In *Can* v. *Austria*, however, the Commission did in fact apply this formula: 'The accused must have the opportunity to organise his defence in an appropriate way and without restriction as to the possibility to put all relevant defence arguments before the trial court and thus to influence the outcome of the proceedings': § 53.   [133] Stavros (1993) 185.
[134] See e.g. the cases of *Artico* v. *Italy* and *Goddi* v. *Italy*.

preliminary investigation?'[135] The question was left open. The early case-law was
generally rather prudent in this respect—the right of access was considered to
arise, at the very latest, from the moment that the indictment was presented.[136]
Since then, this has evolved considerably—even the results of the very first steps
in an investigation must be revealed: the reference to different 'phases of the
proceedings' in *Jespers* v. *Belgium*[137] makes it clear that parts of the file cannot be
shielded from the defence for the sole reason that they consist of material
stemming from a police inquiry.

After *Lamy* v. *Belgium*, this issue appears in a new light. In this case which
concerned habeas corpus proceedings, the applicant complained that he had not
had access to the entire file, in particular to two reports. According to Belgian
law, the file remained inaccessible to the defence for the first thirty days of
detention on remand. The applicant had been arrested on 18 February 1983 and
appeared before the *chambre du conseil* four days later, on the 22nd. The Court
found that '[a]ccess to these documents was essential for the applicant at this
crucial stage in the proceedings...it would...have enabled counsel for
Mr. Lamy to address the court on the matter of the co-defendants' statements
and attitudes'. The Court found a violation of Article 5 § 4 as the proceedings
had not been 'truly adversarial'.[138]

Three further judgments have strengthened this position.[139] While the facts
are not rendered in an unequivocal way in this regard, it appears that the Court
grants a right of access to the file at the very beginning of the arrest, even before a
defendant is brought before a judge pursuant to Article 5 § 3—at any rate,
counsel for the defence asked for a hearing before the district court and for leave
to consult the investigation files.[140] This was refused as it was feared that it might
endanger the purpose of the investigation. The Court said this with regard to
habeas corpus proceedings: 'The proceedings must be adversarial and must
always ensure "equality of arms" between the parties, the prosecutor and the
detained person. Equality of arms is not ensured if counsel is denied access to
those documents in the investigation file which are essential in order effectively
to challenge the lawfulness of his client's detention'.[141] With regard to the
Government's objection that opening the file to the defence might have
endangered the investigation, the Court replied: 'The Court acknowledges the
need for criminal investigations to be conducted efficiently, which may imply
that part of the information collected during them is to be kept secret in order

---

[135] *Bonzi* v. *Switzerland* Application 7854/77. See also *Kröcher and Möller* v. *Switzerland* Application 8463/78.
[136] *X* v. *Austria* Application 1816/63; *Neumeister* v. *Austria* Application 6422/70; *X* v. *Austria* Application 7138/75; Trechsel (1979) 353; Vogler (1995) N 491. In *Mattoccia* v. *Italy*, §§ 48, 64, this was described as being the rule in Italy.
[137] *Guy Jespers* v. *Belgium* Application 8404/78, § 65.
[138] *Lamy* v. *Belgium*, § 29; confirmed e.g. in *Nikolova* v. *Bulgaria*, §§ 58, 63.
[139] *Garcia Alva* v. *Germany*; *Lietzow* v. *Germany*; and *Schöps* v. *Germany*.
[140] *Lietzow* v. *Germany*, § 9.   [141] Ibid., § 44.

to prevent suspects from tampering with evidence and undermining the course of justice. However, this legitimate goal cannot be pursued at the expense of substantial restrictions on the rights of the defence. Therefore, information which is essential for the assessment of the lawfulness of a person's detention should be made available in an appropriate manner to the suspect's lawyer'.[142]

This sweeping statement seems to go a long way towards favouring the defence. However, on closer scrutiny considerable problems appear. What the Court proposed is nothing less than to separate the accused from his counsel. It is all right to keep the file from the suspect but it must be open to his lawyer. It is very doubtful whether a conscientious lawyer would accept such a compromise. Confidence is the essential prerequisite for effective assistance. If the lawyer is forced to conceal information from his client, this confidence is undermined. Apparently the prosecuting authority is to decide which information is to be kept secret and which is 'essential for the assessment of the lawfulness of a person's detention'. The Court seemed to take it for granted that these qualifications will never apply to the same information. This rule is definitely incompatible with the principle of equality of arms.

Could it be assumed that the prosecuting authority must only disclose material on which it wishes the judge to base his or her decision on the detention? Eberhard Kempf, Mr Lietzow' lawyer, answers in the negative.[143] In fact, it would not be easy to operate such a separation. However, the following solution would appear fair: the prosecutor selects the material which is to be put before the court—and before the defence. He or she withholds material which he or she considers ought still to be kept secret. Thereby the prosecutor runs a risk: the judge might, for example, not be convinced that there is a 'reasonable suspicion' against the defendant, and release him or her. The prosecution would have to put up with this. Still, there must be the possibility of some control of the file lest material favourable to the detainee be withheld.

Lamy and the other cases referred to only apply Article 5 § 4, not Article 6 which does not, as such, apply in habeas corpus proceedings.[144] What is their significance for the interpretation of Article 6 § 3(b)? For one, on a merely pragmatic level, they provide a basis for counsel to insist on seeing the file: declare that one plans to file a habeas corpus petition. This is what German authors recommend.[145]

Walischewski is of the opinion that the *Lamy* ruling is equally applicable to defendants who are left at liberty.[146] There is a passage in the judgment which seems strongly to support that assumption: 'The appraisal of the need for a remand in custody and the subsequent assessment of guilt are too closely linked for access to documents to be refused in the former case when the law requires it in the latter case'.[147]

---

[142] Ibid., § 47.   [143] Kempf (2001) 207.   [144] *Neumeister* v. *Austria*, § 22.
[145] Schlothauer and Wieder (2001) N 422.   [146] Walischewski (1999) 93.
[147] *Lamy* v. *Belgium*, § 29.

The issue is, however, not that obvious. One could oppose this suggestion by pointing out that deprivation of liberty is a particularly serious interference with fundamental rights and therefore calls for particularly strong protection; to the extent that the detention is justified by the danger of the detainee meddling with the evidence, that danger is considerably reduced by the detention, therefore there is much less danger associated with granting access to the file to a person behind bars than to an accused who is at liberty; there may also be doubts as to whether there is already a need to prepare the defence at such an early stage in the proceedings.

In favour of Walischewski's opinion, one could recall the famous adage according to which 'the Convention is intended to guarantee not rights that are theoretical or illusory but rights that are practical and effective; this is particularly so of the rights of the defence in view of the prominent place held in a democratic society by the right to a fair trial, from which they derive'.[148] Furthermore, there is *Imbrioscia* v. *Switzerland*, where the Court accepted the principle that a defendant must have the right to assistance by counsel during police interrogations. This is implied by the fact that it first found that such assistance had not been granted in Zurich and then stated that 'the applicant did not at the outset have the necessary legal support'.[149] The accused can only make effective use of his right to put questions to witnesses if he is aware of the actual stage of the investigation which, in turn, presupposes access to the file. Also, participation of the defence at the first hearing of a witness is particularly important, as witnesses, when questioned at a later stage in the proceedings, tend to repeat as closely as possible their earlier statement in order not to create suspicion as to their honesty.

Weighing up these arguments against each other, I come to the conclusion that access to the file ought to be granted right from the beginning of the proceedings, i.e. from the moment that a person is 'charged', i.e. arrested or otherwise substantially affected by the proceedings.[150] However, it is doubtful whether the Court would follow this approach. It will be difficult to convince it that the defence actually needed the access right from the earliest stages of the investigation. On the other hand, it is clear that the right also applies during appeal proceedings—*Melin* v. *France* is a striking example.[151]

The access to the file at the very beginning of an investigation must, however, be qualified. The danger of tampering with the evidence and collusion may and must be taken into account. In particular, it must be possible to keep undisclosed the intentions and plans of the prosecuting authority. To the extent that it is

---

[148] *Artico* v. *Italy*, § 33.

[149] *Imbrioscia* v. *Switzerland*, § 41; the Court found no violation, because the applicant's lawyer had not asked to be present.

[150] In the same vein, see Harris, O'Boyle, and Warbrick (1995) 253; Merrills and Robertson (2001) 121.

[151] *Melin* v. *France*; there are many more examples, such as *Vacher* v. *France*, or *Mattoccia* v. *Italy*.

permissible to imprison a person in the interests of the prosecution, it is basically also justified to restrict access to the file unless the fact of the accused's detention makes disclosure possible. We are faced here with a particularly sensitive issue for which simple 'recipes' will not be found.

Of course the provision is mainly designed with a view to trials at first instance. Yet, according to the Court it is possible that the failure to grant adequate time and facilities for the preparation of the defence at first instance can be remedied on appeal.[152] This presupposes that the superior jurisdiction is competent to re-examine without any restriction, both the facts and the application of the substantive law, as to the guilt or innocence of the accused.[153] The Commission had come to the conclusion that there had been a violation of Article 6 §§ 1 and 3(a) and (b).

Taking into account the deeper meaning of the exhaustion rule and the principle of subsidiarity the Court's solution can be accepted. Still, it is not entirely satisfactory from a rule-of-law perspective. In fact, the applicant is entitled to two fair hearings when domestic law provides for a full appeal. If there was a violation of rights of the defence at first instance, this ought to lead to quashing that judgment. If the right is granted for the first time on appeal, this means that the accused 'loses an instance'. This is not quite satisfactory.[154]

(d) Various Issues

Access to the file can be regulated in a variety of ways. It is legitimate for the authorities to insist that the file must remain on their premises, providing that the defendant and/or counsel may look at it or take notes or make copies. The latter will generally be at the expense of the defence.[155] This must, of course, be modified in the case of indigent defendants. Economic difficulties may not lead to a curtailment of the right to a fair trial, regardless of whether the accused is assisted by counsel or not.

An accused who is detained on remand and not assisted by counsel must be given the possibility of consulting the file, if need be under supervision.

Scientific evidence may be of crucial importance as is illustrated, for example, by the cases of *Bönisch* v. *Austria* and *Brandstetter* v. *Austria*. In *Bricmont* v. *Belgium* the Court conceded that an audit would have been desirable although, in that case, '[t]he Belgian courts could . . . reasonably have believed that such an audit would not have served any useful purpose'.[156]

---

[152] *Du Bois* v. *Netherlands* Application 36986/97.

[153] *Dallos* v. *Hungary*, §§ 50 et seq. See also the similar cases of *Serves* v. *France*, §§ 48 et seq. and *Twalib* v. *Greece*, § 41, where, however, the Court noted that the applicant had not asked for a retrial. In *Pélissier and Sassi* v. *France*, § 62, on the contrary, the court of appeal did not heal the defects complained of; this was also the case in *Mattoccia* v. *Italy*, § 69, where the necessary facilities were precisely denied by the court of appeal.

[154] Judge van Dijk made a very similar point in his dissenting opinion in *Twalib* v. *Greece*.

[155] See e.g. the reformed regulation regarding the French *Cour de Cassation* as described in *Foucher* v. *France*, § 37.   [156] *Bricmont* v. *Belgium*, § 91.

Another facility is the right to be present during on-site inspections. This issue was raised in a recent decision on admissibility, but the Court did not address it.[157]

B. Other Facilities

It is a matter of course that there can be no limited catalogue of facilities which might be useful for the defence. The following are just a few examples which can be found in the case-law.

1. Access to Legal Materials

A defendant representing himself on appeal may need to consult legal materials. The applicant Ross complained that he was not provided with such materials despite repeated requests. The Commission implicitly accepted that this request was covered by the term 'facilities' but found that the materials furnished— the authorities had bought two textbooks for the applicant—were 'adequate'. The Commission also stressed that there were 'practical limits to the steps which the prison authorities could reasonably be expected to undertake to find materials for the applicant's research'.[158]

2. A Reasoned Judgment[159]

The right to adequate facilities to enable preparation also operates at the appeal stage of the proceedings. If the appeal requires the appellant to present a reasoned criticism of the judgment against which the appeal is directed, it is obviously necessary for him to have a copy of the text of the reasoned judgment. This was not the case in *Hadjianastassiou* v. *Greece*. The applicant had been convicted by a courts-martial appeal court. He had five days to appeal to the Court of Cassation. However, he did not receive a copy of the reasoned judgment before the expiry of that time limit. The Court needed no further arguments to conclude that there had been a violation of Article 6 § 3(b).[160] In some legal systems where, for instance, a jury is responsible for determining guilt, the issuing of a reasoned judgment will be impossible. In *R* v. *Belgium* the Commission declared inadmissible a complaint relating to such a procedure, noting that the duty to give reasons must accommodate jury-trial procedure.[161]

As to the quality of the reasoning, the Court has accepted rather low standards. In *Twalib* v. *Greece*, only an abridged version of the judgment was available. The Court noted that it addressed the issues raised by the defence,

---

[157] *Svinarenkov* v. *Estonia* Application 42551/98 (inadmissible).

[158] *Ross* v. *United Kingdom* Application 11396/85.

[159] This subject is discussed in detail in Chapter 4, section IV above.

[160] *Hadjianastassiou* v. *Greece*, §§ 29 et seq.   [161] *R* v. *Belgium* Application 15957/90.

although the items of evidence were not enumerated. However, the applicant had not challenged the evidence.[162]

3. Notification of Consular Rights

Article 36 (1)(b) of the Vienna Convention on Civil and Consular Relations (VCCR) provides that:

if he so requests, the competent authorities of the receiving State shall, without delay, inform the consular post of the sending State if, within its consular district, a national of that State is arrested or committed to prison or to custody pending trial or is detained in any other manner. Any communication addressed to the consular post by the person arrested, in prison, custody or detention shall be forwarded by the said authorities without delay. The said authorities shall inform the person concerned without delay of his rights under this subparagraph.

The argument that this right to information and access to the consular official were part of the facilities referred to in Article 6 § 3(b) has consistently been rejected by the Commission.[163]

In its judgment in the LaGrand case (*Germany* v. *US*),[164] this question was discussed,[165] but the International Court of Justice (ICJ) stated that it did not consider it necessary to give an answer to the question whether the right set out in Article 36 § 1 of the VCCR was also a human right.[166] Yet, it appears that it nevertheless tacitly answered in the affirmative as it accepted the existence of a link between the omission complained of and the conviction and execution of the LaGrand brothers. As far as the Convention is concerned, the obligation under the VCCR cannot be regarded as a 'facility' within the meaning of Article 6 § 3(b). Even assuming that the VCCR grants individual rights, such rights are dependent upon ratification of the VCCR by the countries involved. They lack the universal and fundamental character of human rights.

4. Access to Medical Examination

So far, there is no decision which would include the right to an independent and impartial medical examination as a 'facility' under Article 6 § 3(b). However, the 'facilities' must also include medical evidence. In *Campbell and*

---

[162] *Twalib* v. *Greece*, §§ 45 et seq.

[163] Application 1184/61, mentioned by Fawcett (1969) 169, n. 1; Gollwitzer (1992) N 180; Partsch (1994) 163; Vogler (1986) 480.

[164] *Germany* v. *US*, judgment of 17 June 2001 (ICJ). See also *Arena and other Mexican Nationals* (*Mexico* v. *United States of America*), judgment of 31 March 2004. In this judgment, the ICJ still does not answer the question whether the Vienna Consular Convention protects human rights, as Mexico alleged, but observed 'that neither the text nor the object and purpose of the Convention, nor any *travaux préparatoires*, support the conclusion that Mexico draws from its contention in that regard'; § 124   [165] See, in particular, the pleadings of this author in *LaGrand*.

[166] Ibid., § 78.

Fell v. *United Kingdom*, the Commission did not regard the applicant's claim in
this respect as being well founded[167] and it was not maintained before the
Court.[168] The Commission recognized 'that in personal-injury cases questions
of medical evidence may be of great importance, and considers that in certain
circumstances a refusal to allow a prisoner facilities for medical examination might
raise an issue under Article 6 § 1'. However, the right was not an 'automatic' one.
'Article 6 does not guarantee, as such, any right of access to an independent
doctor'. In fact, the Commission did not really conclude that in that case the
right ought not to have been granted but, in reality, considered that the issue
was covered by the finding of a violation of the right to correspondence under
Article 8.[169]

In *Calogero Diana*, medical evidence was sought by the injured party which
could not rely on Article 6 § 3. However, it is quite conceivable that a defendant
could require medical expertise for the preparation of his or her defence,
for example, the opinion of a psychiatrist as to his or her responsibility.

It cannot be denied that access to an independent medical examination may
also be of crucial importance, for example, when an accused claims that confessions were made under torture. The judgment in *Aksoy* v. *Turkey* illustrated
rather drastically how unreliable official medical examinations can be.[170]

5. The Right to a Hearing[171]

In *T* v. *Austria* the applicant had been found guilty of abuse of process despite
the fact that he had neither been informed of the charge nor afforded the chance
to have a hearing. He appealed, but the Regional Court dismissed the appeal,
again without a hearing. The Court found this to constitute a violation of
Article 6 §§ 1 and 3(a) and (b).[172]

C. Exceptions

We have already seen that the right to adequate facilities for the preparation of
the defence is not absolute. An inherent limitation is already incorporated in the
term 'adequate'.

However, there are also some further restrictions or exceptions which cause
considerable problems. The most difficult problems arise in the area of security.
A person suspected of espionage may have been caught in the net of an anti-
espionage measure. Traces of those measures may have found their way into the
file. In this case, a conflict between the public interest in maintaining such
information secret and the interests of the defence is likely to arise. The easy

---

[167] *Campbell and Fell* v. *United Kingdom*, Report of the Commission, § 78.
[168] Ibid., §§ 117 et seq.   [169] This approach was also taken in *Calogero Diana* v. *Italy*.
[170] Cf. *Aksoy* v. *Turkey*, §§ 11, 16, 19, and 49.
[171] This issue will be discussed in detail in Chapter 10 below.
[172] *T* v. *Austria*, §§ 71 et seq.

answer to that problem is to say that the principle of proportionality has to be applied. However, on closer inspection it appears that such a weighing of interests is hardly possible in this area. It will be nearly impossible for the Strasbourg Court to form a well-founded opinion as to what is necessary in the interests of national security in a specific state.

The Court has shown its comprehension for matters of security, for instance, in the case of *Klass* v. *Germany*. It stated that as a rule, anyone affected by wire-tapping must be informed after the termination of the measure so that he can exercise the right to an effective remedy under Article 13. However, it accepted that some information may be omitted: 'Secret surveillance and its implications are facts that the Court, albeit to its regret, has held to be necessary, in modern-day conditions in a democratic society, in the interests of national security and for the prevention of disorder or crime'.[173]

Under Article 6 § 3(b) it appears that, so far, the question has only come up in one application, *Haase* v. *Germany*. The applicant had been sentenced to eleven years of imprisonment for espionage. He complained that he had not had access to all the documents in his case. While his lawyers had access, 'some protection was necessary for security reasons'. The Commission was of the opinion that this was acceptable.[174] Stavros finds the decision 'totally unacceptable'.[175] This is too harsh a judgment. The state cannot accept an alternative according to which there is an option of letting spies go unsanctioned or giving access to secret information to the person against whom criminal proceedings have been instituted because that person tried unlawfully to obtain that same information. The rights of the defence are undoubtedly very important but they do not constitute absolute values, but allow for a certain degree of flexibility. It is not evident, from the decision in *Haase*, what relevance the documents in question would have had; there are no allegations to that effect, which is understandable, as the defence never saw them. Still, there is the pos-sibility of a compromise in such a situation. As stated above, a system ought to be available, where a totally neutral person, such as the head of the Bar association or an ombudsman, examines the documents in question. That person will be bound by secrecy. To the extent that the file contains material that must remain secret, there must be safeguards against the use of such documents as a sub-stantial ground for the conviction.

More recently, the Court has dealt with the possible limitation on the access to the file under the general guarantee of Article 6 § 1. In *Atlan* v. *United Kingdom* it said that 'it may in some cases be necessary to withhold certain evidence so as to preserve the fundamental rights of another individual or to safeguard an important public interest. However, only such measures restricting the rights of

---

[173] *Klass and others* v. *Germany*, § 68. [174] *Haase* v. *Germany* Application 7412/76.
[175] Stavros (1993) 183. The German approach is also characterized by an extreme reluctance to accept an exception to the right of access to the file in cases concerning matters of national security; see e.g. Dahs (1999) N 252.

the defence which are strictly necessary are permissible under Article 6 § 1. Moreover, in order to ensure that the accused receives a fair trial, any difficulties caused to the defence by a limitation on its rights must be sufficiently counter-balanced by the procedures followed by the judicial authorities'.[176]

Unfortunately, when it comes to actually drawing limits, the wording of the Court becomes very vague. It is true that the general formula just quoted uses relatively precise terms, such as 'strictly necessary', but in the end, this precision is eroded by unspecific references to the need to 'counterbalance' any difficulties.

In the following paragraph of the judgment we read this: 'In cases where evidence has been withheld from the defence on public interest grounds, it is not the role of this Court to decide whether or not such non-disclosure was strictly necessary since, as a general rule, it is for the national courts to assess the evidence before them'. There goes whatever assistance could be found in the words 'strictly necessary'. And the next sentence is downright strange: 'Instead, the Court's task is to ascertain whether the decision-making procedure applied in each case complied, *as far as possible*, with the requirements of adversarial pro-ceedings and equality of arms and incorporated adequate safeguards to protect the interests of the accused'.[177]

Shortcomings 'must be counterbalanced', was the general guideline. Now, however, it appears that this is only required 'as far as possible'. Is it for the national authorities to decide on that possibility? Not to the extent that they reccive a *carte blanche*.

In the present case the prosecution had repeatedly denied that any documents had been withheld—the applicant suspected that a police informer had been involved. Four years later, on appeal, they admitted, however, that they had indeed withheld material. This, in the Court's view, was 'not consistent with the requirements of Article 6 § 1'. The Court of Appeal refused to order that they be disclosed. The Strasbourg Court said: 'the trial judge [sc. as opposed to the judge sitting on an appeal] is best placed to decide whether or not the non-disclosure of public interest immunity evidence would be unfairly prejudicial to the defence. Moreover, in this case, had the trial judge seen the evidence he might have chosen a very different form of words for his summing up to the jury'.[178] Therefore there was a violation of Article 6 § 1.

The Court referred frequently to *Rowe and Davis* v. *United Kingdom* where it also stressed the importance of an adversarial character for the fairness of proceedings.[179] The Court referred to 'competing interests, such as national security or the need to protect witnesses at risk of reprisals or keep secret police

---

[176] *Atlan* v. *United Kingdom*, § 40; *Rowe and Davis* v. *United Kingdom*, § 61.

[177] *Atlan* v. *United Kingdom*, § 41; *Rowe and Davis* v. *United Kingdom*, § 62 (emphasis added).

[178] *Atlan* v. *United Kingdom*, § 45. In *Rowe and Davis*, § 65, the Court furthermore rightly pointed out that full information is also important for the questioning of witnesses.

[179] *Rowe and Davis* v. *United Kingdom*, §§ 59 et seq.

methods of investigation of crime, which must be weighed against the rights of the accused'. In both cases the Court was not satisfied that the violation had been healed on appeal.

As far as the result is concerned, both judgments merit approval. What is unsatisfactory is the vague wording used in the general outline of the law.

Chapter 10

The Right to Defend Oneself and to Have the Assistance of Counsel

I. INTRODUCTION

A. The Texts

3. [In the determination of any criminal charge against him, everyone shall be entitled to the following minimum guarantees, in full equality:] . . .
(d) To be tried in his presence, and to defend himself in person or through legal assistance of his own choosing; to be informed, if he does not have legal assistance, of this right; and to have legal assistance assigned to him, in any case where the interests of justice so require, and without payment by him in any such case if he does not have sufficient means to pay for it;

ICCPR, Art. 14 § 3

3. [Everyone charged with a criminal offence has the following minimum rights:] . . .
(c) to defend himself in person or through legal assistance of his own choosing or, if he has not sufficient means to pay for legal assistance, to be given it free when the interests of justice so require;

ECHR, Art. 6 § 3

2. . . . [During the proceedings, every person is entitled, with full equality, to the following minimum guarantees:] . . .
(d) the right of the accused to defend himself personally or to be assisted by legal counsel of his own choosing, and to communicate freely and privately with his counsel;
(e) the inalienable right to be assisted by counsel provided by the state, paid or not as the domestic law provides, if the accused does not defend himself personally or engage his own counsel within the time period established by law;

AHRC, Art. 8

All three texts feature the right of an accused to defend him- or herself and to have the assistance of counsel (in this Chapter: 'the right to a defence') as one of the minimum rights or guarantees of every accused. The Covenant is the only instrument which expressly mentions the right of the accused to be present at the hearing, although this, as we shall see, is also implicitly protected by the other norms. Furthermore, it is the only text which extends the protection to cover the right to be informed of this guarantee.

On the other hand, only the American Convention includes the right of the accused to communicate with counsel in private. Yet, unlike the other texts, it does not expressly regulate legal aid leaving it for domestic law to determine whether the state will pay for legal-aid counsel. In reality, the other texts do not regulate this aspect either, but they limit the right to receive legal aid to those cases where the accused has insufficient means to pay for it, an element which is absent in the American text. The ACHR can furthermore be distinguished on the basis that it devotes two sub-paragraphs to the issue and refers to the right to state-appointed counsel as 'inalienable'. This implies that the other rights are 'alienable', a strange idea, and one which is difficult to understand. There is a clear suggestion that this expression is of a merely rhetorical character.

However, the differences between the texts are negligible. In essence all three instruments guarantee the right of an accused to defend him- or herself in person, to retain defence counsel and to be provided with, if the interests of justice so require, a state-appointed counsel. The only difference in substance is that the American Convention does not limit the right to assistance by state-appointed counsel to cases where this is required by the interests of justice.

B. The Origins of the Guarantee

The right to legal aid was vividly discussed during the preparation of the UDHR in 1947. However, as there was some controversy as to how it was to be drafted and specifically whether it should apply to civil, or criminal, or indeed to both types of proceedings, it was ultimately dropped from the text—the official argument being that such a detailed approach would have been inappropriate in the context of the Universal Declaration.[1]

In the work on the Covenant, the first references to counsel were not very specific—even the term itself was changed to the less specific notion of the 'qualified representative' by the working group in view of the third session of the drafting committee.[2] The next discussion took place during the sixth session of the Commission. At this stage Belgian lawyers proposed restricting the requirement that a lawyer be appointed to those cases where this was required in the interests of justice. Furthermore, counsel was only to be appointed free of charge if the accused was unable to pay the fees.[3]

C. The Structure of Article 6 § 3(c) of the ECHR

Three main elements are at the core of the right to a defence as formulated in Article 6 § 3(c) of the ECHR: the right to defend oneself in person, the right

---

[1] Weissbrodt (2001) 12 et seq.   [2] Ibid., 46.   [3] Ibid., 57.

to counsel of one's own choosing, and the right to counsel at the expense of the state.[4] While the first two aspects seem to be unlimited, the third is dependent on the presence of certain conditions. There is a difference between the French and the English text. The French text links the second and the third guarantee with '*et*' ('and'), while the English text reads 'or'. In *Pakelli*, the Court made it quite clear that the French version is the one which best expresses the meaning of the Convention.[5] If the English text had been taken literally, it would have meant that the authorities could decide freely which of the three rights to grant in a specific case.[6] This could not be the true meaning of the guarantee.

Hereafter, the three aspects will be examined in turn. There will also be chapters on the contingent right to contact with counsel and the right to an *effective* defence. First, some general observations must be made, particularly with regard to the purpose of the guarantee, its absolute character and its scope of application.

It will be noted that the right guaranteed by Article 6 § 3(c) has two aspects which are not always clearly distinguished. Following the Swiss terminology, it is possible to differentiate between the formal and the substantive aspects of the right to a defence.[7] In the substantive sense, it means something which may seem very banal: every defendant has the right to act in his or her own favour and to defend his or her interests, to propose evidence, to challenge judges for bias, to question the credibility of witnesses, to plead, etc. We shall see that these elements often come up in the case-law, particularly with regard to the first of the three guarantees under consideration, the right to defend oneself. Furthermore, they correspond to '*les droits de la défence*' as defined in the French legal system, which include the right to adequate time and facilities for the preparation of the defence, the right to call and to question witnesses, the right to the assistance of an interpreter, etc.[8] The right to a defence in the formal sense means the right to have the professional assistance and services of counsel and in practice this is the main thrust of Article 6 § 3(c).[9]

1. The Purpose of the Right to a Defence

The purpose of the right to a defence in the substantive sense causes few problems—its role is self-evident. The purpose of the right to a defence in the formal sense, however, is more complex. Four different aspects fall to be distinguished, although they have not all been recognized by the Court.

---

[4] See e.g. *Pakelli* v. *Germany*, § 31; Haefliger and Schürmann (1999) 226. Villiger (1999) 327 instead counts as a fourth guarantee the right to the effectiveness of the assistance.

[5] *Pakelli* v. *Germany*, § 31.   [6] See also Haefliger and Schürmann (1999) 226.

[7] See e.g. Hauser and Schweri (2002) 146; Schmid (2004) N 476.

[8] Verniory (2005) Ch. 1.

[9] For a very elaborate treatise on this aspect of the right to a defence, see Spronken (2001).

(a) The Technical Aspect

The first aspect is the most obvious one, it can be referred to as the *technical* aspect: counsel for the defence provides the accused with the technical skills necessary to enable him or her to make full use of the rights afforded by criminal-procedure law, including the fundamental rights guaranteed by the constitution or by international law. The assistance of counsel is, as it were, the key which opens the door to all the rights and possibilities of defence in the substantive sense of the term.[10] There is no need to elaborate on this. It is clear that the law—substantive as well as procedural—is a rather complicated matter, which is often unintelligible to the layperson.

One does not need to be especially poetic to compare criminal proceedings to a perilous journey. Regularly, it leads to crossroads, where decisions have to be taken. Failure to act decisively may lead to the definite forfeiture of a right. The wrong decision may cause irreparable damage. Reliable knowledge of law and practice is required in order to assess the consequences of such decisions. Usually, the defendant will not be able to make such an assessment. Moreover, this difficult situation is compounded by the fact that the defendant is surrounded (if not persecuted) by experts in the field of criminal proceedings, from the police, investigating authorities, and the public prosecutor, to the judge or members of the tribunal. Reference must be made here to the principle of 'equality of arms'.[11] Even in cases where, as is rather common in continental Europe, the law requires the investigating and prosecuting authorities to be neutral and to respect or even promote the rights and interests of the defence, practice shows that the knowledgeable assistance of a lawyer is by no means superfluous.[12]

One aspect which must not be neglected is the ability of the lawyer to supervise and control the activities of the authorities. His or her know-how is needed in order to ascertain whether the accused is treated correctly, and whether the rules of procedure are respected.

In other words, the purpose is to provide the defendant with the best chance of securing the most favourable outcome of the proceedings.

(b) The Psychological Aspect

The second aspect can be referred to as the *psychological* element of the guarantee: the arguments set out in the preceding paragraphs will not always be relevant. There may be relatively easy cases which do not require any sophisticated knowledge of legal matters. On the other hand, the defendant may be a lawyer, perhaps even a specialist in criminal law and procedure, and thus will not need technical assistance. Still, such a defendant may have a very legitimate interest in having professional assistance. The danger, which he or she faces, lies in the loss of objectivity through excessive interest in the case. This can result in

---

[10] See e.g. Poncet (1977) 161.   [11] See Chapter 4 above.
[12] There appears, however, to be a lack of empirical research on the effective utility of the assistance of counsel.

generally reasonable and well-controlled persons losing their capacity for rational analysis and insight into the consequences of their actions as soon as they are themselves emotionally involved in a dispute. Chapman, an author who was convicted of murder and sentenced to death (and who was eventually executed), said rightly that 'He who defends himself has a fool for counsel'. There is widespread if not unanimous agreement with this view. Still, in the *Melin* judgment[13] the Court seems not to have had this principle in mind when it declared the application of a lawyer who had defended himself and not made use of all the possibilities at his disposal for obtaining a copy of the reasoned judgment against him or precise information as to the date of the hearing in his case before the court of cassation to be ill-founded.[14] Similarly, in *Franquesa Freixas* v. *Spain* the Court agreed with the Government's argument and seemed even to reproach the applicant, who was a lawyer, for having chosen not to defend himself. He had disagreed with the appointment of a legal-aid lawyer who he felt was a specialist in labour law and thus not competent to act for him in his criminal case. The Court noted that in the absence of plausible reasons supporting his assertions that the lawyer who had been appointed was incompetent, and in view of the fact that as a lawyer he could have represented himself, there was no violation of the provision.[15]

While it has a different remit from the first purpose, the psychological aspect still aims to promote the best possible outcome of the proceedings for the defendant.

(c) The Humanitarian Aspect

The third purpose of the right to counsel is the one which is not generally recognized. I would call it the *humanitarian* aspect. Even the mere fact of being involved in criminal proceedings will be a source of enormous stress on all but a few strong and/or experienced defendants. Despite the various rights to information, there will often be a feeling similar to that which Franz Kafka has so aptly described in his famous novel *The Trial*. The feelings of forlornness and desperation are particularly strong whenever the accused is arrested and detained on remand. It may involve problems with employment, the family, or other social ties. It is true that certain defendants will be unemployed and have few or no social ties. Still, the case where a person can 'take it easy' after having been arrested must be the exception rather than the rule. The assistance of counsel, in my view, also serves the humanitarian aim of providing the defendant with a human companion, to lessen the feeling that he or she has been abandoned by the world only to be 'processed' by the judicial machinery which can be perceived as distant and cold, if not downright hostile.[16] The Commission generally accepted this aspect in its report in *Can* v. *Austria*.[17]

---

[13] *Melin* v. *France*, § 24.   [14] See Chapter 9 above.   [15] *Franquesa Freixas* v. *Spain*.
[16] See also Verniory (2005) 137 who, however, rightly warns that the lawyer ought not to assume the role of a social worker.   [17] *Can* v. *Austria* (friendly settlement) Annex p 18 § 55.

This purpose, unlike that of the other two, is not at all outcome-oriented. It concerns the means rather than the end. Acceptance of this view will have consequences which will be discussed later.

(d) The Structural Aspect of the Right to a Defence

The fourth purpose can be called the *structural* aspect: the right to a defence ensures that the accused has an active role in the proceedings, the role of a subject rather than an object. The right of an accused to defend him- or herself or with the assistance of counsel, enables the accused to influence the course of the proceedings. In this sense, it is also a manifestation of the personal dignity of the accused. As the Court put it in *Granger*, granting legal aid 'would in the first place have served the interests of justice and fairness by enabling the applicant to make an effective contribution to the proceedings'.[18]

2. The Absolute Character of the Right to a Defence

The right to a defence is sometimes referred to as an absolute right,[19] although the Court, without further explanation has taken a different view.[20] This epithet can have no less than four quite different meanings; however, not all are convincing.

(a) A Right without Any Restrictions?

First, it could mean that there are no restrictions on the right. This is true to a certain extent. For instance, the complete exclusion of the right to be assisted by a lawyer in a certain type of criminal proceedings would not be compatible with the Convention. The same applies *a fortiori* to the first part of the guarantee, to the extent that it covers the substantive aspect of the right to a defence. On the other hand, the third aspect of the right is obviously a relative one as it refers to two specific conditions for the granting of legal aid.

Things get more complex, however, as soon as we look at the provision in more detail. Does the first right guarantee to the defendant a right *not* to be assisted by counsel? We shall see that this is a disputed issue and that there are other limitations on the right to defend oneself. Nor is the second right without limitations; there are, for example, restrictions on the people permitted to act as counsel, and possibly on the number of defence counsel who may act in a single case.

---

[18] *Granger* v. *United Kingdom*, § 47 with reference to *Pakelli* v. *Germany*, § 38.

[19] See e.g. Frowein and Peukert (1996) Art. 6 N 192, for the second right.

[20] *Poitrimol* v. *France*, § 34: 'Although not absolute, the right of everyone charged with a criminal offence to be effectively defended by a lawyer, assigned officially if need be, is one of the fundamental features of a fair trial'. In fact, however, it is very difficult to imagine any limitations on this right unless one regards the possibility of waiver or the restriction of the number of counsel admitted as a limitation.

(b) No Derogation in Times of War?

A fundamental right can be regarded as 'absolute' if it is not subject to derogation in times of war or other public emergencies, such as those covered by Articles 3 or 7 of the ECHR. However, Article 6 is not among the guarantees singled out in Article 15 § 2 of the ECHR.[21] Still, this does not mean that any derogation from a freedom not mentioned in this paragraph is automatically acceptable. On the contrary, the recent case-law of the Court demonstrates that there have been violations of Article 5 in areas under emergency rule in Turkey notwithstanding the fact that there were valid declarations under Article 15 for the area concerned.[22] So far, there does not seem to have been any analogous case-law stemming from Article 6 § 3(c). However, it can be assumed that the Court would at least be prepared to examine in detail whether, in a specific case, there were compelling reasons to deny a defendant these elementary rights of the defence.

(c) Is a Violation Possible in the Absence of Prejudice?

The term 'absolute' can relate to the question of whether or not, in order for the Court to find a violation of the guarantee, the applicant has to show a link between the violation of the right to a defence and the outcome of the proceedings. The Court gave a resounding answer to this question in *Artico*. The applicant had not been assisted by counsel in his appeal to the court of cassation, but the Italian Government held the view that 'for there to be a violation of Article 6 § 3(c), the lack of assistance must have actually prejudiced the person charged with a criminal offence'. In the Court's opinion, 'the Government are asking for the impossible since it cannot be proved beyond all doubt that a substitute for Mr. Della Rocca would have pleaded statutory limitation and would have convinced the Court of Cassation'.[23] The right to a defence is therefore absolute in the sense that an applicant does not have to establish that he or she has suffered any disadvantage because it was denied. It is doubtful whether the question as to the scope of action of counsel may be raised at all. The Commission did this in its report in *Quaranta*.[24] The question was whether legal aid ought to have been granted during the investigative phase; in this context it was possible to decide the issue without contradicting *Artico*. However, if the result had been that there was a right to legal aid during the preliminary phase of the proceedings, the Commission ought to have criticized such an absence of possibilities of defence rather than saying that in this case legal assistance was not necessary.

(d) Is a Violation Possible if the Accused was Finally Acquitted?

If one accepts the humanitarian element of the purpose of the right to counsel, the absolute character can be taken one step further: there could in fact be a

---

[21] The same is true for the ICCPR, Arts. 14 and 4 § 2, and the ACHR, Arts. 8 and 27 § 2.
[22] See e.g. *Cakıcı* v. *Turkey*, § 104.   [23] *Artico* v. *Italy*, § 35.
[24] *Quaranta* v. *Switzerland*, Report of the Commission, § 70.

violation even in cases where a defendant was finally acquitted. The violation would consist of the fact that the applicant had to go through the ordeal of the proceedings alone, without the support to which he or she was entitled under the Convention. It is my personal opinion that Article 6 § 3(c) ought to be interpreted in this way, but so far this view has not been accepted by the Strasbourg organs.

3. The Scope of the Application of the Right to a Defence

The scope of the application of the right to a defence is, of course, identical to the scope of the application of Article 6 as far as proceedings relating to a 'criminal charge' are concerned. Still, a number of questions specific to the right to a defence arise: the right to a defence may be extended beyond the criminal sphere; it arises long before the trial itself starts and it falls to be distinguished from other aspects of assistance to a defendant.

(a) The Right to Legal Assistance Outside Criminal Proceedings

(i) The Right to Legal Assistance in Proceedings on 'Civil Rights and Obligations'   According to the clear wording of the Convention, Article 6 § 3(c) only benefits defendants in a criminal case. However, the right to a defence is also an element of the general right to a fair trial. There cannot be the slightest doubt that both the plaintiff and the defendant in civil proceedings have the right to defend their interests in person and to retain the services of the lawyer of their choice.[25] The issue of the right to free legal aid is less obvious. In the *Airey* judgment, the Court came to the following conclusion: '... despite the absence of a similar clause for civil litigation, Article 6 § 1 may sometimes compel the State to provide for the assistance of a lawyer when such assistance proves indispensable for an effective access to court either because legal representation is rendered compulsory ... or by reason of the complexity of the procedure or of the case'.[26]

(ii) The Right to Legal Assistance in Habeas Corpus Proceedings   Article 6, including paragraph 3(c), does not, at least not as such, apply to proceedings for habeas corpus under Article 5 § 4.[27] Still, under special circumstances, the effective use of that right may require the assistance of a lawyer. The Commission and the

---

[25] There may be exceptions to the admission of lawyers in certain legislation for a limited number of issues, e.g. arising out of employment contracts or rental agreements, at least at first instance. This is not the place, however, to address the question of whether such restrictions are compatible with Art. 6 of the Convention as this question only arises in non-criminal disputes.

[26] *Airey* v. *Ireland*, § 26; the applicant, Ms Johanna Airey, had complained that she had no possibility to obtain a decree of judicial separation in the absence of legal aid; divorce was not available in Ireland.

[27] *Neumeister* v. *Austria; Winterwerp* v. *Netherlands*, § 60; *De Wilde, Ooms & Versyp* v. *Belgium*, § 78; *Megyeri* v. *Germany*, § 22; *Woukam Moudefo* v. *France* Application 10868/84, Harris, O'Boyle, and Warbrick (1995) 257.

Court both found that the required conditions existed in the case of *Megyeri* v. *Germany*, because the applicant was not in full possession of his mental capacities;[28] the Commission had actually allowed him to be present and to address it at the hearing, and it could ascertain that he was indeed in need of such assistance.

Similarly in *Bouamar* v. *Belgium*, the Court ruled that a minor was entitled to the 'effective assistance of his lawyer' at a hearing where he was challenging his detention.[29]

(b) The Right to Legal Assistance During Different Phases of the Proceedings

(i) Before the Trial   It is very important that the right to a defence is not limited to the trial itself. This is equally true for the fully adversarial proceedings of the Anglo-Saxon legal system, where the defence has a greater role in preparing for the trial and presenting the evidence, and for the continental system. Although, under the continental system, the preparation of the trial is mainly the task of the authorities, the defence has the right to propose witnesses, to present documents, to comment on questions to be put to experts, and so forth. In fact, the assistance of counsel during the pre-trial proceedings is particularly important in proceedings where most of the evidence is only heard by an investigating officer, a member of the public prosecutor's office, or an investigating judge. Often, the trial court will mainly rely on the records of that investigation.[30]

Several aspects must be distinguished when we approach this issue. A distinction must certainly be made between the three aspects of the guarantee. As to the first, there are certainly not many limitations on an accused person's right to defend himself in person. In a way he may even do so before the proceedings have started. In fact, many codes of criminal procedure contain provisions which ensure that the perpetrator of an offence will not be prosecuted for actions he or she takes in order to avoid being caught, such as, to take a very simple example, wiping fingerprints off a glass surface in the victim's apartment.[31] The second part of the guarantee will not be subject to any limitations either—anybody may retain a lawyer at any time, even when there are not yet any proceedings pending. The problem becomes acute with regard to the third aspect, legal aid. Yet another distinction must be made, namely that between *having* a lawyer and having *free access* to that lawyer. We shall return to this problem later on; similar problems arise in relation to the question of effective assistance.

So far, there have not been any judgments which have given a clear answer to the question as to the point in time at which the right to legal aid arises. However, in my view the answer is quite simple: the right to a legal-aid counsel

---

[28] *Megyeri* v. *Germany*.   [29] *Bouamar* v. *Belgium*, § 60.
[30] See e.g. Hauser and Schweri (2002) 202 et seq.
[31] Of course, they do not need a lawyer for that; however, advocates may face punishment if they commit comparable acts!

arises as soon as there is any room for effective assistance. It is particularly likely, for instance, that assistance will be required if the accused is detained on remand. If the prerequisites are fulfilled and the suspect asks for a lawyer, there will normally be no justification for ruling that this request is premature. This means that postponing the appointment of legal-aid counsel will only be acceptable as long as it is not clear whether the person will actually be charged or whether the interests of justice will require the services of counsel. An exception might be tolerated where, for example, the request is made at a point in time when the competent authority decides to drop the charges and where the defendant is awarded full compensation. Even in such cases, however, the competent authority will have to examine carefully whether the accused was able to determine the issue of compensation freely and on the basis of sufficient information.

(ii) Proceedings on Appeal   It is fair to say that, as a rule, appeal proceedings tend to be more technical than proceedings at first instance. Thus, in such proceedings there is an increased likelihood that the 'interest of justice' will require that the accused be assisted by counsel. A typical example of such a case is *Pakelli* v. *Germany*.[32] The applicant had been convicted and sentenced to a term of imprisonment for a drug-related offence. On appeal, a number of rather complicated, technical issues regarding the representation of the appellant arose. The Federal Criminal Court decided to hold a hearing—a route taken only very exceptionally. Counsel for the defence asked to be officially appointed as a lawyer for Mr Pakelli, but this request was rejected. Both the Court and Commission came to the conclusion that there had been a violation of Article 6 § 3(c).

II. THE RIGHT TO DEFEND ONESELF

A. The Right of the Accused to Act in His or Her Defence

1. The General Rule

As was set out above, the part of Article 6 § 3(c) which is 'relatively absolute'[33] is the right of the accused to act in his or her defence. This aspect of the guarantee is not affected by the fact that a lawyer may have been appointed against the will of the accused. It may still be possible for the accused to act personally. This does not mean that *all* defence activities may be carried out by the accused in person. There may be, for instance, highly justified exceptions in rape cases. In a situation where the opinion of the accused runs contrary to that of counsel, the accused's will must prevail. This, however, does not impose a duty on a lawyer

[32] *Pakelli* v. *Germany*.
[33] 'Relatively absolute' is, of course, a contradiction in terms. A reservation is necessary for the question of whether compulsory assistance by a lawyer is compatible with the guarantee.

to act in a manner which is contrary to his or her professional opinion. In a case against Switzerland, the Commission held that the Convention did not 'entitle the accused to require his lawyer to adopt a particular defence strategy' which the latter regarded as impossible to maintain, especially if the accused had been given the opportunity to address the court himself, as was the case here.[34] Similarly in a case brought against the United Kingdom, the Commission noted that an accused person could not require counsel to disregard basic principles of his professional duty in the presentation of the defence.[35] Thus, if such behaviour resulted in the accused having to conduct his own defence, then any 'consequent inequality of arms can only be attributable to his own behaviour'.[36]

In the case of *Wick* v. *Austria*[37] a misunderstanding had arisen between the defendant, who was not aware that he continued to be assisted, and his counsel. The result was that the lawyer, who had initially filed a notice of intention to appeal and a plea of nullity, eventually withdrew the plea of nullity, while Mr Wick declared that he wanted to introduce a plea of nullity but waived the right to appeal. The court rejected both remedies. This case ended with a friendly settlement—there is reason to assume that the Commission would have reached the opinion that the withdrawal of the plea of nullity was invalid as it went against the declared will of the defendant; at the same time, it could have found the declaration that he did not wish to appeal to be invalid because it had been made without consultation with the lawyer.[38]

An entirely different question, that of whether there is a right *not* to be assisted by counsel, will be dealt with later on.

2. The Right to be Present at the Hearing

(a) The General Principle

'Although this is not expressly mentioned in paragraph 1 of Article 6, the object and purpose of the Article taken as a whole shows that a person "charged with a criminal offence" is entitled to take part in the hearing'.[39] This principle, set out in *Colozza*, applies to all trials at first instance and is generally recognized.[40]

---

[34] *X* v. *Switzerland* Application 9127/80.

[35] *X* v. *United Kingdom* Application 8386/78.

[36] This is also the approach adopted by the HRC; see *Earl Pratt and Ivan Morgan* v. *Jamaica*, § 222.

[37] *Alexander Wick* v. *Austria* Application 15701/89, Report of the Commission of 10 Mar. 1994.

[38] Cf. *Pfeifer and Plankl* v. *Austria*, § 38.

[39] *Colozza* v. *Italy*, § 27; confirmed in *Monnell and Morris* v. *United Kingdom*, § 56; *Barberà, Messegué and Jabardo* v. *Spain*, §§ 78, 34; *Brozicek* v. *Italy*, § 45; *FCB* v. *Italy*, § 33; *T* v. *Italy*, § 26; *Zana* v. *Turkey*, § 68; *Belziuk* v. *Poland*, § 37. The Court only hesitated in one case, *Ekbatani* v. *Sweden*, § 25, when it said that the defendant ought to be heard at first instance 'as a general principle'. However, such a restriction was not mentioned in the later judgments and must be regarded as a mistake; cf. van Dijk and van Hoof (1998) 433. See also *Widmaier* v. *Netherlands* Application 9573/81 (friendly settlement).

[40] See e.g. Frowein and Peukert (1996) Art. 6 N 94; Poncet (1977) 46.

In *Stanford*, the Court elaborated further: 'Article 6, read as a whole, guarantees the right of an accused to participate effectively in a criminal trial. In general this includes, inter alia, not only his right to be present, but also to hear and follow the proceedings'.[41]

(b) Exceptions for Disciplinary Reasons

A conflict may arise when a defendant does not conform to the rules of behaviour set up to enable the hearing to proceed in an orderly way. The defendant may disturb the proceedings by speaking and shouting, by acting violently, or by appearing in a state of intoxication. Theoretically it might be possible to react to such behaviour by using force, gagging, and restraining the person or using drugs to calm him or her down. However, the normal course of proceedings would still be disturbed and the dignity of the accused, as well as that of the court and all persons present, would suffer. It must therefore be possible to remove such persons from the courtroom. The Commission has declared applications against such measures to be manifestly ill-founded.[42] However, removal from the courtroom may not be used as punishment—the person must again be admitted to the hearing if he or she promises to behave properly and lives up to such a promise.

(c) Trial *In Absentia*

Is it compatible with the right to a fair trial that a defendant be tried in his or her absence? There are a number of reasons why trials *in absentia* are generally undesirable.

Participation is not only necessary for the purposes of the defence, it also gives the court an opportunity to get a personal impression of the defendant, and to hear any statement that he or she is prepared to make. Moreover it enables the defendant to control the fairness of the proceedings in person. Furthermore, one may ask what the value of a conviction and sentence is if the person concerned is absent, because as long as this is the case it will not be possible to enforce the judgment, at least to the extent that sanctions such as imprisonment are imposed.

One argument in favour of trial *in absentia* is that the statute of limitation for the prosecution of an offence may be shorter than that for the execution of the sentence.[43] There is also an interest in determining the charge while the evidence is still available.[44]

---

[41] *Stanford* v. *United Kingdom*, § 26: the applicant had complained that he could not hear what was said during the hearing because he was placed in a glass-fronted dock. The Court accepted that he had 'difficulties in hearing some of the evidence given during the trial'. However, the applicant did not bring these difficulties to the attention of the trial judge, nor did his (experienced) lawyer. The Court therefore found no violation. The Court also referred to the fact that the applicant was represented by solicitor and counsel (§ 30); this argument is unfortunate—it is essential that the defendant be in a state to follow the proceedings himself within the limits of his or her physical and mental capacities.   [42] *X* v. *United Kingdom* Application 8386/78.

[43] See e.g. Austrian PC, §§ 57 and 59; German PC, §§ 78 and 79; Swiss PC, Arts. 70 and 73.

[44] *Colozza* v. *Italy*, § 29.

At any rate, in several continental criminal-procedure systems there are rules accepting, under certain circumstances, trials *in absentia*; the Convention is not a revolutionary instrument and is not to be interpreted in a way which would entirely overthrow the traditions of national legislation. Consequently the case-law has concentrated on the conditions under which such trials may still be accepted as fair rather than banning them altogether. This issue has also been examined by the Committee of Ministers of the Council of Europe which has adopted a Resolution on the subject.[45]

While the ICCPR explicitly states that the accused has a right to appear at trial, the HRC has noted that Article 14 'cannot be construed as invariably rendering proceedings in absentia inadmissible irrespective of the reasons for the accused person's absence'.[46]

The rules emerging from the European case-law are as follows.

(i) Possibility of a Retrial A trial *in absentia* does not create any problems with regard to fairness as long as it is possible either for the person convicted to obtain a full retrial merely by asking for it, or for a retrial to be ordered automatically.[47] In other words, there is no need to show that there were valid reasons for the accused not appearing for trial. There will usually be a short time

---

[45] Res (75) 11 of 21 Mar. 1975:

1. No one may be tried without having first been effectively served with a summons in time to enable him to appear and to prepare his defence, unless it is established that he has deliberately sought to evade justice.
2. The summons must state the consequences of any failure by the accused to appear at the trial.
3. Where the court finds that an accused person who fails to appear at the trial has been served (*atteint*) with a summons, it must order an adjournment if it considers personal appearance of the accused to be indispensable or if there is reason to believe that he has been prevented from appearing.
4. The accused must not be tried in his absence, if it is possible and desirable to transfer the proceedings to another state or to apply for extradition.
5. Where the accused is tried in his absence, evidence must be taken in the usual manner and the defence must have the right to intervene.
6. A judgement passed in the absence of the accused must be notified to him according to the rules governing the service of the summons to appear and the time-limit for lodging an appeal must not begin to run until the convicted person has had effective knowledge of the judgement so notified, unless it is established that he has deliberately sought to evade justice.
7. Any person tried in his absence must be able to appeal against the judgement by whatever means of recourse would have been open to him, had he been present.
8. A person tried in his absence on whom a summons has not been served in due and proper form shall have a remedy enabling him to have the judgement annulled.
9. A person tried in his absence, but on whom a summons has been properly served is entitled to a retrial, in the ordinary way, if that person can prove that his absence and the fact that he could not inform the judge thereof were due to reasons beyond his control.

[46] *Daniel Monguya Mbenge* v. *Zaire*, § 76. For an examination of the international scope of this provision, see Marauhn (1998) 763.

[47] The latter applies in France by virtue of FCCP, Art. 639; *B* v. *France* Application 10291/83.

limit which begins from the moment when the convicted person has been formally notified of the judgment. The Court has made this clear by stating that '[w]hen domestic law permits a trial to be held notwithstanding the absence of [the defendant], that person should, once he becomes aware of the proceedings, be able to obtain, from a court which has heard him, a fresh determination of the merits of the charge'.[48] If he or she fails to make use of this possibility, this will be regarded as a waiver.

In *Haser* the applicant chose to file an appeal directly rather than avail himself of the possibility of a new trial. The Court rightly stressed again the importance of the presence of the accused at the hearing and declared the application inadmissible.[49]

(ii) Conditions for a Trial In Absentia *Without the Possibility of a Retrial* The Court has consistently noted a difference between a trial *in absentia* resulting from the deliberate decision of the accused not to appear,[50] and a failure to appear which is a consequence of circumstances beyond the control of the accused.[51] However, despite this distinction, the Court has continually insisted that '*le droit à être effectivement défendu par un avocat figurait parmi les éléments fondamentaux du procès équitable et qu'un accusé ne pouvait en perdre le bénéfice du seul fait de sa non comparution*'.[52]

The courts must exercise a reasonable amount of diligence in their attempts to contact the accused. This diligence had been lacking in the case of *Colozza* where the new address of the accused was in no way concealed—both the prosecutor's office and the police were aware of it.[53] The accused 'must not be left with the burden of proving that he was not seeking to evade justice or that his absence was due to *force majeure*'.[54] In other words, it is for the court (in Strasbourg proceedings, for the government) to show that the person concerned was aware of the date of the trial'.[55]

The second part of the Court's statement in *Colozza* appears, however, to be far too sweeping. If it is clearly established that the accused received the summons and then failed to turn up for trial, it is legitimate to require the latter to provide the court with convincing evidence that his or her absence was due to circumstances beyond his or her control and should not be interpreted as a waiver.

(iii) Waiver and its Limitations It is also possible for an accused to waive, explicitly or implicitly, his or her right to be present at the trial.[56] Misbehaviour

---

[48] *Colozza* v. *Italy*, § 29.   [49] *Haser* v. *Switzerland* Application 33050/96.
[50] *Poitrimol* v. *France*, §30; *Van Geyseghem* v. *Belgium*, § 29.
[51] e.g. *Goddi* v. *Italy; Colozza* v. *Italy; Krombach* v. *France*.
[52] *Goedhart* v. *Belgium*, § 26; *Van Geyseghem* v. *Belgium*, § 34; *Lala* v. *Netherlands*, § 33; *Pelladoah* v. *Netherlands*, § 40; *Stroek* v. *Belgium*; and *Krombach* v. *France*.
[53] *Colozza* v. *Italy*, § 28.   [54] Ibid., § 30.
[55] *FCB* v. *Italy*, § 35. See further Chapter 8 above.
[56] In *Colozza* v. *Italy*, § 28, the Court left open the question whether this was possible.

as described above can be interpreted as an implicit waiver if the accused is capable of acting responsibly. However, as with other rights of the defence, any waiver 'must be established in an unequivocal manner'.[57]

The *right* to appear at the hearing marks a second element of the principle, namely the *obligation* on the accused to appear. In certain legal orders a person who does not appear for trial is regarded as being in contempt of court ('*contumax*'). The attitude of the court towards these persons can be extremely negative to the point that they become non-persons and their property is confiscated. One of the possible sanctions in such a case is the forfeiture of the right to defend oneself. This was the case in *Poitrimol* v. *France*. The Aix en Provence court of appeal denied the accused the right to be defended by counsel because he had not turned up in spite of a warrant being issued for his arrest.[58] Here, although the applicant had expressed his wish not to attend the hearings, he had nevertheless clearly stated that he intended to instruct counsel. The question for the Court was thus whether an accused 'who deliberately avoids appearing in person remains entitled to "legal assistance of his own choosing" '.[59] The Court did not exclude the possibility that some sort of sanction could be applied against an accused who wilfully refused to appear for trial: 'It is of capital importance that a defendant should appear ... The legislature must accordingly be able to discourage unjustified absences'.[60] However, the Court noted that it was certainly disproportionate to deny an accused the right to legal assistance as a sanction for his or her failure to appear.

In France, draconian rules govern access to the court of cassation. In one case, an appellant, who had been sentenced to a term of imprisonment, had to give himself up (and thus was remanded in custody); failure to do so would result in the forfeiture of his right to appeal. Again, the Court considered this sanction to be excessive.[61] However, this case was not dealt with as raising an issue of the right to defend oneself, as the Court instead regarded it as an unacceptable restriction on the right of *access to court*.[62] The same approach was followed in *Khalfaoui* which concerned an appeal on points of law—the Court did not find convincing reasons to distinguish this case from those concerning the appeal to the *Cour de Cassation*.[63]

Furthermore, 'in the case of procedural rights a waiver, in order to be effective for Convention purposes, requires minimum guarantees commensurate to its importance'.[64] With regard to trial *in absentia* these guarantees lie primarily in the way the accused is summoned.

---

[57] *Neumeister* v. *Austria*, § 36; *Le Compte, Van Leuven, and De Meyere* v. *Belgium*, § 59; *Albert and Le Compte* v. *Belgium*, § 35; *Colozza* v. *Italy*, § 28; and *Zana* v. *Turkey*, § 70.
[58] A similar problem arose in the cases of *Lala* and *Pellandoah* (both v. *Netherlands*) and *Van Geyseghem* v. *Belgium*.   [59] *Poitrimol* v. *France*, § 32.
[60] Ibid., § 35.   [61] Ibid., § 38; this was confirmed in *Omar* v. *France* and *Guérin* v. *France*.
[62] Ibid., § 38.   [63] *Khalfaoui* v. *France*, §§ 46 et seq.
[64] *Peifer and Plankl* v. *Austria*, § 37; *Poitrimol* v. *France*, § 31; see also *Deweer* v. *Belgium*, § 49.

(d) The Right to be Present at a Hearing on Appeal

While the right to be present at the hearing at first instance is not controversial, rather complex rules have been developed by the Court regarding the rights of accused (or convicted) persons to be present at proceedings on appeal.

At the outset it may be recalled that in one of its first judgments the Court took the opportunity to state the basic principle for the application of Article 6 in appeal proceedings: 'Article 6 para. 1 is indeed applicable to proceedings in cassation. The way in which it applies must, however, clearly depend on the special features of such proceedings'.[65] More recently, the Court has stressed that, as compared to the trial at first instance, 'the personal attendance of the defendant does not necessarily take on the same significance for an appeal or nullity hearing as it does for the trial. Regard must be had in assessing this question to, inter alia, the special features of the proceedings involved and the manner in which the defence's interests are presented and protected before the appellate court, particularly in the light of the issues to be decided and their importance for the applicant'.[66]

The criteria applied by the Court are as follows.

(i) Whether there was a Full Hearing at First Instance   The Court often stresses that there was a full public hearing attended by the defendant at first instance.[67] This is rather surprising because, if such a hearing had not taken place, one would have to assume that there had already been a violation of Article 6 at that stage.

(ii) Whether there is a Full Re-examination of the Case   Normally, the person concerned must be given the chance to attend the hearing if the court of appeal is empowered fully to re-examine the case *in fact and law*, and in particular if it is competent to examine and evaluate the evidence.[68]

There are, however, exceptions to this rule.[69] They are exemplified by the cases of *Jan-Åke Andersson* and *Fejde*. Here, the Court embarked upon a perilous journey. It examined the details of the case and then concluded that the court of appeal could decide the relevant issues on the basis of the documents and submissions before it.[70] This is rather delicate, because the requirement that the Court hypothetically repeat the tasks of the domestic courts, implicitly puts the Court in the position of a court of 'fourth instance'. However, some clarification

---

[65]   *Delcourt v. Belgium*, § 26.

[66]   *Pobornikoff* v. *Austria*, § 24. See also *Belziuk* v. *Poland*, § 37; *Josef Prinz* v. *Austria*, § 34; *Michael Edward Cooke* v. *Austria*, § 35; *Ekbatani* v. *Sweden*, § 25; *Helmers* v. *Sweden*, § 31; *Kremzow* v. *Austria*, § 58; *Monnell and Morris* v. *United Kingdom*, § 56; *Sutter* v. *Switzerland*, § 28; *Pakelli* v. *Germany*, § 29; *Delcourt* v. *Belgium*, § 26; *Jan-Åke Andersson* v. *Sweden*, § 22; *Fejde* v. *Sweden*, § 26.

[67]   See e.g. *Helmers* v. *Sweden*, § 32.

[68]   This was the case, e.g. in *Pobornikoff* v. *Austria; Michael Edward Cooke* v. *Austria; Josef Prinz* v. *Austria; Kremzow* v. *Austria; Belziuk* v. *Poland; Helmers* v. *Sweden*; and *Ekbatani* v. *Sweden* with regard to the appeal proceedings (as opposed to the plea of nullity or cassation proceedings). Frowein and Peukert (1996) Art. 6 N 94, go one step too far by saying that the right always applies when there is an appeal in the strict sense of the term.   [69]   See e.g. *Belziuk* v. *Poland*, § 37.

[70]   *Jan-Åke Andersson* v. *Sweden*, § 29; *Fejde* v. *Sweden*, § 33.

of the context of these judgments is required: both concerned petty offences for which the sanction was only a moderate fine. Here, to some extent, the *de minimis* rule is applied. As the Court is frequently faced with cases where applicants complain of the length of proceedings, it is anxious to balance, to some extent, the interest in expeditious proceedings with those of extensive opportunities of an accused to be heard in person: '... there are other considerations, including the right to trial within a reasonable time and the related need for expeditious handling of the courts' case-load, which must be taken into account in determining the need for a public hearing at stages in the proceedings subsequent to the trial at first instance'.[71]

(iii) What was at Stake for the Applicant Similarly, the Court refers to the question of what is at stake for the person concerned.[72] This is a rather unfortunate element; the importance of the issue is already taken into account 'negatively', as it were, in that participation is not required in cases involving minor offences. The criterion mentioned here ought to have no other meaning than that cases involving minor crimes do not necessitate a hearing with the participation of the accused, even if the court of appeal can examine the facts.

(iv) Whether there was a Risk of Reformatio in Peius A valid criterion could be the question as to whether the result of the appeal could worsen the situation for the accused. Here, we are faced with a real 'win-or-lose-alternative'. The risk is considerably reduced in cases where the prohibition of *reformatio in peius* operates, which leads to a mere 'win-not-win-alternative'. The Commission could have applied this argument in one case, but based its decision on the fact that the applicant had not requested an oral hearing. So far the issue has not been dealt with by the Court.

(v) Whether the Prosecutor Attended the Hearing Governments sometimes seek to justify the absence of the accused at the hearing by referring to the fact that as the prosecutor was not heard either, there was no violation of the *equality of arms*. The Court correctly rejects this argument by saying that equality of arms is 'only one feature of the wider concept of a fair trial in criminal proceedings'.[73] Quite obviously, if there is a violation of this principle, the question of whether the accused took part in a hearing or not becomes redundant. The absence of one violation of the right to fair trial can certainly not prevent the existence of a different violation.

(vi) Whether the Appeal is Limited to Questions of Law Appeals limited to an examination of questions of law, such as the classical plea of nullity ('*recours en*

---

[71] *Jan-Åke Andersson* v. *Sweden*, § 27; *Fejde* v. *Sweden*, § 31.
[72] See e.g. *Botten* v. *Norway*, §§ 51, 52; *Helmers* v. *Sweden*, § 38; *Kremzow* v. *Austria*, §§ 67, 68.
[73] See e.g. *Ekbatani* v. *Sweden*, § 30; *Monnell and Morris* v. *United Kingdom*, § 62.

cassation') do not normally require the presence of the accused.[74] Exceptionally, in *Tripodi*, the Court even concluded that in the circumstances of the case the absence of the *lawyer* did not constitute a violation of Article 6 §§ 1 and 3(c).[75] The label attached to an appeal is not decisive. The Court's approach, as we have seen, is one of great flexibility and each case will be examined on its own merits. Faced with remedies of a mixed character, such as in hearings on a *recours en réforme*[76] which is primarily an appeal in cassation but which also allows for a new judgment to be passed under certain circumstances, the presence of the accused will still be required if an assessment of his or her personality is made.

The Court will itself decide whether the issue involved merely questions of law. It decided that this was not the case in *Botten* where the applicant was charged with having negligently killed a man because he had tried to rescue him using a rubber dinghy rather than a dory. The Court was of the opinion that this was not just a question of law but that the Supreme Court 'had to some extent to make its own assessment for the purposes of determining whether they provided a sufficient basis for convicting the applicant'.[77]

(vii) Whether the Accused was Given a New Sentence   If the appeal also concerns the severity of the sentence, the interests of justice may require the presence of the applicant. This was the case in *Kremzow*.[78] The applicant was a judge accused of having killed a lawyer. At first instance he had been sentenced to twenty years' imprisonment. He had filed a plea of nullity and the public prosecutor had appealed against the sentence. One of Mr Kremzow's complaints was that he had not been present at the hearing before the Supreme Court. As far as the plea of nullity was concerned, the Strasbourg organs found no violation of the Convention because mainly questions of law were at issue. However, with regard to the prosecutor's appeal against sentence which had been successful, they did find a violation of Article 6 §§ 1 and 3(c). In the Court's words, '[t]hese proceedings were . . . of crucial importance for the applicant and involved not only an assessment of his character and state of mind at the time of the offence but also his motive'.[79] It was therefore essential that he had the possibility to appear in person together with his counsel in order to be able to 'defend himself in person'. On the other hand, in *Kamasinski* there was no risk of a more severe

---

[74] *Pobornikoff* v. *Austria*, § 26; *Josef Prinz* v. *Austria*, § 34; *Michael Edward Cooke* v. *Austria*, § 35; *Kremzow* v. *Austria*, § 63. In *Pakelli* v. *Germany*, the *Bundesgerichtshof* exceptionally held a public hearing although a technical legal question had to be answered; the fact that the defendant was denied legal assistance for this hearing, however, led to a violation of Art. 6.

[75] *Tripodi* v. *Italy*, §§ 28 et seq. In particular, the lawyer had known that there would be a hearing which he could not attend but failed to take any action with a view to having it postponed. The case of *Alimena* v. *Italy*, § 20 did not present special features and therefore a violation was found.

[76] Canton of Vaud (Switzerland) Code of Criminal Procedure of 12 Sept. 1967, Arts. 415 et seq.; the statute is accessible at www.safari.vd.ch/.   [77] *Botten* v. *Norway*, § 49.

[78] *Kremzow* v. *Austria*, §§ 57 et seq.   [79] Ibid., § 67.

sentence, and no consideration of the personality and character of the accused; therefore his absence could not have been considered as discriminating against him when compared to the situation of a defendant at liberty.[80]

It is not legitimate for the authorities to put obstacles in the way of an accused who chooses to defend him- or herself in person. In *Foucher* the applicant had been denied access to the file for the preparation of the trial and the appeal. Neither the Commission nor the Court hesitated in ruling that this constituted a violation of the right to fair trial.[81]

(viii) Leave-to-Appeal Proceedings Leave-to-appeal proceedings do not call for a hearing in the presence of the accused. They do not involve a re-examination of facts. This is true even in cases where the appellant is detained and the court of appeal does not count the days spent in pre-trial detention as contributing towards the eventual sentence, with the effect that the total period spent in detention is increased.[82]

(ix) The Obligation on the Defence to Act Diligently Normally, the defence is expected to exercise a certain amount of diligence; it is not legitimate to complain in Strasbourg of the denial of a right which was not requested during the domestic proceedings.[83] This could mean, for instance, that where domestic law dictates that an accused must expressly request to be allowed to be present during appeal proceedings, the accused must follow this domestic procedure before being able to raise the complaint in Strasbourg.[84] However, here the Court has applied stricter rules, referring to the duty of the authorities, and in particular that of the court of appeal, to secure by positive measures the presence of the accused at the hearing, once it had concluded that his or her presence was necessary in order for the proceedings to be compatible with the standard of fairness under Article 6.[85]

---

[80] *Kamasinski* v. *Austria*, §§ 104 et seq. The applicant had invoked Art. 6 in conjunction with Art. 14 which prohibits discrimination. Despite the principle '*iura novit curia*' which the Court otherwise recognizes (cf. e.g. *Guzzardi* v. *Italy*, §§ 58–63), no examination of the facts under Art. 6 alone was undertaken. The Commission had found a discrimination. In my view there was a violation of Art. 6 as such because the Court could be called upon to re-examine the sentence; cf. my separate opinion, p. 67. [81] *Foucher* v. *France*.

[82] *Monnell and Morris* v. *United Kingdom*, §§ 55 et seq. The Commission had come to the conclusion that there had been a violation of Art. 6 because the proceedings had led to a supplementary period of detention. The Court was prepared to accept the argument that this was necessary in order to discourage unmeritorious applications for appeal. This is certainly a legitimate aim; but is the sanction proportionate? There remain considerable doubts. Are not the leave-to-appeal-proceedings designed precisely to decide whether an appeal merits being heard? If such detention had been ordered directly as a disciplinary sanction for having abused the right—not even to appeal, but only to ask for leave to appeal—the application of the criteria developed by the Court for the delimitation of the field of application of Art. 6 in criminal matters must have led to the conclusion that this was a 'criminal sanction' with the result that Art. 6 applied. See further Chapter 2 above. [83] See e.g. *Imbrioscia* v. *Switzerland*.

[84] Cf. e.g., *mutatis mutandis, Schuler-Zgraggen* v. *Switzerland*, § 58.

[85] *Botten* v. *Norway*, § 53; *Kremzow* v. *Austria*, § 68.

In one case, however, the Court departed from this principle.[86] The applicant, Mr Melin, was a lawyer who complained of the fact that he did not have the opportunity to file a memorial to the French court of cassation. The judgment which he wanted to appeal against had not even been served on him, but the Court accepted that three courses of action were available to him. He could have consulted the original copy of the judgment at the registry of the court; if he was refused a copy, he could have repeated the request; finally, he could have made enquiries to the Court of Cassation's registry. The Court concluded: 'the applicant cannot claim that the authorities made it impossible for him to produce a memorial'.[87] There is certainly a stark contrast between this finding and the rulings in *Kremzow* and *Botten* which suggest that the authorities are under a duty to take positive measures to ensure the attendance of the accused—the fact that Mr Melin was a lawyer can hardly justify such a strict approach.[88]

A similar situation arose in *Foucher*—where the applicant was not a lawyer but had, in conformity with French law, conducted his own case. This was the main reason why the Court found a violation.[89] In *Voisine* the Court clearly and rightly stated that the fact that persons choose to defend themselves is no reason to deprive them of the benefits of other rights of the defence.[90]

3. The Limitation to Lawful Defence Activities

It is rather self-evident that the defence can only be permitted to undertake lawful activities. In fact, Article 6 § 3(c) only allows the person concerned to exercise defence activities permitted by law within the framework of paragraph 3(b) of the same Article. In the words of the Court: 'the Court observes in the first place that Article 6 para. 3(c) does not provide for an unlimited right to use any defence arguments'.[91] The defence must, for instance, respect the rights of other persons. The fact that a defendant acts in his or her defence does not justify attacks on the honour of third persons, or declarations that an innocent person committed the crime. In *Brandstetter*[92] where the applicant was convicted of defamation because of comments that he had made alleging that the inspectors who had taken wine samples had acted irregularly, 'the Court observe[d] in the first place that Article 6 para. 3 (c) does not provide for an unlimited right to use any defence arguments . . . It would be overstraining the concept of the right of defence of those charged with a criminal offence if it were to be assumed that they could not be prosecuted when, in exercising that right, they intentionally arouse false suspicions of punishable behaviour concerning a

---

[86] *Melin* v. *France*, § 24.   [87] Ibid., § 25.
[88] The judgment was passed by five votes to four! The Commission had been unanimous in finding a violation of Article 6 § 1 taken in conjunction with para. 3(b) and (c).
[89] *Foucher* v. *France*, § 35 (the main issue concerned access to the file).
[90] *Voisine* v. *France*, §§ 32, 33.   [91] *Brandstetter* v. *Austria*, § 52.   [92] Ibid., § 51.

witness or any other person involved in the criminal proceedings'.[93] On the other hand, any sanction for unlawful activities on the part of the defence must be proportionate. While the Court found that a prosecution for defamation was within the discretion of the domestic authorities, it accepted that the freedom of expression of the defence could be impaired if the sanctions were 'unduly severe'. In particular, 'the mere possibility of an accused being subsequently prosecuted on account of allegations made in his defence cannot be deemed to infringe his rights under Article 6 para. 3(c). The position might be different if it were established that, as a consequence of national law or practice in this respect being unduly severe, the risk of subsequent prosecution is such that the defendant is genuinely inhibited from freely exercising these rights. Mr Brandstetter has not, however, alleged that this is the case in Austria. Moreover, Mr Brandstetter might have been indirectly inhibited if, when he made his allegations, he had been threatened with the possibility of prosecution for defamation'.[94]

It appears that the Court applies a differentiated rule. On the one hand, the right to a defence does not allow the accused to commit offences against third persons. Yet, if such an offence would be sanctioned very severely or if there is an attempt at intimidating the defence, this constitutes an unacceptable restriction. This is a rather strange argument, particularly if one takes into consideration the position of the third party. The Court is in fact suggesting that if there is a very severe sanction in case of defamation and the defence is warned accordingly, this constitutes an unlawful limitation of the rights of the accused, and the third party cannot take action for the protection of his or her rights. This does not seem to make much sense. At most, it can be accepted in very special and extreme cases.

4. Formalities Must be Respected

A typical feature of procedural law is its insistence on compliance with various formalities and procedural rules, thereby ensuring that the proceedings are organized in a clear and predictable way. Time limits, for instance, can be set to govern the period within which the parties have to present evidence or to file appeals. The defence must respect these deadlines unless they are so unreasonable as to interfere with the very essence of the right.

Such time limits were at issue in the case of *Claudel*.[95] French law required that a plea of nullity to the *cour de cassation* be presented either by the appellant in person or by a lawyer specially qualified to act before that jurisdiction. In this case, the applicant had filed an appeal which was signed by his defence counsel who was not competent to plead before that court; it was consequently rejected. The Commission accepted the restriction. One might wonder, however, whether this decision is really convincing. Formal rules must undoubtedly be reasonable,

---

[93] *Brandstetter v. Austria*, § 52.   [94] Ibid., § 53.
[95] *Claudel v. France* Application 23038/93. See also *Meftah v. France*, § 47.

and it is difficult to understand why the appeal would have been admissible if the applicant had signed it himself, but inadmissible, if signed by an 'ordinary' lawyer. It would certainly be more logical to accept only appeals presented by the specially qualified lawyers. Such restrictions serve to limit the number of appeals to the highest courts which all tend to be overburdened with cases.

A number of formal procedural rules exist which seem difficult if not impossible to justify. Good examples include the requirement (for example, in the United Kingdom and in Germany, though not in the German-speaking part of Switzerland) that lawyers wear robes. States are free to impose such rules, the Convention does not forbid them.[96] One particularly scurrilous case involved Germany: the Berlin *Kammergericht* had rejected the grounds for appeal submitted by the applicant's lawyer (and thereby declared the appeal itself inadmissible) on the basis that the lawyer's signature was unsatisfactory— they accepted that it did not have to be legible but it was essential that they could recognize the name. The request of a second lawyer that the decision be reconsidered, was rejected for the same reason. To add insult to injury, the decision of the *Kammergericht* itself bore signatures which were impossible to decipher. I regret that the Commission declared this case inadmissible. It is, in my view, a typical example of excessive formalism, if not an abuse of power.[97]

B. The Right of the Accused to 'Defend Himself in Person'

The difficult question in this context is whether it is possible to impose counsel upon an accused who declares that he or she would prefer not to have one. Does the accused have a right *not* to be assisted by counsel? The problem lies on the border between the 'liberal' and 'social' conceptions of the administration of criminal justice. The 'liberal' approach places the main emphasis on the pre-ferences of the accused; the 'social' approach on the other hand would oblige states not only to refrain from interfering with rights of the individual, but also, when necessary, to take positive action to protect them.[98]

Counsel can also be imposed if the accused shows disruptive behaviour or abuses in any other way his or her position. This was also the issue in the trial against Slobodan Milosevic although no intention to sabotage the trial was alleged. Bad health, in particular high blood pressure, had led to the medical finding that he was not fit to defend himself without causing considerable delay due to the fact that the Trial Chamber would only be able to sit one day per

---

[96] *X and Y* v. *Germany* Applications 5217/71 and 5367/72.

[97] *K* v. *Germany* Application 12304/86. The case was most probably a consequence of some personal feud between the court and the lawyers, but I find it particularly objectionable that the applicant had to bear the consequences.

[98] The Court found the root of this obligation in Art. 1 of the Convention according to which states 'shall secure to everyone . . . the rights and freedoms defined in . . . this Convention'; see e.g. *Ireland* v. *United Kingdom*, § 239.

week. The Appeals Chamber upheld the imposition of counsel but found that
the restrictions imposed by the Trial Chamber were too strict. Primarily,
Milosevic continues to be entitled to act in his own defence.[99]

As a rule, however, it will only be justified in exceptional cases to take action to
protect an individual against his or her own will.[100] It is also rather doubtful
whether the assistance of counsel can serve any useful purpose if the accused is
strictly opposed to it. Where a dispute arises between the lawyer and the client,
the tribunal will have to give preference to the position of the client rather than
that of the lawyer. Thus, there are quite a number of arguments in favour of
accepting the will of the accused not to be assisted by counsel.

There are weighty arguments for the opposite view too. It may safely be
assumed that as a rule even an accused who is fully conversant with criminal law
and procedure will rarely be in a position objectively to appreciate the situation
and to act effectively in his or her own defence. Furthermore, although the
lawyer acting for the accused is not to be regarded as an auxiliary of the court but
has the obligation to act exclusively in the interest of her or his client, the task of
the tribunal is facilitated if a knowledgeable person acts intelligently and
rationally in the interests of the defence.

This situation prompted the Commission in the early years of its existence
to leave a large margin of appreciation to states in solving the problem.[101] In
a different context, the 'Independent Experts' called upon by the Secretary
General of the Council of Europe to determine whether certain detainees in
Azerbaijan were political prisoners or not were very reluctant to accept proceedings as fair where the accused had allegedly waived the assistance of counsel
despite the threat of capital punishment or a very long prison sentence.[102]

The Court followed the Commission's approach and rather laconically stated:
'The requirement that a defendant be assisted by counsel at all stages of
the ... proceedings (...)—which finds parallels in the legislation of other
Contracting States—cannot, in the Court's opinion, be deemed incompatible
with the Convention'.[103] This quotation is taken from the *Croissant* case, where
the complexity of the situation was exacerbated by the decision of the accused,

---

[99] Appeals Chamber of the International Criminal Tribunal for the Prosecution of Persons
Responsible for Serious Violations of International Humanitarian Law Committed in the Territory
of Former Yugoslavia since 1991, case no. IT -02-54-AR73.7, *Slobodan Milosevic* v. *Prosecutor*,
Decision of 1 Nov. 2004.

[100] An exceptional case arises e.g. where persons of unsound mind, who are unable freely to take
any reasoned decision, are concerned.

[101] *X* v. *Austria* Application 2676/65; *X* v. *Norway* Application 5923/72; *Scheichelbauer* v. *Austria*
Application 2645/65; *X* v. *Austria* 7138/75; *Ensslin, Baader and Raspe* Applications 7572/76,
7586/76, and 7587/76, § 21; *X* v. *United Kingdom* Application 8295/78.

[102] For a background to this operation, see Trechsel (2002) 203. The decisions taken by the
Independent Experts will probably be declassified and accessible on the Internet.

[103] *Croissant* v. *Germany*, § 27; Harris, O'Boyle, and Warbrick (1995) 258; see also *Philis* v.
Greece Application 16598/90.

himself a lawyer, to retain two attorneys. The Court saw no problem with the *ex officio* appointment of a third lawyer, but stressed, that 'before nominating more than one counsel a court should pay heed to the accused's views as to the number needed, especially where . . . he will in principle have to bear the consequent costs if he is convicted. An appointment that runs counter to those wishes will be incompatible with the notion of fair trial under Article 6 § 1 if, even taking into account a proper margin of appreciation, it lacks relevant and sufficient justification'.[104]

This can be regarded as being too sweeping a statement; it is acceptable in the specific context of the *Croissant* case and with regard to the appointment of an *ex officio* counsel where the defendant has already chosen one or more lawyers. However, it probably also means that legislation which provides for the obligatory appointment of a defence lawyer, in serious cases and even against the will of the accused, is still compatible with the Convention.

It is true that in *Foucher* the Court made a statement which could lead, and indeed has led,[105] to a different interpretation: 'Mr Foucher chose to conduct his own case, which he was entitled to do both under the express terms of the Convention and under domestic law'.[106] In my opinion this sentence only means that the Convention does not prohibit a regulation which allows an accused to choose to defend himself in person—this is in any case clear. But it does not mean that it prohibits the compulsory appointment of defence counsel. Finally, in *Lagerblom* v. *Sweden*, there was a clear answer: 'A legal requirement that an accused be assisted by counsel in criminal proceedings cannot be deemed incompatible with the Convention'.[107] Furthermore, 'when appointing defence counsel the courts must certainly have regard to the accused's wishes but these can be overridden when there are relevant and sufficient grounds for holding that this is necessary in the interests of justice'.[108]

This makes for a relatively complex chain of rules and exceptions:

1. states may insist that in certain proceedings the accused is assisted by counsel at all times;
2. if the defendant does not choose a lawyer, the authorities may appoint one *ex officio*;
3. there is no rule prohibiting the appointment of more than one lawyer or the appointment of a further lawyer or lawyers even though the defendant has already retained one or more counsel;
4. however, it is not in line with the concept of fair trial under Article 6 § 1, in particular as specified in Article 6 § 3(c), to do so if the accused has not been consulted—his or her views must be taken into consideration;
5. the fourth rule does not necessarily apply if there is no possibility that the accused will ultimately have to pay the costs;[109]

---

[104] *Croissant* v. *Germany*, § 27.   [105] Verniory (2005) 181.   [106] *Foucher* v. *France*.
[107] *Lagerblom* v. *Sweden*, § 50.   [108] Ibid., § 54.
[109] See, on the cost of legal-aid counsel, section IV below.

6. an appointment which runs counter to the wishes of the accused may nevertheless be compatible with the Convention if it is based on a relevant and sufficient justification; the domestic authorities enjoy 'a proper margin of appreciation' in determining whether such justification exists.[110]

The situation is clearer under the Covenant. The HRC had to consider a communication against Spain where the applicant alleged that the assistance of counsel had been imposed on him against his will. The Committee recalled:

that Michael Hill insists that he wanted to defend himself, through an interpreter, and that court denied this request. The State party has answered that the records of the hearing do not show such a request, and that Spain recognized the rights of Auto defence 'pursuant to the Covenant and the European Convention of Human Rights, but that such defence should take place by competent counsel, which is paid by the State when necessary', thereby conceding that its legislation does not allow an accused person to defend himself in person, as provided for under the Covenant. The Committee accordingly concludes that Michael Hill's right to defend himself was not respected, contrary to article 14, paragraph 3(d), of the Covenant.[111]

The majority of legal scholars express a preference for the accused's freedom to choose either way.[112] As already indicated, both solutions are acceptable: they reflect fundamentally different attitudes about the relationship between the authorities and the individual. In my view, therefore, the Court is right in leaving a broad margin of appreciation to the states.

III. THE RIGHT TO THE ASSISTANCE OF COUNSEL OF ONE'S OWN CHOOSING

A. A 'Practically Absolute' Right

The 'most (but not entirely) absolute' right of Article 6 § 3(c) is the right of the accused 'to defend himself... through legal assistance of his own choosing'.[113] A defence which is conducted with the assistance of chosen counsel is certainly the best of the three alternatives offered by Article 6 § 3(c).[114]

In an early judgment, *Engel and others* v. *Netherlands*, the Court seems to have had some doubts in this respect. It recognized that the legal assistance which the applicants had received was 'limited to dealing with the legal issues in dispute'. This implies, rightly, that such limitations are not in line with the right to defence under the Convention. However, the Court added: 'In the circumstances of the case, this restriction could nonetheless be reconciled with the interests of justice

---

[110] This corresponds to the finding of the Appeals Chamber in the Milosevic case noted above.
[111] *Michael and Brian Hill* v. *Spain*, § 14.2.
[112] Poncet (1977) 169; Harris, O'Boyle, and Warbrick (1995) 258; Haefliger and Schürmann (1999) 226; Vogler (1986) Art. 6 N 494; Velu and Ergec (1990) N 597; Verniory (2005) 181.
[113] See also Frowein and Peukert Art. 6 N 192; Vogler (1986) N 511, 514.
[114] *Goddi* v. *Italy*, Report of the Commission, 25.

since the applicants were certainly not incapable of personally providing explanations on the very simple facts of the charges levelled against them'.[115]

The Swiss canton of Basel-Stadt used to have a rule excluding the assistance of counsel in cases involving minor offences. Initially the Federal Court had accepted this limitation, but later correctly found it to be incompatible with the Convention.[116]

There can be no doubt, that the view expressed by the Court in *Engel* must be rejected.[117] Less obvious is the question as to how far the judicial authorities must go in order to facilitate the active participation of counsel. One answer is clear from the outset: as a general rule the lawyer ought to take the initiative. Counsel must have the opportunity to attend the examinations of the accused and witnesses during pre-trial proceedings, but he or she must ask to be informed of the venue and to be permitted to attend.[118]

In one case counsel had been unable to attend the hearing and another lawyer terminated the mandate shortly before it was due to take place, which meant that the applicant was without legal assistance.[119] The Commission rejected the application on the basis that the case was not so difficult as to make it impossible for the accused to defend himself. Again, this argument is unacceptable.[120] The situation is less simple in cases where the Court is faced with improper use of procedure, such as where a lawyer systematically withdraws from a case in order purposely to sabotage the proceedings. This kind of problem arose in Germany at the time of proceedings against alleged members of the so-called RAF (*Rote Armee Fraktion*). The authorities acted in a prudent way by appointing additional counsel.[121] This represents, of course, a compromise. The system prevents the accused from appearing before the tribunal unassisted, it avoids endless postponements of the hearing, but counsel will not be the lawyer chosen by the defendant. Yet, this is not incompatible with the right to a fair trial. It is a general rule of law that the abuse of a right will not be protected. This principle is expressed in Article 17 of the ECHR which falls to be applied by analogy in cases of clear abuse.[122]

B. Limitations as to the Persons Eligible as Counsel

Qualitative or quantitative limitations on the persons who are eligible to act as counsel for the defence are generally acceptable.[123] It is, in fact, quite normal that

---

[115] *Engel and others* v. *Netherlands*, § 91; by mentioning the 'circumstances of the case' the Court referred to the fact that it concerned military disciplinary proceedings.

[116] See Trechsel (1979) 365 et seq. and Haefliger and Schürmann (1999) 227 et seq., both with further references.

[117] See Triffterer and Binner (1977) 136 at 142; Trechsel (1979) 356 et seq.

[118] See e.g. *Imbrioscia* v. *Switzerland*, § 42.   [119] Application 7368/76.

[120] See also Trechsel (1979) 355 et seq.; Vogler (1986) N 515.

[121] The authorities also opted for this course of action in *Croissant* v. *Germany*.

[122] See also ICCPR, Art. S § 4 and ACHR, Art. 29 (a).

[123] See e.g. Van Dijk and Van Hoof (1998) 471.

any (at least any professional) defence activity is restricted to persons who have qualified as lawyers, who are permitted to practise law in the particular jurisdiction, and who are certified as capable of effectively appearing before the competent courts.[124] Furthermore, it is also acceptable for the representation of the accused before the highest courts of the country to be restricted to a limited number of particularly qualified lawyers as is the case in France.[125]

Lawyers may be obliged to respect the rules of their code of ethics[126] and may be ordered to step down from their function if they are needed as a witness in the case.[127] However, states ought to be reluctant to exclude a lawyer chosen by the defendant.[128]

The IACtHR had to consider a strange problem. A decree passed in Peru prohibited lawyers from defending more than one case concerning certain terrorist crimes. The applicant complained that this limited his right to the lawyer of his choosing who, being already involved in such a case, was barred from taking him as a client. The Court's response is not really satisfactory: 'While the law that prohibits an attorney from assisting more than one defendant at the same time does have the effect of limiting the accused's choices of defense attorneys, it does not represent, *per se*, a violation of Article 8(2)(d) of the Convention'.[129]

C. Limitations as to the Number of Counsel

In the case of *Ensslin and others*,[130] the Commission regarded as compatible with Article 6 § 3(c) a regulation which stated that a maximum of two lawyers could act in the case. While this number might be too small for complicated cases, the principle of restrictions on the number of lawyers in a case is certainly legitimate. Extending the number of counsel to, for example, one hundred, may be of some meaning in a case where the defendant is an opponent of an authoritarian regime and the Bar decides to demonstrate its support for the rule of law. In ordinary criminal cases, an excessive number of counsel may lead to technical difficulties and could even interfere with the successful course of the trial. It can be compared to the abuse of freedom of expression by filibuster. As with any abuse of a right, it merits no protection (cf. *mutatis mutandis* Article 17 of the ECHR).

---

[124] *V* v. *United Kingdom* Application 11465/85; in fact, a lawyer can be replaced while a witness cannot.   [125] *Claudel* v. *France* Application 23038/93.
[126] A judgment of the Supreme Court of the Ukraine declared unconstitutional a statute which limited the defence activities to lawyers admitted to the Bar. This causes consternation with the members of the Bar who fear that lawyers not bound by a code of ethics nor by professional secrecy will undermine the confidence needed by counsel for the defence.
[127] *K* v. *Denmark* Application 19524/92 (1993).
[128] Harris, O'Boyle, and Warbrick (1995) 260.
[129] IACtHR, *Petruzzi et al* v. *Peru*, judgment of 30 May 1999, Series C No. 52, § 147; the court nevertheless found a violation because of difficulties in communication.
[130] *Ensslin and others* v. *Germany* Applications 7572, 7586, and 7587.

D. Confiscation of Assets and the Right to Counsel of the Accused's Choosing

A difficult situation may arise if a person is accused of crimes which brought economic gain and the authorities seize his or her entire assets, leaving no means to pay for a lawyer of the suspect's own choosing. It is sometimes alleged, that the purpose of the confiscation of the assets is to make an effective defence impossible. The problem has not yet arisen in the European case-law.

It will hardly ever be possible to establish that the prosecuting authority has abused its powers. However, the seizure of all of a suspect's assets might conflict with the presumption of innocence. The general principle of fairness prohibits the prosecution from making it impossible for the defence effectively to exercise its rights. A reasonable part of the suspect's assets must therefore be left for the purposes of financing an effective defence, in cases where doubts as to the lawful owner persist. Another sensitive aspect is that the authorities will have to determine the amount of money that ought to be set aside; it is legitimate to prevent the suspect from abusing such facilities in order to secure some of the alleged loot for himself. At any rate, there is always the possibility of legal aid.

On the other hand, the interests of the victim of the crime cannot entirely be disregarded. Can a person who has been the victim of an economic crime reasonably be expected to accept that the criminal uses money stolen from her or him for the purposes of paying his or her defence lawyer's fees?

Even from a general point of view there is a need for caution. If a person has engaged in illegal activities, such as drug trafficking, large-scale fraud or money laundering, that person has gravely jeopardized his or her economic situation. Persons who engage in illegal economic activities 'contaminate' their assets. After some time, all their property falls to be regarded as illegally acquired and therefore risks to be seized in view of an eventual confiscation. Although such persons benefit from the presumption of innocence, it would not be equitable if they could use 'suspicious' money in order to retain the assistance of the best-skilled lawyers at enormous expense. They become, at least technically and provisionally, poor and will not have 'sufficient means to pay for legal assistance'. To exempt from seizure the sums claimed for the purposes of the defence would open the door to abuses and lead to an unjustified privilege compared to defendants who are 'naturally poor'.

This is not the only problem which a lawyer might have to deal with in such a case. If a lawyer accepts payment from money which was obtained through the criminal activities of his or her client, there is a risk that he or she might be prosecuted for money laundering, at least in the rather excessive interpretation this offence has been given in certain jurisdictions.[131]

---

[131] Cf. e.g. Burgstaller (2001) 574; Wohlers (2002) and further articles referred to there; *Bundesgerichtshof* (Germany), 2nd Senate, in 21 StV 506, 509 (2001). On the other hand, the German Government did not, apparently, see a problem when they suggested that legal aid should not be granted to a person who had dealt with drugs and could therefore be supposed to have money: *Pakelli* v. *Germany*, § 32.

International human-rights law provides no assistance for accused persons involved in such cases. Each Contracting State has the discretion to decide whether or not to prosecute persons for receiving stolen goods, money laundering, or other similar offences. Moreover, the criminal-procedure law of each state will regulate whether, and under what conditions, the (suspected) proceeds of crime may be seized pending a final determination of the charge. The international instruments provide assistance only insofar as they guarantee that the accused has the right to effective assistance of counsel. Such assistance will not always be of the same quality as that which the accused may have chosen, but the international norms cannot and should not be expected to guarantee the best possible defence.

IV. THE RIGHT TO LEGAL AID

It is a sad joke that 'the law, like the Ritz Hotel, is open to all'. In theory and ideally, judges are absolutely impartial; the so-called continental legal tradition obliges them actively to seek the truth, while the prosecutor is also expected to act with a view to obtaining justice and to take into account all the facts that militate in favour of the suspect. Still, in reality, prosecutors see it as their main duty to avoid unjustified acquittal of the guilty and the judge will largely depend on the evidence and arguments presented by the parties. The right of a suspect to defend himself with the assistance of counsel is designed to counter-balance the odds against her or him, but it will often be a theoretical possibility because the accused is indigent and cannot pay for a lawyer.

Here, legal assistance comes in: the state will—paradoxically—pay for a lawyer whose task will be to frustrate the efforts of the public prosecutor who is equally paid by the state. This means that the administration of criminal justice resembles something of a state-organized sporting event in which it sponsors both teams. However, it is one of the fundamental features of the rule of law that the state is not allowed to pursue its goals—*in casu*, the fight against criminality—using a fully utilitarian approach.

The fundamental value of fairness must be upheld and it requires behaviour which, at first sight, appears to be rather irrational, if not downright contradictory. The solution is not quite ideal. Legal-aid counsel may, but will not necessarily, be the lawyer of the defendant's choice. It will, in fact, not always be a top lawyer. Sometimes he or she will not even be paid at all, in other instances the pay will be below that of the chosen lawyer. This may have an influence upon the motivation of counsel—a fact that may provide some explanation for the cases of *Artico* and *Goddi* where the legal-aid counsel had no right to any remuneration.[132] The institution of legal aid reduces injustice, but only to a certain extent. The advantages enjoyed by rich defendants—mirrored of course

[132] Trechsel (1978) at 577: adequate remuneration of legal-aid counsel is an important element to secure an effective defence. I am not aware of any international decision accepting (or rejecting)

by the advantages enjoyed by them in everyday life—will never be entirely eliminated. However, the problem should not be over-dramatized. For instance, chosen counsel may also turn out to be inadequate while the *ex officio* counsel may sometimes be exceptionally good.

There is a slight difference between the French and the English text. In the English version of Article 6 § 3(c) and Article 14 § 3(d) of the ICCPR, the right is to 'legal assistance', while in the French version the reference is to '*un avocat d'office*', '*un défenseur*'. One might interpret this as a limitation to one counsel only. Yet, the singular is also used for the chosen lawyer, '*un défenseur de son choix*' in both texts. This definitely does not limit the number of lawyers to one. It must also be possible to have more than one counsel in cases where a legal-aid lawyer is appointed. In complex proceedings one person alone may not be able to cope with the task. For instance, it is hardly possible to examine a witness and take notes at the same time.

The guarantee set out in Article 6 § 3(c) of the ECHR is to legal assistance where the defendant 'has not sufficient means to pay for legal assistance, to be given it free when the interests of justice so require'; Article 14 § 3(d) ICCPR has exactly the same meaning. There are, then, two prerequisites for legal aid, an economical one and a legal one.[133]

A. The Economic Prerequisite

For a long time there was only scarce and imprecise case-law on this point. However, the Convention organs themselves have a practice of granting legal aid to indigent applicants. In this respect they rely primarily on the rules of the national law governing the provision of legal aid in domestic proceedings.[134] The rules are not very strictly applied—legal aid is only rarely refused for the reason that an applicant has sufficient means to pay for it him- or herself.

The first judgment where the problem was addressed was *Pakelli*.[135] The applicant was back in Turkey when the case was examined by the Court; the German Government contested his assertion that he had insufficient means to pay, referring to the fact that he had dealt in drugs;[136] the Court accepted the Commission's view that it was hardly possible to prove in 1983 whether the applicant had the means to pay for a lawyer back in 1977; there were, however, a number of rather strong indications in support of his statement. '[W]hile these particulars [were] not sufficient to prove beyond all doubt that the applicant was

that principle. However, *Van der Mussele* v. *Belgium* is another example which shows that often legal-aid counsel are expected to work *pro deo*.

[133] *Pham Hoang* v. *France*, § 39; *R D* v. *Poland*, § 43.

[134] On this system of legal aid, see e.g. Harris, O'Boyle, and Warbrick (1995) 590; Starmer (2001) N 30.40 et seq.; Ravaud (1995) 727 et seq. See also the Rules of the Court.

[135] *Pakelli* v. *Germany*, §§ 32–4.

[136] There appears also a certain amount of cynicism in the argument that counsel ought to be paid with money earned through dealing with drugs!

indigent at the relevant time' and in view of his offer to prove to the Federal Court his lack of means, the Court accepted that this first requirement was fulfilled. In *Twalib* the wording is if anything slightly more open: 'indications, although not conclusive of the issue of ineffective assistance by counsel, . . . confirm to [the Court's] satisfaction that the applicant was indigent'.[137] The onus of proof stays, however, with the accused.[138]

The Court had the opportunity to address the issue more thoroughly in a case concerning civil proceedings, *Kreuz* v. *Poland*. The applicant had asked to be exempted from court fees but this request was refused. The Court stated that it could not evaluate the financial situation of the applicant but found a violation because the Polish authorities had not bothered seriously to examine the matter.[139] In *RD* v. *Poland* the Wrocław Court of Appeal had first granted legal aid but then went on to refuse it in connection with the applicant's cassation appeal, as his economic situation had not changed. The Court held that there could be no justification for this change of attitude. The Court was satisfied that the applicant did not have sufficient means to pay for legal assistance.[140]

The rule therefore is that the domestic authorities have a considerable margin of appreciation in assessing whether a defendant has or lacks sufficient means to pay for legal assistance. Their decision must, however, be supported by a reasonably serious examination of the case and must be accompanied by reasons.

B. The Interests of Justice

The expression 'when the interests of justice so require' is somewhat misleading—it could be read as meaning that the decisive element is not the interests of the defendant but the public interest in the good administration of justice.[141] This view seems to have been held, at least to some extent, by Fawcett and van Dijk and van Hoof.[142] Harris, O'Boyle, and Warbrick suggest that such a consideration might be present in the *Pakelli* judgment, namely the interest in developing the case-law.[143] However, this can hardly be correct in view of the fact that the rights guaranteed in Article 6 only benefit 'the accused'. The Convention protects human rights, not the interests of a proper development of the case-law. The argument is, however, rather theoretical—it is difficult to see how a defendant could complain of the granting of legal aid if it was only required in the interests of justice. It would, however, be incompatible with the Convention to refuse legal aid by arguing that it was *not* required in the interests of justice when it was necessary in the interests of the accused.

The decisive question is whether the proceedings could still be regarded as 'fair' in the absence of counsel for the defence—after all, we are faced with one of

---

[137] *Twalib* v. *Greece*, § 51.   [138] Harris, O'Boyle, and Warbrick (1995) 261.
[139] *Kreuz* v. *Poland*, §§ 63–7.   [140] *RD* v. *Poland*, § 46.
[141] Haefliger and Schürmann (1999) 230.
[142] Fawcett (1969) 170; Van Dijk and van Hoof (1998) 473.
[143] Harris, O'Boyle, and Warbrick (1995) 262, n. 15.

the elements of fairness.[144] This is clearly stated in *RD* v. *Poland*: 'There is . . . a primary indispensable requirement of the "interests of justice" that must be satisfied in each case. That is the requirement of a fair procedure before courts, which, among other things, imposes on the State authorities an obligation to offer an accused a realistic chance to defend him- or herself throughout the entire trial'.[145]

The Court has set out a number of more specific criteria by which to assess whether the interests of justice require that legal aid be granted. Unfortunately, they are neither applied in a very systematic manner, nor easy to distinguish. Generally more than one criterion is referred to even if one of them has already been found to be present.[146] It is quite clear though that *domestic law* is *not relevant*, at least to the extent that it is more restrictive than the Convention law as interpreted by the Strasbourg organs.[147] In a rather old decision the Commission found that it was primarily for the national authorities to determine whether the interests of justice called for legal-aid counsel;[148] however, there is no trace of this approach in the later case-law of the Court.

It is possible to distinguish four types of criteria: the seriousness of the offence, the complexity of the case, equality of arms, and the personal situation of the accused. Problems will often arise in the context of appeal proceedings, but there is no need to examine the problems associated with first-instance and appeal proceedings separately. It is sufficient to note that here the Court repeats its general approach according to which 'the manner in which paragraph 1, as well as paragraph 3(c), of Article 6 is to be applied in relation to appellate or cassation courts depends upon the special features of the proceedings involved; account must be taken of the entirety of the proceedings conducted in the domestic legal order and of the role of the appellate or cassation court therein'.[149] The need for legal assistance is particularly acute when, like in Poland (and contrary to the position in France[150]) access to the court of cassation is only possible through the assistance of a lawyer.[151]

1. The Seriousness of the Offence and the Severity of the Punishment

The seriousness of the offence was established as the first consideration in *Quaranta*.[152] In this case, the question arose as to how the severity was to be

---

[144] See e.g. *Granger* v. *United Kingdom*, § 47; *Pham Hoang* v. *France*, § 39; *Quaranta* v. *Switzerland*, § 27; *Twalib* v. *Greece*, § 46.   [145] *RD* v. *Poland*, § 49.

[146] Cf. e.g. *Benham* v. *United Kingdom*, §§ 61, 62; *Perks and others* v. *United Kingdom*, § 67.

[147] Commission report in *Quaranta* v. *Switzerland*, § 63, judgment, § 32. On the other hand, in *Artico* the Government pleaded that legal aid was not necessary in spite of the fact that it had been granted in accordance with Italian law by a domestic court—an argument which it is difficult to regard as serious; see *Artico* v. *Italy*, § 34.   [148] *Bell* v. *United Kingdom* Application 12322/86.

[149] See e.g. *Granger* v. *United Kingdom*, § 44; *Monnell and Morris* v. *United Kingdom*, § 56; *Maxwell* v. *United Kingdom*, § 34; *Tripodi* v. *Italy*, § 27; *Twalib* v. *Greece*, 46.

[150] *Vacher* v. *France*, § 30.   [151] *RD* v. *Poland*, §§ 50, 51.

[152] *Quaranta* v. *Switzerland*, § 33.

assessed. The Government proposed to rely on the sentence which the accused realistically incurred (not above eighteen months' imprisonment), while the Court held that the abstract maximum possible sentence (three years) was decisive.[153] Ultimately, the accused received six months.

The Court's approach was criticized in Switzerland[154]—in my view, the criticism is justified. The Convention rights are meant to be practical, not theoretical;[155] this does not only work for the applicant but also for the domestic authorities. The observation of the Court, that the anticipated maximum penalty was 'no more than an estimation', betrays a certain lack of experience in the administration of criminal law.

My criticism, however, is not focused on the *result* of the judgment. In fact, even the estimated punishment was, in my view, clearly beyond the limit up to which legal assistance could be dispensed with, but rather on the reasoning: 'The Court agrees with the Commission that where deprivation of liberty is at stake, the interests of justice in principle call for legal representation'.[156] Two questions must therefore be answered: what is meant by deprivation of liberty, and what are the exceptions?

With regard to deprivation of liberty, the criterion must be understood to mean actual imprisonment as opposed to a suspended sentence or a sentence to imprisonment on probation;[157] however, legal aid will then be required if and as soon as a decision on the execution is to be taken. This solution may not be entirely satisfactory. In fact, it is possible for irreparable mistakes to have occurred at the trial which might have been avoided had the assistance of defence counsel been granted. However, the Convention ought not to be interpreted as requiring maximum rights—after all, it guarantees *minimum* standards. Yet, as soon as a substantial sentence, even if it is suspended, is to be expected, the interests of justice require that counsel be appointed. The case-law gives no indication as to what the limit might be, but it is, in my view reasonable to envisage that it would be somewhere between three and six months.

The Court refers to the possible *sanction*, not to deprivation of liberty in the course of the proceedings. In my view, if a person is arrested under Article 5 § 1(c), but released before the short period referred to in Article 5 § 3 of the ECHR elapses, there is no absolute requirement that legal-aid counsel be appointed. If, however, a person is brought before a judge with a view to being taken into detention on remand, the interests of justice will normally require the assistance of counsel.

It is rather difficult to imagine cases where, exceptionally, the interests of justice do not call for legal aid despite the fact that the accused faces an

---

[153] *Quaranta* v. *Switzerland*, § 33.
[154] Haefliger and Schürmann (1999) 232; BGE 120 Ia 45.   [155] *Artico* v. *Italy*, § 33.
[156] *Benham* v. *United Kingdom*, § 61; *Perks and others* v. *United Kingdom*, § 67. In other cases, heavy sentences were at issue, e.g. eight years in *Boner* v. *United Kingdom*.
[157] Haefliger and Schürmann (1999) 231; BGE 120 Ia 45 reject this strict criterion.

unconditional sentence of imprisonment. There will be an exception where two requirements are fulfilled: the sentence is short, not exceeding, for example, one to three months; and at the same time the case is so simple that the accused can defend him- or herself adequately without the assistance of counsel. An example might be a case where a repeat offender is caught shoplifting *in flagrante*. Elements such as the intelligence of the accused and his or her familiarity with similar situations may be taken into account. While it may be tempting to require that legal-aid counsel be made available in practically all cases,[158] one has to take into account the limited possibilities of the states, including budgetary constraints. There is also a certain danger that the excessive use of legal-aid counsel might lower the quality of the services rendered. In other words, it might have an effect of inflation.[159] Sometimes the Court simply refers—in addition to other criteria—to the importance of the appeal proceedings for the applicant.[160] The Commission rejected an application because only petty fines were involved and the legal issue was absolutely trivial.[161]

2. The Complexity of the Case

Whenever legal questions of some difficulty are at issue, the defendant will normally not be able to defend him- or herself in person. It is not surprising, therefore, that in most of the cases it dealt with, the Court also referred to the complexity of the case,[162] even if a case 'may not have been particularly complex'.[163] In particular, the Court thinks that 'to attack in appeal proceedings a judge's exercise of discretion in the course of a trial . . . requires a certain legal skill and experience'.[164]

3. The Particularities of the Proceeding

Legal assistance is furthermore called for in specific procedural situations, particularly if the public prosecution will be represented—in such cases equality of arms is at issue, even if it is not expressly mentioned by the Court.[165]

---

[158] Such a proposal was made, e.g. by Bemmann, Grünwald, Hassemer, Krauss, Lüderssen, Naucke, Rudolphi, and Welp (1979) § 3 (1).

[159] The United Kingdom Government argued in *Boner* v. *United Kingdom* (§ 42) and *Granger* v. *United Kingdom* (§ 39) that if requirements were too strict in appeal proceedings, the automatic right to appeal under Scots law might be abolished 'thereby effectively diminishing the rights of the accused'! [160] *Quaranta* v. *Switzerland*, § 34.

[161] *Y* v. *Germany* Application 11777/85: the case concerned a foreigner who had left the district assigned to him without authorization.

[162] *Benham* v. *United Kingdom*, § 62; *Perks and others* v. *United Kingdom*, § 67; *Boner* v. *United Kingdom*, § 41; *Pham Hoang* v. *France*, § 40; *Twalib* v. *Greece*, § 41; *RD* v. *Poland*, § 48, etc.

[163] e.g. *Boner* v. *United Kingdom*, § 41; *Maxwell* v. *United Kingdom*, § 38.

[164] *Boner* v. *United Kingdom*, § 41.

[165] See e.g. *Pakelli* v. *Germany*, § 39; *Granger* v. *United Kingdom*, § 47; *Monnell and Morris* v. *United Kingdom*, § 62 (*e contrario*).

In view of the judgment in *Monnell and Morris*, it could be expected that the Court would deny the right to legal aid in cases where the applicant wanted to file an appeal which had only a very small chance of success: 'The interests of justice cannot, however, be taken to require an automatic grant of legal aid whenever a convicted person, with no objective likelihood of success, wishes to appeal after having received a fair trial at first instance in accordance with Article 6'.[166] However, in a number of later judgments the Court saw no reason to refuse legal aid in cases where the applicants had been advised that the chances of their appeals succeeding were slim.[167] As a matter of principle, I find it acceptable that legal aid be refused for frivolous appeals which have no chance of success.

4. The Particularities of the Accused

Even if a case is neither particularly serious nor particularly complex and there is no one to appear before the court to oppose the accused, there may be some other reason why legal assistance may be required. It may be a physical or a mental handicap or simply a lack of necessary skills. This issue has arisen in the Court's case-law primarily with regard to foreigners who are often unfamiliar with the language and the legal system of the country.[168]

C. The Choice of the Lawyer

Basically, it is for the authority who will pay for the lawyer to appoint him or her. This was also the position in the early case-law of the Commission.[169] Originally, the Commission did not even require that the accused be consulted.[170] This view has been adopted by the Court without restriction: 'The Court reiterates first that, according to the established case-law of the Convention institutions, Article 6 § 3(c) does not guarantee the right to choose an official defence counsel who is appointed by the court, nor does it guarantee a right to be consulted with regard to the choice of such counsel'.[171] This attitude seems to cast doubt on, and even invalidate, the Court's reasoning in other cases. In *Pakelli* the Court could be understood to have interpreted Article 6 § 3(c) differently. After discussing the differences between the English and the French versions of the Convention—the English one links the three limbs of the paragraph with the word 'or', while the French text uses '*et*' between the second and the third limb—it concluded: 'a "person charged with a criminal offence"

---

[166] *Monnell and Morris* v. *United Kingdom*, § 67.
[167] Cf. *Boner* v. *United Kingdom*, § 11.
[168] Cf. *Quaranta* v. *Switzerland*, § 35; *Twalib* v. *Greece*, § 53; *Biba* v. *Greece*, § 29.
[169] See, among many others, *X* v. *Germany* Application 6946/75.
[170] Application 125/55.
[171] *Franquesa Freixas* v. *Spain* Application 53590/99, with reference to the Commission's decision in *X* v. *Germany* Application 6946/75.

who does not wish to defend himself in person must be able to have recourse to legal assistance of his own choosing; if he does not have sufficient means to pay for such assistance, he is entitled under the Convention to be given it free when the interests of justice so require'.[172] 'Such assistance', grammatically, refers to 'assistance of his own choosing'. Taken literally, this means that the Court requires that the legal-aid counsel must also be of the accused's own choosing.

However, it is not quite clear whether this is actually what the Court wanted to say; it had no reason to address the question—there was no allegation that the authorities wanted to appoint a different lawyer from the one chosen by the applicant. Van Dijk and van Hoof interpret the passage as departing from the Commission's approach.[173] According to them the statement was confirmed in *Croissant* where it is said that 'when appointing defence counsel the national courts must certainly have regard to the defendant's wishes'.[174] Here, the conclusion is indeed supported, because the Court referred to the domestic law, DStPO, § 142, which states that 'in so far as possible, the President of the court shall designate the lawyer . . . The accused shall be offered the opportunity of indicating a lawyer of his choice within a prescribed time-limit. Unless there are important reasons for not doing so, the President shall appoint the lawyer indicated by the accused'.[175]

In my view it would be desirable for the Court to return to its own case-law and follow the German rule. The question then arises as to what constitutes special circumstances justifying, exceptionally, the designation of a lawyer other than that chosen by the accused. Such reasons could be, for example, the fact that the lawyer lives a considerable distance away from the court, which would result in excessive travel expenses, or that he or she is not trustworthy in the specific case, perhaps because of prior involvement in the matter or a conflict of interests. While it can, as a matter of principle, be accepted that the defendant cannot be entirely free to choose his or her legal-aid counsel, there is no justification for failing to consult him or her. The principle ought to be that only specific reasons will justify a departure from the wishes of the accused.

In this context a further question arises: is it acceptable for a trainee lawyer ('*avocat stagiaire*') to be appointed? The Swiss Federal Tribunal is of the opinion that this is in conformity with the ECHR.[176] This is certainly correct even though the essential issue is not the formal position of the person but her or his competence.[177]

D. 'Free'

To be granted legal aid means that the defence lawyer will be 'free', i.e. that the accused will not have to pay for his or her services. There are two possible

---

[172] *Pakelli* v. *Germany*, § 31.   [173] Van Dijk and van Hoof (1998) 471.
[174] *Croissant* v. *Germany*, § 29.
[175] Translation of the Court, cf. *Croissant* v. *Germany*, § 20.   [176] BGE 126 I 194.
[177] See also Verinory (2005) 130.

interpretations of this aspect of the guarantee: it may mean that there will never be a lawyer's bill for the accused, but it may also mean that the accused, for the time being, does not have to worry about the legal costs, but that he or she may be required to pay in the future if his or her economic situation improves.

While the first interpretation was adopted with respect to interpreters' fees under Article 6 § 3(e), it is the second which applies in relation to lawyers' fees. This is easy to understand: contrary to paragraph 3(e), paragraph 3(c) makes the exoneration dependent upon the economic situation of the accused. The free services of an interpreter are meant to put the accused who is not conversant with the language used in court on an equal footing with the other accused; legal aid aims at putting the indigent accused on an equal footing with the economically stronger defendant. It would be rather absurd to ask an accused to reimburse the interpreter's fees after that person has learned, for example, while serving sentence, the language; however, it makes good sense to ask a person who is enjoying a considerably better economic situation after the trial, to pay back the lawyer's fees. The Court left this question open in *Croissant*.[178]

In some countries, for example, in Germany, it is customary to charge a convicted person with the costs of the proceedings including the costs of legal aid. The Commission has found that this does not constitute a violation of Article 6 § 3(c) provided that this debt is only enforced if the defendant's economic situation improves to such an extent that legal aid would no longer be justified.[179]

V. THE RIGHT TO CONTACT WITH COUNSEL

A. The Principle

As long as a defendant is at liberty, no problem with regard to his or her contact with counsel arises. This changes, however, as soon as the defendant is arrested.

As all contacts between the prisoner and the outside world are controlled, some cooperation with the authorities is vital to enable effective contact with counsel, be it in person, via mail, telephone, or some other means of communication. Furthermore, such contacts must be confidential. There can be no effective defence activity unless the accused can trust his or her lawyer. One of the fundamental elements of this trust is the element of secrecy. The client must be able to confide any information to counsel in the secure knowledge that none of what he or she tells counsel will come to the knowledge of the authorities.

---

[178] *Croissant* v. *Germany*, § 34. The criticism raised by Van Dijk and van Hoof (1998) 472 seems to be based on a misunderstanding: The Court only refers to the case where an applicant had been indigent at the time of the trial, not at the time of the enforcement proceedings.

[179] *X* v. *Germany* Application 9365/81. Some authors had held that this was contrary to the Convention, e.g. Schubarth (1973) 263; Poncet (1977) 164.

The criminal law assists this aspect of the attorney–client relationship in that it makes the violation of the professional duty of confidentiality an offence.

On the other hand, prosecuting and investigating authorities often fear the influence of counsel. They assume that such assistance might make their task more difficult in that it will strengthen the self-assurance of the accused and permit her or him to establish and follow useful defence strategies such as making use of the right to silence. They will therefore wish to supervise any contact between the accused and counsel. On the other hand, lawyers will generally refuse to have any interview with a client when representatives of the authorities are listening in; they consider the danger of damaging the climate of confidence, which is of paramount importance, to be too high.

Article 8 § 2(d) of the ACHR specifically guarantees the right to free and private contact with counsel. In the Covenant this rule can be found annexed to the right to adequate time and facilities for the preparation of the defence. In the context of the European Convention, the matter was left to the interpretation of the Court. I have chosen to deal with it in the context of the right to a defence with the assistance of counsel.

The leading case on this issue is the Commission's report in *Can* where it was first noted that, contrary to Article 14 § 3(b) of the ICCPR, the ECHR does not guarantee free communication between the accused and counsel.[180] It also referred to Rule 93 of the Standard Minimum Rules for the Treatment of Prisoners[181] and to the European Agreement Relating to Persons Participating in Proceedings of the European Commission and Court of Human Rights[182] which states that interviews with legal advisers may be 'within sight but not within hearing', of a representative of the authorities. 'These texts reflect the fundamental importance which many legal systems attach to the right of the accused to communicate in private with his lawyer'.

Contrary to Article 6 § 3(b), which, in the French version, refers to the time and facilities 'necessary' for the preparation of the defence, Article 6 § 3(c) 'gives the accused a more general right to assistance and support by a lawyer throughout the whole proceedings' because the Convention guarantees are meant to be 'practical and effective'.[183] The Commission then examined the functions of counsel in criminal proceedings:

They include not only the preparation of the trial itself, but also the control of the lawfulness of any measures taken in the course of the investigation proceedings, the identification and presentation of any means of evidence at an early stage where it is still

---

[180] Annexed to *Can v. Austria*, Series A, No. 96, § 51. See also *Kempers v. Austria* Application 21842/93; *Lanz v. Austria*, § 50.

[181] Resolution (73) 5 of the Committee of Ministers of the Council of Europe; the same guarantee figures in Rule 93 of the *revised* European Prison Rules, Recommendation No. R(87) 3 of the Committee of Ministers. See also UN Basic Principles on the Role of Lawyers (UN GA Res. 45/121, 45/166, 1990).   [182] ETS No. 67.

[183] *Can v. Austria*, report, § 54 with reference to *Artico v. Italy*, § 33.

possible to trace new relevant facts and where the witnesses have a fresh memory, further assistance to the accused regarding any complaints which he might wish to make in relation to his detention concerning its justification, length and conditions, and generally to assist the accused who by his detention is removed from his normal environment. Several of these functions are interfered with or made impossible if the defence counsel can communicate with his client only in the presence of a court official . . . Therefore it is in principle incompatible with the right to effective assistance by a lawyer . . . to subject the defence counsel's contacts with the accused to supervision by the court.[184]

In *S* v. *Switzerland* the Court confirmed this finding with much the same reasoning.[185] During the tense situation when Germany was trying to control the so-called RAF, particularly strict measures were imposed to control the defence lawyers, such as searching them and their briefcases. The Commission agreed that, in principle, such measures were not compatible with the rights guaranteed in Article 6 § 3(c). However, they were held to be exceptionally justified by the specific circumstances of the case.[186] In fact, later on it turned out that the pistol used in the killing of Baader, Ensslin, and Raspe in Stammheim had been smuggled into the prison in a lawyer's file.

The case-law has been confirmed and summed up in the judgment of the First Section of the Court in the case of *Öcalan* v. *Turkey* in the following terms:

The Court refers to its settled case-law and reiterates that an accused's right to communicate with his legal representative out of hearing of a third person is part of the basic requirements of a fair trial in a democratic society and follows from Article 6 § 3 (c) of the Convention. If a lawyer were unable to confer with his client and receive confidential instructions from him without such surveillance, his assistance would lose much of its usefulness, whereas the Convention is intended to guarantee rights that are practical and effective (. . .). The importance to the rights of the defence of ensuring confidentiality in meetings between the accused and his lawyers has been affirmed in various international instruments, including European instruments (. . .). However, as stated above (. . .) restrictions may be imposed on an accused's access to his lawyer if good cause exists. The relevant issue is whether, in the light of the proceedings taken as a whole, the restriction has deprived the accused of a fair hearing.[187]

The right of private access to the lawyer does not only apply to face-to-face meetings but also to other forms of communication. Here, the right to respect for correspondence also applies and the problem arises as to whether the issue ought to be examined in the light of one or the other of the Articles or both together.[188] The right to correspondence will normally be in the foreground whenever civil proceedings are at issue, as in such cases only paragraph 1 of Article 6 applies. Instead of regarding a special feature of fair trial for criminal

---

[184] *Can* v. *Austria*, report, §§ 55–8.

[185] *S* v. *Switzerland*, § 48; the Court does not mention the ICCPR (which does not expressly refer to 'privacy' of the communication) but Art. 8 § 2(d) of the ACHR.

[186] *Ensslin, Baader, and Raspe* v. *Germany* Applications 7572, 7586, 7587/76.

[187] *Öcalan* v. *Turkey*, § 146. (At the time the manuscript was finalized, the case was under examination by the Grand Chamber.)   [188] See further Chapter 20 below.

proceedings as contained also in paragraph 1, as the Commission and Court did in *Airey*, it is more natural and easier to apply Article 8.[189]

So far, the Court seems mainly to have followed the approach of each applicant and dealt with the cases under the Article invoked. This was the case in *Schönenberger and Durmaz* where the request to forward a letter from the first applicant (a lawyer) to the second applicant (his imprisoned client-to-be) was denied—the letter only contained general information on the rights of a defendant and the tactical choice he had to make in respect of the decision whether or not to remain silent. The Court found there to have been a violation but did not refer to Article 6 at all. This may be explained by the fact that, when the letter was handed over to the *Bezirksanwalt*, it was accompanied by a power of attorney still to be signed by Mr Durmaz—formally Mr Schönenberger was not yet the representative; but this argument would have been rather formalistic.[190]

In a relatively old decision the Commission accepted that the inspection of correspondence between lawyer and client was an inherent feature of detention on remand.[191] Van Dijk and Van Hoof rightly criticize this decision which can no longer be regarded as valid.[192] Both Commission and Court also found a violation of Article 8 in the *Campbell and Fell* case because of the interference with the applicants' correspondence to their solicitors.[193]

B. Exceptions

In a number of early decisions, later confirmed by the Court in *Öcalan*, the Commission indicated that the right to confidential communication with counsel was not immune from restrictions.[194] It subsequently confirmed this approach in its report in *Can*.[195] In *S* v. *Switzerland* the Court agreed in principle (but not as regards the facts as presented in that case) that some restrictions could be justified, in particular if there existed a risk of collusion or if the 'professional ethics' of the lawyer or the 'lawfulness of his conduct were at any time called into question in this case'.[196]

The issue is delicate and far from clear. In *S* v. *Switzerland* the Government pointed out that the case was a serious one, involving more than one accused, and that counsel might agree on a common defence strategy. The Court accepted the fact but said that this was perfectly legitimate. It might be different in a case where there existed a danger that the lawyer would, on the instructions of the

---

[189] Cf. e.g. *Silver and others* v. *United Kingdom* and *Golder* v. *United Kingdom*.
[190] *Schönenberger and Durmaz* v. *Switzerland*, §§ 20 et seq.   [191] Application 2375/64.
[192] Van Dijk and Van Hoof (1998) 470, n. 1051.
[193] *Campbell and Fell* v. *United Kingdom*, §§ 108–10.
[194] *Bonzi* v. *Switzerland* Application 7854/77; *Schertenleibv* v. *Switzerland* Application 8339/78; *Kröcher and Möller* v. *Switzerland* Application 8463/78; and *G* v. *United Kingdom* Application 9370/81.
[195] *Can* v. *Austria*, report § 52. See also *John Murray* v. *United Kingdom*, Report of the Commission, § 70.   [196] *S* v. *Switzerland*, § 49.

accused, interfere with the evidence by influencing witnesses or destroying documents. However, this hypothesis seems to accept the assumption that lawyers are not always trustworthy. It is very doubtful whether the administration of justice can function properly on such a basis. My opinion today is that, in principle, it cannot.[197] The state must not only organize the judiciary but also ensure that only persons who are trustworthy will be allowed to act as lawyers. While it is true that the strict supervision of the legal profession by the state would impair its independence, there must be legislation regulating the organization of the legal profession and investing it with the necessary powers to control who can become (and remain) a member of the profession.

If in a specific case, and due to exceptional circumstances, doubts persist, an intermediary system of control might be acceptable: the president of the Bar could appoint a senior lawyer to accompany the defence counsel in conversations with his or her client or receive correspondence between the lawyer and his client. This method would provide an effective protection against abuse while the prosecuting authority or the court would not be able to interfere with the attorney–client relationship. The same system could be used for monitoring other forms of communication.

C. The Right to Contact with Counsel During the Police Investigations

Another controversial issue is the moment from which a person under arrest is entitled to have contact with counsel. The Court has consistently held that the guarantee of the right to a fair trial should not be confined to the trial stage, but should apply to the proceedings as a whole, more precisely, 'in so far as the fairness of the trial is likely to be seriously prejudiced by an initial failure to comply with it'.[198] 'The manner in which Article 6 §§ 1 and 3 (c) is applied during the investigation depends on the special features of the proceedings and the facts of the case. However, this right, which is not explicitly set out in the Convention, may be subject to restrictions for good cause'.[199]

Campbell and Fell was a relatively clear case. The applicant, Father Fell, was a so-called 'category A' (high-security) prisoner, and thus had to wait for two weeks before being allowed privileged contact with his solicitor. Without any hesitation the Court, like the Commission, found that this constituted a violation of Article 6 § 1.[200] The situation in the case of *John Murray* was less clear.[201]

---

[197] Less strict: Trechsel (1981) 243; against any restrictions: Frowein (1980) 445.

[198] *Imbrioscia* v. *Switzerland*, § 36; *John Murray* v. *United Kingdom*, § 62; *Öcalan* v. *Turkey*, § 140. The HRC has also held that the ICCPR is violated when a detainee is refused access to his lawyer and where he confesses during pre-trial detention; see e.g. *Conteris* v. *Uruguay*. For a comparative examination of the international mechanisms relating to pre-trial detention, see Grote (1998).   [199] *Öcalan* v. *Turkey*, § 140.

[200] *Campbell and Fell* v. *United Kingdom*, §§ 111–13.

[201] *John Murray* v. *United Kingdom*, §§ 59 et seq.

The applicant had been arrested in Northern Ireland under the Prevention of Terrorism (Temporary Provisions) Act 1989.[202] Despite asking to see a lawyer, contact was delayed for a period of forty-eight hours. The Court first observed that the application of Article 6 at this initial moment of the proceedings was not contested, but it recalled that 'the manner in which Article 6 § 3 (c) is to be applied during the preliminary investigation depends on the special features of the proceedings involved and on the circumstances of the case'.[203] In this specific case the special feature consisted of the rule that the judge could draw inferences, under certain circumstances, from the applicant's silence.[204]

This led the Court to conclude that there had been a violation because the accused had had to make a difficult decision which would have influenced the continuing proceedings.[205] The decisive part of the judgment is contained in paragraph 67: 'National laws may attach consequences to the attitude of an accused at the initial stages of police interrogation which are decisive for the prospects of the defence in any subsequent criminal proceedings. In such circumstances Article 6 will normally require that the accused be allowed to benefit from the assistance of a lawyer already at the initial stages of police interrogation'. The Court added a reference to restrictions which is worded like the one that it later used in *Öztürk*.

The first sentence betrays, in my opinion, the limited familiarity of the Court with criminal-procedure law. In fact, the behaviour of the suspect immediately after the arrest will *always* have consequences. While the consequences here are specific to the legislation at issue, they are not fundamentally different under the continental system. There, too, the decision has to be taken as to whether to make a statement or not, and the defendant will normally not have sufficient knowledge, experience, or sufficient self-confidence to make the best choice without the advice and support of a lawyer. Even if statements made to the police cannot later be used in evidence, they will still be recorded and joined to the file; in the course of the proceedings they will be quoted in order to clarify contradictions between that and later statements.

The question then arises as to the 'good cause' which might justify an exception. The Court did not specify this. As so often, it retreated behind the rather vague statement that the trial as a whole must be such as to ensure that the accused will have had a fair hearing. This is incompatible with the (in particular, the *English*) text of Article 6 § 3 which states that the paragraph guarantees 'minimum rights'.

The problem is much the same as with the right to private communication in general. The rule must be that the person arrested is entitled to contact counsel as soon as technically possible. There ought to be a warning in line with *Miranda* which makes it clear that the person who has been arrested has the right to

---

[202] See also Fitzpatrick and Walker (1999) 29.
[203] *John Murray* v. *United Kingdom*, § 62 with reference to *Imbrioscia* v. *Switzerland*, § 38.
[204] See further Chapter 13 below.   [205] *John Murray* v. *United Kingdom*, §§ 64 et seq.

remain silent and consult with a lawyer before making a statement.[206] The police and other prosecuting authorities tend to be opposed to this because it may impair their chances of reaching a quick solution to the case. Yet, this is an argument which is generally irreconcilable with respect for human rights in criminal proceedings and which lacks legitimacy.

In a series of more recent judgments against the United Kingdom, the Court has had to consider the role of legal assistance during the questioning of suspects in police custody. As in *John Murray*, these cases have raised questions as to the applicability, *inter alia*, of the privilege against self-incrimination, the presumption of innocence, and the right to assistance of counsel. In *Magee* v. *United Kingdom*, the applicant was detained for forty-eight hours without access to a solicitor, and finally made a signed confession. The Court held that the conditions in which the applicant had been detained, and his exclusion from outside contact were intended to be psychologically coercive, and thus to equalize this atmosphere the accused ought to have been able to have access to a solicitor.[207] Similarly in *Averill* v. *United Kingdom*, the Court held that failure to allow a defence lawyer access to the applicant for twenty-four hours during police interrogation, combined with the reliance by the court on inferences drawn from his silence, was incompatible with Article 6 § 3(c).[208]

These cases are interesting not just for their confirmation of the importance of access to a lawyer in order to ensure that the trial is fair, but also because they signify an extension of the principles of Article 6 into the pre-trial phase.[209] In *Magee* for instance the Court noted, 'Article 6—especially paragraph 3—may be relevant before a case is sent for trial if and so far as the fairness of the trial is likely to be seriously prejudiced by an initial failure to comply with its provisions'.[210] This is in line with the approach of the Court in the case of *John Murray* and also in *Teixeira de Castro* v. *Portugal*, a case concerning incitement by the police, where the Court noted that the 'intervention and its use in the impugned criminal proceedings meant that, right from the outset, the applicant was definitively deprived of a fair trial'.[211]

The pragmatic and utilitarian approach of the Court is further illustrated by the case of *Brennan*. The police had deferred access to a solicitor for twenty-four hours. This deferral 'was made in good faith and on reasonable grounds, namely, that there was a risk of alerting persons suspected of involvement in the offence as yet not arrested, or of making it more difficult to secure the apprehension of such a person or persons'. After the end of this period, but before having had an interview with the lawyer, the applicant made 'incriminating admissions'. The Court found that there had been no violation because the deferral could not be invoked to explain the admissions, and the fact that the lawyer had not

---

[206] *Miranda* v. *Arizona* 384 US 436 (1966).   [207] *Magee* v. *United Kingdom*, § 59–61.
[208] *Averill* v. *United Kingdom*, § 61. The Court noted, however, that there had been no violation of Art. 6 § 2.   [209] See Ashworth (2000) 681–2.
[210] *Magee* v. *United Kingdom*, § 41.   [211] *Teixeira de Castro* v. *Portugal*, § 39.

seen the applicant earlier was not 'attributable to any measure imposed by the authorities'.[212]

The pragmatism was however pushed beyond acceptable limits in two cases against Turkey. The applicants had been in police custody for twenty days without the possibility of seeing a lawyer. The Court however referred to its unfortunate 'global formula' according to which the proceedings must be assessed as a whole. It noted that the applicant rejected the statements which he had made during police custody but admitted that he had been involved in various crimes of kidnapping and arson. As the applicant, at the trial itself, had had the benefit of legal assistance and could discuss the case, the Court concluded that he had enjoyed, overall, a fair trial.[213]

Verniory sees in the other judgments a 'shocking rupture with the previous development of the case-law'—I fully agree.[214] These judgments entirely disregarded the fact that the fairness of a trial cannot be assumed when the accused was found guilty and the trial hearing itself appears to have been faultless—the evaluation 'as a whole' should not be abused to permit very serious shortcomings in the elemental aspects of fairness. It is clearly unacceptable for an accused to be detained—illegally, i.e. in violation of Article 5 § 3 of the ECHR—for twenty days in police custody without having the chance to see a lawyer. One cannot help wondering whether in this case the same methodology was used as in cases concerning the United Kingdom where the Court counted hours. The Court also seemed to disregard the fact that the fairness of a trial is a value in itself.[215] In my view, it is essential that a lawyer be allowed to be present from the first interrogations of a suspect.[216]

Fortunately, in *Öcalan* we find an entirely different approach. The applicant was denied access to his lawyers for seven days and the Court found a violation.[217] In the same case, the Court also considered it unacceptable that interviews with lawyers were limited to two hours per week—it did not accept the excuse that Mr Öcalan was imprisoned on an island with limited transport facilities: 'It notes that the Government have not explained why the authorities did not permit the lawyers to visit their client more often or why they failed to provide more adequate means of transport, thereby increasing the length of each individual visit, when such measures were called for as part of the "diligence" which the Contracting States must exercise in order to ensure that the rights guaranteed by Article 6 are enjoyed in an effective manner'.[218]

The IACtHR has also held there to be a violation of Article 8 § 2(d) when an accused is held *incommunicado*.[219]

[212] *Brennan* v. *United Kingdom*, §§ 46–8 with reference to *O'Kane* v. *United Kingdom* Application 30550/96, and *Harper* v. *United Kingdom* Application 33222/96.
[213] *Sarikaya* v. *Turkey*, §§ 67, 68. See, in the same vein, *Mamaç and others* v. *Turkey*, §§ 48, 49.
[214] Verniory (2005) 148.   [215] Cf. e.g. Trechsel (1997).
[216] For solid arguments, see Verniory (2005) 153–60; see also *Arquint; Soluiri*.
[217] *Öcalan* v. *Turkey*, §§ 141–3.   [218] Ibid., § 155.
[219] *Suaréz Rosero* v. *Ecuador*, judgment of 12 Nov. 1997, Series C No. 35, § 83.

VI. THE RIGHT TO THE EFFECTIVE ASSISTANCE
OF COUNSEL[220]

A. The Quality of the Defence

By ratifying the Convention, states agree to grant certain rights to individuals. However, the Convention does not bind individuals. Therefore it is not possible for an applicant to complain to the Strasbourg Court about his or her lawyer's unsatisfactory representation.[221] The Commission declared many applications inadmissible on the basis that they were in fact directed against counsel.[222] However, it did not exclude the possibility that the state, or more particularly the court, might bear some responsibility for ensuring the effective performance of counsel in a specific case. A typical response is that ' . . . in so far as the above complaints give rise to the question whether the Regional Court failed to ensure that, in the criminal proceedings against the applicant, his defence was properly carried out by his lawyer with the consequence that he was not given a fair hearing within the meaning of Article 6 of the Convention, an examination of the case as it has been submitted, including an examination ex officio, does not disclose any appearance of a violation of this right'.[223]

The Court's task in this area is particularly delicate. It need not be stressed that the independence of lawyers is an important element of the rule of law. The state is not authorized to supervise directly the quality of their services or to intervene if it deems them to be unsatisfactory. As the Strasbourg authorities are one step further removed from the actual proceedings, even more reluctance is to be expected. In fact, when the case of *Goddi* was taken before the Court, the Council of the Rome Bar Association sought leave to take part in the proceedings because they feared that the Court might come to a conclusion which would affect their independence; however, the request was belated and therefore denied[224]—it turned out that the fears of the profession were anyway unfounded.

In fact, the cases of *Artico* and *Goddi* were characterized by the absence of any defence activity. In *Artico* the appointed lawyer flatly refused to defend the applicant whose multiple, dogged appeals to the president of the court had no chance of success. In *Goddi* neither the accused nor the lawyer who would have acted on his behalf were correctly summoned to the hearing before the court of appeal. Although the prosecution moved to postpone the hearing because they wanted to hear two witnesses, the hearing was held in the absence of both.

---

[220] Certain rights of the defence, e.g. access to the file, are considered as 'facilities' within the meaning of Art. 6 § 3(b) and are discussed in Chapter 9 above.

[221] Although the English solicitor is regarded as an 'officer of the court' he or she is not an official of the United Kingdom Government; *X* v. *United Kingdom* Application 6956/75.

[222] The earliest one is Application 172/56; for further references to the early case-law, see Trechsel (1974) 85, n. 68.

[223] *X* v. *Germany* Application 2516/655; further references in Trechsel (1974) 86, n. 73.

[224] *Goddi* v. *Italy*, §§ 7, 31.

Instead, the court called in a lawyer who happened to walk by in the corridor of the court building to act as counsel for the defence. As this lawyer was totally uninformed, he simply referred back to the grounds of appeal which had been drafted by a different lawyer.

In both cases the Court found a violation of Article 6 § 3(c). It rightly stressed in *Artico* that this norm guaranteed the 'assistance', not just the 'appointment' of a lawyer; more generally, it stressed 'that the Convention is intended to guarantee not rights that are theoretical or illusory but rights that are practical and effective'.[225]

While Mr Artico had, from the outset, a legal-aid counsel, Mr Goddi had retained counsel of his own choosing. Thus, the argument made by Peukert that the duty to ensure that an accused can mount an effective defence only arises in cases where the lawyer has been appointed (or is, at least, paid) by the court, is not correct.[226] The case of *Kamasinski* was definitely less extreme. The Applicant complained of the

non-attendance of the lawyer at the indictment hearing and the brevity of the lawyer's pre-trial visits to the prison. He accused the lawyer of failing to acquaint him with the prosecution evidence prior to the trial. He criticised the lawyer's performance at the trial on a number of counts, for example in agreeing to the introduction of written statements by out-of-court witnesses, in omitting to make certain motions in order to preserve the right to lodge a plea of nullity and in asking in the concluding speech for a lenient judgment ('*mildes Urteil*'). In his submission, after the incident following which defence counsel made an unsuccessful request to withdraw from the case, he was 'without the benefit of any legal assistance at all'. The lack of tangible evidence of effective assistance was, so he contended, demonstrated by the incomplete file which Dr Steidl had handed over to Dr Schwank, the legal aid defence lawyer appointed for the purpose of the appeal and nullity proceedings.[227]

The Court's response to these allegations was relatively brief: Mr Kamasinski was never undefended, counsel was replaced twice in his interest; it recalled that 'a State cannot be held responsible for every shortcoming on the part of a lawyer appointed for legal aid purposes';[228] the authorities only have to intervene 'if a failure by legal aid counsel to provide effective representation is manifest or sufficiently brought to their attention in some other way'.[229] This may not be a very appropriate formulation, because the essential element seems to be that the shortcomings are brought to the attention of the authorities; the decisive aspect is, in fact, that the shortcomings are so blatant as to prevent there being the possibility of 'effective representation'. The requirement that this lack of effectiveness be brought to the attention of the competent authorities is very much of secondary importance. The Court then goes on to list the activities of

---

225   *Artico* v. *Italy*, § 33.   226   Frowein and Peukert (1996) Art. 6 N 198.
227   *Kamasinski* v. *Austria*, § 63; references omitted.   228   *Artico* v. *Italy*, § 36.
229   *Kamasinski* v. *Austria*, § 65.

the lawyer in question and finds that he did quite a lot, at any rate, enough. Even if counsel acts contrary to the wishes of the accused this does not mean that the latter remains unrepresented.[230]

The issue of effective legal representation has also arisen under Article 14 § 3(d) of the ICCPR.[231] The HRC has held that states only have a duty to intervene and replace counsel if it is manifest to the court that the behaviour of the legal representative is incompatible with the interests of justice.[232] The HRC has adopted a stricter approach in capital cases. It has noted that in cases where the death penalty is available there is an obligation on the state to ensure that the representation is effective.[233] The state has an obligation to ensure that 'the conduct of the case by the lawyer is not incompatible with the interests of justice'. It has noted that while it is not its task to question counsel's professional judgement, if counsel for the accused concedes that there is no merit in the appeal, the court should, particularly in a capital case, ascertain whether counsel has consulted with the accused and informed him accordingly. If not, the court must ensure that the accused is so informed and given an opportunity to engage other counsel. In the instant case the applicants 'should have been informed that their legal aid counsel was not going to argue any grounds in support of the appeal so that they could have considered any remaining options open to them', the failure of such communication meant that the applicants were not effectively represented on appeal and thus there had been a violation of Article 14 § 3(d).[234]

B. Effective Assistance During Pre-trial Proceedings

What are the possibilities for a lawyer to assist her or his client during pre-trial proceedings? The question arose with regard to the assistance provided during the interrogation of an accused in *Imbrioscia*. The applicant had been arrested under the suspicion of involvement in a drugs offence. He retained counsel but the latter did not attend the various interrogations of his client. The applicant complained that counsel had not been invited to attend, whereas the Government objected that it was for the accused and/or counsel to react.[235]

The important passage in the judgment is this: ' . . . the applicant did not at the outset have the necessary legal support . . . '.[236] This can only be understood in one way: the applicant needed support from the start of the proceedings, including, in particular, during the police interrogations. The police are not always prepared to accept this. They fear being 'outsmarted' by trained lawyers,

---

[230] *Kamasinski* v. *Austria*, § 70.   [231] See de Zayas (1998) 685.
[232] See e.g. Views on *Michael Adams* v. *Jamaica*.
[233] *Kelly* v. *Jamaica* and *Reid* v. *Jamaica*.   [234] *Morrison and Graham* v. *Jamaica*, § 10.5
[235] According to the Court, 'Zurich cantonal legislation and practice did not require her to be present', § 39. This is slightly euphemistic to the extent that interrogations before the police are at issue. In fact, in Zurich neither the law nor the practice allow for the presence of counsel at that stage of the proceedings, cf. ZH StPO § 14 para 1 *e contrario*; see e.g. Trechsel (2001); Arquint (2001); Albrecht (2002); Schmid (2002).   [236] *Imbrioscia* v. *Italy*, § 41.

and encountering increased difficulties in trying to encourage the defendant to make a statement, if possible a full confession. Yet, the rights of the defence require that there be a possibility for the lawyer to be present.

The remaining issue was whether the state could be held responsible for the shortcomings of the successive defence lawyers of the applicant. A minority answered in the affirmative.[237] In their view any interrogation had to take place in the presence of a lawyer, at least in cases where the accused requested the presence of counsel. It may well be true, as Judge Lopes Rocha held, that this 'is the most perfect embodiment of the rights of the defence and therefore of fair proceedings intended to secure for the accused an ever stronger and more effective position as a party to the trial'.[238] However, the Convention is not an instrument designed to enforce 'best solutions'. The obligatory presence of counsel during preliminary proceedings could cause serious delays even in the absence of any dilatory aims of the defence.

The majority of the Court, like the Commission, came to the conclusion that there had been no violation of the Convention. It would have been possible for the lawyers, and they could be expected to have known this, to request that they be allowed to be present during the interrogations and informed of the time and place where they were held. The state could not be held responsible for the fact that they did not avail themselves of this possibility.

This case is highly unsatisfactory in that the Court was not made aware of the fact that, as far as the police interrogations were concerned, there was, from the outset, no right for counsel to assist the accused. Therefore, according to the Court's own criteria, it can only be concluded that this constituted a violation of the Convention.

Finally, the Court had the opportunity to address the issue. In the first case, *Daud*, the Commission held that there had been a violation of Article 6 § 3(c) because the first counsel to be appointed had remained entirely inactive, and the second had not prepared adequately for the hearing—a fact that was not contested. The Court, however, did not concentrate on the special provision but, while fully agreeing with the finding of the Commission, found a violation of Article 6 § 1 'in conjunction with paragraph 3(c)'.[239]

The problem came up again in *Czekalla*. Here the lawyer had committed a procedural error in filing an appeal which, therefore, was inadmissible. Although the Court was slightly more cautious, its response was nevertheless clear: 'in certain circumstances negligent failure to comply with a purely formal condition cannot be equated with an injudicious line of defence or a mere defect of argumentation. That is so when as a result of such negligence a defendant is deprived of a remedy without the situation being put right by a higher court. It should be pointed out in that connection that the applicant was a foreigner who

---

[237] Judges Pettiti, De Meyere, and Lopez Rocha.   [238] *Imbrioscia* v. *Italy*, § 20.
[239] *Daud* v. *Portugal*.

did not know the language in which the proceedings were being conducted and who was facing charges which made him liable to—and indeed led to—a lengthy prison sentence'.[240] '[T]he decisive point is the officially-appointed lawyer's failure to comply with a simple and purely formal rule when lodging the appeal on points of law to the Supreme Court. In the Court's view, that was a "manifest failure" which called for positive measures on the part of the relevant authorities. The Supreme Court could, for example, have invited the officially-appointed lawyer to add to or rectify her pleading rather than declare the appeal inadmissible.'[241] The Court also found the argument of the Government that the judicial authorities were bound to respect the independence of the lawyers 'unpersuasive'. The judgment is to be applauded not just for the finding that there had been a violation of Article 6 §§ 1 and 3(c) of the Convention, but also for the satisfactory reasoning that led to this result.

However, it also creates considerable difficulties on the domestic level. Rules governing appeals are usually rather strict, particularly with regard to the requirement that time limits be respected. It may be necessary for certain states to amend their criminal-procedure codes in order to protect an appellant against the negligence of his or her lawyer.

[240] *Czekalla* v. *Portugal*, § 65.   [241] Ibid., § 68.

Chapter 11

The Right to Test Witness Evidence

I. INTRODUCTION

A. The Texts

[3. In the determination of any criminal charge against him, everyone shall be entitled to the following minimum guarantees, in full equality:] ...
  (e) To examine, or have examined, the witnesses against him and to obtain the attendance and examination of witnesses on his behalf under the same conditions as witnesses against him;

ICCPR, Art. 14 § 3(f)

[3. Everyone charged with a criminal offence has the following minimum rights:] ...
  (d) to examine or have examined witnesses against him and to obtain the attendance and examination of witnesses on his behalf under the same conditions as witnesses against him;

ECHR, Art. 6 § 3(d)

[2. ... During the proceedings, every person is entitled, with full equality, to the following minimum guarantees:] ...
  (f) the right of the defence to examine witnesses present in the court and to obtain the appearance, as witnesses, of experts or other persons who may throw light on the facts;

ACHR, Art. 8 § 2(f)

While the texts of the ICCPR and the ECHR are, with the exception of the introductory formula and the use of commas, identical, the ACHR has its own wording. It only refers to witnesses 'present in the court', which limits the application of the provision to the trial stage. The second part of the sentence expresses an aspect which is also implicit in the other texts, namely, that there is only a right to examine witnesses whose evidence may be of value in establishing the facts. This would exclude legal experts, a facility easily dispensed with in view of the principle *iura novit curia*. On the other hand, experts are mentioned in the second, but not in the first part of the sub-paragraph. However, this can hardly be understood as excluding a right to question experts present at the trial.

B. The Origins of the Guarantee

The right to examine and to call witnesses is not expressly stated in Article 11 of the UDHR. Ms Roosevelt had proposed that such a guarantee be introduced, but Professor Cassin objected on the basis that such principles had no place in a declaration which was concerned with setting out the principles rather than applying principles of fairness.[1]

The United States then presented a proposal for the Covenant which included 'the right to be confronted with the witnesses against him' and 'the right of compulsory process for obtaining witnesses in his favour'.[2] In essence, this right is contained in the Covenant today—subsequent changes to the text are of little, if any, relevance in relation to the interpretation of the right. The right to summon and to question witnesses was thus, right from the beginning of the work on the Covenant, regarded as an essential element of a fair trial. It is also important to note the fact that the guarantee was proposed by the United States which suggests that it has its roots in the common-law system of criminal procedure. In fact, this right has no significant tradition on the European continent.

An interesting amendment was proposed by the Group of Experts at the seventh session: the right 'to challenge all charges and examine all evidence' was to be added to the right to examine witnesses in order to 'clarify and slightly expand' the article.[3] As can be seen, the proposal was not accepted.

C. The Purpose of the Guarantee

The guarantee in paragraph 3(d), like the other 'minimum' rights of the defence prescribed by Article 6 § 3, forms part of the right to a fair trial as set out in Article 6 § 1. While, in a very early case, the Court looked at the specific right in isolation,[4] it has since regularly amalgamated the rights, and generally puts Article 6 § 1 in the foreground.[5] The standard phrase used runs something like this: the Court 'first notes that the guarantees in Article 6 § 3(d) of the Convention are specific aspects of the right to a fair trial set forth in the first paragraph of this Article. Consequently, the complaint will be examined under the two provisions taken together'.[6]

More particularly, the guarantee has a role in ensuring that the adversarial character of the proceedings is upheld.[7] The defence must be given a fair chance to challenge evidence against the accused and to bring its own evidence. This must be granted under the same conditions as those applicable to the prosecution, which serves the general principle of equality of arms.

---

[1] Weissbrodt (2001) 17.   [2] Ibid., 45.   [3] Ibid., 61.
[4] *Engel and others* v. *Netherlands*, § 91.   [5] See e.g. *Bönisch* v. *Austria*, §§ 29, 35.
[6] *SN* v. *Sweden*, § 43; *Asch* v. *Austria*, § 25 and many others.
[7] See also Chiavario (2001) N 7.4.1.2.

On a more fundamental level, the right to question witnesses and to present evidence ensures that the accused is an active participant in the trial. He or she cannot just be characterized as the passive target of the prosecution which must be protected against the power of the state. The accused is regarded as an active participant, a subject. The rights provided for in Article 6 § 3(d) enable him or her to influence the course of the proceedings and the direction which they will take.

While the provision clearly operates to protect the interests of the defence, it also serves justice in a more general way. Discourse assists the establishment of the truth. Questions put by the defence will not only influence the assessment of the credibility of the witness, they may also bring to light further elements of fact which may be of relevance for the final decision of the court, be it in relation to the conviction or in sentencing.[8]

D. The Character of the Guarantee

There are a number of reasons why the right to examine witnesses stands out among the various rights of the defence, identified by the international norms. It is rather more detailed than rights such as the right to time and facilities for the preparation of the defence. It has a particularly close connection to two aspects of the right to a fair trial, namely the right to be heard and the principle of the equality of arms. Two inter-linked characteristics call for more detailed comment: the proximity of the provision to the establishment of the facts and the relative nature of the guarantee.

1. The Proximity to the Establishment of the Facts

The right to question witnesses is the only guarantee in Article 6 which refers and relates directly to the administration of evidence. The essential aspect of the guarantee is not expressed in the text, even though these rights are clearly of considerable importance, but is rather the consequence of non-compliance. What happens if the defence do *not* have the opportunity to examine a witness who has made a statement which has been recorded? What if a witness appears for the trial but, for one reason or another, cannot be questioned by the accused?

These are fundamental questions in criminal proceedings, and they relate to the admissibility of evidence. The admissibility of such evidence, in turn, will regularly be decisive to the question of whether to convict or to acquit. The finding of a violation of this right is tantamount to the international organ saying that the victim of such violation was wrongly convicted. The European Court is very reluctant to make such a finding and repeats again and again the following formula:

The Court reiterates that the admissibility of evidence is primarily a matter for regulation by national law and as a general rule it is for the national courts to assess the evidence

---

[8] See also Gollwitzer (1992) Art. 6 N 219.

before them. The Court's task under the Convention is not to give a ruling as to whether statements of witnesses were properly admitted as evidence, but rather to ascertain whether the proceedings as a whole, including the way in which evidence was taken, were fair.[9]

Although this sounds quite convincing, the statement is nevertheless rather rhetorical. In practice, the guarantee *does* call for a decision as to whether the rule was complied with and in the event that it has not been, the logical consequence is that the evidence should not have been admitted. In my view, this is inevitable. Again, the ominous reference to 'the proceedings as a whole' reappears and does nothing to clarify the interpretation of the Convention.

2. The Relative Character of the Guarantee

(a) The Issue *In Abstracto*

It is quite obvious that the right to examine witnesses is a relative guarantee. The mere fact that an accused was not provided with the opportunity to question a witness or that, despite the defence's request, a witness was not called, cannot in itself make the proceedings unfair, even if the defendant was finally convicted. Such an absolute rule would constitute a disproportionate obstacle to the administration of justice and would open the door wide to abuses and sabotage.

The relative nature of the guarantee is closely linked to the administration of evidence. While a guarantee such as the assistance of counsel affects the general character of the proceedings, quite independently of the substantive issues at stake, the opportunity to question witnesses takes its relevance from the specific circumstances of each case.

One specific feature of evidence is that it can be discussed in quantitative terms. The issue is not simply whether evidence exists or not. Evidence can be insufficient, sufficient, or even ample. In criminal proceedings the question is whether the prosecution has presented enough evidence to rebut the presumption of innocence, thus ensuring the safety of the conviction. A witness statement is an element of proof. If there is plenty of other evidence, it may be irrelevant. Alternatively, there may be very little other evidence, in which case the questionable statement of a witness may serve to tip the balance in favour of the conviction.

It is not possible to enforce Article 6 § 3(d) without making decisions on this issue which at least imply that the applicant ought, or ought not, to have been

---

[9] *Van Mechelen and others* v. *Netherlands*, § 50; *Doorson* v. *Netherlands*, § 67; *Visser* v. *Netherlands*, § 43; *Lucà* v. *Italy*, § 38; *Sadak and others* v. *Turkey*, § 63; *Perna* v. *Italy*, § 26; *Vidal* v. *Belgium*, § 34, and many others. This approach had already been taken by the Commission, e.g. *X* v. *Germany* Application 4119/69: it is within the discretion of the national courts to establish whether the hearing of a witness for the defence is likely to be of assistance in discovering the truth and if not to decide against calling the witness. *Austria v. Italy* Application 788/60: Art. 6 § 3(d) 'does not imply the right to have witnesses called without restriction'.

acquitted. This is in essence the problem which makes the successful application of the guarantee difficult.

(b) The Court's Jurisprudence

The Court has followed this unavoidable route, and in so doing has highlighted the problems.

The first cases, *Unterpertinger* and *Asch*, were both directed against Austria and the facts were strikingly similar. In both cases the applicant had had a dispute with his lawful or 'common-law' wife which had resulted in her suffering minor injuries. The victims then complained to the police and a statement was taken. Mr Unterpertinger had also hit his stepdaughter. In both cases there was a medical report in the file.

At the next stage of the proceedings, the victim was questioned by an investigating judge and made aware of her right to refuse to testify. Ms Unterpertinger testified, while Mrs JL, the victim of Mr Asch, went back to the police and told them they were reconciled and that she wanted to withdraw her complaint.

At the first-instance trials both victims availed themselves of their right to refuse to testify. The accused, therefore had no possibility to question them. They were nevertheless convicted after the whole file, including the statements originally made to the police by the victims, had been read out. Both defendants appealed without success.

The Commission was split in *Unterpertinger*, but on the casting vote of the President came to the conclusion that there had been no violation. The Court, however, followed the minority of the Commission and, unanimously, found there to have been a violation of Article 6. In *Asch*, the Commission held that there had been a violation, while the Court, by seven votes to two, found that there had been no violation of paragraphs 1 and 3(d) of Article 6 taken together.

This finding also came as a surprise to the respondent government. A lawyer who had worked on the case referred, at a conference, to the judgment—which had been favourable to her side—as a miscarriage of justice (*'Fehlurteil'*).[10] In fact, the judgment in *Asch* marks an exceptionally weak point in the Court's jurisprudence and must be regarded as an unfortunate mistake.[11] It is surprising to observe that of the judges who took part in both judgments three came to a different conclusion in the second case.[12]

The reasoning in *Asch* is not convincing. The Court found that it was acceptable to rely on the statement that the victim had made to the police. It mentions, as corroborating evidence, the medical certificates and the statements of the police officer before whom the victim had made her statement.[13] It is hard to see how this could substitute the questioning of the victim by the defence.

---

[10] Bernecker (1992) 65.
[11] For criticism, see also Stavros (1993) 235 et seq.; Osborne (1993) 265.
[12] Judges Matscher, Macdonald, and Russo.   [13] *Asch* v. *Austria*, §§ 28–31.

According to Stavros the Court 'appears to have intentionally undervalued the weight of the untested evidence'.[14]

The Court also made an argument which appears rather circular:

All the evidence must normally be produced in the presence of the accused at a public hearing with a view to adversarial argument. This does not mean, however, that the statement of a witness must always be made in court and in public if it is to be admitted in evidence; in particular, this may prove impossible in certain cases. The use in this way of statements obtained at the pre-trial stage is not in itself inconsistent with paragraphs 3(d) and 1 of Article 6, provided that the rights of the defence have been respected. As a rule, these rights require that the defendant be given an adequate and proper opportunity to challenge and question a witness against him, either when he was making his statements or at a later stage of the proceedings.[15]

What the Court failed to say is how in *Asch* 'the rights of the defence have been respected'. The witness had not made a statement at trial nor had the defence had an opportunity to question her.[16] The only way out of this dilemma would have been for the Court to have asserted that the judgment was not based on the statements of the victim. However, it does not go that far, it limits itself to saying that 'Mrs J.L.'s statements, as related by Officer B., did *not* constitute *the only* item of evidence on which the first-instance court based its decision'.[17] The reverse of this statement demonstrates that the Court (quite rightly) believed that the conviction *was* to some extent based on a statement which was obtained in disregard of Article 6 § 3(d).

This cannot be correct. In fact, the Court simply disregarded the guarantee.[18] Fortunately, however, an examination of further development in the case-law reveals that there have been considerable improvements.

(c) The Relevance of the Statement as Evidence

The Court often states that 'no conviction should be based either solely or to a decisive extent' on a statement which was not obtained in accordance with the

---

[14] Stavros (1993) 235; the same, of course, applies to *Artner* v. *Austria*.

[15] *Asch* v. *Austria*, § 27. See also *Barberà, Messegué and Jabardo* v. *Spain*, § 78; *Kostovski* v. *Netherlands*, § 41; *Windisch* v. *Austria*, § 26; *Delta* v. *France*, § 36; *Isgrò* v. *Italy*, § 34; *Saïdi* v. *France*, § 43; *Ferrantelli and Santangelo* v. *Italy*, § 57; *Solakov* v. *the Former Yugoslav Republic of Macedonia*, § 57; *SN* v. *Sweden*, § 44 and, with different wording, *Van Mechelen and others* v. *Netherlands*, § 51. See also the decision of the Commission in *Trivedi* v. *United Kingdom* Application 31700/96.

[16] Grabenwarter (1997) 640 takes the view that the Court did not, here, refer to *all* the rights of the defence; he thinks the Court excluded Art. 6 § 3(d). Such a hypothesis, however, is not permissible in view of the fact that each of the guarantees set out in para. 3 is a 'minimal right'.

[17] *Asch* v. *Austria*, § 30 (emphasis added).

[18] As a marginal comment I wish to draw attention to the fact that in other legal systems, e.g. the Swiss one (SPC, Art. 123 § 1), the offence allegedly committed by Mr Asch could only be prosecuted on the bases of a formal request of the victim; it would have been quite acceptable if the act would have remained unsanctioned in view of the lack of interest of the victim in a prosecution of the alleged perpetrator. In the meantime, the SPC was amended to allow *ex officio* prosecution of violence against a spouse or common-law wife; still, the victim can demand that the prosecution be stopped: SPC, Art. 66ter.

requirements of Article 6 § 3(d).[19] The term 'decisive' also figures in a number of further judgments.[20] Generally, following *Asch* the Court seems to have been more inclined to adopt a more flexible approach.[21]

After repeating its standard phrase, it applies it to the case at issue using terminology which is often slightly different, and not always entirely consistent. In some cases when it holds that there was no violation, it uses the existence of corroborative evidence to justify its decision that the statement at issue could legitimately be used.[22] This is definitely unsatisfactory.[23] Sometimes reference will be made to the fact that the conviction was 'based to a decisive extent'[24] or 'to a material degree'[25] on the untested statement. The most advanced formulation is found in *Birutis*: 'The trial court . . . referred to the anonymous statements to base the first and the second applicants' conviction'.[26] Had this represented the approach which the Court intended to follow, the right in Article 6 § 3(d) would have been very considerably strengthened. Alas, however, the Court returned in *Hulki Günes* to the earlier wording.[27]

(d) Assessment

The evidence in a criminal case can be compared to stones in a mosaic. Often, some stones will be missing, it will in fact hardly ever be possible to have the full picture (the mosaic itself is an abstraction as soon as the stones have a certain size). The evidence is sufficient to rebut the presumption of innocence when the picture is unmistakable—there is no reasonable explanation other than that the accused committed the crime. When is this the case?

It is clear that the decision as to when the evidence is sufficient to justify the conviction cannot be definitively answered *in abstracto*. It is a matter of quantity. The decision must be made by the trial court. It is certainly not enough for Strasbourg to find that there was also other evidence without at the same time weighing it and saying whether it was sufficient. The Court must undertake a hypothetical examination of the case. It must, as it were, remove each stone which originates from the untested and contested statement. If the picture is still unmistakable, then the judgment is not decisively based on this evidence.

---

[19] *Doorson* v. *Netherlands*, § 76; *van Mechelen and others* v. *Netherlands*, § 55; *AM* v. *Italy*, § 25; *Cyprus* v. *Turkey*, § 109; *Visser* v. *Netherlands*, § 43 (quoting *van Mechelen*); *Birutis and others* v. *Lithuania*, § 29; *Lucà* v. *Italy*, § 40; *Sadak and others* v. *Turkey*, § 65; *Solakov* v. *Former Yugoslav Republic of Macedonia*, § 57; *PS* v. *Germany*, § 24; *Hulki Günes* v. *Turkey*, § 86; *Craxi* v. *Italy*, § 86; *Rachdad* v. *France*, § 23.   [20] *Kostovski* v. *Netherlands*, § 44; *Delta* v. *France*, § 37.
[21] Starmer (2001) N 9.11. As Strange (2001) puts it: 'This watering down of the test in *Unterpertinger* [sc. by the *Asch* judgment] has not been followed in subsequent cases on related areas'—there are, however, 'relapses', such as *Artner*.
[22] e.g. *Artner* v. *Austria*, § 23, where that evidence is discussed in detail; *Doorson* v. *Netherlands*, § 80; *Ferrantelli and Santangelo* v. *Italy*, § 52. In *Visser* v. *Netherlands*, § 45, the question is whether the statement played 'a main or decisive role in securing the conviction'.
[23] In the same sense, see Esser (2002) 632.
[24] *Van Mechelen and others* v. *Netherlands*, § 63.   [25] *Lucà* v. *Italy*, § 41.
[26] *Birutis and others* v. *Lithuania*, § 34.
[27] *Hulki Günes* v. *Turkey*, § 86: '*uniquement ou dans une mesure déterminante*'.

As Stavros correctly points out, it is 'extremely difficult to ascertain the weight attached to the untested evidence'.[28]

In conducting such an examination, the Court inevitable makes its own assessment of the whole evidence and thereby strays into 'forbidden territory'.[29] It is easy to understand why the Court shies away from such an exercise.

For the domestic courts, the lesson is simple enough: the judgment should not refer to the untested statement. This is the safe method to avoid the finding of a violation of Article 6 § 3(d). Esser criticizes this as presenting an opportunity for the manipulation or abuse of the provision.[30] I disagree. Why is the obligation on the domestic court to omit reference to the contested statement problematic? If the remaining evidence is insufficient, it will have to acquit.

Under the common law, where the verdict of the jury is not reasoned, this 'way out' is not available. There must be a finding of a violation if 'contaminated evidence' is admitted.

(e) The Possibility of Waiver: Requirements of Diligence

In view of the relative character of the right to question witnesses, it is obvious that the right can be waived. Yet, the case-law of the Court causes some difficulties in this respect, because, in some cases, it displays a certain rigidity requiring that a waiver be made expressly, while, in others, it implicitly accepts a tacit waiver by blaming the applicant for not having taken the necessary steps to secure the exercise of his or her right.[31]

The possibility of waiving the right has repeatedly been accepted by both the HRC[32] and the European Court. The latter (normally) insists, however, that the waiver be declared explicitly, and adds that the state has a positive duty to display the necessary diligence in order to secure the attendance of witnesses so that they can be questioned by the accused.[33] The duty (and the possibility!) to compel witnesses to testify is, however, limited. It may be necessary to respect the interests of others, particularly where the case involves persons close to the accused who refuse to testify.[34]

On the other hand, the Court also expects the accused to exercise a certain diligence. It will not find a violation if the defence never sought the attendance and examination of a person whose statement was taken into account by the court.[35] Similarly in *SN* v. *Sweden*[36] the Court found that there had been no violation of Article 6 § 3(d) on account of the defence counsel being absent

---

[28] Stavros (1993) 236, n. 742 in connection with *Bayer* v. *Austria* Application 13866/88.
[29] Wąsek-Wiaderek (2000) 29.   [30] Esser (2002) 647.
[31] See, on this issue, the discussion of Esser (2002) 639 et seq.
[32] *Compass* v. *Jamaica; Pratt and Morgan* v. *Jamaica; Adams* v. *Jamaica.*
[33] *Sadak and others* v. *Turkey*, § 67. The requirement that the authorities exercise a certain diligence had earlier been stressed in *Barberà, Messegué and Jabardo* v. *Spain*, § 75.
[34] See e.g. *Unterpertinger* v. *Austria*, § 30.
[35] *Brandstetter* v. *Austria*, § 49 with regard to members of a wine-tasting panel.
[36] *SN* v. *Sweden*, § 49.

because counsel had consented to this absence and had accepted the manner in which the interview was to be conducted. The expectation that the defence show some interest in questioning the witness was again evident in *S* v. *Austria* where the Commission, in dismissing the application, noted *inter alia* that the applicant had 'not shown that he filed a request with the Court to put certain questions to the witness A'.[37]

This, in my view, was clearly taken too far in *Cardot* where, contrary to the Commission, the Court concluded that the applicant had not exhausted domestic remedies because he had failed to express any wish that evidence should be heard from his former co-defendants at first instance and on appeal.[38] When the Court concluded that 'Mr Cardot did not provide the French courts with the opportunity which is in principle intended to be afforded to Contracting States by [former] Article 26, namely the opportunity of preventing or putting right the violations alleged against them',[39] it showed little familiarity with the continental system of criminal procedure in which the courts have a duty to call the evidence *ex officio*.[40]

E. The Model of Full Compliance with the Guarantee

The practical significance of the rule prescribed by Article 6 § 3(d) is best understood if one first describes proceedings which fully comply with the guarantee and then identifies the possible exceptions and potential restrictions on these exceptions.

As the Court repeats in practically every case relating to Article 6 § 3(d), '[a]ll evidence must normally be produced in the presence of the accused at a public hearing with a view to adversarial argument'.[41] This relates in the first place to the trial which is the central aspect of criminal proceedings. The evidence must be produced 'live' before the body called upon to assess the case and determine the facts. This applies in particular to witness evidence. The defence must be able to question witnesses in open court.

---

[37] Application 12262/86. See also *O and T* v. *Netherlands* Applications 17631/91 and 17632/91: 'The Commission notes that the applicants have never submitted a request to the courts dealing with their case that the anonymous witnesses be examined by the courts. The Commission, therefore, considers that under these circumstances no issue arises under Article 6 para. 3(d) of the Convention'.   [38] *Cardot* v. *France*, §§ 34–5.

[39] Ibid., § 36.

[40] See also the criticism of Stavros (1993) 235: 'the accused should not be routinely made to assume responsibility for the failure of the national authorities to ensure respect for his procedural rights'. On the other hand, the blunt statement of van Dijk and van Hoof (1998) 477, that 'the court need not call witnesses of its own accord' cannot be accepted; it is based on decisions of the Commission which are outdated, *X* v. *United Kingdom* Application 5281/71; *X* v. *United Kingdom* Application 4782/71.

For the duty of the 'continental judge', see e.g. Charrier (2002) Art. 6 N 89 with reference to French case-law.

[41] See e.g. *SN* v. *Sweden*, § 44. Gollwitzer (1992) Art. 6 N 225 cannot be followed when he asserts that the Convention does not guarantee a right of confrontation.

Despite this clarity, it is important not to be lulled into a false sense of security. The Court has also said that '[i]n itself, the reading out of statements in this way cannot be regarded as being inconsistent with Article 6 §§ 1 and 3(d)'.[42] In order to reconcile these two statements, the second one must be seen as an exception which requires to be convincingly justified. The Court did not make this sufficiently clear when it added that 'the use made of them as evidence must nevertheless comply with the rights of the defence'.[43] This statement is entirely banal—it is difficult to envisage circumstances which would legitimize non-compliance with the rights of the defence.

F. The Problems Arising with the Guarantee

An analysis of Article 6 § 3(d) and the case-law reveals a prolific number of problems, beside that already discussed.

First, it is essential to distinguish the two rights set out in the provision: the right to question witnesses for the prosecution, and the right to call witnesses or to propose that witnesses be summoned in favour of the defence. The first aspect has dominated the case-law, although the second one has also been found to have been disregarded in a few cases. It will be dealt with separately at the end of this chapter which will concentrate primarily on the first aspect. An important question relates to the moment at which the first of these rights arises. Ideally, as is stated in the provision, witnesses should be questioned at the trial, but in certain circumstances the right may also be validly exercised during the investigation.

Questions also arise in relation to the nature of the interrogation; here, the relationship between the accused and counsel is of particular importance.

The most difficult aspect involves situations where there is a barrier to the implementation of the guarantee, often because of the conflicting interests of the witnesses. The discussion will examine when such protection is justified, the methods of protection, and the safeguards for the defence. In the same section, I shall also deal with the problems which arise whenever a witness cannot be questioned by the defence because he or she has died, disappeared, or refuses to testify.

Before examining these issues, it is essential at the outset to clarify the term 'witness'.

II. DEFINING THE TERM 'WITNESS'

In order to understand the scope of Article 6 § 3(d) a definition of the notion of 'witness' is required. Does the witness 'belong' to the defence or to the prosecution? Such a distinction reveals the origin of the rule. In common-law

---

[42] See e.g. *Unterpertinger* v. *Austria*, § 31.   [43] Ibid.

systems the parties have to present their evidence. In relation to witness evidence this means that after witnesses have been examined by the party which called them they will be directly cross-examined by the other side.

To those schooled in European continental criminal procedure this is a strange concept. Even though the inquisitorial model has been successively adapted to more adversarial models, the court still has the primary responsibility for the administration of evidence. Witnesses are supposed to be neutral and are, as a rule, interrogated by the presiding judge, although the parties or their representatives have the opportunity to ask complementary questions, be it directly, be it through the judge acting as an intermediary.[44] At any rate, statements of persons supposed to have some knowledge relevant to the cause generally begin at the pre-trial stage. Often it is only when the result of the interrogation is known that one can say whether the witness is 'for the prosecution' or 'for the defence'.[45]

This phenomenon in itself raises doubts as to whether defining the notion of 'witness' for the purposes of an international instrument for the protection of human rights makes much sense. There is another perhaps even more fundamental difference: on the European continent an essential quality of the witness is that he or she is not a party to the proceedings.[46] As a matter of course and definition the parties cannot be compelled to testify as witnesses, they are *a priori* considered to be biased and therefore not likely to tell the objective truth. No such rule exists in the common law. While the continental approach is influenced by psychological considerations, the presumption that every person is animated by a strong sense of self-preservation and should not be confronted with the dilemma of either making a statement which can be harmful or risking a penalty for perjury,[47] the Anglo-Saxon approach is a normative one—the accused is free to decide whether or not to take the witness stand, but if he or she so decides, this entails the obligation to tell the truth or face a possible prosecution for perjury.

It is therefore no surprise to find that the Court has not taken any firm stand on who falls to be considered as a witness. A number of observations can, however, be made.

A. The Autonomous Notion of 'Witness'

In determining who can be classed as a witness the Court is not influenced by domestic law; instead, as is its general approach, it will apply an autonomous notion.[48] In *Lucà*, the Court said that 'where a deposition may serve to a

---

[44] e.g. FCCP, Art. 331. This characteristic is also referred to by Strange (2001) 16.3.
[45] Grabenwarter (2003) § 24.   [46] See e.g. Hauser (1974) 38.
[47] See further Chapter 13 below.
[48] See e.g. *Kostovski* v. *Austria*, § 40; *Windisch* v. *Austria*, § 23; *Delta* v. *France*, § 34; *Isgrò* v. *Italy*, § 33; *Asch* v. *Austria*, § 25; *Artner* v. *Austria*, § 19; *Lüdi* v. *Switzerland*, § 44; *Vidal* v. *Belgium*, § 33; *Pullar* v. *United Kingdom*, § 45; *Lucà* v. *Italy*, § 41; *Solakov* v. *The Former Yugoslav Republic of Macedonia*, § 57; *SN* v. *Sweden*, § 45; *Perna* v. *Italy (GC)*, § 29.

material degree as the basis for a conviction, then, irrespective of whether it was made by a witness in the strict sense or by a co-accused, it constitutes evidence for the prosecution to which the guarantees provided by Article 6 §§ 1 and 3(d) of the Convention apply.'[49] Stavros takes this into account when he uses the term 'declarant'[50].

B. The Classical Notion of Witness

The continental classification of witnesses depends on two distinct aspects: substance and form. As far as substance is concerned, the witness is a person who has personally made an observation, optically, acoustically, or otherwise, which is relevant for the establishment of a fact and who is not a party to the proceedings. As to form, the person must be told that he or she is a witness and that the failure to tell the truth may result in the imposition of serious sanctions. There may or may not be an oath.

Neither of these criteria have been adopted in the context of the application of Article 6 § 3(d). It is particularly interesting to note that the Court has not attached any importance to formal procedural rules.[51]

C. Parties as Witnesses

There is no example in the Court's case-law of a case in which the accused gave or wanted to give evidence as a witness—the hypothesis seems rather absurd, but it has come up before the Commission which declared the application inadmissible.[52] However, there is a case where the accused asked for the plaintiff in defamation proceedings to be heard as witness.[53] Co-accuseds can also be witnesses in the sense of Article 6 § 3(d),[54] and the same applies to plaintiffs in civil proceedings.

D. Informants as Witnesses

It is not necessary, in order to be classed as a witness, for the person concerned to be questioned in court.[55] The only question is whether he or she made a statement which has been taken into account by the court in the evaluation of

---

[49] *Lucà* v. *Italy*, § 41; see also *Kostovski* v. *Netherlands*, § 40. This very broad and untechnical definition has been approved by scholars, e.g. Chiavario (2002) N 7.4.

[50] Stavros (1993) 230.   [51] *Olsson* v. *Sweden*, § 79 (a case concerning civil proceedings).

[52] *X* v. *Austria* Application 1092/61; Morrisson (1967) 125, an American author, found the decision surprising!

[53] *Perna* v. *Italy*, § 29; no violation was found, but the Court expressly accepted that the guarantee applied.

[54] e.g. *Isgrò* v. *Italy*, § 33; *Ferrantelli and Santangelo* v. *Italy*, § 52; *Lucà* v. *Italy*, § 41.

[55] e.g. *Asch* v. *Austria*, § 25; *SN* v. *Sweden*, § 45; *Delta* v. *France*, § 34; *Windisch* v. *Austria*, § 23; *Isgrò* v. *Italy*, § 33.

the evidence.[56] In *Kostovski* the Court made it clear that it is even irrelevant whether the statement was read out in court.[57]

Nor is it essential for the statement to be related to the merits of the proceedings. In *Pullar* the issue was whether one of the jurors could be regarded as impartial.[58]

E. Expert Witnesses[59]

Expert witnesses are different from other witnesses in that they are not summoned to tell what they have personally witnessed about the facts of the case. It is their task to assist the court—or one of the parties, as the case may be—through the application of their specialized knowledge. Their task usually combines observation and the application of the laws of science.

Two consequences follow from this difference between the role of the expert and that of a witness. First, while the witness is unique, the expert is replaceable. Second, while the witness must be heard whatever his or her character or attitude to the case or the parties involved may be, the expert must be neutral, free of bias, more or less as the judge must be impartial.[60] This is required in particular in cases where the expert has a privileged position in the proceedings. Grabenwarter correctly points out that an expert's lack of neutrality can be compensated by effective equality of arms which allows the defence to present its own expert(s).[61]

The Court has never taken a clear stand as to whether expert witnesses are to be considered as 'witnesses' within the meaning of Article 6 § 3(d). However, in practice the same rules do apply. This became evident in *Doorson* where the Court did not comment at all on the difference.[62] In the first case, where the question arose, the Court still showed some reluctance. It noted that '[r]ead literally, sub-paragraph (d) of paragraph 3 relates to witnesses and not experts'. It continued by noting 'that the guarantees contained in paragraph 3 are constituent elements, amongst others, of the concept of a fair trial set forth in paragraph 1' and avoided the issue by deciding 'that it should examine the applicant's complaints under the general rule of paragraph 1'.[63]

---

[56] Esser (2002) 630 is critical of the requirement that the statement must be taken into account by the court—in his view this bears no relevance to the status of a witness; however, the Court's approach is reasonable because under the perspective of the protection of fundamental rights the statement is of no interest as long as it has not been taken into account for a conviction.

[57] *Kostovski v. Netherlands*, § 40.   [58] *Pullar v. United Kingdom*, § 45.

[59] The Court has also decided a number of issues regarding experts in the context of civil proceedings; for this case-law, see Esser (2002) 693 et seq.

[60] There are, however, differences—closeness to the institute which contributed to the initiation of the proceedings was not regarded as justifying a fear of bias in *Brandstetter v. Austria*, § 44; whereas in *Sramek v. Austria*, § 41 a similar connection led to the conclusion that the tribunal was not impartial. See also Grabenwarter (1997) 633; this author gives a very thorough analysis of the issues under Art. 6 § 3(d) in Austrian administrative law at 643–65.

[61] Grabenwarter (1997) 632; see also the discussion of this issue by Stavros (1993) 244 et seq.

[62] *Doorson v. Netherlands*, §§ 81, 82.

[63] *Bönisch v. Austria*, § 29; the same approach was taken in *Brandstetter v. Austria*, § 42.

The point at issue in the two cases concerning the testimony of experts was their neutrality. In *Bönisch*, the Director of the Federal Food Control Institute had first filed a report alleging that Mr Bönisch had acted unlawfully; he was later appointed as an expert. The Court accepted that 'it is easily understandable that doubts should arise, especially in the mind of an accused, as to the neutrality of an expert when it was his report that in fact prompted the bringing of a prosecution'.[64] It agreed with the applicant that the expert was rather to be regarded as a witness for the prosecution. This was no obstacle to his being heard, but required equal treatment. However, the Director was heard as an 'expert'.[65] 'By reason of this, his statements must have carried greater weight than those of an "expert witness" called, as in the first proceedings, by the accused'. He also held a privileged position in other respects as he was allowed to attend the entire hearing and ask questions of the accused and other witnesses and comment upon them, rights which were denied to the expert witness called by the defence. The Court found a violation of Article 6 § 1 which dispensed it from also examining the issues under Article 6 § 3(d).[66] Stavros welcomes this approach as the sign of a 'new maturity in the case-law'.[67]

On the other hand, in *Brandstetter* (which concerned wine, *Bönisch* had involved smoked meat) the Court saw no objective justification for doubting the expert's neutrality simply because he was employed by the institute from which the incriminating report had emanated. Therefore he did not fall to be regarded as a witness for the prosecution.[68]

F. Application of Article 6 § 3(d) to Evidence Other than that of Witnesses

Finally, there are some clear indications in the case-law that Article 6 § 3(d) could potentially be applied to evidence other than that of witnesses. The Commission seemed to take this approach in *Edwards*, which concerned the prosecution's failure to disclose various pieces of evidence which could have benefited the defence.[69] Although the Court in *Edwards* did not follow this approach, the Court has subsequently adopted the idea.

In *Perna* the fact that two press articles were not joined to the file was discussed without any further comment under Article 6 §§ 1 and 3(d).[70] Finally, in *Papageorgiou* the issue was that the cheques which had allegedly been forged had not been available. It was held that the guarantee illustrates a typical aspect of the right to fair trial, the right to adversarial proceedings.[71] As such, it can and must be extended to mean that no evidence may be used as the basis of a conviction

---

[64] *Bönisch* v. *Austria*, § 32.
[65] The inverted commas are also used by the Court; ibid., § 33.   [66] Ibid., §§ 33–5.
[67] Stavros (1993) 243.
[68] *Brandstetter* v. *Austria*, §§ 44, 45; Esser (2002) 702 is right in criticizing this attitude of the Court.   [69] *Edwards* v. *United Kingdom*, § 32. See further Chapter 9 above.
[70] *Perna* v. *Italy (GC)*, §§ 25–32.   [71] See further Chapter 4 above.

unless the defence has had the opportunity to challenge its validity and to comment upon its relevance.[72]

III. THE RIGHT TO QUESTION WITNESSES AT DIFFERENT STAGES OF THE PROCEEDINGS

A. At the Trial

The Court's standard reminder that the evidence must normally be examined at the trial has already been mentioned.[73] It is of paramount importance. Here lies the nucleus of what, in German, is called the '*Unmittelbarkeitsprinzip*'—the principle of immediacy.[74] It is well known that the evidence, and particularly the statements of witnesses, can be the source of many errors. These can occur at the time that the observations are made, or later on in the process. Distortions may occur at the point at which the observation is memorized. Or when it is reproduced, it may be misunderstood, the record may not be quite precise—this list is not comprehensive. To determine the case solely on the basis of entries in the file is therefore a very risky matter. My reading of the Court's insistence on repeating that the evidence be examined at trial is that, as a matter of principle, the *Unmittelbarkeitsprinzip* is rooted in Article 6.[75] Some authors and also the Swiss Supreme Court, however, reject this view.[76] In the common law this is much less of an issue. There may be a dispute as to whether certain documents are admissible at trial and whether and to what extent hearsay evidence can be relied upon, but the decision-maker, whether it be a judge sitting alone or a jury, does not have access to the file, it must make its decision solely on the basis of evidence presented at trial.

One of the main arguments advanced against strictly respecting the immediacy principle is that it makes the administration of criminal justice exceedingly onerous and results in costly and lengthy trials. All criminal-justice systems have therefore developed strategies to cope with the problem. In the United States, for instance, plea-bargaining is the solution to the vast majority of criminal cases. In admittedly polemic terms, the administration of justice can be said to have been

---

[72] This disproves Gollwitzer (1992) Art. 6 N 211, who says Art. 6 § 3(d) does not apply to documents.

[73] *Isgrò* v. *Italy*, § 43; *Lüdi* v. *Switzerland*, § 27; *Saïdi* v. *France*, § 43; *Asch* v. *Austria*, § 27; *van Mechelen and others* v. *Netherlands*, § 51; *AM* v. *Italy*, § 25; *Lucà* v. *Italy*, § 40; *Solakov* v. *Former Yugoslav Republic of Macedonia*, § 57; *PS* v. *Germany*, § 21; *Birutis and others* v. *Lithuania*, § 28; *SN* v. *Sweden*, § 44; *Hulki Günes* v. *Turkey*, § 86. In other, both older and more recent judgments, the term 'in principle' is used: *Barberà, Messegué and Jabardo* v. *Spain*, § 78; *Kostovski* v. *Netherlands*, § 41; *Windisch* v. *Austria*, § 26; *Delta* v. *France*, § 36; *Sadak and others* v. *Turkey*, § 64; *Craxi* v. *Italy*, § 85; *Rachdad* v. *France*, § 23.

[74] Krauss (1986) 73 et seq.; Hauser and Schweri (2002) § 51 N 6; Roxin (1998) § 44; Schäfer (1976) 13.62; Geppert (1979).

[75] Trechsel (2000) 1368 et seq.; the same view is held, e.g. by Grabenwarter (1997) 638.

[76] Haefliger and Schürmann (1999) 239; BGE 113 Ia 419 et seq.; 116 Ia 291; 115 II 133.

replaced by a type of business negotiation. There is certainly the possibility, even probability, that the defendant will be coerced into accepting a reduced sentence in order to avoid a (possibly erroneous) conviction by a jury.

There are some indications in continental Europe of similar developments in this direction. In Germany, for instance, a considerable proportion of criminal cases are 'settled' in application of section 153a of the Criminal Procedure Code: the Public Prosecutor's Office, under the supervision of the court, refrains from bringing forward an indictment; the accused, in turn, accepts to fulfil certain conditions which may include the payment of damages and of a sum of money for the benefit of a charitable organization or the state.

There is also at the same time a tendency of increasingly allowing courts to rely on the file rather than live evidence. It is my view that this is not compatible with the spirit of the various international human-rights instruments and, more particularly, with the case-law of the Court. Of course, in some situations compromises will have to be accepted where there are good reasons justifying the use of evidence gathered in the investigation, but these must be the exception. Those who have the responsibility for deciding the guilt or innocence of an accused, ought, in principle, to be able personally to hear witnesses and assess their trustworthiness.

The rule that witnesses must be heard during the trial also has a function which goes beyond that of the safeguarding of fairness and the establishment of the truth in a specific case. For one, it must be seen in conjunction with the requirement that the trial be public.[77] This becomes somewhat farcical if the evidence is heard in the secrecy of preliminary proceedings.[78] On the other hand, the proceedings also serve an important role as the forum for the determination of justice, thereby upholding public confidence in the reliability and just character of court proceedings.[79]

Still, there are exceptions[80] and it is important to define them as precisely as possible. The Court has done so only at a rather late point in its jurisprudence, and this is compounded by its inconsistency. In *Craxi* the Court said that it may be necessary to have recourse to witness statements made during the investigation where it is impossible to hear the witness at the trial because, for example, he or she has died or in order to protect the right of the witness not to incriminate him- or herself.

B. During Pre-trial Proceedings

The exercise of the right to question witnesses during the pre-trial investigation is of considerable relevance. It is of great importance that the right be granted as

---

[77] The same view is expressed by Charrier (2002) Art. 6 N 86.
[78] This seems also to be the view of the Court; cf. *Riepan* v. *Austria*, § 40; *Stefanelli* v. *San Marino*, § 20.
[79] See in particular Luhmann (1975); also Trechsel (2000) 1366.
[80] The Court said so expressly, e.g. in *Lucà* v. *Italy*, § 39.

early as possible. It is a well-known fact that a witness who has been interrogated several times in the course of proceedings will be anxious to answer all questions in such a way as to ensure compatibility with the substance of his or her earlier statements and thus is not primarily interested in ensuring that the answers reflect the true content of his or her observations.[81] The defence therefore has a strong interest in being able to be present at the very first interrogation of the witness and to put questions from the very start. At a later stage in the proceedings it may be virtually impossible to influence the statement through further questioning. On the other hand, however, it is equally important, as has just been demonstrated, that the witness make his or her statement in open court at the trial. Logically, four possibilities can be distinguished:

- the witness is questioned during the investigation but not at the trial;
- the witness is questioned at the trial but not during the investigation;
- the witness is questioned during the investigation and at the trial;
- the witness is not heard at all.

1. The Witness is Only Questioned During the Investigation

The Court regularly refers to this situation after having reaffirmed that the evidence must be presented at the trial: 'However, the use in evidence of statements obtained at the stage of the police inquiry and the judicial investigation is not in itself inconsistent with §§ 1 and 3(d) of Article 6, provided that the rights of the defence have been respected. As a rule, these rights require that the defendant be given an adequate and proper opportunity to challenge and question a witness against him either when he was making his statements or at a later stage of the proceedings'.[82]

On the other hand, the Court has also positively commented on the application of the guarantees of fairness to earlier stages of the proceedings. 'Certainly, the primary purpose of Article 6 as far as criminal matters are concerned is to ensure a fair trial by a "tribunal" competent to determine "any criminal charge", but it does not follow that Article 6 has no application to pre-trial proceedings... Other requirements of Article 6—especially of paragraph 3—may also be relevant before a case is sent for trial if and in so far as the fairness of the trial is likely to be seriously prejudiced by an initial failure to comply with them.'[83] Although this quotation is taken from a case which concerned the right to be assisted by counsel during police questioning, it was later repeated in connection with Article 6 § 3(d).[84]

In stating that witness evidence obtained in the course of pre-trial proceedings may be used as a basis for a conviction, the Court in effect devalued its previous

---

[81] See e.g. Kohlbacher (1978) 129 et seq.
[82] *SN* v. *Sweden*, § 44, referring to *Saïdi* v. *France*, § 43 and *AM* v. *Italy*, § 43. See also e.g. *Birutis and others* v. *Lithuania*, § 28.   [83] *Imbrioscia* v. *Switzerland*, § 36.
[84] *Pisano* v. *Italy*, § 27.

statement: exceptions to the rule that evidence be presented in open court are acceptable without any further condition other than that there has been a confrontation with the defence. In other words, the right to question witnesses can also be granted in the course of a police inquiry or a preliminary invest-igation. If this was done, there is no need to repeat the interrogation before the court. The Court did not comment on whether, where there has been a con-frontation at a prior stage in the proceedings and the witness is heard again at the trial, the defence is allowed to ask further questions. This must certainly be permissible. It is essential that the credibility of the witness be tested in the presence of those who decide on the facts.

The addition of the expression 'as a rule' to the requirement that the defence must be able to question and challenge the witness is rather troublesome. This formulation seems to leave room for exceptions. What these could entail was not specified by the Court. In *Unterpertinger*, it said that such use of the evidence must comply with the rights of the defence, especially when the defendant had not had 'an opportunity at any stage in the earlier proceedings to question the persons whose statements are read out at the hearing'.[85] It is not clear how else the rights of the defence could have been respected.

Fortunately, the later case-law gives a clear answer: there is no other way. The more recent formulation is this: 'In particular, the rights of the defence are restricted to an extent that is incompatible with the requirements of Article 6 if the conviction is based solely, or in a decisive manner, on the depositions of a witness whom the accused has had no opportunity to examine or to have examined either during the investigation or at trial.'[86] Van Dijk and van Hoof write that the case-law 'does not seem to leave much room for exceptions to this rule'[87]—in truth, the only exception concerns cases where there is sufficient other evidence. In adopting this view, the Court gave back to Article 6 § 3(d) its proper value and weight.

2. The Right to Question a Witness During Pre-trial Proceedings

An entirely different question from that dealt with in the context of Article 6 § 3(d) is whether the accused has the right to be present or represented and to put questions, or to request that questions be put, to witnesses during the pre-trial proceedings, irrespective of whether such witness will also be heard at the trial.

---

[85] *Unterpertinger* v. *Austria*, § 31.

[86] *AM* v. *Italy*, § 25 (author's translation). See also *Lucà* v. *Italy*, § 40; *Sadak and others* v. *Turkey*, § 65; *Solakov* v. *Former Yugoslav Republic of Macedonia*, § 57; *Hulki Günes* v. *Turkey*, § 86; *Craxi* v. *Italy*, § 86; *Rachdad* v. *France*, § 23. The formulation 'as a rule' did not immediately disappear after *AM* v. *Italy*; it turns up in *SN* v. *Sweden*, § 44—probably a lapse due to insufficient coordination between the Chambers.

[87] Van Dijk and van Hoof (1998) 474; more positively, on the next page, they agree that there is no exception to the rule that no untested evidence can be the sole or decisive evidence for a conviction.

In the early jurisprudence the Commission rejected such suggestions.[88] This may explain Harris, O'Boyle, and Warbrick's opinion which is to the same effect.[89] The question must be approached from the perspective of Article 6 § 3(c) as is shown in the *Imbrioscia* case.[90] Here, the Court's finding that there was no violation, was due to the failure of the applicant's counsel to request that he be allowed to be present during the police interrogations. In my view this can only be understood as meaning that, as a matter of principle, there is a right to be present and to question witnesses from the beginning of the proceedings.[91]

C. In Appeal Proceedings

Finally, the right to question witnesses may also be of relevance in the context of appeal proceedings, although this will be rather exceptional. Yet, to the extent that a court of higher instance is competent to look at the facts and to re-examine freely that part of the lower-instance court's judgment, it may also hear witnesses. It will then have to grant the defence the right to put questions. This also means that in such cases the court of appeal is in a position to heal the shortcomings of the earlier instance(s). The Court made this implicitly clear when, in *Engel and others*, it noted that the applicant had not asked the Supreme Military Court to hear witnesses.[92]

IV. THE EXERCISE OF THE RIGHT

A. Who is Entitled to Exercise the Right to Question Witnesses?

The right to question witnesses can be exercised by the accused, by counsel for the accused, or by the accused and counsel jointly, i.e. by counsel in the presence and under instruction of the accused.

1. Counsel and the Accused

The only fully satisfactory way of exercising the right to question witnesses is when this is carried out by counsel in the presence and under the instruction of the accused. The situation is analogous to that of examining the file. The accused is not trained in asking the proper questions, particularly under the common law where there are many formal rules to be respected. On the other hand, counsel will not have a detailed knowledge of the facts. At least in cases where the accused was to some extent involved in the activities leading to the

---

[88] *X v. Germany* Application 8414/78; *X v. Germany* Application 6566/74.
[89] Harris, O'Boyle, and Warbrick (1995) 266 with reference to *Schertenleib* v. *Switzerland* Application 8339/78.   [90] *Imbrioscia* v. *Italy*.
[91] This view seems to be shared by Charrier (2002) Art. 6 N 89.
[92] *Engel and others* v. *Netherlands*, § 91; see also e.g. *Isgrò* v. *Italy*, § 35.

criminal charge, it will be important that he or she is able to use this knowledge to influence the direction which the questioning takes.

However, the Court has also accepted, without limitations it seems, that it is legitimate that the right only be exercised either by the accused or by counsel; there is no right to insist that both be able to ask questions.

2. The Accused Alone

The leading case where an accused was confronted with an important witness in the absence of his lawyer is *Isgrò*. In this case the Commission had come to the conclusion that there had been a violation because the prosecution and the defence had not been put on an equal footing. The prosecuting authorities and the investigating judge had questioned the witness D in the absence of the accused and his lawyer. While there had been a confrontation between the applicant and the witness, there was no evidence in the record that the accused had put any questions either directly to the witness or through the investigating judge. This, in the view of the majority of the Commission, meant that the accused had not had an 'adequate and proper opportunity to challenge and question a witness against him' (D did not turn up at the trial).[93]

The Court, however, found that the applicant had indeed been confronted with the witness and had had the chance to put questions directly to him. It saw no inequality because at the confrontation the public prosecutor had not been present. Rather unconvincingly the Court asserted that 'the purpose of the confrontation did not render the presence of Mr Isgrò's lawyer indispensable; since it was open to the applicant to put questions and to make comments himself, he enjoyed the guarantees secured under Article 6 para. 3(d) to a sufficient extent.'[94] This implies that the absence of counsel did not negatively affect the defence's case, an argument which had correctly been rejected in *Artico*.[95]

There seems to be a certain contradiction between *Isgrò* and the *Hulki Günes* case. In the latter case, the Court mentioned the fact that no defence counsel had assisted the applicant during the preliminary proceedings when a confrontation took place.[96] However, this is formulated as *obiter dictum*, as a supplementary argument to say that the witnesses in question ought to have been heard at the trial.

3. Counsel Alone

On the other hand, the Court has made it clear that the exercise of the right by counsel satisfies the requirements of Article 6 § 3(d). It expressed itself in particularly clear terms in *Kamasinski*: 'For the purposes of Article 6 § 3(d)

---

[93] *Isgrò* v. *Italy*, Report of the Commission §§ 55–59; the same view was held by the Swiss Supreme Court in BGE 116 Ia 289.   [94] *Isgrò* v. *Italy*, §§ 35, 36.
[95] *Artico* v. *Italy*, § 35. For a critical view on *Isgrò*, see also Osborne (1993) 256.
[96] *Hulki Günes* v. *Turkey*, § 92.

Mr Kamasinski must be identified with the counsel who acted on his behalf, and he cannot therefore attribute to the respondent State any liability for his counsel's decisions in this respect'.[97] This corresponds to the general rule that the defendant is to a considerable extent in the hands of his lawyer and must put up with his or her failings, such as missing the time limits for an appeal.[98]

In *Compass*, the HRC expressed the same opinion.

B. How is the Right to be Exercised?

The most natural way of exercising the right to put questions to witnesses is through cross-examination, which also served as the model for the guarantee. The opportunity for lawyers directly to conduct interrogations is by no means a typical feature of criminal-procedure systems in continental Europe. One exception is the jury trial according to the Code of Criminal Procedure of the canton of Zurich, a code which is destined to be abolished following the introduction of a federal codification.[99] Generally it is the presiding judge who puts the questions—a practice which stems from the old inquisitorial model.

This must be the explanation for the alternative 'or have examined' which figures both in the ICCPR and the ECHR, but not in the ACHR.[100] The obligation on states under Article 6 § 3(d) is satisfied if the defence has the right to suggest questions for the presiding judge to put to the witness. The presiding judge will have a certain discretion to admit or to refuse a question, a possibility which also exists in the common law if the other party raises an objection. Under the continental system, however, the position of the defence is considerably weaker. It is a practical disadvantage if questions must be put indirectly, because this gives the witness extra time to prepare an answer. As long as the same rule applies to the prosecution, however, it must be considered as being compatible with the requirements of the international human-rights instruments.

If the witness lives abroad, it is possible for him or her to be heard on the basis of commissions rogatory. It is true that the Court has taken a rather strong position against submitting questions in writing: 'according to the Government, the applicant could have put written questions to the women, had he so requested at the trial. These possibilities cannot, however, replace the right to examine directly prosecution witnesses before the trial court'.[101] In this case, however, there was an additional obstacle in that the witnesses were anonymous.

The testimony of witnesses questioned by means of a letter rogatory in the United States was at issue in the *AM* and *Solakov* cases. In *Solakov*, the Court stressed that the applicant 'had not expressly given any questions that he would

[97] *Kamasinski* v. *Austria*, § 91. See also *Kurup* v. *Denmark* Application 11219/84; *X* v. *Denmark* Application 8395/78. For a critical comment, see Chapter 9 above.
[98] See e.g. Application 9671/82; Frowein and Peukert (1996) Art. 26 N 22, n. 87.
[99] Schmid (2004) N 853.
[100] In the same sense, see Gollwitzer (1992) Art. 6 N 230; Nowak (1993) Art. 14 N 53.
[101] *Windisch* v. *Austria*, § 28.

have liked to be put to the witnesses'.[102] This can be understood in the sense that the Court accepted, at least in certain circumstances, the indirect exercise of the rights. In *AM*, the violation seemed rather to be based on the fact that the prosecutor had stated that no lawyer was to be allowed to attend the requested examinations—the issue of written questions was not addressed.[103]

The possibility of having questions put to the witness was also at issue in a case concerning a sexual offence where it was not possible for the defence directly to question the victim/witness; counsel later had the possibility to verify whether this had been done correctly by means of a tape recording and a transcript. The Court seems to have been influenced by the fact that counsel had accepted the procedures.[104]

The effective exercise of the right under Article 6 § 3(d) presupposes access to the file. In order to be able to find weak points regarding the credibility of the witness, it is important to know every statement that he or she has previously made in those, and perhaps even in other, proceedings. The HRC rightly found a violation in a case where the records of such statements had been withheld from the defence.[105]

A number of situations which are recognized as creating an obstacle to the normal exercise of the right to question witnesses require examination. Under such circumstances special rules may apply to the exercise of the guarantee.

V. LIMITATIONS OF THE RIGHT TO TEST WITNESS EVIDENCE

A. General Observations

The central difficulty with the right to question witnesses arises in the context of exceptions to the principle. Such exceptions typically arise in four types of situation. *First*, in cases where the witness cannot be heard either because he or she does not turn up and cannot be brought to the trial; *second*, where there is an interest in keeping the identity of the witness secret—such as for example where undercover agents are involved; *third*, where the witness is intimidated by the accused or fears reprisals; finally, *fourth*, in cases involving victims/witnesses of sexual offences who risk being further traumatized by confrontations with the alleged perpetrator of the offence.[106]

---

[102] *Solakov v. The Former Yugoslav Republic of Macedonia*, § 62.

[103] *AM v. Italy*, § 27. On the rights of the defence in rogatory interrogations, see also *X, Y and Z v. Austria* Application 5049/71; this is also criticized by Vogler (1986) N 555.

[104] *SN v. Sweden*, § 50.   [105] *Peart v. Jamaica*.

[106] This phenomenon has been described very impressively in the novel *The Women's Room* (1997) by Marilyn French.

If the respondent government bases its argument on one of these exceptional situations, the Court proceeds in three steps.[107] *First*, it examines whether the reason invoked as an exception actually existed, and whether it had been subject to serious examination by the national authorities. *Second*, it asks whether the restrictions on the defence rights were kept to a very minimum, and whether they were strictly necessary in order to satisfy the legitimate aim of protection. *Finally*, there is an examination of whether the rights of the defence were adequately compensated for the shortcomings.

Now and then, regrettably, the Court uses arguments which are entirely irrelevant or cryptic. Thus, it sometimes stresses that the defence had the possibility to discuss the statement,[108] or to contest the statement.[109] Every accused has the right critically to comment on the evidence and on the arguments presented by the prosecution. Here, the point at issue is the right to confront the witness in person, not to present arguments to the Court. There is no merit to the Court's argument.

Another formula which is rather weak is the warning that untested evidence must be 'treated with extreme care'.[110] It is by no means clear what the Court means by this. Either the evidence is used or it is not. A benevolent interpretation would lead to the conclusion that the domestic courts must show particular scepticism *vis-à-vis* such statements. But is there ever evidence which must *not* be critically and carefully evaluated?

A rather doubtful method, in my view,[111] is the balancing of the failings of the evidence against its importance for the conviction: 'In the Court's view, in assessing whether the procedures involved in the questioning of the anonymous witness were sufficient to counterbalance the difficulties caused to the defence due weight must be given to the above conclusion that the anonymous testimony was not in any respect decisive for the conviction of the applicant'.[112] This seems to be akin to saying that the conditions for testing the reliability of the witness are admittedly a bit worse than normal, but, this is not really critical because the testimony is itself a bit less important for the conviction. Such an approach cannot be said to reach the standard of precision and reliability expected of legal rules. It provides an opening for immaterial subjective preferences or dislikes.[113]

---

[107] A fourth step, which, however, ought to be the first one, is the question whether and to what extent the conviction is based upon the untested witness statement.   [108] *Asch* v. *Austria*, § 29.

[109] *Craxi* v. *Italy*, § 86.

[110] *Doorson* v. *Netherlands*, § 76; *Visser* v. *Netherlands*, § 44; *SN* v. *Sweden*, § 53.

[111] For a positive comment, see Grabenwarter (1997) 641.

[112] *Kok* v. *Netherlands*, decision of 4 Apr. 2000, Reports 2000-VI 599, at 625, repeated in *Visser* v. *Netherlands*, § 46.

[113] Stavros (1993) 248 holds a much more radical view. According to him, 'Art. 6 . . . does not allow for limitation to protect conflicting interests'.

B. Typical Situations Justifying Exceptions

1. Absent Witnesses

As has already been noted, witnesses must normally be heard at a public trial in the presence of the accused. This is the issue where, in practice, shortcomings can most frequently be observed. Many criminal cases concerning minor offences are dealt with by way of alternative methods of prosecution which do not involve a public hearing. This is an indispensable way of speeding up the proceedings and is based upon the accused's consent, in other words, on his or her waiver.

A considerable number of exceptions are caused by the atrophy of, or non-reliance on, the 'principle of immediacy' in continental Europe.

The solution to the problem was set out by the Court in its first Article 6 § 3(d) cases: 'In itself, the reading out of statements in this way cannot be regarded as being inconsistent with Article 6 §§ 1 and 3(d) of the Convention, but the use made of them as evidence must nevertheless comply with the rights of the defence, which it is the object and purpose of Article 6 to protect'.[114] Such compliance consists essentially in the possibility for the defence to question the witness. This is a straightforward rule. It was applied in the cases of *Unterpertinger, Windisch, Delta, Saïdi,* and *Rachdad.* In *Asch* and *Artner* it should, in my view, also have been applied. However, the Court preferred instead to find that there was no violation on the basis that the conviction had not been exclusively or decisively based on the critical witness statements.[115]

In *Artner* the Court made a statement which must be expressly rejected; it said that the fact that the only witness could not be found, 'did not in itself make it necessary to halt the prosecution'.[116] One gets the impression that the Court thinks that an offender ought not to be acquitted just because the central witness cannot be found. Such an approach would be unacceptable. As a matter of course, a suspect must be acquitted or the proceedings must be postponed if the central element of evidence is not available.[117]

Criticism must also be voiced with regard to a passage in *Doorson.* The Court found that it had been impossible to secure the attendance of witness R at the hearing and concluded that: 'In the circumstances it was open to the Court of Appeal to have regard to the statement obtained by the police, especially since it could consider that statement to be corroborated by other evidence before it'.[118] It is necessary to repeat that there is no logic in a rule according to which an

---

[114] *Unterpertinger* v. *Austria,* § 31; *Windisch* v. *Austria,* § 26.
[115] The same approach was taken in a case concerning rape; there was hardly any other evidence—one victim had been heard in the presence of counsel who could ask questions, the other had not; the application was declared inadmissible; *Verdam* v. *Netherlands* Application 35253/97.
[116] *Artner* v. *Austria,* § 21.
[117] See also the dissenting opinion of Judges Walsh, Macdonald, and Palm.
[118] *Doorson* v. *Netherlands,* § 80.

untested statement of a witness may be accepted as evidence because that witness is not available at the hearing.

In a number of cases the Court raised the question as to whether the authorities were to be blamed for the absence of the witness. In *Isgrò*, for instance, it referred to the efforts made by the courts to secure the presence of witness D.[119] On the other hand, in *Sadak* and *Hulki Günes* the responsibility lay clearly with the authorities.[120] In my view, the argument is partly pertinent. If the prosecution is responsible for not bringing the relevant witnesses to the trial, untested statements made by them in an earlier phase of the proceedings should not be accepted as evidence. In *Ferrantelli and Santangelo* the authorities would have had the possibility to hold a confrontation over a period of two years; the Court nevertheless allowed the statement to be used as evidence. This is particularly regrettable as the allegation that the witness V committed suicide appeared highly unlikely—V had only one arm and would hardly have been able to hang himself. He was also found gagged, something which hardly speaks for the argument that he had committed suicide.[121] The opposite conclusion, however, cannot be sustained. The fact that the authorities cannot be blamed for the absence of the witness does not mean that a conviction can be based on his or her prior statement(s). In *Sadak and others* the Court stressed the 'positive' side of Article 6 § 3(d): it imposes upon states a certain obligation of diligence.[122]

There is, of course, a further possibility, namely that the accused or persons close to her or him takes action to prevent the witness from appearing at the trial—the most drastic course of action would be the physical elimination of the witness.[123]

The case of a witness who refuses to testify must be dealt with in exactly the same way as that of a witness who does not appear.[124]

2. The 'Precious' Witness

Nowadays, states frequently have recourse to undercover agents and similar types of informants in the fight against organized crime, for example, in areas such as drug trafficking, trafficking in human beings, counterfeiting of money, or terrorism. It takes considerable efforts to prepare and train specialized agents for this purpose, which makes them a particularly valuable instrument in the context of police investigations. The essential condition for the operation of such agents is that their identity and function remain secret. This creates problems if the agent has to give evidence. Normally, this ought to be avoided. The agent ought to arrange things so that at a crucial moment the regular police can intervene and secure, at the same time, the principal suspects and the necessary evidence.

[119] *Isgrò* v. *Italy*, § 35; see also *Delta* v. *France*, § 37; *Craxi* v. *Italy*, § 86.
[120] *Sadak and others* v. *Turkey*, § 44, 67; *Hulki Günes* v. *Turkey*, § 88. In the latter case the prosecution refused to bring the police officers who had been summoned to testify with the excuse of the dangers of the road ('*pour des raisons de sécurité routière*').
[121] See also the criticism of Esser (2002) 652.   [122] *Sadak and others* v. *Turkey*, § 67.
[123] See Friedmann (2001).   [124] See e.g. *Lucà* v. *Italy*.

If an undercover agent's testimony is needed to secure a conviction, exceptions to the basic rule of Article 6 § 3(d) are, to a limited extent, acceptable. The Court dealt with this problem in *Lüdi*.[125] The Court accepted as legitimate the concerns of the Government that the identity of the agent remain undisclosed. However, as the Commission had done, it observed that the accused had met the agent, 'Toni', several times. He certainly knew what he looked like. Therefore, it was possible to hear the witness without his identity being revealed. His identity could remain protected in that his real name and address would not be mentioned in open court—it would also have been possible to exclude the public.

3. The Intimidated Witness

The most important category in this context is made up of cases where the witness is scared of the accused and/or his or her associates.[126] The Court gave a convincing line of argument to explain why it was justified to take this problem into account:

> It is true that Article 6 does not explicitly require the interests of witnesses in general, and those of victims called upon to testify in particular, to be taken into consideration. However, their life, liberty or security of person may be at stake, as may interests coming generally within the ambit of Article 8 of the Convention. Such interests of witnesses and victims are in principle protected by other, substantive provisions of the Convention, which imply that Contracting States should organise their criminal proceedings in such a way that those interests are not unjustifiably imperilled. Against this background, principles of fair trial also require that in appropriate cases the interests of the defence are balanced against those of witnesses or victims called upon to testify.[127]

The response of the authorities to this danger may consist of special witness-protection programmes, such as those applied in the United States.[128] The witness will, after the trial, receive an entirely new identity and be assisted in building up a new existence in another part of the country or abroad.[129] Such programmes are extremely onerous and expensive. They can only work in a large country where everyone speaks the same language. In other parts of the world it is hardly possible successfully to disguise and hide a person. Therefore, as it appears impossible to guarantee the safety of an identified witness, recourse is taken to anonymity.[130]

The Court is aware of the dangers associated with this anonymous testimony and has made it clear that the Convention, while admitting the use of anonymous informants at the stage of the police inquiry, prohibits a state from

---

[125] *Lüdi* v. *Switzerland*, §§ 45–50; the principle was reaffirmed in *van Mechelen* v. *Netherlands*, § 57.
[126] A detailed analysis of the intimidated witness in court is given by Fyfe (2001) 113 et seq.
[127] *Doorson* v. *Netherlands*, § 70, repeated in *van Mechelen* v. *Netherlands*, § 53.
[128] Cf. e.g. Fyfe (2001) 15 et seq.   [129] Earley and Schur (2003).
[130] For a discussion of witness protection in English, German, and Polish law, see Wąsek-Wiaderek (2000) 34 et seq.

basing a conviction 'solely or to a decisive extent on anonymous evidence'.[131] On the other hand, the use of anonymous statements is not 'in all circumstances incompatible with the Convention', but the difficulties it causes to the defence must be adequately counterbalanced.[132]

Wąsek-Wiaderek refers to the 'well-developed case law' of the Court.[133]

(a) The Justification for Anonymity

In *Kostovski* the Court quoted Chief Superintendent Alferink of The Hague Municipal Police as saying: 'Consultations take place before anonymous witnesses are interviewed. It is customary for me to ascertain the identity of the witness to be interviewed in order to assess whether he or she could be in danger. In this case the anonymous witnesses were in real danger. The threat was real'.[134] This finding was accepted without further discussion.[135]

In its later jurisprudence, however, the Court began to verify whether the reasons invoked for the witnesses' fear could be held to be convincing. It is not quite clear whether the decisive criterion is a subjective or an objective one. Must a real threat be established or is it sufficient that the witness *is* afraid of reprisals if he or she testifies? The answer must be analogous to that used in the context of the impartiality of the judge; an approach which the Court calls the subjective aspect of a judge's impartiality. The essential element is that the witness's apprehension is based on objective facts.

In *Doorson*, the Court found that the fears of witnesses Y.15 and Y.16 was a relevant reason to grant them anonymity, but wondered whether it was sufficient. Two elements led to a positive answer: the experience 'that drug dealers frequently resorted to threats or actual violence against persons who gave evidence against them' and the fact that one of the witnesses had actually suffered such violence on a previous occasion.[136]

The Court reached a different conclusion in *van Mechelen*, where the witnesses were police officers. The Court recognized that while the safety of the witnesses and their families also deserved protection, they owed 'a general duty of obedience to the State's executive' which might include the duty to give evidence in court.[137] Furthermore, the Court doubted whether the domestic court 'made sufficient effort to assess the threat of reprisals against the police officers or their families'.[138] Finally, the Court pointed out that a civilian witness had made statements identifying one of the applicants and he had not been threatened.[139] Although it also criticized the methods used, the decisive element which led to

---

[131] *Kostovski* v. *Netherlands*, § 44; *Doorson* v. *Netherlands*, § 76; *van Mechelen* v. *Netherlands*, § 55; *Visser* v. *Netherlands*, § 43; *Birutis and others* v. *Lithuania*, § 29.

[132] *Doorson* v. *Netherlands*, § 72; *van Mechelen* v. *Netherlands*, § 54; *Visser* v. *Netherlands*, § 43; *Birutis and others* v. *Lithuania*, § 29. The topic of 'counterbalance' was first brought up in *Kostovski* v. *Netherlands*, § 43.　　　　　　　　　　　　　　[133] Wąsek-Wiaderek (2000) 39.

[134] *Kostovski* v. *Netherlands*, § 19.　　　[135] On Kosovski, see also Callewaert (1990).

[136] *Doorson* v. *Netherlands*, § 71.　　　[137] *Van Mechelen* v. *Netherlands*, § 56.

[138] Ibid., § 61.　　　[139] Ibid.

the finding of a violation seems to have been the fact that the witnesses were police officers.[140] The Court's reference to the fact that police officers are often called to hearings as witnesses, however, does not seem very pertinent—it could be an incentive for criminal organizations to eliminate them. The only relevant criterion is the danger to their families and, to a lesser extent, to themselves, because by entering the police force they have accepted certain dangers which other citizens do not have to face.[141]

In *Visser*, the Court again criticized the domestic authorities' lack of scrutiny: 'The investigating judge apparently took into account the reputation of the co-accused in general, but his report does not show how he assessed the reasonableness of the personal fear of the witness either as this had existed when the witness was heard by police or when he or she was heard by the investigating judge nearly six years later'; moreover no 'examination into the seriousness and well-foundedness of the reasons for the anonymity of the witness' had been carried out by the court.[142] The Court, therefore, was not convinced that the anonymity could be justified and as a consequence, logically, did not find it necessary 'to examine further whether the procedures put in place by the judicial authorities could have sufficiently counterbalanced the difficulties faced by the defence as a result of the anonymity of the witness'.[143]

The opposite result was reached in *Birutis*—which involved a prison riot and where the use of anonymous evidence had not been contested as such.[144]

(b) The Methods for Counterbalancing Anonymity

The handicap caused by the anonymity of a witness is considerable—it varies, of course, with regard to the specificity of each case. Ignorance of a witness's identity makes it difficult to assess whether the witness is reliable, whether there exist elements justifying a suspicion of bias, animosity, hatred, or other motives for lying. In particular, it is not possible to establish whether any links to the suspect, to the victim, or to other witnesses exist. Moreover, where eyewitness testimony is at issue, it may not be possible to assess whether the victim could actually see what he or she claims to have seen; concealing the identity may, at the same time, prevent a precise indication of the place from which the witness observed the crime.

Furthermore, anonymity will regularly result in the witness's physical appearance being disguised. Thus, the defence will not be able fully to observe his or her demeanour while testifying.

For these reasons, special measures to counterbalance these disadvantages are required. The Court accepted that such redeeming features were in place in just one case, namely *Doorson*.[145] In this case the anonymous witness had been

---

[140] *Van Mechelen* v. *Netherlands*, § 64.

[141] This is a principle also applied in criminal law with regard to the defence of necessity (*Notstand*); see Trechsel and Noll, (2004) § 27 B 1 (d). See also Esser (2002) 661.

[142] *Visser* v. *Netherlands*, § 47.   [143] Ibid., § 51.

[144] *Birutis and others* v. *Lithuania*, § 30.   [145] *Doorson* v. *Netherlands*, § 73.

heard during appeal proceedings by an investigating judge who knew his or her identity and who also filed a report on her observations regarding the reliability of the witness.[146] Counsel had been present at the hearing and had had the opportunity to ask any questions that he wished, providing that it was not designed to find out the identity of the witness. Furthermore, the anonymous witness had identified the accused when shown his photograph. This did not, of course, entirely eliminate the handicaps faced by the defence—but any lingering concerns were eradicated through reference to supplementary evidence.

In *Kostovski* almost no action had been taken to counterbalance the disadvantage encountered by the defence. One of the anonymous witnesses had been heard by an investigating judge but the identity of the witness was not even revealed to this judge.[147] It is rather obvious that the possibility of questioning the police officers and investigating magistrates did not constitute a valid alternative to hearing the witnesses.

On the other hand, considerable efforts had been made in *van Mechelen*. Here, the accused and counsel were placed in an adjacent room where they could acoustically follow what happened at the hearing; they also had the possibility to put questions to the witness. This method was regularly used by the European Commission of Human Rights when its delegates took evidence under what was formerly Article 28(b) of the ECHR.[148]

The Court found this insufficient, because the defence were 'not only unaware of the identity of the police witnesses but were also prevented from observing their demeanour under direct questioning, and thus from testing their reliability'.[149] The Court cautiously referred to an explanatory memorandum which accompanied new legislation in the Netherlands which suggested measures of protection 'such as making the police officer unrecognisable by the use of make-up or disguise or preventing eye contact between the accused and the police officer'.[150] In my view, this slightly tips the balance too far in favour of the defence. The Commission did not follow this approach and declared inadmissible an application in which the same method had been applied.[151] The notion that a witness could be disguised in order to maintain his or her anonymity, while, at the same time, enabling the defence reliably to observe his or her demeanour, does not convince me as being very realistic.[152] There is also a danger of bringing an atmosphere of carnival into the hearing, if false beards, wigs, and fake glasses are being used. On the other hand: is it really decisive that

[146] As Esser (2002) 668 points out, however, the value of that report is open to doubt as it was drafted nine months after the interrogation and the investigating judge had to admit that her memory was not flawless.   [147] *Kostovski v. Netherlands*, § 43.

[148] See e.g. *Cyprus v. Turkey*, Report of the Commission of 5 June 1999, § 37.

[149] *Van Mechelen v. Netherlands*, § 59.   [150] Ibid., §§ 42, 60.

[151] *SE v. Switzerland* Application 28994/95.

[152] See also the criticism of Esser (2002) 671; Renzikowski (1999) 605, 612, n. 79; Corstens and Pradel (2002) N 359 find the judgment 'awkward'.

the defence be able to observe the witness? It is certainly helpful in that counsel can point out specific observations to the court. But it is mainly and finally for the judges to assess the reliability of the testimony. Anyway, the voice itself carries a wealth of information on the speaker's state of mind.

From a more general perspective, there is a legitimate interest in preventing criminal organizations from frustrating criminal prosecutions by intimidating witnesses. I fully agree that the aim cannot justify the means and that accused persons who are suspected of hideous crimes must not lose their right to a fair trial. However, in certain areas, such as the protection of witnesses, it must be possible to adapt these rights. It is interesting to note that there has never been any serious criticism of the methodology used by the delegates of the Commission (in any case it does not seem that the Court itself ever objected)[153] in conducting witness hearings, a methodology which was the same as that used in *van Mechelen*.

In *Birutis* one of the applicants had been convicted exclusively on the basis of anonymous statements—this constituted a clear violation.[154] With regard to the other two applicants, a suspicion had been raised that their testimony could have been brought about by improper pressure or promises; the court had not examined this matter properly and the accused had not had an opportunity to question the witnesses. This also led to a finding of a violation.[155]

4. The Vulnerable Witness

Finally, witnesses who have been the victims of sexual offences are often extremely reluctant to be confronted with the suspect because they risk severe emotional suffering if forced to relive in a very painful way the offence and the feelings of helplessness, exposure, and shame associated with it.[156] It is the most recent category of cases where the problem of restrictions on the rights under Article 6 § 3(d) have arisen. The Court has accepted that '[s]uch proceedings are often conceived of as an ordeal by the victim, in particular when the latter is unwillingly confronted with the defendant'.[157]

Initially, the Commission showed a strong tendency towards protecting victim-witnesses. In *Baegen* a rape victim had been warned by her attacker not to tell the police. She therefore asked to remain anonymous. However, at one point she was confronted with the applicant. There was also further evidence—another witness was also granted anonymity. Counsel could, however, put questions in writing. The applicant pretended never to have had intercourse with the victim, but refused a blood or saliva test which could have proved this point.

---

[153] Of course, the proceedings under the Convention are not criminal proceedings (Art. 6 of the Convention does not apply); nor can they be in all respects compared to criminal proceedings.
[154] *Birutis and others* v. *Lithuania*, § 31.   [155] Ibid., §§ 32–4.
[156] Wąsek-Wiaderek (2000) 33; Sanders and Young (1994) 26; *Baegen* v. *Netherlands*, report of 20 Oct. 1994, § 77; see also *MK* v. *Austria* Application 21155/93.   [157] *SN* v. *Sweden*, § 47.

The Commission found no violation. The case was brought before the Court, but the applicant did not pursue the case and it was therefore struck off the list.[158]

The applicant Finkensieper had been the director and senior medical officer of a psychiatric ward for minors. Several former patients had complained of having been sexually abused by him. The witnesses, who were all victims, were heard by an investigating judge in the presence of counsel who could put questions.[159] One witness did not appear due to psychological problems.

There was, however, considerable supporting evidence which led to the conclusion that there had been no violation.[160]

While vulnerable witnesses are anxious to remain anonymous because they do not want to be seen, the victims of sexual offences shy away from seeing the accused. Therefore, there is generally no obstacle to hearing them in such a way as to ensure that they cannot see the accused while the latter can follow the interrogation by way of closed-circuit television.[161]

So far, the Court has dealt with the issue in two cases. In *PS* v. *Germany* the applicant was accused of having sexually abused an eight-year-old girl. Neither he nor the judge ever had an opportunity to question her. The court decided not to hear her 'in order to protect her personal development' as, according to her mother, she had meanwhile repressed her recollection of the event and would seriously suffer if she were to be reminded of it.[162] The Court accepted that this was 'a relevant consideration' but found that the reasons given by the district court for rejecting the request to question the girl and to order an expert opinion were 'rather vague and speculative'. As far as the issue of questioning is concerned, this is a rather surprising statement. The regional court did then order an expert opinion on the girl's credibility, but the Court criticized this on the basis that the opinion was only prepared eighteen months after the alleged offence.[163] As with the case of *van Mechelen*, I am of the opinion that in this case the interests of the victim ought not to have been overridden by those of the defence. The argument that the expert opinion was seriously flawed by delay is not very convincing. However, it would certainly have been possible to improve the situation of the defence without damaging the position of the victim-witness.

This was successfully managed in *SN* v. *Sweden*. The applicant was suspected of having committed sexual acts with an eleven-year-old boy. The victim was not prepared to testify as a witness at the court hearing. His first interview with the police was recorded on videotape. The defence could see the tape and put forward questions in view of a second one. On that occasion, although counsel

---

[158] Van Dijk and van Hoof (1998) 476 doubt whether the Court would have come to the same conclusion. The decision in *Verdam* confirms those doubts.
[159] This possibility had also been given in *Slobodan* v. *Netherlands* Application 29838/96.
[160] *Finkensieper* v. *Netherlands*, report of 17 May 1995. See also *S* v. *Austria* Application 2262/86, which, at the present stage of the development of the case-law, would probably have led to the finding of a violation of Art. 6 § 3(d) in conjunction with Art. 6 § 1.
[161] This was the method employed in *Hols* v. *Netherlands* Application 25206/94.
[162] *PS* v. *Germany*, § 27.　　　[163] Ibid., §§ 28, 29.

was not allowed to be present or to follow the hearing from another room, he had nevertheless consented to such a set-up. The interview was audio taped and counsel for the defence could later listen to the recording and read the transcript. In this way he could verify that his questions had actually been put to the boy. The recordings of both interviews were also presented during the hearing. Although these circumstances were not really optimal, the Court found no violation.

The lesson to be learned from this case-law is as follows: it is possible to reconcile the protection of the victim and the effective right of the accused to question her or him. The best way to achieve this is to record the first hearing on videotape. That tape should then be made available to the accused and counsel who will be given the opportunity to formulate questions. There should then be a second interview which the accused and counsel can follow via closed-circuit television. Ideally there should be an audio connection between the defence and the person who interviews the child, using the technique applied, for example, for communication between a director and a cameraman in live TV reporting. This enables the defence to suggest, without even being heard by the witness, further questions and to react immediately, though only through the intermediary of the agent, who must be a person specially trained for the task. The recordings can then be played at the hearing.[164]

C. Hearsay Evidence

In the common law the admissibility of hearsay evidence is a well-known, and controversial issue. On the European continent, however, it is of marginal importance but accepted in most countries—exceptions include Italy and Portugal.[165] In Germany it is the subject of considerable debate, but is certainly not *a priori* excluded.[166]

Starmer rightly observes that under the Convention 'nothing prevents a court from relying on hearsay evidence'.[167] The author links this issue closely to that of the untested evidence which may only be relevant for a conviction to the extent that its flaws are properly counterbalanced by specific safeguards. In my view no special issue arises per se in international human-rights law.

VI. THE RIGHT TO CALL WITNESSES

While Article 14 § 3(e) of the ICCPR, Article 6 § 3(d) of the ECHR, and Article 8 § 2(f) of the ACHR all guarantee two distinct rights, the practical

---

[164] For the use of new technologies, see also Chiavario (1996) 121 et seq.; Renucci (2002) 291; Strange (2001) N 16.5.1.3.   [165] An overview is given by Pradel (2002) NN 319 et seq.
[166] See, for the German law, e.g. Roxin (1998) § 44 B IV.
[167] Starmer (2001) N 9.5; see also Strange (2001) N 16.4.

relevance of the second right, namely to call witnesses (and experts), has remained in the background.[168] In the European system, there is only one case in which a violation was found.[169] This is not surprising if one keeps in mind the particularities of this right.

The text says 'witnesses on his behalf', but, as Grabenwarter rightly points out, there must also be a right to call 'neutral' witnesses or even prosecution witnesses whose credibility the defence wishes to challenge in the presence of the court.[170] The words 'on his behalf' should be understood as meaning no more than the fact that the witness is called upon the initiative of the defence.

On the other hand, the same author cannot be followed when he restricts the right to those cases in which a hearing on the merits is held.[171] The defence must also be able to request the hearing of witnesses at the pre-trial stage, particularly in cases where due to illness, impending departure, or other reasons it is unlikely that the person will be heard at the trial.

A. The Particularities of this Right

The right to call witnesses is a special aspect of a more general right to present evidence.[172] It is a very important right as it gives an active role to the defence, and in particular the possibility to contribute in shaping the proceedings. While it is a fundamental element in common-law criminal proceedings, where the parties are responsible for presenting their evidence, it is only of secondary importance in systems, which are common on the continent, where the evidence is called by the court. Here, it is the court which not only decides what evidence is to be heard at the hearing but which also organizes the administration of evidence, by issuing, on its own initiative, summons for witnesses, experts, etc. While it is not entirely free in deciding what evidence is to be heard, it certainly enjoys a very broad margin of appreciation.[173]

Of course, the continental system also recognizes a right of the defence to influence this process by proposing witnesses. Such a proposal will, however, be evaluated critically by the presiding judge or the court. Considerations of economy are no strangers to such an evaluation. The court has a strong interest in keeping expenditure to a minimum. It will therefore carefully examine whether the proposal to hear one or several persons is justified.[174] Three questions are essential. Is the point which the defendant wishes to establish by the hearing of the witness relevant for the decision in the case? If so, is it necessary to hear the proposed (additional) witness in order to accept the point? And is hearing the proposed witness likely actually to assist the court in deciding the issue?[175]

---

[168] This observation was already made in 1979; cf. Trechsel (1979) 371.
[169] *Vidal* v. *Belgium.*   [170] Grabenwarter (2003) § 24 N 75.   [171] Ibid.
[172] On this right, see Pieth (1984).   [173] Nowak (1993) Art. 14 N 52.
[174] Restrictions are also accepted by the HRC; see e.g. *Denroy Gordon* v. *Jamaica*, § 816.
[175] *Huber* v. *Austria* Application 5523/71. See also *Doorson* v. *Netherlands*, § 81.

An essential prerequisite for the effective exercise of this right is, therefore, that the accused gives a precisely reasoned argument answering these questions.[176] In particular he or she must show that the refusal to hear the witnesses made the trial unfair.[177] Stavros is critical of the requirement that the accused must, in a way, show that the trial would have had a more favourable outcome had the witness been heard.[178] However, this requirement must be taken *cum grano salis*, i.e. it must suffice to show that there was a certain likelihood that hearing the person would have improved the chances of the defence.

B. The Discretion of the Presiding Judge

It is rather obvious and has already been mentioned that in taking this decision the presiding judge (or the full court, as the case may be) has a large margin of appreciation. A particularly sensitive consequence of this is that he or she will be called upon to make an anticipated evaluation of the evidence proposed. Needless to say that it is also an evaluation which is very closely related to the specific features of the case to be decided and that it goes to the heart of the merits of that case.

C. The Reluctance of the Strasbourg Court

Consequently, the Strasbourg authorities have shown a great reluctance to intervene in this area. In a number of cases the Court followed a path already sketched out by the Commission which involved withdrawing behind the curtain of the equality of arms. A passage in the *travaux préparatoires* indicates that equality was what was primarily intended.[179] One author took this aspect to extremes by comparing the number of witnesses for and against the accused and even the time spent on hearing them,[180] a view expressly rejected by the Commission.[181] Generally, however, the case-law has met with rather harsh criticism.[182]

The Court first dealt with Article 6 § 3(d) in *Engel*, where it said that 'this provision does not require the attendance and examination of every witness on the accused's behalf. Its essential aim, as is indicated by the words "under the same conditions", is a full "equality of arms" in the matter. With this proviso, it leaves it to the competent national authorities to decide upon the relevance of

---

[176] *Perna* v. *Italy (GC)*, § 29, with reference to *Engel and others* v. *Netherlands* and *Bricmont* v. *Belgium*. See also Stavros (1993) 239.

[177] Application 9457/81; Application 4501/70; Application 8375/78.

[178] Stavros (2003) 239.

[179] Rapporteur Stryckens, Doc. CM/WP4(59)19, *Travaux préparatoires* III 653.

[180] Poncet (1977) 46; similarly Antonopoulos (1967) 154; contra Gollwitzer (1992) Art. 6 N 215; Grabenwarter (1997) 631; Velu and Ergec (1990) N 610.

[181] *AJ* v. *France* Application 11794/85, reported by Frowein and Peukert (1996) Art. 6 N 203, n. 868.   [182] Jacobs (1975) 119; Kohlbacher (1979) 96.

proposed evidence insofar as is compatible with the concept of a fair trial which dominates the whole of Article 6'.[183] The Court has recently taken up this line of argument.[184]

In *Bricmont* the Commission had found a violation with regard to one witness whom the domestic courts had refused to hear without giving any reasons; the Court's answer, however, was harsh: 'It is normally for the national courts to decide whether it is necessary or advisable to call a witness. There are exceptional circumstances which could prompt the Court to conclude that the failure to hear a person as a witness was incompatible with Article 6 but in the instant case it does not have sufficient grounds to form the view that such circumstances exist'.[185]

The Court's reluctance is easy to understand. It involves the proximity of such a decision to the merits of the case, and the danger of the Court being (ab)used as a court of fourth instance. The Commission's similarly unenthusiastic attitude was described by Harris, O'Boyle, and Warbrick as ' "relaxed" and a "hands off" approach'.[186]

The general attitude of the Court to evidence, based on Article 19, is that

it is not its function to deal with errors of fact or of law allegedly committed by a national court unless and in so far as they may have infringed rights and freedoms protected by the Convention. While Article 6 guarantees the right to a fair hearing, it does not lay down any rules on the admissibility of evidence as such, which is therefore primarily a matter for regulation under national law (. . .) It is not the role of the Court to determine, as a matter of principle, whether particular types of evidence—for example, unlawfully obtained evidence—may be admissible or, indeed, whether the applicant was guilty or not. The question which must be answered is whether the proceedings as a whole, including the way in which the evidence was obtained, were fair.[187]

D. The Further Development of the Case-law

While the reluctance of the Court is still—rightly so—considerable, a certain opening up of its attitude can be observed.

In *Vidal* the Court repeated what it had said in *Engel*, but it added an important passage which can be regarded as a turning point: 'The concept of "equality of arms" does not, however, exhaust the content of paragraph 3(d) of Article 6'.[188] In this case it was convinced that there were no valid reasons to reject the hearing of the proposed witnesses. The specific features of this case certainly contributed to the finding of a violation. The applicant had been

---

[183] *Engel and others* v. *Netherlands*, § 91.   [184] *Pisano* v. *Italy*, § 40.

[185] *Bricmont* v. *Belgium*, § 89. For a critical view of the Court's decision, see also Stavros (1993) 239.   [186] Harris, O'Boyle, and Warbrick (1995) 268.

[187] *Khan* v. *United Kingdom*, § 34 and countless others.

[188] *Vidal* v. *Belgium*, § 33; this passage is also repeated in *Pisano* v. *Italy*, § 21, although it appears that the Court then 'forgot' it again in § 23 of the same judgment which strongly stressed the equality-of-arms aspect.

acquitted at first instance and the conviction on appeal was based entirely on the file.[189] However, as Esser[190] rightly says, these particularities have no relevance to the decision on whether the court must grant the request to hear a witness.

There can be no doubt that the Court will continue to be very cautious in assessing whether the refusal to hear a witness proposed by the defence was justified, but it is important to recognize that the possibility to challenge its refusal exists. This should encourage lawyers to argue such proposals with particular care, to force courts to give convincing reasons if they decide to refuse them. It can reliably be said that the Court's attitude in *Bricmont* has disappeared.

VII. THE EQUALITY-OF-ARMS ASPECT

As mentioned above, the element of equality of arms is particularly evident in Article 6 § 3(d).[191] In fact this is the only place in the Convention where it is expressly mentioned. This element of a fair trial is examined in its own right[192] and there is no need to deal with it in the present context.

---

[189] A similar situation arose in *Sigurþor Arnarsson v. Iceland*.   [190] Esser (2002) 636.

[191] It is often (mis-)presented as the essential element, e.g. by Chiavario (2001) N 7.4.1; Frowein and Peukert (1996) Art. 6 N 200; Grabenwarter (2003) § 24 N 71; Peters (2003) § 20 IV 1; Corstens and Pradel (2002) N 359; van Dijk and van Hoof (1998) 473; Villiger (1999) N 516; Vogler (1986) N 548. In relation to the Covenant, see Nowak (1993) Art. 14 N 52. In my view, the approach which puts the adversarial character of proceedings in the foreground is to be strongly preferred; see e.g. Sudre (2003) 356; Reed and Murdoch (2001) N 5.132.

[192] See Chapter 4 above.

Chapter 12

The Right to the Free Assistance of an Interpreter

I. INTRODUCTION

A. The Texts

[3. In the determination of any criminal charge against him, everyone shall be entitled to the following minimum guarantees, in full equality:] . . .
> (f) to have the free assistance of an interpreter if he cannot understand or speak the language used in court;

ICCPR, Art. 14 § 3(f)

[3. Everyone charged with a criminal offence has the following minimum rights:] . . .
> (e) to have the free assistance of an interpreter if he cannot understand or speak the language used in court;

ECHR, Art. 6 § 3(e)

[2. . . . During the proceedings, every person is entitled, with full equality, to the following minimum guarantees:] . . .
> (a) the right of the accused to be assisted without charge by a translator or interpreter, if he does not understand or does not speak the language of the tribunal or court;

ACHR, Art. 8 § 2(b)

The texts of the Covenant and the European Convention are identical. The provision in the American Convention is more complicated than that of the others, although the meaning of the guarantee is essentially the same. Interestingly, the provision refers not only to an interpreter but also to a translator, who works in writing rather than orally. This accentuates the fact that the right is not limited to assistance in the course of oral communication.

B. The Origins of the Guarantee

Although the right to an interpreter was included in the early drafts of the ICCPR,[1] the express requirement that it be provided free of charge first appeared,

---

[1] Weissbrodt (2001) 48.

apparently without any controversy, in the thirteenth draft at the end of the Commission's fifth session.[2]

C. The Purpose of Article 6 § 3(e)

1. *The Character and Purpose of the Right to an Interpreter*

The right to be assisted by an interpreter may be seen as part of the right to be heard which, in turn, is an essential element of the right to a fair trial.[3] It would be absurd to reduce the right to be heard to its acoustic aspect—one is not 'heard' in the sense of procedural law unless one is understood. In *Stanford*, the Court stated that Article 6 'guarantees the right of an accused to participate effectively in a criminal trial. In general this includes, *inter alia*, not only his right to be present, but also to hear and follow the proceedings'.[4] While that case concerned problems with the acoustics, the same principle applies in relation to language as an indispensable instrument of communication.

It is very important to recognize that the right to an interpreter is not only a right of the defence but also an essential prerequisite for the proper functioning of the administration of justice. The interest in having an interpreter is shared by all who are involved in the proceedings, i.e. in addition to the accused, the prosecutor, any private plaintiff, and the tribunal itself. This is clearly demonstrated if one considers the possibility of the applicant waiving the right to an interpreter. Where an accused is conversant with the language used in court to a limited degree, a waiver appears acceptable; the same applies if the translation of a specific document is waived because the defence knows its contents.[5] However, it is equally conceivable that a court will, in spite of the waiver, appoint an interpreter. Where, for instance, an accused wants to waive the services of an interpreter for political reasons, i.e. because he or she insists in communicating with the court in a minority language, the court will have to appoint an interpreter *ex officio* in order to ensure that the process can function properly.

Moreover, the authorities will be entitled to charge the applicant, who would have been able to communicate in the language used at the trial, with the expenses, because the prerequisite for the right to an interpreter free of any charge is not given. The insistence of an accused, for reasons unrelated to his or her language abilities or the needs of the proceedings, on using a different language and thus necessitating the appointment of an interpreter, constitutes an abuse of the right.

---

[2] Weissbrodt (2001) 54.

[3] As the Commission put it in *Roos* v. *Sweden* Application 19598/92: 'In general [the right to a fair trial] includes not only his right to be present but also to hear *and follow* the proceedings' (emphasis added). The Court adopted this wording in *Stanford* v. *United Kingdom*, § 26. In the *Alejandro Ramírez* case (Ohio State, US) the lack of adequate interpretation led to the accused's conviction being overturned; see Framer (2000).   [4] *Stanford* v. *United Kingdom*, § 26.

[5] *Kamasinski* v. *Austria*, § 80.

On the other hand, it is difficult to agree with Stavros when he writes that 'it falls in the first place on the accused to request such services'.[6] However, in certain cases it will be for the accused to complain that he or she cannot follow the hearing. It is also for the accused to intervene if he or she feels that the interpretation is inadequate, although the court must react *ex officio* if the inadequacy is gross and obvious.[7] Indeed, recent case law suggests that the trial judge 'as the ultimate guardian of fairness' has an obligation to ensure that the accused does not encounter difficulties stemming from a lack of interpreting facilities.[8] Although counsel had declared that the appointment of an interpreter was not required as they could 'get by' without one, the Court found a violation of Articles 6 § 1 taken in conjunction with Article 6 § 3(e) of the Convention; it held that '[t]he onus was ... on the judge to reassure himself that the absence of an interpreter at the hearing on 26 January 1996 would not prejudice the applicant's full involvement in a matter of crucial importance for him'.[9]

The wording of the provision is not entirely satisfactory to the extent that it only speaks of an 'interpreter' which in some languages, and indeed in the tradition of the Council of Europe, implies oral translation. In fact the Court has interpreted the provision as requiring not just interpretation during the oral hearing—but also translation of important documents.[10] As we shall see, the qualifications of the person who establishes the linguistic bridge between the accused and the other persons involved in the proceedings have not yet raised any serious issues.

Some suggest that the guarantee was designed to secure equality of arms.[11] This is not entirely convincing. Of course the assistance by an interpreter facilitates the communication between the accused and his or her adversaries in the proceedings on the one hand, and the communication of both with the court on the other. To this extent one can say that it helps to eliminate, at least to some extent, a disadvantage which makes the defence more difficult for someone who does not understand or speak the language used in court. But this is only a secondary effect. Primarily the services of an interpreter constitute the key which opens the door of communication between the accused and the judge. This function, cannot, in my view be regarded as an element essentially designed to establish equality of arms.

It is also interesting to examine what is *not* protected by Article 6 § 3(e). This guarantee is strictly tied to the requirements of criminal proceedings, it bears no relation to the problems associated with linguistic minorities.[12] Therefore, it

---

[6] Stavros (1993) 257; he refers to the fact that a member of the HRC had reservations about a system which relied on a request by the accused. See *Griffin* v. *Spain*, § 9.5.

[7] *Kamasinski* v. *Austria*, § 74; *Emile Delcourt* v. *Belgium* Application 2689/65; Application 8124/77. [8] *Cuscani* v. *United Kingdom*, §§ 38–40.

[9] Ibid., § 38. [10] *Luedicke, Belkacem, and Koç*, § 48.

[11] Merrills and Robertson (2001) 131; Starmer (2000) N 8.37; HRC: *Guesdon* v. *France*, § 10.2; Stavros (1993) 256 is undecided.

[12] *Isop* v. *Austria* Application 808/60; *Bideault* v. *France* Application 11261/84. The HRC has interpreted the corresponding provision of the ICCPR similarly; see *Guesdon* v. *France* and *MK* v. *France*.

does not extend to the question of whether the trial ought to be held in one language rather than in another.

The 'language used in court' is a given entity which does not, in principle,[13] fall to be critically commented upon in the light of the Convention. Nor does it grant the accused the right to use a specific language if he or she is sufficiently conversant with that which is used by the court.[14] Again, it is important to observe another negative aspect: there is no right for an accused to use his or her mother tongue. The interpretation only serves the communication. It is therefore satisfactory if the proceedings are translated into a language which the accused can understand and speak, even if it is not his or her first language.[15] Therefore there was no violation in a case where the Turkish authorities had not provided an interpreter for a Kurdish accused who was able to speak Turkish.[16] Moreover, it goes without saying that there could be no violation in a case where the applicant was French and all the procedure took place in French.[17] In this case, it was the victim who did not speak the language and thus the application was manifestly ill-founded.

2. The Meaning and Purpose of the Right to the Free Assistance of an Interpreter

Two questions arise in this context: Why should the services of an interpreter have no financial consequences for the accused? And what is the meaning of 'free'?[18] The answer to the first question depends upon the answer given to the second.

First of all it must be determined whether there is any link between the obligation to pay for the services of an interpreter and the fairness of the proceedings. The answer must be that there is not. The fairness of the proceedings is not a guarantee designed to bring financial advantage to or to avert expenses from the accused. Of course, there would be serious problems for both the court and the defendant, if a defendant could not afford an interpreter. Here we are faced with quite a familiar situation—indeed one which resembles Article 6 § 3(c) with regard to the right to counsel. Still, there is a difference. The court can deal with a case even if the accused has no counsel—it is in no way the task of counsel to assist the court; the position of the interpreter is, as we have seen, somewhat different.

---

[13] One should not entirely exclude the possibility of exceptions, e.g. if the authorities, for some whimsical reason, were to decide that the trial be held in an exotic language not spoken in the country.

[14] See *D* v. *France* Application 10210/82; *Bideault* v. *France* Application 11261/84; Application 2264/64; Application 8124/772. See also the jurisprudence of the ICCPR, above and the view of the HRC in *Domukovsky, Tsiklauri, Gelbakhiani, and Dokvadez* v. *Georgia*.

[15] See also the opinion of the HRC in *Guesdon* v. *France*, § 10.2.

[16] *Zana* v. *Turkey* Application 18954/91.   [17] *C* v. *France* Application 17276/90.

[18] It is obvious that this only refers to the accused, not to third persons who, as a consequence, cannot complain of an alleged violation of Art. 6 § 3(e); *Fedele* v. *Germany* Application 11311/84.

Further, the exemption from interpretation costs is designed to place accused persons who do not speak the language used in court on an equal footing with the accused who do. *Prima vista* this is entirely separated from the issue of fairness, but on closer scrutiny the link becomes visible: in criminal proceedings the accused has to take a number of decisions which may entail additional expenses. This may involve asking for witnesses to be summoned or summoning them him or herself, or even deciding whether or not to challenge the impartiality of a judge or whether or not to file an appeal. It is quite accepted and acceptable that the consideration of costs is a factor the accused will have to take into account. However, there ought not to be any difference depending on whether he or she does or does not understand and/or speak the language used in court.[19] It is true that the Court, in its leading judgment, *Luedicke, Belkacem, and Koç* also relied on other methods of interpretation. It referred to the Vienna Convention on the Law on Treaties of 23 May 1969[20] and came to the conclusion that the term 'free'/'*gratuitement*' means a 'once and for all exemption or exoneration'.[21] Nevertheless, the teleological approach was, in my view, decisive.

In view of these considerations it is clear that only exoneration once and for all is compatible with the meaning of the guarantee. In fact, there is clear case-law to the effect that costs for the services of interpreters and translators in criminal proceedings may never be charged to the accused.[22]

D. The 'Relative' and the 'Absolute' Character of the Guarantee

Does the right to the free assistance of an interpreter belong to those rights that are of an absolute character, i.e. where the violation is per se incompatible with the Convention? Or does it have a more relative character, i.e. where a violation of the Convention will only be found if it has been shown that the defence was in some way disadvantaged?

Stavros tentatively asserts that the guarantee is of an absolute character. He draws this conclusion from *Luedicke, Belkacem, and Koç* which, in his view, rests 'on a more profound philosophical basis to the effect that differences in

---

[19] *Luedicke, Belkacem, and Koç* v. *Germany*, § 42, confirmed in *Öztürk* v. *Germany*, § 58; *Zengin* v. *Germany* Application 10551/83; *Akdogan* v. *Germany* Application 11394/85, Res. CM of 10 Nov. 1988.   [20] Entered into force on 27 Jan. 1980, 8 ILM 679.
[21] *Luedicke, Belkacem, and Koç* v. *Germany*, § 40.
[22] *Luedicke, Belkacem, and Koç* v. *Germany; Öztürk* v. *Germany*, § 58; *Zengin* v. *Germany* Application 10551/83; *Akdogan* v. *Germany* Application 11394/85; *Shanmukanathan* v. *Germany* Application 14261/88 (friendly settlement); *K* v. *Germany* Application 13402/87 (friendly settlement). (On ratifying the Convention, Switzerland made a declaration according to which it asserted that Art. 6 § 3(e) was satisfied as long as the accused did not have to pay in advance for the interpretation. In *Temeltasch* v. *Switzerland* Application 9116/80, the Commission accepted this declaration as a reservation. The subsequent case of *Belilos* v. *Switzerland* made it clear, however, that the Court would not follow suit as the requirements of former Art. 64 of the ECHR had not been met; see also Haefliger and Schürmann (1999) 236 et seq.; Wagner and Wildhaber (1983) 145.)

treatment on the ground of language spoken are fundamentally repugnant to the notion of a fair trial'.[23]

In my view, the answer to our question must be two-fold, in accordance with the two-fold guarantee set out in Article 6 § 3(e). The guarantee is absolute in its financial aspect. Interpreters' costs must be borne by the state, possibly by a private plaintiff, but never by the accused. It is of no importance whatsoever whether the proceedings ended with an acquittal or with a conviction. Even in a case where the accused prepared an objection to a regulatory fine order but withdrew his objection before the hearing, it was not possible to let him bear the expenses for the interpretation.[24]

However, with regard to the right to assistance as such, the picture we gain from the case-law is quite different. An applicant who complains of the refusal to translate certain parts of the file or to appoint an interpreter, despite speaking and understanding the language used in court to some extent, will have to establish that he or she was hindered in mounting a defence. This part of the guarantee is not absolute.

E. The Relationship of Article 6 § 3(e) to other Rights of the Defence

1. The Relationship to Article 5 § 2 and Article 6 § 3(a)

While Article 6 § 3(e) gives the accused the right to be assisted by an interpreter, Article 5 § 2 and Article 6 § 3(a) guarantee the right to be informed of the reasons for the arrest and the charge respectively 'in a language which he understands'. In other words, these guarantees cover the substantive part of Article 6 § 3(e) but remain silent about the financial aspect. In my view there can be no doubt that the interpretation or translation costs for conveying this information may not be imposed upon the defendant.

2. The Relationship to Article 6 § 3(c)

The right to the free assistance of an interpreter complements the right to counsel. It has certain parallels: Both counsel and interpreter assist the communication between the accused and the authorities. The interpreter, however, has a limited, purely technical role—he or she does not interfere with the substance of the communication. Counsel, on the other hand, provides assistance by virtue of his special knowledge of the law. Law can be seen as a language in itself—it is the level on which counsel communicates with the authorities; in addition he or she acts, at least in part, under his or her own responsibility, and this goes beyond merely 'translating' for the accused. This has at least two further consequences.

---

[23] Stavros (1993) 256.   [24] *Zengin* v. *Germany* Application 10551/83.

First, the primary right under Article 6 § 3(c) is that of defending oneself—it makes no sense to look for a parallel to this in Article 6 § 3(e). Accordingly, as shown above, there is, at most, very limited room for a waiver; it is suggested that the possibility to waive is more restricted in the latter case.

Second, another essential difference lies in the fact that Article 6 § 3(e) does not mention any right to a free choice of an interpreter. This can easily be explained. Counsel is an assistant who acts unilaterally for the defence and may or even ought to, therefore, be biased in favour of the accused. The interpreter, however, acts as a neutral intermediary who may not in any way appear as a person with his or her own opinions. There is no particular relationship of confidence between the interpreter and his or her client.

Finally, as we have noted, there is a difference in the financial area between a legal-aid counsel and interpreter. As far as the former is concerned, subsequent imposition of costs will be permissible if it is based on the improved economic situation of the person concerned.[25]

3. The Relationship to Article 6 § 3(d)

Communication at the trial is, as stated before, polygonal. It involves everyone who participates, including witnesses. In this context a number of problems may arise.

Article 6 § 3(e) definitely covers the case where the accused speaks a foreign language while the witness speaks the language used in court. The same must apply when both the defendant and the witness speak different languages neither of which is the one used at the trial.

What if the defendant speaks the language used in court but the witness speaks a different language? This case is not covered by Article 6 § 3(e). Although there is no difference in the wording of Article 14 § 3(f) of the ICCPR, the Committee has, as it were, expanded the scope of that guarantee to a right to an interpreter 'for himself and his witnesses'.[26]

As far as the substance is concerned, I can agree. However, I am unhappy with the approach. It is true that both the Convention, in Article 6 § 3(d), and the Covenant, in Article 14 § 3(f) refer to witnesses 'on his behalf'.[27] However, it must be stressed that not all legal orders distinguish different classes of witnesses according to which party hopes they will testify in their favour. Further, why should the right be limited to witnesses for the defence when it can be crucial for the defence effectively to cross-examine witnesses for the prosecution?

In my view there is no need for elaborate argument to say that there must be interpretation of the statements of witnesses whenever they speak a language different from that used at the trial unless all participants explicitly declare that they do not need it. This may be the case in a multilingual country such as

---

[25] See Chapter 10 above.   [26] HRC *Guesdon* v. *France*, §§ 10.2–10.4 and 11, para. 10.2.
[27] A formulation which Art. 8 § 3(e) ACHR fortunately avoided.

Belgium, Canada, or Switzerland. The source of that right can be found in
Articles 6 § 3(d) or 14 § 3(e) of the ICCPR.

II. THE NEED FOR INTERPRETATION

A. The Lack of Linguistic Proficiency

The right to interpretation arises when the defendant 'cannot understand or
speak the language used in court'. This is, as it were, one of the 'soft spots' of the
guarantee. Obviously, the issue arises only in cases where the court does not use
the mother tongue of the accused. No difficulty arises where the defendant does
not know the language used by the court at all; here the need for an interpreter
is clear. There is a problem, however, where the accused is, to some extent,
conversant with the language, but affirms that he or she still needs interpretation. It is, of course, possible to measure the linguistic abilities of a person, at
least to a certain extent. However, in the present context, we are faced with three
difficulties:

First, it is not just the knowledge of everyday language that is required, but
also a certain understanding of the legal language which forms part of that
language which is used in court proceedings and may remain quite foreign to
someone who gets along reasonably well in everyday life.

Second, it is difficult to measure the knowledge in an objective way. What
should the standard be? This will often depend upon the case at issue, for
example, whether the facts are relatively simple as in an ordinary theft or
burglary, or whether they are complicated, as in cases of economic crime.

Third, it is quite likely that the accused will not cooperate. This means that it
will not be possible to test his linguistic proficiency. The court will have to hear
evidence on the subject, examine letters and/or other texts written by him, hear
witnesses who have spoken with him in the language used in court, etc. It will
have to be decided case-by-case whether this is worthwhile. At any rate, the
Commission was ready to accept the findings of the domestic authorities that
they had seriously examined the issue.[28] In a case where the applicant had lived
in the United Kingdom for thirteen years, the Commission was also satisfied that
his knowledge of the language was sufficient.[29]

---

[28] See e.g. *SEK* v. *Switzerland* Application 18595/91: 'The Commission notes further that the
Court of Appeal, in its judgment of 8 March 1989, dealt extensively with the applicant's complaint
that he had no sufficient command of German and concluded that the applicant did sufficiently
understand German. These findings were confirmed by the Court of Cassation and the Federal
Court in their respective judgments. The Commission also notes that there is no indication that at
the time of his interrogation by the police, the applicant had asked for the assistance by an
interpreter, especially after having been assisted by counsel'.
[29] *Santa Cruz Ruiz* v. *United Kingdom* Application 26109/95. It would be wrong, however, to
accept any general rule to the effect that, after a stay of so much time, a person can be considered to

As a matter of course, it is only the linguistic deficiency of the *accused* which is at issue. Where a witness does not speak the language of the proceedings and the interpretation is unsatisfactory, this may, as I have said, raise an issue under Article 6 § 3(d) but not under sub-paragraph (e).[30] Also, there is no reason why the costs ought not be imposed upon the convicted defendant in such a case—they are not caused by the specific 'status' of the accused.

B. The Lack of Acoustic Abilities

A situation analogous to that of an accused unversed in the language used in court is that where an accused's hearing is impaired.[31] Of course, only oral proceedings then call for assistance, there is no problem with regard to documents. At the same time the element of discrimination is linked to a quality which, contrary to 'language', is not mentioned in Article 14 of the ECHR. So far, the Court has not yet had the opportunity to state whether the fact of being disabled could be regarded as falling under the category of 'other status' within the meaning of Article 14.[32]

In *Roos*, the Commission examined in detail the complaints of an applicant who was hard of hearing: 'The Commission recalls that during these proceedings the applicant moved around in the court room in order to be close to the person speaking and, when not in the court room, had to make arrangements so as to be very close to the loudspeaker in order to hear the statements by his wife and his daughter'.[33] It did not find a violation—the case seems to mark the limit of what a defendant can be expected to tolerate. The Commission did not say, at any rate, that it had applied Article 6 § 3(e).

We are another step further away from this guarantee in a case where the acoustics made it difficult to follow the proceedings. This was the situation in *Stanford*, but the Court came to the conclusion that the obstacle was not so serious as to affect the fairness of the proceedings as a whole.[34]

be conversant with the language spoken by the population and also used in court. One can observe that some immigrants, particularly women, live a secluded life and have contact almost exclusively with their family and other immigrants from the same country.

[30] *PSV* v. *Finland* Application 23378/94. See also *C* v. *France* Application 17276/90 where the Commission declared the application inadmissible for other reasons.

[31] Art. 102, sub-para. 3 of the French CCP, to give but one example, regulates the interpretation for persons hard of hearing at the same time as that for persons of a foreign tongue. See also the Austrian CCP, § 164; German CCP, § 259m, sub-para. 2 etc.

[32] See *Botta* v. *Italy*, confirmed in *Zenhalova et Zehnal* v. *Czech Republic* Application 38621/97 where the Court refused to apply Art. 8 to enable handicapped persons to claim a right of access to the beach and public buildings; consequently Art. 14 was equally inapplicable.

[33] *Roos* v. *Sweden* Application 19598/92.

[34] *Stanford* v. *United Kingdom*, § 29; the applicant had been in a glass cage—the Court stressed that he was assisted by a solicitor and counsel, an argument which is hardly convincing in view of the fact that the right to follow the proceedings is a personal right of the accused which cannot be exercised, as it were, by proxy through counsel.

III. THE MODALITIES OF THE RIGHT TO AN INTERPRETER

A. The Application at Various Stages of the Proceedings

The text of Article 6 § 3(e), by referring to the language 'used in court' (*'employée à l'audience'*), gives the impression that this guarantee only applies to court hearings, not to preliminary proceedings. Such an interpretation was proposed by the German Government in *Luedicke, Belkacem, and Koç*—it was rightly rejected by the Court.[35] In *Kamasinski* the Court made it quite clear that the right of the accused to an interpreter also applies to the 'pre-trial proceedings'.[36] On the other hand, Harris, O'Boyle, and Warbrick state that the right does 'not benefit suspects being questioned by the police prior to their being "charged" in the sense of Article 6(1)'.[37] If by this they mean that Article 6 only applies where a 'criminal charge' exists, the observation is entirely redundant. On the other hand, what would such a limitation mean? The absence of an interpreter would surely render any questioning useless. That during the pre-trial proceedings the accused must bear the interpretation costs? How could that be justified? The remark cannot be approved.

B. The Application *Ratione Materiae*: The Objects of Interpretation and Translation

The term *'ratione materiae'* in connection with the right to a free interpreter refers here to the different objects which fall to be translated: the court proceedings, preliminary proceedings, documents, and the conversations between the accused and counsel.

1. Interpretation at the Trial

As the text of Article 6 § 3(e) indicates, the right to an interpreter arises primarily during court hearings. This covers proceedings at first instance as well as on appeal. The interpretation must not necessarily be simultaneous— consecutive interpretation is acceptable[38] and probably also the rule. Of course, the services of an interpreter are only needed to the extent that the defendant actually takes part in the hearing. The accused who did not to turn up for the trial and who had to pay the cost for an interpreter who had been summoned to

---

[35] *Luedicke, Belkacem, and Koç*, § 48.

[36] *Kamasinski* v. *Austria*, § 74, confirmed tacitly in §§ 76 et seq.

[37] Harris, O'Boyle, and Warbrick (1995) 270.

[38] *Kamasinski* v. *Austria*, § 83. Sometimes double translation will be required; indeed the European Commission, when inquiring into cases against Turkey, regularly used double translation from English or French to Turkish and then from Turkish to Kurdish and back. On this point, see also *R.* v. *West London Youth Court, ex parte N* [2000] 1 WLR 2368 where the Divisional Court held double translation to be lawful and *R* v. *Iqual Begum* (1986) 83 Cr App R 96, where the Privy Council reached the same conclusion.

assist him did not, in the Commission's view, suffer a violation of the guarantee.[39] It may appear rather absurd that a defendant does not have to pay for the services of an interpreter of which he or she makes use, while payment is required if the interpreter did not provide any assistance. In fact, it is rather logical that expenses for the preparation of a trial can basically be awarded against the accused and that there is no reason for making an exception for costs which would have been free had the accused made use of the service.

As a rule all the proceedings must be interpreted, not just questions addressed to the accused and his answers. The accused must be able to follow the trial from start to finish and be able to understand every sentence that is uttered, even if it does not directly concern him or her. In *Kamasinski*, the applicant complained that questions to the witnesses had not been translated. The Court said that this 'in itself does not suffice to establish a violation of sub-paragraphs (d) or (e)'.[40] This is a finding which is based on the relative nature of the guarantee—the applicant failed to show how the lack of the interpretation constituted an obstacle to the effective presentation of his defence. As a matter of principle, however, the view cannot be approved: it is also important for the defendant to understand the questions put to the witness as it will be difficult to assess the answers without having understood the questions. Also, the way an interrogation is conducted inevitably betrays, to some extent, preconceived opinions of the interrogator who, in continental proceedings, is often the presiding judge. The Court must have been aware of this, because it admitted, very vaguely, that the lacunae in the interpretation 'is one factor along with others to be considered'. In the case of *Kamasinski* it may also be of some relevance that the defence did not complain at the trial of inadequate interpretation.

2. Interpretation During the Pre-trial Proceedings

As indicated above, the right to free services of an interpreter also applies to pre-trial proceedings, as the Court expressly stated in *Kamasinski*.[41] This does not call for further comment. It is enough to note that in different jurisdictions the importance of those proceedings may vary greatly. It would lead to unjustified inequality if in a country where the administration of evidence takes place during preliminary proceedings the accused had to pay a considerable amount for the interpreter's fees, while an accused living in a country where the evidence is examined at the trial hearing did not have to pay.

In *Luedicke, Belkacem, and Koç* the Court mentions a number of instances where free interpretation must be available: the appearance before the judge,[42] review of the detention,[43] translation of the indictment.[44]

---

[39] *Fedele* v. *Germany* Application 11311/84.
[40] *Kamasinski* v. *Austria*, § 83.   [41] *Kamasinski* v. *Austria*, § 74.   [42] Cf. Art. 5 § 3.
[43] Cf. Art. 5 § 4.   [44] Cf. Art. 6 § 3(a); *Luedicke, Belkacem, and Koç*, § 49.

3. Translation of Documents

As with the previous issue, the relationship between documentary evidence and oral evidence may vary in different jurisdictions—excluding them from the right to free translation would create unjustified inequalities. At least in continental-type proceedings, where the file plays an important role, it is rather obvious that the right to free interpretation must also cover the right to have documents translated. The Court had already recognized this in *Luedicke, Belkacem, and Koç*[45] and confirmed it in *Kamasinski*.[46]

With regard to written material, however, we find a limitation. Not all the documents connected to the criminal proceedings fall to be translated, but only those 'which it is necessary for him to understand or to have rendered into the court's language in order to have the benefit of a fair trial'.[47] Here, the applicant faces the difficulty that he or she must show, at least *prima facie*, that his or her defence was hindered by the fact that one or several documents were not translated. So far, no case has been brought successfully on this basis.

One 'borderline' example is given, again, in *Kamasinski*. The applicant had not been given a translation of the judgment which he wanted to appeal against. The Court concluded that 'as a result of the oral explanations given to him, Mr. Kamasinski sufficiently understood the judgment and its reasoning to be able to lodge, with the assistance of [counsel] an appeal against sentence and an extensive plea of nullity challenging many aspects of the trial and the judgment'.[48] As a rule, Stavros is certainly right when he calls for a translation of the judgment at least in those cases where there is a possibility of appeal.[49]

4. Communication with Counsel

As the accused must be assisted by an interpreter to the extent that it is necessary for him to have a fair trial, the services of the interpreter must also be available to enable him to communicate with his counsel. As Harris, O'Boyle, and Warbrick quite rightly stress, the authorities must provide an interpreter if they appoint counsel who does not speak the language of his client.[50] In a way this view finds confirmation in the Court's *Lagerblom* judgment.[51] In that case the applicant complained that a lawyer, S, who could speak Finnish, the language of the applicant, was not appointed to replace H, his appointed counsel. The Court based its finding of no violation on the fact that the applicant was able to speak and understand 'street Swedish'. It therefore could not 'find that

---

[45] *Luedicke, Belkacem, and Koç*, § 48.   [46] *Kamasinski v. Austria*, § 74.
[47] *Luedicke, Belkacem, and Koç*, § 48; *Kamasinski v. Austria*, § 74.
[48] *Kamasinski v. Austria*, § 85; see also Application 3117/67; *Harward v. Norway* Application 14170/88. The Commission also followed a very restrictive line in *Buitrago Montes and Perez Lopez* v. *United Kingdom* Application 18077/91.   [49] Stavros (1993) 254 and 255.
[50] Harris, O'Boyle, and Warbrick (1995) 271; the Commission was certainly wrong when it found that Art. 6 § 3(e) only guaranteed free services of an interpreter for the communication between the accused and the judge in *X* v. *Austria* Application 6185/73.
[51] *Lagerblom v. Sweden*.

he was so handicapped that he could not at all communicate with H. or understand him'.

This implies that, had communication not been possible, the right for an interpreter or to a change in counsel would have existed. As the conversation between an accused and counsel, contrary to the communication during the trial, takes place in an informal setting where it is possible to ask that something be repeated if one has not understood what the other said, the solution is acceptable.

What if the accused decides in favour of a counsel 'of his own choosing' with whom he or she is unable to communicate in a common language? If the lawyer comes from a foreign jurisdiction—for example, a German defendant accused in France chooses a famous Italian lawyer who speaks French but not German—it is only fair that the defendant pay for the interpretation. The Commission even thought that he ought to pay for the necessary interpreter if he chooses a French lawyer who does not speak German.[52] I disagree. This narrows the right to the free choice of a lawyer in an unacceptable way. It is of the foremost concern that the accused has full trust in his legal counsel; an accused ought not to be under an obligation to choose a lawyer in whom he or she does not have confidence, just because the lawyer knows his or her language.

C. The Qualifications of the Interpreter

The domestic legislation usually has rules concerning the nomination of interpreters. They have to be sworn in,[53] there exist rules of incompatibility[54] and they can be challenged if their impartiality is open to doubt.[55]

No such formalities are called for under international human-rights law. As a matter of fact, the case-law does not indicate any limits as to who can function as an interpreter. The only thing that matters is that the accused can understand what is going on and can make himself understood. The judgment in *Kamasinski* provides some illustration.[56] At one police interrogation a prisoner served—inadequately—as interpreter; on another occasion there was an interpreter who was not a registered interpreter. However, the Court did not consider this to constitute a violation of Article 6 § 3(e).

This ought to be viewed as quite acceptable. The freedom of movement and global mobility of today's world means that legal systems might have to deal with foreigners who speak rare languages. It may be difficult to find anybody capable of serving as an interpreter. It may, moreover, be downright impossible to find anybody with formal qualifications. Here the effectiveness of the administration of justice must take precedence over circumstances which while desirable cannot be considered as essential.

---

[52] *X* v. *Germany* Application 10221/82; Harris, O'Boyle, and Warbrick (1995) 271 seem to approve.　　　　[53] e.g. German *Gerichtsverfassungsgesetz*, § 189; Austrian CCP, § 100.
[54] French CCP, Art. 344, sub-para. 3; Italian CPP, Art. 144.
[55] German CCP, § 191; French CPP, Art. 344, sub-para. 2; Italian CPP, Art. 145.
[56] *Kamasinski* v. *Austria*, §§ 11, 76.

Chapter 13

The Privilege Against Self-incrimination

I. INTRODUCTION

A. The Texts

[3. In the determination of any criminal charge against him, everyone shall be entitled to the following minimum guarantees, in full equality:] . . .

(g) Not to be compelled to testify against himself or to confess guilt.

ICCPR, Art. 14 § 3(g)

No corresponding guarantee.

ECHR

[2. . . . During the proceedings, every person is entitled, with full equality, to the following minimum guarantees:] . . .

(g) the right not to be compelled to be a witness against himself or to plead guilty;

3. A confession of guilt by the accused shall be valid only if it is made without coercion of any kind.

ACHR, Art. 8 §§ 2(g) and 3

In comparing these texts, the most striking feature is the absence of any guarantee in the European Convention. This is particularly noticeable as efforts were made to align the rights guaranteed by the Convention with those of the Covenant which was adopted sixteen years later. The omission of a corresponding provision in Protocol No. 7 cannot, however, be characterized as an oversight. It was agreed that the right formed part of the general fair-trial guarantee.[1]

Furthermore, there is an important difference between the text of the ICCPR and that of the ACHR. The latter features a second guarantee which is set out in a sub-paragraph of its own, i.e. on an equal level with the 'collective' guarantee of rights of the defence. In my view this does not add any substance to what one finds in the Covenant, but it does demonstrate the particular attention given to the problem of forced confessions.

---

[1] Schlauri (2003) 82; see also Chapter 14, section I below for further explanations.

The remaining differences, 'testify' and 'be a witness', 'confess guilt' or 'plead guilty' are only differences in style.

B. Terminology

The privilege against self-incrimination is certainly one of the most complex guarantees in the entire body of fundamental rights applicable in the context of criminal proceedings. While the basic problem is clear, many specific issues are contested and there is no agreement on the structure of the guarantee. This is evidenced by problems in finding the appropriate terminology. One author is so hesitant that every reference in her study to *'le droit de ne pas s'auto-incriminer'* is accompanied by inverted commas (with the sole exception of the title!).[2]

Expressions which are currently in favour include, apart from the title chosen for this chapter, 'right to silence' or 'right not to incriminate oneself'. These expressions are so short that they risk distorting the meaning. What is meant is the right not to be *compelled* to incriminate oneself, to be protected against any pressure to make a statement. The Latin expression *'nemo tenetur se ipsum accusare vel prodere'* is very popular—the right is sometimes referred to as the 'nemo tenetur principle'. However, it expresses rather the basic philosophy behind the guarantee than a precise 'right'. I have opted for the term 'privilege', short for 'privilege against self-incrimination', because it refers to the situation of someone who enjoys enhanced protection. To simplify the linguistic expression, the term 'privilege' will be used unless the discussion focuses more precisely on a specific aspect of the guarantee.

C. The Origins of the 'Privilege'

In view of the above it will come as little surprise that the origins of the 'privilege' have been the subject of in-depth study and lively controversy.[3] The principle that a person ought not to be compelled to act against his or her own interests and in particular be able to refrain from implicating him- or herself in a crime has been traced back to Talmudic law.[4] However, it might be difficult, or quite probably impossible, to trace the modern procedural guarantee back to such a source. It is perhaps preferable to think of the principle as having its origins in the development of common law. Although some authors refer to developments in the eleventh and twelfth century, the birth of the right is generally traced back to 1641 when both the Star Chamber and the High Commission were abolished and the *ex officio* oath procedure forbidden.[5]

---

[2] Bouissou (2002–3), see also p. 8 on the terminology. I had this excellent paper at my disposal and shall refer to it even though it is not (yet) easily accessible.

[3] Helmholz, Gray, Langbein, Moglen, Smitz, and Alschuler (1997); Moglen (1994) 1086; Rogall (1977) 67 et seq; Schlauri (2003) 39 et seq; O'Boyle (2000) 1021.

[4] Schlauri (2003) 39 et seq.   [5] Ibid., 56, 60. See also O'Boyle 1021.

D. The Character of the Guarantee

1. *Right to Silence and the Privilege Against Self-incrimination*

One might be tempted, perhaps even seduced, by the rather loose terminology into assuming that the 'right to silence' and the 'privilege against self-incrimination' are one and the same thing. However, the two guarantees must be seen as being represented by two partly overlapping circles. The right to silence is narrower in that it refers to acoustic communication alone, the right not to speak. The privilege clearly goes further in that it is not limited to verbal expression. As the cases of *Funke* v. *France* and *JB* v. *Switzerland* illustrate, it also protects against pressure to produce documents.

On the other hand, the scope of the right to silence goes beyond that of the privilege as it does not only protect against the pressure to make statements detrimental to the person concerned, but any declaration at all.[6] This is illustrated by the case of *Saunders* where the applicant had made no admissions at all during the investigation by the inspectors. Here it becomes apparent that the texts reproduced above may be formulated in too narrow a way—they only mention the danger that an accused be forced to make statements 'against himself'. Such a restriction, however, does not make much sense. Practical experience shows that sometimes interrogations even on seemingly unimportant questions, are particularly risky for an accused. If he or she does not pay particular attention, the risk of unwise admissions or contradictory statements increases. These, in turn, will serve to weaken the position of the suspect and may well affect the credibility of his or her declarations on important points.

It is therefore important that the right to silence be retained in its pure and absolute form, and not interpreted through a rigid adherence to the texts. In this respect the absence of an express guarantee in the ECHR may have a certain advantage.

2. *Right to Silence and Freedom of Expression*

In a case settled after the Commission had adopted its report, and thus before the Court had an opportunity to express a view, the right to silence was linked to the freedom of expression.[7] This is in fact a view with which I still sympathize.[8]

The applicant was accused before the District Court in Linz of having bought three grams of heroin from a couple, M and Ch W, who were being prosecuted in separate proceedings before the Regional Court in Linz. The applicant was charged with having bought and possessing drugs, *inter alia*, from this couple. M and Ch W were charged with drug dealing. The applicant pleaded not guilty

---

[6] Judge Martens defines the 'privilege' as the 'right not to be obliged to produce evidence against oneself', the broader right encompassing the right to silence: dissenting opinion in *Saunders* v. *United Kingdom*, § 4.   [7] *K* v. *Austria*.

[8] See my separate opinion in the Commission's report in *Serves* v. *France*.

and was then summoned to give evidence at the trial of M and Ch W. It can be assumed that in the witness stand he would have had two choices: either to lie or to say that he had in fact bought drugs from the defendants, and thus at the same time, necessarily admit that he had committed an offence. This would certainly have amounted to a confession and would have been incompatible with his right not to incriminate himself and to remain silent. The Commission, however, found that in the proceedings against M and Ch W, K could not be considered to be an accused and thus could not claim any rights under Article 6.

In this situation it applied the negative aspect of Article 10 and came to the conclusion 'that the right to freedom of expression by implication also guarantees a "negative right" not to be compelled to express oneself, i.e. to remain silent'.[9]

Interpreting this right in the light of Article 6 it found that while there were situations in which a person could be compelled to make a statement, i.e. when there was a basis in law, a legitimate aim in conformity with Article 10 § 2, and a pressing social need for the compulsion—such as the duty to testify as a witness—a person, even outside the scope of criminal proceedings or in a different role than that of the accused, could not be compelled to make statements which were self-incriminatory. In particular, the Commission 'noted that the principle of protection against self-incrimination is, like the principle of presumption of innocence, one of the most fundamental aspects of the right to a fair trial'.[10]

This view has met with criticism. O'Boyle, in discussing the case of *Funke* v. *France* suggests that the 'privilege' ought to be seen 'as a free-standing specific guarantee contained in Article 6 . . . once a person is considered to be charged'. In support he mentions the fact that no proceedings had yet been brought against Mr Funke for breaching the exchange-control legislation when he was asked to produce documents or risk a criminal sanction. However, this argument is hardly convincing as Mr Funke's home had already been searched and he was made aware that he was suspected of unlawfully having transferred money abroad.[11] However, the Commission did not follow the 'freedom-of-expression approach' in *Serves* as the applicant could be regarded as also being the *de facto* accused.[12]

3. Absolute or Relative Right?

There has also been some discussion as to whether the 'privilege' can be characterized as an absolute or a relative right. In *Saunders* the Court did not find it

---

[9] *K* v. *Austria*, § 45.   [10] Ibid., § 49.

[11] In the same sense, see Naismith (1997); Schlauri (2003) 88. For a critical approach, see O'Boyle (2000) 1030 et seq; Verniory (2005) 313.

[12] In *Serves* v. *France* an officer was questioned in connection with a murder trial in which, technically, he was not an accused, although he still seemed to be under suspicion of being somehow involved in the crime.

necessary to determine this issue[13] although it seems to give an affirmative answer—at least this is how the judgment was interpreted by Judges Martens and Pettiti in their dissenting opinions. The Commission had boldly stated: 'It cannot be compatible with the spirit of the Convention that varying degrees of fairness apply to different categories of accused in criminal trials. The right of silence, to the extent that it may be contained in the guarantees of Article 6, must apply as equally to alleged company fraudsters as to those accused of other types of fraud, rape, murder or terrorist offences. Further, there can be no legitimate aim in depriving someone of the guarantees necessary in securing a fair trial'.[14]

The answer depends on what is meant in this particular context by the term 'absolute'. I recall that it is possible to distinguish two aspects. 'Absolute' can mean that there are no exceptions; but it can also mean that there can be a violation even if it is not established that the failure to respect the right to silence has contributed to the conviction.

In this latter sense the right was certainly given an absolute quality in *Saunders*. It may be recalled that the applicant, who was a director and the chief executive of Guinness plc, was suspected of acting unlawfully in the course of a takeover bid. There was first an investigation by inspectors of the Secretary of State for Trade and Industry and the applicant was under a legal obligation to answer their questions. Later there were also criminal proceedings in which the transcripts of many of the interviews were used in evidence.

The Government emphasized, 'that nothing said by the applicant in the course of the interviews was self-incriminating and that he had merely given exculpatory answers or answers which, if true, would serve to confirm his defence'. In their submissions 'only statements which are self-incriminating could fall within the privilege against self-incrimination'. The Court did not fully agree, but stressed that

the right not to incriminate oneself cannot reasonably be confined to statements of admission of wrongdoing or to remarks which are directly incriminating. Testimony obtained under compulsion which appears on its face to be of a non-incriminating nature—such as exculpatory remarks or mere information on questions of fact—may later be deployed in criminal proceedings in support of the prosecution case, for example to contradict or cast doubt upon other statements of the accused or evidence given by him during the trial or to otherwise undermine his credibility. Where the credibility of an accused must be assessed by a jury the use of such testimony may be especially harmful. It follows that what is of the essence in this context is the use to which evidence obtained under compulsion is put in the course of the criminal trial.[15]

It was sufficient for the Court, that the transcripts were used in the criminal proceedings with an aim of incriminating the applicant.

---

[13] *Saunders* v. *United Kingdom*, § 74.

[14] *Saunders* v. *United Kingdom*, Report of the Commission, 71. Boissou (2002–3) 75 also supports the position that the guarantee be interpreted as being of an absolute character.

[15] *Saunders* v. *United Kingdom*, §§ 70, 71.

This is a refreshing contrast, for example, to the way in which the Court examines whether the testimony of witnesses, whom the accused had no opportunity to question, had been instrumental in securing his conviction. There is no reference in *Saunders* to other evidence which could have justified the judgment against him.

The *Saunders* judgment also affirms another aspect of absoluteness. The Government had claimed that the particular nature of 'white-collar crime' necessitated the existence of exceptions to the principle. The Court however rejected the 'argument that the complexity of corporate fraud and the vital public interest in the investigation of such fraud and the punishment of those responsible could justify such a marked departure as that which occurred in the present case from one of the basic principles of a fair procedure. Like the Commission, it considers that the general requirements of fairness contained in Article 6, including the right not to incriminate oneself, apply to criminal proceedings in respect of all types of criminal offences without distinction from the most simple to the most complex. The public interest cannot be invoked to justify the use of answers compulsorily obtained in a non-judicial investigation to incriminate the accused during the trial proceedings'.[16] Again, the Court took a clear stand and this has met with approval.[17]

However, the case of *John Murray* somewhat blurs this picture. This applicant was found by the police in a house where a person kidnapped by the IRA was held prisoner on the first floor. The applicant came down the staircase when the police entered the building. It is the first case which concerns legislation permitting inferences from the silence of a suspect under certain circumstances—it shall be discussed in more detail later on.

In its report the Commission stated that 'whether a particular applicant has been subject to compulsion to incriminate himself in such a way as to render the criminal proceedings unfair . . . will depend on an assessment of the circumstances of the case as a whole'.[18] The Court addressed the issue squarely:

What is at stake in the present case is whether these immunities are absolute in the sense that the exercise by an accused of the right to silence cannot under any circumstances be used against him at trial or, alternatively, whether informing him in advance that, under certain conditions, his silence may be so used, is always to be regarded as 'improper compulsion'.

On the one hand, it is self-evident that it is incompatible with the immunities under consideration to base a conviction solely or mainly on the accused's silence or on a refusal to answer questions or to give evidence himself. On the other hand, the Court deems it equally obvious that these immunities cannot and should not prevent that the accused's

---

[16] Ibid., § 74. The Commission had expressed the same philosophy in even stronger terms; see *Saunders* v. *United Kingdom* Application 19187/91, § 71 (annexed to the judgment).

[17] See e.g. Stessens (1997); Bouissou (2002–3) 60.

[18] *John Murray* v. *United Kingdom* Application 18731/91, Report of 14 Oct. 1991 (annexed to the judgment), § 56.

silence, in situations which clearly call for an explanation from him, be taken into account in assessing the persuasiveness of the evidence adduced by the prosecution.

Wherever the line between these two extremes is to be drawn, it follows from this understanding of 'the right to silence' that the question whether the right is absolute must be answered in the negative.[19]

This is a clear answer and one with which I agree. It does not mean, that in certain cases the right does not apply at all or that different levels of protection apply to different types of criminality.[20] The relativity of the guarantee is intrinsic in the sense that it is impossible to draw sharp borders. How much pressure on a suspect is acceptable? It is hardly possible to dictate that the accused be put under no pressure at all.[21]

This becomes immediately apparent when one looks at the realities of criminal proceedings. Even if one puts aside the danger of adverse inferences being brought on account of the accused's silence, it is probable that if an accused refuses to speak more time will be taken and more costs will be accumulated, costs which, in the event of a conviction, will be imposed on the accused. The decision as to whether or not to speak often presents the accused with something of a dilemma—if he or she decides to remain silent, it will be more difficult for the other side to establish proof, but at the same time there will then be no chance to explain, or to plead for understanding and mitigation. There is also a psychological aspect which should not be underestimated. To maintain one's silence in the face of questions is an affront, a clearly unfriendly act, and is behaviour which draws no sympathy. The argument that an accused has the right to remain silent, could to some extent be deemed rather theoretical, but the very situation he or she is in constitutes pressure, every question is more than a neutral, emotionless sentence. It is an invitation to answer.

The pressure becomes even more acute when the defendant is detained because the authorities assume that there is a danger of him or her tampering with the evidence. A confession would result in the release of the accused. The guilty suspect therefore 'pays' for the better chance of acquittal in the 'currency of personal liberty'.

4. Direct and Indirect Effects of the Guarantee

It is obvious that the right to remain silent and the right not to be compelled to contribute to one's own conviction have two distinct aspects.

The direct aspect concerns the situation of the person who is expected to give some sort of reaction to questions or requests. At its extreme, this means that it is definitely forbidden to have any recourse to torture in order to obtain a statement, whether self-incriminating or not.

[19] *John Murray* v. *United Kingdom*, §§ 46, 47.
[20] Bouissou (2002–3) 60; Stessens (1997) 50.   [21] Cf. Dennis (1995).

The indirect aspect concerns the use of any material obtained in violation of the right not to be compelled to make a statement, including the drawing of adverse inferences from the silence of an accused.

5. The Rationale of the Guarantee

The rationale of the right to silence has been addressed by the Court in a number of cases. The theory is rather complex—I shall refer to the various arguments one by one.

(a) The Starting Point

The Court started out by asserting that 'the right to silence and the right not to incriminate oneself are generally recognised international standards which lie at the heart of the notion of a fair procedure under Article 6'.[22] In other words, the central idea is that proceedings which do not respect the 'privilege' are not fair. The fact that this guarantee figures both in the ICCPR and, with particular insistence, in the ACHR, lends plausibility to the reference to 'international standards'.[23] Of course, the rule can also be found in the domestic laws of many countries.[24]

(b) The Link to Outcome-related Justice

Next, the Court found the rationale 'inter alia, in the protection of the accused against improper compulsion by the authorities thereby contributing to the avoidance of miscarriages of justice and to the fulfilment of the aims of Article 6'. No less than three justifications are mentioned in this sentence. That the privilege protects against improper compulsion is rather tautological. The question would be: what type of compulsion is 'improper'? Or rather: where are the limits of proper compulsion? This remains entirely unclear.

The second point is more precise. It highlights the possibility that compulsion may well lead to an accused making a statement. This is problematic primarily because compulsion involves the danger of untruthful answers. If the facts are not correctly established, the potential for a miscarriage of justice increases. This is a functional argument which, as it were, works both ways. It is not only in the interests of the accused, but also of the state to avoid both potential miscarriages of justice as well as methods which hinder the emergence of the truth.

Finally, it is rather strange that a guarantee which 'lies at the heart of the notion of a fair procedure' is designed to contribute 'to the fulfilment of the aims of Article 6'. If disregarding the privilege tarnishes proceedings with the stigma

---

[22] *Saunders* v. *United Kingdom*, § 68; *John Murray* v. *United Kingdom*, § 45; *Serves* v. *France*, § 46; *Quinn* v. *Ireland*, § 40; *Heaney and McGuinness* v. *Ireland*, § 40; *Allan* v. *United Kingdom*, § 44; *JB* v. *Switzerland*, § 64. *Condron* v. *United Kingdom* and *Averill* v. *United Kingdom* refer to *John Murray*. The quotations immediately following are all from the same identical paragraph.

[23] Judge Martens, in his dissenting opinion at § 9 criticizes this view.

[24] For a very thorough comparative analysis of the law in Germany and in the United States, see Schlauri (2003).

of unfairness, how can it be said that the privilege (only) contributes to making the trial fair? I fear that this statement is merely an unfortunate rhetorical turn which contributes little to the understanding of the provision.

(c) The Presumption of Innocence

The Court went on to mention a much more substantial link: 'The right not to incriminate oneself, in particular, presupposes that the prosecution in a criminal case seek to prove their case against the accused without resort to evidence obtained through methods of coercion or oppression in defiance of the will of the accused. In this sense the right is closely linked to the presumption of innocence contained in Article 6 para. 2.' It is the task of the prosecution to prove the guilt of the accused. The latter thus does not have to establish his or her innocence. *A fortiori* there is not the slightest duty on the defence to contribute to a conviction or, for that matter, to contribute in any way to the proceedings. This is indeed a fully satisfactory justification for the existence of the privilege. In one case the topic of 'right to silence' was brought and dealt with directly and exclusively under Article 6 § 2.[25]

(d) Respecting the Will of the Accused

Finally, and at the beginning of the following paragraph, the Court introduced a further aspect: 'The right not to incriminate oneself is primarily concerned, however, with respecting the will of an accused person to remain silent.'[26] This passage has led to animated discussion. The fact that there is indeed a certain link between the privilege and Article 3 is particularly convincing. It is degrading to be forced to act against one's own interests; it is likely to cause feelings of humiliation, inferiority, debasement—in short, there is a degrading element to it, although it will not normally reach the gravity required for the finding of a violation of Article 3.[27] At the same time it can also be understood as constituting a lack of respect for private life as set out in Article 8.

Judge Martens in his dissenting opinion does not deny such a link but objects that it is too absolute. However, this is not a convincing argument—it is rather obvious that life is much too complicated for giving such notions as 'degrading' an absolute character.[28] Bouissou even doubts whether the Court really wanted to base the privilege on the need to respect the will of the accused not to incriminate him- or herself.

In my view, the passage becomes very clear when it is read in the context of the case at issue. The starting point must be the criticism of *Funke*. Some authors

---

[25] *Telfner* v. *Austria*, §§ 15 et seq. In *Averill* v. *United Kingdom*, § 54, the Court, having found no violation of the right to silence, saw no reason also to examine the issue under Art. 6 § 2. Schlauri (2002) 83 doubts whether the Court derives the privilege from the presumption of innocence—I do not think that these doubts are justified.   [26] This passage is missing in *Serves*.
[27] On the notion of 'degrading treatment', see e.g. *Tyrer* v. *United Kingdom*, § 30.
[28] Cf. the telling title of a study by Callewaert (1995).

feared that this judgment would also affect the requirement that an accused submit to a blood test or other similar methods of investigation. I shall return to this issue shortly.

6. The Scope of the Guarantee

(a) Application *Ratione Materiae*
The privilege applies only within the context of criminal proceedings. The state may request that individuals provide many types of information and often the information can have a negative effect, one need only think about tax returns. There can be no doubt that the privilege does not apply outwith the criminal law—a fact evidenced by the very term self-in*crim*ination. In *Saunders* the Court made it quite clear that the fact that the applicant was under an obligation to answer the questions of the inspectors did not create any problems under the Convention.[29]

(b) Application *Ratione Personae*
Consequently, only a person who is subject to a 'criminal charge' is entitled to the privilege.[30] However, as far as the direct effect is concerned, I doubt whether this really constitutes a limitation in the sense that before being charged a person cannot invoke the privilege. It should be recalled that the term 'charge' has been given an autonomous interpretation by the Court—the criterion is whether a person is 'substantially affected' by a suspicion held against him or her.[31] However, as soon as somebody is confronted with questions or with a request for documents which could result in self-incrimination, that person is *de facto* 'charged' within the meaning of Article 6.

In the case of *K* v. *Austria*, referred to above, the Commission did not follow this approach, but instead accepted the fact that the applicant had been questioned as a witness. With hindsight, it might have been preferable to say that notwithstanding his formal position under Austrian criminal-procedure law, he fell to be regarded *de facto* as a person charged with a criminal offence even when he was asked to testify as a witness in the proceedings against the W couple. In fact, this is exactly what the Court did in *Serves*.[32]

The privilege can also be invoked by a legal person if it is the target of criminal proceedings.[33]

---

[29] *Saunders* v. *United Kingdom*, § 67.
[30] Bouissou (2002–3) 40; Schlauri (2003) 85 et seq.   [31] See further Chapter 2 above.
[32] *Serves* v. *France*, § 42. Bouissou (2002–3) 40 is of the opinion that there exists an exception from the rule that only persons who are 'accused' are entitled to the privilege in cases where somebody has to testify as a witness—that person, in her view, can directly invoke Art. 6. In effect, there is no difference to the proposal made here.
[33] Bouissou (2002–3) 42 et seq, referring to *Société Sténuit* v. *France*, Report of the Commission of 27 Feb. 1992, § 66; the Court struck the case off the list. See also O'Boyle (2000) 1033.

II. THE DIRECT EFFECT OF THE PRIVILEGE

A. The Right to Remain Silent

1. Protection Against Immediate Physical Pressure

In a way, the right to silence is a very obvious and fundamental guarantee. In fact, provided that a person is determined not to answer a question, there is no method which could reliably extract the truth. And there is certainly no method which would be compatible with the most elementary human-rights standards. What comes to mind in this context is torture,[34] and, as Viorney rightly asserts, the privilege in this area does not add anything to the prohibition of torture or inhuman or degrading treatment; the latter can consist of the administering of drugs which weaken the power of self-control.[35] The HRC speaks of 'the absence of any direct or indirect physical or psychological pressure from the investigating authorities'.[36]

However, there must at least have been some threat. The mere fact that an accused was urged to tell the truth does not violate his or her right to remain silent.[37] A very delicate question arises in relation to the 'lie detector', which is said to indicate whether a person is telling the truth. In my view, forcing someone to submit to such a procedure would constitute a degrading treatment. However, it is not unusual for persons who affirm their innocence to request the use of such an apparatus to strengthen the credibility of their defence. In my view, even in such a case the request ought not to be granted; in fact, I see a danger in that if the possibility existed, the refusal to take the test would be held against the accused.

2. Protection Against the Use of Deception

Does the privilege also protect against deception and entrapment? The Court, taking its inspiration from a judgment of the Canadian Supreme Court, gave a positive answer in *Allan* v. *United Kingdom*.

The applicant was suspected of murder committed in the course of a robbery in a supermarket. He chose to remain silent. As the police strongly suspected that he had committed the crime and were positive that normal questioning would not prove successful, they used technical devices to produce acoustical and optical recordings of the suspect's behaviour in his cell and in the reception area of the prison where he was held. The use of these means had no legal basis and therefore violated Article 8.[38] This alone, however, did not constitute a violation

---

[34] An example is IACtHR *Cantoral-Benavides* v. *Peru*, judgment of 18 Aug. 2000, Series C No. 69, §§ 132, 133.   [35] Verniory (2005) 316.

[36] *Berry* v. *Jamaica* (HRC).

[37] IACtHR, *Castillo Petruzzi et al* v. *Peru*, judgment of 30 May 1999, Series C No. 52, § 167.

[38] *Allan* v. *United Kingdom*, §§ 34–6; the same result had been reached in *Khan* v. *United Kingdom*, §§ 26–8, where listening devices were secretly installed in a private house.

of Article 6—the Court maintained the approach which it had initiated in *Schenk* v. *Switzerland*.[39]

However, the police also used a police informer whom they coached and instructed to 'push him for what you can'. The Court accepted that the privilege did not only protect against the use of pressure:

> While the right to silence and the privilege against self-incrimination are primarily designed to protect against improper compulsion by the authorities and the obtaining of evidence through methods of coercion or oppression in defiance of the will of the accused, the scope of the right is not confined to cases where duress has been brought to bear on the accused or where the will of the accused has been directly overborne in some way. The right, which the Court has previously observed is at the heart of the notion of a fair procedure, serves in principle to protect the freedom of a suspected person to choose whether to speak or to remain silent when questioned by the police. Such freedom of choice is effectively undermined in a case in which, the suspect having elected to remain silent during questioning, the authorities use subterfuge to elicit, from the suspect, confessions or other statements of an incriminatory nature, which they were unable to obtain during such questioning and where the confessions or statements thereby obtained are adduced in evidence at trial.[40]

It then goes on to quote the Canadian Supreme Court on the limits beyond which a violation of the right to a fair trial occurs—in accordance with its general approach it 'depends on all the circumstances of the individual case':[41]

> the Canadian Supreme Court expressed the view that, where the informer who allegedly acted to subvert the right to silence of the accused was not obviously a State agent, the analysis should focus on both the relationship between the informer and the State and the relationship between the informer and the accused: the right to silence would only be infringed where the informer was acting as an agent of the State at the time the accused made the statement and where it was the informer who caused the accused to make the statement. Whether an informer was to be regarded as a State agent depended on whether the exchange between the accused and the informer would have taken place, and in the form and manner in which it did, but for the intervention of the authorities. Whether the evidence in question was to be regarded as having been elicited by the informer depended on whether the conversation between him the accused was the functional equivalent of an interrogation, as well as on the nature of the relationship between the informer and the accused.[42]

The doctrine is not entirely convincing. At any rate, the criteria for establishing a link between the state and the informer must not be too formal. On the other hand, assuming that one is prepared to maintain the rule that the use of evidence obtained in violation of a Convention right does not make a trial unfair, it is justified to insist on the requirement that the gathering of evidence is not limited to recording conversations of a spontaneous nature.

---

[39] See further Chapter 20 below.   [40] *Allan* v. *United Kingdom*, § 50.
[41] Ibid., § 51.   [42] The case referred to is *R* v. *Hebert* [1990] 2 Supreme Court Reports 151.

In the present case it was then obvious that the Court had to find a violation because the informer had in fact more or less 'interrogated' the suspect informally and without any of the safeguards normally respected in ordinary proceedings.

3. A Right to be Warned?

The right to remain silent is not necessarily known to every accused. Does it entail a right to be warned? '*Miranda*' has become a household word throughout the world, not only for lawyers but also for those who watch American detective movies. It refers to a case, or rather a small group of cases, decided by the US Supreme Court in 1966.[43] According to *Miranda*, every suspect, upon arrest, must receive a formal warning, or else his depositions cannot be used in evidence. He must be told 'that he has the right to remain silent, that anything that he says can be used against him in a court of law, that he has the right to the presence of an attorney, and that if he cannot afford an attorney one will be appointed for him prior to any questioning if he so desires'.[44] Does international human-rights law demand the same?

It is astonishing to see that this question is not discussed more intensely. It is not addressed, for example, by Esser or by Viorney—Schlauri only deals with it in the context of US law.[45]

Although there can be hardly any doubt that such information is an important element of the right to a fair trial and may be indispensable to the realization of the right to remain silent, I have some hesitations about giving a positive answer.[46] This hesitation does not have ethical or doctrinal reasons, but quite practical ones. In fact, it is not easy to imagine a case which could give the Court in Strasbourg the opportunity to find a violation of the right to a fair trial due to the absence of a proper warning. The applicant would have to claim that the decision to answer the questions, constituted a waiver of the right to remain silent, but that this waiver was not valid because he or she had not been properly informed.

According to the Court's case-law, the waiver of a right guaranteed by the Convention . . . must be established in an unequivocal manner . . . Moreover, . . . in the case of procedural rights a waiver, in order to be effective for Convention purposes, requires minimum guarantees commensurate to its importance.[47]

In order to be successful the applicant would have to claim that he or she was mainly convicted on the basis of statements made during the first interrogations. In view of the fact that the reluctance of the Court to interfere with the

---

[43] *Miranda* v. *Arizona* 384 US 436 (1966).   [44] Ibid., 479.
[45] Schlauri (2003) 219 et seq.; see however, Wyss (2001).
[46] There are still doubts, however, whether the warning really takes the pressure out of custodial interrogation; cf. Schlauri (2003) 264.   [47] *Pfeifer and Plankl* v. *Austria*, § 37.

admissibility of evidence characterizes its approach to Article 6, it is rather improbable that it would go so far as to follow the US Supreme Court.

The situation is much easier for the HRC. It even has the possibility to interpret the Covenant by way of 'General Comments'. In fact, it *has* commented on Article 14 § 3(g) of the ICCPR in General Comment 13.[48] However, to my knowledge it has never called for the general introduction of the *Miranda*-style warning.

It is clear that the ACHR does not require that such a warning be given, as the Court found no violation even in a case where the alleged victims were 'urged' to tell the truth.[49]

B. The Right Not to Hand Over Documents

1. *The Judgment in* Funke v. France

The leading European case concerning the right to silence is *Funke* v. *France*. The applicant was suspected of having bank accounts abroad. Customs officers questioned him about this and asked him to present the corresponding documents, which he declined to do. On 3 May 1982 the customs authorities summoned him before the Strasbourg police court seeking to have him sentenced to a fine and a further penalty of 50 French francs a day until such time as he produced the bank statements. Later on he was also punished with a fine for not having produced certain other documents. He complained of a violation of the privilege. The majority of the Commission found there to have been no violation, but the Court followed the impressive dissenting opinion of the minority (written by Mr Soyer)—although its reasoning was less inspiring.

In fact, the Court answered in a rather sparse way:[50]

The Court notes that the customs secured Mr Funke's conviction in order to obtain certain documents which they believed must exist, although they were not certain of the fact. Being unable or unwilling to procure them by some other means, they attempted to compel the applicant himself to provide the evidence of offences he had allegedly committed. The special features of customs law . . . cannot justify such an infringement of the right of anyone 'charged with a criminal offence', within the autonomous meaning of this expression in Article 6, to remain silent and not to contribute to incriminating himself.

Ms Bouissou certainly has a point when she refers to this judgment as 'brutal'.[51]

---

[48] General Comment No. 13, 1984, § 14 where the HRC stressed that legislation ought to exclude the admissibility as evidence of all statements obtained in violation of the privilege.

[49] IACtHR, *Castillo Petruzzi et al* v. *Peru* judgment of 30 May 1999, Series C No. 52, § 167.

[50] O'Boyle (2000) 1025 rightly refers to a 'noticeable absence of argument'; he also mentions the fact that the ECJ had been equally laconic when deciding *Orkem*, judgment of 18 Oct. 1989 374/87 [1989] ECR I-3343 et seq.

[51] Bouissou (2002–3) 19. The Commission had found no violation—it considered that the duty to provide information corresponded to the fact that the state did not control all transfer of capital across the border.

The Court later made up for these failings by addressing the theoretical issues in *Saunders*, which did not concern documentary evidence—this has already been discussed above. The next case which involved a situation like the one which arose in *Funke* was *JB* v. *Switzerland*. The Federal Tax Administration found evidence of investments made by the applicant, which he had failed to declare in his tax return. Mr JB was therefore ordered to present all the documents concerning this subject. As the applicant did not comply, he was repeatedly fined. This clearly constituted a violation of the privilege—the Swiss Government had no serious arguments which would have given rise to a fresh discussion.

C. Exceptions

1. Non-testimonial Contributions

The judgment in *Funke* has not only been labelled 'brutal', it has also been criticized as being too wide.[52] The suggestions that *Funke* might constitute a bar to the taking of blood samples for an analysis of the degree of intoxication of a driver or samples of saliva for the purpose of a DNA analysis are however founded on a misunderstanding.

The privilege only covers assistance from the suspect which could not be substituted by employing direct force. In American law the term 'testimonial' is used, meaning that the contribution must be comparable to testifying.[53] This is the justification for the Court's statement that the privilege primarily exists to ensure that the will of the accused is respected. It has expressly explained this argument: the privilege 'does not extend to the use in criminal proceedings of material which may be obtained from the accused through the use of compulsory powers but which has an existence independent of the will of the suspect such as, inter alia, documents acquired pursuant to a warrant, breath, blood and urine samples and bodily tissue for the purpose of DNA testing'.[54]

It is questionable whether or to what extent this also applies to the production of documents. An exception is discussed in relation to cases where the authorities have secure knowledge of the existence of the documents—this is said to justify the compulsion to produce them. Schlauri has discussed this aspect in detail and arrives convincingly at the conclusion that such an exception ought not to be accepted.[55]

2. Disclosure of One's Identity

No one who is accused in criminal proceedings is obliged to say anything. To this, however, there is a generally accepted exception: there is no right to remain

---

[52] See e.g. Butler (2000) 461 et seq.; Dennis (1995); Stessens (1997); and Judge Martens' dissenting opinion in *Saunders* v. *United Kingdom*, § 11.   [53] Cf. Schlauri (2003) 107 et seq.
[54] *Saunders* v. *United Kingdom*, § 69.   [55] Schlauri (2003) 15 et seq., 183 et seq.

anonymous and therefore a person can legitimately be compelled to reveal his or her identity. This is not set out in international human-rights treaties, but is expressly stated in the Third Geneva Convention on prisoners of war: 'Every prisoner of war, when questioned on the subject, is bound to give only his surname, first names and rank, date of birth, and army, regimental, personal or serial number, or failing this, equivalent information'.[56]

I find it reasonable to assume that this fundamental rule also applies outside the context of war. There can, in my view, be no right to conceal one's identity, no right to anonymity. Man as an *ens sociale*, a social being, needs relations with others and such relations cannot be meaningful if a person refuses to reveal his or her identity.

However, the importance of this issue must not be overstated. In practice, a general duty to disclose one's identity to the authorities simply means that certain types of coercion can be applied in order to motivate the person concerned. According to Geneva Convention III, '[p]risoners of war who refuse to answer may not be threatened, insulted, or exposed to unpleasant or disadvantageous treatment of any kind'.[57] However, if the prisoner withholds that elementary information, 'he may render himself liable to a restriction of the privileges accorded to his rank or status'.[58] It is not easy to extrapolate potential equivalent sanctions in peacetime. I would suggest that it could take the form of a regulatory fine, which must not be imposed more than once, perhaps short-term deprivation of liberty in the sense of Article 5 § 1(b) would be acceptable. The importance of this issue lies less with the administration of criminal law than with controlling immigration. Alleged refugees sometimes destroy their identity papers and make no or false statements as to their nationality which can make their expulsion almost impossible.[59]

III. THE INDIRECT EFFECT OF THE PRIVILEGE

A. Introduction

The right to silence would be useless if the tribunal were entirely free to interpret the refusal of the accused to answer. There must also be safeguards against the use of statements as evidence even if they have been made under pressure. This rule is expressly set out in Article 15 of the Convention against Torture and Other Cruel, Inhuman or Degrading Treatment or Punishment:[60] 'Each State Party shall ensure that any statement which is established to have been made as a result of torture shall not be invoked as evidence in any

---

[56] Convention (III) Relative to the Treatment of Prisoners of War, Geneva, 12 Aug. 1949, Art. 17, para. 1.   [57] Ibid., Art. 17, para. 4, 2nd sentence.
[58] Ibid., Art. 17 para. 2.
[59] Cf. the case of *Manitu Giama* v. *Belgium* (friendly settlement).
[60] Adopted by the General Assembly of the United Nations on 10 Dec. 1984.

proceedings, except against a person accused of torture as evidence that the statement was made'.

The text of Article 8 § 3 of the ACHR which addresses the same issue is both wider and narrower. It is narrower in that it only refers to a confession. This notion ought to be interpreted in a broad sense so as to include any self-incriminatory statement made by the accused. On the other hand it is wider in that it excludes not only those statements which are made under torture but also those which were made under (a lesser degree of) coercion.

B. Adverse Inferences from Silence

1. John Murray v. United Kingdom

The basic principle that the right to remain silent encompasses a prohibition on the court from drawing any negative conclusions from such silence is uncontested. What the psychological effect of the attitude of a silent witness on the mind of the judge will be in a specific case cannot be assessed. In practice the rule means that the *reasoning of the judgment* may not refer to the accused's silence in any way which implies that it was considered as an element supporting the findings against him or her.

In the United Kingdom attempts to combat terrorism in Northern Ireland led to the adoption of legislation which marked a certain distance from that principle. Article 3 of the Criminal Evidence (Northern Ireland) Order 1988 states as follows:

Circumstances in which inferences may be drawn from accused's failure to mention particular facts when questioned, charged, etc.

(1) Where, in any proceedings against a person for an offence, evidence is given that the accused—

    (a) at any time before he was charged with the offence, on being questioned by a constable trying to discover whether or by whom the offence had been committed, failed to mention any fact relied on in his defence in those proceedings; or

    (b) on being charged with the offence or officially informed that he might be prosecuted for it, failed to mention any such fact, being a fact which in the circumstances existing at the time the accused could reasonably have been expected to mention when so questioned, charged or informed, as the case may be, paragraph (2) applies.

(2) Where this paragraph applies—

    (a) the court, in determining whether to commit the accused for trial or whether there is a case to answer,

    (b) . . .

    (c) the court or jury, in determining whether the accused is guilty of the offence charged, may—

        (i) draw such inferences from the failure as appear proper;

> (ii) on the basis of such inferences treat the failure as, or as capable of amounting to, corroboration of any evidence given against the accused in relation to which the failure is material . . .[61]

This legislation was at the centre of several judgments, including the leading case, *John Murray*. Police had found the applicant in a house where a person had been unlawfully imprisoned by the IRA as he was suspected of being a police informer. The applicant was seen coming down the stairs—the prisoner was upstairs. The applicant was informed about his right to remain silent and did not make any statements during the police investigations or at the trial. He had been warned: 'You do not have to say anything unless you wish to do so but I must warn you that if you fail to mention any fact which you rely on in your defence in court, your failure to take this opportunity to mention it may be treated in court as supporting any relevant evidence against you. If you do wish to say anything, what you say may be given in evidence'.[62]

Despite remaining silent, he was eventually convicted. The judge stated *inter alia*: 'I am further satisfied that it is an irresistible inference that while he was in the house [the applicant] was in contact with the men holding L. captive and that he knew that L. was being held a captive. I also draw very strong inferences against [the applicant] under Article 6 of the 1988 Order by reason of his failure to give an account of his presence in the house when cautioned by the police on the evening of 7 January 1990 under Article 6, and I also draw very strong inferences against [the applicant] under Article 4 of the 1988 Order by reason of his refusal to give evidence in his own defence when called upon by the Court to do so'.[63]

Taking part in the proceedings as *amicus curiae*, Amnesty International submitted that 'permitting adverse inferences to be drawn from the silence of the accused was an effective means of compulsion which shifted the burden of proof from the prosecution to the accused and was inconsistent with the right not to be compelled to testify against oneself or to confess guilt because the accused is left with no reasonable choice between silence—which will be taken as testimony against oneself—and testifying'.[64]

The Court admitted that there was 'a certain level of indirect compulsion' if the defendant is warned that his silence could be used in evidence against him. Yet, like the Commission, it found that there had been no violation.

Typically, the Court began its judgment by stating that it was not its 'role to examine whether, in general, the drawing of inferences under the scheme contained in the Order is compatible with the notion of a fair hearing under Article 6'.[65] It then reiterated its general acceptance of the privilege: the accused is protected against 'improper compulsion'. With reference to the specific case,

---

[61] Quotation taken from *John Murray* v. *United Kingdom*, § 27. [62] Ibid., § 11.
[63] Ibid., § 25. [64] As referred to in *John Murray* v. *United Kingdom*, § 42.
[65] This and the following quotations are taken from paras. 44 et seq. of the judgment.

the Court continued:

What is at stake in the present case is whether these immunities are absolute in the sense that the exercise by an accused of the right to silence cannot under any circumstances be used against him at trial or, alternatively, whether informing him in advance that, under certain conditions, his silence may be so used, is always to be regarded as 'improper compulsion'. On the one hand, it is self-evident that it is incompatible with the immunities under consideration to base a conviction solely or mainly on the accused's silence or on a refusal to answer questions or to give evidence himself. On the other hand, the Court deems it equally obvious that these immunities cannot and should not prevent that the accused's silence, in situations which clearly call for an explanation from him, be taken into account in assessing the persuasiveness of the evidence adduced by the prosecution.

Although, as mentioned above, the Court did accept that there had been a certain degree of compulsion, it did not find it to be 'decisive'. In its view the other safeguards, such as the warning and the requirement on the prosecution to present a *prima facie* case, were sufficient. The essential argument seems to be the following:

The question in each particular case is whether the evidence adduced by the prosecution is sufficiently strong to require an answer. The national court cannot conclude that the accused is guilty merely because he chooses to remain silent. It is only if the evidence against the accused 'calls' for an explanation which the accused ought to be in a position to give that a failure to give any explanation 'may as a matter of common sense allow the drawing of an inference that there is no explanation and that the accused is guilty'. Conversely if the case presented by the prosecution had so little evidential value that it called for no answer, a failure to provide one could not justify an inference of guilt. In sum, it is only common-sense inferences which the judge considers proper, in the light of the evidence against the accused, that can be drawn under the Order.[66]

The Court found that the presence of Mr Murray in the house strongly called for an explanation and that it was reasonable to assume that his silence meant that he had no 'innocent' explanation.

In the Commission, Mr Busuttil dissented, mainly because he found the *prima facie* case to have been too weak. In the Court, there were five votes against the finding. The separate opinion of Judge Walsh relied predominantly on English and American law, while Judge Pettiti also referred to some comparative legal elements. Both seemed to reject any exception to the right to remain silent, although neither added a more theoretical dimension to the argument than that of the majority.

2. The Case-law after John Murray

The Court came to the same conclusion in *Averill* v. *United Kingdom* which concerned murder. In *Condron* v. *United Kingdom* a couple were convicted of

---

[66] *John Murray* v. *United Kingdom*, § 51.

drug offences. Here the applicants, on the advice of their solicitor, had chosen to remain silent. They later made a statement at the trial and gave an explanation for their previous silence. The reason their solicitor gave for his advice was his concern about their capacity to follow questions put to them during interview. The judge, however, told the jury that they were free to rely on the silence of the accused during the investigation. In this case, and with the use of some very elaborate reasoning, the Court came to the conclusion that there had been a violation. It reached the same result in *Beckles* v. *United Kingdom*.

The only case in this series which has concerned continental Europe is *Telfner* v. *Austria*. The applicant's car had been involved in an accident. He denied having driven it and his mother and sister who lived at the same place availed themselves of their right to refuse to testify. He was convicted because he was the person who mainly used this car and because he had been absent from home that whole day and his whereabouts were unknown. He had also refused to make a statement. Here, contrary to *John Murray*, the evidence was not 'such that the only common-sense inference to be drawn from the accused's silence [was] that he had no answer to the case against him'.[67] The case had been brought under Article 6 § 2 and the Court found a violation of that guarantee.

Finally, in two cases against Ireland, the violation was rather clear-cut. The Court found 'that the "degree of compulsion" imposed on the applicants by the application of section 52 of the 1939 [Offences Against the State] Act with a view to compelling them to provide information relating to charges against them under that Act in effect destroyed the very essence of their privilege against self-incrimination and their right to remain silent'.[68] In both cases the Court found a violation of Article 6 §§ 1 and 2.

3. Assessment

The implementation of the right to silence by the ECHR is relatively recent and extremely complicated—a view which is shared by other authors.[69] Having participated in the adoption of the Commission's report in *John Murray* and voted with the majority, I still approve of the decision.[70] However, the issue is a very sensitive one indeed. There is a thin dividing line between the creation of an unfair dilemma for the accused and the facilitation of the conscientious appreciation of the evidence. In fact, if one considers the evidence in *John Murray* or in *Averill*, one can well imagine that a judge could reach the unimpeachable conviction that the accused were guilty without needing to refer to their silence.

---

[67] *Telfner* v. *Austria*, § 17.
[68] *Heaney and McGuinness* v. *Ireland*, § 55; *Quinn* v. *Ireland*, § 56.
[69] Bouissou (2002–3) 19, 85; O'Boyle (2000) 1037; Verniory (2005) 312.
[70] See, however, the criticism of Schlauri (2003) 366 et seq.

Chapter 14

The Right to Appeal

I. INTRODUCTION

A. The Texts

> Everyone convicted of a crime shall have the right to his conviction and sentence being reviewed by a higher tribunal according to law.
>
> ICCPR, Art. 14 § 5

> Right to appeal in criminal matters
>
> 1. Everyone convicted of a criminal offence by a tribunal shall have the right to have his conviction or sentence reviewed by a higher tribunal. The exercise of this right, including the grounds on which it may be exercised, shall be governed by law.
> 2. This right may be subject to exceptions in regard to offences of a minor character, as prescribed by law, or in cases in which the person concerned was tried in the first instance by the highest tribunal or was convicted following an appeal against acquittal.
>
> ECHR Protocol No. 7, Art. 2

> 1. . . . During the proceedings, every person is entitled, with full equality, to the following minimum guarantees: . . .
>   the right to appeal the judgment to a higher court.
>
> ACHR, Art. 8 § 2(h)

A comparison of the texts makes it clear that the scope of the guarantee differs in the respective texts. The ACHR is very brief, the ICCPR barely more precise, while the ECHR specifies the need for legal regulations and sets out three exceptions. Yet, the practical consequences of the difference has not left any traces in the case-law.

B. The Origins

The right to appeal makes a late appearance in the debate on the codification of international human-rights law. It was first proposed during the fourteenth session of the Third Committee of the General Assembly by the Israeli Delegate Mr Baror. He drew particular attention to the need for an examination of whether the right to a fair trial under Article 14 had been respected. Answering a question raised by Mr Tchobanov of Bulgaria he made it clear that he did not have a specific remedy in mind, such as an appeal at which new evidence could be presented, but instead envisaged a more general right of review. While he had first proposed an exception for petty offences, this was later dropped because it was feared that no uniform universal definition could be achieved.[1]

The fact that this session was held in 1959 explains why no analogous right was adopted by the ECHR. Some of those responsible for drafting the ECHR had also been involved in the drafting of the ICCPR, most notably René Cassin, who had taken over the *acquis* of 1950. Six years after the adoption of the ICCPR, the Council of Europe began the process of comparing the texts. The Committee of Experts charged with this task produced a report which mentioned no less than thirty variations in the substantive part of the two treaties although some of them, it must be admitted, concerned insignificant details.[2]

The Parliamentary Assembly then decided that the ECHR should be amended so as to mirror the standards set out in the ICCPR.[3] This was by no means a quick process. It took four years before the Committee of Ministers was formally charged with preparing this step.[4] Following consultations with, *inter alia*, the Court and the Commission, Protocol No. 7 was adopted. It did not meet with much enthusiasm.[5] In view of the fact that thirty differences had been pinpointed, the addition of just five Articles adding substantive rights might seem somewhat meagre. It must not be forgotten, however, that it could have been dangerous to codify every right not expressly set out in the Convention. A good example to illustrate this point is the privilege against self-incrimination which is set out in Article 14 § 3(g) of the ICCPR. The Commission and Court would later on hold that this right was implicit in the right to a fair trial guaranteed by Article 6 § 1. Had it been incorporated into Protocol No. 7, it would have been difficult to say that it was already covered by Article 6 and to apply it to states, such as the United Kingdom, which had not ratified the Seventh Protocol.

---

[1] Weissbrodt (2001) 74.

[2] Report of the Committee of Experts to the Committee of Ministers, *Problems Arising from the Co-existence of the United Nations Covenants on Human Rights and the European Convention on Human Rights: Differences as Regards the Rights Generated* (Strasbourg, 1970), Doc. H (70) 7 (this report can be accessed from the shared catalogue of the Council of Europe's libraries (WEBCAT) at www.coe.int).

[3] Resolution 683 (1972), Action to be Taken on the Conclusion of the Parliamentary Conference on Human Rights, 24th Session of the Parliamentary Assembly, second part.

[4] Recommendation 791 (1976), Protection of Human Rights in Europe, 28th Session of the Parliamentary Assembly, second part.

[5] Opinion 116 (1983), Draft Protocol to the Convention for the Protection of Fundamental Rights and Freedoms Extending the List of Political and Civil Rights Set Forth in the Convention, 35th Session of the Parliamentary Assembly, second part.

Despite criticism, the Protocol was opened for signature on 22 November 1984. States proved reluctant to ratify it and it was not until 1988 that enough ratifications were submitted to enable the Protocol to come into force.[6] While most of the Member States of the Council of Europe have since ratified it, there are still a number which have not: Andorra, Belgium, Germany, Liechtenstein, Netherlands, Portugal, Spain, Turkey, and the United Kingdom—nine out of forty-five. It may seem surprising that none of the former communist countries are on this list. The explanation is however quite simple: the Council of Europe now makes membership of the organization conditional upon ratification of the entire 'parcel' of rights set out in the ECHR and its protocols. All those who have not yet ratified the Seventh Protocol have, however, ratified the ICCPR, with the exception of Andorra.

C. The Purpose of the Right to Appeal

Generally, appeals serve two purposes. First, they function as a mechanism whereby parties can obtain a more favourable outcome to the proceedings. Second, appeals promote ideals such as consistency and fairness and regulate uniform interpretation of the law.

Within the framework of human rights, only the first of these aspects can be of relevance for the individual—international human-rights law is not concerned with the uniform and correct application of national law, it will only react if domestic law has been applied in an entirely arbitrary way.

It should be noted that an appeal will not necessarily render a more advantageous result than the original judgment. In most European countries, the public prosecutor is entitled to appeal against an acquittal or against a judgment which he or she deems to be too lenient. On the other hand, the Convention does not contain any prohibition against *reformatio in peius*, it does not protect an appellant from a more severe judgment on appeal.[7] Thus, it is difficult to construe the right to appeal simply in terms of benefiting the defence.

Still, the possibility of obtaining a more favourable judgment from a higher tribunal can nevertheless be regarded as providing an element of hope. Furthermore, indirect advantages with the potential to influence the fairness of the proceedings are undeniable. The fact that the judgment is subject to further examination has a preventive effect in that it constitutes a strong motivation for judges to work conscientiously and to avoid errors or arbitrariness. In this sense, it is linked to the right to a reasoned judgment. Finally, there is a clear

---

[6] Seven signatures were required. The Protocol came into force on 1 Nov. 1988.

[7] This is implicit in *Monnell and Morris* v. *United Kingdom*. See also *X* v. *Germany* Application 3347/67 and *Luksch* v. *Austria* Application 370735/97. In its decision in *Magharian* v. *Switzerland* Application 23337/94, the Commission said that the prohibition of *reformatio in peius* is not guaranteed by the Convention although it did not discuss whether it could be construed as being implicit in Art. 6.

connection between the right to appeal and the right to an effective remedy as set out in Article 2 § 3(a) of the ICCPR, Article 13 of the ECHR, and Article 25 of the AHRC. In their earlier jurisprudence, the Strasbourg authorities maintained that Article 13 of the ECHR did not apply in cases where Article 6 was at issue. This was based on the fact that application to such cases would have amounted to providing a right to appeal in civil proceedings, something which would have been impossible as the right was clearly limited to criminal cases. Furthermore, Article 13 does not necessarily require a judicial remedy; yet the judgment of a court can only be reviewed by another court. Thus, in cases where the Court had found a violation of Article 6 on the basis of the length of proceedings, it did not go on to examine the further complaint that the applicant had had no opportunity to challenge the delay.[8] The jurisprudence has since been partially modified. The Court was so worried about the large number of cases alleging excessive delays in (mainly) civil proceedings that it decided to interpret Article 13 as requiring that there be a remedy for some, but not all, of these cases. In particular, cases concerning denial of access to court were held not to require an Article 13-type remedy.[9]

The right of appeal had to be added to the Convention as it could not be derived directly from the right to a fair trial. The Court had already ruled in very early judgments that the Convention did not cover that right.[10]

II. THE PREREQUISITES FOR THE RIGHT TO APPEAL

The right to an appeal arises when somebody has been 'convicted of a criminal offence by a tribunal'. The terms 'criminal offence', 'convicted', and 'by a tribunal' thus fall to be discussed.

A. The Term 'Criminal Offence' in the Right to Appeal

It would perhaps be legitimate to expect that the term 'criminal offence' have the same meaning in both Article 6 and Article 2 of Protocol No. 7.[11] The issue does not even arise in the context of the ICCPR or the ACHR as the analogous guarantees are found within the same Article. The position is similar with regard to the ECHR, in that generally the term has the same meaning in both provisions although some states, including Italy and France, have made reservations which have limited the scope of application of the right to appeal.[12]

---

[8] Cf. e.g. *Tripodi* v. *Italy*, § 15. [9] *Kudła* v. *Poland*, §§ 148 et seq.
[10] *Case 'relating to certain aspects of the laws on the use of languages in education in Belgium' (Belgian Linguistics case)*, § 9; *Delcourt* v. *Belgium*, § 25; Spangher (2001) 944.
[11] Grabenwarter (2003) § 24 N 100.
[12] See *Borrelli* v. *Switzerland* Application 17571/90; *Demel* v. *Austria* Application 30993/96; *Simonnet* v. *France* Application 23037/93; and *CB and AM* v. *Switzerland* Application 17443/90; see also Trechsel (1988) 202.

France ensured that the guarantees of Arts. 2–4 of Protocol No. 7 would only apply to 'those offences which under French law fall within the jurisdiction of the French criminal courts', and Italy declared in a letter that the rules only applied to 'offences, procedures and decisions qualified as criminal by Italian law'.[13] This can easily be explained as a reaction to the tendency of the Strasbourg organs to apply a broad, 'autonomous' interpretation of the term 'criminal offence'.

B. The Notion of 'Conviction' in the Right to Appeal

By limiting the right to appeal to persons who have already been convicted, the Protocol follows a fundamental principle of procedural law.[14] It is generally presumed that the interest in an appeal disappears following an acquittal. A person not yet convicted cannot be seen to be a 'victim' in the sense of Article 34 of the ECHR. Yet, the issue is not quite as simple as that, although it has not yet arisen in the case-law.

First, it is possible that although a person is convicted, no sanction is imposed. In such a case the right to appeal still applies because the person concerned may have a legitimate interest in restoring the presumption of innocence which has been rebutted by the conviction.

Conversely, an acquittal may be accompanied by negative consequences for the accused, such as the confiscation of assets or the imposition of costs. In such cases, despite the existence of an interest, there is no right to appeal. In fact such interests can be seen as being similar to those of a party in civil proceedings. The right to appeal however applies exclusively in the context of criminal proceedings and in view of the relatively precise wording it is difficult to imagine how it could be extended to cover civil proceedings.[15]

Finally, difficult questions may arise if an accused has been acquitted for lack of criminal responsibility but committed to a mental hospital or similar institution. In my view the Convention ought to be interpreted in a strictly literal sense: no conviction, no right to appeal. This does not leave the person concerned without protection. In such a case Article 5 § 4, the right to *habeas corpus* proceedings, would apply. Although the procedural safeguards contained within this provision are not quite as rigorous as those guaranteed by Article 6, they are nevertheless significant. Furthermore, there is a right to regular review of the detention at intervals of no more than one year.

Unfortunately, the Court has shown little regard for such subtle distinctions in its jurisprudence. In the *Welch* case, it did not hesitate to label a sanction

---

[13] Reservations can be accessed online on the website of the Council of Europe treaty office; see conventions.coe.int/Treaty/EN/cadreprincipal.htm.

[14] Including legal persons; cf. *Fortum Oil & Gas OY* v. *Finland* Application 32559/96.

[15] This can be contrasted with the position regarding the right to legal assistance; cf. *Airey* v. *Ireland*.

(confiscation order and subsequent detention for being in default of payment) as a punishment even though it was not conceived as such.[16] It cannot be excluded, therefore, that in a similar case the Court would have recourse to the autonomous interpretation of Convention terms and hold such a judgment to be a 'conviction' even in cases where the accused has been acquitted.

C. Conviction *by a Tribunal*

Except for a few linguistic points the only difference in the drafting of the right to appeal is that the Convention specifies that the appeal must be against conviction by a tribunal.[17] The meaning of this is somewhat unclear as any conviction which is not the product of a tribunal would violate Article 6. I have been unable to find any normative content in these words.[18]

The case-law does not make the matter any clearer. It shows, however, that the Court will examine whether there has been a conviction by a tribunal.[19] A number of applications against Austria concerned cases where the original decision had been taken by an administrative authority which had imposed a fine on the applicant. The applicants then had the possibility to bring the case before a judicial authority. Consequently, the decision of the judicial authority constituted a 'conviction by a tribunal' against which there was a right of appeal.[20]

Both Van Dijk and van Hoof and Merrills and Robertson seem to regard the reference to a tribunal as a restrictive element because conviction at first instance by a body which is not a tribunal is compatible with Article 6 if the accused waives that right.[21] However, as I would regard such a waiver as also covering the right to appeal, their argument does not, in my view, provide a convincing justification for this view.

III. THE REVIEW

A. The Discretion Left to the Contracting States

Another difference between the ECHR and the ICCPR is that those responsible for drafting the Convention thought it necessary to add a sentence stressing that the exercise of the right to appeal 'shall be governed by law'. This wording

---

[16] *Welch* v. *United Kingdom*.

[17] The ICCPR says 'conviction *and* sentence', whereas the Convention uses '*or*'.

[18] See also Trechsel (1988) 202.

[19] An affirmative answer was given in *Fortum Oil & Gas OY* v. *Finland* Application 32559/96, for the Competition Council; and *Didier* v. *France* (decision) Application 58188/00, for the Financial Markets Board.

[20] See *Hubner* v. *Austria* Application 34311/96; *HS* v. *Austria* Application 26510/95; *Horst* v. *Austria* Application 25809/94; *Hauser* v. *Austria* Application 26808/95.

[21] Van Dijk and van Hoof (1998) 686; Merrills and Robertson (2001) 264, n. 96; see also Harris, O'Boyle, and Warbrick (1995) 567.

differs from that found in other Articles of the Convention. While it could be understood as imposing an obligation on states to set up legal rules governing appeals, if one looks at the case-law one gets the impression that it is mainly meant to stress the freedom of the states in regulating the matter.

The discretion left to the states in this area can be explained by the fact that, as the Commission has stressed in a number of cases, there are a wide variety of types of appeal in Europe: 'The Commission notes that different rules govern review by a higher tribunal in the member States of the Council of Europe. In some countries such review is in certain cases limited to questions of law such as the "recours en cassation" (in French law) or "Revision" (in German law). In other countries there is a right to appeal against findings of fact as well as on questions of law; and in some States a person wishing to appeal to a higher tribunal must in certain cases apply for leave to appeal'.[22]

The states are said to enjoy 'a wide margin of appreciation',[23] 'discretion' ('*faculté de décider*'),[24] a '*pouvoir discrétionnaire*',[25] or to retain the power to decide ('*conservent la faculté de décider*').[26] These terms clearly demonstrate that this discretion is not the same as that normally implied by the term 'margin of appreciation' when it is applied, for instance, in the context of Articles 8–11. In fact, the Explanatory Report to the Protocol states that the various forms of appeal, even a request for leave to appeal, are all sufficient to satisfy the demands of the Protocol. This is a rather restrictive interpretation of the right to appeal, particularly in view of the fact that the leave-to-appeal proceedings may actually prevent the operation of the very right that they are supposed to satisfy.[27] The aim of the Convention is not to oust important rules of criminal procedure; it is especially important to allow courts to limit their case-load. The ECtHR is particularly sensitive to this issue as it currently has more than 80,000 pending cases.[28] Yet van Dijk and van Hoof sound an important warning: leave-to-appeal proceedings will not satisfy the requirement of Article 2 if the higher tribunal is

---

[22] *Peterson Sarpsborg AS and others* v. *Norway* Application 25944/94; *Hubner* v. *Austria* Application 34311/96; *HS* v. *Austria* Application 26510/95; *Jakobsen* v. *Denmark* Application 22015/93; *Lantto* v. *Finland* Application 27665/95; *Demel* v. *Austria* Application 24208/94.

[23] *Krombach* v. *France*, § 96. See also e.g. *Didier* v. *France* (decision) Application 58188/00; *Meischberger* v. *Austria* Application 51941/99; *Fortum Oil & Gas OY* v. *Finland* Application 32559/96; *Sawalha* v. *Sweden* Application 64299/01.

[24] *HS* v. *Austria* Application 26510/95; *Poulsen* v. *Denmark* Application 32092/96.

[25] *Haser* v. *Switzerland* Application 33050/96; *Altieri* v. *France, Cyprus, and Switzerland* Application 28140/95.

[26] *De Lorenzo* v. *Italy* Application 69264/01; *Guala* v. *France* Application 64117/00; *Mariani* v. *France* Application 43640/98; *Loewenguth* v. *France* (decision) Application 53183/99; and *Deperrois* v. *France* Application 48203/99.

[27] See also the criticism expressed by Spangher (2001) 949. Ovey and White (2002) 197 and Grabenwarter (2003) § 24 N 101 also doubt whether the request for leave to appeal satisfies the Protocol. The HRC considered that the introduction of leave-to-appeal proceedings in Sweden might raise concern; Weissbrodt (2001) 150.

[28] For plans to reform the Convention in order to face this challenge, see Protocol No. 14 to the Convention for the Protection of Human Rights and Fundamental Freedoms, Amending the Control System of the Convention of 13 May 2004.

competent to refuse leave to appeal for the simple reason of expediency.[29] This also seems to be the attitude of the HRC which found a violation of Article 14 § 5 of the ICCPR in a case where leave to appeal had been refused without reasons.[30]

This is in contrast to the Strasbourg jurisprudence. In some cases applicants complained that they only had a remedy with limited powers of the higher tribunal at their disposal, for example, merely to control whether the law was applied correctly or whether there had been procedural mistakes. Leave to appeal was at issue, for example, in a number of cases from Scandinavia—their applications were all declared manifestly ill-founded.[31]

The same fate befell a considerable number of applicants who had misunderstood Article 2 of the Protocol as guaranteeing the right to a full appeal in the sense of a second hearing as to both facts and law. The Commission and the Court declared their applications inadmissible.[32]

So far, there has been just one case, *Krombach* v. *France*, which has led to the finding of a violation by the Court. The applicant had been convicted and sentenced *in absentia* by the Paris Assize Court—he had been aware that the proceedings were taking place but had chosen to remain in Germany. His complaint was that by virtue of Article 636 of the Code of Criminal Procedure he was absolutely excluded from appealing to the Court of Cassation.

The Court held that the Contracting States enjoy a wide margin of appreciation in regulating appeals, but it also stated that the right to appeal had to be regarded as an aspect of the right of access to a court as guaranteed by Article 6 § 1. Although this right is not unlimited, any restriction must 'pursue a legitimate aim and not infringe the very essence of that right'.[33] In this case the Court attached particular importance to the fact that the applicant had wanted to raise a procedural issue, namely that his lawyers were not allowed to plead because of his absence.[34]

According to the ECHR the appeal can concern 'conviction *or* sentence', whereas the ICCPR applies to 'conviction *and* sentence'. The text of the ECHR is potentially misleading and may have misled van Dijk and van Hoof as they

[29] Van Dijk and van Hoof (1998) 687.   [30] *Reid* v. *Jamaica.*
[31] *Peterson Sarpsborg AS and others* v. *Norway* Application 25944/94; *EM* v. *Norway* Application 20087/92; *Näss* v. *Sweden* Application 18066/91; *CPH* v. *Sweden* Application 20959/92.
[32] Cf. Austria (supreme court): *Sinowatz* Application 18962/91; *Hannak* Application 70883/01; *Pesti and Frodl* (decision) Applications 27618/95 and 27619/95. Austria (administrative court): *Weh and Weh* Application 38544/97; *Hauser* Application 26808/95; *IH, MeH, RH & MuH* Application 42780/98; *Hubner* Application 34311/96; *Demel* Application 24208/94; *Horst* Application 25809/94. France (*cour de cassation*): *Guala* Application 64117/00; *Feldmann* Application 53426/99; *Mariani* Application 43640/98; *Loewenguth* (decision) Application 53183/99; and *Deperrois* Application 48203/99. Italy (*corte di cassazione*): *De Lorenzo* Application 69264/01; *Kwiatkowska* Application 52868/99; *Emmanuello* Application 35791/97. Luxembourg (*cour de cassation*): *NW* Application 19715/92. Switzerland (*Corte di cassazione e di revisione penale del Cantone del Ticino*): *Haser* 33050/96; *Waridel* Application 39765/98. The same solution was also adopted by the HRC, *Perera* v. *Australia.*   [33] *Krombach* v. *France*, § 96.
[34] Ibid., § 100 with reference to *Poitrimol* v. *France*, § 38.

seem to assume that states may limit the review to one or the other of these.[35] It would be rather absurd and would serve to undermine the purpose of the guarantee if the provision only guaranteed an appeal against conviction. The text can only be interpreted as meaning that it is possible to limit an appeal to the issue of sentencing alone. This may be the case when an applicant has pleaded guilty.[36] Such a plea may not be regarded as a waiver of the right to appeal against the sentence.

The discretion of the states extends, *a fortiori*, to the way in which the appeal is exercised, for example, to such issues as written form, requirement of reasoning, and time limits.[37] The conditions may not, however, be so restrictive as to 'infringe the very essence of the right'.[38]

B. The 'Higher Tribunal'

Little substance is to be found in the requirement that the appeal be considered by a 'higher tribunal'. In accordance with Article 6 there must already have been a conviction by a tribunal. It would be incompatible with the right to an independent and impartial court if a conviction could be reviewed by any instance other than a tribunal with analogous qualifications.[39] In the case-law this criterion has not played a decisive role. In a case against France the Court found that 'when reviewing decisions . . . , the *Conseil d'Etat* is competent to deal with all aspects of the case, so that in that respect it too is a "judicial body that has full jurisdiction", and thus a "tribunal" '.[40]

The essential point is that it would not be sufficient if the remedy led to a new examination of the case by the same tribunal. This had been the case in a communication to the HRC directed against Colombia.[41]

IV. THE EXCEPTIONS

In contrast to the ICCPR and the ACHR, the Protocol sets out three exceptions to the right of appeal.

A. Petty Offences

The first exception concerns 'offences of a minor character' a point which, as we have seen, was mooted during the drafting of the ICCPR but later rejected. It

---

[35] Van Dijk and van Hoof (1998) 686.
[36] See *Nielsen* v. *Denmark* Application 19028/91; *Jakobsen* v. *Denmark* Application 22015/93.
[37] Spangher (2001) 946.   [38] *Krombach* v. *France*, § 96.
[39] Before the HRC, however, the representative for Iraq pretended that the appeal to the President satisfied Art. 14 § 5; McGoldrick (2001) 10.21.
[40] *Didier* v. *France* (decision) Application 58188/00, referring to *Diennet* v. *France*, § 34.
[41] *Consuelo Salgar de Montejo* v. *Colombia*, § 168.

embodies to some extent the maxim '*de minimis non curat praetor*', and exists to serve the principle of expediency in criminal proceedings. The exception must be 'prescribed by law'; it cannot be left to the discretion of the authorities to decide in each case whether the character of a specific offence is 'minor' or not.

The criteria can either be abstract or specific. According to the abstract model, the decisive element is the penalty that the offence carries according to the law. Often there are specific categories, for example, misdemeanours, regulatory fines, *contraventions*, or *Ordnungswidrigkeiten*. The Explanatory Report endorses this approach when it states that 'an important criterion is the question of whether the offence is punishable by imprisonment or not'.[42] According to the specific model, on the other hand, the legislation would rely on the sanction pronounced in a specific case, for example, a fine of up to 100 euros. In this respect again the states would still have to enjoy a rather wide margin of appreciation.

If one evaluates the two models, the first seems to have potential drawbacks. The maximum penalty even for the categories just mentioned may be relatively high. On the other hand, a fine can sometimes be imposed for an offence which, technically, qualifies as a felony, *crime*, or *Verbrechen*. The model is thus highly dependent on the legislative style of each country. It would therefore be difficult to fix a limit valid for the forty-five Member States which make up the Council of Europe.[43] The specific model is perhaps preferable because the judgment at issue will have set a specific sentence. The danger is that it might invite abuse—in cases where the conviction is dubious the judge might decide to exclude the possibility of a remedy by fixing the sentence below the level which would allow an appeal.

The case-law is of little help in finding a clear answer to these issues, let alone in setting precise limits. When Denmark ratified the Protocol, it made a declaration that defined 'minor' cases as those 'where only sentences of fines or confiscation of objects below the amount or value established by law are imposed'.[44] The Commission has regarded a number of cases as being of a 'minor' character. These have included a fine of 200 CHF (130 euros)[45] imposed on an applicant as her dogs had caused excessive noise;[46] a fine of 100 CHF (65 euros) for assault, even though the offence was classified as a 'misdemeanour' and carried a sentence of up to three months' imprisonment;[47] and a fine of 2,000 AS (145 euros)

---

[42] Explanatory Report, § 21; according to Spangher (2001) this would mean that '*contravenzioni*' which carry only a pecuniary sanction are 'minor' offences.

[43] In reality it would be even more as in some states the regions, *Länder, Cantons, Krai*, etc. have their own criminal laws. For a critical view of the abstract method, see also Charrier (2002) Art. 2 of Protocol No. 7 N 3; Frowein and Peukert (1996) Art. 2 of Protocol No. 7 N 3; Grabenwarter (2003) § 24 N 102; van Dijk and van Hoof (1998) 687.

[44] The reservations can be accessed online from the Council of Europe's treaty office; see conventions.coe.int/Treaty/EN/cadreprincipal.htm.

[45] All monetary conversions are approximate and have been calculated as at June 2004.

[46] *Von Arx-Derungs* v. *Switzerland* Application 23269/94.

[47] *LKD* v. *Switzerland* Application 20320/92.

imposed on a member of the public for disrupting court proceedings—the maximum sanction was detention of up to eight days.[48]

In this case the Commission appeared to follow the 'specific method' and accepted that cases where a sanction of a few hundred euros were imposed can be regarded as 'minor'—it paid no attention to the abstract possibility of a custodial sentence.

It should also be noted that the Convention organs employ two limits: First, there is a level of seriousness below which there is not even a 'criminal offence' within the meaning of Article 6; second, there is the (higher) limit below which there is a right to the guarantees of Article 6 but not to those of Article 2 of Protocol No. 7.

While the ICCPR does not have a similar exception, the following excerpt from General Comment No. 13 is of interest: 'Article 14, paragraph 5, provides that everyone convicted of a crime shall have the right to his conviction and sentence being reviewed by a higher tribunal according to law. Particular attention is drawn to the other language versions of the word "crime" ("infraction", "delito", "prestuplenie") which shows that the guarantee is not confined only to the most serious offences'.[49] It certainly leaves open an interpretation which would exclude truly 'minor' offences and thus allow for a similar approach as that employed by the ECHR.[50] Furthermore, the drafting history would support this view.[51]

B. The Highest Court Sitting at First Instance

Particular problems arise when the highest officers of a state, such as the president, ministers, or members of the supreme or constitutional courts are suspected of having committed criminal acts. Not only are there usually special procedures to lift immunity, but there may also be special rules for the competent court. The Strasbourg organs have had to deal with such problems, for example, in cases against Italy[52] and Belgium[53] where the highest courts were involved in first-instance proceedings. As in such cases, the senior members of the judiciary have already been involved in the first-instance proceedings, it is understandable that no further appeal lies—there is simply no higher instance left. Charrier misunderstands the exception when he suggests that in France there is, even from the 'highest tribunal', an appeal to the *Cour de Cassation*.[54]

Switzerland made a reservation in this respect when ratifying the Covenant;[55] however, this was unnecessary because there did exist a remedy against judgments

---

[48] *Reinthaler* v. *Austria* Application 19360/92; see also *Putz* v. *Austria* Application 18892/91 where the fine was higher.   [49] General Comment No. 13, § 17.
[50] The same view is held by McGoldrick (2001) 10.50.   [51] Nowak (1993) Art. 14 N 67.
[52] *Crociani and Others* v. *Italy* Applications 8603/79, 8722/79, 8723/79, and 8729/79.
[53] *Coëme and others* v. *Belgium*.   [54] Charrier (2002) Art. 2 Protocol No. 7 N 3.
[55] See Haefliger and Schürmann (1999) 365, n. 68.

of the Federal Criminal Court, even though its scope was limited. Legislative change has made the reservation redundant.[56]

C. Conviction on Appeal after Acquittal

If one were to apply Article 2 § 1 of the Protocol or the corresponding Articles of the other instruments literally, an awkward situation could arise in the event that a person acquitted at first instance, was then convicted following an appeal by the prosecution. A third instance would be called for. If a person was originally charged with three crimes, acquitted at first instance, convicted on one count on appeal and acquitted on two counts, it is possible that at third instance that person is convicted for the first time for the second count. That would mean that there must be a fourth instance. The example may be slightly far-fetched, but the Convention makes it clear that the right to a remedy is a right to one appeal only.

This is certainly not satisfactory and it may be significant that the Court shows some reluctance in applying it.[57] A somewhat atypical example was *Lannto*. The applicants had been convicted by the District Court, but on appeal the Court of Appeal held that the District Court had not been impartial. Instead of quashing the judgment, however, it simply passed a new one convicting the applicants for a second time. Leave to appeal was refused. The Court rejected the application on the basis that leave-to-appeal proceedings satisfy the requirements of Article 2.[58] It would have been preferable, in my view, to rule either that the applicant had already had access to an appeal and that the guarantee did not grant a third degree of jurisdiction[59] or to have ruled that the District Court's judgment could be regarded as null and void, and that the third exception of paragraph 2 applied. In fact, the applicants were deprived of one instance and respect for the administration of justice ought to have dictated that the judgment be quashed. An entirely typical case against Italy was dealt with—as an *obiter dictum*—in an analogous way.[60] Finally, in two cases the exception was expressly applied.[61]

The HRC has taken a much more liberal approach in interpreting Article 14 § 5 of the ICCPR. It found that wherever the domestic law provided for a third level of appeal, access to that remedy must be granted effectively. In *Henry* v. *Jamaica* the further appeal was rendered ineffective because the court of appeal had failed to produce reasons for its judgment.[62]

---

[56] On the reservations made by other European countries, see Nowak (1993) Art. 14 N 69.

[57] See also van Dijk and van Hoof (1998) 687 who rightly stress that the exception will not apply if the first acquittal was pronounced by a body other than a tribunal.

[58] *Lannto* v. *Finland* Application 27665/95.

[59] The French title (added with the adoption of Protocol No. 11) is '*Droit à un double degré de juridiction en matière pénale*'. It is not clear why Renucci (2002) N 139 believes that the text does not expressly guarantee this.   [60] *Emmanuello* v. *Italy* Application 35791/97.

[61] *Botten* v. *Norway* Application 16206/90; and *Partouche* v. *France* Application 25906/94.

[62] *Henry* v. *Jamaica*; see also *Little* v. *Jamaica*. Similar problems with delays can be found in *Earl Pratt and Ivan Morgan* v. *Jamaica*, § 222 and *Pinkey* v. *Canada*, § 101.

Chapter 15

The Right to Compensation for Wrongful Conviction

I. THE TEXTS

When a person has by a final decision been convicted of a criminal offence and when subsequently his conviction has been reversed or he has been pardoned on the ground that a new or newly discovered fact shows conclusively that there has been a miscarriage of justice, the person who has suffered punishment as a result of such conviction shall be compensated according to law, unless it is proved that the non-disclosure of the unknown fact in time is wholly or partly attributable to him.

ICCPR, Art. 14 § 6

When a person has by a final decision been convicted of a criminal offence and when subsequently his conviction has been reversed, or he has been pardoned, on the ground that a new or newly discovered fact shows conclusively that there has been a miscarriage of justice, the person who has suffered punishment as a result of such conviction shall be compensated according to the law or the practice of that State concerned, unless it is proved that the non-disclosure of the unknown fact in time is wholly or partly attributable to him.

ECHR, Protocol No. 7, Art. 3

Every person has the right to be compensated in accordance with the law in the event he has been sentenced by a final judgment through a miscarriage of justice.

ACHR, Art. 10

There are only slight differences between the text of the ICCPR and that of the ECHR. The European version puts the words 'or he has been pardoned' between commas and adds to the reference to 'the law' the alternative 'the practice of that State concerned'. The American text is more concise. It refers neither to domestic law nor to the requirement that there be a finding that there was a miscarriage of justice. This could be misinterpreted as suggesting that it applies to the international authorities. This would hardly reflect the meaning of the ACHR as it would give the IACommHR and IACtHR the function of a court competent to reopen proceedings. The conciseness of the text probably reflects the belief that the additional aspects of the other instruments were, in any case, implicitly contained in Article 10.

II. THE ORIGINS OF THE GUARANTEE

The right to compensation was first introduced in connection with the protection of personal liberty, in other words, it was limited to cases of 'wrongful arrest'.[1] The first proposal that an analogous right be established for cases involving a miscarriage of justice came from Mr Ingles (Philippines) at the fifth session of the Commission on Human Rights in May 1949[2] and became the subject of repeated debate. According to Nowak it was 'the most controversial provision' in Article 14.[3] The proposed text stated: 'Every one who has undergone punishment as a result of an erroneous conviction of crime shall have an enforceable right to compensation. This right shall accrue to the heirs of a person executed by virtue of an erroneous sentence'. Mrs Roosevelt objected because she believed—mistakenly—that the issue was already covered by the right to compensation for unlawful deprivation of liberty.

The discussion continued at the fifth session and finally the US and the Philippines jointly agreed to drop the proposal. A vote had, however, already been scheduled and a majority voted in favour of keeping it.[4]

At the sixth session discussions centred around a new French draft proposal: 'In any case where by a final decision a person has been convicted of a criminal offence and where subsequently a new or newly discovered fact shows conclusively that there has been a miscarriage of justice, the person who has suffered punishment as a result of such conviction shall have an enforceable right to compensation'.[5] Again the US proposed to delete the guarantee because Mrs Roosevelt thought that it was difficult to implement and of minor importance. One of the subjects for discussion was whether to set out specific criteria to define a miscarriage of justice requiring compensation. Such a course of action would most probably have had an influence on the national law on reopening proceedings in the Contracting States. The Philippines, for example, proposed to restrict the operation of the provision to cases where the real perpetrator of the crime confessed or where it had been proven that the offence could not have been committed, for example, where the alleged victim of a murder was shown to be alive. Following a proposal by Afghanistan, the words 'according to law' were added.

Continuing the discussion at the eighth session of the Commission, Mrs Roosevelt proposed limiting the provision to cases where there had been an acquittal at a new trial. During this session a clause denying a convicted person deemed to be responsible for the miscarriage of justice the right to compensation was introduced, as was, upon a proposal from the Belgian delegate, Mr Nisot, the possibility of a pardon.[6]

---

[1] Nowak (1993) Art. 14 N 70; Weissbrodt (2001) 26.   [2] Weissbrodt (2001) 49.
[3] Nowak (1993) Art. 14 N 70.   [4] Weissbrodt (2001) 53.   [5] Ibid., 59–60.
[6] Ibid., 67 et seq.

When the draft was voted on at the General Assembly, there was a proposal, introduced by Argentina, the Netherlands, and the United Kingdom to delete the entire paragraph. It passed, however, with a clear majority.[7]

Although the draft had been discussed several times before the ECHR was created, no parallel guarantee was adopted at that time. In fact, the attitude of the Member States was rather ambivalent and, as is shown by the proposals to drop this right to compensation, it was by no means certain that such a guarantee would figure in the final version of the ICCPR. It is also possible that the drafters of the ECHR had in mind that the Court would have the possibility to grant compensation for violations of the ECHR[8]—an option not available under the ICCPR. So far, there is no indication that the provision answered an urgent need.

III. THE PURPOSE AND SIGNIFICANCE OF THE GUARANTEE

The purpose of the right to compensation does not raise any problems and has even been referred to as being 'rather self-explanatory'.[9] A person who has clearly suffered gross injustice ought to be compensated in order to re-establish the balance of justice. In this sense it is little more than a branch of tort law.

An examination of the drafting process of Article 14 § 6 demonstrates not just ambivalence but also inconsistency in the treatment of the provision. At one point it was said that not to grant a right to compensation to the heirs of a person wrongfully executed 'would be a flagrant injustice',[10] while on the other hand there were repeated proposals that it be dropped altogether.

In my view, it is precarious to legitimize the right to compensation by labelling it a human right. Unlike other human rights which can be used to seek acknowledgement that a wrong has been done, the right to compensation only becomes relevant after the original mistake has been recognized and rectified by way of an acquittal. In this sense it resembles the cream on the top of the dessert rather than the dessert itself. Is it really an essential requirement for the preservation of human dignity that financial compensation be awarded?

The case-law confirms this scepticism. As far as I can see, there has never been a finding of a violation under either the ICCPR, the ECHR, or the ACHR. All eight applications to the European Commission were declared inadmissible.[11]

---

[7] Weissbrodt (2001) 73; for details, see Nowak (1993) Art. 14 N 70.
[8] ECHR, Art. 50, now Art. 41.
[9] Ovey and White (2002) 197.
[10] Mr Nisot (Belgium) and Mr Juvigny (France), quoted in Weissbrodt (2001) 68.
[11] *B* v. *Germany* Application 14219/88; *FN* v. *France* Application 18725/91; *Gharib* v. *Suisse* Application 24198/94; *YM* v. *France* Application 24948/94; *Pechanec* v. *Slovak Republic* Application 30904/96; *Stamoulakatos* v. *Greece* Application 42155/98; *Georgiou* v. *Greece* Application 45138/98; *Nakov* v. *Former Yugoslav Republic of Macedonia* Application 68286/01.

There is only one reported case under the ICCPR, but similarly no violation was found.[12]

IV. THE PREREQUISITES OF THE RIGHT TO COMPENSATION FOR WRONGFUL CONVICTION

Van Dijk and van Hoof set out seven prerequisites which must be fulfilled in order for the right to compensation under Article 14 § 5 of the ICCPR and Article 3 of Protocol No. 7 to the ECHR to arise.[13] On my count there are nine, as set out below.

A. Convicted of a Criminal Offence

The rules under consideration use the term 'criminal offence'. In the absence of any indication to the contrary this must be interpreted in the same way as the notion of 'criminal charge' in Articles 14 § 1 of the ICCPR and 6 § 1 of the ECHR.[14]

Consequently compensation is required both in cases concerning petty offences and in those which in domestic law would not be classified as belonging to the 'criminal law'.[15] Several countries, for example, Belgium or France, do not allow for a *'révision'* in cases involving a *'contravention'*, which make up the lowest class of offences.[16]

B. A Conviction

The person concerned must have been 'convicted'. This term is broad enough to include cases where the accused has agreed to pay a fine rather than face a court hearing or has accepted a plea-bargain. An acquittal following such a fine, plea bargain, or indeed guilty plea would, of course, be quite unusual as it would imply that the criminal charge was based on facts which later turn out to have been erroneously or willingly accepted by the accused.

C. The Conviction Must Have Been Final

There must have been a *final* decision convicting the applicant. A decision is final 'if, according to the traditional expression, it has acquired the force of *res judicata*. This is the case when it is irrevocable, that is to say when no further ordinary remedies are available or when the parties have exhausted such remedies

---

[12] *Paavo Muhonen* v. *Finland*, § 164.
[13] Van Dijk and van Hoof (1998) 688. Art. 10 of the ACHR being clearly less specific will not be commented on.   [14] See also van Dijk and van Hoof (1998) 688; Nowak (1993) N 73.
[15] See further Chapter 2 above.   [16] Pradel (2002) N 498.

or have permitted the time-limit to expire without availing themselves of them'.[17] It should be noted that there is in fact one further possibility, namely the case where a person withdraws an appeal which he or she had lodged.

This definition is generally accepted.[18] Frowein and Peukert's assertion that a conviction is final when all remedies have been exhausted is wrong; this is obviously not required.[19]

This element is not hugely relevant but it does serve to exclude cases in which a person is acquitted in the course of appeal proceedings. This is not entirely satisfactory, because it is certainly possible that the conviction at first instance constituted a miscarriage of justice and that the appeal has brought new facts to light. In such a case, even if the person had started to serve a custodial sentence, there is no right to compensation. Similarly, a person who, after having been detained on remand, is acquitted or not even indicted will have no ('human') right to compensation. The discussion surrounding this guarantee has shown that it can be regarded as a marginal, barely legitimated fundamental right. This may explain its evident narrowness.

The Explanatory Report mentions one exception where the reversal of a judgment following an appeal may give rise to compensation.[20] This involves the very peculiar 'appeal out of time' which is found, for example, in English law. In fact, despite its name this must be regarded as a specific kind of remedy which allows for proceedings to be reopened.

D. The Punishment

The person concerned must have 'suffered punishment'. No right to compensation arises out of a *mera condemnatio*, a conviction without sanction.[21] What about measures taken to protect public safety? If the measure consists of confinement to a mental hospital, no compensation is due. If, however, it involves imprisonment 'at Her Majesty's pleasure',[22] compensation is due because this is a *de facto* deprivation of liberty which also, to some extent, serves retributive purposes.

E. The Execution of the Sentence

The sentence must have been at least partly served[23]—this element is not mentioned by van Dijk and van Hoof, but is clearly set out in the Explanatory Report. The person must 'have *suffered* punishment as a result of such

---

[17] Commentary on Article 1.a: Explanatory Report of the European Convention on the International Validity of Criminal Judgments, publication of the Council of Europe, 1970, 22, which is also quoted in para. 22 of the Explanatory Report to Protocol No. 7.

[18] Van Dijk and van Hoof (1998) 668; Esposito (2001) 953; Merrills and Robertson (2001) 266; Charrier (2002) 531; Harris, O'Boyle, and Warbrick (1995) 568 et seq.

[19] Frowein and Peukert (1996) Protocol No. 7 Art. 3 N 1.   [20] Explanatory Report, § 22.

[21] Van Dijk and van Hoof (1998) 688.

[22] cf. the cases of *Hussain* v. *United Kingdom* and *Singh* v. *United Kingdom*.

[23] Esposito (2001), 954; Nowak (1993) Art. 14 N 77; Villiger (1999) N 663.

conviction'.[24] In fact, there will be no suffering as long as the sanction remains on paper. But what does execution of a sentence mean in the case of probation or a suspended sentence? In my view this is also a form of serving a sentence. The wrongfully convicted person will certainly be affected not least by the fact that the possibility of a revocation hangs, like Damocles' sword, over him. This certainly has the potential to create anxiety and suffering. Therefore, even a suspended sentence must be sufficient to justify compensation under Article 14 § 5 of the ICCPR and Article 3 of Protocol No. 7, although it may be much less than in the case of actual imprisonment.

F. The Decision to Convict Must Have Been Set Aside

The right to compensation is justified by the existence of a miscarriage of justice, a fact which leaves the original judgment open to serious criticism. It is not sufficient, therefore, for the mistake to have come to light. Even if a person thought to have murdered reappears, this will be insufficient in itself to entitle the person wrongly convicted of murder to compensation. The person concerned, possibly the heir or next of kin if he or she cannot do so herself or himself, will have to start proceedings in order to get the conviction formally set aside. This may appear overly formalistic if the facts are as drastic as those in the example above, but most cases are likely to be less clear and subject to dispute. It must be accepted therefore that the human-rights instruments make the right to compensation dependent upon these formal requirements.

What is somewhat surprising is the fact that pardon is mentioned along with the setting aside of a conviction which must, of course, be the work of a judicial authority.[25] The reason is that each state has a different system for dealing with the situation where new facts show that a conviction is unsafe. Although, as a rule, pardon is an instrument of clemency and ought not be used in any way that could be regarded as criticism of the courts, it appears that certain countries use it to correct flagrant miscarriages of justice.[26]

In the case of *Muhonen*[27] a conscientious objector had been sentenced to imprisonment because the authorities were not convinced of his motivation for avoiding military service. He was later pardoned. The HRC came to the conclusion, however, that he was not entitled to compensation because the pardon did not constitute a reversal of the judgment but was simply a measure of clemency.

G. The Reversal Must be Based on New Facts

A further restrictive condition is that the quashing of the judgment must be based on new or newly discovered facts, *propter nova*. In domestic criminal-procedure

---

[24] Explanatory Report, § 22 (emphasis added).
[25] See also Koering-Joulin (1995) Art. 3, 1091.
[26] Van Dijk and van Hoof (1998) 689; Nowak (1993) Art. 14 N 74.
[27] *Paavo Muhonen v. Finland*, § 164.

law, this is not the only reason for reopening proceedings. Other grounds include, for instance, the discovery that the judgment was influenced by a criminal act, for example, corruption on the part of a judge, public officer, witness, expert, or perjury, or the use of forged documents. Another possible reason would be the existence of another judgment which is irreconcilable with the one at issue.[28]

What if new evidence such as a witness, document, or DNA analysis appears which serves to exclude the convicted person as the perpetrator of the crime? In my view no difference can sensibly be made between the appearance of new facts and new evidence. New evidence must be regarded as equivalent to new facts and a right to compensation will arise when the convicted person is acquitted for the latter reason.

H. No Responsibility for Non-disclosure

In order to ensure the respect of the principle '*nemo audietur propriam turpi-dudinem allegans*' (no one can obtain an advantage due to a mistake he made himself), the guarantee excludes the right to compensation in cases where the convicted person is responsible for having withheld evidence or concealed the facts which finally led to the quashing of the judgment. This could occur for instance where a person gave a false alibi in order to conceal something, for example, where a married man wanted to conceal the fact that he was visiting his mistress at the time of the crime.[29]

I. The Establishment of Innocence

Finally, the new facts must have established that the person was innocent—it is not enough that they lead to prove the existence of mitigating circumstances.[30] Compensation is due, however, if there has been an acquittal in one of several counts on which the person was convicted, for example, one of two murders.

It would also be insufficient if the new facts were to tip the balance of the evidence so that, when taken into account, there is an acquittal in application of the guarantee set out in Article 6 § 2, *in dubio pro reo*.[31] One may wonder whether this is quite compatible with that principle.[32] One has to bear in mind, however, that the Convention does not grant any right to compensation in the case of an acquittal, whether *in dubio* or because the innocence of the accused has been established. Having regard to the rather extraordinary character of the right to compensation, the restrictions must be accepted—they go along with the other defects of the guarantee.

Still, a situation where the judge in effect says to a defendant in proceedings which have been reopened: 'Well, the new facts really increase the doubts about

[28] Cf. Pradel (2002) N 498.   [29] See also Merrills and Robertson (2001) 267.
[30] Explanatory Report, § 25.   [31] Ibid. See also Merrills and Robertson (2001) 267.
[32] I have expressed doubts in Trechsel (1988) 206.

your guilt, so I shall acquit you; but you will not get any compensation because it is in no way established that you are innocent', is hard to reconcile with the spirit of the Convention. It is possible that in such a case the HCR and/or the Court would be prepared to 'correct' the text of the guarantee and give precedence to the presumption of innocence.

Finally, in this context it may be recalled that the right to compensation does not have any connection with the right to a retrial which only exists in domestic law.

V. THE RIGHT TO COMPENSATION

A. The Substance of the Compensation

The texts do not give any indication as to what form the compensation ought to take. It seems to be assumed, however, that it will be mainly of a pecuniary nature. In the first place, substantive damages must be paid. Here, the substantial case-law of the ECHR provides some guidelines, although the 'just satisfaction' afforded under international law does not necessarily follow the same pattern as the compensation referred to here—it tends to be rather more restrictive. If the sentence was just a fine, the sum must be repaid with interest; the same, of course, must go for any costs and the expenses incurred by the defence. This is not sufficient in cases where the person has been detained—the compensation will have to take into account the damage caused during this period, such as loss of earnings.

In addition, compensation for non-pecuniary damage is due.[33] Here the example of the Court must *not* be followed. It often concludes that the finding of a violation constitutes sufficient satisfaction.[34] This finding cannot be applied on the domestic level under this guarantee.

B. The Beneficiary of the Right to Compensation

At one point during the drafting process a specific right was inserted to provide for compensation for the heirs of persons executed after a miscarriage of justice. It was later removed. The text could have been drafted in such a way as to have avoided such a lacuna. The right could have been provided for persons who had suffered *from* or *under* the punishment. This would have included spouses and other members of the family of the ex-convict. However, the wording 'suffered punishment' clearly excludes this. Only someone who has been wrongly convicted is entitled to compensation.

---

[33] Frowein and Peukert (1996) Art. 3 Prot. 7 N 3; Trechsel (1988) 206; Villiger (1999) N 693.
[34] e.g. *Benthem* v. *Netherlands; Brogan and others* v. *United Kingdom.*

C. According to the Law (or the Practice) of the State Concerned

Some discussion has arisen in relation to the reference to the fact that the compensation must be in accordance with the law. It is quite obvious that the reference here has an entirely different meaning from that in those Articles which require that any exceptions to fundamental rights have a basis in law. Here, the states are obliged to introduce legislation which provides for and regulates a right to compensation. The HRC has expressly reminded states of this duty.[35]

What it means is that the states are permitted to regulate the manner in which the provision is to be applied. However, they are not entirely free in doing so, and they must certainly protect the very essence of the right to compensation.[36]

---

[35] Nowak (1993) Art. 14 N 78 with reference in n. 210.
[36] Charrier (2002) 361; Esposito (2001) 954.

Chapter 16

The Protection Against Double Jeopardy

I. INTRODUCTION

The guarantee of *ne bis in idem* is rather complex. In 2002 the Court observed that its case-law on this subject was not especially well developed,[1] a fact which can be explained not only by the small number of cases which have come before the Strasbourg organs,[2] but also by some obvious contradictions in the jurisprudence. This chapter will open with a comparison of the texts of the different normative instruments followed by a general overview of the development of the guarantee as a human right. Thereafter the aim and purpose of the right, its relationship with Article 6 § 1, the scope of its application, and the exceptions to the principle will be discussed.

A. The Texts

No one shall be liable to be tried or punished again for an offence for which he has already been finally convicted or acquitted in accordance with the law and penal procedure of each country.

ICCPR, Art. 14 § 7

Right not to be tried or punished twice[3]

1. No one shall be liable to be tried or punished again in criminal proceedings under the jurisdiction of the same State for an offence for which he has already been finally acquitted or convicted in accordance with the law and penal procedure of that State.
2. The provisions of the preceding paragraph shall not prevent the reopening of the case in accordance with the law and penal procedure of the State concerned, if there is evidence of new or newly discovered facts, or if there has been a fundamental defect in the previous proceedings which could affect the outcome of the case.

---

[1] *Göktan v. France*, § 44: '*La Cour note, en premier lieu, que sa jurisprudence relative à la règle non bis in idem n'est pas très fournie*'.
[2] The Court has had to rule on this principle in just six cases, five other cases were struck off the list.   [3] The title was introduced by Protocol No. 11.

3. No derogation from this Article shall be made under Article 15 of the Convention.

ECHR, Protocol No. 7, Art. 4

An accused person acquitted by a nonappealable judgment shall not be subjected to a new trial for the same cause.

ACHR, Art. 8 § 4

Although the essence of the provisions is the same, there are quite a number of differences between the texts.[4] Only the ECHR, for example, places the guarantee among those that cannot be derogated from, even in a state of emergency—this may be explained by the fact that the other two instruments have integrated the guarantee in the more general context of the right to a fair trial which, as such, does not enjoy that enhanced protection under the ECHR.[5] Furthermore, only the ECHR expressly mentions exceptions to the principle.

B. The Origins of the Guarantee

The principle guaranteed by Article 4 of Protocol No. 7 has several names. While on the European continent the Latin expressions '*ne bis in idem*' or '*non bis in idem*' are normally used (the full maxim being '*bis de eadem re non sit actio*'[6]), in common-law countries a number of different terms including *res judicata*,[7] double jeopardy,[8] *autrefois acquit*,[9] as well as *ne bis in idem* are employed.

The guarantee made a late appearance into the respective international normative instruments on human rights. It was absent from the original texts of both the ECHR[10] and the ICCPR. The question as to its inclusion in the latter was first raised in the Human Rights Commission charged with drafting the Covenant by the Government of the Philippines in 1951, but this did not provoke a response and there is no mention of the principle in the draft of 1954. Later, Italy and Japan initiated another proposal; their text was somewhat amended and then introduced jointly by Canada, Ceylon, Iran, Italy, Japan, Jordan, and Pakistan.[11]

The issue was hotly debated by the Third Committee of the General Assembly and indeed it has remained controversial. This is to some extent evidenced by the variations between the respective texts.

---

[4] See also Spangher (2001), Art. 14, N 80.   [5] On this issue, see Stavros (1992) 343.
[6] Roxin (1998) § 50 B I. 1; Hauser and Schweri (2002) § 84 N 17.
[7] e.g. Scotland; see Walker and Walker (1964) § 50, quoting Dickson (1887) § 385. When *res judicata* applies in a criminal case, the accused is said to have 'tholed his assize'.
[8] e.g. England and USA.   [9] e.g. Canada; see Pradel (2002) N 501.
[10] It was introduced in 1984 by way of Article 4 of the Seventh Protocol which came into force for certain Member States on 1 Nov. 1988.
[11] Weissbrodt (2001) 63, 74; Nowak (1993), Art. 14 N 80, n. 213.

II. THE AIM AND PURPOSE OF THE GUARANTEE

Throughout its tortuous case-law the Court has consistently used a standard formula for the aim of the Article: 'to prohibit the repetition of criminal proceedings that have been concluded by a final decision'.[12] This is a rather banal statement with little jurisprudential substance.

If we look at the issue more closely and from a comparative perspective, we find that the principle fulfils different aims and is subject to different expectations in different jurisdictions. In the common-law tradition, the protection against double jeopardy is mainly seen as an individual right, therefore a retrial does not appear to constitute a threat if it operates in favour of the convicted person.[13]

In more recent times, however, other aspects of the principle, such as its role in promoting finality, have also been acknowledged in England, where a thorough reform of the law on double jeopardy is currently being discussed.[14]

On the European continent, *ne bis in idem* has traditionally been understood as serving two purposes. Apart from the protection of the individual it is also seen as an important guarantee for legal certainty.[15] In French 'finally' (*jugement définitif*) as used in Article 4 means that the judgment has attained *'l'autorité de la chose jugée'*, i.e. the authority of the judgment itself is at stake—as well as the authority of the court which passed that judgment. A court is not independent and impartial within the meaning of Article 6 § 1 unless its decisions are binding on other organs of the state, including other courts,[16] with the exception, of course, of appeals to a court of second or third instance.

While it might be said that the first aspect is the only one likely to have any relevance under the Convention, the second aspect should not be overlooked. To the extent that it protects the independence of the judge, it is not at all devoid of 'human-rights substance'.

The difference between these two approaches is not merely academic or theoretical. Admittedly for the finality aspect, it is definitely irrelevant, whether the first judgment has acquitted or convicted the person 'tried again'. Still, if the second judgment is clearly more lenient than the first, there will be no violation

---

[12] *Gradinger* v. *Austria*, § 53, referring to Application 15963/90, § 68. See also *Franz Fischer* v. *Austria*, § 22; *WF* v. *Austria*, § 7; *Sailer* v. *Austria*, § 53; *Göktan* v. *France*, § 47; *Manasson* v. *Sweden* Application 41265/98, § 95. Strangely, the passage was not introduced into *Oliveira* v. *Switzerland*.
[13] Ovey and White (2002) 196. See also the Scottish authority Hume: 'The prime benefit of absolvitor is, that the panel can never again be challenged or called in question, or made to thole an assize (as our phrase for it is) on the matter or charge that has been tried. The ground of which maxim lies in this obvious and humane consideration, that a person is substantially punished, in being twice reduced to so anxious and humiliating a condition, and standing twice in jeopardy of his life, fame or person' Hume (1844), vol. II, ch. XVII, 465. More recently, the perspective has widened. The Law Commission also recognizes the importance of finality in litigation; Dennis (2000) 940. [14] See in particular Fitzpatrick (2002); Roberts (2002) 393.
[15] Koering-Joulin (1995) 1093; Renucci (2002) N 3950.
[16] Cf. *Benthem* v. *Netherlands*, § 37 et seq.

of the individual rights of an applicant because he or she will not be aggrieved, i.e. will not be able to claim to be a 'victim' within the meaning of Article 34.

Although there would still be a violation of the principle of *res judicata*, a human-rights body would not look at this, because it is not its task to protect general principles of criminal procedure, even if they are of considerable importance. The philosophy according to which *ne bis in idem* also pursues an aim in the public interest means, moreover, that the finding of a violation is regarded as a sanction against the authorities for their negligence during the first proceedings. An example would be a case where a driver was only prosecuted for having been under the influence, as the prosecuting authorities did not realize that another offence, for example, causing bodily harm, was also committed. They are not allowed to 'fire a second shot'—they have missed their chance and their errors will serve to benefit the defendant. In other words, the risk of any mistakes made by the prosecuting authority, or indeed the court, must be borne by the state and must not be remedied at the expense of the individual concerned.[17] The same idea is expressed by Wils who examines the economic justification for the *ne bis in idem* principle.[18]

III. *NE BIS IN IDEM* AS AN ELEMENT OF THE RIGHT TO A FAIR TRIAL?

Under the ICCPR and the IACHR the protection against double jeopardy forms an element of the right to a fair trial. That it has been set out in a separate protocol under the ECHR is due to the fact that it constitutes a later addition to the treaty.

Before the adoption of the Seventh Protocol the question had arisen whether the guarantee could be derived from the general guarantee of the right to a fair trial under Article 6 § 1. Such an extensive and constructive interpretation was made with regard to the protection against self-incrimination. Yet, there is an important difference between that right and the one we are dealing with here. The very fact that the guarantee was expressly introduced in a special additional protocol is indicative of the opinion that it was needed and that, contrary to the guarantee against self-incrimination, it was not covered by Article 6 § 1.[19]

The Commission dealt with this question in a number of admissibility decisions.[20] In some of them it stated clearly that *ne bis in idem* was not covered by Article 6; in others, it left the question open.[21] In my view it cannot entirely

---

[17] Esser (2002) 98; Roxin (1998) § 50 B II. 2. [18] Wils (2003) 138.
[19] Trechsel (1988) 195, 209; Nowak (1985) 240 at 241.
[20] See e.g. Harris, O'Boyle, and Warbrick (1996) Art. 6 N 173; Stavros (1993) 296.
[21] *X* v. *Austria* Application 1519/62; *X* v. *Austria* Application 4212/69; *X* v. *Germany* Application 7680/76; *S* v. *Germany* Application 8945/80, concerning a German citizen who had been punished for a drug offence for which he had already received a lenient sentence in the Netherlands; *X* v. *Netherlands* Application 9433/81.

be excluded that this right constitutes an element of the right to a fair trial, but that would presuppose a much more innovative approach than that of including the protection against self-incrimination. In both Article 14 § 3(g) of the ICCPR and in Article 8 § 2(g) of the IACHR the privilege against self-incrimination figures among the rights of the defence within the meaning of 'fair trial' in criminal proceedings, whereas the protection against double jeopardy is placed in a paragraph of its own. It is not a guarantee which requires a specific quality of the trial, but leads to the consequence that there should be no trial at all in specific circumstances.

Has the question become redundant with the introduction of Protocol No. 7? Starmers implicitly suggests that it has not, as he expects the issue to be determined by the Court.[22] In fact, the issue could arise with regard to countries which have not ratified Protocol No. 7.[23]

Still it is, in my view, extremely unlikely that the Court would satisfy this expectation. In the interpretation of international treaties, as with domestic law, the principle of '*effet utile*' or '*ut res magis valeat quam pereat*' is applied: the interpretation must be such as to avoid rendering redundant part of the existing text.[24] If the Court were to say that the guarantee is already covered by Article 6 this would make Article 4 of the Protocol, in essence, superfluous.

IV. THE SCOPE OF APPLICATION OF THE GUARANTEE

A. Territorial Application

The ECHR makes it very clear that the double-jeopardy principle can only be applied at national level. In other words, from the perspective of the ECHR, a person may legitimately be tried again for an offence which has already been the object of conviction and sentencing in a different state.[25]

The ICCPR is not clear in this respect[26]—Koering-Joulin thought it bore the promise of international application.[27] The Committee, however, opted for the

---

[22] Starmer with Byre (2001) N 8.58.

[23] It is a rather surprising list: Andorra, Belgium, Germany, Liechtenstein, Netherlands, Portugal, Serbia and Montenegro, Spain, Turkey, and the United Kingdom. On the other hand, quite a number of states have made reservations regarding Art. 14 § 3(g) when ratifying the ICCPR: Austria, Denmark, Finland, France, Iceland, Netherlands, Norway, and Sweden. Cf. McGoldrick (1994/2001) N 10.23.   [24] Bernhardt (1963) 96.

[25] *X* v. *Austria* Application 1519/62; *X* v. *Austria* Application 1592/62; *X* v. *Austria* Application 4212/69; *X* v. *Germany* Application 7680/76; *S* v. *Germany* Application 8945/80; *Baragiola* v. *Switzerland* Application 17265/90; *Manzoni* v. *Italy* Application 15521/89; *Gestra* v. *Italy* Application 21072/92.

[26] This was also the conclusion of the Committee of Experts on Human Rights who drafted a report to the Committee of Ministers on *Problems Arising from the Co-existence of the United National Covenants on Human Rights and the European Convention on Human Rights* (Strasbourg, Sept. 1970), Council of Europe Doc. H (70) 7.   [27] Koering-Joulin (1995) 1094.

reasonable solution which corresponds to that of Protocol No. 7.[28] Renucci seems to assume that the rule applies to the relationship between domestic jurisdiction and that of the European Union, where conflicts occur, for example, in the area of competition law.[29] However, there can hardly be any doubt that here we are (still) dealing with two jurisdictions. Generally, it must be recalled that, at the time when the Protocol was drafted (and even more when the Covenant was elaborated), international criminal jurisdiction was practically non-existent. Otherwise, instead of 'State' the term 'jurisdiction' would have to be chosen. Yet, this is an area in which the law is undergoing changes at a breathtaking speed.[30] With the entering into force of the regulation of the European arrest warrant, judgments passed in one Member State are valid for all other Member States. Therefore the European Union will have to be considered as a 'state' as far as the protection against double jeopardy is concerned.

Furthermore, Article 50 of the Charter of Fundamental Rights of the European Union states:

No one shall be liable to be tried or punished again in criminal proceedings for an offence for which he or she has already been finally acquitted or convicted within the Union in accordance with the law.[31]

The Explanatory Notes accompanying the Charter explain that the provision 'corresponds to Article 4 of Protocol No. 7 to the ECHR, but its scope is extended to European Union level between the Courts of the Member States'.[32] Thus the principle applies not only within the jurisdiction of one state but also between the jurisdictions of several Member States.[33] One will recall that the Charter is not (yet) a legally binding document. Still it can be expected that within a few years the guarantee will apply within the EU on both levels: state–EU and state–state.

Leaving aside the very special case of the European Union, it would not be realistic to expect a human-rights instrument to impose upon states a general and global duty to recognize foreign judgments in criminal matters. This is rather obvious with regard to the complexity of the law of international cooperation in criminal matters. Even within the European Union the implementation of the *Corpus Juris* meets with considerable difficulties[34] and German professors of criminal law have launched an appeal against the adoption of the European arrest warrant.

---

[28] *AP* v. *Italy* (ICCPR). See also *AR J* v. *Australia* (ICCPR); Nowak (1993) 273; Spangher (2001) 958; Weissbrodt (2001) 147.

[29] Renucci (2002) N 140, 295. On this subject, see also Esser (2002) 99.

[30] See e.g. Wils (2003).   [31] Art. II-110 of the Constitution of the EU; see also ibid., 135.

[32] Council of the EU, Charter of Fundamental Rights of the European Union: Explanations Relating to the Complete Text of the Charter, Dec. 2000, p. 76 available at www.europarl.eu.int/charter/.   [33] Ibid., 69.

[34] Cf. e.g. the four volumes of Delmas-Marty and Vervaele (eds.) (2000–1); more generally on problems regarding *ne bis in idem* and the EU, see Schomburg (1998).

Further regulation for states belonging to the Council of Europe can be found in a number of important special conventions.[35] However, it must be borne in mind that these all deal with cases where a person is abroad and the state needs cooperation with another state in order to prosecute him or her or when two states cooperate in pursuance of the goal of judging a person or executing a sentence. They are without any bearing in cases where a person who is prosecuted is found in the prosecuting state.

Even if the principle can not always be applied extraterritorially, it would be realistic to expect that any time served or fine paid pursuant to a conviction in another state be taken into account in calculating or executing the second sentence.[36]

B. The Scope of Application *ratione materiae*

In Article 4 of the Protocol we find the expression 'criminal proceedings'/ '*poursuivi pénalement*' which clearly echoes the terms 'criminal charge'/'*accusation en matière pénale*' found in Article 6 § 1. Indeed, these terms are to be understood in the same way.[37] In *Hangl* the applicant alleged that he had been punished twice.[38] In fact, apart from being criminally sanctioned, the applicant had had his driving licence withdrawn for a period of two weeks. The Court simply referred to *Escoubet* where it had held that the immediate withdrawal of the licence constituted a preventative measure for the safety of road users and not a repressive sanction, so that Article 6 did not apply; consequently, said the Court, Article 4 of Protocol No. 7 did not apply either.[39] Similarly, in *Göktan* the question arose whether deprivation of liberty with a view to enforcing (or rather replacing) the payment of a confiscation order ('*contrainte par corps*') constituted a criminal sanction.[40] The Court again referred to a previous case where the question had been answered in the context of Article 6.[41] Charrier expresses the fear that governments (he has the French Government in mind) might abuse this limitation by having recourse to measures of security such as the expulsion of foreigners considered dangerous, after they have served their sentence.[42] However, expulsion is certainly not a sanction which calls for the

---

[35] European Convention on Extradition of 13 Dec. 1957, ETS No. 24, Art. 9; European Convention on the International Validity of Criminal Judgments of 28 May 1970, ETS No. 70, Arts. 53–5; European Convention on the Transfer of Proceedings in Criminal Matters of 15 May 1972, ETS No. 73, Arts. 35–7.

[36] The suggestion is also made by Stavros (1993) 298 and is widely accepted.

[37] See also Charrier (2002) 352; Esser (2002) 95; Harris, O'Boyle, and Warbrick (1995) 569; van Dijk and van Hoof (1998) 690; Wils (2003) 134.

[38] *Hangl* v. *Austria* Application 38716/97.

[39] *Escoubet* v. *Belgium*, § 32 et seq.; see also *Mulot* v. *France* Application 37211/97.

[40] *Göktan* v. *France*, § 44.

[41] *Jamil* v. *France*, § 32; cf. also *Welch* v. *United Kingdom*, §§ 27 et seq. where the question was discussed in the context of Art. 7.　　　　　　　　　　　　　　　[42] Charrier (2002) 252.

guarantees of Article 6 etc., as can be implied *e contrario* from Article 1 of Protocol No. 7. There is no risk of a violation of *ne bis in idem*.

As the field of application *ratione materia* in relation to the protection against double jeopardy is the same as that under Article 6, reference can be made here to what has been explained above in this respect and there is no need for further elaboration.

V. THE FIRST TRIAL

The operation of *ne bis in idem* presupposes a first trial which, according to the text of both the Convention and the Covenant, must fulfil two prerequisites: It must have led to an acquittal or a conviction and it must be final. The words 'in accordance with the law and penal procedure of that State', which are common to both instruments, also call for comment.

A. Acquittal or Conviction

The texts of both Article 4 of Protocol No. 7 to the ECHR and Article 14 § 7 of the ICCPR seem to be strict: the proceedings at first instance must have ended with a court judgment acquitting or convicting the applicant. In fact, the case of a mistrial resulting from a hung jury will not preclude the reopening of the proceedings.[43] In *Smirnova and Smirnova* the Court had to examine a complaint that the double-jeopardy principle had been violated by the reopening of proceedings which had earlier been discontinued. It declared this complaint inadmissible: 'The discontinuance of criminal proceedings by a public prosecutor did not amount to either conviction or an acquittal, and therefore Article 4 of Protocol No. 7 finds no application'.[44]

In practice, the term 'judgment' is necessarily interpreted with some flexibility. Thus, in *Oliveira* the principle applied even though the first 'judgment' which sentenced the applicant to a fine of 200 CHF had been issued by the Zurich District Office ('*Statthalteramt*'),[45] an authority which could in no way be regarded as a judge. Still, in this respect the judgment merits full approval because the 'judgment', which was in fact a transactional fine comparable to that in the *Deweer* case,[46] became final as the applicant failed to ask for a trial before a court.

In my opinion, the question must be addressed in view of the second element, the 'final' character of the decision. It will depend upon the way in which the domestic law deals with the decision in question. If domestic law allows for the proceedings to be reopened, after a decision not to prosecute has been made, that decision does not fall to be considered as 'final' in the sense of the Convention

---

[43] Pradel (2002) N 501.

[44] *Yelena Pavlovna Smirnova and Irina Pavlovna Smirnova* v. *Russia* Applications 46133/99 and 48183/99, § 3.   [45] *Oliveira* v. *Switzerland*, §§ 9, 10.

[46] *Deweer* v. *Belgium*.

or Covenant. However, if the domestic legislation says that the decision is 'final', it ought to be regarded as an acquittal within the meaning of the international guarantee. In fact, it cannot be the task of the Court to deny protection which the domestic law would grant.[47] Charrier, writing from a French perspective, refers to '*une ordonnance mettant fin à une information, qu'il s'agisse d'un non-lieu ou d'une déclaration de non-culpabilité*'.[48] As a matter of fact, in *Gradinger* the Court did not apply a very demanding test as to the form of an 'acquittal'. In this case, the applicant had first been charged with causing death by negligence. He was convicted but found guilty only of the ordinary offence, not of the qualified offence of being intoxicated to a degree of a minimum of 0.8‰. The fact that the court had rejected the qualification and the more serious offence was regarded as being tantamount to an acquittal although it is not even mentioned in the operative part of the judgment[49] and despite the fact that on the continent, only the operative part of a judgment can attain the quality of *res judicata*, not the reasoning.

Gradinger also illustrates the fact that the expression 'acquittal' ('*autrefois acquit*') must not be read in too literal a sense. The guarantee also applies where a person who has already been convicted faces another trial for aggravated charges. Article 8 § 4 of the IACHR limits the right to those persons who have been 'acquitted'—this ought to be interpreted as including persons convicted of a lesser crime or convicted of and sanctioned to a more lenient penalty.

B. The 'Final Character' of the Decision

Ne bis in idem presupposes that the first decision has attained a definite character, i.e. that it has become *res judicata*.[50] Otherwise there would be a contradiction between paragraphs 2 and 4 of Protocol No. 7.[51] The link between these two guarantees leads to the definition of 'final': an acquittal or a conviction is final where there is no further possibility of appeal.[52] There are thus four possible scenarios:

- The domestic law does not provide a right to appeal; in the present context it is irrelevant whether the offence belongs to one of the categories for which an appeal is not required under Article 2 § 2 of Protocol No. 7;
- all appeals have been exhausted;
- the time limit for an appeal has expired and no appeal was filed; or
- an appeal was first filed but later withdrawn or there was a waiver of right.

---

[47] Cf. ECHR, Art. 53.   [48] Charrier (2002) 352.
[49] *Gradinger* v. *Austria*, §§ 8, 14, and 55.   [50] Van Dijk and van Hoof (1998) 691.
[51] ICCPR, Art. 14 §§ 5 and 7 or ACHR, Art. 8 §§ 2(7) and 4.
[52] Charrier (2002), 352; Ovey and White (2002), 196; Nowak (1993), 272. See also the explanatory notes accompanying the Protocol which refer to the European Convention on the International Validity of Criminal Judgments which states that a decision is final 'if according to the traditional expression, it has acquired the force of res judicata. This is the case when it is irrevocable, that is to say when no further ordinary remedies are available or when the parties themselves have exhausted such remedies or have permitted the time limit to expire without availing themselves of them', Article 1.a, Explanatory Report of the European Convention on the International Validity of Criminal Judgments, publication of the Council of Europe, 22.

The details such as time limits, the need to give reasons etc., are determined by domestic law[53] but it is not the terminology which is decisive. In Switzerland, for example, legal force ('*Rechtskraft*') is attained after exhaustion of all cantonal remedies.[54] However, the judgment can often be the subject of an appeal to the Federal Court. Therefore, in the light of international human-rights law such cantonal judgments are not 'final'. In practice, this is of little interest because the time limit for the federal appeal is short. New proceedings would hardly be introduced during that interval.

In my opinion, there is a very simple test which indicates whether we are faced with an ordinary remedy that would prevent the judgment from becoming final, or another remedy, namely the existence of a time limit.[55] Appeals which are not tied to the decision by a strict temporal limitation cannot prevent it from becoming *res judicata*. Otherwise legal certainty would suffer intolerable damage.

The reference to *res judicata* also means that there is 'no prohibition . . . on the prosecution right of appeal'.[56]

C. 'In Accordance with the Law and Penal Procedure of that State'

The words 'in accordance with the law and penal procedure of that State' were added to the ICCPR following a proposal from the Ecuadorian representative, Mr Romero, who feared that the terms 'finally convicted or acquitted' might be interpreted too broadly (it is not quite clear to me what this means). He stressed that the qualification only applied to the words 'finally convicted or acquitted',[57] and the amendment was adopted by a narrow majority.[58]

The meaning of this passage is still rather unclear. It may have been misunderstood, for example, by Koering-Joulin who relates it to the words 'conviction' and 'acquittal' and suggests that these must have been lawful.[59] However, this can hardly be correct. The very essence of the guarantee is that judgments become final once they have acquired legal force, even if they are not entirely 'lawful', i.e. even if certain errors of fact and/or law have occurred. If it were otherwise, the effect of *res judicata* would be lost.

These words simply stress that the conditions for a judgment to become final are set out exclusively in domestic law. Nowak's suggestion, that they might also be interpreted as limiting the rule to judgments emanating from the same state is not really convincing, especially in view of the express formulation of this exception in the European Convention.[60]

---

[53] Spangher (2001) 959.
[54] Hauser and Schweri (2001) § 84 N 5; Schmid (2004) N 585.
[55] See also van Dijk and van Hoof (1998) 691.   [56] Dennis (2000) 937.
[57] Weissbrodt (2001) 75.   [58] Nowak (1993) 272.
[59] Koering-Joulin (1995) 1093.   [60] Nowak (1993) 272/3.

VI. THE SECOND TRIAL

A person finally acquitted or convicted must not be 'tried or punished again'.[61] What does the formula 'tried' and 'punished' mean?

There is certainly a violation if a new judgment is passed, unless it is clearly more lenient than the original one. The difference must be such as to compensate the hardship caused by a second trial. Yet, there is more, as the text does not say 'nobody shall be tried . . . again', but 'no one shall be liable to be tried . . . again'. In French, there is no equivalent to 'liable to', the text is simply *'poursuivi ou puni'*. The violation occurs as soon as the person *'autrefois aquit'* or *'autrefois convict'* again becomes the object of a criminal prosecution.

According to the case-law of the Commission and the Court, the provision 'does not . . . apply before new proceedings have been opened'.[62] This is somewhat surprising. Should the provision not apply from the very moment that the first decision has become final? In my view, the wording of that passage is defective. It would have been more correct to say that there will be a violation only on the commencement of a new prosecution.

However, the unfortunate formulation must be read in the context of the case at issue, *Gradinger*. The question was whether the Commission and Court were competent to examine the complaint. The new proceedings had started before the Protocol had entered into force for Austria, but ended after this had happened. The Government had claimed that they were not yet bound by Protocol No. 7. It was right to affirm competence *ratione temporis* because the violation continues for the duration of the new proceedings, i.e. until the final judgment.

There is no justification for introducing a new notion in this respect—the criterion must be the same as that applied in relation to Article 6; the person concerned must be 'substantially affected' by the activity of the authorities preparing for new proceedings.[63]

VII. IDENTICAL OFFENCES

The most controversial aspect of the protection against double jeopardy concerns the criteria which link the first trial to the second one. A number of aspects fall to be considered including the aim of the prosecution, the person, the facts (*'état de faits'/'fatto'/'Sachverhalt'*), in particular the conduct of the person concerned, and the charge or offence.[64] It is irrelevant whether the jurisdiction is the same or not, the application of the principle is not affected by the fact that

---

[61] The ACHR says 'prosecuted again'; this is a better form of words because it certainly encompasses trial and conviction and already bars any inquiry or investigation.

[62] *Gradinger* v. *Austria*, § 53; *Sagir* v. *Austria* Application 32054/96.

[63] *Corigliano* v. *Italy*, § 34.   [64] Cf. e.g. Piquerez (2000) N 3966–72.

a case is brought before a different jurisdiction, for example, military courts after civilian justice.[65]

A. An Identical Aim

It is possible that parallel prosecutions will further different aims, for instance, in *Gradinger* one provision was designed to protect public safety, the other to ensure the smooth flow of traffic.[66] This is not in itself sufficient, however, to prevent the operation of the principle. To the extent that the difference concerns the essence of the proceedings (retribution, discipline, securing mentally ill persons), it is already covered by the term 'criminal'.

B. Same Person

Again, in the present context this is rather obvious: if several persons have been involved in criminal activities and one of them has been convicted and sanctioned, the others cannot invoke the double-jeopardy guarantee.

On the other hand, the *victim* need not necessarily be the same. If a person has, by a single act, caused damage to a number of other persons and has been convicted for his deed, new proceedings would be barred, even if brought by a person who was not involved in the first trial and whose name as a victim had not been mentioned in the judgment. Needless to say, this would not interfere with that victim's civil claim for damages.

One could be tempted to interpret a decision of the Commission in a case against Switzerland as being contrary to this view.[67] The applicant had been prosecuted for tax offences committed against the federal state and the (half-) canton of Obwalden. One and the same tax return form was at issue. The Commission declared the application inadmissible, not because of the formality that the form had different columns for the two sets of information, but because the rules governing tax assessment were also different and, mainly, because the legal basis of the offences differed. This was held to be sufficient to constitute separate offences.

C. Same Conduct

In *Gradinger*, the Court held the identical nature of the conduct (the facts) to be the determining factor, noting: '. . . both impugned decisions were based on the same conduct. Accordingly there has been a breach . . .'.[68]

---

[65] ICCPR, Concluding Observations Regarding Cameroon, A/55/40 vol. I, (2000) 35, §§ 215 and 216.   [66] *Gradinger* v. *Austria*, § 54; the distinction, in my view, is not very convincing.
[67] *HB* v. *Switzerland Application* 28332/95.
[68] *Gradinger* v. *Austria*, § 55. The Commission had taken the same view; see *Gradinger* v. *Austria* Application 15963/90, § 75. See also *Marte and Achberger* v. *Austria* Application 22541/93, § 41 (the case was settled in Court); and *Oliveira* v. *Switzerland*, Application 25711/94, § 47, where the result was twenty-four votes to eight.

Conduct is also the criterion applied by the IACtHR.[69] It considered that the wording of Article 8 § 4 of the IACHR, 'the same cause', was broader than that of the ICCPR. It even went so far as to declare that the Peruvian Decree-Laws Nos. 25,659 and 25,485 violated the IACHR because they covered largely the same conduct, namely 'terrorism' and 'treason'. The applicant had been acquitted of one crime but was subsequently prosecuted for the other thus there was a violation of the double-jeopardy principle.

This seems to be a clear-cut rule. Still, a number of further distinctions must be borne in mind.

1. 'Natural' and 'Legal' Unity of Conduct

The term 'conduct' can be seen from at least two perspectives: as an ontological, even scientifically observable phenomenon, or as a normative notion. In fact, it is rather difficult to define an event, or conduct in merely scientific terms. For example, the act of shooting a person, consists, *inter alia*, of at least two elements, pointing and pulling the trigger. Together, they constitute a unity which is defined by the result, causing the death of a person.

On the other hand, a series of distinguishable successive acts may be, as it were, forged in an artificial unity by law or legal practice. Thus, a multitude of blows may constitute one beating; a large number of thefts over a period of time may constitute one offence of theft; several acts of offering sexual services for money may amount to prostitution.[70]

In my view, it is not for the Court in Strasbourg to interfere with the way in which these matters are dealt with in domestic law. One country may have a system which would deal with a certain set of facts as constituting *one* crime, whereas in another country each single act would be regarded individually. Similarly, it must be left to the states to determine their system of meting out the sentence. In one country a system of accumulation will be used (with the possibility of letting prison terms run consecutively or concurrently), in another the sentence of the most serious crime may be taken as a starting point and then increased within a certain limit with regard to the other penalties, or the sentence for the most serious crime may be considered to absorb any further sentence. The Court ought to bear in mind these possibilities and accept whatever a state has adopted, unless it is faced with a clear case of abuse. This means that there can be no violation of *ne bis in idem*, even though the several single acts would be regarded as a unity in other states.

2. Conduct or Result?

Another question is whether a distinction must be made between the conduct of the person concerned and the result of such conduct. A person may set out to

---

[69] *Loayza Tamayo* v. *Peru*, judgment of 17 Sept. 1997, Series C No. 22 (IACtHR).
[70] Cf. e.g. Schomburg (2000) 1833 at 1835.

kill another by administering poison. Over a period of two months the victim is given small portions, none of them lethal in itself, but which together result in death after ten weeks. Or a terrorist explodes a bomb in a coffee shop and kills fourteen people. Do these cases fall to be regarded as a unity?

In my view the answer in the first example must be affirmative. It is the result which defines the offence. To put it rather bluntly: a person can be killed only once.

In the second example, the solution is less obvious. However, in relation to the requirement that the same persons be involved, both cases come to the conclusion that this is not in fact a decisive element—there is unity of conduct even if damage is caused to more than one person. Therefore, if, after the terrorist has been finally convicted for the murder of some of the victims, while others only die later or their bodies are only discovered later, the ban on retrial applies.

D. The Same Offence

Article 14 § 7 of the ICCPR and Article 4 of Protocol No. 7 to the ECHR link the two cases by reference to the term 'offence'. This was first stressed by the dissenting members of the Commission in its *Gradinger* report[71] and later accepted by the Court which in *Oliveira* also regarded the offence, not the conduct, as decisive.[72] The Court has remained faithful to this opinion in all of its subsequent jurisprudence.[73]

E. Is the Court's Case-law Consistent?

1. *Gradinger* and *Oliveira*

The relationship between the cases of *Gradinger* and *Oliveira* is puzzling. Both cases involved road-traffic offences. In the first, the applicant was initially charged with and convicted of causing death by negligent driving, although found not guilty of the aggravated charge of being under the influence of alcohol at the time. Later he was fined for contravening the Road Traffic Act by driving while under the influence, a conviction which stemmed from the same incident. In *Oliveira* the applicant had caused a traffic accident—the car she was driving slid on ice and hit another car whose driver was seriously injured. She was first fined 200 CHF for driving with excessive speed and losing control of her vehicle. Later, she was fined another 2,000 CHF for having caused grievous bodily harm by negligence; the fine was later reduced first to 1,500 CHF and

---

[71] Members Liddy, Soyer, Rozakis, Cabral Barreto, Bratha, Herndl, and Bieliunas in one opinion, Loucaides in another.   [72] *Oliveira* v. *Switzerland*, § 26.

[73] *Franz Fischer* v. *Austria*, § 23; *WF* v. *Austria*, § 9; *Sailer* v. *Austria*, § 11. See also the admissibility decisions in *Ponestti and Chesnel* v. *France* Applications 36855/97 and 41731/98; *Brigitte Maier* v. *Austria* Application 70579/01; *Manasson* v. *Sweden* Application 41265/98.

then to 1,300 CHF following the deduction of the first fine. In the first case, the Court found a violation, in the second it did not.

The Court took into account the fact that Ms Oliveira was not punished twice as the fine paid in the first proceedings was deducted from that imposed in the 'second round'.[74] However, that aspect cannot be decisive because Article 4 of the Protocol protects against repeated trial *or* punishment. Even if there has been no double punishment, there has indeed been a second prosecution and trial.

Even the Court admitted that its approach appeared 'somewhat contradictory'—a rather surprising confession.[75] A certain contradiction between *Gradinger* and *Oliveira* was also detected by academic writers. Esser, to give an example, laments that in *Oliveira* the Court abandoned an attitude which was favourable to the accused.[76] In fact, in *Gradinger* the Court clearly declared the existence of identical facts to be the relevant criterion. This was in line with the continental approach to *ne bis in idem*.[77] Convictions first for an offence against life and limb and then for an offence against the Road Traffic Act—both based on the same conduct—led to the finding of a violation.

However, the Court did not compare the two offences as such, but only the qualifying element of the first one as compared to the second. It took the fact that the element of intoxication was not found to be present in the first decision as a *de facto* acquittal of a charge of drunken driving and examined whether the aggravating factor in Article 81 § 2 of the Criminal Code was identical to the offence of driving while intoxicated under the Road Traffic Act. The answer was clearly in the negative. 'The Court is fully aware that the provisions in question differ not only as regards the designation of the offences but also, more importantly, as regards their nature and purpose'.[78] Clearly, what led to the finding of a violation was 'the same conduct'.

In *Oliveira* the Court operated a 180-degree turn, at least as far as its doctrine was concerned. Here, there were again two convictions based on the same facts. However, the Court failed to proceed in its customary method, setting out the principle first. It ventured into the area of criminal law and stated that it was

---

[74] *Oliveira* v. *Switzerland*, § 25; the Court was quite explicit on this in *Franz Fischer v. Austria*, § 30 where the sentence had been reduced by a pardon.

[75] *Franz Fischer* v. *Austria*, § 23. The dissenting judge in *Oliveira*, Mr Repik, had the same impression—in his view, in *Oliveira* 'the Court chose exactly the opposite solution'.

[76] Esser (2002) 97. See also Haefliger and Schürmann (1999) 357 N 71; Jennings (2001) N 14.19.

[77] See, to give but a number of random examples, Art. 647 of the Italian CCP, Frowein and Peukert (1996); Art. 4 of the 7th Protocol, N 2, Piquerez (2000) N 3970 et seq.; Renucci (2002) 140; Koering-Joulin (1995) 1093 (referring to French law); Pradel (2002) N 501; Roxin (1998) § 50 B II 2.

[78] *Gradinger* v. *Austria*, §§ 8–16, 54, 55: whereas Art. 81, para. 2 of the Criminal Code punished homicide committed while under the influence of drink, section 5 of the Road Traffic Act punished the mere fact of driving a vehicle while intoxicated. The former was designed to penalize acts that cause death and threaten public safety, the latter to ensure a smooth flow of traffic. This assessment, with due respect, is wrong. Driving under the influence is regarded as conduct extremely dangerous to life and limb!

faced with 'a single act constituting various offences (*concours idéal d'infractions*)' a situation where 'one criminal act constitutes two separate offences'.[79] Without giving reasons, the Court added that since Article 4 of Protocol No. 7 'does not preclude separate offences, even if they are all part of a single criminal act, being tried by different courts, especially where, as in the present case, the penalties were not cumulative, the lesser being absorbed by the greater . . . The instant case is therefore distinguishable from the case of *Gradinger* cited above, in which two different courts came to inconsistent findings on the applicant's blood alcohol level'.[80] It may be interesting to note that not a single judge sitting on *Oliveira* had also participated in *Gradinger*!

(As an aside: according to Swiss criminal law [Art. 68 of the Criminal Code] in cases of *concours idéal d'infractions* one penalty does *not* absorb the other, but the greater is aggravated. In *Oliveira* the national proceedings had not run in accordance with domestic law nor is it normal for the first fine to be fully deducted from the second.)

2. Consolidation of the Case-law

No wonder, then, that the Court took the opportunity of a similar case to *Gradinger, Franz Fischer*, to clarify its position. Here, we find a statement which is in diametrical contrast to what it had said in *Gradinger*, although the con- tradiction remains veiled: 'In the *Gradinger* case the essential elements of the administrative offence of drunken driving did not differ from those constituting the special circumstances of Article 81 § 2 of the Criminal Code, namely driving a vehicle while having a blood alcohol level of 0.8 grams per litre or more'.[81] It also made it clear that 'while it is true that the mere fact that a single act constitutes more than one offence is not contrary to this Article, the Court must not limit itself to finding that an applicant was, on the basis of one act, tried or punished for nominally different offences'.[82] For this case, 'a closer examination shows that only one offence should be prosecuted because it encompasses all the wrongs contained in the others'. Such an examination led in *Ponsetti and Chesnel*, to a differentiation being made on the basis of *mens rea* between the non-declaration of income and tax fraud, as the latter was deemed to require that the accused had acted voluntarily—a conclusion which cannot be said to be very convincing.[83]

3. Understanding Criminal Law

In domestic criminal law in Switzerland, Germany, and Austria, the relationship between several offences committed by the same person is a much debated point, popular in law-school exams. If a person commits one or more acts

---

[79] *Oliveira* v. *Switzerland*, § 26.   [80] Ibid, § 27.   [81] *Franz Fischer* v. *Austria*, § 27.
[82] Ibid., § 25.   [83] *Ponsetti and Chesnel* v. *France* Applications 36855/97 and 41731/98.

corresponding to more than one offence, the conviction may, under certain circumstances, only cover the most serious one, with the others being 'absorbed' ('*concurrence imparfaite*').[84] The Court in Strasbourg awards itself the competence to decide such delicate issues of criminal law on a case-by-case basis. The different assessment of the same issues in *Gradinger* and in *Franz Fischer* ought to have taught it prudence. To pretend that the aggravation of assault by intoxication (the element of intoxication to be taken in isolation) and drunk-driving are 'essentially the same', with due respect, is wrong. Both, it is true, reprove drunkenness. However, the aggravating element in connection with causing death by negligence is not specifically related to traffic. It does not cover the essential element of the offence of drunken driving, namely the fact that the driver also endangered the safety of *other* road users. The relationship between the two offences, at least in Swiss law, is not one of '*concurrence imparfaite*', at least when other persons were also endangered.[85]

Still, the fact remains that the Court has now switched to a different approach to *ne bis in idem*, requiring not only identical facts, but also identical offences. This approach had already been used in the admissibility decision in *Ponsetti and Chesnel*.[86] A number of judgments simply repeat *Franz Fischer*.[87] The decision on admissibility in *Brigitte Maier* is, finally, quite laconical: '[T]he applicant does not complain that she was tried or punished again for an offence of which she had already been finally acquitted or convicted. Her complaint relates to her conviction for different offences based on a single act in the course of one set of criminal proceedings. Accordingly, Article 4 of Protocol No. 7 does not apply.'[88]

4. Evaluation

While the way in which the Court has developed its jurisprudence clearly falls to be criticized and, in view of the apparent contradiction between the two judgments, it is quite puzzling to see *Gradinger* and *Oliveira* quoted side by side as if they were congruent, the result is not so obviously negative.

In fact, the Anglo-Saxon approach to double jeopardy is focused on the offence rather than conduct.[89] Judge Loucaides in his 'separate', but not 'dissenting', opinion in *Oliveira* makes a very strong point in favour of this approach.

---

[84] See e.g. Killias (2001) N 1118.   [85] Schwarzenegger (2003) N 7.

[86] *Ponsetti and Chesnel* v. *France* Applications 36855/97 and 41731/98.

[87] *WF* v. *Austria* Application 38275/97; *Sailer* v. *Austria* Application 38237/97; *Manasson* v. *Sweden* Application 41265/98.

[88] *Brigitte Maier* v. *Austria* Application 70579/01. See also *Göktan* v. *France*, § 51. The Swiss Federal Court has adopted the *Oliveira* doctrine and denied a violation in cases where somebody was first prosecuted for tax withdrawal ('*Steuerhinterziehung*') and then for tax fraud ('*Steuerbetrug*'): BGE 122 I 257, although the general opinion in Switzerland was to the contrary.

[89] Merrills and Robertson (2001) 268; with some hesitations, Stavros (1993) 297; Spangher (2001) 959, disregarding domestic Italian law, also accepts identity of the offence as a criterion. Dennis (2000) 929, points out, however, that English courts might prefer the narrower view of Article 4 § 1.

If we compare the two options—'conduct' versus 'offence'—we must first observe that the latter is closer to the text which actually refers to 'offence'. The second variant also gives better protection to the state and the public interest in ensuring that all offences are prosecuted. However, there are also elements militating in favour of the first alternative. For one, it is clearly more favourable to the individual concerned. This, in itself, is not, however, a convincing argument.

What really assists in deciding the issue, is the focus on the quality of the protected interest. It is not simply that of inflicting as few penal sanctions as possible. The central point is that at the end of the trial, the accused knows that that was *it*, that now everything is settled. The sentence still has to be executed, but otherwise the period of uncertainty (which is itself limited by the right to be tried within a reasonable time) is over and the future, if not bright, is at least to some extent visible and foreseeable. For the individual, his own conduct is his experience, not its legal evaluation. We conceive our behaviour as a series of acts, not as a realization of abstract concepts such as theft, forgery, etc.

Once an offender is at the hands of the administration of justice, he or she may expect that the authorities will deal with the matter not only speedily but also thoroughly, bringing the case to a close in one go. As long as the accused knows that he or she has also done things not yet known to the authorities, she or he will remain anxious in this respect. Once everything is on the table the person concerned is entitled to feel relieved and expect a final solution to the problem. If a state decides to split up an occurrence into multiple offences,[90] which it is free to do, the organs of that state must bear the risk that, if the authority make errors, the *ius puniendi* will have been exercised incompletely.[91]

For these reasons it is regrettable that the Court has not stuck to the correct approach it took in *Gradinger*, namely to interpret Article 4 of Protocol No. 7 as prohibiting a second trial with regard to the facts that formed the basis of earlier proceedings which ended with a decision having acquired the force of law.

Coming back to *Gradinger* and *Oliveira*, the Court has created considerable confusion by saying one thing and doing another. In *Gradinger* it said that conduct was the criterion and relied, in fact, on offence. A contradiction only exists in this respect—in both judgments the decisive element was the offence. It then made a second mistake in its interpretation of Austrian criminal law.

5. Proposal

The Court, in my view, would be well-advised to follow the US Supreme Court which, in *Blockburger* v. *United States*,[92] said that prosecution for two offences arising from the same act will constitute a violation of the principle *ne bis in*

---

[90] e.g. burglary can consist of trespass/unlawful entry, damage to property and theft.
[91] See also Esser (2002) 98.
[92] *Blockburger* v. *United States* 284 US 299 (1932); see also *United States* v. *Dixon* 113 S. Ct. 2849, 2856 (1993).

idem unless 'each provision requires proof of an additional fact which the other does not'. This would be considerably more precise than the ECtHR's test which rests on whether one offence encompasses all the wrongs contained in the others or has 'the same essential elements'.[93] The Court does in fact mention the criterion of 'speciality' used by the US Supreme Court, but only as 'an obvious example'. Its approach therefore remains enveloped in an almost impenetrable cloud of fog.

VIII. 'PUNISHED AGAIN'

Article 4 of Protocol No. 7 as well as Article 14 § 7 of the ICCPR says that nobody shall be 'tried or punished again'. This reference to punishment has not been subject to much examination.

A violation was alleged in *Sagir* v. *Austria* where the applicant's complaint related to the sentencing at his first trial—a matter clearly outside of *ne bis in idem*.[94]

The Court has dealt with this issue very superficially in an admissibility decision.[95] Again, the offence was driving while intoxicated. The Road Traffic Office withdrew the applicant's driving licence for a period of four months. Later, the judicial authorities formally convicted him and imposed a suspended prison sentence and a fine. The application was found to be manifestly ill-founded for the following reasons: '[T]he Court notes that the Swiss authorities were merely determining the three different sanctions envisaged by law for such an offence, namely a prison sentence, a fine, and the withdrawal of the driving licence. These sanctions were issued at the same time by two different authorities, i.e. by a criminal and by an administrative authority. It cannot, therefore, be said that criminal proceedings were being repeated contrary to Article 4 of Protocol No. 7 within the meaning of the Court's case-law'.

Three aspects are puzzling. First, the sanctions were, of course, not all issued at the same time.[96] Second, *ne bis in idem* means 'one act/offence, one trial'. The Court implicitly accepted a system where, for three sanctions, three different proceedings are acceptable. Third, it also implied that the matter would be different if, a considerable time after the original trial, a second set of proceedings were held with a view to imposing on the convict a new additional penal sanction.

The problem is currently relevant in both Germany and Switzerland. Psychiatrists are of the opinion that certain persons sentenced to a fixed term of imprisonment for dangerous crimes may have to be released despite the fact that

---

[93] *Franz Fischer* v. *Austria*, § 25.

[94] *Sagir* v. *Austria* Application 32054/96; see also HRC, *Schweizer* v. *Uruguay* referred to in McGoldrick (1994/2001) N 10.54.   [95] *RT* v. *Switzerland* Application 31982/96.

[96] The licence was withdrawn by a decision taken on 11 May 1993 which did not become final until 31 May 1995, whereas the fine was pronounced on 9 June 1993.

they still constitute a considerable danger to society. The proposal therefore has been made, and adopted in certain German regions ('*Länder*'), to introduce preventative detention which would apply after the sentence has been served.[97] It is highly doubtful whether this is compatible with the double-jeopardy principle.[98] In my view, two possibilities fall to be distinguished.

First, it is possible that the person concerned has come to suffer some form of mental defect such as could be regarded as a 'mental illness' within the meaning of Article 5 §1(e). In that case, the proceedings would not be criminal and there would be no violation of fundamental rights. The main focus would be on therapy and care, just as if some other (mental) illness had befallen the prisoner.

Second, the prisoner is *not* mentally ill. This is not an entirely unlikely hypothesis. In such a case, imposing continued deprivation of liberty for an unlimited amount of time would amount to a new punishment. The further detention would correspond to that which constitutes the prison sentence after the 'tariff period' in the law of the United Kingdom which falls to be considered as a penalty, even if the punitive motive is no longer decisive. If one were to reject this view, the detention would not be acceptable at all because sheer preventative detention is not compatible with human-rights law.[99]

IX. THE EXCEPTIONS

Of the three texts referred to in this chapter only the ECHR mentions exceptions, although the others certainly do not exclude new proceedings *in favour* of the convicted person. Beyond this, however, the *lacuna* is not easy to interpret—do the ICCPR and the IACHR entirely exclude a retrial against an acquitted person even if the judge and the witnesses were 'bought' by the defence, the evidence forged, or the prosecution intimidated?

At any rate, the solution of the ECHR seems to respect domestic law. To varying degrees several Member States allow for a retrial in the case of acquittal. Where domestic law does not provide for such a possibility, the ECHR could not be invoked. The exception only serves to diminish the obligations of the state

---

[97] See e.g. Kinzig (2001) 1455; with further references.

[98] This question was also raised in the HRC when it examined the Report of Costa Rica in 1980. It appeared that judges had the possibility 'to impose security measures if they felt that the penalty imposed had not helped in the rehabilitation of the convicted person'; CCPR A/35/40 (1980) § 361. See also ibid., § 345.

[99] *Lawless* v. *Ireland* (*No. 3*), § 14, where, with regard to preventative detention, the Court held that if 'anyone suspected of harbouring an intent to commit an offence could be arrested and detained for an unlimited period on the strength merely of an executive decision without its being possible to regard his arrest or detention as a breach of the Convention . . . such an assumption, with all its implications of arbitrary power, would lead to conclusions repugnant to the fundamental principles of the Convention'. What the Court failed to see is that the Convention does not have any place for preventative detention based on a judicial decision either; cf. the cases of *Guzzardi* v. *Italy* and *Ciulla* v. *Italy*, and, in particular, *Jéčius* v. *Lithuania*, § 50.

but does not create a basis for any individual rights. The following discussion is limited to the reopening of proceedings *against* a person acquitted or convicted of and sentenced to a clearly lesser offence. This possibility is foreign to the common-law tradition. However, the Law Commission is considering its introduction in England and Wales, for cases where new evidence is available.[100] To some extent the possibility of 'appeal out of time' leads to the same result.

According to the Protocol the reopening of proceedings is possible in two cases: when there are new or newly discovered facts and where there was a fundamental defect in the first proceedings.

A. New Facts

New facts will rarely justify the reopening of proceedings against a person, but this is not outwith the bounds of possibility. One example might be a case where a person is convicted of the attempted murder of her husband, but where, after the conclusion of the proceedings, he dies and it turns out the poison used by the wife had a very slow active force. According to the Court's approach the proceedings could then be reopened. However, this would probably also be regarded as a new offence, so the guarantee would not apply at all.

Perhaps more likely is the appearance of facts that were not known at the time of the trial. It must be added that only new facts which could not be known at the first trial can justify a retrial. The potential for abuse would be too great if the prosecution could withhold certain facts 'in reserve' so as to keep open the option of a retrial in the event that the first attempt at securing a conviction failed. Nor would it be consistent with the spirit of the protection against double jeopardy if the prosecution were able, as it were, to subsequently 'repair' their own negligence. This proposition finds a certain support in Article 3 of Protocol No. 7 which guarantees a right to compensation for a miscarriage of justice. The applicant has no such right when 'it is proved that the non-disclosure of the unknown fact in time is wholly or partly attributable to him'.

A valid reason for new proceedings is the subsequent confession of the accused. It is tantamount to a newly disclosed fact: that the accused was actually guilty.

While the Strasbourg organs have not yet been called upon to examine the issue of exceptions, the HRC stressed that the government must indicate what the new evidence is.[101]

B. Procedural Defects

Only *fundamental* defects in the proceedings will justify a retrial. This is not surprising—'normal' violations of criminal-procedure law will give rise to an

---

[100] Dennis (2000) 933; James, Taylor, and Walker (2000).
[101] *Laura Almirati Garcia on behalf of her father Juan Almirati Nieto* v. *Uruguay* (ICCPR). For details on 'new evidence', see Dennis (2000) 947.

appeal. It would undermine the protection of *ne bis in idem* if, in addition, its application could lead to the reopening of proceedings.

'Fundamental' defects can be characterized as defects which result in the acquittal appearing as a travesty of justice. The main example will be where criminal acts, such as coercion, false testimony, or bribery have influenced the trial.[102] In the United Kingdom 'tainted acquittals' can be challenged in the High Court 'where there has been an offence of interference with, or intimidation of, a juror or witness'.[103]

X. ABSOLUTE CHARACTER

Finally, unlike the other instruments, paragraph 3 places the protection against double jeopardy among the absolute rights within the meaning of Article 15 of the ECHR—an enhanced protection which means that the provision cannot be derogated from, even in times of war or other public emergency.

---

[102] Cf. e.g. ACCP, § 365, GCCP, § 362; the French and Italian criminal codes do not provide for the possibility of reopening proceedings to the detriment of the accused.

[103] Criminal Appeal Act 1968, s. 7, quoted from James, Taylor, and Walker (2000). See also Dennis (2000) 949 et seq.

Part Four

Measures of Coercion

Chapter 17

Liberty and Security of Person:
The Rules on Imprisonment

I. INTRODUCTION

The last part of this book deals with the measures of coercion most commonly applied in the context of criminal proceedings. The focus, in the first place, will be on deprivations of liberty. The character of the human rights involved in this context differs markedly from those in relation to the guarantee of a fair trial. This is due to the fact that we are not faced here primarily with an obligation on the state to organize proceedings and generally ensure that an effective defence can be mounted. Human rights in this context serve to limit the rights of the state to interfere with fundamental values of the individual. It is not entirely wrong to say that in criminal proceedings the interference with fundamental freedoms is 'normal', although, in theory, it ought only to occur in exceptional circumstances. The intervention of the human-rights instruments is designed to restrain the prosecution authorities, to ensure that measures such as detention, wire-tapping, and search and seizure are based on appropriate legal regulations, and to restrict any interference to a degree which can reasonably be accepted as 'necessary'.

A. General Observations

1. The Texts

> 1. Everyone has the right to liberty and security of person. No one shall be subjected to arbitrary arrest or detention. No one shall be deprived of his liberty except on such grounds and in accordance with such procedure as are established by law.
>
> ICCPR, Art. 9

> Article 5 Right to liberty and security
> 1 Everyone has the right to liberty and security of person. No one shall be deprived of his liberty save in the following cases and in accordance with a procedure

prescribed by law:

(a) the lawful detention of a person after conviction by a competent court;
(b) the lawful arrest or detention of a person for non-compliance with the lawful order of a court or in order to secure the fulfilment of any obligation prescribed by law;
(c) the lawful arrest or detention of a person effected for the purpose of bringing him before the competent legal authority on reasonable suspicion of having committed an offence or when it is reasonably considered necessary to prevent his committing an offence or fleeing after having done so;
(d) the detention of a minor by lawful order for the purpose of educational supervision or his lawful detention for the purpose of bringing him before the competent legal authority;
(e) the lawful detention of persons for the prevention of the spreading of infectious diseases, of persons of unsound mind, alcoholics or drug addicts or vagrants;
(f) the lawful arrest or detention of a person to prevent his effecting an unauthorized entry into the country or of a person against whom action is being taken with a view to deportation or extradition.

ECHR, Art. 5

Article 7. Right to Personal Liberty

1. Every person has the right to personal liberty and security.
2. No one shall be deprived of his physical liberty except for the reasons and under the conditions established beforehand by the constitution of the State Party concerned or by a law established pursuant thereto.
3. No one shall be subject to arbitrary arrest or imprisonment.

ACHR, Art. 7

In view of the fact that the Covenant, the Convention, and the American Convention all have their origins in the same preparatory work, it is not surprising that they share similarities in both their structure and their wording. Yet, a number of important differences are also evident.

All three start with a declaratory sentence, a proclamation of the right. The wording is almost identical—I cannot detect any difference in their meaning. The first paragraph of the ACHR is limited to this sentence, whereas the two other texts add further requirements; the ACHR gives them slightly more weight than the Covenant in that they are given their own paragraph.

In the part which sets out the exceptions to the right to personal liberty there is a remarkable difference between the European and the two other instruments. All three texts require that any interference be in accordance with the law. This requirement has a substantive aspect, in the form of the justification for arrest and detention in law, and a procedural aspect in that certain—in the words of the American text—'conditions' must be followed. Furthermore, both the ICCPR and the ACHR outlaw 'arbitrary' arrest and detention.

It is in this respect that the ECHR differs. There is no reference to arbitrariness, but the Court repeats in almost every judgment concerning Article 5 that the purpose of this fundamental right is 'to protect individuals from arbitrariness'.[1] In fact, the protection here is much stronger in that paragraph 1 contains a list which, in six sub-paragraphs (a) to (f) sets out—depending on how one counts—thirteen to fifteen exceptions. It is an exhaustive list and although it appears rather extensive there have been cases where a violation was found because the deprivation of liberty did not fit any of these exceptions.[2]

All three instruments establish a right to be informed of the reasons for the arrest and to take habeas corpus proceedings. In all three there is also a right to be brought promptly before a judge. Explicitly, or implicitly in the case of the ACHR, this right is only granted to persons detained on the suspicion of having committed an offence.[3] The Covenant and the Convention grant a right to compensation in the event that a deprivation of liberty is found to be unlawful.[4]

2. The Importance of Personal Liberty in Criminal Proceedings

One of the most frequently invoked human rights is the right to personal liberty. This is of little surprise as the interference with this right certainly causes considerable suffering. Moreover, contrary to the right to life and to physical integrity, it is a right which the authorities regularly and lawfully interfere with, particularly in the context of crime control. It is the most serious measure of coercion permitted both by domestic and international criminal-procedure law and by the international human-rights instruments.

Of course, these instruments have been drafted by politicians and there is no question of them abolishing all deprivation of liberty—far from it! For instance, there is so far no protection against life imprisonment.[5] It is possible to identify two goals of the guarantee. The *first* and foremost is to prevent any form of arbitrary imprisonment. Deprivation of liberty must always have a basis in law, although this will depend to a certain extent on the type of detention and the case under consideration. *Second*, the international instruments aim to limit the duration of certain forms of detention, in particular detention on remand.

---

[1] See e.g., to take examples at random, *Nowicka* v. *Poland*, § 58; *DG* v. *Ireland*, § 75 with further references.   [2] e.g. *Ciulla* v. *Italy*.
[3] The implication in the ACHR lies in the reference to 'charges' and to 'guarantees to assure his appearance for trial'.
[4] Furthermore, all three instruments prohibit detention because of the inability to fulfil contractual obligations; ICCPR, Art. 11; ACHR, Art. 7 § 5; ECHR, Protocol No. 4, Art. 1.
[5] In one admissibility decision, however, there is an *obiter dictum* which suggests that the Court considered that life imprisonment without the slightest prospect of release might be contrary to Art. 3 of the ECHR; *Einhorn* v. *France*, § 27, Application 71555/01, decision of 15 Oct. 2001, unreported.

3. The Scope of the Present Chapter

As this study is focused on human rights in criminal proceedings, it would not be feasible to examine all of the problems which arise in the field of personal liberty. Yet, most of the issues are in one way or another relevant to our subject and fall to be addressed. This introductory chapter will begin with an examination of the scope of the protection of personal liberty in the international human-rights instruments and the basic elements of the terms 'personal liberty', 'arrest', and 'detention'. Thereafter I shall deal with the preconditions for detention. Chapter 18 will address the rights of all persons deprived of their liberty, while the specific rights of persons detained on remand will be examined in Chapter 19.

4. The Construction of the Guarantee

In all three instruments the right to personal liberty is constructed in a rather complicated way. They begin with a general, positive declaration of the right to liberty and security of person and then set out the legitimate exceptions. This is not extraordinary. The texts of the ICCPR and the ACHR, practically resemble a *carte blanche* which enables states to decide in which circumstances they want to detain persons, as long as they promulgate statutes sufficiently precise to avoid arbitrariness. The text of the ECHR sets out an exhaustive list of situations in which arrest and detention is allowed. The reference to a legal basis is integrated into the exceptions contained in paragraph 1(a)–(f) of the English version. In the French version it was omitted from paragraph 1(c), although this has not affected the interpretation of the provision.[6]

Paragraphs 2[7] and 4[8] then set out specific rights guaranteed to all persons deprived of their liberty, while paragraph 3[9] contains two specific safeguards which only apply to paragraph 1(c), arrest and detention of a person on the suspicion of having committed an offence. Finally, paragraph 5[10] guarantees the right to compensation for everyone whose rights under the preceding paragraphs of Article 5 have been violated.

B. The Right Guaranteed

1. The Notion of Personal Liberty

Personal liberty, as referred to in non-technical, everyday language, is a very vague concept. It is possible that it could be understood as covering the right of an individual to do whatever he or she wants to do.[11] There are no

---

[6] According to Fawcett (1969) 6, this must be due to an oversight.   [7] For the ACHR, § 4.
[8] For the ACHR, § 6.   [9] For the ACHR, § 5.
[10] There is no parallel in the ACHR.
[11] The Swiss Federal Court, for instance, has extended the notion of personal liberty to include integrity of the person and the freedom to determine one's own will; see BGE 90 I 29 (1964); BGE 102 Ia 279 (1976); BGE 104 Ia 35 (1978).

misconceptions, however, as to what is protected by Article 5: it is the classical *liberté d'aller et de venir* ('the physical liberty of the person').[12] In practice, the term can be further defined by reference to what it protects against, namely arrest or detention.[13]

2. The Notion of Security of Person

As well as personal liberty the international instruments also grant a right to 'security'. It is not clear what is meant by this and specifically whether it can in fact be regarded as a substantive value to be protected in its own right.[14] As Nowak points out, its origins, which can be traced to the time of the French Revolution, lay in ensuring protection from other individuals.[15] So far, it can safely be stated that the reference to security has no practical relevance at all, and might as well be eliminated. This is a rather harsh judgment which requires justification.

First, it must be noted that the *travaux préparatoires* give hardly any indication as to what 'security' should encompass.[16] In the first drafts of the Convention, security was used in connection with personal integrity and legal remedies.[17] When Article 5 was drafted in more detail, the first sentence was not originally included.[18] It first appears in the draft before the Conference of Senior Officials in June 1950,[19] when the declaratory and definitive methods were combined. *Second*, for a long time the case-law of the Court did not deal with the notion of security of person, whereas that of the Commission provided only unsatisfactory answers. In the *Agee* decision it was stated that: 'The Commission considers that the protection of "security" of person guaranteed by Article 5 is concerned with arbitrary interference by a public authority with an individual's personal "liberty". Accordingly any decision taken within the sphere of Article 5 must, in order to safeguard the individual's right to "security of person", conform to the procedural and substantive requirements laid down by an already existing law'.[20]

In *Arrowsmith* the Commission added that 'security' is a 'guarantee against arbitrariness in the matter of arrest and detention'. Problems could arise where 'the law in question is so vague as to allow an arbitrary arrest or detention of people'.[21]

---

[12] *Engel and others* v. *Netherlands*, § 58; *Gusinskiy* v. *Russia*, § 52.
[13] See further section I.C below.   [14] See also Nowak (1993) Art. 9 N 7.   [15] Ibid.
[16] See also Nowak (1993) Art. 9 N 8. It was introduced in the discussion of the Covenant only after adoption of the Convention.
[17] Doc. A 116 of 29 Aug. 1949, *Collected Edition of the* Travaux Préparatoires, vol. I, 168.
[18] cf. e.g. ibid., vol. IV 52, 58.   [19] Ibid., 218.
[20] *Agee* v. *United Kingdom* Application 7729/76, § 11. See also *X* v. *Germany* Application 5573/72; *Arrowsmith* v. *United Kingdom* Application 7050/75; *Dyer* v. *United Kingdom* Application 10475/83.
[21] *Arrowsmith* v. *United Kingdom* Application 7050/75, § 64. See also *Winer* v. *United Kingdom* Application 10871/84.

This case-law cannot be read as attributing any specific meaning to the guarantee of 'security of person'. The text of Article 5 makes it clear that, in order to be compatible with the Convention, deprivation of liberty must always be lawful in substance and also follow a procedure prescribed by law. Furthermore, the very concept of 'law' presupposes a certain degree of precision, as the Court has made clear in the *Sunday Times* case.[22]

In an isolated passage, the Commission stated that '[t]he "right of security" of person is guaranteed in absolute terms. This means that there can be no violation of Article 18 in conjunction with this right'.[23] However, it must be assumed that this was in fact wrong.[24]

In a few instances, the Commission examined whether 'security' could be understood in its ordinary meaning as denoting safety from unlawful attacks.[25] In the case of a stateless couple from India who had been refused leave to enter the United Kingdom, the Commission found that there was 'no indication that the persons of Mr. and Mrs. X are insecure in India. If they had faced insecurity, it was insecurity of property, not insecurity of person'.[26]

In a case against Ireland,[27] the applicant complained that the authorities failed to provide him with adequate protection against the IRA, which had allegedly been responsible for an attack during which he was shot in the back and leg. Here, security was indeed the issue. However, the Commission, having 'found that Article 2 did not impose a positive obligation on States to give individuals personal protection of the kind sought by the applicant', came to the conclusion 'that neither can Article 5 § 1 be considered to impose on States such an obligation'.[28]

The Court first dealt with the notion of 'security' in *Bozano*.[29] After having repeated that 'any measure depriving the individual of his liberty must be compatible with the purpose of Article 5, namely to protect the individual from arbitrariness', it stated: 'What is at stake here is not only the "right to liberty" but also the "right to security of person"'. The applicant having been deprived of his liberty in what 'amounted in fact to a disguised form of extradition', the deprivation of liberty 'was neither "lawful", within the meaning of Article 5 § 1(f)

---

[22] *Sunday Times* v. *United Kingdom*, § 49; confirmed in *Malone* v. *United Kingdom*, § 67; *Silver and others* v. *United Kingdom*, §§ 88, 89; *Kruslin* v. *France*, § 30; *Huvig* v. *France*, § 29; *Ezelin* v. *France*, § 45; and *Müller and others* v. *Switzerland*, § 29.

[23] *Kamma* v. *Netherlands* Application 4771/71.

[24] Frowein and Peukert (1996) Art. 5 N 4, n. 7 agree with this view; see also Alkema (1978) 58.

[25] Thus, in *X* v. *Germany* Application 8334/78, it stated that 'the applicant's right to security of person could only be infringed if he had been threatened with arbitrary or unjustified detention' (which was not the case).

[26] *X* v. *United Kingdom* Application 5302/71; Alkema (1978) 58, feared that the Commission might apply 'security' to cases involving asylum seekers which, however, did not happen.

[27] *X* v. *Ireland* Application 6040/73.

[28] In *McQuiston and others* v. *United Kingdom* Application 11208/84, the Commission also rejected the claim that integrating republican and loyalist prisoners at HM Prison Magilligan affected the applicants' right to security.

[29] *Bozano* v. *France*, §§ 54 and 60; on this case see the thorough analysis by Sudre (1987) 533.

nor compatible with the "right to security of person" '. In view of this finding, the Court did not deem it necessary to examine the same issue under Article 18. This may lead to the conclusion that it regards the right to 'security' as providing a special protection against any abuse of the derogations from personal liberty set out in Article 5 § 1. However, it does not become clear what the reference to 'security' adds to 'protection of liberty' taken alone or in conjunction with Article 18.

More recently, 'security' has been referred to in the context of an arrest in which the law on international cooperation in criminal matters was wilfully ignored. In *Öcalan* the Court affirmed that 'an arrest made by the authorities of one State on the territory of another State without the consent of the latter, affects the person's individual rights to security under Article 5 § 1'.[30] However, the fact that the Court used the plural 'rights' indicates clearly that it has in mind the guarantees surrounding personal liberty rather than a separate right to security.

In legal writing, we do not find more convincing answers. Van Dijk and van Hoof suggest that '[t]he contracting States will also have to give guarantees against other encroachments on the physical security of persons and groups by the authorities as well as individuals, for instance against unnecessary threats to the physical integrity of spectators during police action or against incitement to action against a particular group of persons. However, such protection might, under specific circumstances, be called for under the duty of the State to "secure" the right to life and to the respect of physical integrity (Art. 3) or of private life (Art. 8)'.[31] The authors fail to explain in which way a specific (but unspecified) right to 'security' could add anything to that protection.

Castberg, Ouchterlony, and Opsahl remain unsatisfactorily vague when they speculate: 'Apparently, "security of person" must have an independent meaning besides "liberty", but . . . its scope remains to be settled'.[32]

In conclusion, it must be accepted that the reference to 'security of person' in Article 5 § 1 does not add anything to the protection of personal liberty or to any other right guaranteed by the Convention.[33]

The situation is somewhat different in relation to the ICCPR. In one case a Columbian teacher complained that his life was threatened because of the fact that his political and religious opinions did not conform to those of the Catholic Church and the Government. A colleague of his had been shot and he had not only been threatened but also attacked. The HRC raised Article 9 of the ICCPR *ex officio* and concluded:

The first sentence of article 9 does not stand as a separate paragraph. Its location as a part of paragraph one could lead to the view that the right to security arises only in the context

---

[30] *Öcalan* v. *Turkey*, § 88 referring to *Stocké* v. *Germany*, § 167.
[31] Van Dijk and van Hoof (1998) 345.
[32] Castberg, Ouchterlony, and Opsahl (1984) 92; for further references to older publications, see Trechsel (1974) 176 et seq.
[33] See also Fawcett (1987) 37; Frowein and Peukert (1996) Article 5 N 4–8.

of arrest and detention. The *travaux préparatoires* indicate that the discussions of the first sentence did indeed focus on matters dealt with in the other provisions of article 9. The Universal Declaration of Human Rights, in article 3, refers to the right to life, the right to liberty and the right to security of the person. These elements have been dealt with in separate clauses in the Covenant. Although in the Covenant the only reference to the right of security of person is to be found in article 9, there is no evidence that it was intended to narrow the concept of the right to security only to situations of formal deprivation of liberty. At the same time, States parties have undertaken to guarantee the rights enshrined in the Covenant. It cannot be the case that, as a matter of law, States can ignore known threats to the life of persons under their jurisdiction, just because that he or she is not arrested or otherwise detained. States parties are under an obligation to take reasonable and appropriate measures to protect them. An interpretation of article 9 which would allow a State party to ignore threats to the personal security of non-detained persons within its jurisdiction would render totally ineffective the guarantees of the Covenant.[34]

While this passage indicates a clear difference in the technical approach to the problem, it does not, in my view, mean that the ICCPR offers stronger protection than the ECHR. The Strasbourg Court would most probably approach an analogous case by applying Article 2 of the ECHR, the right to life, combined with Article 1, the duty to 'secure' the rights set out in the Convention to everyone under their jurisdiction.[35]

C. The Interference: Arrest and Detention

1. The Definition

The text of Article 5 expressly refers to the deprivation of liberty, arrest, and detention, giving thus a clear indication as to what kind of interference it is intended to regulate. Although no definition of these terms is given in the Convention or in the case-law of the Convention organs, it can be accepted that deprivation of liberty is a measure taken by a public authority by which a person is kept against his or her will for a certain amount of time within a limited space and hindered by force, or a threat of the use of force, from leaving that space.[36]

The Court insists on an autonomous interpretation of the notion of deprivation of liberty, as it does in other areas.[37] Each of the elements of the definition referred to leaves room for interpretation—the space and time elements, and the degree of coercion.[38] In addition, the various elements must be given simultaneous consideration as they may influence each other.[39] Therefore, 'the starting point must be the concrete situation of the individual concerned and

---

[34] *William Eduardo Delgado Páez* v. *Colombia*.　　　[35] Cf. e.g. *Osman* v. *United Kingdom*.

[36] Frowein and Peukert (1996) Article 5 N 9; Khol (1989) at 487; both with reference to German constitutional law.

[37] For a discussion of this phenomenon, see e.g. Ost (1989) 405 at 448–58.

[38] *Lavents* v. *Latvia*, § 62; *Amuur* v. *France*, § 42; *Guzzardi* v. *Italy*, § 92.

[39] See also Rosenmayr (1988) at 154 et seq.

account must be taken of a whole range of criteria such as the type, duration, effects, and manner of implementation of the measure in question'.[40] Article 5, however, does not regulate the conditions of detention.[41] In particular, the amount of (dis)comfort associated with the situation of the detainee is of no relevance.[42]

Matters change, however, when the deprivation of liberty is justified by a condition of which the person suffers, such as for example mental illness: '[T]here must be some relationship between the ground of permitted deprivation of liberty relied on and the place and conditions of detention ... in principle, the "detention" of a person as a mental health patient will only be "lawful" for the purposes of sub-paragraph (e) of paragraph 1 if effected in a hospital, clinic or other appropriate institution'.[43]

A systematic reading of the Convention shows that mere restrictions on the liberty of movement are not covered by Article 5: such restrictions fall under Article 2 § 1 of Protocol No. 4.[44] However, the distinction between the restriction of movement and the deprivation of liberty is 'merely one of degree or intensity, and not one of nature or substance'.[45]

2. Space

It is not surprising, after what has just been said, that it is impossible to define the border which marks the limit between deprivation and restriction of liberty precisely in square metres. Confinement to a cell is usually considered to be a deprivation of liberty. The same applies to house arrest,[46] to the stay of a person detained on remand in a hospital,[47] and to the confinement to churches, schools, stadiums, garages, hotels, and similar detention centres,[48] even if the persons concerned can move about freely within such locations.[49] Of course, the place of detention may itself move, such as the car in which Mr Bozano was taken to the Swiss border.[50] By contrast, a curfew is only a restriction of movement.[51]

---

[40] *Amuur v. France,* § 42; *Shamsa v. Poland,* § 44; *Ashingdane v. United Kingdom,* § 41; *Engel and others v. Netherlands,* § 59; *Guzzardi v. Italy,* § 92.

[41] *D v. Germany* Application 11703/85.   [42] *Lavents v. Latvia,* § 64.

[43] *Morsink v. Netherlands,* § 65; *Brand v. Netherlands,* § 62; *Hutchison Reid v. United Kingdom,* § 48; *Aerts v. Belgium,* § 46; *Ashingdane v. United Kingdom,* 46.

[44] *Ashingdane v. United Kingdom,* § 41; *Engel and others v. Netherlands,* § 58.

[45] *Ashingdane v. United Kingdom,* § 41; *Guzzardi v. Italy,* § 93.

[46] *Vachev v. Bulgaria,* § 64; *CN v. Italy (No. 1),* § 33; *Vittorio and Luigi Mancini v. Italy,* § 17; *Lavents v. Latvia,* § 63 (where the applicant was also under surveillance); EComHR, *The Greek Case* (1969) 12 Yb 134 et seq., §§ 283–7; *Cyprus v. Turkey,* § 286.   [47] *Lavents v. Latvia,* § 63.

[48] *Cyprus v. Turkey,* report of 10 July 1976, §§ 285–8.

[49] *X v. Switzerland* Application 8500/79.

[50] In *Bozano v. France* the question was not even discussed by the Court as it had never been contested; ibid., p. 32 (report of the Commission). See also the case of a person held on a ship on the Danube, discussed by Rosenmayr (1988) 155.

[51] *Cyprus v. Turkey* Applications 6780/74 and 6950/75, report of 10 July 1976, §§ 234–6.

Regrettably, the Court does not always take a clear stand. In *Manzoni* it first found that the parties disagreed as to whether 'detention at home' constituted a deprivation of liberty. It referred to a number of measures figuring in the Italian Penal Code which 'all restrict individual liberty to a greater or lesser extent' and then found that there was no violation of the Convention because 'the public prosecutor's office acted in accordance with the legislation'.[52] It might at least have said that the distinction was not relevant; the simple reference to conformity with domestic law is in stark contrast to the frequent repetition of the principle that such conformity is 'not always a decisive element'.[53]

The most critical borderline case decided so far on this issue is *Guzzardi*.[54] The applicant, a suspected member of the Mafia, was confined to a camp on the small island of Asinara off the coast of Sardinia. Together with others he could, during the day, move about freely in an area of some 2.5 square kilometres. While the applicant was from time to time given permission to travel to the small town of Porto Torres on Sardinia, such excursions were always under the strict supervision of the police. The Court relied, in particular, on the fact that 'there were few opportunities for social contacts available'; that he could not 'leave his dwelling between 10 p.m. and 7 a.m. without giving prior notification to the authorities' to whom he had to report twice a day; that he had to indicate the identity of the person he was calling when he used the telephone; and that he had to live under these conditions for more than sixteen months.[55] The fact that his wife and son initially lived with him and, from time to time, also his parents-in-law and a nephew, did not stop the Court from holding that Mr Guzzardi had been deprived of his liberty.

3. Coercion and Waiver

In the 'Vagrancy' case, we find the following sentence: 'Detention might violate Article 5 even though the person concerned may have agreed to it'.[56] This sentence, in my view, is misleading and contradictory in that the very notion of detention implies the absence of consent. The passage reveals its meaning, however, when read in its context: detention cannot be justified by relying on the fact that the person concerned *initially* agreed to enter and stay in a particular institution if he or she later wishes to leave. As long as a person stays at a certain place of his or her own free will there exists no deprivation of liberty. Such consent can, however, as a rule, be withdrawn at any time.[57] An exception might nevertheless be envisaged where the person concerned foresees an intermediate period during which, under duress, he or she might falter in his or her

---

[52] *Giulia Manzoni* v. *Italy*, §§ 22–3.
[53] *Kawka* v. *Poland*, § 48. See also e.g. *Berktay* v. *Turkey*, § 195; *NC* v. *Italy*, §§ 40–2; *Assenov* v. *Bulgaria*, § 139; *Jėčius* v. *Lithuania*, § 56.   [54] *Guzzardi* v. *Italy*.
[55] Ibid., § 95.   [56] *De Wilde, Ooms and Versyp* v. *Belgium ('Vagrancy' case)*, § 65.
[57] See also e.g. Rosenmayr (1988) 156.

determination and thereby miss the goal of the internment. This might be the case where, for example, an addict calls for 'cold turkey' treatment to attain a state of health which allows for constructive therapy.

Of course, consent must be given on the basis of full information and by a person with full mental capacity. This was exactly the question which arose in the *Nielsen* case.[58] A twelve-year-old boy had been committed to the child psychiatric ward at a hospital by his mother although he was not suffering from a true mental disorder. The Commission had considered that, although the mother was legally entitled to make the decision, such a right was not unlimited and that the applicant as 'a normally developed 12-year-old . . . was capable of understanding his situation and to express his opinion clearly'.[59] He had therefore been deprived of his liberty within the meaning of Article 5. The Court disagreed by nine votes to seven.[60] The majority accepted 'that the rights of the holder of parental authority cannot be unlimited and that it is incumbent on the State to provide safeguards against abuse'.[61] However, in the present case there was no deprivation of liberty because the mother had, in the Court's view, exercised her powers in a responsible way. I agree with Velu and Ergec who criticize this judgment.[62]

The element of coercion must not be taken too literally—handcuffs are not a necessary prerequisite. It is quite sufficient that there is a threat of the use of force. House arrest, for example, does not necessarily mean that the door is locked or that electronic surveillance and detention devices are used to confine the applicant.

In two cases, however, the Court and Commission have attached weight to the fact that the room in which the applicants had to stay was not locked. In *Engel*[63] the Court considered this fact to be the decisive element when it determined that 'strict arrest' did not constitute a deprivation of liberty, whereas the Commission relied on this detail in the case of two schoolgirls who were made to wait at a police station.[64] In my view, this case-law places too much emphasis on physical constraint and insufficient emphasis on psychological coercion. I would suggest that it suffices if the person concerned is under the impression that he or she could not leave the room to which he or she is confined without serious consequences, including that of being returned by force.[65] It must be kept in mind that certain modern open prisons have no walls and no bars.

A special problem with regard to the element of coercion has arisen in relation to prospective immigrants who are accommodated at airport buildings. A first application was declared inadmissible because the applicants were free to leave

---

[58] *Nielsen* v. *Denmark*.   [59] Ibid., § 128, p. 43.

[60] Judges Thór Vilhjálmsson, Pettiti, Russo, Spelmann, De Meyer, Carrillo Salcedo, and Valticos dissenting.   [61] *Nielsen* v. *Denmark*, § 72.

[62] Velu and Ergec (1990) N 306, p. 254.

[63] *Engel and others* v. *Netherlands*, § 62. In its Report of 19 July 1974, § 75, the Commission had reached the opposite conclusion.   [64] *X* v. *Germany* Application 8819/79.

[65] See also the detailed considerations of the Commission in *Nielsen* v. *Denmark*, pp. 39–40.

the airport and fly abroad.[66] This approach was, however, abandoned in the case of *Amuur*. The applicants had reached Paris via Syria—they feared persecution after the overthrow of the regime of President Siyad Barre. They were held in the transit zone, on a floor specially reserved for such purposes at the Hôtel Arcade. The Court observed that such constraints constituted a mere restriction of liberty if it only lasted for a short while. Here, the applicants were, however, held for twenty days. The Court rejected the argument of the Government and a majority of the Commission that there was no deprivation of liberty because they were free to leave France. This possibility was illusory because they had no chance to travel to a country which would offer comparable protection.[67]

4. Time

Deprivation of liberty constitutes an interference with a fundamental right which is necessarily linked to the element of time. It may roughly be asserted that there exists a certain relationship between the intensity of the elements of space and coercion on the one hand, and the duration of the interference on the other. Thus, as we have seen, in the *Guzzardi* case the Court took into consideration the fact that the applicant was held on the island of Asinara for over sixteen months. It concluded that, despite the relative freedom of movement and the possibility for rather extensive social contacts, he had been deprived of his liberty.[68] On the other hand, if somebody is asked to follow a police officer to a police station in order to answer a few questions, the half hour he or she 'loses' would probably not constitute an 'arrest' in the sense of Article 5. This might, however, be different if the person were handcuffed.[69]

Deprivation of liberty which only lasts for a short period of time raises, however, more complex problems which have been studied in detail by Koschwitz.[70] These problems are twofold. First, at the time of the drafting and adoption of the Convention the legislation of several High Contracting Parties provided for short-term police arrest in cases which are not covered by any of the exceptions listed in Article 5 § 1. The police may be authorized, for example, immediately before or during a violent demonstration to arrest persons they believe to be dangerous, even though they are neither suspected of having committed an offence nor of being about to commit one. Second, some of the

---

[66] *SS, AM and YSM* v. *Austria* Application 19066/91.

[67] *Amuur* v. *France*, §§ 43–9; see also *Shamsa* v. *Poland* (transit zone at the airport).

[68] Similarly, the duration of twenty days led to the conclusion that the initial restriction of liberty had become a deprivation in *Amuur* v. *France*, § 43. In *Shamsa* v. *Poland* fourteen days led to the same result.

[69] Cf. *X and Y* v. *Germany* Application 8819/79. Two children were questioned at a police station about an alleged theft in the classroom. The Commission denied the existence of a deprivation of liberty *inter alia* because the girls were only held for a short time and it was not really the intention of the authorities to deprive them of their liberty (the door was not locked). The reliance on such intent of the authorities has been rightly criticized by Rosenmayr (1988) 154 et seq. and Velu and Ergec (1990) N 305, 253.   [70] Koschwitz (1970).

specific guarantees for persons deprived of their liberty, such as the right to be promptly brought before a judge or to take habeas corpus proceedings, have no meaning with respect to deprivation of liberty of short duration, that is to say, less than four days.[71] In fact, '[n]o violation of Article 5 § 3 can arise if the arrested person is released "promptly" before any judicial control would have been feasible',[72] nor is there a breach of Article 5 § 4 if a person is set free before any judicial control could become operative.[73]

While this rule is quite convincing in cases such as *Fox, Campbell and Hartley* where the persons concerned were in fact released, there remains an uneasy feeling regarding cases such as the Commission's decision in *X and Y v. Sweden*.[74] In this case the Swedish authorities decided to expel the applicants, and instead of being released they were put on an aircraft which was to take them to Japan. It is doubtful whether the transfer to the jurisdiction of another state, particularly if it is not a Contracting Party to the Convention, can be equated to release.[75]

The fact that certain phenomena regarding short-term deprivation of liberty are lawful or used in administrative practice in some High Contracting States is more difficult to deal with. It would certainly be unfortunate if, in order to avoid conflict, Article 5 (in particular paragraph 1(b)) were to be interpreted in an excessively broad way. So far, it is satisfying to see that the Convention organs have not embarked upon such a course.[76]

5. Relativity of the Notion of Deprivation of Liberty

Whether a specific situation constitutes a deprivation of liberty may depend on the living conditions of the person concerned and the degree of freedom he or she has previously enjoyed. Thus, when a prisoner serves a disciplinary sanction which means that he or she is confined to a less comfortable prison cell, the difference to his or her prior situation is relatively small, and the measure does not constitute a (separate or additional) deprivation of liberty.[77] The same applies if a prisoner is serving a sentence and is additionally detained on

---

[71] This originally led to the proposal that Art. 5 be construed in such a way that it does not cover short-term deprivation of liberty. See also van Bemmelen (1966) 701; Trechsel (1974) 185 et seq. At the outset, however, the second argument is not convincing. I have abandoned my original opinion in Trechsel (1980).

[72] *Brogan and others v. United Kingdom*, § 58; *De Jong, Baljet and Van den Brink v. Netherlands*, § 52.

[73] *X and Y v. Sweden* Application 7376/76; *Fox, Campbell, and Hartley v. United Kingdom*, § 44.

[74] *X and Y v. Sweden* Application 7376/76; van Dijk and van Hoof (1998) 290 approved, however, of the decision.

[75] At the time the decision was taken Protocol No. 7 was not yet in existence and the Commission, therefore, was not called upon to examine whether Art. 1 of that Protocol had been complied with.

[76] The Austrian Constitutional Court has, by comparison, given a rather narrow interpretation to the term 'deprivation of liberty' in relation to prospective immigrants held for a security check at the airport; XVII YB 629 (1974). Swart (1978) 265 and n. 39; and Alkema (1978) 57 seem to regard such interferences as being covered by Art. 5 § 1(d), (e), or (f). In some states, however, there is no legal basis in domestic law.   [77] *X v. Switzerland* Application 7754/77.

remand, even though the arrest warrant places additional restrictions on the detainee.[78]

This case-law has recently evolved. Two applicants complained that they were kept in prison from 7 to 13 January 1998—despite the fact that their sentence had been changed to house arrest—because of a shortage of personnel to oversee the modification of the sentence. Although it was not contested that house arrest also constituted a deprivation of liberty, the Court found a violation of Article 5 § 1. In comparison to *Ashingdane* it considered that the difference between the type of interference was considerable in that, 'replacing detention in prison with house arrest [. . .] entails a change in the nature of the place of detention from a public institution to a private home. Unlike house arrest, detention in prison requires integration of the individual into an overall organisation, sharing of activities and resources with other inmates, and strict supervision by the authorities of the main aspects of his day-to-day life'.[79] Therefore, the additional time spent in prison fell to be regarded as 'detention' within the meaning of Article 5.

The decisive factor is the factual situation of the person concerned. If a habitual offender is placed 'at the Government's disposal' but not actually detained[80] or if a criminal who has been sentenced to life imprisonment is released on license,[81] these persons are *de facto* not detained and any decision to recall them therefore constitutes a deprivation of liberty. Again, if, in the United Kingdom, a prisoner is subject to a disciplinary sanction of loss of remission by which his earliest release date is postponed, such a sanction amounts to an extra deprivation of liberty even though, in law, the whole prison term would be covered by the judgment.[82]

The most difficult problem in the area discussed here arose in the context of military disciplinary sanctions. The leading case affirms that 'the Convention applies in principle to members of the armed forces and not only to civilians'.[83] 'Nevertheless, . . . the Court must bear in mind the particular characteristics of military life and its effects on the situation of individual members of the armed forces'.[84] Military service, though it imposes serious limitations on servicemen, 'does not on its own in any way constitute a deprivation of liberty'.[85] The decisive element consists of the fact that a person has been locked up.[86] The Court said, however, that committal to a disciplinary unit, which was also a

---

[78] *D* v. *Germany* Application 11703/85.   [79] *Vittorio and Luigi Mancini* v. *Italy*, § 19.
[80] *Van Droogenbroeck* v. *Belgium*, § 34.   [81] *Weeks* v. *United Kingdom*, § 40.
[82] This is what the case of *Campbell and Fell* v. *United Kingdom*, § 72, amounts to; the issue concerned the application of Art. 6 to the disciplinary proceedings. The Commission had earlier reached a different conclusion in *Kiss* v. *United Kingdom* Application 6224/73. See further Chapter 2 above.
[83] *Engel and others* v. *Netherlands*; see also the Commission's report in *Santschi and others* v. *Switzerland* Applications 7668/76, 7938/77, 8018/77, 8106/77, 8325/78, and 8778/79; for comments on *Engel*, see e.g. Trechsel (1993) 94, n. 15.
[84] *Engel and others* v. *Netherlands*, § 54.   [85] Ibid., § 59.   [86] Ibid., §§ 61–4.

supplementary punishment under the criminal law, also constituted a deprivation of liberty because of the fact that the soldiers serving this sentence could not leave the establishment for a month or more. The finding is not entirely clear because the Court also referred to the fact that the applicants spent the night locked in a cell.[87] This certainly constitutes a deprivation of liberty, but more details would have to be examined in order to come to the same conclusion with regard to the service during the day.

Finally, Article 5 is—in principle[88]—only concerned with the fact of deprivation of liberty, not with the modalities of its execution which might raise problems under, for example, Articles 3, 8, 9, 10, 11, or 12. However, in *Ashingdane*[89] the Court stated that 'there must be some relationship between the ground of permitted deprivation of liberty relied on and the place and condition of detention'.[90]

II. THE EXCEPTIONS TO LIBERTY OF PERSON

A. General Aspects

1. The Structure of the Second Sentence of Paragraph 1

While the first sentence of paragraph 1 of Article 5 contains a general declaration of the right to liberty and security of person, the second sentence sets out a general prerequisite and an exhaustive list of six ways in which detention may legitimately be imposed.

It is interesting and, in my view, important to compare the way in which the Convention regulates these interferences with the provisions in paragraphs 2 of Articles 8–11 of the ECHR which serve an analogous function. There, in order to be in accordance with the Convention, any interference with the right guaranteed must satisfy three conditions. First, it must be 'in accordance with the law' or 'prescribed by law'; second, it must pursue one of the legitimate aims listed in broad terms[91] in the paragraph; and, third, it must be 'necessary in a democratic society'.

In Article 5, the first prerequisite figures twice, namely with reference to the procedure followed and to the substantive legal basis for the deprivation of liberty.[92] The second prerequisite, the legitimate aim, is split up into six different and very specific categories in the ECHR. At first sight, the third element, which is, in practice, the most discussed one, is missing—there is no reference to 'necessity in a democratic society' in Article 5. This is surprising if one considers

---

[87] Ibid., § 64.
[88] Although obviously there is an exception in the case of detention on remand and house arrest.
[89] *Ashingdane* v. *United Kingdom*, § 44.
[90] The problem is dealt with as one of the 'lawfulness' of detention.
[91] e.g. 'the protection of public order' in Art. 9 § 2.   [92] See further section II.2.(b) below.

the fact that deprivation of liberty is a particularly serious interference with the rights of the individual. I shall return to this subject shortly.

2. The Requirement of Lawfulness

(a) The Meaning of 'Law' in the Convention

It can safely be said that the Convention presupposes that the signatory states are both democratic and based on the rule of law. This means, at the outset, that no interference with any fundamental right of a person under their jurisdiction can be deemed to be acceptable unless it is in accordance with law. Consequently, a legal basis must exist and this basis must have been respected. Accordingly, the definition of 'law' is of the greatest importance for the interpretation of most of the substantive guarantees of the Convention. It also leads to the conclusion that the term must have the same meaning throughout. The definition of the term 'law' is, therefore, of considerable importance.

Nevertheless, I shall not deal with this issue in detail in the context of Article 5 but return to it when discussing the guarantee of privacy.[93] It is sufficient to note that the Convention organs apply a substantive rather than a formal notion of 'law', which is not entirely satisfactory.[94]

(b) The Various Elements of 'Lawfulness' in Article 5, paragraph 1

The text of Article 5 § 1 clearly refers to a double test of legality—any arrest or detention must be 'lawful' and respect a 'procedure prescribed by law'. In this respect, 'the Convention refers back essentially to national law and lays down the obligation to conform to the substantive and procedural rules thereof'.[95] To this, the Court added: 'However, it requires in addition that any deprivation of liberty should be consistent with the purpose of Article 5, namely to protect individuals from arbitrariness'. In *Bouamar*, 'lawfulness' is related to a further element: it 'also implies that the deprivation of liberty is in keeping with the purpose of the restrictions permissible under Article 5 § 1 of the Convention'.[96] This formula, which first appeared in *Winterwerp*[97] and was referred to in *Thynne, Wilson and Gunnell*,[98] was replaced by a simple reference to 'arbitrariness' in other cases, although they were of a similar nature.[99]

---

[93] For a detailed study of the question, see Malinverni (1990) 401–9; and Matscher (1991).

[94] See Trechsel (1980) 100 et seq.; criticism is also voiced by Frowein and Peukert (1996) Art. 5 N 25; and Velu and Ergec (1990) N 309. In the case of *Drozd and Janousek* v. *France and Spain*, § 107, the Court even accepted 'Franco-Andorran custom' as having 'sufficient stability and legal force to serve as a basis for the detention in issue'.

[95] *Wassink* v. *Netherlands*, § 24. The formula turns up in most of the cases dealing with Article 5 § 1, e.g. *Van der Leer* v. *Netherlands*, § 22; *Bouamar* v. *Belgium*, § 47. Different wording is used in *Weeks* v. *United Kingdom*, § 42; *Bozano* v. *France*, § 54; *Ashingdane* v. *United Kingdom*, § 44; and *Winterwerp* v. *Netherlands*, §§ 39 and 45.   [96] *Bouamar* v. *Belgium*, § 50.

[97] *Winterwerp* v. *Netherlands*, § 39.

[98] *Thynne, Wilson and Gunnell* v. *United Kingdom*, § 70.

[99] *Van Droogenbroeck* v. *Belgium*, § 40; and *Weeks* v. *United Kingdom* § 49.

The latter formulation is to be preferred as there is a danger of blurring the notion of 'lawfulness' if it is also used to express conformity with the scope of the deprivation of liberty. In my view, it would be preferable to use it exclusively with reference to the conformity with national law.

As far as the criterion of arbitrariness is concerned, the Court has correctly stated that an arbitrary deprivation of liberty could never be 'lawful'.[100] The question must, however, be turned the other way: could detention which is in conformity with procedural and substantive national law and follows one of the aims set out in Article 5 § 1 ever be arbitrary? In my view, this could only be the case where such a deprivation of liberty fails the test of necessity which would be more precise than that of 'arbitrariness'. The Court has, for its part, indicated that in considering arbitrariness it 'attaches great weight to the circumstances' in which the detention occurs.[101]

Another formulation used in *Winterwerp* was absent from the Court's jurisprudence for a long time. In this case the Court gave substance to the words 'in accordance with a procedure prescribed by law' in stressing that 'the law must itself be in conformity with the Convention, including the general principles expressed therein. The notion underlying the term in question is one of fair and proper procedure, namely that any measure depriving a person of his liberty should issue from and be executed by an appropriate authority . . .'.[102] This passage reappeared in *Kemmache (No. 3)* and was quoted by the Court more recently in *Ilascu*.[103]

(c) The Degree of Scrutiny Exercised by the Court

Having found that the 'lawfulness' in Article 5 (and elsewhere in the Convention) refers to national law, the question arises to what degree the Convention organs will examine whether a legal basis exists and whether the requirements of national law were complied with. The most complete answer to this question is found in the *Bozano* judgment: 'Where the Convention refers directly to domestic law, as in Article 5, compliance with such law is an integral part of Contracting States' "engagements" and the Court is accordingly competent to satisfy itself of such compliance where relevant (Article 19); the scope of its task in this connection, however, is subject to limits inherent in the logic of the European system of protection, since it is in the first place for the national authorities, notably the courts, to interpret and apply domestic law'.[104] It is not

---

[100]   *Winterwerp* v. *Netherlands*, § 39; see also *Ashingdane* v. *United Kingdom*, § 44.

[101]   *Bozano* v. *France*, § 59 where the Court refers to the fact that the applicant was arrested at night without previous warning, handcuffed and driven immediately to the Swiss border.

[102]   *Winterwerp* v. *Netherlands*, § 45.

[103]   *Kemmache* v. *France (No. 3)*, 37; *Ilascu* v. *Moldova and Russia*, § 461. Judge Velaers in his dissenting opinion in *Conka* v. *Belgium*, § 2 also refers to this passage from *Winterwerp*. The insufficiency of national law concerning Art. 5 § 3 was criticized in the case of *De Jong, Baljet and van den Brink* v. *Netherlands*, § 48.

[104]   *Bozano* v. *France*, § 58. See also e.g. *Bouamar* v. *Belgium*, § 49; *Wassink* v. *Netherlands*, § 25; *Luberti* v. *Italy*, § 27; *Winterwerp* v. *Netherlands*, §§ 40 et seq. In other (similar) cases, the formula is not recalled, e.g. *Van der Leer* v. *Netherlands*, §§ 22, 23.

possible to state in general terms what this means in practice, because two groups of cases have to be distinguished.

The first one concerns those cases where the issue of 'lawfulness' is linked to the substance, in particular to the aim of the deprivation of liberty. Thus, where a person is confined on the basis of a mental illness, compliance with domestic law will usually coincide with the fulfilment of the prerequisite set out in the exception relied upon. This was the Court's approach in *Bouamar*.[105] In such a case—although the Court does not mention it—the national authorities 'are to be recognized as having a certain margin of appreciation', like in those cases where the Court examines whether an applicant could be regarded as a person of unsound mind.[106]

The second group consists of those cases where it is alleged that the deprivation of liberty was not 'in accordance with a procedure prescribed by law'. Here, particular weight is given to the prevalent opinion on the domestic law in the state concerned. The Court actually asks whether it is given 'sufficient reason' for finding that the procedural rules were not complied with,[107] which amounts to applying *in dubio pro reo* in favour of the respondent Government.

A recurring problem concerns the respect of time limits for the renewal of detention orders. In *Winterwerp,* the Court's answer sounded rather helpless when, after accepting the Government's explanation, it added that 'the interval of two weeks [sc. which is contrary to domestic law!] . . . can in no way be regarded as unreasonable or arbitrary'.[108] In *Koendjbiharie* the Commission had found a violation of Article 5 § 1 because of a delay of sixty-six days, but the Court avoided the issue.[109] Nevertheless, as soon as a violation of national procedural rules is clearly established and recognized on the domestic level, there is also a violation of the Convention,[110] even though such violation has not been shown to be causal to the deprivation of liberty.[111]

It is interesting to note that violations of Article 5 § 1 have so far been found mainly in connection with procedural problems.[112]

---

[105] *Bouamar* v. *Belgium*, § 50 concerning the detention of a minor for the purpose of educational supervision.

[106] *Luberti* v. *Italy*, § 27. See also *Weeks* v. *United Kingdom*, § 50; *Winterwerp* v. *Netherlands*, §§ 39 et seq.; *X* v. *United Kingdom*, § 43. In other cases the Court has only said that its task was 'limited to reviewing under the Convention the decisions taken by the national authorities': *Ashingdane* v. *United Kingdom*, § 37; *Wassink* v. *Netherlands*, § 25. See also *De Wilde, Ooms, and Versyp* v. *Belgium*, § 67 in fine concerning vagrancy.

[107] *Winterwerp* v. *Netherlands*, § 48. In *Wassink* v. *Netherlands*, § 26, the Court relied heavily on the opinion of the Attorney General.

[108] *Winterwerp* v. *Netherlands*, § 49; see also *Egue* v. *France* Application 11256/84.

[109] *Koendjbiharie* v. *Netherlands*, opinion of the Commission §§ 55–8, judgment of the Court § 25—see, however, the dissenting opinion of Judge Bernhardt.

[110] *Van der Leer* v. *Netherlands*, § 23 (failure to hear the applicant before authorizing her confinement); *Wassink* v. *Netherlands*, § 27 (absence of a registrar at the hearing).

[111] The opinion I had expressed in Trechsel (1980) 106 must therefore be revised.

[112] Exceptions are e.g. *Bouamar* v. *Belgium; Bozano* v. *Italy*; and *Fox, Campbell and Hartley* v. *United Kingdom*.

B. Detention on Remand: Article 5, paragraph 1(c)

The most important case of deprivation of liberty in connection with criminal proceedings is pretrial detention. It is essentially detention on remand, although different stages of preliminary detention can be distinguished, in particular:

- 'stopping' by the police; it serves the purpose of verifying the identity of a person or conducting a search[113] and lasts normally less than an hour;
- police detention; unless very special circumstances of emergency prevail, it may not last more than four days;
- detention on remand during the investigation;
- detention on remand after the investigation awaiting the trial hearing;
- detention on remand during appeal proceedings;
- detention on remand after the final trial awaiting the beginning of the sentence.

Departing from the order in Article 5 § 1, which starts with detention following conviction, I shall take a chronological approach and deal first with pre-trial detention. As neither of the two other international texts which are examined in this study detail the cases when deprivation of liberty is allowed, this chapter will continue to deal mainly with the ECHR.

Paragraph 1(c) can probably be awarded the unfortunate distinction of being the most inadequately drafted provision in the whole Convention.[114] Despite this, its application in practice has not caused substantial difficulties. This might, *inter alia*, be due to the fact that the laws of the Member States governing detention on remand are frequently drafted in stricter terms than those set out in the Convention.[115] Pre-trial detention is characterized by certain prerequisites and a specific formal aim. The detention must be based on one of the three substantive prerequisites: suspicion of having committed an offence, necessity to prevent the committing of an offence, or danger of absconding. Moreover, from a procedural perspective, the detention must be to bring the person 'before the competent legal authority'.

1. Reasonable Suspicion

All three eventualities presuppose the existence of 'reasonable suspicion' in the sense of the presumption that a person could have committed an offence. For a long time this condition was not subject to much discussion and the assumption was rather that the test would be met in all but those cases where the suspicion was shown to be of an entirely arbitrary nature.[116] Indeed, the Commission had

---

[113] For an illustration, see *KF* v. *Germany* where the time limit set by domestic law was exceeded by forty-five minutes which meant a violation of Art. 5 § 1.

[114] See also e.g. van Dijk and van Hoof (1998) 260; Frowein and Peukert (1996) Art. 5 N 58; Velu and Ergec (1990) N 324, 326.

[115] Frowein and Peukert (1996) Art. 5 N 58; Trechsel (1980) 114; Velu and Ergec (1990) N 323.

[116] Trechsel (1980) 117.

always been extremely reluctant to question whether the arresting authority had really acted upon reasonable suspicion.[117]

This changed with the case of *Fox, Campbell and Hartley*.[118] The applicants were arrested under section 11(1) of the Northern Ireland (Emergency Provisions) Act 1978 according to which 'any constable may arrest without warrant any person whom he suspects of being a terrorist'. The interpretation of this provision under national law was that the suspicion which needed only to be 'honestly held' was a 'subjective one'. Commission and Court found[119] that Article 5 § 1 was violated because the exception under paragraph 1(c) required 'reasonable', not only *bona fide*, suspicion. Therefore, the Government would have had 'to furnish at least some facts or information capable of satisfying the Court that the arrested person was reasonably suspected of having committed the alleged offence'.[120]

The Court, in later judgments, fully confirmed these findings. It stressed that the suspicion must be 'plausible': the material put forward by the prosecuting authority must be sufficient to persuade an objective observer that the person concerned may have committed the offence—and the facts must be presented by the Government.[121]

On the other hand, the very term 'suspicion' suggests an element of uncertainty. The guilt of the person concerned does not have to be already established, as it is the purpose of the investigation to verify whether such guilt is sufficiently probable to enable the preparation of an indictment.[122] The police do not even need evidence which would be sufficient to enable the bringing of a charge.[123]

In the context of the situation in Northern Ireland, the Court accepted in two later cases that these requirements had been met. In one case the applicant, Ms Murray, had been suspected of being involved in efforts to supply the IRA with weapons. Her brother had been engaged in this business in the USA and she had been there to visit him. The Court also heavily relied on the review which had been carried out on the domestic level.[124] The situation was more difficult in *O'Hara* where the police had relied on evidence that had been given by unidentified informants. But the Court decided that it could rely on the good faith of the police officers involved in the arrest and moreover no suggestion had been made 'that the arrest had been motivated by malice or was an arbitrary

---

[117] Trechsel (1980) 115 et seq. with an extensive quotation from *Deutsch* v. *Germany* Application 7033/75, a very problematic case. The applicant had been a very successful lawyer bringing restitution claims of Jewish clients before German courts for damages caused by Nazi persecution. He was, perhaps somewhat artificially, suspected of having committed fraud when claiming compensation for the art collection of one Mr Hatvany who had made a fortune in sugar.

[118] *Fox, Campbell and Hartley* v. *United Kingdom*.

[119] The vote being seven-to-five and four-to-three respectively.

[120] *Fox, Campbell and Hartley* v. *United Kingdom*, § 34.

[121] *Murray* v. *United Kingdom*, § 60; *KF* v. *Germany*, § 57; *Włoch* v. *Poland*, § 108; *Berktay* v. *Turkey*, § 199; *O'Hara* v. *United Kingdom*, § 34; *NC* v. *Italy*, § 40; *Labita* v. *Italy*, § 155; *Gusinskiy* v. *Russia*, § 53.   [122] *NC* v. *Italy*, § 45.

[123] *Gusinskiy* v. *Russia*, § 53.   [124] *Murray* v. *United Kingdom*, §§ 55–63.

abuse of power'.[125] With regard to the very difficult task of combating terrorism it added that '[t]here may thus be a fine line between those cases where the suspicion grounding the arrest is not sufficiently founded on objective facts and those which are'. As usual in such cases, everything 'depends on the particular circumstances of each case'.[126]

In the area of ordinary criminality the Court found no violation in a case where the applicant had gone to the police in order to complain that he had been a victim of crime and was then arrested on suspicion of having made a false accusation,[127] and another case where the applicant was suspected of rent fraud.[128] The Russian authorities also had enough evidence to suspect Mr Gusinskiy of having fraudulently deprived Gasprom of the right to broadcast television programmes.[129]

On the other hand, a violation was found in *Pantea* where the Government admitted that the reason for the arrest, the danger that the applicant might abscond, was entirely unfounded,[130] and in *Berktay*, where there existed no plausible suspicion for the arrest of the applicant.[131]

(a) The Object of the Suspicion

As we have seen, Article 5 § 1(c) mentions suspicion in relation to three possible situations. This has often been misunderstood, particularly by authors with a continental background, as meaning that detention on remand requires (as it does in a number of legal systems) a double justification. Not only must there be a 'reasonable suspicion', but this must be accompanied by a specific reason justifying the detention ('*Haftgründe*'). There are a limited number of grounds, typically these will include detention to prevent the suspect absconding, tampering with the evidence, or committing new offences. It was quite natural for those used to such a system to look for a parallel in the Convention.

However, this is already excluded for linguistic reasons. In many continental legal systems both suspicion *and* justification are required, whereas the three scenarios mentioned in paragraph 1(c) are presented as alternatives. Furthermore there is no reference to the danger of tampering with the evidence. It cannot be the meaning of the Convention to exclude this legitimate ground for detention on remand. Yet, it would not be compatible with elementary rules of interpretation to interpret the treaty contrary to its text, even if it would lead to the restriction of the scope of an exception. Therefore one has to conclude that the object of the suspicion mentioned in the Convention is limited to the fact of having committed an offence and does not include additional 'dangers'.

On the other hand, the specific '*Haftgründe*' retain their importance for the Convention law in an indirect way: deprivation of liberty must always be lawful—in the sense of being in conformity with domestic law. Therefore, where

---

[125] *O'Hara v. United Kingdom*, § 40.   [126] Ibid., § 41.   [127] *Erdagöz v. Turkey*.
[128] *KF v. Germany*.   [129] *Gusinskiy v. Russia*.   [130] *Pantea v. Romania*.
[131] *Berktay v. Turkey*, §§ 199–201.

a specific element is required under national law for arrest and detention of a suspect to be lawful, the Court will examine whether in the specific case it was also present. Thus, it examined whether there was in fact a danger of absconding[132] or of reoffending.[133]

(b) The Suspicion of Having Committed an Offence

This first alternative is the only one not to cause any particular difficulties—it refers to detention on remand. As no prerequisite other than suspicion is required, the exception is extremely broad. However, as was mentioned above, additional limitations will often be imposed under domestic law. Furthermore, the specific reasons justifying detention on remand are of essential importance in the assessment of the reasonableness of the length of detention under paragraph 3.

The reference to an 'offence' means a specific and concrete offence.[134] Both the Commission and the Court found this condition to be satisfied with regard to section 14 of the British Prevention of Terrorism (Temporary Provisions) Act 1984 which defined terrorism.[135]

It has been argued that only an offence which carries a prison sentence could justify detention on remand, because such detention also serves the purpose of rendering the execution of the sentence possible.[136] However, the text of the Convention does not refer to any such restriction and, in the first place, detention on remand is intended to secure the presence of the accused at the trial. In view of the importance of certain misdemeanours, for example, in the context of the protection of the environment, there may be cases where the public interest is strong enough to justify the detention.[137]

In a number of cases it was doubtful whether the actions which the applicant was suspected of constituted an offence at all and thus whether they could 'be reasonably considered as falling under one of the sections describing criminal behaviour in the Criminal Code'.[138] The Court dealt with this issue as an element of the 'lawfulness' of the detention. In *Lukanov* the Strasbourg institutions were faced with a situation where there had been a clear abuse of power. The applicant, a high-placed politician under the communist regime, was prosecuted for embezzlement. This had allegedly consisted of the Government granting assistance to a number of extremely poor developing countries. There was not even the slightest possibility that this conduct could have constituted an offence.[139]

In *Włoch* the legal situation was very unclear. The applicant had been involved in organizing adoptions and was charged with trading in children under a section of the Criminal Code which had never before been applied. Had the applicant

---

[132] *Pantea* v. *Romania*, §§ 220–3.   [133] *NC* v. *Italy*, §§ 48–50.
[134] *Guzzardi* v. *Italy*, § 102; *Ciulla* v. *Italy*, § 40; it is also implicit in *Brogan and others* v. *United Kingdom*, § 51.   [135] *Brogan and others* v. *United Kingdom*, § 51.
[136] Frowein and Peukert (1996) Art. 5 N 59.
[137] See also Trechsel (1974) 215 and n. 793.   [138] *Włoch* v. *Poland*, § 109.
[139] *Lukanov* v. *Bulgaria*, §§ 42–5.

not been suspected of having committed another offence, the legality of the detention would, according to the rather enigmatic observation of the Court, have been 'doubtful'.[140] Such situations are particularly difficult because the Court is called upon to interpret domestic criminal law, a task which it is not particularly well equipped to do.

The term 'offence' has an autonomous definition. Even in cases where an act is not considered to be a *criminal* offence under domestic law, it may be regarded as an 'offence' within the meaning of Article 5 § 1(c) of the Convention, as happened with 'breach of the peace' in England.[141] Moreover, it is the substance rather than the form which is decisive. In *Douiyeb* a clerical error had led to the offence being wrongly designated—this did not affect the lawfulness of the detention.[142]

(c) When it is 'Reasonably Considered Necessary to Prevent [a Person] Committing an Offence'

The second alternative refers to 'preventative detention' in the narrow sense of the term.

In its very first case the Court stressed that the Convention could not permit detention which generally aimed at preventing a person from committing offences.[143] It later reaffirmed this view in the context of Italian 'measures of security' within the framework of the fight against organized crime. Article 5 § 1(c), the Court said, 'is not adapted to a policy of general prevention directed against an individual or a category of individuals who, like *mafiosi*, present a danger on account of their continuing propensity to crime; it does no more than afford the Contracting States a means of preventing a concrete and specific offence'.[144] Nor can the formula be invoked to justify detention where it is feared that the person concerned might evade other preventative measures which do not constitute a deprivation of liberty.[145] Furthermore, however, the Court has held that any person detained under paragraph 1(c) must eventually be brought to trial.[146] This makes sense only if there also exists a suspicion that the person concerned has actually committed an offence. In view of the first alternative, the second one becomes thereby redundant.[147]

Finally, in *Jėčius*, any lingering doubts about the compatibility of preventative detention with the Convention were dissipated: 'A person may be detained within the meaning of Article 5 § 1(c) only in the context of criminal proceedings, for the purpose of bringing him before the competent legal authority on suspicion of his having committed an offence'.[148] I cannot see, therefore, any substance in the second alternative of paragraph 1(c) of Article 5.

---

[140] *Włoch* v. *Poland*, §§ 111–14, 115.
[141] *Steel and others* v. *United Kingdom*, §§ 46, 48, 49.
[142] *Douiyeb* v. *Netherlands*, § 51; *Nikolov* v. *Bulgaria*, §§ 57–65.
[143] *Lawless* v. *Ireland (merits)*, § 14.   [144] *Guzzardi* v. *Italy*, § 102; *Ciulla* v. *Italy*, § 40.
[145] *Ciulla* v. *Italy*, § 40.   [146] *Lawless* v. *Ireland (No. 3)*, § 14, p. 53 with reference to § 3.
[147] This also results from *Ireland* v. *United Kingdom*, § 196.
[148] *Jėčius* v. *Lithuania*, § 50; see also *Włoch* v. *Poland*, § 108.

(d) When it is Reasonably Considered Necessary to Prevent a Person from Fleeing after Having Committed an Offence

This third alternative obviously does not add anything to the first one. It is difficult to reconcile with Article 6 § 2 as it presupposes, as a fact, that the person concerned *has* committed an offence. It can only be assumed that the drafters intended to cover a scenario where the suspect was 'caught in the act' ('*in flagrante*', '*flagrant délit*'). However, there is certainly no question of this constituting a legitimate exception from the requirements of the presumption of innocence.

2. The Purpose of Bringing the Person Concerned 'Before the Competent Legal Authority'

Detention on remand presupposes an intention to bring the person concerned 'before the competent legal authority'. The Court has repeatedly stressed that this applies to all three variants set out in paragraph 1(c)[149] but, as we have seen, two of them are without any normative meaning. The problem here is that the text leaves some doubt as to the meaning of the term 'competent judicial authority'.

There are two possibilities. First, the reference may be to the 'judge or other officer authorized by law to exercise judicial power' mentioned in paragraph 3. The Court adopted this view in several cases,[150] with the explanation that Article 5 §§ 1(c) and 3 have to be read as a whole. The rather vague term of 'competent legal authority' as compared to 'judge' or 'court' supports this idea. However, detention on remand must continue to be fully in conformity with paragraph 1(c), even after the person who has been arrested has been brought before the judge or other officer.[151] If that step were the fulfilment of the intention required, any detention thereafter would not be in conformity with Article 5 § 1(c) any more—an absurd result. Therefore, the purpose must be interpreted as referring to the trial judge, the judge who will decide on the merits.[152]

As paragraph 1(c) speaks of 'purpose', it does not require that the person concerned be actually brought to trial or even before the 'judge or other officer'. There is no violation of the Convention if he or she is released 'promptly' or if the investigation is discontinued as long as the deprivation of liberty was ordered 'in good faith'.[153] The Convention does forbid however any detention which is

---

[149] *Lawless v. Ireland (No. 3)*, § 14, p. 51; *De Jong, Baljet, Van den Brink v. Netherlands*, § 44.

[150] *Schiesser v. Switzerland*, § 29; *Guzzardi v. Italy*, § 102; *De Jong, Baljet, Van den Brink v. Netherlands*, § 44.

[151] This aspect is neglected in the dissenting opinions of Judges Bindschedler-Robert and Matscher in *Guzzardi v. Italy*, pp. 58 and 63 et seq. See, however, *mutatis mutandis*, *Bouamar v. Belgium*, § 46.

[152] This was already the Court's opinion in *Lawless v. Ireland*, §§ 14, 52 et seq., confirmed in *Ireland v. United Kingdom*, § 199; *Ciulla v. Italy*, § 38; and *Brogan and others v. United Kingdom*, § 53. See also Frowein and Peukert (1996) Art. 5 N 67. It is also implied quite clearly in *Ječius v. Lithuania*, § 50.

[153] *Brogan and others*, § 53; *Murray v. United Kingdom*, § 67; *KF v. Germany*, § 61; *Erdagöz v. Turkey*, § 51.

pursued in order to facilitate a 'fishing expedition', i.e. only for the purposes of interrogation.[154]

The term 'competent' refers to the function of the legal authority, not to the assignment of a judge to the task under paragraph 3 in accordance with internal rules on the distribution of cases.[155]

3. Specific Aspects of Lawfulness of Detention on Remand

No deprivation of liberty is compatible with the Convention unless it is lawful. The Court repeats the same standard formula again and again:

> The Court recalls that the expressions 'lawful' and 'in accordance with a procedure prescribed by law' . . . essentially refer back to national law and state the obligation to conform to the substantive and procedural rules[156] thereof. However, 'lawfulness' of detention under domestic law is not always the *decisive* element. The Court must in addition be satisfied that detention during the period under consideration was compatible with the purpose of Article 5 § 1 of the Convention, which is to prevent persons from being deprived of their liberty in an arbitrary fashion. The Court must moreover ascertain whether domestic law itself is in conformity with the Convention including the general principles expressed or implied therein.[157]

As to the degree of scrutiny exercised by the Court, there is also a standard formula:

> It is in the first place for the national authorities, notably the courts, to interpret and apply the domestic law. However, since under Article 5 § 1 failure to comply with domestic law entails a breach of the Convention, it follows that the Court can and should exercise a certain power to review whether this law has been complied with.[158]

One aspect of lawfulness has already been discussed, namely, the existence of an 'offence' under domestic law which the person concerned is suspected of having committed. Three further issues are to be discussed, the foreseeability of the law, the legality of detention of a person who was arrested outside the jurisdiction of the state, and delays in releasing a detainee.

(a) Insufficient Certainty of the Law

The requirement that deprivation of liberty must be 'lawful' presupposes a situation in law which satisfies the criteria first developed in the *Sunday Times (No. 1)* judgment, particularly as to the general principle of certainty. Adapting the general rule to the issue here under consideration, the Court said: 'It

---

[154] Cf. *Murray* v. *United Kingdom*, §§ 65–6.

[155] *X* v. *Germany* Application 9997/82, strongly criticized by van Dijk and van Hoof (1998), 263.

[156] In the French text of the Convention, the corresponding word '*régulier*' is missing, but this is of no relevance; *Kemmache* v. *France (No. 3)*, § 42.

[157] *Stasaitis* v. *Lithuania* § 58, referring to *Jėčius* v. *Lithuania*, § 56, and many others.

[158] *Öcalan* v. *Turkey*, § 87, referring to *Benham* v. *United Kingdom*, § 41; and *Bouamar* v. *Belgium*, § 49; and many others.

is . . . essential that the conditions for deprivation of liberty under domestic law should be clearly defined and that the law itself be foreseeable in its application'; it must be possible 'to foresee, to a degree that is reasonable in the circumstances, the consequences which a given action may entail'.[159]

In Poland persons detained on remand were regularly kept in prison after expiry of the detention order, because it was considered that with the lodging of a bill of indictment the detainee was placed at the disposal of the regional court. There was no legal basis for this practice, the legislation lacked clear rules and, in particular, no judicial decision authorizing the detention had been passed. The Court commented with reference to the general rule

that for the purposes of Article 5 § 1 of the Convention, detention which extends over a period of several months and which has not been ordered by a court or by a judge or any other person 'authorised . . . to exercise judicial power' cannot be considered 'lawful' in the sense of that provision. While this requirement is not explicitly stipulated in Article 5 § 1, it can be inferred from Article 5 read as a whole, in particular the wording in paragraph 1(c) ('for the purpose of bringing him before the competent legal authority') and paragraph 3 ('shall be brought promptly before a judge or other officer authorised to exercise judicial power'). In addition the habeas corpus guarantee contained in Article 5 § 4 further supports the view that detention which is prolonged beyond the initial period foreseen in paragraph 3 necessitates 'judicial' intervention as a safeguard against arbitrariness.[160]

A similarly unclear situation existed in Lithuania. In a whole series of cases, beginning with *Jėčius*, the Court found violations of Article 5 because persons had been detained without judicial warrant or a clear legal basis.[161]

The problem is not limited to former communist countries. In *Laumont* the Indictment Division ('*chambre d'accusation*') had ordered further investigations without, at the same time, ordering the continued detention of the applicant. However, there was clear case-law of the court of cassation according to which the fact of ordering further investigations meant, at the same time, that the imprisonment was to continue. Therefore, the Court found no violation.[162]

In the United Kingdom the case of *Steel and others* raised the question of legal certainty with regard to the notion of 'breach of the peace'. A person was deemed to have breached the peace 'when he or she behaved in a manner the natural consequence of which was that others would react violently'.[163] The applicants argued that this left the police too much discretion. The Court, however, found it well established that a breach of the peace was only committed 'when an individual causes harm or appears likely to cause harm, to persons or property or

---

[159] *Baranowski* v. *Poland*, § 52; *Kawka* v. *Poland*, § 49; *Steel and others* v. *United Kingdom*, § 54; *Laumont* v. *France*, § 45; and many others.

[160] *Baranowski* v. *Poland*, § 57; quoted verbatim in *Kawka* v. *Poland*, § 51.

[161] See the cases of *Jėčius* v. *Lithuania*; *Grauslys* v. *Lithuania*; *Stasaitis* v. *Lithuania*; and *Butkevicius* v. *Lithuania*.   [162] *Laumont* v. *France*, §§ 50, 51.

[163] *Steel and others* v. *United Kingdom*, § 52.

acts' likely to provoke violent reactions. This test constituted sufficient guidance.[164] Thus, it was clear that to walk in front of a hunter, and prevent him from shooting, or to stand in front of a mechanical digger in order to prevent a road from being built, would constitute a breach of the peace.[165]

However, the Court also found that the prerequisites were not present in the case of three applicants who were arrested for distributing leaflets.[166] On the one hand, this finding somehow contradicts the general assessment of the English law by the Court, because it demonstrates that 'breach of the peace' can provide a pretext for unjustified arrest of peaceful protesters. On the other hand, the Court seems to take on the role of a court of fourth instance by actually determining whether a certain form of behaviour fell to be regarded as a breach of the peace or not.

(b) *Male Captus Bene Iudicatus?*

States are able to exercise their jurisdiction within their territory. If the person they want to prosecute, or some evidence they want to gather, is located in another state, they will have to request the assistance of the relevant state. Such assistance, by way, for instance, of extradition or letters rogatory, will be granted on the basis of multilateral or bilateral international treaties or ad hoc agreements.[167] In any case, certain procedural safeguards exist. Mutual assistance in criminal matters, which was originally regarded as a matter affecting only the interests of the states concerned, has in recent years become increasingly focused on the individual.[168] The most spectacular judgment of the Court in this field is *Soering*, where it was found that the extradition of the applicant to the United States, where he risked suffering from the so-called 'death row phenomenon', would violate his rights under Article 3 of the ECHR.

In a number of cases the Commission and the Court were called upon to decide whether a person who had been brought under the jurisdiction of a respondent state by irregular procedures could be regarded as being lawfully detained there—an issue sometimes referred to by the Latin expression '*male captus bene iudicatus*', which means that despite an irregular arrest, the later conviction and enforcement of sentence are lawful.

For the purposes of Article 5 § 1(c), the question is whether such deprivation can be regarded as being based on a 'procedure prescribed by law' ('*selon les voies légales*').[169]

---

[164] Ibid., § 55.   [165] Ibid., §§ 58, 59.   [166] Ibid., § 64.

[167] For a collection of sources, see C. van den Wijngaert, *International Criminal Law: A Collection of International and European Instruments*, 3rd edn. (Leiden and Boston: Nijhoff, 2005).

[168] On this subject, see O. Lagodny, *Internationale Rechtshilfe in Strafsachen* (Munich: Beck, 2003).

[169] For a negative answer, see Trechsel (1987) 75 et seq.; Trechsel (1992) 633 et seq. For the case-law of the US Supreme Court, see e.g. *United States* v. *Duarte-Acero*, 296 F. 3d 1277, cert denied, 123 S.Ct. 573, US Court of Appeals for the Eleventh Circuit, 12 July 2002, and Sloss (2003).

While the Commission, for a long time, declared such cases inadmissible,[170] the Court, in *Öcalan*, accepted the principle that 'an arrest made by the authorities of one State on the territory of another State, without the consent of the latter, affects the person's individual rights to security under Article 5 § 1'.[171] Even this principle, however, is phrased in rather vague terms. What do the words 'affect . . . the rights to security' mean?

Until now, the question whether a deprivation of liberty was 'in accordance with a procedure prescribed by law' was only examined with regard to the law of the Contracting State where the applicant had been deprived of his or her liberty. What if a person is detained in state B after having been apprehended in state A in a way which is not in accordance with the law of that state? In other words, does the Convention support the thesis of *male captus bene detentus* (or *judicatus*)?[172]

It would seem that it does. The Commission declared inadmissible the application of *Altmann (Barbie) v. France*, where the applicant claimed to have been unlawfully kidnapped in Bolivia.[173] Likewise, the Court found no violation in *Stocké*,[174] although the applicant had been (quite unlawfully) induced to board a plane in France and later arrested in the Federal Republic of Germany where he had been taken against his will.[175] The question has been addressed by the Court in *Öcalan*.

The applicant, leader of the PKK, had briefly found refuge in Kenya, in the Greek embassy, after a journey which had taken him from Syria to Greece, Russia, Italy, and again to Russia and Greece, in search of asylum. The Kenyan authorities did not want him there either and they eventually handed him over to Turkish officials at Nairobi airport. The Court's approach was to ask whether Turkey, by conducting the arrest on a Turkish aeroplane in the international zone of Nairobi airport, had violated Kenyan sovereignty. It found that this had not been the case as the Kenyan authorities had been keen to cooperate.[176] The Court concluded:

101. In the light of these considerations and in the absence of any extradition treaty between Turkey and Kenya laying down a formal procedure to be followed, the Court holds that it has not been established beyond all reasonable doubt that the operation carried out in the instant case partly by Turkish officials and partly by Kenyan officials amounted to a violation by Turkey of Kenyan sovereignty and, consequently, of international law.

---

[170] *Freda v. Italy* Application 8910/80; *Klaus Altmann (Barbie) v. France* Application 10689/83; *Luc Reinette v. France* Application 14009/80; *Illich Sanchez Ramirez ('Carlos') v. France*.
[171] *Öcalan v. Turkey*, § 88; referring to the Commission's report in *Stocké v. Germany*, § 167. *Stocké v. Germany* was not decided on the merits in that the Court found the facts not established; the same applied in *Egmez v. Cyprus*.　　　　　　　　　　[172] Velu and Ergec (1990) N 319.
[173] *Altmann v. France* Application 10689/83.
[174] *Stocké v. Germany*, §§ 49, 54; the Court found that an involvement of the German authorities was not proven.　　　[175] The question arises in *Drozd and Janousek v. France and Spain*.
[176] *Öcalan v. Turkey (1st Section)*, §§ 96 et seq.

102. The Court holds, lastly, that the fact that the arrest warrants were not shown to the applicant until he was detained by members of the Turkish security forces in an aircraft at Nairobi Airport does not deprive his subsequent arrest of a legal basis under Turkish law.

At the time of writing, the case is pending before the Grand Chamber. It seems therefore premature to discuss the judgment of the First Section in detail. However, it is not quite convincing that the respect of the applicant's rights under Article 5 of the Convention should depend on the question whether the sovereignty of Kenya has been respected. Kidnapping suspects abroad cannot be compatible with the rule of law.

(c) Delayed Release

It would appear rather obvious that a person has to be set free as soon as the reasons on which her or his detention is based cease to exist, particularly after there has been an acquittal or a decision to release.[177] The jurisprudence of the Court demonstrates that this is not always the case.

In the first judgment dealing with this problem, *Quinn* v. *France,* there seems to have been a clear abuse of power. The chamber responsible for preparing the indictment ('*chambre d'accusation*') had ordered the immediate release of the applicant, but the public prosecutor did not execute this order because he was expecting a demand for extradition which duly arrived that evening. The criminal proceedings thus continued and the applicant was forced to remain in custody awaiting extradition. The Court acknowledged that 'some delay in executing a decision ordering the release of a detainee is understandable', but the continuation for eleven hours after the decision which was not even notified to him 'was clearly not covered by sub-paragraph (c) of paragraph 1 of Article 5 and did not fall within the scope of any other of the sub-paragraphs of that provision'.[178]

Later cases seem to involve administrative inactivity and carelessness rather than deliberate, improper acts. Most, though not all, of the judgments are quite persuasive. In *K and F* v. *Germany,* where the delay was limited to forty-five minutes, it was decisive that the German law was very precise on this point.[179] In *Nikolov* the authorities attempted to explain the delay by referring to difficulties in contacting the applicant's mother—an excuse which was not at all convincing.[180]

In *Labita* the Court detailed some reasons which may justify delay, namely 'the need for the relevant administrative formalities to be carried out'.[181] It is legitimate to wonder, however, how prolonged detention can be justified by the need to carry out such formalities. So far, the Court seems not to have addressed this question which is, however, of particular importance. In *Mancini* the

---

[177] e.g. *Pantea* v. *Romania,* § 225, where the Government agreed that there had been a violation.
[178] *Quinn* v. *France,* § 42.   [179] *K-F* v. *Germany,* §§ 69–72.
[180] *Nikolov* v. *Bulgaria,* §§ 83, 84; the Court found it particularly serious that there was no 'strict account of the relevant events, hour by hour'.   [181] *Labita* v. *Italy,* § 172.

Government claimed that the delay was due to the fact that it had taken three days for the decision to be served on the detainees—the Court left this point unanswered.[182] There can be no doubt, however, that such a delay is entirely unacceptable.

In contrast to these judgments, *Manzoni* must be regarded as being an unfortunate mistake. The applicant had been released after a delay of seven hours. The Court was not informed of any details of her imprisonment but accepted that there had been avoidable delays. Nevertheless, and without really explaining why, it found that 'that is not a ground for finding that there has been a breach of the Convention'.[183] The Court seemed to apply the *de minimis non curat praetor* rule. A few months later a delay of forty-five minutes (sic!) was held sufficient to constitute a violation.[184] *Erdagöz* must be similarly criticized. The applicant had complained of the fact that he had been kept in detention beyond the legal limit for detention in police custody. The Court did not answer this allegation as the applicant had not complained to the Commission of a violation of Article 5 § 3.[185] Such a formalistic approach is, fortunately, rather exceptional. It seems rather obvious that the applicant was in fact kept unlawfully imprisoned for thirteen hours and had complained of this fact in substance—the later case-law has not supported this approach which is hard to reconcile with the scope and spirit of the Convention.

One of the most serious violations of the right to liberty, if the disappearance of persons is excluded, is documented in the *Assanidze* case where a prisoner was kept in a small cell in Adjaria, Georgia for over three years after the court had ordered his release.[186] Here, the difficult political situation, which has since improved, was to blame for this patently unsatisfactory situation.

4. Necessity

We have seen that no requirement of the deprivation of liberty being 'necessary in a democratic society' found its way into Article 5 of the ECHR.[187] It would be tempting to regard this as a glaring oversight. Upon closer scrutiny, however, it becomes clear that the reason for its absence is based on the different types of detention covered by the provision.

In relation to Article 5 § 1(a) which concerns detention following conviction, it is quite obvious that any test of necessity would be quite inappropriate. Not only must the Convention organs assume that it is generally necessary to give effect to penal judgments, but they have no competence to examine the diverse, and sometimes complicated, rules on remission, release on parole, '*semi-liberté*', and so forth which, under national law, may affect the enforcement of a prison sentence or other criminal sanctions implying deprivation of liberty. It would be

---

[182] *Vittorio and Luigi Mancini v. Italy*, §§ 22, 25. [183] *Giulia Manzoni v. Italy*, § 25.
[184] *KF v. Germany.* [185] *Erdagöz v. Turkey*, § 50.
[186] *Assanidze v. Georgia.* [187] Nor into ICCPR, Art. 9 or ACHR, Art. 7.

even less appropriate for an international body called upon to implement human rights to enter into a discussion on the severity of sentences or on necessity of the use of detention as a criminal sanction.[188]

Similarly, most, if not all, of the Contracting States have concluded treaties on extradition. These treaties may oblige them to arrest the person who is the subject of an extradition request. In this respect, although excluding issues relating to the length of the detention, there is hardly any room for a test of necessity.[189] On the other hand, such a test is called for, at least to some extent, with regard to detention on remand under paragraph 1(c). At any rate, such detention may not exceed a reasonable period of time in order to ensure compatibility with paragraph 3.

As far as the other cases listed in paragraph 1 are concerned, I would suggest that they must be read as if the element of necessity were an integral part of them.[190] In fact, any such deprivation of liberty which cannot be regarded as 'necessary', that is, as satisfying a 'pressing social need' and as being proportional to the aim pursued, must be regarded as arbitrary and thereby in violation of the Convention. Of course, 'necessity' must always be assessed with regard to the specific case at issue. The question, therefore, requires further elaboration in the context of the different exceptions. At any rate, the fact that the necessity requirement was not written into the text of the exception does not exclude its relevance for their interpretation.

In *NC* v. *Italy* we find, however, an interesting sentence: 'It does not suffice that the deprivation of liberty is executed in conformity with national law; it must also be *necessary* in the circumstances'.[191] The sentence is rather surprising. Despite the reasons given above, they show that the Court is prepared to retain a requirement of 'necessity' in cases where it is appropriate.

Unfortunately, so far there seems to have been no repetition of this rule nor have there been any cases where lack of necessity led to the finding of a violation of Article 5. Such an approach might have led to a different result in a rather puzzling case, *Kemmache* v. *France*.

The applicant was to be tried before the Alpes-Maritimes Assizes Court. Having been at liberty, he surrendered and was taken into custody in conformity with Article 215-1 of the FCCP. The hearing was adjourned but he was nevertheless kept in custody. This was explained by a fear that he might abscond or bring pressure upon witnesses. The Court refused to criticize these explanations, referring to the 'fourth instance formula'.[192] The Commission had earlier found a violation. Indeed, any test of necessity would have failed miserably in this case. It is entirely illogical to pretend that there is a danger of flight or of meddling with the evidence in the case of a person who, after the investigation, was

---

[188] This is, however, challenged by the abolitionist movement.
[189] See further section II.G.2.(b) below.
[190] Cf., *mutatis mutandis*, *Van der Mussele* v. *Belgium*, § 43.
[191] *NC* v. *Italy*, § 41 (emphasis added).   [192] *Kemmache* v. *France (No. 3)*, §§ 44–5.

liberated and then surrenders of his free will before the trial. In fact, the very rule of the French law which requires such surrender can hardly be accepted as following a pressing social need.

C. Detention after Conviction: Article 5, paragraph 1(a)

1. General Characteristics

Article 5 § 1 begins with a practically uncontested exception to personal liberty—the serving of a sentence.[193] Although, at the outset, this might seem to be a straightforward and simple matter, a surprising number of problems have arisen in this context. Although the justification is of a formal character, the terms 'conviction' and 'competent court', as well as the relationship between conviction and detention (expressed simplistically by the term 'after'), need further explanation. While the implementation of a custodial sentence cannot be regarded as forming part of criminal proceedings, it is so closely linked to the latter that its inclusion in the present study seems justified.

2. Conviction

(a) Definition

In comparing Article 5 § 1(a) with Articles 6 § 2 and 7 § 1, the Court found 'that for Convention purposes there cannot be a "condemnation" (in the English text: "conviction") unless it has been established in accordance with the law that there has been an offence—either criminal or, if appropriate, disciplinary... Moreover... that word implies a finding of guilt'.[194] Furthermore, 'conviction' refers to 'the imposition of a penalty or other measure involving a deprivation of liberty'.[195] In the case of a fine or a similar pecuniary sanction which is liable to be converted into a prison sentence in event of non-payment, there are two possibilities. First, if the fine has been imposed by a court and that same court or clear legal provisions determine from the outset the length of deprivation of liberty incurred in the case of non-payment, the detention itself may then be ordered by an administrative authority. Alternatively, if these conditions are not fulfilled, the decision to commute the fine must be taken by a court.[196]

The existence of a conviction was challenged in *Steel and others* where environmental activists refused to comply with a 'binding over' order. They had been fined for breach of the peace and were asked to sign a declaration promising 'to keep the peace and be of good behaviour for a period of twelve months, subject to a recognizance of GBP 100'. The Court rightly concluded that the

---

[193] Chiavario (1998) 2 N 1.2.

[194] *Guzzardi* v. *Italy*, § 100, confirmed *inter alia* in *X* v. *United Kingdom*, § 39; *Van Droogenbroeck* v. *Belgium*, § 35; the inclusion of disciplinary convictions was first mentioned in *Engel and others* v. *Netherlands*, § 68.   [195] *Van Droogenbroeck* v. *Belgium*, § 35.

[196] Trechsel (1974) 301 et seq.

committal to prison for refusing to sign this order fell under the exception of Article 5 § 1(b) rather than (a).[197]

A person sentenced to life imprisonment cannot invoke the Convention to obtain release on probation.[198] However, if a prison pre-release system is operated, this must be done without discrimination.[199]

(b) Guilt

There can only be said to be a 'conviction' if the person concerned has been found guilty of a criminal offence. If, due to mental illness, there has been an acquittal and the person has been committed to an institution for therapy, care, or safety, then the detention falls under paragraph 1(e).[200] This means, in my view, that it is legitimate for a non-judicial body, such as a chamber of indictment ('*Anklagekammer*'), or even the public prosecutor's office, to commit a defendant who would have to be acquitted at a trial directly to a mental institution; this would not violate the Convention.[201] The necessary judicial control would then be secured by habeas corpus proceedings.

(c) Final Judgment

As the deprivation of liberty must be lawful, and 'lawfulness' refers to domestic law, it would seem that any deprivation of liberty could only be based upon a conviction if and insofar as the execution of the sentence is possible under national law. As a rule, this will be the case when the judgment becomes final.

The Court, however, does not follow this chain of thought. Since one of its first judgments,[202] it has been of the opinion that, irrespective of the rules under domestic law, detention after the judgment at first instance, even if there is an appeal pending, always falls to be considered as detention in the sense of paragraph 1(a), with the consequence that the time restraints imposed by paragraph 3, do not apply.[203] The main reason for this is the fact that national legislation varies in this respect and, therefore, in some states detention pending appeal would have to be concluded within a 'reasonable time' while in other states it would not. This issue will be discussed in more depth in the context of Article 5 § 3.

(d) Material Justification

It has sometimes been suggested that the execution of a prison sentence could only be lawful if the conviction itself were in substance well founded or, at least, in conformity with Article 7.[204] However, this proposition cannot be correct. I do not find it necessary to develop an advanced theory in order to prove this

---

[197] *Steel* v. *United Kingdom*, §§ 69–70.
[198] *Christinet* v. *Switzerland* Application 7648/67; *G* v. *Germany* Application 14289/88.
[199] *W* v. *United Kingdom* Application 12118/86.
[200] *Luberti* v. *Italy*, § 25; *Herczegfalvy* v. *Austria*, § 66; and, *e contrario*, *Bizzotto* v. *Greece*, § 32.
[201] *X* v. *Belgium* Application 5973/73.   [202] *Wemhoff* v. *Germany*, § 9.
[203] This jurisprudence was confirmed in *B* v. *Austria*, §§ 36–9.
[204] Van Dijk and van Hoof (1998) 256; Jacobs (1975) 47; Velu and Ergec (1990) N 313.

opinion—a simple consideration of the procedural situation should be entirely convincing.

Any violation of Article 7 would occur at the time of the conviction and can, according to Article 35 § 1 of the ECHR, only be brought before the Court within six months of the final judgment. This six-month rule would be frustrated if the question could still be raised at a later point in time via a 'detour' by complaining of the custodial sentence which the convict is serving. Legal certainty, which is served by the time limit, would be severely jeopardized.

On the other hand, paragraph 1(a) is of a formal character[205] and does not, as a matter of principle, empower the Convention organs to test the conviction itself.[206] However, the argument relating to the procedural aspect just referred to suggests that there must be an exception to the rule. In fact, there is no danger of Article 35 § 1 being ignored if the 'conviction' was imposed by a jurisdiction not bound by the Convention. If such a judgment were to be enforced by a Contracting State, even though it was passed in clear violation of Article 7, this could constitute a violation of the Convention.[207]

Another exception applies if the conviction is so blatantly unlawful as to be characterized as arbitrary. This was the case in *Tsirlis and Kouloumpas*.[208] The applicants were ministers of the Jehovah's Witnesses which meant that they were exempt from military service. Nevertheless the Recruitment Office ordered them to report for duty at a military training centre. On refusal, they were convicted for insubordination and sentenced to four years' imprisonment. Their appeals failed. They were only released after having served thirteen and twelve months in prison respectively.

The Court accepted that the detention was 'after conviction by a competent court' but concluded that it was not 'lawful'. While it is in the first place for the national authorities to interpret domestic law, the Court must exercise a certain power to review this, because failure to comply with domestic law entails a breach of the Convention.[209] More specifically, the Court described its task as follows: 'detention will in principle be lawful if it is carried out pursuant to a court order. A subsequent finding that the court erred under domestic law in making the order will not necessarily retrospectively affect the validity of the intervening period of detention. For this reason, the Strasbourg organs have consistently refused to uphold applications from persons convicted of criminal offences who complain that their convictions... were found... to have been based on errors of fact or law'.[210] In the present case, however, the military

---

[205] Velu and Ergec (1990) N 313.   [206] *Krzycki* v. *Germany* Application 7629/76.
[207] The facts would have to be assessed not only in the light of Art. 5 § 1(a), but also of Art. 7 read together with Art. 1 ('shall secure'). In its report on Application 12747/87, *Drozd and Janousek* v. *France and Spain*, § 120, the Commission held that Art. 5 § 1(a) also applies to the execution of foreign judgments, whereas the Court took a somewhat more reserved stand in para. 110 of the judgment.   [208] *Tsirlis and Kouloumpas* v. *Greece*.
[209] Ibid., § 57; *Bouamar* v. *Belgium*, § 49.
[210] *Tsirlis and Kouloumpas* v. *Greece*, § 57; with reference to *Benham* v. *United Kingdom*, § 42.

authorities had 'blatantly ignored' the law. It is remarkable that the Court does not limit itself to finding that the detention had not been lawful but uses the word 'arbitrary' which can only been read as emphasizing the Court's belief that this was a particularly serious violation.[211] It also awarded the applicants compensation which almost amounted to the full amount which they had asked for.[212]

(e) Compliance with Article 6

A similar question arises with regard to the proceedings which have led to the conviction—do they have to satisfy the requirements of Article 6? Again, the answer must in principle be 'no', and the same argument as used in relation to Article 35 § 1 still holds.[213] In *Engel* the Court went so far as expressly to say that as Article 5 § 1(a) was an 'autonomous provision' its 'requirements are not always co-extensive with those of Article 6'.[214] The question was again at issue in the case of *Drozd and Janousek*. The Commission had stressed that 'it is hardly possible to scrutinize thoroughly' whether a foreign judgment had been passed in respect of the guarantees as set out in Article 6, but added that 'the detention of a person by virtue of a sentence passed following criminal proceedings in which the essential guarantees of the rights of the defence have not been respected could be regarded as not "lawful"'.[215] The Court set somewhat narrower limits:[216] assistance in criminal matters by way of execution of sentence must only be refused 'if it emerges that the conviction is the result of a flagrant denial of justice'.[217] It found that the present case did not meet this standard. This is far from ideal. For one, the standard is too low—detention must be lawful, not just 'not arbitrary'. In addition, the problem with the judgment was that it was passed by a tribunal which did not satisfy the requirements of Article 6 § 1 and fell to be regarded as null and void. It seems that the enforcement of such a judgment would indeed amount to a flagrant denial of justice.[218]

The judgment may also take the form of a penal order, that is, a proposal issued by a judge or an administrative authority (including a public prosecutor) which becomes enforceable unless the accused objects.[219]

---

[211] *Tsirlis and Kouloumpas* v. *Greece*, § 62.   [212] Ibid., § 78–80.

[213] Van Dijk and van Hoof (1998) 257 seem to hold the opposite view, based on what, in my view, is an erroneous reading of *Wemhoff* v. *Germany*, § 9, p. 24.

[214] *Engel and others* v. *Netherlands*, § 68.

[215] *Drozd and Janousek* v. *France and Spain* Application 12747/87, §§ 148, 149. See also *X* v. *Germany* Application 1322/62, criticized by Jacobs (1975) 47 et seq.

[216] *Drozd and Janousek* v. *France and Spain*, § 110.

[217] cf. also *Soering* v. *United Kingdom*, § 113.

[218] Judges Cremona, Macdonald, Bernhard, Pekkanen, and Wildhaber, in dissenting opinions to *Drozd and Janousek* v. *France and Spain*, objected that France ought at least to have exercised effective control.

[219] Trechsel (1988) 135 at 137. It must be pointed out, however, that penal orders ought not to be the form in which prison sentences are passed; cf. Resolution R(87)18, adopted by the Committee of Ministers on 17 Sept. 1987.

3. Competent Court

The notion of 'court' in paragraph 1(a) must be given the same meaning as in Article 6 § 1.[220] Although the Court has stated that the term implies 'also the guarantee of judicial procedure',[221] the scrutiny of the Convention organs on that point is strictly limited, for the reasons set out above.

Competence falls to be examined *ratione loci, personae, temporis,* and *materiae.* Again, however, the Court will not examine in detail whether the domestic law was correctly applied and will interfere only in cases of an obvious lack of competence.[222] An example is deprivation of liberty as a disciplinary sanction. In two cases against Switzerland the Commission found a violation of Article 5 § 1 because the applicants concerned had not been convicted by 'a competent court'.[223]

4. The Link Between Conviction and Detention: 'After'

As the Court has frequently and correctly stated, 'the word "after" in sub-paragraph (a) does not simply mean that the detention must follow the "conviction" in point of time: in addition, the detention must result from, follow and depend upon or occur by virtue of the "conviction" '.[224] This was clearly not the case in *Bozano*.[225] In this case, the applicant had been sentenced to life imprisonment in Italy; he had fled to France which then refused to extradite him because the judgment had been passed *in absentia.* One night, however, Bozano was brought unlawfully to the Swiss border where he was arrested by the Swiss police; later on he was extradited to Italy. The detention in France was not based on the conviction.

The link was also clearly missing in *Steel* where the applicants had been fined for breach of the peace and then imprisoned for refusing to be bound over.[226]

Difficult questions have also arisen with regard to the link between conviction and detention in cases where measures of security or prison sentences of indeterminate duration had been pronounced. These will often concern mentally ill offenders or criminals considered to constitute a danger to society. Indeterminate or life sentences are not as such contrary to the Convention.[227] However, insofar as the sentence has been justified by reference to a specific condition in the convicted person's personality and such a condition is subject to change with the

---

[220] *De Wilde, Ooms and Versyp* v. *Belgium,* § 76.   [221] Ibid.
[222] *R* v. *Germany* Application 11506/85; Velu and Ergec (1990) N 519.
[223] *Santschi and others* v. *Switzerland* Application (1981) 31 DR 5 (report); *Eggs* v. *Switzerland* Application 7341/76, § 72. For the situation after reform, see *Borrelli* v. *Switzerland* Application 17571/90.
[224] *Monnell and Morris* v. *United Kingdom,* § 40; *Weeks* v. *United Kingdom,* § 42; *Bozano* v. *France,* § 53; *van Droogenbroeck* v. *Belgium,* § 35; *X* v. *United Kingdom,* § 39; *B* v. *Austria,* § 38.
[225] *Bozano* v. *France,* § 53.   [226] *Steel and others* v. *United Kingdom,* § 68.
[227] Frowein and Peukert (1996) Art. 5 N 40.

course of time, it is conceivable that the connection might break.[228] Two distinct problems arise in these cases, the conformity of the deprivation of liberty with Article 5 § 1(a) and the right to habeas corpus proceedings—here we are only concerned with the former.

The cases which were examined by the Commission and the Court are all characterized by an additional particularity: the detention had been interrupted by provisional release, but on breaching the terms of the licence permitting the release, the applicant was then recalled to prison by an administrative authority.[229] In the older cases, the Strasbourg authorities concluded that a causal link between conviction and detention still existed.[230]

In the *Stafford* case, the Court went a step further. It abandoned its usual tendency of carefully shaping its jurisprudence to ensure that it can be applied to all the different legal systems of the states party to the Convention,[231] in favour of a more active approach. This judgment is solidly imbedded in the legal system of the United Kingdom and it is difficult to speculate how it will be applied in other legal systems. On the continent, the court will normally opt for a sentence which it deems to be proportionate to the guilt of the convicted person, even if other aspects such as the dangerousness of the person or the importance of reintegration may also be considered. As a consequence of the ontological approach to crime, the birth of criminology, in particular Cesare Lombroso and the school of *défence sociale*, a binary system developed. The arsenal of criminal law was enriched by the introduction of so-called 'measures of security' which were independent of any guilt of the criminal.[232] They served the purpose of permitting to cure mental defects including addiction, and/or to protect society against dangerous persons.

In the United Kingdom the same effect was pursued in a somewhat oblique way by use of a complex sentencing procedure, at least in relation to life sentences.[233] A life sentence has two components, a punitive one, which serves the dual aims of retribution and deterrence, and a further element which may be imposed in the interests of public safety. Although nominally it may be thought otherwise, with regard to the sentence of life imprisonment, there is usually no serious intention to keep the person concerned behind bars until he or she dies. On the contrary, in *Weeks* the judge stressed that the applicant might be released earlier on the basis of a life sentence than if he were sentenced to a number of

---

[228] *Van Doogenbroeck* v. *Belgium*, § 40; *Weeks* v. *United Kingdom*, § 46.

[229] In addition to *Van Droogenbroeck* v. *United Kingdom* and *Weeks* v. *United Kingdom*, see also *Christinet* v. *Switzerland* Application 7648/76.

[230] See e.g. *X, Weeks, Singh, Hussain, Wynne, Thynne, Gunnell and Wilson*, and *Stafford*, all v. *United Kingdom*.

[231] See for a striking though not very convincing example, the judgments of *Kruslin* v. *France*, § 29 and *Huvig* v. *France*, § 28.   [232] Kaenel (1981).

[233] Detention 'at Her Majesty's pleasure', however, which was at issue in *Singh* v. *United Kingdom* and *Hussain* v. *United Kingdom* corresponds largely to a continental-type 'measure of security'.

years in prison.[234] The time to be served under the title of retribution is called the 'tariff period'.

For quite some time, the tariff was fixed by the Home Secretary. However, this was not compatible with Article 6 § 1 which requires that not only the conviction, but also the sentence, be decided by an independent and impartial tribunal.[235] At first only the discretionary life sentence was regarded as being comprised of these two parts. In *Wynne* the Court considered that the mandatory life sentence meant indeed detention for the rest of the convicted person's life.[236] However, this turned out to be erroneous and in *Stafford* the Court held that even part of such sentences involved public-safety considerations.

The applicant in *Stafford* had been convicted of murder in 1967 and sentenced to life imprisonment. He was released on licence in 1979. However, in violation of the conditions imposed on him he went to South Africa and the licence was revoked. When he returned to the United Kingdom he was arrested and fined for having used a false passport. He remained in custody due to the revocation of his licence.

The Court came to the conclusion that this detention violated Article 5. It could not be justified under paragraph 1(a) because by 1979 the applicant had already served that part of his sentence which was covered by the 'tariff', i.e. the time to be served for the purposes of retribution and deterrence. Any further detention could only be justified by dangerousness. The Court accepted that there might have been a danger that the applicant would commit fraud. However, this was irrelevant because the original sentence had been passed to punish a violent crime and only the risk of further violent crimes could be regarded as covered by the life sentence.

It is much more difficult, however, to follow the Court's reasoning in *Monnell and Morris* which concerned an entirely different matter. Here, the Commission had come to the conclusion, by ten votes to one, that there had been a violation of Article 5 § 1; the Court however disagreed.[237] In this case the Court of Appeal had ordered loss of time for the detention which the applicants had served pending appeal, which 'effectively impose[d] a period of imprisonment in addition to that which would result from the sentence',[238] a period which, in my view, must be considered as arbitrary, since it was in no way related to the conviction and its duration could not be influenced by the applicants. The purpose of this detention was to discourage misuse of appeal proceedings, which is undoubtedly a legitimate aim. I fail to understand, however, why it should be regarded as detention 'after conviction' within the meaning of paragraph 1(a).[239]

---

[234] *Weeks* v. *United Kingdom*, §§ 14, 15.
[235] For a concise description of the development of the domestic law, see *Stafford* v. *United Kingdom*, §§ 70–80; see also *Easterbrook* v. *United Kingdom*.
[236] *Wynne* v. *United Kingdom*, § 32.   [237] *Monnell and Morris* v. *United Kingdom*.
[238] Ibid., § 43; see also *Gerger* v. *Turkey*, § 68.
[239] See also the criticism expressed by Velu and Ergec (1990) N 315a.

The solution which was adopted by the Commission in no way implies that detention on remand or pending extradition must be counted towards sentence under the Convention,[240] the domestic law is decisive in this respect.[241] However, it must be compatible with one of the grounds set out in Article 5 § 1.

5. The Duration of Imprisonment

It is obvious that any detention which exceeds the time to be served will lead to a violation of Article 5. In this respect, the case of *Grava* is particularly clear.[242] The applicant was in a rather complicated situation. He had been sentenced in one judgment to six years' imprisonment which had however been reduced to four. Having fled, he was arrested in Romania with a view to extradition, which was finally granted. After his return to Italy he applied for a further remission of the sentence to which he was entitled by law. The court of appeal of Trieste refused this request for reasons which do not appear to have been from the outset unfounded. However, the Court of Cassation came to a different conclusion. It found that the applicant ought to have been released two months earlier. He had in fact spent an additional two months and four days in prison. The Strasbourg Court considered that this detention was unjustified and also awarded non-pecuniary damages of 8,000 euros. It gave no weight to the authorities' assertion that they had kept the applicant in detention in good faith.

D. Detention for Non-compliance with a Court Order or to Secure the Fulfilment of a Legal Obligation: Article 5, paragraph 1(b)

Paragraph 1(b) deals with two unrelated exceptions to personal liberty, which must be dealt with separately. They may be of relevance in the context of criminal proceedings, particularly as a measure of discipline against, for example, recalcitrant witnesses.

1. Detention 'for Non-compliance with the Lawful Order of a Court'

In the case of non-compliance with a court order, the Convention introduces a third reference to lawfulness in that the order in question must itself be lawful. It is clear that this refers not only to domestic law but also to compatibility with the Convention. A court order might be, for example, incompatible with Article 5 if it required an interference with private life which is not as such justified according to the criteria set out in Article 8 § 2[243] or if it required the person to incriminate him- or herself.

---

[240] See e.g. *C* v. *United Kingdom* Application 10854/84.
[241] Cf. e.g. *Grava* v. *Italy*, §§ 24 et seq.   [242] *Grava* v. *Italy*.
[243] See also Protocol No. 4, Art. 1.

According to the text, only the order to do or to omit to do something has to be made by the court, while the detention itself could be decided by an administrative authority.[244] This solution is, however, potentially problematic as it might leave too large a margin of appreciation to non-judicial authorities. The clause, in my view, should be interpreted in the sense that the court must not only make the order but also fix the duration of any detention in case of non-compliance. It could be left to an administrative authority to decide whether the order was complied with or if detention is required.

While, in early writing, the meaning of Article 5 § 1(b) was quite contested,[245] no difficult issues have arisen in relation to its application on the European level.[246] The Court only briefly addressed the issue in *Bouamar* to say that the imprisonment of an 'adolescent with a disturbed personality owing mainly to family problems' did not fall to be justified under paragraph 1(b).[247]

2. Detention 'in Order to Secure the Fulfilment of any Obligation Prescribed by Law'

According to general rules, all exceptions to fundamental rights must be interpreted 'very narrowly'.[248] This is particularly so for the second alternative in paragraph 1(b) which could potentially be applied in such a manner as to evade the strict requirements in paragraph 1(a) and (c).[249]

In its first judgment, the Court, following the Commission, stated that the legal obligation could not be that of not committing 'offences against public peace and public order or against the security of the State', but only 'specific obligations imposed by law'.[250] It could definitely not justify the long-term imprisonment of the applicant just because he was suspected of connections with a terrorist organization. The formula becomes more precise in *Engel*, where the Court rightly concluded that military disciplinary punishment is not a measure to secure the fulfilment of a legal obligation, because this presupposes 'a specific and concrete obligation which [the person concerned] has until then failed to satisfy'.[251] This presupposes that the person in question was first warned and

---

[244] Frowein and Peukert (1996) N 54; Trechsel (1974) 203. Velu and Ergec (1990) N 321, while accepting the proposition, point out that Belgian law is stricter and must prevail by virtue of (former) Art. 60.

[245] For a detailed discussion of opinions expressed before 1974, see Trechsel (1974) 202.

[246] For the cases decided by the Commission, see Frowein and Peukert (1996) Art. 5 N 53; Trechsel (1980) 113; Velu and Ergec (1990) N 321.   [247] *Bouamar* v. *Belgium*, § 44.

[248] *McVeigh, O'Neill and Evans* v. *United Kingdom* Applications 8022/77, 8025/77, and 8027/77, § 162 (report). The Commission referred to *Winterwerp* v. *Netherlands*, § 37, where the Court only spoke of 'narrow interpretation'; in fact, the Commission then went on to give Article 5 § l(b) a particularly broad interpretation. In other judgments the Court used the term 'strictly', e.g. in *Ciulla* v. *Italy*, § 41.

[249] *Engel and others* v. *Netherlands*, § 69; see also van Dijk and van Hoof (1998) 259.

[250] *Lawless* v. *Ireland (No. 3)*, § 9, p. 47. See also *Guzzardi* v. *Italy*, § 101; *Ciulla* v. *Italy*, § 36.

[251] *Engel and others* v. *Netherlands*, § 69; the Court also rightly stressed that the detention must not be punitive.

given an opportunity to comply but neglected or refused to do so.[252] Obviously, the obligation must, then, have existed before the detention.[253]

A good example can be found in the *Johansen* case where the applicant was detained to enforce his obligation to perform civil service.[254] The Commission also accepted as 'specific' the duty to prove one's identity.[255]

Unfortunately, the Commission extended the scope of the application considerably and vaguely in the *McVeigh, O'Neill and Evans* case to 'other limited circumstances of a pressing nature which warrant detention in order to secure fulfilment of an obligation'.[256] The applicants had been held for almost two days for identification and, in particular, examination on their arrival from Ireland to Liverpool under the Prevention of Terrorism (Temporary Provisions) Act 1976 and the Prevention of Terrorism (Supplemental Temporary Provisions) Order 1976. Here, in my view, paragraph 1(b) was invoked to circumvent the requirement of 'suspicion' in paragraph 1 (c).[257]

E. Detention of a Minor: Article 5, paragraph 1(d)

1. 'Minor'

Paragraph 1(d) gives the Contracting State 'far-reaching powers'[258] to deprive young persons of their liberty for educational purposes. So far, the Convention organs have not had to determine what is meant by the term 'minor'. In the first place, regard must be had to domestic law;[259] otherwise the measure would not be 'lawful'. On the other hand, however, the term might have to be given an autonomous interpretation if the limit set by domestic law is too high. Resolution (72)29 of the Committee of Ministers, according to which the age limit that brings full legal capacity should be lowered to eighteen, is in no way binding for the Court.[260]

2. The Educational Purpose

Deprivation of liberty under paragraph 1(d) must always serve an educational purpose, either directly or indirectly, such as where the minor is first to be

---

[252] *McVeigh, O'Neill and Evans* v. *United Kingdom* Applications 8022/77, 8025/77, and 8027/77, §§ 173, 190 (report).   [253] *Ciulla* v. *Italy*, § 36.
[254] *Johansen* v. *Norway* Application 10600/83; for further (hypothetical) examples, see Trechsel (1974) 205.   [255] *B* v. *France* Application 10179/82.
[256] *McVeigh, O'Neill and Evans* v. *United Kingdom* Applications 8022/77, 8025/77, and 8027/77, § 175, confirmed in *Harkin* v. *United Kingdom* Application 11539/85.
[257] See my dissenting opinion, p. 54, and the criticism expressed by Velu and Ergec (1990) N 232, 267; see also *Fox, Campbell and Hartley* v. *United Kingdom*, §§ 29–36.
[258] Van Dijk and van Hoof (1998) 265; Velu and Ergec (1990) N 328, 274.
[259] Trechsel (1974) 209.
[260] On this issue, see also Frowein and Peukert (1996) Art. 5 N 68; Velu and Ergec (1990) N 238, 274 et seq.

brought before the competent legal authority which will decide on the educational measures to be taken. It must be conceded that the term 'educational' is vague and mainly characterized by the purpose of exercising, by the application of pedagogical methods, a beneficial influence on the development of the minor. This excludes a purely punitive action and requires appropriate institutional facilities and staff with educational training.[261]

However, paragraph 1(d) also covers detention which is not (yet) in itself educational, but which involves detention while the transfer of the minor to the place where the educational supervision can be exercised is arranged.[262] The Commission went very far when it accepted as legitimate the detention of a 15-year-old in an observation centre for eight months.[263] It must, however, be accepted that the observation may not only have been necessary to find out what the best method of education might be, but would have also had in itself an educational effect or goal.

3. Detention of a Minor on Remand

Paragraph 1(d) also makes provision for detention on remand, although it differs dangerously from paragraph 1(c) in that there is no requirement that there be suspicion that an offence has been committed and the safeguards of paragraph 3 do not apply. That the educational supervision of a minor may be justified and even necessary without any connection to criminal behaviour is self-evident. However, the clause must be interpreted in a similar way to the way outlined by the Court in the slightly different context of detention for the purpose of educational supervision[264]—such detention must be strictly limited in time.

4. The Implementation of Deprivation of Liberty of a Minor

The Convention does not have any rules concerning the conditions of juvenile detention. The ACHR does not expressly refer to personal liberty but, under the title 'Right to Humane Treatment', commands that '[m]inors while subject to criminal proceedings shall be separated from adults . . .'.[265] The Covenant has an analogous rule: 'Accused juvenile persons shall be separated from adults . . .'.[266]

This separation must in particular be observed if the minor is detained on remand. This rule which is rigidly applied has been contested in the Third Committee of the General Assembly.[267] Indeed, it is not entirely persuasive.

---

[261] *Bouamar* v. *Belgium*, § 52; where the Court rightly held that the repeated internment of a juvenile delinquent in a remand prison did not comply with para. 1(d).

[262] *Bouamar* v. *Belgium*, § 50.   [263] *X* v. *Switzerland* Application 8500/79.

[264] *Bouamar* v. *Belgium*, § 50.   [265] ACHR, Art. 5 § 5.

[266] ICCPR, Art. 10 § 2(b).   [267] Nowak (1993) Art. 1 N 19 with references.

The principle is certainly legitimate to the extent that it prevents young people from being held together with hardened criminals where they risk not only being exposed to the 'wrong elements of society', but also being physically assaulted, intimidated, or sexually abused. On the other hand, there are cases where a juvenile girl can positively benefit from sharing a cell with a motherly prisoner who looks after her and keeps her company. The principle ought to be applied with a certain flexibility.

F. Detention for the Prevention of the Spreading of Contagious Diseases and of the Socially Maladjusted: Article 5, paragraph 1(e)

Paragraph 1(e) refers to 'the lawful detention of persons for the prevention of the spreading of infectious diseases, of persons of unsound mind, alcoholics or drug addicts or vagrants'. The Court has referred to these categories (except for 'infectious diseases') as comprising persons 'who are socially maladjusted'.[268] This might not be quite true in relation to the mentally or contagiously ill as it suggests that, with some effort, adjustment might be possible. The important point however is the Court's understanding of the basis of the provision: 'The reason why the Convention allows [the persons concerned] to be deprived of their liberty is not only that they have to be considered as occasionally dangerous for public safety but also that their own interest may necessitate their detention'.[269]

Again, the reference to lawfulness refers primarily to domestic law. As far as proceedings are concerned, the Convention does not require that the decision be taken by a judicial authority, but judicial control after arrest, and later on at reasonable intervals, is required by Article 5 § 4. Where irregularities in proceedings for the continuation of the deprivation of liberty are alleged, the Court examines them in the context of that provision.[270] If, however, the initial proceedings were unlawful, it rightly declines to examine other allegations.[271]

1. Detention for the Prevention of the Spreading of Infectious Diseases

So far, there is no Strasbourg case-law dealing with this type of detention category, which is the only one in paragraph 1(e) which is not defined by the characteristics of the person concerned. It is therefore correct to assume that not only persons who are actually infected can be detained, but also those persons who it is feared will contract and then spread a contagious disease.[272] It must also be possible to arrest a person in order to find out whether he or she is infected. In these cases, however, only short-term detention—for the period of incubation, for example, will be acceptable.

---

[268] *Guzzardi* v. *Italy*, § 98.   [269] Ibid.
[270] *Keus* v. *Netherlands*, § 20; *Koendjbiharie* v. *Netherlands*, § 25.
[271] *Van der Leer* v. *Netherlands*, § 24.
[272] Frowein and Peukert (1996) N 72; Velu and Ergec (1990) N 330.

The implicit general requirement of 'necessity' leads to the obvious conclusion that the disease in question must be a dangerous one—the Convention cannot justify the deprivation of liberty of a person because of influenza.[273] At present, one of the most well-known contagious diseases is acquired immune deficiency syndrome (AIDS). However, unlike tuberculosis or yellow fever, the infection is only transmissible in a limited number of ways and protection is to a large extent effectively possible. Only in the case of totally irresponsible persons could internment therefore be justified.

This exception has practically no relevance to criminal proceedings.

2. Persons of Unsound Mind

(a) General Observations
Detention gives rise to a number of specific problems in the context of persons of unsound mind. If they are really suffering from mental illness, it may be in their interests to be hospitalized and to receive treatment. However, eccentricity and other behaviour considered as deviant may raise an unjustified suspicion of mental disturbance, and such a diagnosis tends to reduce the subjects concerned to objects of (perhaps compassionate) interest who are no longer taken seriously. It is therefore particularly important to supervise carefully the legality of their confinement which may also be ordered in the course of criminal proceedings.

(b) The Three Prerequisites
The Court has set three minimum conditions which must be fulfilled in order for a person to be considered of unsound mind and deprived of his or her liberty: '[H]e must be reliably shown to be of unsound mind; the mental disorder must be of a kind or degree warranting compulsory confinement; and the validity of continued confinement depends upon the persistence of such a disorder'.[274] Furthermore, in determining these issues, 'the national authorities are to be recognized as having a certain margin of appreciation since it is in the first place for the national authorities to evaluate the evidence adduced before them in a particular case'.[275]

(c) The Evidence for Mental Illness
The Court has never undertaken the hazardous if not impossible task of defining mental illness.[276] It has, however, referred to the definition used in English law, namely: 'a person suffering or appearing to be suffering from a mental disorder', that is, 'mental illness, arrested or incomplete development of mind, psychopathic disorder or any other disorder or disability of mind.'[277] Here, although mental

---

[273] For a list of dangerous diseases, see e.g. Douraki (1986) 32.
[274] *Luberti* v. *Italy*, § 27; see also *X* v. *United Kingdom*, § 40; *Winterwerp* v. *Netherlands*, § 40.
[275] *Luberti* v. *Italy*, § 27; *X* v. *United Kingdom*, § 43; *Winterwerp* v. *Netherlands*, § 40.
[276] *Winterwerp* v. *Netherlands*, § 37.
[277] *X* v. *United Kingdom*, § 41; see also *Winterwerp* v. *Netherlands*, § 38.

illness is not defined it is put on equal footing with similar conditions under a psychological-functional perspective. From this it can perhaps be assumed that mental illness is a physiological affliction of the brain which seriously affects its functions. At any rate, the meaning of the term 'persons of unsound mind' 'is continually evolving as research in psychiatry progresses, an increasing flexibility in treatment is developing and society's attitude to mental illness changes . . .'.[278]

Another way to define mental illness would consist of referring to international systems of diagnostics such as the *DSM-IV* (the *Diagnostic and Statistical Manual of Mental Disorders*)[279] and *ICD-10* (the WHO's international classification of diseases).[280] However, even such a classification does not provide more than a label. The essential element lies in the second condition, the necessity for an in-patient intervention.

It may seem paradoxical that the presence of such a vague condition must be 'reliably shown', but in fact only the formal requirement of an expert opinion can provide any reliable guarantee. In all cases it examined so far, the Court found this condition to be satisfied.[281] Where the person has committed an offence, it is essential that the condition be present when the measure is adopted.[282] The Court also recognizes that exceptionally a situation of emergency may occur which warrants immediate internment and does not leave time for prior thorough medical examination.[283] In such a case, however, no further delay in the examination is permissible after confinement.[284] The exception also covers detention for the purpose of observation.[285]

(d) The Element of Danger

When the Court requires that the disorder 'must be of a kind or degree warranting compulsory confinement', it clearly refers to danger towards him- or herself and/or to others. It also seems to distinguish between 'kind' and 'degree', as it links the two terms by the word 'or' whereas it might have been preferable to use the conjunctive 'and'. Like the existence of an eventual illness, the 'danger' must be reliably shown to exist by medical evidence.

[278] *Winterwerp* v. *Netherlands*, § 37.

[279] See e.g. American Psychiatric Association, Task Force on DSM-IV, *Diagnostic and Statistical Manual of Mental Disorders* ('DSM-IV-TR' [Text Revision]).

[280] World Health Organization, *The ICD-10 Classification of Mental and Behavioural Disorders* (Geneva, 1992).

[281] *Winterwerp* v. *Netherlands*, § 41; *X* v. *United Kingdom*, § 44; *Luberti* v. *Italy*, § 28 (see however my dissenting opinion to the report of the Commission, p. 31.); *Wassink* v. *Netherlands*, § 25. See also *Dhoest* v. *Belgium* Application 10448/83. In *Gordon* v. *United Kingdom* Application 10213/82, the Commission also accepted the fact that the Secretary of State took more than a year to consider conditional discharge after it had been fully recommended by the responsible medical officer.

[282] The Court referred to this element in *Luberti* v. *Italy*, § 28, without clearly stating the principle; it flows, however, clearly from the third condition, namely that the disorder must persist throughout the confinement.

[283] *Winterwerp* v. *Netherlands*, § 39; see also *X* v. *United Kingdom*, § 45.

[284] In *Winterwerp* v. *Netherlands*, § 42, the Court felt 'some hesitation' in the face of a six-week period.   [285] *B* v. *France* Application 10179/82.

(e) The Element of Continuation

It follows from what has just been outlined that a person detained as being mentally ill must be released as soon as the basic conditions cease to prevail. Therefore, the 'third element' does not really add anything to the other two. In practical terms, it is, however, of great importance that, in addition to, and independent of, the periodic control within the framework of paragraph 4, there be a continuous concern of the medical staff involved in assessing the detainee's progress. The task is a difficult one: 'The termination of confinement of an individual who has previously been found by a court to be of unsound mind and to present a danger to society is a matter that concerns, as well as that individual, the community in which he will live if released'.[286]

3. The Place of Detention

In *Ashingdane* the Court accepted 'that there must be some relationship between the ground of permitted deprivation of liberty relied on and the place and condition of detention. In principle the "detention" of a person as mental health patient will only be "lawful" . . . if effected in a hospital, clinic or other appropriate institution authorised for that purpose. However, subject to the foregoing, Article 5 § 1(e) is not in principle concerned with suitable treatment or conditions'.[287] In that case, the Court found no violation, although the applicant could have been treated in an 'open' clinic but had to stay for an additional two years in Broadmoor Hospital because the nurses' union of Oakwood hospital opposed his admission. The Court was satisfied that in Broadmoor 'qualified staff displayed a constant preoccupation with the applicant's treatment and health'.[288] The judgment is not convincing.

There may be exceptions to the rule in cases of very dangerous 'patients' with a psychopathic disorder who are not amenable to treatment and can only be securely confined in a prison.

Paragraph 1(e) also covers detention in an observation clinic with a view to ascertaining whether the person concerned is of unsound mind.[289]

4. Addicts

The possibility to confine alcoholics and other drug addicts is similarly problematic. The Convention organs have not yet had to deal with this exception.

---

[286] *Luberti* v. *Italy*, § 29, p. 14. In *Herczegfalvy* v. *Austria* Application 10533/83, the Commission found a violation of para. 1 as continued detention was not justified by medical evidence. The Court, however, came to the opposite result in *Herczegfalvy* v. *Austria*, § 68—in both bodies the vote was unanimous!

[287] *Ashingdane* v. *United Kingdom*, § 44; the right to treatment was already denied in *Winterwerp* v. *United Kingdom*, § 51. See also *Dhoest* v. *Belgium* Application 10448/83.

[288] *Ashingdane* v. *United Kingdom*, § 47.

[289] Van Dijk and van Hoof (1998) 268, reject this possibility and would prefer to apply sub-para. (b). However, in my view the same reasoning as discussed above with sub-para. (d) arises.

Again, they will have to define criteria and insist on the requirement of a danger for the person concerned and/or others. The relevance for criminal proceedings is, at most, marginal. The same applies to the next group.

5. Vagrants

The exception concerning vagrants must be regarded as outdated. The Court has accepted the definition of Article 347 of the Belgian Criminal Code according to which vagrants are 'persons who have no fixed abode, no means of subsistence and no regular trade or profession'.[290] The fact that this provision is to be found in a penal code raises the suspicion that their confinement is justified by the assumption that these people, in order to survive, must be stealing—an attitude difficult to reconcile with the presumption of innocence as long as no theft is proven.

In *Guzzardi,* the Court seemed to have narrowed the scope of the exception by pointing to the similarity with other categories covered by paragraph 1(e): '[T]heir own interest may necessitate their detention'.[291] However, as 'vagrants' are (supposedly) of sound mind and not addicted to alcohol or other drugs, surely it ought to be their decision where they want to stay.[292] The Court rightly rejected the argument presented by the Italian Government that a person suspected of connections to the Mafia could for that reason be regarded as a 'vagrant'.[293]

G. Detention to Prevent an Unauthorized Entry or with a View to Deportation or Extradition

1. Detention to Prevent Unauthorized Entry

So far, the Convention organs have not been called upon to decide many cases alleging a violation of Article 5 § 1 in cases of 'arrest or detention of a person to prevent his effecting an unauthorised entry into the country' although a substantial number of measures of coercion to control unlawful immigration are being applied. An exception is *Amuur* v. *France* which has already been discussed. There it was the lack of a legal basis for the detention which led to the finding of a violation.[294]

It may be doubted whether this first alternative of Article 5 § 1(f) has any independent meaning, as persons certainly cannot be imprisoned indefinitely to

Furthermore, in *X* v. *United Kingdom,* § 41, the Court seemed to have accepted the definition in the UK Mental Health Act 1959, s. 147(1), according to which also a person '*appearing* to be suffering' (emphasis added) is regarded as a 'patient'.

[290] *De Wilde, Ooms and Versyp* v. *Belgium,* § 68.   [291] *Guzzardi* v. *Italy,* § 98.
[292] This is in fact what had happened initially in the case of the Belgian 'vagrants'; see *De Wilde, Ooms and Versyp,* §§ 16, 17, 23, 24, 28, and 29.   [293] *Guzzardi* v. *Italy,* §§ 97 et seq.
[294] *Amuur* v. *France,* §§ 52–4.

prevent them from entering the country. In fact, detention can only be justified for the time used to determine whether entry could be permitted. If it is not, such persons will be deported. The deprivation of liberty could therefore also be justified under the second alternative.

There might, nevertheless, be an exception in cases where it is not possible to deport or extradite a person who cannot be permitted to stay in the country—for example, where a person would be deported to a state where he or she would run a serious risk of ill treatment and there is no alternative country prepared to take the person or where the country of origin is not known. It might be necessary to submit such foreigners, at least for some time, to a regime of detention amounting to deprivation of liberty.[295]

2. Arrest or Detention with a View to Deportation or Extradition

(a) The Formal Character of the Exception
The main exception to the right to liberty under paragraph 1(f) is contained in the second alternative: arrest or detention 'of a person against whom action is taken with a view to deportation or extradition'. This covers not only deprivation of liberty pending the decision as to whether or not the person should be deported, but also that which is associated with the enforcement of such a decision—arrest and transportation to the border.[296]

It is important to note that the mere intention possibly to remove the person[297] suffices to justify arrest and detention; it is therefore irrelevant whether the intention will finally become a decision and the decision is executed or not.[298] Furthermore, just as detention on remand may be justified even though the person suspected is innocent, detention with a view to deportation or extradition must logically be accepted even though it may finally turn out that the deportation would not be lawful. In the words of the Commission, 'the lawfulness of the deportation order is not a prerequisite for the detention to be in conformity with Article 5 (1)f'.[299]

There are, however, certain restrictions to this principle. Thus, 'a legal situation may occur, where... national law makes the lawfulness of detention dependent on the lawfulness of the deportation'; in such a case, the 'scope of the

---

[295] See also Velu and Ergec (1990) N 334 p. 282, with further references.

[296] See the facts of *Bozano* v. *France*.

[297] 'Removal' may also consist of surrendering the person to a foreign state without removing him or her across the border; *C* v. *United Kingdom* Application 10427/83.

[298] *Caprino* v. *United Kingdom* Application 6871/75 (decision on admissibility); the situation is thus similar to that under Art. 5 § 1(c), discussed above.

[299] *Caprino* v. *United Kingdom* Application 6871/75 (Report of the Commission); the Commission had first taken a different view in its decision on admissibility where it discussed compatibility with EEC Directive No. 64/221, XXI Yb 284 at 288 ff. (1978)—see also the dissenting opinion of Mr Melchior added to the Report at p. 14. The opinion expressed by Velu and Ergec (1990) N 314, 282, is based on the decision on admissibility which was disapproved by the Report. See also Labayle (1991) 296 at 307; Nowak (1991) 388 at 393 et seq.

Commission's review is limited to examining whether there is a legal basis for the detention and whether the decision of the courts on the question of lawfulness could be described as arbitrary in light of the facts of the case'.[300] In particular, the deprivation of liberty is arbitrary if it is made pursuant to an aim different from that invoked in the decision, for example, if a 'deportation' amounts 'in fact to a disguised form of extradition designed to circumvent' a decision by which extradition was refused.[301]

Van Dijk and van Hoof certainly exaggerate when they write that it 'is obvious . . . that in reviewing the lawfulness of the detention, the lawfulness of the deportation or extradition will often also be in issue'.[302] But it is necessary to make a distinction: as long as no decision on deportation or extradition has been taken, it is sufficient for the national authorities that there exists a *bona fide* intention to come to such a decision, and no issue can arise under the Convention as to the lawfulness of any hypothetical removal. Once the decision has been made, however, the Convention organs will at least have to determine whether the decision is arbitrary. This calls for slightly closer scrutiny than is required in cases under paragraph 1(a).[303]

(b) Limitations to the Length of Detention under Sub-paragraph (f)

While there exists a certain similarity between detention of a suspect with a view to extradition and detention on remand, the limitation in time guaranteed in paragraph 3 does not apply to detention covered by paragraph 1(f). However, in a series of decisions launched in the aftermath of the decision in *Lynas*,[304] the Commission held that 'only the existence of extradition [or, as the case may be, deportation] proceedings justifies deprivation of liberty in such a case. It follows that if, for example, the proceedings are not conducted with the requisite diligence . . . it ceases to be justifiable under Article 5 § 1 (f). Within these limits the Commission might therefore have cause to consider the length of time spent in detention pending extradition'.

With one exception, the Commission has never come to the conclusion that detention pending extradition was excessive—it even declared inadmissible an application where it had lasted for over five years.[305] The explanation for this lies in the conflict of interests which is typical in such cases: a person opposing extradition may have an extremely strong motivation, for example, if they are facing life imprisonment under abominable conditions or even capital

---

[300] *Zamir* v. *United Kingdom* Application 9174/80; see also *X* v. *United Kingdom* Application 9403/91.   [301] *Bozano* v. *France*, § 60.
[302] Van Dijk and van Hoof (1998) 269.   [303] See earlier discussion above.
[304] *Lynas* v. *Switzerland* Application 7317/75; see also *Z* v. *Netherlands* Application 10400/83; *S* v. *France* Application 10965/84; *Kolompar* v. *Belgium* Application 11613/85. It is regrettable that in *Kolompar* v. *Belgium* a different solution was reached.
[305] *Osman* v. *United Kingdom* Application 15933/89; see also *B* v. *France* Application 13706/88 with a detention of three years and three months—the French authorities had used much time to get assurances that capital punishment would not be executed in Morocco.

punishment, not to be extradited. Detention in the requested state with some hope of eventually being released may therefore be regarded as the lesser evil. In the case of *Osman* the applicant had stated in a press release that he would fight extradition even if it meant staying in prison for fifty years. Persons in such a situation will avail themselves of every possibility to delay a negative decision and the enforcement of the extradition. This may lead to long periods of detention for which, however, the respondent government cannot be held responsible.

In *Kolompar*, the Commission came to the conclusion that the Government had not acted with the diligence required under paragraph 1(f).[306] The Court, however, found that the long time spent in detention was due to the applicant's conduct and that, therefore, Article 5 § 1 had not been violated.[307]

---

[306] *Kolompar* v. *Belgium* Application 11613/85.   [307] Ibid., §§ 40–3.

Chapter 18

The Rights Guaranteed to all Persons
Deprived of their Liberty

I. THE RIGHT TO BE INFORMED OF THE
REASONS FOR THE ARREST

A. Introduction

1. The Texts

> 2. Anyone who is arrested shall be informed, at the time of arrest, of the reasons for his arrest and shall be promptly informed of any charges against him.
>
> ICCPR, Art. 9 § 2

> 2. Everyone who is arrested shall be informed promptly, in a language which he understands, of the reasons for his arrest and of any charge against him.
>
> ECHR, Art. 5 § 2

> 4. Anyone who is detained shall be informed of the reasons for his detention and shall be promptly notified of the charge or charges against him.
>
> ACHR, Art. 7 § 4

Despite the obvious similarities between these texts, quite a number of differences can be observed, particularly in relation to the references to promptness. The ICCPR calls for information 'at the time of arrest', the ECHR obliges the authorities to convey the information 'promptly', and the ACHR makes no reference to time in the obligation to inform of the reasons of arrest. All three texts require that information be given in relation to any charges. This must occur 'promptly' in all three cases. The ECHR is the only instrument which refers to language. The American Convention seems to imply that a charge will always accompany an arrest, whereas the other ones, by using the phrase '*any* charge', make it clear that the duty to give reasons for the detention also arises in cases of arrest based on other grounds than a suspicion. Finally, the ACHR refers to 'detention', whereas the other two concern persons who have been 'arrested'.

2. The Purpose of the Guarantee

All three texts guarantee in practice the right of anyone arrested to be informed promptly of the reasons for his or her arrest. This guarantee has mainly been seen as an instrument for ensuring the effectiveness of habeas corpus proceedings in the sense of paragraph 4.[1] In fact, it is almost impossible for someone to challenge the lawfulness of his or her detention, if he or she does not know the justification invoked by the authorities. In an early case, the Court concluded that there was no point in examining an allegation brought under Article 5 § 2 when a violation of paragraph 4 had been found as the former was 'absorbed' by the latter.[2]

This doctrine was justly abandoned in the *van der Leer* judgment where the Court found first a violation of paragraph 2 and, later on in the judgment, also examined the issue under paragraph 4. Unlike the Commission it did not use the same argument to find a violation of the right to habeas corpus proceedings, reaching its result on the basis of other reasons.[3]

The question is, however, whether this is the only justification for the right to information about the charge. In my view, it is not. In addition to the operational and technical purposes, the right to be informed of the reason for one's arrest also pursues a humanitarian goal. Besides the possibility of challenging the lawfulness of his or her detention, the person who has been arrested has a fundamental need to know what is happening—a need most dramatically illustrated in the famous novel *The Trial* written by Franz Kafka. An arrest will often come as a surprise and it undoubtedly has a dramatic effect on the everyday life of the person concerned. The suffering is considerably enhanced if, in addition, he or she remains ignorant of what is going on. Such ignorance will not only prevent the effective use of habeas corpus proceedings, but will generally have a paralysing effect. I find it important to accept this elementary 'need to know' as a legitimate purpose of the right under paragraph 2, as merely utilitarian considerations may lead to quite unsatisfactory results.

3. The Characterization of the Right by the European Court

The European Court, in *Fox, Campbell and Hartley*, coined a formula which it quoted in many of its later judgments on the matter. It is therefore useful to reproduce it here:

Paragraph 2 of Article 5 contains the elementary safeguard that any person arrested should know why he is being deprived of his liberty. This provision is an integral part of the scheme of protection afforded by Article 5: by virtue of paragraph 2 any person

---

[1] *X* v. *United Kingdom*, § 66; *van der Leer* v. *Netherlands*, § 28; *Fox, Campbell and Hartley* v. *United Kingdom*, § 40.

[2] *X* v. *United Kingdom*, § 66; see, however, the dissenting opinion of Judge Evrigenis.

[3] *Van der Leer* v. *Netherlands*, §§ 31, 34; see also the Commission's report in the case of *Fox, Campbell and Hartley*, § 66, p. 30.

arrested must be told, in simple, non-technical language that he can understand, the essential legal and factual grounds for his arrest, so as to be able, if he sees fit, to apply to a court to challenge its lawfulness in accordance with paragraph 4 . . . Whilst this information must be conveyed 'promptly' (in French: 'dans le plus court délai'), it need not be related in its entirety by the arresting officer at the very moment of the arrest. Whether the content and promptness of the information conveyed were sufficient is to be assessed in each case according to its special features.[4]

B. The Elements of the Right to Information

1. The Scope of the Right to be Informed of the Reasons for the Arrest

Both the ICCPR and the ECHR state that the right to receive information about the charge is guaranteed to '[e]veryone who is arrested', while the ACHR uses the term 'detained'. Nowak finds this strange.[5] Indeed, 'arrest' generally signifies the moment at which someone is apprehended by the police and, in the case of those suspected of having committed a crime, the period before he or she has been brought before a 'judge or other officer . . . '. However, as the drafters of international conventions are not normally conversant with the technical details of the law on criminal procedure, it would be wrong to attach too much weight to such terminological deviations.

A brief glance at the ECHR demonstrates that of the exceptions listed in Article 5 § 1, three, namely paragraphs (a), (d), and (e), do not mention arrest at all. A purely literal interpretation of the text could easily lead to the mistaken belief that Article 5 § 2 does not apply to detention falling under these categories, as it speaks exclusively of arrest. However, such an interpretation would be manifestly wrong. The Court has applied paragraph 2 to cases of detention of persons of unsound mind without even commenting on this aspect.[6] Information about the detention must be provided whenever a person is arrested, even if there was no actual arrest per se. This may be the case when the legal basis for the detention changes, for instance where a person serving a sentence becomes mentally ill[7] and is committed to a psychiatric hospital, or where a patient in such an institution is suspected of having committed an offence and is transferred to detention on remand. Information is also required if a person who had been released on probation is then recalled to prison.[8]

2. The Nature of the Information to be Conveyed

The information which must be conveyed to a person who has been arrested must cover 'the reasons for his arrest and . . . any charge against him'. This can

---

[4] *Fox, Campbell and Hartley* v. *United Kingdom*, § 40, referring to *van der Leer* v. *Netherlands*, § 28. The passage is reproduced in *Murray* v. *United Kingdom*, § 72; *Dikme* v. *Turkey*, § 53; *HB* v. *Switzerland*, § 47; *Conka* v. *Belgium*, § 50.   [5] Nowak (1993) Art. 9 N 32, n. 86.
[6] *X* v. *United Kingdom*, § 66; *van der Leer* v. *Netherlands*, §§ 27–8.
[7] *X* v. *United Kingdom* Application 6840/74, § 105 (report).   [8] *X* v. *United Kingdom*, § 66.

be compared to the duty of the authorities under Article 6 § 3(a) to inform everyone 'charged with a criminal offence . . . in detail, of the nature and cause of the accusation against him'. The two guarantees are, however, not identical. The difference relates to, and can be explained by, the different purposes of the guarantees and by the fact that they arise at different stages in the proceedings. Both share a common humanitarian aspect. While the duty to inform under Article 5 must enable the person concerned to make effective use of proceedings under paragraph 4, the guarantee provided for in Article 6 § 3(a) exists to enable him or her to mount an effective defence at trial. The information provided under Article 6 § 3(a) must therefore be more specific (all three texts call for information 'in detail') with regard to both the facts and their legal basis.[9] Yet, as the 'standard formula' reproduced above states, in both cases the information must refer to facts and to the law. As a rule, it can, consequently, be said that the information to be given under Article 5 § 2 must be sufficient to allow for the lawfulness of the detention to be challenged effectively. It follows that the degree of specificity cannot be described in general terms but depends on the ground invoked to justify the detention in question.

Under Article 5 § 1(a) there will normally be no right to habeas corpus proceedings.[10] In such cases Article 5 § 2 simply calls for the identification of the sentence which the convicted person is to serve. In cases under paragraph 1(b), the respective court order or the violation of the legal obligation must be named.[11]

The main field of application is detention on remand to which the words 'and of any charge against him' refer.[12] In this respect, the Court found a reference to the arrest being made 'pursuant to the emergency legislation' to be insufficient.[13] The Commission was satisfied with information limited to the legal basis for the offence.[14]

In cases under paragraph 1(d), the reasons for the authorities' belief that the minor is in need of educational supervision must be stated. In cases where the detention is based on paragraph 1(e), there must be an indication of whether and why a person is considered to fall under one of the categories mentioned therein, and if the reason is mental illness, the illness that he or she is suspected of suffering from must be identified. Furthermore, the information must also cover the reasons why it is deemed necessary to confine the person concerned.[15]

---

[9] See e.g. *Nielsen* v. *DK* Application 343/57; *X* v. *United Kingdom* Application 4220/69.

[10] See further section II below.

[11] *McVeigh, O'Neill and Evans* v. *UK* Applications 8022/77, 8025/77, and 8027/77, §§ 209–11: obligation to submit to further examination was sufficient.

[12] *Van der Leer* v. *Netherlands*, § 27.

[13] *Ireland* v. *United Kingdom*, § 198. See also *Fox, Campbell and Hartley* v. *United Kingdom*, § 41. The HRC follows the same approach: *Adolfo Drescher Caldas* v. *Uruguay*, § 80 where the person arrested had only been told 'that he was being arrested under the prompt security measures'.

[14] *X* v. *Belgium* Application 1105/61; this seems not to be in line with the Court's finding in the case of *Fox, Campbell and Hartley* v. *United Kingdom*, § 66.

[15] Of course, a voluntary patient must also be informed of the fact that an order to confine him has been made; *Van der Leer* v. *Netherlands*, §§ 30, 31.

There has been some dispute about the information which is required in cases involving arrest and detention based upon paragraph 1(f). In its admissibility decision in the case of *Caprino*,[16] the Commission, in view of the formal character of the exception, found that it is enough for the person concerned to learn that extradition or deportation proceedings are in process against him or her, while the reasons for such action need not be disclosed.[17] Commentators take a stricter approach and suggest that information on the merits of the extradition or deportation ought to be conveyed to the detainee.[18] The precise nature of the information required will depend upon the circumstances of each case. All in all, the information will be deemed to be sufficient if it enables the detainee to 'judge the lawfulness of the measure and take steps to challenge it if he sees fit, thus availing himself of the right guaranteed by Article 5 (4)'.[19]

In the event that there are no valid reasons for the arrest one must, somewhat cynically, conclude that there can be no issue under Article 5 § 2—at any rate, in such cases the finding of a violation of Article 5 § 1 leaves no room for a further examination under Article 5 § 2.[20]

3. The Addressee of the Information

In the first place, it is obviously the person who has been arrested who must be informed of the reason for his or her arrest. This may, however, not be possible in cases involving a person suffering from mental illness. It is possible—in cases relating to juveniles and children—that the person will not be able, intellectually and/or emotionally, to understand the information. This could not, of course, justify a decision by the authorities simply to neglect to give any reasons for the arrest; rather, they will have to inform the person who is taking care of, and competent to act for, the patient or child, for example, a guardian, or a lawyer.[21]

Even if the arrestee is not mentally ill, it may be *sufficient* to inform his or her lawyer,[22] provided, however, that the latter has the possibility to inform his or her client immediately.

4. The Time Element

While Article 9 § 2 of the ICCPR requires that the information be given 'at the time of arrest', the other instruments use the word 'promptly' ('*dans le plus court*

---

[16] *Caprino* v. *United Kingdom* Application 6871/75. The relevant passage is not reproduced in the Decisions and Reports, which has only an extract of the decision. See, however, 6 EuGRZ 74 at 78 (1979).   [17] See also *K* v. *Belgium* Application 10819/84.

[18] Frowein and Peukert (1996) Article 5 N 91; Velu and Ergec (1990) N 335.

[19] *McVeigh, O'Neill and Evans* v. *United Kingdom* Applications 8022/77, 8025/77, and 8027/77, § 208. See also *Fox, Campbell and Hartley* v. *United Kingdom*, § 40.

[20] *Raninen* v. *Finland*, § 51.

[21] cf. the opinion of the Commission as reflected in the *X* v. *United Kingdom* case, § 65.

[22] *X* v. *Sweden* Application 7170/75.

délai', '*sin demora*'). In the English version of the ECHR the term is identical to the one used in paragraph 3, but there is a difference in the French text, where paragraph 3 uses '*aussitôt*'. Keeping in mind that the time period referred to in paragraph 3 can be extended to up to four days, it must be concluded that paragraph 2 uses the term 'promptly' in a different sense. As a matter of fact, nobody could ever be arrested without pre-existing reasons known to the person who executes the arrest. It would therefore have been realistic to adopt the solution which was chosen for the ICCPR.[23] The only inevitable delay occurs when an interpreter must first be found or if, for any other reason such as intoxication, the person is incapable of understanding the information. Where the person who has been arrested absconds, it is sufficient if he or she is informed of the reasons on first contact with the authorities.[24]

The Convention organs, particularly the Commission, have, however, been reluctant to impose strict limits. The Commission accepted delays of over five hours,[25] over thirty-two hours,[26] and even two days.[27] In the Court's case-law we find periods of a few hours being regarded as acceptable.[28] It has also accepted a system which combined insufficient information at the time of the arrest with subsequent indirect information obtained a few hours later through interrogation.[29] A delay caused by the flight of the detainee—he claimed that the authorities ought to have informed his lawyer—cannot be imputed to the state.[30]

5. The Form of the Information

The Convention contains just one (superfluous) indication as to the form which the reasons given to the person who has been arrested must take: it must be 'in a language which he understands'. In fact, this is already implied in the very notion of 'information'. There is, however, no right to request that the information be conveyed in a specific language, such as a minority language. The Convention is not concerned with solving linguistic disputes but only with the effective protection of the individual.[31] Where an arrest warrant stating reasons for the arrest exists, it is sufficient that it be translated orally,[32] as, at any rate, oral information is adequate.[33]

It has been argued that the costs of an interpreter should not be charged to the person who has been arrested.[34] However, such a right cannot be inferred

---

[23] This interpretation of Art. 5 § 2 is proposed by Grigori (1979) 95.
[24] *Keus* v. *Netherlands*, § 22.   [25] *X* v. *Denmark* Application 8828/79.
[26] *X* v. *Belgium* Application 4502/70.   [27] *Skoogström* v. *Sweden* Application 8582/79.
[28] *Fox, Campbell and Hartley* v. *United Kingdom*, § 42; *Murray* v. *United Kingdom*, § 78.
[29] *Fox, Campbell and Hartley* v. *United Kingdom*, § 41.   [30] *Keus* v. *Netherlands*, §§ 21, 22.
[31] On the relationship between human rights and minority rights, see Trechsel (2000).
[32] *Delcourt* v. *Belgium* Application 2689/65.
[33] See e.g. the uncontested argument of the Belgian Government in *Lamy* v. *Belgium*, § 31.
[34] Velu and Ergec (1990) N 337.

from Article 5 § 2.[35] Whether Article 6 § 3(e) finally applies in cases under paragraph 1(c) is a matter which falls to be discussed elsewhere. In the other cases, it is impossible to see how the imposition of the costs of interpretation could have repercussions on the exercise of any other rights.[36] It is, however, important that the reasons for the arrest be given 'in simple, non-technical language'.[37] What is quite unsatisfactory in the case-law of the Commission and the Court is that it does not call for even the most rudimentary elements of formal qualities. The Commission saw no problem where the person who had been arrested was not informed, either orally or in writing, of the reasons for his arrest, but could be expected to infer them from the ensuing interrogation, or could, given the circumstances, be able to deduce why he or she was arrested.[38] In the case of *Fox, Campbell and Hartley*, the Commission found, however, that 'given the elementary nature of the safeguard, Article 5 § 2 places a direct burden on the arresting authorities to provide a detainee with adequate information as to the reasons for his arrest at the time of the arrest or as soon as it is practicable thereafter'.[39] The Court did not follow this approach and found that there was 'no ground to suppose that [the interrogations following arrest] were not such as to enable the applicants to understand why they had been arrested'.[40]

This approach was maintained in later judgments. In *Murray* the Court held that questions concerning the applicant's stay in America and financial matters ought to have enabled the applicant to understand that she was suspected of collecting money for the IRA.[41] Mr Dikme was arrested in possession of false papers and could have 'gained some idea of what he was suspected of'.[42] Mr Egmez had been caught in *flagrante delicto*[43] and another applicant 'was well aware of the prosecuting authorities' interest in the B company' which 'enabled [him] to file a hand-written complaint' with the court of appeal.[44] These cases show that the Court will not impose any formal requirements on domestic authorities. This is far from ideal—the essence of the duty to give reasons for the arrest is, in my view, to prevent the person concerned from having simply to guess but to get a clear answer to the question 'why have I been arrested?'

This problem is less critical in relation to the case-law of the Covenant where some complainants have been left ignorant of the charges against them for over two years.[45]

---

[35] Trechsel (1974) 231.   [36] Cf. *Luedicke, Belkacem and Koç* v. *Germany*, § 42.

[37] *Fox, Campbell and Hartley* v. *United Kingdom*, § 40.

[38] *Neumeister* v. *Austria* Application 1936/63; *B* v. *France* Application 10179/82. For references to critical comments, see Trechsel (1974) 231, n. 872; Velu and Ergec (1990) N 335.

[39] *Fox, Campbell and Hartley* v. *United Kingdom*, § 68.   [40] Ibid., § 41.

[41] *Murray* v. *United Kingdom*, §§ 76–7.   [42] *Dikme* v. *Turkey*, § 56.

[43] *Egmez* v. *Cyprus*, §§ 85–6.   [44] *HB* v. *Switzerland*, § 48.

[45] e.g. *Hiber Conteris* v. *Uruguay*, at 196, § 10.

II. THE RIGHT TO HABEAS CORPUS PROCEEDINGS

A. Introduction

1. The Texts

Anyone who is deprived of his liberty by arrest or detention shall be entitled to take proceedings before a court, in order that [the] court may decide without delay on the lawfulness of his detention and order his release if the detention is not lawful.[46]

ICCPR, Art. 9 § 4

Everyone who is deprived of his liberty by arrest or detention shall be entitled to take proceedings by which the lawfulness of his detention shall be decided speedily by a court and his release ordered if the detention is not lawful.

ECHR, Art. 5 § 4

Anyone who is deprived of his liberty shall be entitled to recourse to a competent court, in order that the court may decide without delay on the lawfulness of his arrest or detention and order his release if the arrest or detention is unlawful. In States Parties whose laws provide that anyone who believes himself to be threatened with deprivation of his liberty is entitled to recourse to a competent court in order that it may decide on the lawfulness of such threat, this remedy may not be restricted or abolished. The interested party or another person in his behalf is entitled to seek these remedies.

ACHR, Art. 7 § 6

The right to a habeas corpus-type review is expressed in almost identical terms in the English versions of the ICCPR and the ECHR, a similarity which is even more pronounced in the French versions.[47] The wording of the ACHR differs from that of the others in that it includes a reference to *amparo* proceedings. The drafters seem to have been of the opinion that express reference to these proceedings, which had proven both effective and successful, was required in order to prevent Article 7 § 6 from being used as a pretext to lessen their importance.

2. The Origin and Purpose of the Right

(a) The Origin of the Right to Habeas Corpus Proceedings
The origins of the right to take habeas corpus proceedings can be traced back to the Habeas Corpus Act of 1679 which contains the following passage:

... whensoever any person or persons shall bring any habeas corpus directed unto any sheriff or sheriffs, gaoler, minister or other person whatsoever, for any person in his or

---

[46] The article 'the' before 'court' is missing from the original text.
[47] Art. 9 § 4 ICCPR (ECHR variations in square brackets): '*Quiconque se trouve privé [toute personne privée] de sa liberté par arrestation ou détention a le droit d'introduire un recours devant un tribunal[,] afin que celui-ci [qu'il] statue sans [à bref] délai sur la légalité de sa détention et ordonne sa libération si la détention est illégale*'.

their custody, and the said writ shall be served upon the said officer, or left at the gaol or prison with any of the under-officers, under-keepers or deputy of the said officers or keepers, that the said officer or officers, his or their under-officers, under-keepers or deputies, shall within three days after the service thereof as aforesaid (unless the commitment aforesaid were for treason or felony, plainly and specially expressed in the warrant of commitment) upon payment or tender of the charges of bringing the said prisoner, to be ascertained by the judge or court that awarded the same, and endorsed upon the said writ, not exceeding twelve pence per mile, and upon security given by his own bond to pay the charges of carrying back the prisoner, if he shall be remanded by the court or judge to which he shall be brought according to the true intent of this present act, and that he will not make any escape by the way, make return of such writ; (3) and bring or cause to be brought the body of the party so committed or restrained, unto or before the lord chancellor, or lord keeper of the great seal of England for the time being, or the judges or barons of the said court from which the said writ shall issue, or unto and before such other person or persons before whom the said writ is made returnable, according to the command thereof; (4) and shall then likewise certify the true causes of his detainer or imprisonment, unless the commitment of the said party be in any place beyond the distance of twenty miles from the place or places where such court or person is or shall be residing; and if beyond the distance of twenty miles, and not above one hundred miles, then within the space of ten days, and if beyond the distance of one hundred miles, then within the space of twenty days, after such delivery aforesaid, and not longer.

This guarantee was deemed to be too detailed to be included in the Universal Declaration, but it did in fact appear in the first drafts of the Covenant. There had even been some discussion about using the Latin, i.e. common-law, term, but these proposals were not taken up—rightly so, in my opinion.[48] The use of terms that have, or are at least perceived to have, strong ties to a specific legal order or national legal tradition can prove remarkably problematic. It would not be commendable if an international treaty were to use a term that is so strongly tied to the legal order of a specific country or group of countries.

(b) The Purpose of the Guarantee

Personal liberty could be described as a 'preferential freedom' because it is equipped with two instruments of protection which the other rights contained in the international treaties do not enjoy. One of them is the guarantee which we are concerned with here, namely the right to a specific remedy. The other is the right to compensation for unlawful interference with the right. These guarantees are set out in Article 9 §§ 4, 5 of the ICCPR, Article 5 §§ 4, 5 of the ECHR, and Article 7 § 6 of the ACHR—the right to compensation for unlawful detention was not included in the American Convention. The inclusion of a specific right to take proceedings to review the lawfulness of detention might appear superfluous in the light of the existence of the general right to an effective remedy set out in Article 2 § 3(a) of the ICCPR, Article 13 of the ECHR, and Article 25 of the ACHR. The protection of persons deprived of their liberty, however, goes

---

[48] See also Nowak (1993) Art. 9 N 14 with references.

further than the right to a general remedy in at least two respects: it provides for access to a *judicial* authority[49] and it requires that the decision be given *speedily and effectively*. This notion of effectiveness dictates that it be possible to obtain immediate release which considerably enhances the protection on the domestic level. The purpose of habeas corpus proceedings is not just to verify whether the detention can be justified as such, but also to examine whether other formal guarantees, such as those concerning persons detained on remand, have been respected.

The right under consideration is the *lex specialis* in relation to the general right to an effective remedy.[50]

Experience on the European level demonstrates that the guarantee also has a considerable practical importance; it is often invoked and a relatively high number of complaints have been upheld.[51] As we are dealing here with a relatively abstract and formal guarantee, the Court is much less reluctant to censure the domestic authorities than when it supervises the substantive justification of a deprivation of liberty. The purpose of habeas corpus proceedings is not just to verify whether the detention can be justified as such, but also to examine whether other formal guarantees, such as those concerning persons detained on remand, have been respected. The importance of the guarantee is evidenced by the wealth and breadth of the case-law, both on the European and on the national level. It seems quite justified to speak of this guarantee as forming the cornerstone of the protection of personal liberty.

3. The Issues to be Discussed

The right to habeas corpus raises a number of interesting questions. First, the scope of the provision has proven somewhat controversial, and it will be shown that much of this controversy has stemmed from the Court's reluctance to sanction the application of the guarantee to persons who have been detained following conviction. The discussion of this subject will thus take us slightly outside the normal scope of criminal proceedings. A number of issues concerning the time period in which the guarantee must be applied also require consideration. This will be followed by an analysis of the effectiveness of the remedy and finally a detailed examination of the case-law concerning the procedural requirements which accompany the guarantee.

B. The Scope of the Right to Take Habeas Corpus Proceedings

Every person deprived of his or her liberty has the right to take habeas corpus proceedings. This sentence in itself demonstrates that the guarantee has a very

---

[49] This is also a requirement in ACHR, Art. 25.
[50] *De Jong, Baljet and Van den Brink* v. *Netherlands*, § 60; *Chahal* v. *United Kingdom*, § 127.
[51] See e.g. *Toth* v. *Austria*, § 67.

wide scope of application. The application of the guarantee is subject to a number of restrictions and these can be divided into four categories: restriction of the guarantee to persons actually detained; restrictions involving time; the exception for detention after an appropriate court decision; and the exceptions to this exception. Before addressing these four issues, however, it is important to examine the autonomous character of the guarantee.

1. The Autonomous Character of the Guarantee

Although the right to habeas corpus ('Everyone who is deprived of his liberty...') is framed in different terms from the guarantee to an effective remedy ('Everyone whose rights...are violated'), there was originally some uncertainty as to whether the right under Article 5 § 4 should be granted even in the case of lawful detention.[52] The question has, however, been correctly answered in the affirmative by the Court.[53] Moreover, the Commission and Court will examine an alleged violation of paragraph 4 even when they have already found a breach of paragraph 1.[54] In fact, it would defy logic if a remedy were only granted in those cases where it would also be successful—the very purpose of these proceedings is to ascertain whether the detention is or is not lawful, therefore the latter cannot be a prerequisite for the guarantee to apply.

One could be forgiven for fearing that the judgment in *Minjat* v. *Switzerland* marked a return by the Court to the errors of the past.[55] The applicant had complained to the Federal Court that he had not received reasons justifying the decision of the cantonal authority to detain him. The Federal Court had indeed found that the lack of reasons had violated the right to personal liberty but had sent the case back to the earlier instance rather than ordering the applicant's immediate release. The applicant, in this case, *did*, in fact, have the benefit of habeas corpus proceedings. His complaint related not to the lack of such proceedings, but rather to the decision of the Federal Court and, in particular, to the fact that he was not released. As the Federal Court had found that in spite of the procedural defects, the detention was clearly lawful, he could not claim that he ought to have been released. In fact, the Strasbourg Court had itself come to the conclusion that his detention was lawful.

---

[52] See the dissenting opinion of Judges Holmbäck, Rodenbourg, Ross, Favre, and Bilge in *De Wile, Ooms and Versyp* v. *Belgium*, p. 75. Originally, the Commission also held that Art. 13 only applied when somebody's rights had actually been violated. The Court, following a dissenting opinion in the Commission's Report, set this right in *Klass* v. *Germany*, § 64.

[53] *De Wile, Ooms and Versyp* v. *Belgium*, § 73. See also *Winterwerp* v. *Netherlands*, § 53; *Luberti* v. *Italy*, § 30; *Kolompar* v. *Belgium*, § 45; *Douiyeb* v. *Netherlands*, § 57; and *Esser* (2002) 328.

[54] *Bouamar* v. *Belgium*, § 55. See also *Ireland* v. *United Kingdom*, § 200. In *Koendjbiharie* v. *Netherlands*, § 31, however, the Court held unconvincingly that it was unnecessary to examine para. 1 as it had already found a violation of para. 4.   [55] *Minjat* v. *Switzerland*, §§ 50–3.

2. The Condition of Being Deprived of One's Liberty

The wording of paragraph 4 makes it quite clear that the right to take habeas corpus proceedings only applies while a person is either under arrest or while he or she is detained. This interpretation is confirmed by the reference to the power to release. This paragraph cannot therefore be invoked in order to seek a retrospective control of the lawfulness of an earlier period of detention.[56] In such a case Article 13 would be the applicable provision. Nor can a person who has been provisionally discharged claim a right to be permanently released under this guarantee.[57]

3. The Scope of Application in Time

With regard to the time element, two questions arise: first, does the right to a review arise immediately after an arrest or only after a certain amount of time has elapsed? And second, what is the effect on habeas corpus proceedings if the prisoner is released after having filed a request but before the court has taken a decision?

(a) Immediate Applicability

The right to apply for judicial control of the lawfulness of any deprivation of liberty arises immediately after the arrest or detention.[58] There can be no justification for any delay. Thus, the Court found a violation of paragraph 4 in a case where some Dutch conscientious objectors had to wait six, seven, and thirteen days respectively before they could challenge the legality of their detention before a court.[59] In cases of detention on remand under paragraph l(c), this means that paragraph 4 becomes operative even before the person who has been arrested has been brought before a judge or other officer in compliance with paragraph 3, of which paragraph 4 is fully independent.[60] In fact, it may be of particular practical importance to ensure the involvement of a judicial authority in cases where the requirements of paragraph 3 have not been complied with.[61]

---

[56] *Baranowski* v. *Poland*, § 69; see also *X* v. *Sweden* Application 10230/82.

[57] *L* v. *Sweden* Application 10801/84 (report). Esser (2002) 363 concludes from *Bouamar* v. *Belgium* that there might be an opening, in the future, for a control of lawfulness after release. He quotes the Court as saying that after release the habeas corpus request is 'inadmissible because devoid of purpose'; *Bouamar* v. *Belgium*, § 63. I cannot follow this argument.

[58] Eryilmaz (1999) 360.

[59] *De Jong, Baljet and Van den Brink* v. *Netherlands*, § 58; *Ireland* v. *United Kingdom*, § 200. See also *Igdeli* v. *Turkey*, §§ 32–6 (seven days); *Gündoğan* v. *Turkey*, §§ 24–8 (nine days of police custody); *Zeynep Avcı* v. *Turkey* (twenty-one days in police custody).

[60] *De Jong, Baljet and Van den Brink* v. *Netherlands*, § 57; the dissenting opinion of the minority of the Commission (including myself) on this issue was rightly rejected by the Court. See, however, also *Bezicheri* v. *Italy*, § 20; *E* v. *Norway*, § 64.

[61] cf. the facts in the decision on admissibility in *Sargın and Yağcı* v. *Turkey* Applications 14116/88 and 14117/88.

A period of twelve or more days is quite excessive,[62] although in its jurisprudence the Court has even been faced with periods of thirty days.[63]

One might expect a different solution in cases where confinement to a psychiatric institution has been ordered in judicial proceedings. This had been the case in *Luberti* where the applicant applied for judicial control barely three days after the judgment. The Court referred to the notion of 'incorporation' and 'reasonable interval', but also noted that Italian law did not oblige the applicant to wait—excessive delays led, nevertheless, to the finding of a violation of Article 5 § 4.[64]

(b) Release Pending Habeas Corpus Proceedings

Does the right to habeas corpus proceedings persist even after the detainee has been released? In order to answer this question, a distinction between two eventualities must be made.

The first concerns cases where an applicant files an appeal to challenge his detention, but is set free before the '*bref délai*' has expired. This person has had all the success that he or she could hope for and cannot therefore continue to claim to be a victim of a violation of Article 5 § 4. This was the case in *Brogan*. The Court found no violation, but followed the Commission in basing its finding on the fact that the law provided for a remedy which satisfied the requirements of Article 5 § 4.[65] I do not regard that approach as particularly satisfactory. It constitutes an examination of the law *in abstracto* which is neither representative of the Court's usual approach, nor justified. All of the applicants were released within seven days. Even assuming that they had immediately asked to be released, it could not be said that a court decision would, or ought to have, intervened at a considerably earlier point in time. This consideration also leads to the conclusion that there was no violation.

The Court has clearly taken a different stand in other cases where it has found that if the person concerned manages to escape after having applied for habeas corpus, but before his or her request has been determined, he or she remains entitled to a speedy decision[66] in such circumstances, though it would not be possible to complain of delays caused by the fact that he or she was unavailable for psychiatric examination.[67] The Court even went so far as to say that the

---

[62] *Sakık and others* v. *Turkey*, § 51; see also *Mamaç and others* v. *Turkey*, §40; *Sarıkaya* v. *Turkey*, § 59.   [63] *Taş* v. *Turkey*, § 86.

[64] *Luberti* v. *Italy*, §§ 34, 37; the finding may have been influenced by the fact that Mr Luberti had already been detained for more than seven years.

[65] *Brogan and others* v. *United Kingdom*, §§ 64–5.

[66] *Van der Leer* v. *Netherlands*, § 35—the applicant had escaped and was granted probationary leave some time later but was not informed of this decision. *Keus* v. *Netherlands* concerned an applicant who, due to his escape, could not attend the hearing on the extension of his confinement; he ought to have had a remedy after his renewed detention (§ 27). See also *Zamir* v. *UK* Application 9174/80. The Commission made an exception, however, in a case where the applicant was released within a short period of time; *X* v. *United Kingdom* Application 9403/81.

[67] *Luberti* v. *Italy*, §§ 35 et seq.; *Herz* v. *Germany*, § 68, where the detention had ended.

guarantee would lose its effect if there was no possibility to have the lawfulness of detention reviewed after the measure had ceased to be executed.[68]

I do not regard this as entirely convincing. The aim of the right to a speedy review of the lawfulness of any deprivation of liberty is twofold, encompassing a theoretical and a more pragmatic objective. The theoretical aim requires a determination of the lawfulness of the deprivation of liberty; the pragmatic one seeks liberty. The primary aim should be the pragmatic one. Once a person has been released, there may still be a certain interest in knowing whether the detention was lawful, for instance, for the purposes of compensation, but this is in any case covered by the general guarantee of an effective remedy (ECHR, Art. 13; ICCPR, Art. 2 § 3(a)). This would mean that Article 5 § 4 would not be violated by the discontinuation of habeas corpus proceedings after release. Of course, it must effectively lead to liberty. If a person opposes deportation to another country and is detained, release after transport to that country can be no substitute for liberation in the country in which the arrest occurred.[69]

What if after the filing of habeas corpus proceedings the detainee is convicted and, from that moment on, serves his sentence in the sense of Article 5 § 1(a)? This was the case in *König*, where the request for release was dealt with at the same time as an appeal against the supreme court judgment. The Court decided that this was not legitimate. It found that the regional court of Kosice had not ruled on the request for release and that, therefore, the applicant was still detained on remand.[70] This is indeed hard to understand and difficult to reconcile with the Court's doctrine according to which detention on remand is brought to an end by a conviction at first instance.[71] Judge Borrego Borrego in his dissenting opinion rightly stressed that the conviction and sentence of imprisonment must be regarded as an implicit rejection of the request. It is indeed highly unrealistic to assume that in this situation there was even the most tenuous chance of the convict being released.

4. Habeas Corpus where the Detention was Ordered by a Court

Contrary to the guarantee in paragraph 3 of both Articles 9 of the ICCPR and 5 of the ECHR, paragraph 4 of both Articles is applicable to all types of detention. Yet, in the so-called 'Vagrancy case' the Court made an exception and established what is known as the 'incorporation doctrine'.[72] This doctrine has, over time, been softened and more and more exceptions have been developed.

(a) The 'Doctrine of Incorporation'
The applicants de Wilde, Ooms, and Versyp were persons without regular income or fixed abode and were thus classed as 'vagrants' under Belgian law. At

---

[68] *Herz* v. *Germany*, § 68.   [69] *Conka* v. *Belgium*, § 55.   [70] *König* v. *Slovakia*, § 20.
[71] e.g. *B* v. *Austria*. See further Chapter 19 below.
[72] *De Wilde, Ooms and Versyp* v. *Belgium*, § 76.

one point in time they agreed to be committed to a closed institution where they were effectively imprisoned. Later, when they requested that they be freed from this institution, they were denied the opportunity to have their detention reviewed by a judicial authority. The Government argued, *inter alia*, that their imprisonment had been ordered by a judge and that therefore Article 5 § 4 did not apply.

The Court agreed in principle with this proposition, referring in particular to Article 5 § 1(a), which permits detention in the case of a person serving a sentence. Indeed, at first sight, it seems rather obvious that a person in that situation cannot invoke Article 5 § 4 in order to have his or her judgment reviewed.[73] It found that recourse to a court was required in cases where the decision to deprive someone of his or her liberty was taken by an administrative authority, and added that 'there is nothing to indicate that the same applies when the decision is made by a court at the close of judicial proceedings. In the latter case the supervision required by Article 5 § 4 is *incorporated* in the decision'.[74]

In my view, this doctrine is not at all convincing, especially given the flawed reasoning on which it is based.[75] While it is certainly correct to say that habeas corpus proceedings cannot lead to the re-examination of a judgment, a number of other issues may arise, such as the identity of the prisoner with the person sentenced, or a statute of limitations. It is also difficult to understand why the application of Article 5 § 4 to detention under Article 5 § 1(a) requires to be justified, particularly in view of the clear wording to the contrary. It is the 'opting out' which ought to call for a compelling justification.

Nevertheless, the result of the 'vagrancy' judgment can be regarded as quite satisfactory. The Court found that the applicants had been placed at the disposal of the Government for two years by a police court after having had the chance to be heard. These proceedings however did 'not ensure guarantees comparable to those which exist regarding detention in criminal cases, notwithstanding the fact that the detention of vagrants is very similar in many respects'. While presenting certain judicial features, they 'were not sufficient to give the magistrate the character of a "court" . . . when due account is taken of the seriousness of what is at stake'.[76] This approach also answers a question raised by Esser: is there 'incorporation' in cases where the suspect was arrested on the basis of an arrest warrant issued by a court?[77] In fact this cannot be the case, because there has not been any appropriate procedure—on the contrary, it is the Convention itself which regulates the next step, by requiring in Article 5 § 3 that the person who has been arrested be brought before a judge. (In passing, it may be noted that such incorporation does not attach to the proceedings under Article 5 § 4 themselves!)

---

[73] The right to appeal was only introduced by Protocol No. 7, Art. 2.

[74] *De Wide, Ooms and Versyp* v. *Belgium*, § 76 (emphasis added).

[75] See Trechsel (1974) 234 et seq.; Trechsel (1980) 127 et seq.; van Dijk and van Hoof (1998) 285.   [76] *De Wide, Ooms and Versyp* v. *Belgium*, § 79.

[77] Esser (2002) 333.

This remains the approach followed by the Court. The control of lawfulness of the detention is said to be 'incorporated' in the initial court decision, provided that 'the procedure followed has a judicial character and gives to the individual concerned guarantees appropriate to the kind of deprivation of liberty in question'.[78]

Leaving aside the general criticism of this approach, other judgments and in particular *Drozd and Janousek* and *Iribarne Pérez* have, in my view, produced results which are far from convincing. In these cases the applicants had been tried and sentenced by the 'corts' in Andorra and the proceedings were far removed from the procedural standards required to ensure conformity with the requirements of Article 6. The applicants then served their sentences in France. One of the issues was whether the applicants were entitled to take habeas corpus proceedings. In *Iribarne Pérez* the complaint was rejected on the basis of the incorporation doctrine.[79] In *Drozd and Janousek* Article 5 § 4 had not even been invoked. It is hard to understand how the Court could conclude that the control of the lawfulness of a twelve-year prison sentence could be considered as 'incorporated' in a judgment which was the result of proceedings hardly conforming to the standards required by Article 6 of the Convention.

(b) A Further Development

A particular weakness of the incorporation doctrine is that it does not take into account imprisonment which is at least partly justified by factors unconnected to the formal court decision. A typical example is where a person is deemed to be dangerous; such characteristics are likely to change over time and there would have been considerable scope for injustice had it been ruled that such detention nevertheless fell outwith the scope of the provision. In a series of cases the Commission and Court avoided this by taking such circumstances into account and have thereby made the doctrine considerably more flexible.

5. *The Exceptions to the Incorporation Doctrine*

(a) Confinement Linked to 'Unsoundness of Mind'

Nine years after the 'Vagrancy' judgment, the doctrine of incorporation was first adapted in a case involving imprisonment on mental-health grounds. In *Winterwerp* the Court, in following the Commission, found that it would be contrary to the purpose of paragraph 4 to make confinement for an indefinite period on grounds of mental illness immune from subsequent review, as the reasons initially warranting confinement may cease to exist. The question, however, remained undecided as the decision depriving the applicant of his liberty had not been taken in 'proceedings [before] a court'.[80]

---

[78] *Vodenicarov* v. *Slovakia*, § 33; *Herz* v. *Germany*, § 64.
[79] *Iribarne Pérez* v. *France*, §§ 30–1.   [80] *Winterwerp* v. *Netherlands*, § 55.

Two years later, in *X* v. *United Kingdom*, the Court seemed to rely on *obiter dicta* from that case.[81] The applicant had been convicted by the Sheffield Assizes of wounding with intent to cause grievous bodily harm, and the court had made an order confining him to a high-security mental hospital for the criminally insane. His detention was then covered by both paragraph l(a) *and* (e). The Court gave a rather creative interpretation of what it had said in the 'Vagrancy' case. There, it had held that 'the decision depriving a person of his liberty' could incorporate the control of legality of subsequent detention; now, it concluded that that passage 'does not purport to deal with an ensuing period of detention in which new issues affecting the lawfulness of the detention might subsequently arise'.[82]

'Article 5 para. 4 sometimes requires the possibility of subsequent review of the lawfulness of detention by a court. This usually applies to the detention of persons of unsound mind within the meaning of paragraph 1(e), where the reasons initially warranting confinement may cease to exist: . . . it would be contrary to the object and purpose of Article 5 . . . to interpret paragraph 4 thereof . . . as making this category of confinement immune from subsequent review of lawfulness merely provided that the initial decision issued from a court.'[83] The Court added that the obligation under Article 5 § 4 'will not necessarily be the same in all circumstances and as regards every category of deprivation of liberty; . . . a person of unsound mind compulsorily confined in a psychiatric institution for an indefinite or lengthy period is . . . in principle entitled, at any rate where there is no automatic periodic review of a judicial character, to take proceedings at reasonable intervals before a court to put in issue the "lawfulness" . . . of his detention, whether that detention was ordered by a civil or criminal court or by some other authority'.[84] Of course, the guarantee also applies when an accused has been acquitted of a crime on the basis of a lack of criminal responsibility and has been committed directly to a mental hospital.[85]

This approach has subsequently been extended to cover all detention which is based on mental-health grounds, irrespective of whether the person concerned has committed an offence[86] or not.[87]

(b) Detention of Dangerous Convicts

Perhaps the most innovative development in criminology and criminal law in the second half of the nineteenth century was the recognition that crime was not

---

[81] *X* v. *United Kingdom*, §§ 50 et seq.

[82] Ibid., § 51; see also *E* v. *Norway* where the issue of incorporation was, however, not discussed.

[83] *Iribarne Pérez* v. *France*, § 30; see also *Winterwerp* v. *Netherlands*, § 55; *X* v. *United Kingdom*, § 52; *Luberti* v. *Italy*, § 31.   [84] *X* v. *United Kingdom*, § 52; confirmed in *Konig* v. *Slovakia*, § 19.

[85] *Silva Rocha* v. *Protugal*; and *Magelhães Pereira* v. *Portugal*.

[86] *Luberti* v. *Italy*, §§ 31 et seq.

[87] *Van der Leer* v. *Netherlands*, § 33 (control not incorporated because of insufficient proceedings); *Wassink* v. *Netherlands*, §§ 29 et seq. (control incorporated notwithstanding the fact that the 'procedure prescribed by law' had not been strictly followed—the Commission had found a violation by seventeen votes to one). See also the Commission's report in *Koendjbiharie* v. *Netherlands*, § 65.

just a product of evil, the Devil, but was connected to a number of factors which were not adequately approached with the tools of morality. This lead to a widening of the methods of disposal. Although, traditional, retributive penalties such as imprisonment were maintained, they were joined by new 'measures of security' which were focused less on retribution and more on public safety, hence the term '*défence sociale*'.[88]

Still, it is quite common in many countries for the criminal law to distinguish between these two types of sanctions. Typically, a non-retributive sanction, often imposed on the basis of the perceived dangerousness of the convict, will be of indeterminate length. The detention will not end until the danger is thought to have diminished to such an extent that release, albeit under supervision or certain conditions, is possible.

The Court first had to deal with this issue in the case of *van Droogenbroeck*. The applicant was 'placed at the government's disposal' ('*ter beschikkingstelling aan de regering*'),[89] whereby the minister of justice was able to decide whether he would be detained or not. The Court accepted the Commission's view that his detention was not ordered by the court but by an administrative authority, and thus Article 5 § 4 was applicable.

While this case is still entirely in line with the doctrine of incorporation, a series of cases against the United Kingdom marked a new approach. I have already referred to the case of *X* which concerned a man who as well as having committed an offence was also considered to have been suffering from a mental illness. The position in *Weeks* was rather different. In this case the applicant was a young man who had robbed a pet shop, armed with a starter pistol loaded with blank cartridges. He managed to take just thirty-five pence which he lost as he left the shop. Later he called the police and turned himself in. When they came to arrest him, there was a struggle, shots were fired and an officer was wounded. The judge imposed a life sentence, explaining that:

[L]ife imprisonment in this case at any rate means an indeterminate sentence. If when he gets to prison it then appears after he has been there some time that there are grounds for transferring him to a mental institution for treatment, there are ample powers under the Act which will enable the Home Secretary to do so. Moreover, as soon as it becomes apparent, and it is to be hoped that it may not be long, but one cannot tell, that it is safe from the public point of view and from his own point of view to do so, this boy will be released. At first sight a sentence of life imprisonment, particularly having regard to his age, sounds terrible, but when the factors to which reference has been made are considered it will be seen that this is really in mercy to the boy and will perhaps enable him to be released much sooner than if a long term of imprisonment had been imposed, which was the only other alternative.[90]

The applicant was eventually released on licence, but on breaching the terms of the licence was recalled to prison, whereupon he had no opportunity to

---

[88] cf. Ancel (1981); see also Liszt (1904) 1.
[89] *Van Droogenbroeck* v. *Belgium*, §§ 19 et seq.   [90] *Weeks* v. *United Kingdom*, § 15.

challenge his continued detention by way of habeas corpus proceedings. This led to the finding of a violation of Article 5 § 4 of the ECHR. The Court agreed that the sentence belonged to a 'special category' whereby the young man was 'subject to a continuing security measure in the interests of public safety'.[91] As 'the grounds relied on by the sentencing judges for deciding that the length of the deprivation of Mr. Weeks' liberty should be subject to the discretion of the executive for the rest of his life are by their nature susceptible of change with the passage of time', he was entitled to have the persistence of his dangerousness re-examined.[92]

The next step was taken in the *Thynne, Wilson and Gunnell* judgment. Here, the accused had committed extremely serious crimes which were deemed to be related to a psychological disorder. They were each given a discretionary life sentence, which comprises two elements. The first is called the 'tariff', and 'denotes the period of detention considered necessary to meet the requirements of retribution and deterrence'. The second element consists of any further detention imposed to serve the interests of security.[93] The tariff had originally been set by the Home Secretary, a procedure which the Court has since found to be incompatible with the right to be judged by a tribunal.[94] At any rate, it ruled that once the tariff period had expired, the detainee had the right to take habeas corpus proceedings.

The final step in the development of the jurisprudence led to a similar finding with regard to the mandatory life sentence. For a long time, the Court had consistently refused to apply the guarantees of Article 5(4) to determinate sentences, with the significant exception of sentences relating to children (see below). Claims that a mandatory life sentence ought also be subject to Article 5(4) had fallen on deaf ears as the Court maintained that mandatory sentences belonged to a 'different category from the discretionary sentence in the sense that it is imposed automatically as the punishment for the offence of murder irrespective of considerations pertaining to the dangerousness of the offender'.[95]

Finally, in *Stafford*, the Court changed its approach—although, regrettably, it did not do this in a clear way.[96] It accepted that even a mandatory sentence of life imprisonment consisted of two elements, namely the 'tariff', which was purely punitive in character and did not give rise to the right to a judicial review of the

---

[91] Ibid., § 46.   [92] Ibid., § 58.

[93] *Thynne, Wilson and Gunnell* v. *United Kingdom*, §§ 52–3; see also the similar cases of *Oldham* v. *United Kingdom*; and *Hirst* v. *United Kingdom*.

[94] *Easterbrook* v. *United Kingdom*, §§ 26 et seq.

[95] *Wynne* v. *United Kingdom*, §§ 35 et seq. See also *X* v. *United Kingdom* Application 9089/80; *Hogben* v. *United Kingdom* Application 11653/85.

[96] This is an issue which calls for *obiter dictum*: why does the Court try to change its case-law so surreptitiously? Is it afraid of criticism or of implicitly criticizing earlier judgments? Is the legal community in Europe not entitled to clarity? The questions must remain unanswered, but I wish to express the hope that this undignified practice (cf. e.g. *Huber* v. *Switzerland* and *Borgers* v. *Belgium*) will soon disappear.

detention, and the ensuing period which was justified by the dangerousness of the prisoner, a condition which was subject to change over time and to which Article 5 § 4 applied.[97]

This judgment raises interesting questions, not least whether this approach can be applied to other countries which do not have a 'tariff' system. In many countries, even those serving a life sentence can be released on probation.[98] The release is essentially justified by the expectation that the convict will respect the law. The reverse of this means that the detention of a person beyond the earliest possible release date, amounts to continued detention based on the assumption that the person still constitutes a danger to society. This would mean that the right to take habeas corpus proceedings now arises as soon as a prisoner becomes eligible for release on probation. The Court has not yet had the opportunity to examine this issue, but the jurisprudence would suggest that such an application would be successful, not the least in order to ensure uniform application of the Convention across Europe.

(c) Sentences against Juvenile Offenders

I have already referred to the case of *Weeks*, a 17-year-old juvenile who was considered to be very dangerous. In two other cases concerning juveniles, *Singh* and *Hussain*, the applicants, who were both under eighteen, were detained 'during Her Majesty's pleasure' following convictions for murder. Their sentences also comprised two elements: the tariff period and then a second period during which they could continue to be held if it was believed that they still posed a danger to the public. The situation seems to be very similar to that under a discretionary life sentence. The Court considered that 'an indeterminate term of detention for a convicted young person, which may last as long as that person's life, can only be justified by considerations based on the need to protect the public'. Thus, it was essential to 'take into account any developments in the young offender's personality and attitude as he or she grows older'.[99] Consequently, after the expiry of the tariff period, they were entitled to be able periodically to challenge the legitimacy of the detention.

The cases *T* v. *United Kingdom* and *V* v. *United Kingdom*[100] concerned two boys who had committed the widely publicized murder of a toddler, whom they had kidnapped in full view of a CCTV camera in a shopping centre. They also received an indeterminate sentence. The Court again went one stage further. It noted that in this case the 'tariff' was initially set by the Home Secretary rather than by the sentencing judge. This led to the conclusion that the supervision required by Article 5(4) could not be regarded as having been incorporated into

---

[97] *Stafford* v. *United Kingdom*, § 87; confirmed in *Von Bülow* v. *United Kingdom*, §§ 23–4; *Wynne* v. *United Kingdom* (*No. 2*), §§ 24–6; *Hill* v. *United Kingdom*, §§ 19–22.
[98] e.g. SPC, Art. 38 § 1(1) (after fifteen years); revised SPC, Art. 68 § 5 (after ten years).
[99] *Singh* v. *United Kingdom*, § 61; *Hussain* v. *United Kingdom*, § 53.
[100] *T* v. *United Kingdom*, § 119; *V.* v. *United Kingdom*, § 120.

the trial court's sentence at all. The right to habeas corpus therefore arose as soon as they had been sentenced.

(d) Detention for Non-payment of a Fine

In one case an applicant was detained because he had not been able to pay a customs fine. The Court found that financial solvency had to be considered as a factor that could evolve with the course of time. Where the imposition of a prison sentence is contingent on the applicant's failure to pay a fine, proceedings must be available to enable an examination of the lawfulness of the applicant's imprisonment. In *Soumare* the applicant was sentenced to a ten-year prison sentence and a customs fine, together with an order for imprisonment in case of default. After serving the prison sentence, the applicant was detained for a further period because of defaulting on the fine. The Court held that such detention without adequate review was incompatible with Article 5(4).[101]

C. The Scope of Judicial Control under Paragraph 4

1. General Observations

It is important to recognize that the scope of the obligations under Article 5 § 4 will not be absolutely identical in every case.[102] The essential point is that the review must be wide enough to enable an examination of all the conditions, which are essential for the lawful detention of a person according to Article 5 § 1.[103] This means, taking detention under Article 5 § 1(c) as an example, that the competent court has to examine 'not only compliance with the procedural requirements set out in [domestic law] but also the reasonableness of the sus- picion grounding arrest and the legitimacy of the purpose pursued by the arrest and the ensuing detention'.[104] In cases of mental illness 'the review exercisable by the courts in habeas corpus proceedings will bear solely upon the conformity of the exercise of [the] discretion' left to the administrative authority.[105] It is noteworthy that in this case the very institution of habeas corpus under English law, from which paragraph 4 derives, was held to fall short of the requirements of this guarantee.

---

[101] *Soumare v. France.*
[102] *Bouamar v. Belgium*, § 60; *Chahal v. United Kingdom*, § 127. See also *McVeigh, O'Neill and Evans v. United Kingdom* Applications 8022/77, 8025/77, and 8027/77; and *Caprino v. United Kingdom*, Application 6871/75, § 64.
[103] *E v. Norway*, § 50; *Chahal v. United Kingdom*, § 127; *Jėčius v. Lithuania*, § 101.
[104] See e.g. *Brogan and others v. United Kingdom*, § 65; *Nikolova v. Bulgaria*, § 58; *Jėčius v. Lithuania*, § 100; *Grauslys v. Lithuania*, § 51–5; *Ilijkov v. Bulgaria*, § 94; *Stasaitis v. Lithuania*, § 90; *Butkevicius v. Lithuania*, § 43; *Esser* (2002) 328.
[105] *X v. United Kingdom*, § 56; see also *Weeks v. United Kingdom*, § 69; confirmed in *Thynne, Wilson and Gunnell v. United Kingdom*, § 80; *Ireland v. United Kingdom*, § 200. By contrast, habeas corpus was considered to be adequate in *Brogan and others v. United Kingdom*, § 65; and in *McVeigh, O'Neill and Evans v. United Kingdom* Applications 8022/77, 8025/77, and 8027/77, § 217 (report).

On the other hand, the review required in cases of detention with a view to expulsion or extradition under Article 5 § 1(f) is particularly narrow. Such detention is justified by the Government's decision to expel or to extradite the person concerned and Article 5 § 4 does not require that the domestic courts should have the power to review whether the underlying decision to expel could be justified under national or Convention law.[106]

With regard to the scope of judicial control under paragraph 4, two questions arise: what sort of 'lawfulness' is to be ascertained and what degree of scrutiny is required?

As to the first question, it is obvious that Article 5 must be read as a whole. The 'court' referred to in paragraph 4 must therefore verify whether the detention is 'in conformity not only with domestic law but also with the text of the Convention, the general principles embodied therein and the aim of the restrictions permitted by Article 5 § 1.[107] '[I]n relation to one and the same deprivation of liberty the notion of "lawfulness" should have the same significance in paragraphs 1 . . . and 4.'[108]

2. Ineffective Remedies

The Strasbourg authorities have had to consider a number of remedies which have not met the conditions required for a habeas corpus-type review. Remedies which concentrate on the establishment of the guilt or criminal responsibility of a public official for having failed to attend to complaints about the lawfulness of the detention, rather than on the release of the detainee, will be insufficient to meet the requirements of the provision.[109] The remedy must enable the applicant to obtain a review of the lawfulness of the detention. The mere opportunity to claim compensation will not satisfy the requirements of Article 5 § 4.[110] In *Keus* the Court accepted that '*kort geding*' proceedings before the president of the district court constituted a valid remedy. This must be viewed as being somewhat dubious in light of the fact that the Government had only suggested this route at the hearing before the Court.[111]

The issue of 'lawfulness' must be distinguished from that of arbitrariness. Arbitrariness refers to a decision which no reasonable judge could have taken.

---

[106] *Chahal* v. *United Kingdom*, § 128; *Caprino* v. *United Kingdom* Application 6871/75; *Conka* v. *Belgium*, Report of the Commission, § 38.

[107] *Thynne, Wilson and Gunnell* v. *United Kingdom*, § 61 in fine. See also *Brogan and others* v. *United Kingdom*, § 65; *E* v. *Norway*, § 50; *Weeks* v. *United Kingdom*, § 57; *Van Droogenbroeck* v. *Belgium*, §§ 48 et seq.; and *X* v. *United Kingdom*, §§ 57 et seq.

[108] *Ashingdane* v. *United Kingdom*, § 52.

[109] See e.g. *Van Droogenbroeck* v. *Belgium*, § 51; *Sabeur Ben Ali* v. *Malta*, § 39; see also *Kadem* v. *Malta*, § 52.   [110] *Öcalan* v. *Turkey*, § 75.

[111] *Keus* v. *Netherlands*, § 28. The decision was taken by five votes to four; see the convincing dissenting opinion of Judges Ryssdal, Pettiti, Bernhardt, and Spielmann, at 70 et seq.; the Commission had been unanimous in finding a violation. Alkema (1991) 2630, in his note on the judgment, states that the remedy has in fact not (yet) passed the test of effectiveness.

Therefore a remedy which restricts the tribunal to examining whether the detention was arbitrary, cannot be regarded as 'effective' within the meaning of Article 5 § 4.[112] In *E* v. *Norway*, however, the Court disregarded this principle and considered it sufficient that the domestic courts would have been competent to examine whether the applicant's detention was 'arbitrary'.[113] Furthermore, it did not find fault with the fact that there had 'not so far been any decision by the Norwegian Supreme Court to the effect that an administrative decision taken under Article 39 of the Penal Code can be overruled in judicial proceedings'.[114] In other cases, both in the context of exhaustion of domestic remedies[115] and in other circumstances,[116] the Court has required that the effectiveness of a remedy be demonstrated by reference to prior decisions.[117]

Although the Court will not rule on legislation *in abstracto*, it will consider the application of laws. In *Nikolova*, where the law placed on the applicant the burden of proving beyond reasonable doubt that there did not exist even a hypothetical danger of absconding, reoffending or obstructing justice, the Court noted that the failure of the domestic court to consider the applicant's arguments as relevant to the question of lawfulness violated Article 5 § 4.[118]

It seems that in these two judgments, the Court did not give appropriate weight to the requirement that the available review be clear and certain, particularly in light of the fact that the Convention purports to set out guarantees which are not 'theoretical and illusory but . . . practical and effective'.[119]

Where the domestic law at issue has changed, a situation of uncertainty may arise. This was the case in *Soumare*, where the Paris Court of Appeal had relied on the old case-law. The Court did not accept the Government's argument that counsel for the applicant could and should have familiarized himself with the new case-law.[120]

A particular challenge to the effectiveness of the remedy can lie in the federal structure of a country. The applicant *RMD* was arrested in a Swiss canton. As he was suspected of having committed offences in several cantons, he was, as it were, sent on a tour from one police station to the next. In each canton he instituted habeas corpus proceedings, but before the court had a chance to determine the case he had already been moved to another canton and thus another jurisdiction. While recognizing that the problem here lay in the federal structure of Switzerland, the Court, like the Commission, held that 'it is for the State to

---

[112] See e.g. *Ireland* v. *United Kingdom*, § 200.

[113] *E* v. *Norway*, § 60; the Commission had been unanimous in finding a violation; this dangerous mistake was repeated in *Minjat* v. *Switzerland*, § 48, where the Court was satisfied that the detention was 'not arbitrary'. [114] Ibid.

[115] *De Jong, Baljet and van den Brink* v. *Netherlands*, § 39.

[116] *Van Droogenbroeck* v. *Belgium*, § 54; *Sakık and others* v. *Turkey*, § 53.

[117] See also Esser (2002) 331.

[118] *Nikolova* v. *Bulgaria*, § 61; *Ilijkov* v. *Bulgaria*, §§ 94 et seq.; *Hristov* v. *Bulgaria*, § 117; *Mihov* v. *Bulgaria*, § 103; *Yankov* v. *Bulgaria*, §§ 176–86; *Hamanov* v. *Bulgaria*, §§ 79–85.

[119] *Artico* v. *Italy*, § 33.   [120] *Soumare* v. *France*, §§ 39–43.

organise its judicial system in such a way as to enable its courts to comply with the requirements of' Article 5 § 4.[121] Esser criticizes this judgment—in his view the Court did not pay attention to the fact that on three occasions a judge had confirmed the lawfulness of Mr RMD's arrest.[122] Esser refers however to the decisions taken in relation to Article 5 § 3, which cannot replace habeas corpus proceedings.

Finally, it must be stressed that the detainee is expected to pursue his or her rights with sufficient diligence. As with the exhaustion of domestic remedies, the detainee is expected to follow domestic law in exercising the right to take habeas corpus proceedings.[123] Even if the rules are rather formalistic, their strict application by the domestic authorities is respected by the Court.

3. Issues of National Security

The Court has had to consider situations where Member States have ostensibly had a legitimate interest to interfere with the scope of judicial control. The Court has reviewed a number of cases where, because of national-security or other interests, the domestic courts were unable to review documents relating to the detention of an applicant.[124] The Court has noted that while it recognizes that there may be circumstances where the use of confidential material is unavoidable, this does not free the authorities from the obligation of ensuring that the domestic courts are able to exercise free control.[125] The Court will look for some evidence of attempts by the state to employ techniques which are able both to 'accommodate legitimate security concerns about the nature and sources of intelligence information and yet accord the individual a substantial measure of procedural justice'.[126]

D. Procedural Requirements

1. Introduction

The procedural aspects of habeas corpus proceedings have been the most controversial aspect of Article 5 § 4, attracting the most debate and undergoing the most significant developments. Initially, in the *Neumeister* case, the Court clearly stated that the fair-trial provisions, and in particular the requirements of equality of arms, did not apply to proceedings covered by Article 5.[127] With time, however, the rights of detainees in these proceedings have been extended—and the Article 5 § 4 proceedings now share a number of similarities with those

---

[121] *RMD* v. *Switzerland*, § 54.   [122] Esser (2002) 342.
[123] *Kampanis* v. *Greece*, §§ 50–1.
[124] *Chahal* v. *United Kingdom*, § 130; *Al-Nashif* v. *Bulgaria*, § 94; *X* v. *United Kingdom*, § 61.
[125] *Fox, Campbell and Hartley* v. *United Kingdom*, § 34; *Murray* v. *United Kingdom*, § 58; *Chahal* v. *United Kingdom*, § 131.   [126] *Chahal* v. *United Kingdom*, § 131.
[127] *Neumeister* v. *Austria*, The Law, § 22; see also *Matznetter* v. *Austria*, The Law, § 13.

provided by Article 6. It should be noted that the Court's jurisprudence differs depending on the ground on which the deprivation of liberty is justified. I shall mainly concentrate here on detention on remand.[128]

The decision must, first of all, be taken by a court which is competent to determine the legality of the deprivation of liberty and which has the power to order the release of the applicant. The provision also requires that the court dealing with the matter provides 'guarantees of judicial procedure'. This means that there must be an adversarial hearing, which ensures equality of arms between the detainee and the prosecutor and respect for the rights of the defence.'[129] These issues will be examined in turn.

As the Court has stated, 'the cornerstone guarantee of Article 5 § 4 is that a detainee must have the right actively to seek judicial review of his detention'.[130] Furthermore, the existence of the right must be sufficiently certain.[131]

2. The Right to Access to a Court

(a) Independence and Impartiality

While the text of Article 5 § 4 expressly states that the competent authority must be a 'court', the Strasbourg authorities have not simply referred to Article 6 § 1, preferring instead to create an autonomous notion for the purposes of habeas corpus proceedings: 'The "court" referred to in Article 5 § 4 does not necessarily have to be a court of law of the classic kind integrated within the standard judicial machinery of the country. The term denotes bodies which exhibit not only common fundamental features, of which the most important is independence of the executive and of the parties to the case..., but also the "guarantees" "appropriate to the kind of deprivation of liberty in question"—"of [a] judicial procedure", the forms of which may vary but which must include the competence to "decide" the lawfulness of the detention and to order release if the detention is unlawful.'[132] It is obvious, for example, that a prosecutor cannot be regarded as a 'court', and it is hard to understand why such a claim is raised again and again, by, inter alia, the Turkish Government.[133]

---

[128] A summing up of the case-law can be found in *Megyeri* v. *Germany*, § 22; *Lutz* v. *Germany*, §§ 40–2; *Garcia Alva* v. *Germany*, §§ 40–3; *Schöps* v. *Germany*, § 44; *Lietzov* v. *Germany*, § 45; *Migon* v. *Poland*, §§ 68, 69; *Shishkov* v. *Bulgaria*, § 77; *Nikolov* v. *Bulgaria*, § 97; *Niedbała* v. *Poland*, § 66; *Trzaska* v. *Poland*, § 74.

[129] In a number of judgments the Court has repeated these requirements using more or less identical wording: see e.g. *Lanz* v. *Austria*, §§ 40–2; *Nikolova* v. *Bulgaria*, § 58; *Włoch* v. *Poland*, §125.   [130] *Rakevich* v. *Russia*, § 43; *Musiał* v. *Poland*, § 43.

[131] *Mamaç and others* v. *Turkey*, § 41; *Sakık and others* v. *Turkey*, § 53; *Sarıkaya* v. *Turkey*, § 60.

[132] *Hutchison Reid* v. *United Kingdom*, § 63, referring to *Weeks* v. *United Kingdom*, § 61. See also *de Wilde, Ooms and Versyp* v. *Belgium*, § 78; *X* v. *United Kingdom*, § 53. In *DN* v. *Switzerland*, § 42 the Court again stressed the element of independence, although the case is mainly concerned with impartiality.

[133] e.g. *Dalkılıç* v. *Turkey*; *Murat Satık and others* v. *Turkey*; and *Sakık and others* v. *Turkey*; but also *Varbanov* v. *Bulgaria*, § 58.

This definition is slightly blurred when it is used in connection with the doctrine of incorporation. In *Wassink*, for example, the Court found that '[t]he President of the District Court is undoubtedly a "court" from the organisational point of view, but the European Court has consistently held that the intervention of a single body of this kind will satisfy Article 5 § 4 only on condition that the procedure followed has a judicial character . . .'.[134] This statement could be misunderstood insofar as it links the possibility of one judge forming a 'court' and the requirement that the minimum procedural guarantees be respected. Of course, such procedural guarantees must be respected, irrespective of the number of persons which make up the 'court'.[135]

As far as the practical application of the law goes, it is certainly clear that a minister of justice cannot be construed as a 'court'.[136] Of more significance is the view that the Parole Board is sufficiently independent and impartial to fulfil the requirements of the provision.[137] I disagree with the Court, however, when it accepts—in cases concerning detention on remand—that the investigating judge can constitute a 'court' within the meaning of Article 5 § 4.[138] In fact, even though an investigating judge may, according to the organization of the judiciary in a given state, be independent of the executive and the parties, he or she can hardly be regarded as being impartial. After all, it is his or her responsibility to bring the investigation successfully to an end, and he or she therefore has an interest in keeping the accused from absconding or interfering with the evidence. Furthermore, it is usually the investigating judge who, at the outset, ordered or approved (under Article 5 § 3) the detention and would hence be called upon to review his or her own decision.[139] It remains to be seen whether the case of *HB* v. *Switzerland*, where it was held that the investigating judge could not be regarded as a proper authority to decide on detention under Article 5 § 3, will lead to a modification of the jurisprudence in this area.[140]

A question of 'objective impartiality' was also raised in the case of *DN* v. *Switzerland*.[141] One of the members of the 'Administrative Appeals Commission' ('*Verwaltungsrekurskommission*') which was responsible for determining the applicant's request to be released from a psychiatric hospital, Mr RW, had also acted as *rapporteur* and had prepared a report on the applicant's state of health. The Government and a minority of the Commission had argued that this did not impair the impartiality of the Administrative Appeals Commission and

---

[134] *Wassink* v. *Netherlands*, § 30; see also *Bouamar* v. *Belgium*, 136, § 57. The President of the District Court was also regarded as a 'court' in *Keus* v. *Netherlands*, § 28, and in *Van Droogenbroeck* v. *Belgium*, § 54 (where, however, his competence was not yet established).

[135] Cf. *Sanchez-Reisse* v. *Switzerland*, §§ 46 et seq.   [136] *Keus* v. *Netherlands*, § 28.

[137] *Weeks* v. *United Kingdom*, § 62; confirmed in *Thynne, Wilson and Gunnell* v. *United Kingdom*, § 80. See also with regard to the Belgian Mental Heath Review Board, *X* v. *Belgium* Application 6859/74; and *Dhoest* v. *Belgium* Application 10448/83.

[138] *Bezicheri* v. *Italy*, § 20, with reference to *Lamy* v. *Belgium*, §§ 27–9; *Douiyeb* v. *Netherlands*, § 58.

[139] Cf. *De Cubber* v. *Belgium*, § 124.   [140] *HB* v. *Switzerland*, §§ 55–64.

[141] See further Chapter 6, section I above.

compared the situation to that of members of the European Commission of Human Rights who, as delegates, had taken evidence and informed their colleagues internally of the result. For the Court, the decisive difference lay in the fact that in this case Mr RW had not only informed the other members of the Administrative Appeals Commission, but had also made known his provisional opinion to the applicant:

In the Court's opinion, this situation raised legitimate fears in the applicant that, as a result of R.W.'s position in these proceedings, he had a preconceived opinion as to her request for release from detention and that he was not, therefore, approaching her case with due impartiality . . . The applicant's fears would have been reinforced by R.W.'s position on the bench of the Administrative Appeals Commission where he was the sole psychiatric expert among the judges as well as the only person who had interviewed her. The applicant could legitimately fear that R.W.'s opinion carried particular weight in taking the decision. In the Court's view, these circumstances taken as a whole serve objectively to justify the applicant's apprehension that R.W., sitting as a judge in the Administrative Appeals Commission, lacked the necessary impartiality.[142]

This is not particularly convincing. Why would the fact that Mr RW was the only psychiatrist on the body affect his impartiality? Can the mere fact that the applicant was informed of the provisional opinion of the expert have affected her confidence in his impartiality? Would not the opposite argument be rather more convincing, namely that making the provisional opinion known is an element of fairness, of 'glasnost', which would have assisted the applicant in presenting her case more effectively?[143]

(b) The Power to Release

Only a body which is not restricted to giving advice, but which is also empowered to order release 'if the detention is not lawful', can fulfil the requirements of Article 5 § 4. In this respect, the Parole Board set up under the United Kingdom's Criminal Justice Act 1967,[144] along with the Mental Health Review Tribunal set up by the Mental Health Act 1959,[145] failed to satisfy the provision because they merely had an advisory function.[146] This was also the case with regard to the 'advisory panel' in the *Chahal* case.[147]

In *Benjamin and Wilson* the Mental Health Review Tribunal was at issue. Again, according to the law, it was only able to recommend that the detainee be

---

[142] *DN* v. *Switzerland*, §§ 54–6.

[143] See the dissenting opinion to the Commission's report of Trechsel and Liddy, joined by Busuttil, Geus. Pellonpää, and Nicolini.

[144] Except in cases concerning recall on licence; cf. *Weeks* v. *United Kingdom*, §§ 64 et seq.; *Thynne, Wilson and Gunnell*, § 80; *Hussain* v. *United Kingdom*, § 58; *Singh* v. *United Kingdom*, § 66; *Stafford* v. *United Kingdom*, § 88. After the Court's judgments in *Hussain* and *Singh* the Secretary of State changed the procedure which, from 1 Aug. 1996, conformed to the requirements of Art. 5 § 4; see *Waite* v. *United Kingdom*, §§ 50–2. However, in that case there was still held to be a violation (§§ 58 et seq).   [145] *X* v. *United Kingdom*, § 61.

[146] The problem does not exist any more under the Mental Health Act 1983; *Roux* v. *UK* Application 12039/86.   [147] *Chahal* v. *United Kingdom*, § 130.

released. The Government argued that it was the stated policy of the Secretary of State to follow the Tribunal, but the Court rightly rejected this argument.[148] In fact, it appears quite contradictory for the power to order a detainee's release to be vested in a minister, who in turn is bound by the advisory opinion of a tribunal.

Lack of the power to release also led to the rejection of prosecution for arbitrary detention as a remedy under Article 5 § 4.[149]

The Court was, however, extremely benevolent towards the Norwegian system. While there existed no case-law to confirm the hypothesis, it assumed that a court which had found Article 39 § 1 of the Penal Code to have been unlawfully applied, would 'normally' declare the decision 'invalid' and would have the power to order the detainee's release.[150]

It is important to distinguish the power to release from the actual release of the detainee. In *Assanidze* the Court was faced with a case where the release had been ordered by a court, but where the judgment had not been executed. It considered this to constitute a violation of Article 6 § 1.[151] A number of judges dissented, arguing convincingly that there had been a violation of the *lex specialis* Article 5 § 4.[152]

3. The Procedural Rights

(a) The Right to an Oral Hearing

An important question relates to the character of the proceedings required by the habeas corpus guarantee. The Court has stressed that the guarantees required depend on the kind of detention at issue.[153] However, it appears that there are some general basic requirements and any exceptions to these must be justified. In *Sanchez-Reisse*, the Court had to consider, for the first time since *Neumeister*,[154] whether a detainee had a right to be heard in person by the body responsible for determining the lawfulness of detention. The Court gave a somewhat cryptic, but effectively negative response:

Despite the difference in wording between paragraph 3 (right to be brought before a judge or other officer) and paragraph 4 (right to take proceedings) of Article 5, the Court's previous decisions relating to these two paragraphs have hitherto tended to acknowledge

---

[148] *Benjamin and Wilson* v. *United Kingdom*, §§ 33–8.
[149] *Van Droogenbroeck* v. *Belgium*, § 51.   [150] *E* v. *Norway*, § 62.
[151] *Assanidze* v. *Georgia*, §§ 181–4.
[152] Dissenting opinion of Judges Costa, Bratza, and Thomassen.
[153] See e.g. *Megyeri* v. *Germany*, § 22 (b, c); the origin of this doctrine lies in *De Wilde, Ooms and Versyp* v. *Belgium*, § 76, where the Court found that a court deciding on deprivation of liberty must provide the fundamental guarantees of procedure applying in that field, having regard 'to the particular nature of the circumstances in which such proceedings take place', § 78. See also *Sanchez-Reisse* v. *Switzerland*, § 51; *Bouamar* v. *Belgium*, § 60.
[154] *Neumeister* v. *Austria*, § 24: 'Full written proceedings or an oral hearing of the parties in the examination of such remedies would be a source of delay which it is important to avoid in this field'.

the need for a hearing before the judicial authority... These decisions concerned, however, only matters falling within the ambit of sub-paragraphs (c) and (e) in fine of paragraph 1. And, in fact, 'the forms of the procedure required by the Convention need not... necessarily be identical in each of the cases where the intervention of a court is required'.

In the present case, the Federal Court was led to take into consideration the applicant's worsening state of health, a factor which might have militated in favour of his appearing in person, but it had at its disposal the medical certificates appended to the third request for provisional release from custody. There is no reason to believe that the applicant's presence could have convinced the Federal Court that he had to be released.[155]

The Court has since clarified its opinion, stating unequivocally that: 'In the case of a person whose detention falls within the ambit of Article 5 § 1(c), a hearing is required'.[156]

There is, however, no right to a *public* hearing—in this respect the *Neumeister* judgment still represents the current position: 'Article 6 (1) does not merely require that the hearing should be fair, but also that it should be public. It is therefore impossible to maintain that the first requirement is applicable to the examination of requests for release without admitting the same to be true of the second. Publicity in such matters is not however in the interest of accused persons as it is generally understood'.[157] This argument can be described as being rather paternalistic—after all, the person concerned should be aware of what is, or is not, in his or her interest.

I think that it would be possible to add a public-hearing requirement to the rights of the detainee in habeas corpus proceedings, although with the caveat that the detainee must be able to waive this right. This is necessary as those detained on remand are protected by the presumption of innocence, which may be impaired if the press were able to report such hearings. Moreover, a person confined to a psychiatric institution might legitimately fear that admitting the public to the hearing might result in his or her personal details being discussed in public.[158]

A particular problem arises in cases where the person concerned has escaped. Given the requirement of a speedy decision, the court cannot be blamed if it makes a decision in his or her absence, as long as another remedy exists if the authorities succeed in again securing his or her detention.[159]

---

[155] *Sanchez-Reisse* v. *Switzerland*, § 51.

[156] *Włoch* v. *Poland*, § 126. See also *Assenov* v. *Bulgaria*, § 163; *Niedbala* v. *Poland*, § 67; *Trzaska* v. *Poland*, § 78; *Garcia Alva* v. *Germany*, § 39; *Waite* v. *United Kingdom*, § 59; *Singh* v. *United Kingdom*, § 67; *Grauzinis* v. *Lithuania*, § 33; *Kawka* v. *Poland*, § 57; *Kampanis* v. *Greece*, § 47; *Pantea* v. *Romania*, § 254; *GK* v. *Poland*, § 91; *MB* v. *Poland*, § 65.   [157] *Neumeister* v. *Austria*, § 23.

[158] See further Chapter 5 above.

[159] *Keus* v. *Netherlands*, § 26. In the same judgment the Court held that the fact that the applicant's lawyer was not informed of the hearing was not problematic, because there was no rule in Dutch law which required the authorities to do so; ibid., § 25. The argument is not entirely convincing; see also Alkema (1991) 2630.

(b) Equality of Arms and Adversarial Proceedings

'The proceedings must be adversarial and must always ensure "equality of arms" between the parties, the prosecutor and the detained person.'[160] The requirement for an adversarial procedure means that 'both the prosecution and the defence must be given the opportunity to have knowledge of and comment on the observations filed and the evidence adduced by the other party'.[161] Despite the categorical way in which the Court expressed these principles, it appears to have had some reservations. It stressed that as such proceedings are generally at a preliminary stage and thus differ from the determination of a charge, they 'should *in principle* also meet, *to the largest extent possible under the circumstances* of an on-going investigation, the basic requirements of a fair trial'.[162]

As usual, the question whether the right was granted is answered in a pragmatic way. In *Wassink* the court had based its decision on information obtained in the course of a number of telephone conversations. Although the detainee had only been given a summary of the conversations, the Court had regard to the fact that the judge had acted under emergency procedures and accepted the procedure as being in conformity with Article 5 § 4.[163] On the other hand, there was held to be a violation in *Sanchez-Reisse* where the authority responsible for the detention had filed a brief which was not communicated to the applicant.[164]

There is clearly no equality of arms if the prosecutor attends the hearing, which is held *in camera* and in the absence of the detainee and his or her counsel.[165]

(c) The Right of Access to the File

The leading case on access to the file in habeas corpus proceedings is *Lamy*. In this case the applicant was suspected of having committed a number of offences connected to his bankruptcy and was arrested. For the first thirty days he had no access to the file and he complained that this had prevented him from being able effectively to challenge his detention. The Court agreed, stating that: 'Access to these documents was essential for the applicant at this crucial stage in the proceedings, when the court had to decide whether to remand him in custody or to release him. Such access would, in particular, have enabled counsel for Mr Lamy to address the court on the matter of the co-defendants' statements and attitude . . . In the Court's view, it was therefore essential to inspect the documents in question in order to challenge the lawfulness of the arrest warrant effectively'.[166]

This approach was later confirmed in subsequent jurisprudence; essentially the applicant must have the possibility to respond to any argument brought forward

---

[160] *Garcia Alva* v. *Germany*, § 39. On equality of arms, see further Chapter 4 above.
[161] Ibid.   [162] Ibid. (emphasis added).
[163] *Wassink* v. *Netherlands*, § 33. In *X* v. *Belgium* Application 6859/74, the Commission found it important that the applicant be able to present medical evidence of his own.
[164] *Sanchez-Reisse* v. *Switzerland*, § 51; see also *MB* v. *Poland*, § 66.   [165] *GK* v. *Poland*, § 92.
[166] *Lamy* v. *Belgium*, § 29.

by the detaining authority. This means that any comments of the detaining authority on the request for release must be submitted to the detainee so that she or he can respond,[167] be it in writing[168] or orally.[169] Even though there was an oral hearing in *Włoch*, the right to adversarial proceedings was not granted because there had been no access to the file and the prosecutor remained in the room with the court after the defence had been heard.[170]

On the other hand, this requirement is also presented as an essential element of equality of arms, a broad and sometimes ambiguous concept, frequently referred to by the Court in its Article 6 judgments. In relation to Article 5 § 4, the Court has suggested that equality of arms is not ensured if 'counsel is denied access to those documents in the investigation file which are essential in order to effectively challenge the lawfulness of his client's detention'.[171] The requirement that a person who is detained on remand must have *de facto* access to the entire investigation file is a very far-reaching proposition; this is clearly demonstrated by the *Lamy* case where the documents concerned were mainly records of the applicant's own statements. The Swiss Federal Court subsequently interpreted this judgment rather restrictively.[172] The Strasbourg Court itself showed some flexibility on the issue and in *Włoch* it held that '[t]he opportunity of effectively challenging the statements or views which the prosecution bases on specific documents in the file, *may in certain instances* presuppose that the defence be given access to these documents'.[173] Esser convincingly suggests that the Court ought not to deal with this problem under the paradigm of equality of arms but should apply instead the requirement of fairness directly.[174]

What is remarkable is that access to the file is granted in cases of detention on remand where there may well be a danger of collusion. The German Government stressed this aspect in *Schöps, Lietzow* and *Garcia Alva*. The Court responded to this in the following way:

The Court acknowledges the need for criminal investigations to be conducted efficiently, which may imply that part of the information collected during them is to be kept secret in order to prevent suspects from tampering with evidence and undermining the course of justice. However, this legitimate goal cannot be pursued at the expense of substantial restrictions on the rights of the defence. Therefore, information which is essential for the

---

[167] *Sanchez-Reisse* v. *Switzerland*, § 51; see also *Nedbiała* v. *Poland*, § 67; *Trzaska* v. *Poland*, 78; *Ilijkov* v. *Bulgaria*, § 103.   [168] *Sanchez-Reisse* v. *Switzerland*, § 51.

[169] *Toth* v. *Austria*, § 84.

[170] *Włoch* v. *Poland*, §§ 129–31; *Migon* v. *Poland*, § 61. Later the Government recognized the inadequacy of Polish law in this respect and the Court found a violation of Art. 5 § 4 just by referring to these cases; cf. *Klamecki* v. *Poland*, § 130. See also *Lietzow* v. *Germany*, § 44; *Schöps* v. *Germany*, § 44; and *Garcia Alva* v. *Germany*, § 39.

[171] *Lamy* v. *Belgium*, § 29; *Weeks* v. *United Kingdom*, § 66; *Nikolova* v. *Bulgaria*, § 63; *Niedbała* v. *Poland*, § 67.

[172] 115 la BGE 302 (1989)—an unpublished judgment of 21 June 1991, re N, is more liberal; see also *X* v. *Switzerland* Application 8485/79.   [173] *Włoch* v. *Poland*, § 127 (emphasis added).

[174] Esser (200) 352.

assessment of the lawfulness of a detention should be made available in an appropriate manner to the suspect's lawyer.

In these circumstances, and given the importance in the Berlin Courts' reasoning of the contents of the investigation file, and in particular of the statements made by Mr K., which could not be adequately challenged by the applicant, since they were not communicated to him, the procedure before the said courts, which reviewed the lawfulness of the applicant's detention on remand, did not comply with the guarantees afforded by Article 5 § 4. This provision has therefore been violated.[175]

(d) The Right to Legal Assistance

An interesting development in the jurisprudence on Article 5 § 4 is the increasing emphasis that has been placed on procedural guarantees ordinarily associated with Article 6. One of the most important of these is the right to legal advice or representation to assist a detained person in challenging the legality of his or her detention.[176] It is quite obvious that a detainee may be assisted in habeas corpus proceedings. The Court has confirmed, when examining Article 6 § 3(c), that the right of access to a lawyer does not just apply to the trial itself, but may also have application in earlier stages of the proceedings.[177]

(i) General Rules Concerning Access to Counsel   There is no express right to have the assistance of counsel in order to challenge the legitimacy of the detention. Indeed, Article 5 contains no explicit mention of any right to legal advice. In the *Öcalan* case, however, the Court expressly recognized such a right.[178] In this case the applicant had been held, over a prolonged period of time, in total isolation.[179] The Court held that the applicant could not reasonably have been expected under such conditions to have challenged the lawfulness of his detention without legal assistance.

Proceedings under Article 5 § 4 are judicial proceedings and, therefore, a detainee must have the opportunity to be assisted by counsel. Furthermore, in order that the right to counsel be applied effectively, there must be an opportunity for counsel and client to communicate confidentially.

(ii) The Right to Legal-Aid Counsel   Article 5 § 4 not only requires that a detainee have the assistance of counsel, but also grants a right to legal-aid counsel in certain cases.

The Court has stated that while 'judicial proceedings referred to in Article 5 § 4 need not always be attended by the same guarantees as those required under Article 6 § 1 for civil or criminal litigation', it is nevertheless essential that 'the person concerned should have access to a court and the opportunity to be heard either in person or, where necessary through some sort form of representation'.

---

[175] *Garcia Alva* v. *Germany*, §§ 42, 43. See also, *mutatis mutandis, Lietzow* v. *Germany*, §§ 47–8. For confirmation of this approach, see *Migon* v. *Poland*, § 79; *Shishkov* v. *Bulgaria*, § 77; *Nikolov* v. *Bulgaria*, § 97.   [176] See further Chapter 10 above.
[177] *Imbrioscia* v. *Switzerland*.   [178] *Öcalan* v. *Turkey*, § 73.   [179] Ibid., § 72.

To this end 'special procedural safeguards may prove called for in order to protect the interests of persons who, on account of their mental disabilities, are not fully capable of acting for themselves'.[180]

In *Megyeri* v. *Germany* the applicant, who was confined to a psychiatric institution, argued that the failure of the domestic authorities to appoint him a lawyer in actions concerning his possible release, breached Article 5 § 4.[181] The Court held that this was one instance where the state was under an obligation to ensure that representation was available for the applicant. It stated that as a general rule, 'where a person is confined in a psychiatric institution on the ground of the commission of acts which constituted criminal offences but for which he could not be held responsible on account of mental illness, he should— unless there are special circumstances—receive legal assistance in subsequent proceedings relating to the continuation, suspension or termination of his detention. The importance of what is at stake for him—personal liberty—taken together with the very nature of his affliction—diminished mental capacity— compel this conclusion'.[182] In this case there were no special circumstances, suggesting that the applicant should not receive legal assistance and moreover the Court harboured substantial doubts as to the applicant's capacity adequately to address the legal issues involved in his case by himself. Thus, there was a violation of Article 5 § 4. It is interesting to note that here the wording seems to imply that there is a presumption in favour of legal aid which then requires to be rebutted by arguments to the contrary.

A similar obligation lies on the state where the detainee is a minor. The Court held in *Bouamar* that an applicant, who was under the age of majority during the proceedings, ought to have been represented by counsel.[183] Here the applicant's lawyers were not given notice that the hearing would take place, thus preventing the applicant from receiving the effective assistance of his lawyer.

However, the question has also arisen in other cases, such as *Woukam Moudefo*, where the applicant challenged his detention at the *cour de cassation*. He had asked for a legal-aid counsel and the Bar association had replied that they were considering his request. On the same day, however, the court rejected his appeal. The Commission, by a small majority, came to the conclusion that there had been a violation of Article 5 § 4 because it was not possible for the applicant effectively to defend himself. The case was then settled before it reached the Court.[184]

(e) A Presumption *pro libertate?*

In my view Article 5 § 4 also requires that there be a basic presumption, which functions rather like the presumption of innocence in criminal proceedings,

---

[180] *Winterwerp* v. *Netherlands*, § 60.   [181] *Megyeri* v. *Germany*, §§ 21–7.
[182] *Megyeri* v. *Germany*, § 23, confirmed in *Magelhães Pereira* v. *Portugal*, §§ 57–61.
[183] *Bouamar* v. *Belgium*, § 60.
[184] *Woukam Modefo* v. *France*; see in particular the Commission's Report, §§ 89–91. The question had already been touched upon in *Winterwerp* v. *Netherlands*, § 66. However, there the Court only rejected the argument that the applicant could have asked for a lawyer.

against the existence of specific reasons justifying the detention—a type of *in dubio pro libertate* principle. This concept can be seen to be underpinning the Court's approach when it refers to 'the assumption under the Convention that such detention [scil. detention on remand] is to be of strictly limited duration'.[185]

In *Nikolova* the Court was given the perfect opportunity to set out this principle in clear terms, but regrettably refrained from doing so. In this case the applicant could only have been released if she had proved that there was *no* danger of her absconding, obstructing justice, or reoffending. Thus only in exceptional circumstances would it have been possible to overturn the presumption *pro detentione*. Moreover, the judge had no competency to examine whether the suspicion was sufficient to justify the deprivation of liberty. The Court limited itself to finding that the applicant had presented weighty arguments which the domestic court had failed to address:

While Article 5 § 4 of the Convention does not impose an obligation on a judge examining an appeal against detention to address every argument contained in the appellant's submissions, its guarantees would be deprived of their substance if the judge, relying on domestic law and practice, could treat as irrelevant, or disregard, concrete facts invoked by the detainee and capable of putting in doubt the existence of the conditions essential for the 'lawfulness', in the sense of the Convention, of the deprivation of liberty. The submissions of the applicant in her appeal of 14 November 1995 contained such concrete facts and did not appear implausible or frivolous. By not taking these submissions into account the Regional Court failed to provide the judicial review of the scope and nature required by Article 5 § 4 of the Convention.[186]

The Court returned to the issue in *Hutchison Reid*, where it did indeed adopt the principle.[187] It held that *in dubio pro libertate* had already been considered to be an implicit element of Article 5 § 1. In earlier cases involving detention under Article 5 § 1(e), the Court had stressed that the detention would only be legitimate if it could be 'reliably shown that he or she suffers from a mental disorder sufficiently serious to warrant detention'.[188] In *Hutchison Reid* the applicant complained that he had the burden of proving that he was no longer suffering from a mental disorder requiring detention for medical treatment. The Court was not convinced that the onus of proof placed on the applicant was irrelevant to the outcome and held that: 'It is . . . sufficient to raise a problem concerning the effectiveness of the proceedings as a mechanism for preventing arbitrary or unlawful detention, if, on the state of evidence before the court, the burden of proof placed on the applicant was capable of influencing the decision.

---

[185] *Assenov* v. *Bulgaria*, § 162.

[186] *Nikolova* v. *Bulgaria*, § 61; see also *Ilijkov* v. *Bulgaria*, § 99; *Grauslys* v. *Lithuania*, § 54.

[187] *Hutchison Reid* v. *United Kingdom*, § 70: the applicant had invoked domestic case-law to the same effect, namely *R.* v. *Mental Health Review Tribunal North and East London Region, ex parte H*, Court of Appeal, 28 Mar. 2001 (England) and *Lyons* v. *The Scottish Ministers*, 7 Jan. 2002, First Division of the Court of Session (Scotland).

[188] *Winterwerp* v. *Netherlands*, §§ 39–40; *Johnson* v. *United Kingdom*, § 60.

In the applicant's case, where the issue of treatability was subject to conflicting views, this would appear to be the case'.[189]

(f) A Right to Appeal?

Does the detainee also have a right to appeal against a decision rejecting his request to be released? The Court has clearly indicated that there is no such right. There is no obligation on the authorities to set up a second level of jurisdiction for the examination of the lawfulness of detention and for hearing applications for release. If, however, the domestic law provides for appeal proceedings, these must offer the essential procedural guarantees.[190] This applies in particular to the requirement of speediness.[191]

(g) A Right to Submit Multiple Applications

A general feature of judicial decisions is that they become final. In principle, this must also apply to the determination of the lawfulness of a deprivation of liberty. However, in certain cases the course of time has such a strong impact on the lawfulness of detention that it almost constantly changes the factual situation, with the result that the '*idem*' (as in '*ne bis in idem*') is short-lived, particularly in cases under Article 5 § l(c) and (e).

Detention on remand is limited in time by virtue of Article 5 § 3. The person concerned must therefore have the possibility to repeat applications to a court at 'short intervals; there is an assumption in the Convention that detention on remand is to be of strictly limited duration . . . because its *raison d'être* is essentially related to the requirements of an investigation which is to be conducted with expedition'.[192]

Detention on the basis of mental-health considerations calls for repeated control because of the possibility that the patient's health may improve.[193] The case-law gives few suggestions as to what should be considered 'reasonable' in this context. The Court has considered intervals of between fifteen months and two years as excessive;[194] the Commission and the Court have accepted intervals of six months,[195] ten months[196] and one year.[197] It is a complex issue. On the one

---

[189] *Hutchison Reid* v. *United Kingdom*, § 72.

[190] *Navarra* v. *France*, § 28; *Lanz* v. *Austria*, § 42; *Toth* v. *Austria*, § 28; *Nikolova* v. *Bulgaria*, § 61; *Kampanis* v. *Greece*, § 47; *Niedbała* v. *Poland*, § 66; *Ječius* v. *Lithuania*, § 100; *Grauslys* v. *Lithuania*, § 53; *Grauzinis* v. *Lithuania*, § 32.   [191] *Letellier* v. *France*, § 33.

[192] *Bezicheri* v. *Italy*, § 21; an interval of one month was deemed to be 'not unreasonable'. See also *Letellier* v. *France*, § 56.

[193] *Herczegfalvy* v. *Austria*, § 75; *Oldham* v. *United Kingdom*, § 30. In this context, 'reasonable interval' was referred to in *Winterwerp* v. *Netherlands*, § 55; *X* v. *United Kingdom*, § 52; *Van Droogenbroeck* v. *Belgium*, § 48; *Luberti* v. *Italy*, §§ 31, 32.

[194] *Herczegfalvy* v. *Austria*, § 77; *Hirst* v. *United Kingdom*, §§ 35–44; a *fortiori* periods of up to five years, *Van Droogenbroeck* v. *Belgium*, § 53.   [195] *X* v. *Belgium* Application 6692/74.

[196] *M* v. *France* Application 10272/82.

[197] *Tunbridge* v. *United Kingdom* Application 16397/90; *AT* v. *United Kingdom* Application 20448/92; *Megyeri* v. *Germany*, § 25; *Herczegfalvy* v. *Austria*, §§ 75–8 (in that case the domestic law prescribed a period of one year, whereas the intervals were fifteen months and two years, which led to the finding of a violation.)

hand, the appropriate frequency ought to be assessed with regard to the particular circumstances of each case. On the other hand, reliable indications are called for in the interest of legal certainty. Lately, the Court has opted for the latter approach. It has rejected the idea that 'mental instability and dangerousness' can be considered as being susceptible to change over longer periods than mental illness and has concluded that even in this type of cases a period of two years was excessive.[198] Without saying so expressly, it has indicated that the limit is one year.[199]

In this respect, it must be stressed that domestic law may provide for a substitute to proceedings under paragraph 4 which can be taken at the initiative of the detainee, and constitute an 'automatic periodic review of a judicial character' which 'must comply with both the substantive and procedural rules of the national legislation and moreover be conducted in conformity with the aim of Article 5'.[200]

In *Silva Rocha* the Court even accepted a period of almost two years, which is hard to justify. Even more problematic was the Court's total lack of understanding of the relevant criminal law. The applicant had been accused of aggravated homicide and unlawful possession of arms, but had been held not to have been criminally responsible for his actions. Yet, the Court found that the decision of the national court could be regarded as a 'conviction' and concluded: 'The case involved a homicide committed by a person who could not be held responsible for his actions and who was at the same time dangerous. The seriousness of the offences together with the risk that he represented for himself as well as for others could reasonably justify his being removed from society for at least three years'.[201] Such disregard for both the domestic law and the general doctrine of criminal law is unacceptable. It also contradicts the principle of *nulla poena sine culpa* which the Court seems to have accepted in cases brought under Article 6.[202]

In cases of mental illness, *stricto sensu* the maximum period acceptable would, in my view, be one year. In any case, the right to a remedy must be granted even earlier if new facts, for example, medical evidence, are invoked, such as the castration of a sexual offender.

---

[198] *Oldham* v. *United Kingdom*, §§ 34–7; *Hirst* v. *United Kingdom*, § 41: in § 42 of the latter judgment the Court then continued to examine in some detail the applicant's development and came to the conclusion that he 'had developed significantly during the course of his sentence and could not be considered as a person in respect of whom no further change of circumstance could be envisaged'. This is, in my view, a rather dangerous approach. Does the Court intend to form an opinion on each applicant in an analogous situation and determine whether he or she is likely to develop favourably? This would hardly be compatible with the principle of subsidiarity and would again create considerable uncertainty.   [199] *Hirst* v. *United Kingdom*, § 39.
[200] *Koendjbiharie* v. *Netherlands*, § 27; see also *X* v. *United Kingdom*, § 52; *Keus* v. *Netherlands*, § 24; *Rutten* v. *Netherlands*, §§ 51 et seq.   [201] *Silva Rocha* v. *Portugal*, § 28.
[202] *AP, MP* and *TP* v. *Switzerland*; and *EL, RL* and *JO-L* v. *Switzerland*.

4. The Requirement of Speediness

(a) Issues Related to the Time Element

A very important aspect of the guarantee of habeas corpus lies in the obligation on the court to determine the lawfulness of the detention speedily. This, in the Court's view, is intended to prevent ill-treatment,[203] a fact which emphasizes its relationship to the right to be brought promptly before a judge under Article 5 § 3. Procedural rules may also impose speediness requirements on the detainee, setting short time limits for the filing of an appeal under Article 5 § 4. If such a time limit is too short, however, it may hinder the effectiveness of the remedy.[204]

The period to be assessed starts, in principle, with the introduction of the request.[205] If the applicant has announced that he or she will submit reasons at a later date, it is only with the introduction of such reasons that the period begins.[206] Where the request has to be submitted first to an administrative authority as a prerequisite for the access to a court, the date of the application to the administrative authority is the relevant one.[207] In cases of automatic periodic review, the period starts with the first step taken by the detaining authority to have the competent court decide on the prolongation.[208] Exceptionally, the time spent before an application was filed can count, such as in cases where domestic law excludes the possibility to take habeas corpus proceedings for a certain period.[209]

One particular problem which has frequently arisen in relation to determining the relevant period, concerns cases where the Convention came into force after the review proceedings had been instituted but before a decision had been made.[210] This occurred in the *Musiał* case where the application was made on 16 March 1993, while the Convention only came into force on the 1 May 1993. The Court accepted that the period began to run from the later date but unfortunately omitted to mention the obligation to take into account the fact that the proceedings had already taken some time by then.[211] It is true that this case did not call for such a caution as the decision would not have been taken before 9 January 1995!

The period normally ends when a decision has been made. In *Luberti* the Court did not take into consideration a delay of eleven days between the date on which the decision was taken and the date on which the applicant was released.[212] This could raise doubts about the lawfulness of the detention during this time. In some cases, the Strasbourg authorities took the date on which the

---

[203] *Pantea v. Romania*, § 256, with reference to *Aksoy v. Turkey*, § 76.

[204] This question was raised before the Court in *Farmakopoulos v. Belgium* Application 11683/85, § 52, unreported; however, as the applicant showed no interest, the case was struck from the list.

[205] *Van der Leer v. Netherlands*, § 35; *Pantea v. Romania*, § 250; *Zamir v. UK* Application 9174/80.

[206] *Herz v. Germany*, § 73.   [207] *Sanchez-Reisse v. Switzerland*, § 54.

[208] *Koendjbiharie v. Netherlands*, § 28. In *Egmez v. Cyprus* there were two automatic reviews within a week and the applicant was legally represented, so there was no violation, §§ 94, 95.

[209] *De Jong, Baljet and van den Brink v. Netherlands*, § 58.

[210] This problem has also arisen in a number of cases involving Art. 5 § 3.

[211] *Musiał v. Poland*, § 42.   [212] *Luberti v. Italy*, § 36.

Case-law on 'speedily', Art. 5 § 4 ECHR

Name	Date	Type of Detention	Time	Other Factors	Outcome
Letellier v. France	29/06/91	5 § 1(c)	8 to 20 days		no violation
Herczegfalvy v. Austria	24/09/92	5 § 1(e)	15 months, 2 years		violation
Musiał v. Poland	25/03/99	5 § 1(e)	1 year, 8 months, 8 days	—applicant asked for medical examination at a different institution	violation
Baranowski v. Poland	28/03/00	5 § 1(c)	almost 6 months	—complexity of the case —complexity of medical issues involved —length of appeal meant it had ultimately no legal or practical effect	violation
Trzaska v. Poland	11/07/00	5 § 1(c)	1 year, 23 days	defect of law	violation
Włoch v. Poland	19/10/00	5 § 1(c)	almost 3 months		no violation
Rehbock v. Slovenia	28/11/00	5 § 1(c)	23 days (twice)		violation
GB v. France	30/11/00	5 § 1(c)	32 days	suspected terrorist; two-tier proceedings	violation
MB v. Poland	03/11/00	5 § 1(c)	34 days	suspected terrorist; two-tier proceedings	violation
Jabłoński v. Poland[213]	21/12/00	5 § 1(c)	43 days	only one instance involved	violation

[213] It is astonishing that in this case (§ 94) the Court found that the period of forty-three days 'may prima facie appear not to be excessively long', while in *Rehbock v. Slovenia* twenty-three days were deemed to be so obviously over the limit that the Court did not even provide any reasoning.

Case	Date	Article	Duration	Details	Outcome
Vodenicarov v. Slovakia	21/12/00	5 § 1(e)	33 days		violation
Rutten v. Netherlands	24/07/01	5 § 1(e)	2 months and 17 days	limit set by domestic law: 2 months	violation
Ilowiecki v. Poland	04/10/01	5 § 1(e)	4 months, 3 days; 3 months, 22 days; 2 months, 24 days; almost 7 months; almost 7 months		violation for all five periods
Magelhães Pereira v. Portugal	26/02/02	5 § 1(e)	2 years, 6 months and 18 days	applicant fled and was absent during 7 months	violation
Delbec v. France	18/06/02	5 § 1(c)	1 month	14 days' inactivity	violation
LR v. France	27/06/02	5 § 1(e)	24 days	delay in transmitting request	violation
DM v. France	27/06/02	5 § 1(e)	1 year and 20 days	applicant was released after 3 months	violation
Laidin v. France	05/11/02	5 § 1(e)	over 5 weeks	delay of hospital in sending medical file	violation
Kadem v. Malta	09/01/03	5 § 1(c)	17 days		violation
Nikolov v. Bulgaria	30/01/03	5 § 1(c)	42 days		violation
Hutchison Reid v. UK	20/02/03	5 § 1(e)	3 years, 9 months, 25 days	appeals up to the House of Lords	violation
Pantea v. Romania	03/06/03	5 § 1(c)	3 months, 28 days	delay because hearing was postponed	violation
Herz v. Germany	12/06/03	5 § 1(e)	1 month, 2 days	delay of the applicant in filing observations	no violation

applicant was released as the final date rather than the (later) date of the
decision.[214] This is correct because the best possible result of habeas corpus
proceedings is the release of the applicant. However, this argument does not
work when the detainee escapes because he or she will then be on the run, and
will be likely to be rearrested at any time. In this type of case the time keeps
running,[215] unless his or her absence makes it impossible to make a decision.[216]
The Court has ruled on a number of occasions that where there are proceedings
at different levels of jurisdiction, account must be taken of the 'overall length' of
the proceedings.[217] As noted above, while a state is not compelled to set up a
second level of jurisdiction,[218] if such a system exists, then it must accord
detainees the same guarantees on appeal as at first instance.[219]

At any rate, the '*bref délai*', the acceptable duration of the proceedings cannot
be determined in the abstract but depends on the specific circumstances of
each case.[220]

(b) An Illustration taken from the Case-law

The table on pages 492–3 gives a very approximate illustration of what periods
of time were regarded as sufficiently short or otherwise. Although special features are referred to, a warning is necessary: this table ought not to be consulted
as a reliable 'tariff'.

(c) Plurality of Remedies

A number of legal systems provide for more than one opportunity when the
lawfulness of deprivation of liberty can be determined by a court. In such cases,
'[t]he Court fully accepts the need to take a comprehensive view of the whole
system, as apparent shortcomings in one procedure may be remedied by safeguards available in other procedures'.[221] I have already shown that 'automatic
periodic review' can replace a remedy taken on the initiative of the detainee.
On the other hand, however, proceedings by which the investigating judge
requests a prolongation of detention on remand do not fall to be considered
under Article 5 § 4.[222] Article 5 § 4 becomes relevant whenever a detainee makes a
'request for release'.[223] The Commission was of the opinion that the right under
paragraph 4 'must be seen independent of the possibility of applying to a court
for release on bail'.[224] I doubt whether this opinion is correct—the spirit of

---

[214] *Bezicheri* v. *Italy*, § 22; *Zamir* v. *United Kingdom* Application 9174/80, § 110. See, however, *Bouamar* v. *Belgium*, § 63.   [215] *Van der Leer* v. *Netherlands*, § 35.
[216] *Luberti* v. *Italy*, §§ 35, 36.
[217] Ibid., § 33; *Bouamar* v. *Belgium*, § 61; *Letellier* v. *France*, § 56; *Navarra* v. *France*, § 28.
[218] *De Wilde, Ooms and Versyp* v. *Belgium*, § 76; *Ječius* v. *Lithuania*, § 101; *Grauzinis* v. *Lithuania*, § 32.
[219] See also *Toth* v. *Austria*, § 84; *Navarra* v. *France*, § 28; *Rutten* v. *Netherlands*, § 53; *Ilijkov* v. *Bulgaria*, § 103; and *Hutchison Reid* v. *United Kingdom*, § 77.   [220] *Pantea* v. *Romania*, § 253.
[221] *X* v. *United Kingdom*, § 60; see also *Winterwerp* v. *Netherlands*, § 62; *Weeks* v. *United Kingdom*, § 69.   [222] *Toth* v. *Austria*, § 87.
[223] See e.g. *Neumeister* v. *Austria*, § 22; *van der Leer* v. *Netherlands*, §§ 32 et seq.
[224] *Zamir* v. *United Kingdom* Application 9174/80, § 109.

Article 5 § 3, if not even the wording, suggests that it would be unlawful to continue to detain a person who could be released on bail.[225]

Finally, a difficult problem arises with regard to appeals against decisions on the lawfulness of detention. The Court has transferred its jurisprudence on Article 6 to these proceedings: 'Article 5 § 4 does not compel the Contracting States to set up a second level of jurisdiction for the examination of applications for release from detention. Nevertheless, a State which institutes such a system must in principle accord to the detainees the same guarantee as at first instance'.[226] Even before this judgment, paragraph 4 had been applied several times to appeal proceedings.[227] In *Luberti* the appeal took an excessive amount of time, but the Court was satisfied with the possibility for the applicant to file new applications while the appeal was pending, a possibility which she did in fact avail herself of.[228] Even if it is possible to file new requests pending appeals on an earlier application, the requirement of 'speediness' must apply to the appeal proceedings.

III. THE RIGHT TO COMPENSATION

A. Introduction

1. The Texts

Anyone who has been the victim of unlawful arrest or detention shall have an enforceable right to compensation.

ICCPR, Art. 9 § 5

Everyone who has been the victim of arrest or detention in contravention of the provisions of this article shall have an enforceable right to compensation.

ECHR, Art. 5 § 5

No corresponding right to compensation.

AHRC

The most surprising feature revealed by a comparison of the three instruments is the absence of any guarantee of this kind in the ACHR. This indicates that there

---

[225] While para. 3 is only directly applicable to detention pursuant to para. 1(c), the element of 'necessity' inherent in all exceptions under para. 1 would require the precedence of less stringent substitutes to deprivation of liberty whenever possible.

[226] *Toth* v. *Austria*, § 84, with reference to *Delcourt* v. *Belgium*, § 25 and *Ekbatani* v. *Sweden*, § 24; for exceptions to the rule, see e.g. *Fejde* v. *Sweden* and *Jan-Åke Andersson* v. *Sweden*. The Commission denied a right to appeal in *Dhoest* v. *Belgium* Application 10448/83.

[227] *Luberti* v. *Italy*, § 34; *Bouamar* v. *Belgium*, § 62; see also the Commission's report in *Woukam Moudefo* v. *France*, §§ 42 et seq.

[228] *Luberti* v. *Italy*, § 34; see too *Navarra* v. *France*, §§ 28, 29; *Letellier* v. *France*, § 56. See also the criticism of Esser (2002) 369.

may have been doubts about its justification. The ECHR differs from the ICCPR in that it expressly refers to compliance with Article 5 whereas the latter simply requires 'lawfulness'. This difference, in my opinion, is of no significance in practice.

2. The Origins of the Guarantee

The right to compensation formed part of the 1949 draft of the Covenant.[229] At first, the experts responsible for drafting the ECHR did not want to adopt this right at all.[230] However, the Senior Officials joined it to their draft.[231] The words which now serve to distinguish the guarantee from that of the ICCPR were later added in order to make the text clearer.[232]

3. The Characteristics of the Right

Compensation for damages caused by unjustified interferences with human rights is generally a matter left entirely to domestic legislation. If the Court has found a violation and the domestic law of the state concerned allows only partial reparation or none at all, the Court can afford just satisfaction to the injured party according to Article 41. The *travaux préparatoires* do not provide any answers as to why express inclusion of such a guarantee in cases involving unlawful detention was considered necessary; it is noticeable, for example, that there is no corresponding right to compensation for victims of torture!

The effectiveness of the guarantee is also open to doubt—although in order to draw any compelling conclusions about this, it would be necessary to research the application of the guarantee on the domestic level. As far as the ECtHR is concerned, it may safely be said that paragraph 5 has remained of little interest, even though the Court has, in several judgments, come to the conclusion that it had been violated.[233] In fact, quite a number of these judgments appear downright illogical in that despite the finding that Article 5 § 5 has been violated, compensation under Article 41 (formerly Art. 50) is refused.[234] In other words, the Court tells the applicant: 'Your rights under Article 5 §§ 1–4 have been violated; you therefore have, under paragraph 5, an enforceable right to compensation; here again, domestic legislation falls short of the requirements of the Convention and we therefore find another violation. However, we do not hold

---

[229] Doc. E/1371 19.
[230] First and second meeting of the Committee of Experts, *Collected Edition of the 'Travaux Préparatoires' of the European Convention on Human Rights*, vol. III, 353 and 426 et seq., 449, 491.
[231] Ibid., vol. III, 622.   [232] Ibid., vol. III, 651.
[233] *Ciulla v. Italy*, § 44; *Brogan and others v. United Kingdom*, § 67; *Fox, Campell and Hartley v. United Kingdom*, § 46; *Thynne, Wilson and Gunnell v. United Kingdom*, § 82. A more positive evaluation is given for Italy by Chiavario (1990) at 450.
[234] *Brogan and others v. United Kingdom; Ciulla v. Italy; Fox, Campbell and Hartley v. United Kingdom; Sakık and others v. Turkey; Taş v. Turkey; Rehbock v. Slovenia; SBC v. United Kingdom.*

that the respondent government is to pay any compensation to you as the present judgment "constitutes in itself sufficient just satisfaction"'.

B. The Prerequisites of Compensation

1. Detention which is 'Unlawful'/'in Contravention' of Paragraphs 1–4 of Article 5

(a) In General

The right to compensation under paragraph 5 presupposes, primarily, that a person 'has been the victim of arrest or detention in contravention of the provisions of this Article', that is paragraphs 1–4. As these rules frequently refer to 'lawfulness', a violation of national law also amounts to a violation of Article 5 and, therefore, leads to the right to compensation.[235] The same applies for the ICCPR.

There are two possible kinds of violation. The first concerns a situation where a person was detained even though he or she ought to have been at liberty. This could occur, for example, where the detention was not in conformity with Article 5 § 1, but also where detention on remand exceeded the limits set by paragraph 3. The second scenario concerns mistakes of a formal nature, such as where the suspect was brought before a person who did not qualify as a 'judge or other officer . . .' for the purposes of Article 5 § 3, or where there was a failure properly and 'promptly' to inform the suspect of the reasons for arrest.

Here, the right to compensation differs from the right to a remedy. The latter only requires an *allegation* that the detention was unlawful (ECHR, Art. 6; ICCPR, Art. 14), while paragraph 5 requires that it has been clearly established that this was the case. It follows therefore, that there is no right to compensation when there was no violation of the Convention.[236]

The right to compensation arises in both cases.[237] It must, however, be stressed that only *unlawful*, not merely *unjustified*, detention is covered by paragraph 5. A person who was kept lawfully in detention on remand but was later acquitted is not entitled to compensation under the Convention.[238] On the other hand, of course, even a person who is finally convicted and sentenced to a heavy penalty is entitled to compensation if (part of) the detention on remand was unlawful.

A special situation arose in the case of *Eggs*. The Commission, in its report under Article 31, came to the conclusion that Article 5 had been violated.[239]

---

[235] Frowein and Peukert (1996) Art. 5, N 131; Velu and Ergec (1990) N 351; Trechsel (1974) 266.

[236] *Keus* v. *Netherlands*, § 29; *Murray* v. *United Kingdom*, § 82; *Benham* v. *United Kingdom*, § 50; *Perks and others* v. *United Kingdom*, § 74; *NC* v. *Italy*, § 61; *Bouchet* v. *France*, §§ 50, 51.

[237] Trechsel (1974) 266; Velu and Ergec (1990) N 352. The Court decided to the contrary in *De Wilde, Ooms and Versyp* v. *Belgium*, § 24, but later followed, without any discussion, the opinion expressed here; *Brogan and others* v. *United Kingdom*, § 67; *Fox, Campbell and Hartley* v. *United Kingdom*, § 46; *Thynne, Wilson and Gunnell* v. *United Kingdom*, § 82.

[238] Trechsel (1974) 267, with further references in n. 1032.

[239] *Eggs* v. *Switzerland* Application 10313/85.

In the Committee of Ministers, however, the necessary majority of two-thirds was not reached—the failure to find that there had been a violation, meant therefore that the prerequisite of paragraph 5 was not fulfilled.[240] The Commission, nevertheless, declared the application admissible[241] and a friendly settlement was reached.[242]

(b) Problems Occurring where the Convention is Not Yet in Force

Problems can arise when a state becomes bound by the Convention after the unlawful detention has occurred but before compensation is sought. Does the ratification impose a duty to compensate violations which occurred previously?

The Commission has given a rather strict answer: violations of the guarantees of Article 5 do not give rise to the right under paragraph 5 if they occurred prior to the entry into force of the Convention in the relevant state.[243] There is no such limitation, however, if the Convention was in force, but the right to individual application under Article 25 was recognized only after the deprivation of liberty.[244] As far as the ECHR is concerned, this is quite logical. There *cannot* be a 'contravention of the provisions of this article' as long as the latter does not apply.

(c) Procedural Problems

The right to compensation can be characterized as a kind of 'secondary right', dependent on and at the same time responsible for the extension of the primary right concerning personal liberty. The question then arises as to how the primary violation must be established in order for the secondary one to become operative. James Fawcett, a former President of the Commission, had held the view that first a violation must be established by the Strasbourg organs.[245] Thereupon the applicant would have to seek compensation on the domestic level and 'Strasbourg' would only deal with Article 5 § 5 if that had been unsuccessful.[246] Needless to say, this would not have rendered the guarantee very effective, bearing in mind that proceedings under the ECHR could easily take five years.

Later, the Commission dispensed with the requirement of a prior finding by Convention organs—applications could also be filed after national authorities

[240] Resolution DH(79)7, Collection of Resolutions 1958–83, p. 74. See also Frowein and Peukert (1996) Art. 32 N 4. It is important to note that in the parallel case of *Santschi and others* v. *Switzerland*, the Committee of Ministers *did* in fact, following the Commission, find a violation. Resolution DH(83)5, Applications 7468/76, 7938/77, 8018/77, 8106/77, 8325/78, and 8778/79.
[241] *Eggs* v. *Switzerland* Application 10313/85.   [242] Ibid. (1985) 41 DR 160.
[243] *X* v. *Germany* Application 844/60; *X* v. *Germany* Application 1151/61.
[244] However, the six-month rule of Art. 35 § 1 must be respected. The period starts with the final decision on domestic remedies or, if no remedy (that is, no possibility to claim compensation) exists, with the decision on the alleged violation, in substance, of Art. 5 §§ 1–4.
[245] Fawcett (1969) 119. This had also been the view of the Commission; see *X* v. *Germany* Application 4149/69; *X* v. *Austria* Application 5560/72.
[246] Report in *Wemhoff* v. *Germany*, Series B, vol. 5, § 76, p. 90.

had found, in substance, a violation of Article 5[247] but compensation had been denied on the highest level of domestic remedies.[248] Finally, it accepted that complaints under paragraph 5 could be examined jointly with complaints under paragraphs 1–4 of Article 5,[249] an approach which has been followed by the Court. More importantly, whenever an applicant alleges that there has been a violation of one of the guarantees of Article 5 and invokes paragraph 5, the Court will examine whether or not domestic remedies to obtain compensation have been exhausted.[250]

The main question in these proceedings is whether there was any possibility in domestic law of obtaining compensation. The respondent government will often point to all kinds of remedies and the Court will try to determine whether they are effective.

In the case of *Sakık*, the Turkish Government had alleged that Article 19 of the Constitution granted such a right.[251] However, the Court noted that the Government did not refer to a single case where such compensation had been paid. On the other hand, in *Steel*, it was possible for the applicant to file a civil action for damages against the police, therefore there could be no violation of paragraph 5.[252] Again, in *Tsirlis and Kouloumpas*, the Military Court of Appeals had already stated that the applicants were not entitled under Greek law to any compensation on the ground that their detention had been due to their own 'gross negligence'.[253]

In other cases the Court has accepted the government's argument, sometimes in terms which serve, in my opinion to invert the presumption: 'the evidence provided to the Court does not lead to the conclusion that an action based on Article 1401 of the Netherlands Civil Code would have failed to satisfy the requirements of Article 5 § 5 of the Convention'.[254] In *Steel* it concluded that 'civil actions for damages against the police' could have led to a successful compensation claim.[255]

What is decisive is not the abstract possibility of success but the specific situation of the applicant. If compensation is only possible in the event of an acquittal, and he or she *was* indeed acquitted, the Court will leave it at that; the setting aside of a decision will not necessarily affect the lawfulness of the detention.[256]

2. Damage

In an early admissibility decision, the Commission held that 'the right to compensation contained in Article 5 § 5 does not depend on the existence of any

---

[247] *L* v. *Sweden* Application 10801/85; *Eggs* v. *Switzerland* Application 10313/83; *Eggs* v. *Switzerland* Application 10313/83 (Report); and *Huber* v. *Austria* Application 6821/74.
[248] *Huber* v. *Austria* Application 6821/74; *X, Y and Z* v. *Austria* Application 7950/77.
[249] *X* v. *Germany* Application 6033/75.
[250] See e.g. *Brogan and others* v. *United Kingdom*, § 67.
[251] *Sakık and others* v. *Turkey*, § 59.   [252] *Steel and others* v. *United Kingdom*, § 83.
[253] *Tsirlis and Kouloumpas* v. *Greece*, § 66.   [254] *Wassink* v. *Netherlands*, § 38.
[255] *Steel and others* v. *United Kingdom*, § 83.   [256] *NC* v. *Italy*, §§ 53–6.

damage'.[257] I find this statement misleading, as the Commission must have been referring to material damage only. In fact, paragraph 5 must be read as presuming *de iure* that unlawful detention always generates damage, even if it is not of a pecuniary nature. In fact, the Court will find a violation of Article 5 § 5 before even addressing the issue of damages.

However, the question then comes up under Article 41 according to which the Court 'shall, if necessary, afford just satisfaction to the injured party'. Here, a practice has developed which I consider regrettable. In many cases the Court has concluded that the judgment itself, simply as a result of the finding that there has been a violation of the Convention, constitutes sufficient satisfaction. It has never even sanctioned compensation of a symbolic nature, such as one French franc.

In *Hood* it stated:

The Court recalls that just satisfaction can be awarded only in respect of damage resulting from a deprivation of liberty that the applicant would not have suffered if he had had the benefit of the guarantees of Article 5 § 3. Consequently, in its Huber judgment, for example, the Court found that the evidence did not give any reason to suppose that the pre-trial detention would not have occurred had the making of the detention order been a matter within the competence of a judicial officer who did offer the guarantees of Article 5 § 3. Accordingly, in that case the Court dismissed the claim as regards pecuniary damage and, in the circumstances, it was considered that the judgment would provide sufficient just satisfaction for any non-pecuniary damage suffered (see the Huber judgment cited above, pp. 18–19, §§ 45–46).[258]

This leads to the slightly paradoxical result that the Court finds a violation of the Convention because the applicant could not obtain compensation for unlawful detention, and at the same time finds that there is nothing to compensate. Even taking into account the differences between 'just satisfaction' as guaranteed by Article 41 and 'compensation' for unlawful detention, the situation remains rather unsatisfactory, even in spite of the Court's acceptance that an applicant may have suffered non-pecuniary damage, particularly in cases where he or she was detained for a considerable length of time, without any possibility of habeas corpus proceedings.

C. The Amount of Compensation

One would, in examining the rule under consideration, expect to find some indication as to the amount of compensation due, as well as some explanation of the method used to fix the sum. However, the Court has never given even the slightest hint. There is not a single case where the amount of compensation was at issue. Whenever the Court addresses the question of compensation it relates

---

[257] Resolution DH(83)5, 31 DR 41 (1983); the Commission referred to *Artico* v. *Italy*, § 35.
[258] *Hood* v. *United Kingdom*, § 84.

to Article 41. The question could arise if an applicant complained that he or she had been awarded insufficient compensation.

Such compensation would certainly have to cover any pecuniary damage. In cases of detention contrary to Article 5 § 1 or where the detention on remand has exceeded the 'reasonable time' under Article 5 § 3, loss of income (assuming that the person concerned did have an income at the time of arrest) will be the most obvious damage. There might also be other loss. It will be important to present convincing evidence in this respect.

On the other hand, no pecuniary damages will be due if the applicant was the victim of some formal mistake, such as where he or she was not brought promptly before a judge, where the person responsible for determining the lawfulness of the detention was not a 'judge', or where a petition for habeas corpus was not decided speedily.[259] Many applicants, in such cases, present claims for damages based on the assumption that the detention would not have been ordered at all if the procedural error had not occurred. This, however, is not correct. The Court rightly reiterates again and again that it is not permitted to speculate on the outcome of proceedings had there been no procedural mistake made.[260] A certain amount of speculation is nevertheless possible: in *Weeks* there had been a violation of Article 5 § 4, the right to habeas corpus proceedings. According to the Court it could not be entirely excluded that the availability of the remedy would have led to his earlier release.[261]

There can be no doubt that other damages for non-pecuniary loss may also be due and this is where the real difficulty lies. Again, when it is proven that a period of detention was unlawful, some sum of money will be awarded under Article 41 and must be awarded under Article 5 § 5. The amount will depend on the circumstances, the conditions of detention, the impact it had on the applicant's health, his or her professional, social, and family life, and its duration. In my personal opinion the minimum ought to be around fifty euros per day, the maximum in the region of 1,000 euros. This estimate is both broad and very rough, but it is essential that scope is left to enable the cost of living in the relevant state to be factored into the equation. The most important consideration is that the compensation is substantial enough to highlight the value of personal liberty.

---

[259] This depends on the outcome. If the application is successful, it may be proper to assume that the applicant would have been released earlier if there had been no delay.

[260] *Weeks* v. *United Kingdom*, Art. 50 § 13 (regarding material damage).   [261] Ibid.

Chapter 19

The Special Rights of Persons Detained on Remand

I. INTRODUCTION

A. The Texts

> 3. Anyone arrested or detained on a criminal charge shall be brought promptly before a judge or other officer authorized by law to exercise judicial power and shall be entitled to trial within a reasonable time or to release. It shall not be the general rule that persons awaiting trial shall be detained in custody, but release may be subject to guarantees to appear for trial, at any other stage of the judicial proceedings, and, should occasion arise, for execution of the judgement.
>
> ICCPR, Art. 9 § 3

> 3. Everyone arrested or detained in accordance with the provisions of paragraph 1.c of this article shall be brought promptly before a judge or other officer authorised by law to exercise judicial power and shall be entitled to trial within a reasonable time or to release pending trial. Release may be conditioned by guarantees to appear for trial.
>
> ECHR, Art. 5 § 3

> 5. Any person detained shall be brought promptly before a judge or other officer authorized by law to exercise judicial power and shall be entitled to trial within a reasonable time or to be released without prejudice to the continuation of the proceedings. His release may be subject to guarantees to assure his appearance for trial.
>
> ACHR, Art. 7 § 5

Essentially these texts say the same and even the variations in the wording do not indicate any differences in the meaning. As if it were done on purpose, the paragraphs begin with 'anyone', 'everyone', and 'any person'. However, there follows a difference between the ICCPR and the ECHR on one side, the ACHR on the other. With different words the former refer to detention on remand. The ECHR does it formally by referring to Article 5 § 1(c), the ICCPR speaks of 'on a criminal charge',[1] although the arrestee is not necessarily charged yet at the

---

[1] Nowak (1993) Art. 9 N 37.

time of arrest. The ACHR omits any specification. However, the continuation clearly indicates that this guarantee too is aimed at the arrest and detention of suspects. No other persons have any interest in a trial within a reasonable time or release pending trial.

What is striking is that the first guarantee is framed in identical terms in all three texts.

Finally, the Covenant has a welcome sentence saying that detention ought not to be the rule. It is a sentence of dubious normative value, a recommendation rather than the guarantee of a right. It expresses a thought which is certainly also part of the spirit of the guarantee of personal liberty in the two other instruments.

The Covenant is particularly precise in that it introduces an additional justification for detention on remand: making sure that the accused, in case of conviction and sentence, would be available for the execution of the latter. This makes it clear that the deprivation of liberty may continue after the trial if the convict does not immediately start to serve his sentence of imprisonment. However, the specification is unnecessary. As soon as a person is deprived of his or her liberty after having been sentenced by a court, his detention is, at least in relation to the Convention, justified under Article 5 § 1(a) irrespective of the regime or the place where that person is held.

B. The Justification of Special Safeguards for those Detained on Remand

Article 5 § 1 of the Convention sets out, in six sub-paragraphs, an exhaustive list of legitimate grounds of detention. One of these grounds, set out in sub-paragraph (c), is the subject of two specific guarantees in Article 5 § 3: the right to be brought before a judge and the right to be released within reasonable time; in colloquial language one would say 'as soon as possible'. These specific safeguards also figure in the other texts.

Why are such extra measures required?[2] The answer lies in the fact that detention on remand is meant to be a provisional coercive measure. It is justified purely on the basis of the suspicion of the detainee's involvement in a crime and requires to be extremely carefully monitored precisely because it facilitates an investigation which seeks to prove that this suspicion is justified. In other words, those who order the arrest and detention of a suspect will find their work considerably simplified if the suspect makes a confession. Indeed these two aspects are closely linked; it is assumed that in the isolation of a prison cell, a person will be more inclined to admit involvement than if he or she is free and has the support of family and friends. Of course, this is not the official explanation given in support of detention on remand; yet, one does not have to be a professional psychologist to appreciate that the investigator responsible for the suspect's arrest hopes that this will result in a confession.

[2] See also Pradel and Corstens (2000) N 317.

At any rate, the person who orders or proposes the detention on remand has an interest in ultimately establishing the suspect's guilt, because this will prove that he or she was right. Release without a tangible result will leave the impression that the suspect was unnecessarily locked up.

Even in the absence of a confession, the investigator's task will usually be facilitated if the suspect is safely 'stowed away' and can be 'brought up' any time for questioning. These interests may well influence the perception of reality by the investigator. It is therefore important that a neutral judicial officer is in control of the situation. There is also a need to limit the duration of the detention. The task of bringing to light all the relevant facts of a case may sometimes conflict with the duty to limit interference with the suspect's fundamental rights.

The requirement that detention on remand be used sparingly has a long tradition. Cesare Beccaria wrote in 1764 in his famous treatise, *Dei delitti e delle pene*, that it was only justified in case of danger of absconding and in order to protect the evidence.[3]

These reasons explain why special guarantees were introduced for detention on remand, and in the following sections they shall be examined in some detail.

C. Other Safeguards

Although the Convention only expressly provides for the special guarantees set out in the third paragraph, the Court has introduced another requirement which may be regarded as self-evident, although it is of a somewhat formal nature. The authorities are obliged to *register* every act related to the deprivation of liberty. This problem has turned up in the context of a number of cases brought against Turkey, where prisoners had disappeared and no proper records were found.

The Court expressed this requirement in unequivocal terms: 'Article 5 provides a corpus of substantive rights intended to ensure that the act of deprivation of liberty be amenable to independent judicial scrutiny and secures the accountability of the authorities for that measure. The unacknowledged detention of an individual is a complete negation of these guarantees and discloses a most grave violation of Article 5'.[4] This leads to the conclusion that '[t]he recording of accurate and reliable holding data provides an indispensable safeguard against arbitrary detention, the absence of which enables those responsible for the act of deprivation of liberty to escape accountability for the fate of the detainee'.[5]

In addition, the Court transferred to Article 5 a principle which it had developed in connection with Articles 2 and 3: the *duty to secure* these rights (Art. 1[6]) implies a procedural component. Whenever there is an arguable allegation that death could have been caused unlawfully or that someone has been ill-treated, the authorities are under an obligation to carry out a prompt and

---

[3] Pisani (2001) N 10.6.

[4] *Taş* v. *Turkey*, § 84; see also *Kurt* v. *Turkey*, §§ 122–5; *Çakıcı* v. *Turkey*, § 104.

[5] *Taş* v. *Turkey*, § 85.   [6] cf. in particular *Ireland* v. *United Kingdom*, § 239.

effective investigation.[7] 'Bearing in mind the responsibility of the authorities to account for individuals under their control, Article 5 requires them to take effective measures to safeguard against the risk of disappearance and to conduct a prompt and effective investigation into an arguable claim that a person has been taken into custody and has not been seen since'.[8] In the *Taş* case, the absence of any records and the fact that the detention had been extended twice by a period of fifteen days by the prosecutor led to the finding of a 'particularly grave violation of the right to liberty and security'.[9]

II. THE RIGHT TO BE BROUGHT BEFORE A JUDGE

A. The Purpose and Character of the Right

By virtue of paragraph 3, everyone arrested as a suspect in criminal proceedings must 'be brought promptly before a judge or other officer authorised by law to exercise judicial power'.[10] This is a particularly important guarantee in those states where there exists a specific danger of police brutality or torture. It is also a matter of interest to the Committee for the Prevention of Torture.[11] Although techniques have been developed which make it possible to inflict severe pain or suffering without leaving scars or other traces, there may still be a relatively good chance of finding evidence of ill-treatment on the body within one or two days. Within that time, the arrested person must, therefore, be withdrawn from the absolute control of the police and brought under the protection of the judiciary.[12] This aspect has been mentioned several times by the Court—it is one of the reasons why the control, as we shall see, must happen automatically—in fact, after being tortured a person might well be unable physically and/or mentally to file any kind of application.[13]

Protection against ill-treatment is, however, not the official or even the main purpose of the guarantee. The Court sees this as relevant only within the framework of Article 5 as a whole which 'enshrines a fundamental human right, namely the protection of the individual against arbitrary interferences by the State with his right to liberty'.[14] Deprivation of liberty, in other words, is such a

---

[7] *McCann and others* v. *United Kingdom*, §§ 161 et seq.; *Kurt* v. *Turkey*, § 125; *Taş* v. *Turkey*, § 85.

[8] *Taş* v. *Turkey*, § 84; *Kurt* v. *Turkey*, §§ 122–5; *Çakıcı* v. *Turkey*, § 104.

[9] *Taş* v. *Turkey*, § 87; see also *Kurt* v. *Turkey*, §§ 122–5; *Çakıcı* v. *Turkey*, § 104.

[10] Preventative detention to which Art. 5 § 1 (c) does not apply, gives no right under para. 3; *Ječius* v. *Lithuania*, § 75.   [11] Cf. Reed and Murdoch (1991) 228 and n. 7.

[12] See also Cook (1992) at 29; Pradel and Corstens (2000) N 314.

[13] *Van der Sluijs, Zuiderveld and Klappe Netherlands*, § 46; *De Jong, Baljet and Van den Brink* v. *Netherlands; Duinhof and Duijf* v. *Netherlands*, § 36; *Aquilina* v. *Malta*, § 49; *TW* v. *Malta*, § 43; *Aksoy* v. *Turkey*, § 76; *Dikme* v. *Turkey*, § 64; *Zeynep Avcı* v. *Turkey*, § 46.

[14] This formula is to be found in most of the many judgments dealing with the issue. To give but a few examples, see *Brogan and others* v. *UK*, § 58; *Kurt* v. *Turkey*, § 123; *Aquilina* v. *Malta* § 49; *Niedbała* v. *Poland*, § 50; *Nuray Sen* v. *Turkey*, § 22.

grave interference with a person's fundamental rights that administrative authorities responsible to the executive are only competent to make a provisional decision to detain a person; as soon as possible thereafter, the decision must be scrutinized and confirmed by a member of the judiciary, who has been able to meet the detainee in person. This obligation remains even if there exists an arrest warrant issued by a judicial authority, and even if counsel was present when that order was made.[15]

This requirement may create unforeseen problems for the domestic authorities. Particular rules of domestic procedure law may prove problematic, such as, for instance, a rule that once a person has been brought before a judge, the police lose their power to investigate. In this case, the application of the guarantee leads to a side effect which was neither envisaged nor intended by the Convention. That such conflicts can only be solved by amending the national law, was clearly stressed in a number of cases concerning the investigation of alleged terrorists in Turkey. Thus, in *Demir*, the Court said: 'As to the Government's assertions about the "thorough" and "careful" nature of the police investigation that had to be conducted, they do not provide an answer to the central question at issue, namely for what precise reasons relating to the actual facts of the present case would judicial scrutiny of the applicants' detention have prejudiced the progress of the investigation. In respect of such lengthy periods of detention in police custody it is not sufficient to refer in a general way to the difficulties caused by terrorism and the number of people involved in the inquiries'.[16] If the domestic law presents an obstacle to the implementation of the Convention it will have to be amended—there can be no doubt about that.

The judicial authority responsible for determining the lawfulness of the detention is defined in a rather enigmatic way—the issue will be dealt with below, along with that of promptness (section III below) and the requirements of the proceedings.

It is important to note that the third paragraph is relatively formalistic: first, the person concerned must be brought physically—if necessary *manu militari*—before the judge;[17] of course the judge could also go to the place where the person is detained, for instance, if the detainee is in hospital.[18] Second, the rights cannot be waived—this highlights a general distrust of the police authorities and concerns as to whether such a waiver would truly be voluntary.[19]

During this first hearing, the representative of the judiciary will have to make a *prima facie* evaluation of whether the conditions for detention under paragraph 1(c) (and potentially stricter conditions of domestic law) are fulfilled.

---

[15] *McGoff* v. *Sweden*, §§ 12, 13, 27. The same applies under the ICCPR; see Nowak (1993) Art. 9 N 38.   [16] *Demir* v. *Turkey*, § 52.

[17] *Schiesser* v. *Switzerland*, § 31; *McGoff* v. *Sweden*, § 27. In *D* v. *Netherlands* Application 11013/84 the Commission found it sufficient (without discussing the issue) that the Military Court could hear the 'advisor' of the arrestee—in my view this was an erroneous statement.

[18] This was the case in *Egmez* v. *Cyprus*: the Court followed the view of the Commission that the requirement had been complied with, § 90.   [19] See also Pradel and Corstens (2000) N 314.

The examination will necessarily be of a summary nature, as the investigation may still be at an early stage and it is quite possible that only rudimentary elements of evidence and information will be available. The Court has spoken of 'the obligation of reviewing the circumstances militating for or against detention, of deciding, by reference to legal criteria, whether there are reasons to justify detention . . . '.[20] However, this must not be misunderstood as meaning that only the lawfulness of the detention, in the strict meaning of the term, must be assessed. The 'judicial officer' must also examine whether the detention is justified.[21]

Like the 'court' referred to in Article 5 § 4,[22] the judicial authority must have the power to release the person brought before it if it reaches the conclusion that further deprivation would not be lawful or even expedient (*in dubio pro libertate*).[23] Furthermore, this power must extend to a decision *proprio motu* and 'compliance with Article 5 § 3 cannot be ensured by making an Article 5 § 4 remedy available'.[24]

B. The Judge or 'Other Officer Authorised by Law to Exercise Judicial Power'

1. The Independence and Impartiality of the Authority

While the term 'judge' is rather self-explanatory and does not require further comment in this context, there has been considerable controversy about the meaning of the term 'other officer authorised by law to exercise judicial power'.[25]

A literal approach to the interpretation would suggest that the two terms 'judge' and 'other officer . . . 'mean different things.[26] However, the historical perspective does not support that hypothesis. It appears that the drafters of the Convention did not trust those who would be called upon to apply it. They must have feared that the term 'judge' would be given too narrow and formalistic a meaning. By developing an 'autonomous meaning', the Court has facilitated an interpretation which is centred on substance rather than on terminology.[27] Having this in mind, one can, in my view, safely return to what the Court had said in its very first judgment, namely, that a judge is the only person who can be deemed to be a proper authority,[28] enjoying the unfettered confidence of the

---

[20] *Schiesser* v. *Switzerland*, § 31; *Aquilina* v. *Malta*, § 49; *TW* v. *Malta*, § 43.

[21] *Aquilina* v. *Malta*, § 53, where the Court clearly stated that avoidable detention is not necessarily unlawful under Maltese law; *TW* v. *Malta*, § 47.　　　　　　　[22] See p. 479 above.

[23] *Ireland* v. *United Kingdom*, § 199; *Schiesser* v. *Switzerland*, § 31; *Van der Sluijs, Zuiderveld and Klappe* v. *Netherlands*, §§ 42, 43, and 48.

[24] *Aquilina* v. *Malta*, § 49; *TW* v. *Malta*, § 47; this implicitly contradicts the separate opinion of Frowein et al. to the Commission's Report in *Schiesser* v. *Switzerland*.

[25] See the discussion in Trechsel (1974) 251 et seq. with reference to other authors.

[26] Villiger (1999) N 350; Esser (2002) 264; on the other hand, that same author later affirms that Art. 5 § 3 calls for scrutiny by a judge ('*richterliche Kontrolle*') at 272.

[27] See e.g. Kastanas (1996) 333 et seq.; Yourow (1996) 33 et seq.

[28] *Lawless* v. *Ireland*, The Law, § 9; cf. Esser (2002) 264 et seq., who also discusses the meaning of 'authorized by law'. In my view this is unnecessary as part of the definition of 'judge' requires that the authority is 'established by law' and exercises functions as provided for by law.

Convention.[29] Strong support for this view can be found by examining the drafting history of the Article. René Cassin who had taken a very active part in the drafting of the ICCPR (which was also the source of Article 5 § 3 of the ECHR) reported that the decision to add the words 'other officer...' was adopted at the request of English lawyers who were afraid that the 'magistrate' would not be accepted as a 'judge'.[30]

However, the Court seemed either to have forgotten or to have ignored this when it addressed the issue in the case of *Schiesser*, concerning the Zurich '*Bezirksanwalt*'.[31] This officer is part of the public prosecutor's office. He or she is in charge of the investigation and may, in certain cases, be called upon to exercise prosecutorial functions. The Court stressed the striking dualism of the terms 'judge' and 'other officer'. In this case it reached the conclusion that there was no violation of paragraph 3 as the officer dealing with Mr Schiesser had not later acted as a prosecutor at the trial.[32]

According to the principles established in *Schiesser*, 'the "officer" is not identical to the "judge" but must nevertheless have some of the latter's attributes, that is to say he must satisfy certain conditions each of which constitutes a guarantee for the arrested person. The first of such conditions is that he must be independent of the executive and the parties. This does not mean that the 'officer' may not be to some extent subordinate to other judges or officers provided that they themselves enjoy 'similar independence'.[33] The Court had also considered that a 'literal analysis' meant that this could include 'officials in public prosecutors' departments'.[34]

However, later on in a series of judgments concerning military proceedings, the Court recognized that members of the prosecutor's office are, or are as a rule liable to become, one of the parties to the proceedings and cannot, therefore, be regarded as being independent of the parties.[35] In one case, for instance, the Court considered that a commanding officer who was liable to play a central role in the subsequent prosecution of the case against the accused and who was also responsible for discipline and order could not be objectively held to be independent or impartial.[36] It is, in my view, quite significant that the Court, in this

---

[29] Haefliger and Schürmann (1999) 110. English authors such as Whitaker (2001), N 10.4.2, 11.2.3; and Starmer (2001) N 7.5, say that the arrestee must be brought before a 'court'. Charrier (2002) Art. 5 N 37; and Renucci (2002) 112, also see this guarantee as an aspect of '*le droit au juge*'. Harris, O'Boyle, and Warbrick (1995) 133, say that the term has the same meaning as 'tribunal' in Article 6, which also seems to be the opinion of Picard and Titiun (1995) 215.

[30] Cassin (1970) 628; see also Esser (2002) 264; Pieth (1980) 209; Trechsel (1974) 251 et seq.; Trechsel (1992) 193.   [31] *Schiesser* v. *Switzerland*, §§ 25 et seq.

[32] For a critical appraisal of the judgment, see Pieth (1980); Cohen-Jonathan (1989) 334 et seq.; Cohen-Jonathan (1979); Cohen-Jonathan (1980) 436; Pouget (1989); Starmer (2001) N 7.7.

[33] *Schiesser* v. *Switzerland*, § 31.

[34] Ibid., § 28. Velu and Ergec (1990) N 341, seem to agree with this proposition.

[35] *De Jong, Baljet and Van den Brink* v. *Netherlands*, § 49; *Van der Sluijs, Zuiderveld and Klappe* v. *Netherlands*, § 44; *Duinhof and Duijf*, § 38; *Pauwels* v. *Belgium*, § 37. This change in the jurisprudence was also observed by Velu and Ergec (1990) N 342, 291.

[36] *Hood* v. *United Kingdom*, §§ 57 et seq.; *Stephan Jordan* v. *United Kingdom* (British law has now been amended by the Armed Forces Act 1996).

context, quoted case-law relating to Article 6.[37] It did not come as a surprise, then, that in the case of *Huber*, the Court finally reversed the *Schiesser* ruling with regard to the Zurich '*Bezirksanwalt*'.[38]

The formula actually used by the Court is this: 'Before an "officer" can be said to exercise "judicial power" within the meaning of this provision, he or she must satisfy certain conditions providing a guarantee to the person detained against any arbitrary or unjustified deprivation of liberty. Thus, the "officer" must be independent of the executive and the parties.[39] In this respect, objective appearances at the time of the decision on detention are material: if it appears at that time that the "officer" may later intervene in subsequent criminal proceedings on behalf of the prosecuting authority, his independence and impartiality may be open to doubt'.[40] This passage is taken from a case where an 'investigating judge' ('*Untersuchungsrichter*') had acted as the officer responsible for controlling the lawfulness of the detention.[41] Although the investigating judge is considered in domestic law as a 'judge',[42] he or she is responsible for drawing up a document at the close of the investigation which contains a summary of the facts and the applicable criminal provisions in view of the decision whether to prosecute or not ('*Schlussverfügung*'). The Court rightly considered this to be akin to preparing an indictment and therefore found that the requirements of Article 5 § 3 were not met. Esser correctly points out that it is often the same public prosecutor (or investigating judge) who orders the arrest and who then acts as a judicial officer in the sense of Article 5 § 3; he or she is therefore not the ideal person critically to evaluate that decision.[43]

The result in the *HB* case is to be applauded, although the reasoning used by the Court is far from convincing. In reaching its decision it relied on the *Schiesser* case, which can safely be referred to as one of the least impressive judgments ever produced by the Court.[44] The main defect lies in the Court's reliance on speculation as to whether the officer 'could subsequently have acted against the applicant in criminal proceedings'.[45] The question is not whether possibly, at some point in the future, the officer might find him- or herself in an adversarial position *vis-à-vis* the detainee, but whether at the moment when the suspect is

[37] Namely *De Cubber and Piersack* v. *Belgium*; cf. *Pauwels* v. *Belgium*, § 38. In *Huber* v. *Switzerland*, § 43, a reference to *Hauschildt* v. *Denmark* was added.
[38] *Huber* v. *Switzerland*, §§ 41–3. In *Brincat* v. *Itlay*, § 20, the Court confirmed this ruling and made it perfectly clear that the decisive question is whether the person concerned may later intervene as representative of the prosecuting authority. See also *HB* v. *Switzerland*; *Pantea* v. *Romania*, § 236. For a commentary on *Huber* v. *Switzerland*, see Trechsel (1992) 193 et seq.
[39] The position is similar to that of a judge; Haefliger and Schürmann (1999) 111.
[40] *HB* v. *Switzerland*, § 55. [41] The facts took place in the Swiss canton of Solothurn.
[42] Haefliger and Schürmann (1999) 111 were also of the opinion that it satisfied the requirements of Art. 5 § 3. [43] Esser (2002) 265.
[44] The judgment was highly misleading: Velu and Ergec (1990) N 341 conclude that the public prosecutor could function as 'officer' within the meaning of Art. 5 § 3; Haefliger and Schürmann: 'an unfortunate decision' (my translation). For criticism, see also Charrier (2002) Art. 5 N 37 with further references to French authors; Trechsel (1981) 133 at 135.
[45] Quoted from *Assenov* v. *Bulgaria*, § 149.

arrested the officer's position is such that the suspect can objectively assume that he or she is biased in favour of the prosecution.[46]

Therefore, the judge or other officer must be an authority which is not charged with the investigation. In my opinion the investigating judge would even lack the necessary objectivity if, once the investigation had been terminated, its only further function was to hand over the file to the public prosecutor who would then draft the indictment; the investigating judge would still have pursued a partial aim in the process and thus could not be considered to be institutionally independent of the prosecution. The requirements and attributes of an investigator are incompatible with the neutrality required of an authority charged with supervising a deprivation of liberty.

Thus, it is not entirely clear whether the French *juge d'instruction* or the German *Ermittlungsrichter* would meet the standards required by this provision.[47]

It is very important, particularly with regard to the former communist countries, to stress that the public prosecutor is not, in the light of the Convention law, an impartial authority. In *Niedbała* the Polish Government had pointed out that 'under applicable laws the prosecutors, in addition to exercising a prosecutorial role, also act as guardian of the public interest'; with the requisite clarity the Court replied that this 'cannot be regarded as conferring on them a judicial status'.[48]

2. The Power to Order Release

The 'officer' must hear the individual brought before him in person and must determine, by reference to legal criteria, whether or not the detention is justified. If it is not justified, he or she must have the power to make a binding order for the detainee's release.[49] In *Assenov*, the decision to detain the applicant on remand was taken by an investigator who did not have that power; any decision taken by this officer could be overturned by the prosecutor. In such circumstances, the investigator was not sufficiently independent properly to be described as an 'officer' within the meaning of paragraph 3.[50]

In *Caballero* v. *UK* the power to release was given a particularly strict interpretation. The applicant had committed a very serious crime. Under domestic legislation detention on remand was mandatory. Therefore, the judge before

---

[46] *Huber* v. *Switzerland*, § 43; *Brincat* v. *Italy*, § 21 (in this case, the Court found it 'immaterial that, in the end, the prosecutor was shown to lack territorial jurisdiction').

[47] Esser (2002) 270 suggests that they do.

[48] *Niedbała* v. *Poland*, § 53; *Eryk Kawka* v. *Poland*, § 16; *Dacewicz* v. *Poland*, § 22; *Salapa* v. *Poland*, § 69; *Klamecki* v. *Poland*, §§ 105, 106; *Pantea* v. *Romania*, §§ 238, 239. Surprisingly, Renucci (2002) N 112, 201, considers that the French *procureur de la République* could possibly qualify as a 'judge or other officer . . .'; Picard and Titiun (1995) 216, correctly stated that this would not be the case.

[49] *Schiesser* v. *Switzerland*, § 31; *Ireland* v. *United Kingdom*, § 199; *Assenov* v. *Bulgaria*, § 146.

[50] *Assenov* v. *Bulgaria*, §§ 146 et seq. See also the similar cases of *Nikolova* v. *Bulgaria*, §§ 49 et seq.; *Shishkov* v. *Bulgaria*, § 53.

whom the applicant was brought had no possibility to release him under the specific circumstances. The Commission held by a majority, that this constituted a violation of the Convention. Surprisingly, the UK Government, in the proceedings before the Court, adopted the Commission's view, and the Court, in turn, accepted this concession.[51]

I am of the opinion that this was all wrong, and that it takes the issue too far. Under Article 5 § 3 the authority before whom the arrestee is brought must assess whether the detention is lawful; whether it is in accordance with domestic law. In *Caballero* it was quite clear that the requirements of domestic law had been complied with. Therefore there was no reason in the first place to release the applicant. On the other hand, before the judgment in *Caballero*, the Court's jurisprudence could not have been interpreted as prohibiting rules providing for automatic denial of bail or mandatory detention on remand. Of course, after a short while the need for concrete reasons arise. But that is not yet the case 'promptly' after the arrest. In my view it was even a mistake to say that the judge has no possibility to release in such a case. He or she still has to examine whether there is a reasonable suspicion that the person concerned has committed the crime.

The review of the detention must be 'sufficiently wide to encompass the various circumstances militating for or against detention'. There must be an automatic review[52] of the merits of the detention and thus a magistrate with the power to order release only following the submission of a bail application, did not qualify to exercise functions under Article 5 § 3.[53]

In *Koster*, the question was raised whether the Military Court in the Netherlands satisfied the requirements of paragraph 3.[54] The Court was barred from addressing the issue because it had not been raised before the Commission. The latter had, however, given a positive answer in an earlier case.[55]

C. 'Promptly'/'*Aussitôt*'

By demanding that the detainee be brought 'promptly'/'*aussitot*' before a judge, paragraph 3 introduces a reference to time.

1. The Period to be Considered

First of all it must be determined when the relevant period starts. The answer seems rather obvious: it begins as soon as the person is arrested and deprived of his or her liberty. In the vast majority of cases, this is relatively clear. Problems

---

[51] *Caballero* v. *United Kingdom*, § 21; this was confirmed in *SBC* v. *United Kingdom*, § 22, where the Court also gave a summary of the Commission's report in *Caballero*.

[52] *De Jong, Baljet and Van den Brink* v. *Netherlands*, § 57; *Niedbała* v. *Poland*, § 50.

[53] *Aquilina* v. *Malta; TW* v. *Malta; Sabeur Ben Ali* v. *Malta.*

[54] *Koster* v. *Netherlands*, § 26.

[55] *D* v. *Netherlands* Application 11013/84. For an assessment of the 'advisory committees' and 'commissioners' in Northern Ireland before the interstate application, see *Ireland* v. *United Kingdom*, § 199.

have arisen in cases where a person was arrested before the Convention was applicable in the relevant state, either because it had not yet been ratified or because a reservation under Article 57 of the Convention applied, according to which the public prosecutor continued to be the competent officer under Article 5 § 3 before whom the detainee had to be brought.

This was the case in *Jėčius* v. *Lithuania*. The applicant had been kept in custody from 14 March 1996 until 14 October 1996. The reservation ceased to have effect on 21 June 1996. The applicant alleged that he ought to have been brought before a judge promptly after that date.

The Court quite correctly rejected this claim: 'The Court considers that the reading of the words "brought promptly" in Article 5 § 3 implies that the right to be brought before an appropriate officer relates to the time when a person is first deprived of his liberty under Article 5 § 1(c). The obligation on Contracting States under Article 5 § 3 is therefore limited to bringing the detainee promptly before an appropriate officer at that initial stage'.[56]

The period ends when the person concerned is physically confronted with the competent authority. Of course, the judge will have to take a decision immediately[57]—any delay would have to be regarded as an implicit approval of the detention.[58]

2. The Time Limit

It is more difficult to determine the meaning of the requirement that the detainee be brought 'promptly' before the authority. Article 5 § 3 does not expressly state a time limit[59] and further confusion is caused by a difference in the English and French texts of the Convention.

The Court has pointed out that '*aussitôt*' literally means immediately, while 'promptly' allows for more flexibility. Initially the approach of the Court was unclear. It seemed reluctant to impose an absolute time limit, stating instead that this had 'to be assessed in each case according to its special features'.[60] However, the flexibility in this respect is limited since 'the significance to be attached to [specific] features can never be taken to the point of impairing the very essence of the right guaranteed by Article 5 § 3, that is to the point of effectively negativing [*sic*] the State's obligation to ensure a prompt release or a prompt appearance before a judicial authority'.[61]

---

[56] *Jėčius* v. *Lithuania*, § 84; confirmed in *Grauslys* v. *Lithuania*, § 49; and *Grauzinis* v. *Lithuania*, § 25.   [57] Esser (2002) 276.

[58] Trechsel (1974) 254.

[59] The same applies with the ICCPR; Nowak (1993) Art. 9 N 38. Renucci (2002) N 113 welcomes this flexibility.

[60] *Koster* v. *Netherlands*, § 24. See also *Brogan and others* v. *United Kingdom*, § 59; *De Jong, Baljet and Van den Brink* v. *Netherlands*, § 52; *Van der Sluijs, Zuiderveld and Klappe* v. *Netherlands*, § 49; *Duinhof and Duijf* v. *Netherlands*, § 41.

[61] *Brogan and others* v. *United Kingdom*, § 59; on this case, see Tanca (1990).

The crucial point in the interpretation of this provision was reached in the case of *Brogan and others* where the Court, although refraining from imposing an absolute limit, held that even in an extremely tense situation of fighting against terrorism, a period of four days and six hours 'falls outside the strict constraints as to time permitted by the first part of Article 5 § 3'.[62] Since the *Brogan* case the Court has consistently interpreted the provision as imposing, as a general rule, a maximum limit of four days. Only in exceptional cases would a longer period be justifiable.[63] Such an exception could arise where it is technically impossible to bring the arrestee before the judge in time.[64]

With regard to cases involving alleged acts of terrorism, detention that lasts for longer than this time period has consistently been held to be contrary to the provision.[65] However this does not by any means imply that detention for less than this time will always comply with the promptness requirement of the Convention or the Covenant. It is evident that, in normal cases, the limit must be set far below four days.[66] Renucci suggests that twenty-four hours, with the possibility of one extension, would be realistic and reasonable.[67]

The basic rule ought to be that the detainee is brought before the judge without any undue delay.[68] It may be accepted that the administrative authority first makes some inquiries in order to provide the judicial authority with a more solid basis for its decision. As a rule, however, the person concerned should be brought before the judge no later than on the day following the arrest. Only in extraordinary cases will a further prolongation be acceptable. It remains to be tested whether the upper limit is to be set at four days or less, but detention in excess of four days constitutes a violation of Article 5 § 3.

---

[62] Ibid., § 62. Whitaker misunderstands *Brincat* when he says that the Court there found four days to be too long; the judgment only deals with the problem of 'judge or other officer'.

[63] e.g. *Taş* v. *Turkey*, § 86.

[64] *Rigopoulos* v. *Spain*, where a delay of sixteen days was explained by the fact that the arrest took place at sea and it took a fortnight to sail to Spanish territory; routine military manoeuvres did not suffice in *Koster* v. *Netherlands*.

[65] *Murray* v. *United Kingdom; Brogan and others* v. *United Kingdom; Aksoy* v. *Turkey*, § 78 (fourteen days or more); *Sakık and others* v. *Turkey*, § 45 (twelve and fourteen days); *Demir* v. *Turkey*, §§ 49–58 (twenty-three and sixteen days); *Dikme* v. *Turkey* (sixteen days); *Altay* v. *Turkey*, §§ 64 et seq. (fifteen days); *Günay and others* v. *Turkey*, §§ 21 et seq. (between five and eleven days); *O'Hara* v. *United Kingdom*, § 46 (six days and thirteen hours; the Government agreed that there was a violation); *Zeynep Avcı* v. *Turkey*, § 52 (twenty-one days); *Igdeli* v. *Turkey* (seven days); *Filiz and Kalkan* v. *Turkey* (eight days); *Gündoğan* v. *Turkey* (nine days); *Murat Satık and others* v. *Turkey* (thirteen days); *Öcalan* v. *Turkey* (seven days); *Nuray Sen* v. *Turkey* (eleven days); *Ayise Tepe* v. *Turkey* (fifteen days); *Pantea* v. *Romania* (over four months).

[66] Frowein and Peukert (1996) Art. 5 N 94; Pouget (1989) 88; van Dijk and van Hoof (1998) 275. This limit was clearly overstepped in *McGoff* v. *Sweden*, and in three *Skoogström* cases, one of which was settled in Court, *Skoogström* v. *Sweden*, the others before the Commission, *Skoogström (Nos. 2 and 3)* v. *Sweden* Applications 12867/87 and 14073/88. The Commission regrettably did not share this view—it declared *C* v. *Netherlands* Application 19139/91 inadmissible even though the applicant had been held by the police for over ninety hours without special justification.

[67] Renucci (2002) N 112.

[68] Gollwitzer (1992) Art. 5 N 111; Trechsel (1974) 255; van Dijk and van Hoof (1998) 37. This is the rule in French law: Charrier (2002) Art. 5 N 36.

If this limit is respected, even though a shorter one required by domestic law is ignored, there will be no violation of Article 5 § 3.[69] However, the ensuing detention will no longer be considered to be lawful and will therefore violate Article 5 § 1.

There is, of course, no violation when the detainee is *released* before the period is over.[70]

D. The Procedure Before the Judge

It may generally be said that the function of a judge is inseparably tied to formally regulated procedures, even if the rules are rudimentary. This is also the case with regard to Articles 5 § 3 of the ECHR, 9 § 3 of the ICCPR, or 7 § 5 of the ACHR.[71] The Court expressed this unambiguously in *Brannigan and McBride*, when it ruled that Article 5 § 3, 'like Article 5 para. 4—must be understood to require the necessity of following a procedure that has a judicial character'.[72]

1. The Need for an Oral Hearing

As we have already seen, the detainee must appear in person before the judge responsible for hearing his or her objections to the detention. The judge must 'review, by reference to legal criteria, whether or not the detention is justified'.[73]

2. The Need for Previous Information

It will sometimes be impossible for a detainee to put forward arguments against the detention without first knowing some details about the nature of the suspicion and the reasons invoked by the investigating authorities to justify the detention. The right to such information is expressly set out in Article 5 § 2 which applies to all types of detention.

3. The Right to be Assisted by Counsel

Does the Convention grant the right to be assisted by counsel at the hearing before a 'judge or other officer'? In *Schiesser* the Court clearly decided that it did not; it did 'not consider [the exclusion of assistance by a lawyer] to be

---

[69] Gollwitzer (1992) Art. 5 N 111; Vogler (1977) 773.

[70] *Brogan and others* v. *United Kingdom*, § 58; Application 12422/86; Frowein and Peukert (1996) Art. 5 N 115; Pisani (2001) Art. 5 N 10.3.

[71] Report of the Commission in *Schiesser* v. *Switzerland* of 9 Mar. 1978. The Court followed this approach; see e.g. *Schiesser* v. *Switzerland*, § 31; *De Jong, Baljet and Van den Brink* v. *Netherlands*, § 51; *Van der Sluijs, Zuiderveld and Klappe* v. *Netherlands*, § 46; *Duinhof and Duijf* v. *Netherlands*, § 46.

[72] *Brannigan and McBride* v. *United Kingdom*, § 58.

[73] *Assenov* v. *Bulgaria*, § 146; see also *Pantea* v. *Romania*, § 231.

incompatible with Article 5 para. 3 of the Convention, which does not make a lawyer's presence obligatory'.[74]

Seventeen years later, in *John Murray*, the Court's approach can be seen to have changed markedly. The Court discussed the issue in the light of Article 6 § 1 which undisputedly 'applies even at the stage of the preliminary investigation into an offence by the police'.[75] Although the reference to *Imbrioscia* makes it clear that it does not go as far as to call for the presence of a lawyer throughout the hearing under Article 5 § 3, in *John Murray* the possibility of drawing inferences from the silence of the suspect, meant that it was nevertheless required.[76]

The development goes in the right direction but it is to be hoped that in the future it will go even further.[77] It is difficult to see what considerations would justify the exclusion of legal assistance at the hearing after arrest. The only justification in *Schiesser* was that it was 'consistent with the practice followed in the Canton of Zurich'[78]—an argument which can be seen to have little, if any, weight.

4. The Right to a Reasoned Decision

Finally, if detention is ordered, the judge must give a reasoned decision, although this need not be in writing. These reasons are necessary to enable the detainee effectively to challenge the decision in proceedings under Article 5 § 4.

E. The (Ir)Relevance of Situations of Emergency

Governments have sometimes claimed that longer periods prior to judicial control of deprivation of liberty of a suspect ought to be accepted in times of emergency, for example, in the fight against terrorism. From the beginning the Court has displayed a seemingly flexible attitude towards this issue. It has recognized the difficult situation created by terrorism, but at the same time has stressed that there must be strict limits on the time spent in police custody.[79] Even when there exists a valid derogation under Article 15, bearing in mind that Article 5 does not figure among the absolute guarantees enumerated in paragraph 2, the Court has examined whether the government has established the need for prolonged detention in police custody.

The first case which raised this question followed the judgment in *Brogan and others*. The United Kingdom Government believed that they could not effectively counter terrorism in Northern Ireland without extending the

---

[74] *Schiesser* v. *Switzerland*, § 36.   [75] *John Murray* v. *United Kingdom*, § 62.
[76] Ibid., § 63–4.
[77] For slight criticism, see also Harris, O'Boyle, and Warbrick (1995) 135.
[78] *Schiesser* v. *Switzerland*, § 36.
[79] *Brogan and others* v. *United Kingdom*, § 61. See also *Sakık and others* v. *Turkey*, § 44; *Gündoğan* v. *Turkey*, § 21; *Murat Satık and others* v. *Turkey*, § 22; *Igdeli* v. *Turkey*, § 28; *Filiz and Kalkan* v. *Turkey*, § 24; *Öcalan* v. *Turkey*, § 106.

maximum length of police detention to seven days. The Court examined this question in great detail and came to the conclusion—by a vote of twenty-two to four—that the derogation was valid and that therefore there had been no violation of Article 5 § 3.[80] In the Commission, four Members had been of the opinion that the Government had failed to establish the necessity for such prolonged police detention.[81]

The later cases all concerned Turkey where the time limit was considerably longer—up to thirty days. In each of these cases the Court came to the conclusion that this was not acceptable.[82]

III. THE LIMITATION IN TIME OF DETENTION ON REMAND

A. General Remarks

The length of detention on remand was the first problem under the Convention to occupy the Court with an entire series of cases.[83] It is rather surprising that after its judgment of 16 July 1971, it was not called upon to decide a similar issue until 28 March 1990.[84] The Commission is partly responsible for this interval, as for a long time it took a rather lenient view towards governments, and refrained from bringing cases in which it had found no violation of Article 5 § 3 before the Court, because they did not raise any important issues in law. The position has since changed and there has been a vast increase in the number of such complaints before the Court. A considerable number of cases were also dealt with by the Commission and the Committee of Ministers before the Eleventh Protocol came into force.

The requirement that the length of detention on remand be limited is closely related to the presumption of innocence—there is a clear danger that this detention will be misused;[85] 'its continuation cannot be used to anticipate a custodial sentence'.[86]

While the text of the Convention seems to offer an alternative: either to bring the accused to trial within a reasonable time or to ensure his or her provisional release, it in fact requires that the release be ordered as soon as the 'continuing detention ceases to be reasonable'.[87] The interpretation of this provision as

[80] *Brannigan and McBride* v. *United Kingdom*, §§ 39–74; dissenting votes of Judges Petiti, Walsh, De Meyer, and Makarczyk are joined to the judgment.
[81] Dissenting opinions of Mr Frowein and of Mr Loucaides joined by Ms Thune and Mr Rozakis. [82] *Aksoy* v. *Turkey*, § 78; *Demir* v. *Turkey*, § 41; *Nuray Sen* v. *Turkey*, §§ 25–8.
[83] *Wemhoff* v. *Germany; Neumeister* v. *Austria; Stögmüller* v. *Austria; Matznetter* v. *Austria; Ringeisen* v. *Austria*. For a detailed analysis of this early case-law, see Kramer (1973); Trechsel (1971). [84] *B* v. *Austria*.
[85] See e.g. *Neumeister* v. *Austria*, § 4; *Jabloński* v. *Poland*, § 83.
[86] *Tomasi* v. *France*, § 91. [87] *Jabloński* v. *Poland*, § 83 and many others.

providing for an alternative would, moreover, be incompatible with the right to speedy proceedings under Article 6 § 1.

According to the text of paragraph 3 it seems obvious that only detention on remand, in the sense of detention falling within Article 5 § 1(c), is subject to time limitations. Yet, the Court has sometimes examined the issue of length, even though the detention could also have been justified under a different heading. An example is *Eriksen*, where Article 5 § 1(a) could also have been relied on.[88] Esser concludes that Article 5 § 3 is not restricted to detention on remand,[89] but this is erroneous; the Court erred in addressing the issue—it would definitely not have found a violation on the basis of the duration in detention as the detention was justified under a different heading. Generally, the opinion of Reindl, who stresses that Article 5 § 1(a) and (c) cannot be applied simultaneously, is quite correct.[90]

A delicate problem of competing justifications for provisional detention arose in *Scott*. The applicant was suspected of rape and during these proceedings the United Kingdom requested that Spain extradite the applicant. At one point, after the decision to extradite had been taken but while the investigation was still continuing, the applicant was 'released' from detention on remand but kept imprisoned on the basis of the extradition proceedings. The Court regarded the whole period of detention as falling under Article 5 § 1(c), a decision which is not particularly convincing.[91] Reindl suggests that the essence of the provision could be undermined if detention were justified under another title, even though it also constitutes detention on remand.[92] This assertion seems initially rather persuasive, however, it is essential to note that the point at issue is not a potential conflict between domestic and Convention law, but between the competing exceptions under the Convention itself. It would be rather illogical to grant the special rights set out under Article 5 § 3 in the knowledge both that the detention falls clearly within paragraph 1(a) or (f) and that the detainee's detention would in any case be entirely in conformity with the Convention.

The situation is again different when detention on remand is interrupted in order to allow the suspect to be examined in a psychiatric hospital. The Commission deducted such periods from the time spent under Article 5 § 1(c), on the assumption that this detention was covered by sub-paragraph (e).[93] However, in this situation the examination forms part of the investigation and does not, as a

---

[88] *Eriksen* v. *Norway*, § 92.   [89] Esser (2002) 282.

[90] Reindl (1998) 49; see also the separate opinion of Judge Repik in *Eriksen* v. *Norway*.

[91] *Scott* v. *Spain*. See the separate opinion of Judge Repik who held that detention which, according to domestic law, was not 'detention on remand' should not be categorized as such by the Court. Reindl (1998) 53 thinks that the Court was correct to act in accordance with its approach to 'autonomous' interpretation. In my own dissenting opinion (joined by Members Soyer and Nowicki) to the Commission's report I held the detention to be contrary to Article 5 § 1 because the detention pending extradition could not be justified as such.   [92] Reindl (1998) 55.

[93] *X* v. *Germany* Application 2219/64; *X* v. *Germany* Application 2279/64: see also Frowein and Peukert (1996) Art. 5 N 120; Gollwitzer (1992) Art. 5 N 116.

rule, serve any of the therapeutic purposes envisaged by that exception. Therefore sub-paragraph (c) and, accordingly, paragraph 3 ought to continue to apply.

The task of assessing the reasonableness of the length of detention on remand is often a particularly difficult one.[94] The interests of the detainee have to be weighed against the interests of the effective prosecution of crime, which may be a particularly onerous task, especially in cases of white-collar crime, organized crime, crimes against humanity, or terrorism.

The Convention organs have to 'determine whether the time that has elapsed ... before judgment is passed on the accused [or he/she was released] has at some stage exceeded a reasonable limit, that is to say imposed a greater sacrifice than could, in the circumstances of the case, reasonably be expected of a person presumed to be innocent'.[95] On the other hand, '[i]t should not be overlooked that, while an accused person in detention is entitled to have his case given priority and conducted with particular expedition, this must not stand in the way of the efforts of the judges to clarify fully the facts in issue, to give both the defence and the prosecution all facilities for putting forward their evidence and stating their cases and to pronounce judgment only after careful reflection on whether the offences were in fact committed and on the sentence'.[96]

According to the text of paragraph 3, everyone detained on remand 'shall be entitled to trial within a reasonable time or to release pending trial'. The Court has also had to stress the rather obvious point[97] that the obligation to proceed without unjustified delays continues to apply, by virtue of Article 6 § 1, once the defendant has been released.[98] It must be recognized, however, that greater diligence is required under Article 5 § 3: '[A]n accused person held in custody is entitled to have his case given priority and conducted with special diligence'.[99]

B. The Period to be Assessed

1. The Beginning of the Period

The relevant period usually starts when the suspect is arrested.[100] There are, however, exceptions to this rule. One of them concerns the competence of the

---

[94] See also Haefliger and Schürmann (1999) 113. For measures to prevent excessive length of detention on remand, see Pradel (2002) N 446–52.
[95] *Wemhoff* v. *Germany*, The Law, § 5; Esser (2002) 289 has reservations about the Court's failure to give more weight to this aspect.   [96] *Wemhoff* v. *Germany*, The Law, § 17.
[97] Van Dijk and van Hoof (1998) 278 et seq.
[98] *Wemhoff* v. *Germany*, The Law, § 5; see also *X* v. *United Kingdom* Application 8233/78.
[99] *Matznetter* v. *Austria*, The Law, § 12.
[100] In *De Wilde, Ooms and Versyp* v. *Belgium*, §§ 67, 75 the Court accepted that a preliminary period of deprivation of liberty of up to twenty-four hours did not count towards the whole period of detention. As Esser (2002) 285 suggests, this incomprehensible doctrine has never been upheld. However, contrary to his view, the issue does not create any difficulties as it is of no practical relevance if the detention lasts one day more or less. Cf. in a similar sense the futile issue in *Murray* v. *United Kingdom*, §§ 32, 78 where the applicant quarrelled over a dispute regarding thirty minutes with respect to 'promptly'—the Court did not see any problem.

Court *ratione temporis*. If the respondent state has ratified the Convention during the detention or when, before Protocol No. 11, the recognition of the right to individual application (Article 25) was subject to a temporal limitation, time spent in detention on remand prior to the relative date cannot directly be examined by the Convention organs; nevertheless, the Court will 'take account of the stage of the proceedings reached'.[101]

The other exception occurs when the suspect has already been deprived of his or her liberty for other reasons, such as where he or she was detained in another country, pending extradition. Time spent in detention in that context does not fall under Article 5 § 3[102]—not only because, formally, it is covered by paragraph 1(f) rather than paragraph 1(c), but also because it falls under the jurisdiction of another state.

2. The End of the Period

The period ends when the detainee is either released or convicted.[103] According to the Court's case-law, conviction at first instance is the decisive date, even if the person concerned files an appeal and remains, according to domestic law, detained on remand as the judgment is not final.[104] This view was held for the first time in *Wemhoff*.[105] I have always opposed it and am still of the opinion that it is wrong.[106]

The Court used five arguments to support its view: *First*, after a judgment at first instance, the applicant has had his guilt established in a trial which was in conformity with Article 6; *second*, it is obvious that the detention comes 'after' such conviction and that there exists a causal link between conviction and deprivation of liberty; *third*, the detention after conviction at first instance does not have the purpose of bringing the applicant before the competent judicial authority; *fourth*, if the detention were not based on paragraph 5 (a) it would not be possible to arrest the person concerned at the hearing;[107] *fifth*, regarding the detention after conviction at first instance as detention on remand would create differences between various countries tied to the Convention.

However, these arguments are not convincing and meet with what, in my view, are stronger counter-arguments. It is not correct blindly to assume that the

---

[101] *Jabłoński* v. *Poland*, § 66; *Szeloch* v. *Poland*, § 78; *Kreps* v. *Poland*, § 36; *Stasaitis* v. *Lithuania*, § 80; *Jėčius* v. *Lithuania*, § 91. From the Commission's case-law, see among others e.g. *Ventura* v. *Italy* Application 7438/76, § 178. A corresponding formula is missing in *Kudła* v. *Poland*, §§ 102 et seq.; *Kalashnikov* v. *Russia*, § 111; *Klamecki* v. *Poland*, §§ 70–1; and *Lavents* v. *Latvia*, §§ 65, 66.
[102] Application 5078/76; *Quinn* v. *France*, § 53.
[103] See e.g. *Clooth* v. *Belgium*, § 35; *Toth* v. *Austria*, § 66.
[104] *B* v. *Austria*, §§ 35 et seq.; *Punzelt* v. *Czech Republic*, § 70; *Labita* v. *Italy*, § 147; *Kalashnikov* v. *Russia*, § 110; *Lavents* v. *Latvia*, § 61; *Demirel* v. *Turkey*, § 56. See also *Hauschildt* v. *Denmark* Application 10486/83.
[105] *Wemhoff* v. *Germany*, § 9.
[106] Trechsel (1974) 192 et seq.; see also my dissenting opinion in the Commission's report on *B* v. *Austria*.   [107] This argument only comes up in *Wemhoff* v. *Germany*, The Law, § 9.

applicant will have had a trial which was in conformity with Article 6; the purpose of his or her appeal may be precisely to establish that this was not the case. The observation regarding the causal connection to the judgment is not really correct—what if the applicant was acquitted but the public prosecutor appealed? In such cases it is certainly possible that the detention will continue. It is questionable whether it is justified to treat such deprivation of liberty differently than that which occurs after conviction[108]—detention must always be lawful according to domestic law; where domestic law does not allow for the serving of sentence before a conviction has acquired force of law, any execution of the sentence would clearly be unlawful. Furthermore, the presumption of innocence remains in force until the judgment has become final; there may be complicated solutions with regard to the plea of nullity or for proceedings in cassation, but the ordinary appeal which leads to a retrial is dominated by the presumption of innocence notwithstanding any conviction at first instance. The view proposed here does in no way impede arrest at the hearing; such deprivation would be detention on remand if the proceedings go on at second instance; if there is a temporary obstacle to the execution of the sentence combined with a fear that the person might abscond, the detention could be based on Article 5 § 1(b) as a means 'to secure the fulfilment of any obligation prescribed by law'. It is true that there are countries in which a sentence may be immediately executed after conviction and sentencing, like, for example, England and Wales, as the Court stated in *Monnell and Morris*.[109] However, Article 53 (formerly Article 60) of the Convention gives a clear indication that in such a case the Convention may not be construed as limiting a fundamental right; yet, this is exactly what the Court has done: it disregarded domestic law to lower the level of protection to that prevailing in England and Wales. In *B* v. *Austria* the difference was no less than three years!

What if the first judgment is quashed on appeal? If the detention is regarded as being justified under paragraph 1(a), one would have to find that retrospectively it was unlawful. In such a case, should the detention be reinterpreted as having fallen under paragraph 1(c)? At any rate, this is not the opinion of the Court. It still regards the time spent after the first judgment as serving a sentence, which is very difficult to understand; however, once that judgment is quashed, the detention on remand is resumed.[110] In view of this, the end of the period to take into consideration is an issue which the Court should re-examine.[111]

In cases concerning continuing detention on remand, the Commission assessed the whole period up to the adoption of its Report.[112] The Court was

---

[108] Such criticism is also voiced by Reindl (1998) at 47.

[109] *Monnell and Morris* v. *United Kingdom*, § 41.

[110] *Kudła* v. *Poland*, § 104; *Vaccaro* v. *Italy*, § 31.

[111] For criticism, see also Esser (2002) 289; Reindl (1998) 47; Villiger (1999) N 340. For approval, see Renucci (2002) N 112, 202–3; van Dijk and van Hoof (1998) 275, n. 414. Harris, O'Boyle, and Warbrick (1995) 138, label the decision as 'reasonable' but recognize that it has flaws.

[112] This was expressly accepted by the Court in the *Neumeister* v. *Austria*, § 7, p. 38; see also *Stögmüller* v. *Austria*, § 7; *Matznetter* v. *Austria*, The Law, §§ 4 et seq.

bound by this limit and could not examine the detention after that date.[113] There is now no obstacle to its taking into consideration the whole period right up to the date of its judgment.

3. Interruption of the Period

Finally, the period can be interrupted for various reasons. For instance, the suspect may, during the period of his or her detention on remand, serve a prison sentence;[114] or he or she may have spent some time in liberty between release and rearrest.[115] Such liberty may even have been chosen by way of absconding—estoppel is not the consequence of such disrespect for the law, the 'clean hands' doctrine of international law does not apply.[116]

The Commission also accepted a deduction for time spent in a psychiatric institution for the purpose of psychiatric examination.[117] However, this solution is not convincing, as such detention is also based on suspicion and serves the criminal proceedings. It must be regarded as covered by paragraph 1(c) and (e) and falls also to be assessed under paragraph 3.[118]

Such intervals of time must be deducted from the period between the start and the end of the detention on remand.

Finally, a special question arises when a detainee is to be released on bail and there is an interval between that decision and the actual liberation. Unless the detainee falls to be criticized for lack of diligence in providing the sum needed it is the actual date of release that is decisive.[119]

C. Criteria of Reasonableness[120]

The main difficulty in applying paragraph 3 consists, in practice, of formulating and employing reliable criteria for the notion of 'reasonable time'. The Court's comments made in 1969 still hold true: 'It is admitted on all sides that it is not feasible to translate this concept into a fixed number of days, weeks, months or years, or into various periods depending on the seriousness of the offence.'[121] The least that can be said is that detention on remand may never go beyond the time of a prison sentence realistically incurred in case of

---

[113] *Kemmache* v. *France*, § 44.

[114] e.g. *Toth* v. *Austria*, § 66; *D* v. *Germany* Application 11703/85.

[115] *Letellier* v. *France*, § 34.   [116] *Van der Tang* v. *Spain*, §§ 49, 53.

[117] *X* v. *Germany* Application 2219/64 (1965); and *X* v. *Germany* Application 2279/64; Frowein and Peukert (1996) Art. 5, N 100, approve of the decisions.

[118] The Court has already accepted that detention can be covered by more than one exception, e.g. paras. 1(a) and (c); *X* v. *United Kingdom*, § 39.

[119] *Van der Tang* v. *Spain*, § 57; see also Esser (2002) 286 et seq.

[120] See also Frowein and Peukert (1996) Art. 5 N 122–30 with numerous references to the Commission's case-law.

[121] *Stögmüller* v. *Austria*, The Law, § 4; confirmed in *W* v. *Switzerland*, § 30. At least, when the detention has lasted a long time, e.g. four years and eight months, particularly strong reasons are

conviction.[122] Furthermore, it is not the abstract sentence incurred which is to be taken as a yardstick, but the time the defendant would actually spend in prison, taking into account the possibility of remission, release on probation, and so forth. The Court has recently discussed this approach and warned against premature and exaggerated anticipation of the possible sentence.[123] Its approach is as follows.

It falls in the *first* place to the national judicial authorities to ensure that, in a given case, the pre-trial detention of an accused person does not exceed a reasonable time. To this end they must examine all the circumstances arguing for and against the existence of a genuine requirement of public interest justifying, with due regard to the principle of the presumption of innocence, a departure from the rule of respect for individual liberty and set them out in their decisions on the applications for release. It is essentially on the basis of the reasons given in these decisions and of the true facts mentioned by the detainee in his applications for release and his appeals that the Court is called upon to decide whether or not there has been a violation of Article 5 § 3.

The persistence of reasonable suspicion that the person arrested has committed an offence is a condition *sine qua non* for the validity of the continued detention, but, after a certain amount of time has elapsed, it no longer suffices: the Court must then establish whether the other grounds cited by the judicial authorities continued to justify the deprivation of liberty. Where such grounds were 'relevant' and 'sufficient', the Court must also ascertain whether the competent national authorities displayed 'special diligence in the conduct of the proceedings.'[124]

Thus, the Court's approach is clear: while 'continued suspicion' has, so far, never been at issue, and, therefore, there is no precise indication of how long the 'certain lapse of time' during which suspicion suffices to justify detention on remand may last, the Court has examined in detail, and rather strictly, whether a danger of absconding persisted; whether there was a risk of pressure being brought to bear on witnesses or of evidence being tampered with in other ways; whether there was a risk of repetition of the offence; and whether the continued detention could be justified for the preservation of public order on relevant and sufficient reasons.

The Court has noted that Article 5 § 3 cannot be 'read as obliging the national authorities to release a detainee on account of his state of health. The question of

---

required, and the Court is prepared to make a 'global evaluation'; *PB* v. *France*, § 30, 36. See also *Vaccaro* v. *Italy*, § 44; *Gombert and Gochgarian* v. *France*, § 52; *Richet* v. *France*, § 69; *Erdem* v. *Germany*, § 47.

[122] This criterion is relied on by the Swiss Courts, BGE 107 Ia 256, 116 Ia 137; Haefliger and Schürmann (1999) 114.

[123] In *Klamecki* v. *Poland*, § 122, it referred to the fact that, while the maximum sentence was ten years, the actual sentence was only three years, 'at the lower end of the applicable scale'.

[124] *W* v. *Switzerland*, § 30; *Tomasi* v. *France*, § 84; *Toth* v. *Austria*, § 67. See also *Clooth* v. *Belgium*, § 36; *Kemmache* v. *France*, § 45; *Letellier* v. *France*, § 35 with references to the earlier case-law.

whether or not the condition of the person in custody is compatible with his continued detention should primarily be determined by the national authorities and, as the Court has held in the context of Article 3 of the Convention, those courts are in general not obliged to release him on health grounds or to place him in a civil hospital to enable him to receive a particular kind of medical treatment'.[125] Nevertheless, this does not absolve the authorities of all responsibility for the health of the applicant, and in *Jabloński* v. *Poland* the Court found that there had been a violation where the authorities refused to release an accused who had gone on hunger strike and who had repeatedly inflicted injuries on himself. The Court stated that 'no account was taken of the fact that with the passage of time and given the number and character of the applicant's acts of self-aggression in prison, it became more and more acutely obvious that keeping him in detention no longer served the purpose of bringing him to "trial within a reasonable time" '.[126]

The Court has explicitly rejected the idea, which seemed to be suggested by the Commission in *W* v. *Switzerland*, that Article 5 § 3 implies a maximum length of pre-trial detention. The Court is adamant that the reasonableness of the time period cannot be considered *in abstracto* and must be assessed 'in each case according to its special features'.[127]

1. 'Relevant' and 'Sufficient' Grounds for the Continuing Detention[128]

It is the responsibility of the authorities to ensure that the pre-trial detention of an accused does not exceed a reasonable time. As prolonged detention interferes with the rule of respect for individual liberty, there must be a genuine public interest in the continuing detention of the accused.[129] The authorities must 'examine all the facts arguing for or against the existence of a genuine requirement of public interest justifying, with due regard to the principle of presumption of innocence, a departure from the rule of respect for individual liberty and set them out in their decisions on the applications for release'.[130]

Moreover, they must set out reasons for their decision to prohibit release. It is principally these reasons which the Court will then examine to determine whether one or a combination of these reasons are 'relevant' and 'sufficient' and thus able to justify the prolonged period of detention.[131] The Court limits its examination to reasons actually invoked by the domestic judicial authorities—it

---

[125] *Jabloński* v. *Poland*, § 82; *Kudła* v. *Poland*, § 93. [126] *Jabloński* v. *Poland*, § 84.

[127] *W* v. *Switzerland*, § 30. See, however, the dissenting opinion of Judge Pettiti, which Harris, O'Boyle, and Warbrick (1995) 145 seem to endorse; *Stögmüller* v. *Austria*, The Law, § 4; *Wemhoff* v. *Germany*, The Law, § 10.

[128] See also Cabral Barreto (1999) Art. 5 N 4.2.3; Harris, O'Boyle, and Warbrick (1995) 139–42.

[129] *Tomasi* v. *France*, § 84. [130] *Yağcı and Sargın* v. *Turkey*, § 50.

[131] For a recent summing up of the Court's principles, see *Klamecki* v. *Poland*, §§ 118–19.

will not hear new arguments put forward by the government in the Strasbourg proceedings[132] nor will it substitute the reasons itself.[133]

Although the Court will primarily consider the justifications advanced by the authorities for the detention, it will also take into account the conduct of domestic courts in giving reasons for upholding the detention. In *Mansur* v. *Turkey*, the Court noted that the 'first court's orders confirming the detention nearly always used an identical, not to say stereotyped, form of words, and on three occasions gave no reasons'.[134] This, in itself, raised doubts about the justification with the Court; however the lack of detailed reasoning will not in itself amount to a violation of Article 5 § 3. If a foreigner faces serious charges, the danger of absconding may be evident, as in *Van der Tang* v. *Spain*.[135]

Finally, it is incompatible with Article 5 for the authorities to shift the burden of proof to the detained person. Thus in *Ilijkov* v. *Bulgaria* the Court found a violation when the authorities insisted that the applicant had to prove the existence of exceptional circumstances in order to secure his release.[136] It is particularly important that the authorities take into account the passage of time and demonstrate that the reasons for the detention existed at the beginning of the detention and continued to exist until the point at which the applicant was released or convicted.[137]

(a) Danger of Absconding

The danger of the suspect absconding is an uncontested justification for detention on remand. It is connected to the right to defend oneself in court—trials *in absentia* are an unsatisfactory substitute for a fair trial, leaving aside the consideration that most sanctions cannot be enforced if the convict is absent.[138] Finally, the last sentence of Article 5 § 3 indicates that the main purpose of detention under Article 5 § 1(c) is to secure that the suspect appears for trial.

While the severity of the sentence incurred is an element indicative of the danger of absconding, the Court has pointed out that this danger 'cannot be gauged solely on [that] basis . . . it must be assessed with reference to relevant factors which may either confirm the existence of a danger of absconding or make it appear so slight that it cannot justify detention pending trial'.[139]

---

[132] *Trzaska* v. *Poland*, § 66.   [133] *Ilijkov* v. *Bulgaria*, § 86.

[134] *Mansur* v. *Turkey*, § 55. See also *Kalashnikov* v. *Russia*, § 116 (the Maidan court had not mentioned 'any factual circumstances underpinning its conclusions'); *Lavents* v. *Latvia*, § 73; *Demirel* v. *Turkey*, § 60; *Nikolova* v. *Bulgaria*, §§ 68–9.

[135] *Van der Tang* v. *Spain*, § 60; see also Esser (2002) 296b et seq.

[136] *Ilijkov* v. *Bulgaria*, § 85.

[137] *Labita* v. *Italy*, §§ 159, 163, where the accusations were based on statements by a '*pentito*' witness, a person who, as a Crown witness, gave information about the Italian mafia in exchange for leniency; this was 'evidence which, with time, had become weaker rather than stronger'.

[138] cf. the express reference to this aspect in ICCPR, Art. 9 § 3.

[139] *Tomasi* v. *France*, § 98, citing *Letellier* v. *France*, § 43; *Mansur* v. *Turkey*, § 55; *Ječius* v. *Lithuania*, § 94. In *Ilijkov* v. *Bulgaria*, § 81 the Court also stressed the obvious fact that the estimation of the sentence incurred is based merely on an assessment by the prosecution authorities.

'[C]ontinued detention can be justified in a given case only if there are specific indications of a genuine requirement of public interest which, notwithstanding the presumption of innocence, outweighs the rule of respect for individual liberty.'[140] Therefore, regard must be had in particular to 'the character of the person involved, his morals, his assets, his links with the State in which he is being prosecuted and his international contacts'.[141] In *W* v. *Switzerland*, where the accused had links to many different countries, no family in Switzerland, and considerable financial resources, the Court held that the temptation to evade trial was considerable.[142]

The poor financial situation of the accused may also justify the authority's suspicion. In *Barfuss* v. *Czech Republic*, the Court noted that the applicant had substantial debts in the Czech Republic and the authorities felt that there was a risk that he might try to abscond to Germany.[143] Similarly, where an applicant has previously absconded from earlier proceedings,[144] or where the applicant has already tried to avoid the criminal proceedings by fleeing the country,[145] the authorities are justified in their belief that the danger of him or her absconding is greater. Where the law establishes certain presumptions in favour of continued detention, the necessity must nevertheless be established by specific facts.[146]

Again, however, a reason which justifies detention on remand at the beginning of the proceedings may fade with the course of time; the authorities will have to provide specific reasons demonstrating why a suspect must remain in detention.[147]

(b) Risk of Tampering with Evidence and Suborning Witnesses
The risk of the accused tampering with the evidence (including the danger of collusion) also belongs to the established reasons to keep an accused in detention. In this way the state defends its right (and secures its obligation) to see that justice is done.

The Court considered this ground in a case concerning an applicant who was, at the time of his arrest, Deputy Director of the Civil Secret Service (SISDE) for Sicily, in Palermo.[148] He had previously been, in the same city, Head of the Mobile Unit, Head of the Criminal Investigation Police ('*Criminalpol*'), and Principal Private Secretary to the Anti-Mafia High Commission ('*Alto Commissario Antimafia*'). He was detained on accusations of involvement in a mafia-type organization. In view of the nature of the offence and the applicant's personal connection with many of the witnesses, the fear of the authorities that he would, if released, 'exert pressure on witnesses or tamper with other evidence' was justified.[149]

---

[140] *Ilijkov* v. *Bulgaria*, § 84; *Letellier* v. *France*, §§ 35–53; *Clooth* v. *Belgium*, § 44; *Muller* v. *France*, §§ 35–45; *Labita* v. *Italy*, §§ 152, 162–5; *Ječius* v. *Lithuania*, §§ 93, 94.
[141] *W* v. *Switzerland*, § 33, citing *Neumeister* v. *Austria*, § 10.
[142] See also *Van der Tang* v. *Spain*, § 64.   [143] *Barfuss* v. *Czech Republic*, § 69.
[144] *Punzelt* v. *Czech Republic*, § 76.   [145] *Český* v. *Czech Republic*, § 79.
[146] *Ilijkov* v. *Bulgaria*, § 84, referring to *Contrada* v. *Italy*, §§ 14, 16, 18, 23–30, 58–62.
[147] *Debboub alias Husseini Ali* v. *France*, § 42.   [148] *Contrada* v. *Italy*, § 61.   [149] Ibid.

In *IA* v. *France*, the applicant had staged a burglary in his own house which ought to have led to the elimination of evidence connecting him to the murder of his wife. According to the Court, it could 'easily be understood how an event of that nature could lead the investigating authorities to fear that, if released, the accused might endeavour to conceal other evidence. It appears, however, from the case file that at the stage of the proceedings at which the burglary took place most of the evidence had already been gathered—moreover, on 24 October 1994 the investigating judge ordered the removal of the seals placed on the applicant's house'.[150] Thus the argument had lost much of its force.

(c) The Risk of Collusion

Collusion is a specific form of tampering with the evidence whereby those involved attempt to 'co-ordinate' the testimony of co-accused and witnesses. The Court has been willing to consider collusion as a legitimate ground for prolonging a period of detention.[151] However, here again, it has noted that in the long term, justifications of the investigation no longer suffice and 'in the normal course of events the risks diminish with the passing of time as inquiries are effected, statements taken and verifications carried out'.[152] Moreover, when the investigation phase has been completed and the accused committed to stand trial, the risk of collusion between the persons involved will be deemed to have disappeared.[153]

(d) The Risk of Reoffending

Unlike the previous points, there is disagreement as to whether the risk of reoffending is a legitimate ground for detention. Such detention is of a generally preventative nature, unrelated to the specific investigation. Also, the very term 'reoffending' is not easily reconcilable with the presumption of innocence as it implies that the suspect has in fact already committed one or more offences.[154]

A reference to an accused person's antecedents cannot suffice to justify refusing release.[155] In *Assenov*, where the applicant was charged with sixteen or more robberies and burglaries, a number of which were allegedly committed after the investigations had begun, the Court stated that the national authorities were not unreasonable in fearing that if released he might reoffend.[156] In spite of this the Court found that there had been a violation in this case as the accused was a minor and the authorities failed to exercise the extra special diligence in ensuring that he was brought to trial within a reasonable time. Whitaker believes that the Court is stricter on this point than English law.[157]

---

[150] *IA* v. *France*, § 110.   [151] *Tomasi* v. *France*, § 95; *W* v. *Switzerland*, § 35.
[152] *Clooth* v. *Belgium*, § 43; *W* v. *Switzerland*, § 35; *IA* v. *France*, § 109; *Debboub alias Husseini Ali* v. *France*, § 44.   [153] *Kemmache* v. *France*, § 54; *Muller* v. *France*, § 40.
[154] A lively discussion has surrounded this subject since the first judgments of the Court; cf. Trechsel (1971) 146 et seq., with further references.
[155] *Clooth* v. *Belgium*, § 40; *Muller* v. *France*, § 44.   [156] *Assenov* v. *Bulgaria*, §§ 156 et seq.
[157] Whitaker (2001) N 11.3.3.

(e) Protection of Public Order

The Court has accepted that the gravity of an offence and the reaction of the public to such an offence may 'give rise to public disquiet capable of justifying pre-trial detention, at least for a certain time'.[158] However, it has limited the importance of this ground stating that it can only be regarded as relevant and sufficient if it is 'based on facts capable of showing that the accused's release would actually prejudice public order'. Moreover, the detention would only continue to be legitimate 'if public order remains actually threatened; its continuation cannot be used to anticipate a custodial sentence'.[159]

In *Tomasi* the accused had been charged with being involved in various offences committed by a known terrorist organization, and although the Court was willing to accept that in the beginning there may have been a threat to public order, it held that this threat would dissipate with time. In this regard the psychological state of the accused is also relevant, and the Court found that there had been no violation in a case where the authorities partly justified the detention on the basis of the applicant's mental state and the vulnerability of the victim.[160] The applicant's personality was also deemed to be relevant by the Commission in a case where he had made death threats on a number of occasions against the police and the main witnesses.[161]

(f) The Need to Protect the Applicant

The Court has accepted that 'in some cases the safety of a person under investigation requires his continued detention, for a time at least. However this can only be so in exceptional circumstances having to do with the nature of the offences concerned, the conditions in which they were committed and the context in which they took place'.[162] It might even be necessary, for a limited amount of time, to protect a detainee against her or his own suicidal tendencies.[163]

2. Grounds which are not Relevant or Sufficient to Justify the Continued Detention

(a) The Seriousness of the Alleged Offence

The gravity of the offences with which the accused is charged is one reason which is often put forward to justify continuing detention. The Court has repeatedly stated, however, that 'the existence and persistence of serious indications of guilt of the person concerned undoubtedly constitute relevant factors, but the Court considers, like the Commission, that they cannot alone justify . . . a long period of detention'.[164]

---

[158] *Tomasi* v. *France*, § 91.
[159] *Letellier* v. *France*, § 51; *Kemmache* v. *France*, § 52; *Tomasi* v. *France*, § 91; *IA* v. *France*, § 104.
[160] *Bouchet* v. *France*, §§ 46, 47.   [161] *Deschamps* v. *Belgium* Application 13370/87.
[162] *IA* v. *France*, § 108; the applicant, suspected of having killed his wife, feared being attacked by her family—the Court was not convinced.   [163] Whitaker (2001) N 11.3.5.
[164] *Tomasi* v. *France*, § 89; *Mansur* v. *Turkey*, § 52; *Yağcı and Sargın* v. *Turkey*, § 50; *Jēčius* v. *Lithuania*, § 94.

(b) The Requirements of the Inquiry

Domestic authorities often also refer to the needs or requirements of the inquiry. However, in my view this is not a reason which justifies detention on remand at all. The presumption is always against an interference with a fundamental right. As a matter of course the detention must be connected to an inquiry. However, there must be a convincing explanation *why*, in a specific case, the inquiry calls for the deprivation of the suspect's liberty. The reason must be one of those discussed above.[165]

Often national authorities will detail a whole series of reasons and repeat that list in every decision on the detention, sometimes in a rather stereotypical way. The Court will not be impressed by that kind of reasoning: it will always examine whether there are convincing reasons justifying one of the legitimate grounds of detention. If that is not the case, the length of detention will be found to be unreasonable.[166]

3. 'Special Diligence' and the Conduct of the Proceedings

If the case passes the relevance and sufficiency test, then the Court will turn its attention towards the way in which the authorities dealt with the investigation. In particular, it aims to detect any unjustified delays or periods of inactivity.[167] It displays more reluctance than the Commission did to criticize the way in which an investigation is generally organized,[168] for example, whether it would have been preferable to disjoin proceedings against certain co-accused or with regard to certain elements of the indictment.[169] The Court is anxious to stress that the duty of expediency in cases where the accused is detained on remand should not hamper the investigating authorities in carrying out their task with the requisite care.[170]

Even if the national authorities have invoked relevant and sufficient reasons to justify the detention, and the investigation has been pursued with the necessary diligence and without undue delays, there can still be a violation of Article 5 § 3.[171]

The complexity of the proceedings may contribute to the length of the pre-trial detention. In this regard there is nevertheless a duty on the authorities to process the applicant's case within a reasonable time. Where, however, the contested detention is not attributable either to the complexity of the case or to the applicant's conduct, and the Court considers that there were no adequate other

---

[165] Esser's evaluation (2002) 297 et seq. does not lead to a different conclusion.

[166] See e.g. *Letellier*, § 52; see also Esser (2002) 292 et seq.

[167] See e.g. *Toth* v. *Austria*, § 76; *Barfuss* v. *Czech Republic*, § 72.

[168] See the dissenting opinion of Judge Cremona in *Matznetter* v. *Austria* (*e contrario*).

[169] See e.g. *Ventura* v. *Italy* Application 7438/76 and my dissenting opinion, p. 99, §§ 7 et seq. (*e contrario*).

[170] *Toth* v. *Austria*, § 77; *Debboub alias Husseini Ali* v. *France*, § 46; *PB* v. *France*, § 34; *Gombert and Gochgarian* v. *France*, § 50; *Richet* v. *France*, § 66.

[171] Cf. *Stögmüller* v. *Austria*, The Law, § 5. See also *W* v. *Switzerland* Application 14379/88, Report of 10 Sept. 1991, unreported. In the opinion of the Commission the detention on remand of four years constituted a violation of Article 5 § 3 although there existed a residual danger of absconding and the authorities had made impressive efforts to speed up a very complex investigation of white-collar criminality. The Court did not share this view. By a narrow vote of five to four it found that the applicant was mainly responsible for the length of the investigation.

grounds justifying the length of detention, then there will be a violation of Article 5 § 3.[172]

The complexity of the case may provide a justification for a prolonged period of detention.[173] Conversely, where the case is not particularly complex the continued detention will give rise to a violation of Article 5 § 3.[174] In determining complexity and the length of the detention, the Court will take into account a number of factors including: the size of the case file[175] and the volume of evidence;[176] the joining of the case to a wider investigation;[177] the replacement of judges without the required expediency;[178] the time needed to consult expert witnesses;[179] the period of time taken to deliver a judgment;[180] the court's diligence in successfully summoning witnesses;[181] the number of witnesses involved;[182] and unexplained delays in the proceedings.[183]

An argument frequently invoked by governments is that the detainee is responsible for the length of time spent on remand, because he or she availed him- or herself excessively of legal remedies or refused to cooperate. Under Article 5 § 3, this objection must be weighed with even more reluctance than under Article 6 § 1.[184] The accused is in no way obliged to contribute to his or her own conviction and is entitled to use all remedies and appeals provided for in domestic law. To some extent he or she must, of course, accept an unavoidable delay, but only improper use of such remedies can lead to the exoneration of the authorities.[185]

However, in a number of cases the Court has decided that the applicant contributed to the prolongation of the time period and thus held that there had been no violation.[186] This was the case in *W* v. *Switzerland* where the Court considered that 'the applicant was primarily responsible for the slow pace of the investigation: there had been great difficulties in reconstructing the financial situation of his companies, as a result of the state of their accounts. It stated that things had become even more difficult when he decided to refuse to make any statement, thereby delaying the progress of the case'.[187]

---

[172] *Tomasi* v. *France*, § 102.
[173] *Van der Tang* v. *Spain*, § 75, where once joined to another file the case became part of a complex process involving large-scale drug-trafficking offences which justified the prolonged period of detention. [174] *Scott* v. *Spain*.
[175] Ibid., § 83.   [176] *Contrada* v. *Italy*, §§ 66, 67.   [177] *Van der Tang* v. *Spain*, § 75.
[178] *Muller* v. *France*, § 48.
[179] *Eriksen* v. *Norway*, § 92; *Kreps* v. *Poland*, § 44; *Zannouti* v. *France*, § 46.
[180] *Punzelt* v. *Czech Republic*, § 80; *Ĉeský* v. *Czech Republic*, § 84.
[181] *Trzaska* v. *Poland*, § 68. According to the Court, domestic authorities are expected to impose fines on witnesses who do not appear.
[182] *Stefano* v. *United Kingdom* Application 12391/86.   [183] *Vaccaro* v. *Italy*, § 44.
[184] cf. e.g. Velu and Ergec (1990) N 524.
[185] This was first addressed in the case-law of the Commission: *Bonnechaux* v. *Switzerland* Application 8224/78, § 84; *Schertenleib* v. *Switzerland* Application 8339/78; *Levy* v. *Germany* Application 6066/73, Report of July 1975, §§ 40 et seq. The applicant was held to be responsible for important delays in Application 3576/67; *X* v. *Germany* Application 6541/74. It has also been the position of the Court, e.g. *Richet* v. *France*, § 66.   [186] *Herczegfalvy* v. *Austria*, § 72.
[187] *W* v. *Switzerland*, § 42.

This obviously suggests an underlying conflict with the right of the accused to remain silent and to do nothing to help the prosecution case. It is difficult to see how the Court can balance the right to remain silent which is protected by Article 6 § 1 with the notion that if an accused should choose to exercise this right and refuse to cooperate with the authorities then he is less deserving of the right to liberty as guaranteed by Article 5.

An argument which will not convince the Court is the excessive workload of the prosecuting or investigating authorities or a shortage of staff. States have the duty to organize their judicial systems so that they can cope with the requirements of speedy trial to which they have committed themselves *inter alia* by ratifying the Convention and/or the ICCPR.[188]

Although the figures in themselves are of very limited significance, as an illustration, the cases decided by the Court[189] so far are as follows:

Name	Date	Time	Outcome
Wemhoff v. *Germany*	27/07/68	3 years, 4 months, 29 days	no violation
Neumeister v. *Austria*	27/06/68	2 years, 2 months and 4 days	violation
Stögmüller v. *Austria*	01/11/69	2 years, 1 day	violation
Ringeisen v. *Austria*	16/07/71	2 years and 4 months	violation
B v. *Austria*	28/03/90	2 years, 4 months, 15 days	no violation
Letellier v. *France*	26/06/91	2 years and 9 months	violation
Kemmache v. *France*	27/11/91	2 years, 10 months and 10 days	violation
Toth v. *Austria*	12/12/91	2 years, 1 month, 2 days	violation
Clooth v. *Belgium*	12/12/91	3 years, 2 months and 4 days	violation
Tomasi v. *Austria*	27/08/92	5 years and 7 months	violation
Herczegfalvy v. *Austria*	24/09/92	7 months and 15 days and 6 months and 8 days	no violation
W v. *Switzerland*	26/01/93	4 years and 3 days	no violation
Quinn v. *France*	22/03/95	1 year	no violation
Mansur v. *Turkey*	08/06/95	about 5 years and 3 months	violation
Yağcı and Sargın v. *Turkey*	08/06/95	2 years and 2 months	violation
Van der Tang v. *Spain*	13/07/95	3 years, 1 month and 27 days	no violation
Scott v. *Spain*	18/12/96	2 years and 7 months	violation
Muller v. *France*	17/03/97	almost 4 years	violation
Eriksen v. *Norway*	27/05/97	2.5 months	no violation
Contrada v. *Italy*	24/08/98	2 years, 7 months and 7 days	no violation
IA v. *France*	23/09/98	6 years and 9 months	violation
Assenov and others v. *Bulgaria*	28/10/98	about 2 years	violation
Debboub alias Hussaini Ali v. *France*	09/11/99	4 years, 2 months and 10 days	violation
Labita v. *Italy*	06/04/00	almost 2 years and 7 months	violation

(*Continued*)

[188] *Scott* v. *Spain*, § 83; *Contrada* v. *Italy*, § 67; Esser (2002) 302 et seq.

[189] See also the Commission's reports, e.g. *Ferrari-Bravo* v. *Italy* Application 9627/81 (4 years, 11 months); *Ventura* v. *Italy* Application 7438/78 (4 years, 11 months, 27 days); *Jentzsch* v. *Germany* Application 2604/65 (6 years); *Hauschildt* v. *Denmark* Application 10486/83 (33 months); and *J* v. *France* Application 15932/89 (2 years, 11 months, 17 days). The leniency of the Commission is criticized by Pouget (1989) 93.

Name	Date	Time	Outcome
Punzelt v. *Czech Republic*	25/04/00	2 years, 6 months and 18 days	violation
Český v. *The Czech Republic*	06/06/00	3 years, 3 months and 7 days	violation
Trzaska v. *Poland*	11/07/00	3 years and 6 months	violation
Jēčius v. *Lithuania*	31/07/00	14 months and 26 days	violation
Barfuss v. *Lithuania*	31/07/00	3 years, 5 months and 19 days	violation
PB v. *France*	01/08/00	4 years, 8 months and 3 days	violation
Kudła v. *Poland*	26/10/00	2 years, 4 months and 3 days	violation
Vaccaro v. *Italy*	16/11/00	4 years, 8 months and 2 days	violation
Jabloński v. *Poland*	21/12/00	3 years, 9 months and 7 days	violation
Gombert and Gochgarian v. *France*	13/02/01	4 years, 9 months and 7 days	violation
Richet v. *France*	13/02/01	4 years, 8 months and 14 days	violation
Szeloch v. *Poland*	22/02/01	1 year, 10 months and 3 days	violation
Bouchet v. *France*	20/03/01	1 year, 5 months and 17 days	no violation
Erdem v. *Germany*	05/07/01	5 years and 11 months	violation
Ilijkov v. *Bulgaria*	26/07/01	3 years, 3 months and 27 days	violation
Kreps v. *Poland*	26/07/01	4 years less 12 days	violation
Zannuti v. *France*	31/07/01	5 years, 5 months and 23 days	violation
Ilowiecki v. *Poland*	04/10/01	1 year, 9 months and 19 days	violation
Olstowski v. *Poland*	15/11/01	almost 3 years and 3 months	violation
Stasaitis v. *Lithuania*	21/03/02	3 years, 8 months and 3 days	violation
Klameckiv v. *Poland*	28/03/02	7 months and 3 weeks (some 17 weeks before competence)	no violation
Kalashnikov v. *Russia*	15/07/02	1 year, 2 months and 29 days (2 years, 10 months before competence)	violation
Grisez v. *Belgium*	26/09/02	2 years, 3 months and 19 days	no violation
Lavents v. *Latvia*	28/11/02	6 years, 5 months and 14 days (of which 4 years and 6 months before competence)	violation
Shishkov v. *Bulgaria*	09/01/03	7 months and 3 weeks	violation
Demirel v. *Turkey*	21/01/03	7 years and 20 days	violation
Nikolov v. *Bulgaria*	30/01/03	5.5 months (minor)	violation
Klamecki v. *Poland (No. 2)*	03/04/03	2 years, 3 months and 16 days	violation
Pantano v. *Italy*	06/11/03	2 years, 8 months and 14 days	no violation
Imre v. *Hungary*	02/12/03	2 years, 9 months and 26 days	violation
Matwiejczuk v. *Poland*	02/12/03	2 years, 7 months and 22 days	violation
Yankov v. *Bulgaria*	11/12/03	2 years and almost 4 months	violation
GK v. *Poland*	20/01/04	3 years and 17 days	violation
DP v. *Poland*	20/01/04	about 2 years and 9 months	violation
Ahmet Özkan and others v. *Turkey*	06/04/04	at least 5 years, 6 months and 15 days (Ali Erbek)	violation
JG v. *Poland*	06/04/04	2 years, 2 months and 6 days	violation
Hamanov v. *Bulgaria*	08/04/04	2 years, 7 months and 18 days	violation
Belchev v. *Bulgaria*	08/04/04	4 months and 14 days	violation
Bałi and others v. *Turkey*	03/06/04	1 year, 8 months and 15 days and more	violation
Wesołowski v. *Poland*	22/06/04	3 years, 2 months and 8 days	violation
Pavletić v. *Slovakia*	22/06/04	2 years	violation
Cevizovic v. *Germany*	29/07/04	4 years, 9 months and 3 days	violation

IV. RELEASE ON BAIL

At the end of paragraph 3, a sentence is added: 'Release may be conditioned by guarantees to appear for trial'.[190] There was no need for this, as substitutes for detention would have been justified according to the *a maiore minus* rule. For practical reasons bail is an option almost exclusively in cases where the detention is justified by the danger of the suspect absconding—it would not prove effective in preventing interference with the evidence, the commission of new offences, or disturbance of the public order.[191] On the other hand, bail may only be required as long as reasons justifying detention prevail.[192]

Automatic denial of bail pending trial is incompatible with the guarantees of this provision.[193] The Court agreed with the opinion of the Commission that judicial control of interference by the executive with an individual's right to liberty was an essential feature of the guarantees embodied in Article 5 § 3 and thus the removal of judicial control of pre-trial detention amounted to a violation of the Article.[194]

The amount of bail must be assessed by reference to the detainee, 'his assets and his relationship with the persons who are to provide the security, in other words to the degree of confidence that is possible that the prospect of loss of the security or of action against the guarantors in case of his non-appearance at the trial will act as a sufficient deterrent to dispel any wish on his part to abscond'.[195] When the authorities have reason to assume that the person concerned has considerable means, but the latter refuses to disclose information about his or her assets, it is permissible to fix bail on the basis of the hypothetical assets.[196]

Apart from financial guarantees, other measures of security are possible, for example, restriction of movement.[197] As the fundamental right to liberty is at stake, the authorities must take as much care in fixing appropriate bail as in deciding whether or not the accused's detention is indispensable.[198] In *Iwancuk* the applicant was not released on bail until more than four months after the decision was taken to release him. The Court held that the authorities' handling of the case suggested that they were 'reticent to accept the bail which, in the case of the applicant's non-appearance for the trial would require undertaking certain

---

[190] And for implementation of sentence, cf. the text of ICCPR, Art. 9 § 3.
[191] Grabenwarter (2003) § 21 N 17; Haefliger and Schürmann (1999) 115.
[192] Van Dijk and van Hoof (1998) 380.
[193] *Caballero* v. *United Kingdom*; *SBC* v. *United Kingdom*; *BH* v. *United Kingdom* Application 30307/96. For a discussion of this issue, see Leach (1999).
[194] See *SBC* v. *United Kingdom*, § 22.
[195] *Neumeister* v. *Austria*, The Law, § 14, p. 40; *Iwanczuk* v. *Poland*, § 66; *Moussa* v. *France* Application 28897/95. The amount of costs incurred and a possible fine were invoked by the French authorities in *Kemmache (No. 3)* v. *France*: the Court did not react, but certainly that approach must be rejected.   [196] *Bonnechaux* v. *Switzerland* Application 8244/78, § 74.
[197] *Schmid* v. *Austria* Application 10670/83; such restrictions are justified under Article 3 § 2 of Protocol No. 4. See also Harris, O'Boyle, and Warbrick (1995) 142.
[198] *Schertenleib* v. *Switzerland* Application 8339/78; *Iwanczuk* v. *Poland*, § 66.

formalities in order to seize the assets'.[199] The Court held that this could not be regarded as a sufficient ground on which to maintain for four months the detention on remand which had already been deemed unnecessary by the competent judicial authority; thus there had been a violation of Article 5 § 3.

While there is no absolute right to release on bail under the Convention, the detainee does have, at the least, the right to be heard in this respect. The Court commented critically where a proposal was made by the applicant and the domestic court did not react.[200]

V. POSSIBILITY OF REDRESS

A number of cases have been dealt with by the Commission where domestic courts had acknowledged the excessive length of detention on remand and consequently reduced the sentence. In such cases the Convention organs concluded that the applicant could no longer claim to be a 'victim' within the meaning of Article 34 (formerly Article 25). In order to bring redress, the domestic decision must show two elements: first, there must be a recognition of the violation of the Convention right at issue,[201] and second, some sort of compensation must be granted.[202]

---

[199] *Iwanczuk* v. *Poland*, § 69.   [200] *Szeloch* v. *Poland*, § 94.

[201] This was missing in *Lüdi* v. *Switzerland*, §§ 31–4.

[202] In *Amuur* v. *France* this condition was not fulfilled because the applicants had been hastily deported to Syria, §§ 34–6.

Chapter 20

Other Fundamental Rights Affected by Criminal Proceedings

I. INTRODUCTION

A. The Issues Dealt with in this Chapter

Most of the measures of coercion applied in criminal proceedings constitute intrusions into the private sphere of the suspect and sometimes also third persons.

Another area which is particularly relevant is the interception of communications and the censorship of correspondence. This can take many different forms depending on the type of communication and can involve written correspondence, telephone conversations, or electronic communication such as e-mail. Conversations can be recorded and behaviour can be subjected to surveillance through the use of devices able to record sound and/or images. Other possible interferences include house searches in order to locate suspects or evidence; covert surveillance by undercover agents; the right to property can also be affected where, for instance, assets are confiscated for use in evidence, to prevent them being used dangerously, to secure the payment of fines, damages, costs or other claims, or for some other purpose. This last element will be dealt with at the end of this chapter while a number of general considerations can and must be made collectively for the other issues.

B. The General Approach

The rights involved in this chapter are, especially in relation to the European case-law, of particular complexity. Unlike guarantees such as the right to a fair trial or the right to personal liberty, they have only a marginal link to criminal proceedings. A full analysis of these guarantees would be entirely disproportionate in the context of a work focused on criminal proceedings. I shall therefore limit the examination of these rights to the points necessary to understand the legal structure of the guarantees, and those relating directly to the problems under consideration. In view of the importance of the case-law, the emphasis will be on the jurisprudence of the ECtHR.

II. INTERFERENCE WITH THE RIGHT TO RESPECT FOR PRIVATE LIFE: GENERAL OBSERVATIONS

A. The Basic Structure of the Protection of Private Life

1. The Texts

> 1. No one shall be subjected to arbitrary or unlawful interference with his privacy, family, home or correspondence, nor to unlawful attacks on his honour and reputation.
> 2. Everyone has the right to the protection of the law against such interference or attacks.
>
> ICCPR, Art. 17

> Right to respect for private and family life
>
> 1. Everyone has the right to respect for his private and family life, his home and his correspondence.
> 2. There shall be no interference by a public authority with the exercise of this right except such as is in accordance with the law and is necessary in a democratic society in the interests of national security, public safety or the economic well-being of the country, for the prevention of disorder or crime, for the protection of health or morals, or for the protection of the rights and freedoms of others.
>
> ECHR, Art. 8

> 1. Everyone has the right to have his honor respected and his dignity recognized.
> 2. No one may be the object of arbitrary or abusive interference with his private life, his family, his home, or his correspondence, or of unlawful attacks on his honor or reputation.
> 3. Everyone has the right to the protection of the law against such interference or attacks.
>
> AHRC, Art. 11

These provisions are more specific than the guarantees which are more closely connected to criminal proceedings.[1] This can be explained by the more political nature of the subject matter—and by the fact that it is considerably less 'technical'. The most important difference between the texts is the inclusion in the ECHR of a relatively detailed rule on acceptable (or legitimate) interferences with the right, while the other texts simply prohibit 'arbitrary or unlawful' (ICCPR) or 'arbitrary or abusive' (ACHR) interferences. Unlike Nowak, I regard this as a rather fundamental difference.[2] The ECHR is stricter in that it requires any

---

[1] For a brief history of the European text, see Russo (1995) 305; and Coustirat-Coustère (1995) 323.

[2] Nowak (1993) Art. 17 N 8 opposes 'the hypothesis that Art. 17 permits greater interference than Art. 8 of the ECHR'.

interference with the right to be justified, and to fulfil the conditions set out in paragraph 2. The texts employ a different methodology. Under the ICCPR and the ACHR the interference seems at the outset to be accepted, even normal. There is a violation only if the interference can be characterized as representing one of the stated, negative values.

For instance, if the interference has no legal basis, or only a rather vague one, it could not be criticized by either the ACHR or the ICCPR as being unlawful, but there would be a violation under the ECHR. Under the Covenant and the ACHR the victim must show that the interference is 'unlawful', 'arbitrary', or 'abusive'. In Strasbourg it is enough to show that there was an interference. The government must then establish that the interference had a sufficient legal basis, pursued a legitimate aim, and could be regarded as 'necessary in a democratic society'.

Although I have some reservations as to Nowak's position, I still regard his statements as important: they betray, I believe, the aspiration of the ICCPR not to fall (considerably) behind the standards achieved in Europe.

2. The Elements of the Protection of Private Life [3]

The examination of whether, in a particular case, there has been a violation of Article 8, can be roughly determined by going through five steps.[4]

First, the question arises whether the interference is covered by the scope of the guarantee. For instance, the question has arisen whether a lawyer's office enjoys the protection of 'home'.[5]

Second, there must be an interference with that right. This may be doubtful, for example, if letters to or from a prison inmate are only delayed for a short period of time.

Third, if there has been an interference with the right, it must be confirmed that the conditions set out in paragraph 2 have been fulfilled, starting with the requirement of lawfulness.

Fourth, the lawful interference must be in pursuance of one of the goals set out in the paragraph.

Fifth, and finally, the Court will address the issue of proportionality, the question as to whether the interference could be considered to be necessary in a democratic society, in other words, whether it satisfied a 'pressing social need'. The international organ must not itself ask whether the interference was necessary—this is a task for the domestic authorities. By saying that the interference was necessary, the Court would say that there *had to be* an interference. This would

[3] For a brief but informative description of the right, see Nowak (1993) Art. 17 N 1 et seq.
[4] Harris, O'Boyle, and Warbrick (1995) 304 distinguish an additional step: 'What is required of the state . . . ?' This is not relevant in the context of criminal proceedings.
[5] *Niemietz* v. *Germany*.

not be in line with its obligation to 'ensure the observance of the engagements undertaken by the High Contracting Parties'.[6]

B. The Elements Common to the Protection of Various Aspects of Private Life

While the three texts reproduced vary quite considerably, they are all predominantly concerned with four aspects which fall under the titles of privacy, family life, home, and correspondence in the ICCPR, the ACHR, and the ECHR. Their scope falls to be discussed within the context of the different typical procedural measures by which they may be affected. The same applies to the type of 'interference'. This leaves as common elements the requirements of the lawfulness, scope, and proportionality of the measure. Even here, certain aspects will have to be addressed for each specific interference separately. This is because the Court has given considerable weight to the fact that lawfulness requires certain precise questions to be addressed in the relevant law in order for it to provide the requisite degree of precision.

1. The Requirement of Lawfulness

In order to be compatible with the guarantee, any interference must be 'in accordance with the law'.[7] Although this requirement seems at first sight to be quite simple, it has taken on a more complex shape in the European case-law. In the first place, there must be legislation which generally permits the interference. This legislation must itself fulfil certain requirements. Then, the actual act complained of must have respected the domestic law. This means that the Court will, to a certain extent, have to do what it normally refuses to do: ascertain whether domestic law has been correctly applied.

Several formal and substantive aspects of the notion of 'law' must be distinguished. The formal aspects relate to the origin of the norm, whether it was passed by a parliament or similar legislative assembly, or created by the government or by an administrative body. In this respect one can distinguish 'law in the formal sense' and 'law in the substantive sense'. The former applies when the text has been adopted in pursuance of the constitutional rules for legislation by the parliament or an equivalent body. The latter term has a broader meaning and includes decrees, ordinances, orders, regulations, enactments, etc., as long as they contain a generally applicable abstract norm (as opposed to a single

---

[6] ECHR, Art. 19.

[7] This requirement was already discussed in relation to the right to a 'tribunal established by law' in Chapter 3 above and to deprivations of liberty in Chapter 17 above; however, the Court in Strasbourg is so keen on adapting its doctrines to the specific cases that the issue is not identical under Art. 8.

administrative act aimed at one specific matter). This latter and broader meaning of the term is generally accepted by the Court,[8] with the exception of the requirement of a 'tribunal established by law' set out in Article 6 § 1 of the ECHR.[9] In *Silver and others* the Court seemed to hesitate before concluding that 'directives' of the Home Secretary, in the form of 'Standing Orders' and 'Circular Instructions' could indeed qualify as law. It concluded that 'although those directives did not themselves have the force of law, they may—to the admittedly limited extent to which those concerned were made sufficiently aware of their contents—be taken into account in assessing whether the criterion of foreseeability was satisfied in the application of the Rules' which means that they were regarded *de facto* as 'law'.[10]

The international scope of the guarantees and particularly the need to interpret the Convention—and the same can be said for the two other instruments—in such a way as to ensure that it can be applied both in those legal systems which rely entirely on legislation, and in those based on the common law, has certainly had an impact on its extent. The text seems to fit more naturally to the former, but cannot be understood as excluding the latter.[11] In other words, 'the word "law/loi" is to be interpreted as covering not only written law but also unwritten law'.[12] This certainly merits approval to the extent that it is applied to the common-law system. The problem was discussed in two parallel cases against France where the Government relied on case-law as a legal basis, while the Delegate of the Commission suggested that the recognition of unwritten law or case-law ought not to be extended to continental countries. The Court reaffirmed that it understood 'law' in its 'substantive' sense and concluded that the interference had indeed been 'in accordance with the law', although the law did not satisfy the requirement of foreseeability.[13] I continue, however, to believe that the notion of 'law' ought not to be interpreted in the same sense for the two systems, particularly in view of the fact that in the continental tradition it is very important that the 'law' is laid down in a written text.[14]

On the other hand, as Esser points out, it is surprising that the Court censures domestic law for lacking the required precision while recognizing that detailed norms have been developed by the case-law.[15]

---

[8] See, *inter alia, De Wilde, Ooms and Versyp* v. *Belgium*, § 93; *Kruslin* v. *France*, § 29; *Huvig* v. *France*, § 28.   [9] *Coeme* v. *Belgium*, § 98; see Chapter 3 above.

[10] *Silver and others* v. *United Kingdom*, §§ 26, 88.

[11] The problem presented itself very impressively in the cases of *SW* v. *United Kingdom* and *CR* v. *United Kingdom* in which the applicants complained, under ECHR, Art. 7, of the retroactive application of the criminal law when in 1991 the English courts abolished what remained of the 'marital rape exemption'.

[12] *Sunday Times* v. *United Kingdom*, § 47; *Dudgeon* v. *United Kingdom*, § 44; *Chappell* v. *United Kingdom*, § 52; *Malone* v. *United Kingdom*, § 66.

[13] *Kruslin* v. *France*, §§ 28 et seq.; *Huvig* v. *France*, §§ 27 et seq.

[14] On the contrary, Wildhaber and Breitenmoser (1992) N 548 complain of the Court's silence on the suggestion of MM. Soyer and Martinez who were of the opinion that the interference was based on customary law.

[15] Esser (2002) 152 referring to *Kopp* v. *Switzerland* and *Valenzuela Contreras* v. *Spain*.

The Court requires that the right is clearly protected, there must be some control system which ensures the correct application of the legal rules, especially in view of the relatively wide discretion which must be left to the authorities. 'However, the Court does not interpret the expression "in accordance with the law" as meaning that the safeguards must be enshrined in the very text which authorises the imposition of restrictions.'[16]

A further formal aspect was highlighted by the Court in the *Sunday Times (1)* judgment, namely that the norm is accessible. The law must also provide for safeguards against abuse.[17]

With respect to the substantive aspect, the essential elements are precision and detail. In the same judgment the Court formulated this requirement as follows:

a norm cannot be regarded as a 'law' unless it is formulated with sufficient precision to enable the citizen to regulate his conduct: he must be able—if need be with appropriate advice—to foresee, to a degree that is reasonable in the circumstances, the consequences which a given action may entail. Those consequences need not be foreseeable with absolute certainty: experience shows this to be unattainable. Again, whilst certainty is highly desirable, it may bring in its train excessive rigidity and the law must be able to keep pace with changing circumstances. Accordingly, many laws are inevitably couched in terms which, to a greater or lesser extent, are vague and whose interpretation and application are questions of practice.[18]

While this judgment concerned the right to freedom of expression under Article 10 of the ECHR, the principle is equally applicable to the right to respect for private and family life under Article 8.[19] The formula itself is, of course, relatively open. Yet, it is characterized by a considerable degree of realism. It may well constitute the optimum protection to be attained at an international level. Later on, it was somewhat simplified and the focus became the requirement 'that the quality of the law is such as to provide safeguards against arbitrariness'.[20]

Of course, the authorities are not left with unlimited discretion. Here, however, the rules are no longer of a general nature: 'The degree of precision required of the "law" in this connection will depend upon the particular subject-matter'.[21] We shall therefore return to this aspect when dealing with the specific measures of coercion.

2. The Legitimate Aim

The list of interests which can justify an interference with the right to privacy is varied and drafted in broad terms. In Article 8 § 2 we find, *inter alia*, 'the

---

[16] *Silver and others* v. *United Kingdom*, § 90.   [17] *Silver and others* v. *United Kingdom*, § 90.
[18] *Sunday Times* v. *United Kingdom (1)*, § 49; the HRC also requires a legal basis which is not limited to general principles, *Larry James Pinkney* v. *Canada*, at 95, § 34.
[19] See e.g. *Silver and others* v. *United Kingdom*, § 85; *Malone* v. *United Kingdom*, §§ 66, 67; *Kruslin v. France*, §§ 28, 29; *Huvig* v. *France*, §§ 27, 28.
[20] *PG and JH* v. *United Kingdom*, § 61; see also *Taylor-Sabori* v. *United Kingdom*, § 18.
[21] *Malone* v. *United Kingdom*, § 68, quoted verbatim in *Kruslin* v. *France*, § 30; *Huvig* v. *France*, § 29. See also *PG and JH* v. *United Kingdom*, § 46.

interests of national security, public safety... the prevention of disorder or crime...'. There is no example in the Court's jurisprudence of a case where there was any reason for a substantial discussion about this point.[22] For the purposes of the present study, it will suffice to quote a typical passage: 'The Court shares the opinion of the Government and the Commission and considers that the interference was designed to establish the truth in connection with criminal proceedings and therefore to prevent disorder'.[23] Esser rightly observes that none of these aims really fit the needs of criminal investigations which are not, at least not immediately, directed towards preventing disorder.[24]

3. Necessary in a Democratic Society

While the elements of 'lawfulness' and 'legitimate aim' lend themselves, at least to some extent, to an examination *in abstracto*, the proportionality requirement, expressed by the words 'necessary in a democratic society', can only be assessed in the context of a specific interference. One exception concerns measures which are inhuman or degrading, which are clearly prohibited from the outset by virtue of Article 3 of the ECHR (corresponding to Articles 7 of the ICCPR and 5 § 2 of the ACHR). As a guideline, the Court has specified the following basic principles: 'necessary' means less than 'strictly necessary' but more than 'useful' or 'desirable': the states enjoy a certain margin of appreciation, but the ultimate control lies with the Court; the interference must correspond to a 'pressing social need'; and the exception must be 'narrowly interpreted'.[25]

There are a number of examples in the Court's jurisprudence where the issue of proportionality has been decisive although, quite in contrast to other guarantees such as the right to freedom of expression protected by Article 10 of the ECHR, the main emphasis has been on the element of lawfulness.

III. SURVEILLANCE AND INTERCEPTION OF COMMUNICATIONS

A. Introduction

As soon as the prosecution authorities suspect that an offence has been committed, they will begin to gather information.[26] Various kinds of surveillance may even begin at an earlier stage in order to pursue preventative aims. This is

---

[22] The absence of any question or discussion is mentioned in *Silver and others* v. *United Kingdom*, § 96; see also *Klass and others* v. *Germany*, § 46; *Campbell* v. *United Kingdom*, §§ 41, 60; *Lambert* v. *France*, § 29.   [23] *Lambert* v. *France*, § 29.

[24] Esser (2002) 116.

[25] See e.g. *Handyside* v. *United Kingdom*, §§ 48, 49; *Klass and others* v. *Germany*, § 42; *Silver and others* v. *United Kingdom*, § 97.

[26] For other public needs to interfere with privacy, see Velu and Ergec (1990) N 655.

a classical field of activity for the police, its aim is not to prosecute suspects but to protect people. As the focus of this study is criminal proceedings, I shall deal only marginally with issues involving the prevention of crime.[27] One of the leading cases, however, concerns measures taken in Germany for the protection against espionage and organized crime and will be discussed below.[28]

Once a person has been targeted as a suspect, an act which will often mark the beginning of criminal proceedings,[29] it is quite common for the suspect to be subjected to covert surveillance in order to assist the authorities in obtaining further information. Such surveillance is also discussed in the perspective of the right to protection against self-incrimination.[30] If a person is either detained on remand or serving a custodial sentence, the surveillance will be designed mainly to detect plans for collusion or absconding.

All sorts of communications can be intercepted. Before the introduction of new means of communication the main target was letters and parcels. During the proceedings such interception is done secretly; the suspect ought not to become aware of it.[31] Letters and parcels will be sealed again and forwarded with a minimal delay. This is what the traditional protection of the fundamental right to respect for correspondence refers to. There is a parallel duty of confidentiality on the postal services and all persons working there. A further type of interference does not exactly concern the process of communication but rather, as it were, its frozen result, namely the storage of data concerning somebody's personal life. This will be discussed in section V below.

The protection of correspondence from interference could serve a number of different purposes. It certainly has, in particular with regard to parcels, an economic side to it; it serves the right to express opinions and to obtain information; it may be related to religious freedom and to the right to vote. In the specific context of criminal proceedings, however, it is the right to privacy that stands out. The exchange of ideas and information, in particular the sharing of personal experience and feelings, are fundamental expressions of the human personality and therefore highly personal matters. It is important for the development of the personality that such communication can be carried on in the confidence that from the moment the sender releases the letter until it is in the hands of the addressee it will not be read by third persons. In the case of prisoners the right extends to the exchange of correspondence as such.[32] It is also important of course that the remand prisoner be able to correspond freely with his or her lawyer without having to worry about incriminating him- or herself or compromising the defence. Apart from the general importance of the right to communicate, the prisoner will also have a need to free correspondence with his lawyer.

---

[27] The Court makes this distinction in *Klass and others* v. *Germany*, § 40.
[28] *Klass and others* v. *Germany*.   [29] See p. 137 et seq.   [30] See Chapter 13 above.
[31] Velu and Ergec (1990) N 680 rightly point out that the protection depends on the will of a sender—if he or she uses an open postcard, this signals a lack of any wish to keep the contents secret.
[32] Tulkens (2001) 881.

The technical developments over the half century since the drafting of the instruments call for a wider interpretation of the term 'correspondence'. Telegrams, telex messages,[33] facsimile letters, even correspondence via the Internet (e-mail) are included.[34] More recently, SMS messages must be included, as well as any other transmission of language in written form. The Commission has also regarded magazines that were transferred from one person to another as correspondence, although it would be more appropriate to consider such communication as falling under Article 10.[35]

Pictures which can form a part of traditional correspondence or of digital messages, including via mobile telephones, must also be considered to constitute correspondence.

It is more difficult to add in the term 'correspondence' communication via the telephone,[36] be it by traditional land lines or via mobile (or 'cell') telephones or 'walkie-talkies'.[37] There are two possible answers to this issue: either they can be regarded as a form of correspondence or as emanating directly from the notion of privacy. The results will be identical—the Court referred to both indistinctly in *Klass*—it took 'correspondence' and 'private life' together.[38] Finally, communication in person is not correspondence but simply a manifestation of private life.

B. Interception of Written Correspondence

1. The Case-law[39]

All the cases concerning the freedom from interference with written correspondence which have been decided by the ECtHR have concerned prisoners.[40] The most common problem was the failure to forward letters.

The HRC had to consider a communication against Canada where a racist party and its founder had set up a telephone number which allowed callers to hear an anti-Semitic message. This was forbidden and the Committee accepted 'that the broad scope of the prohibitory order, extending as it does to all mail, whether sent or received, raises a question of compatibility' with, *inter alia*, Article 17 of the ICCPR.[41]

---

[33] *Christie* v. *United Kingdom* Application 21482/93.
[34] Charrier (2002) Art. 8 N 35; Reed and Murdoch (2001) N 6.15.
[35] *X* v. *United Kingdom* Application 7308/75.
[36] *A* v. *France* Application 14838/89 (1991).   [37] *X* v. *Belgium* Application 8962/80.
[38] *Klass and others* v. *Germany*, § 41 (the Court also raised—but left undecided—the question whether there was an interference with the right to the respect of the applicants' home). See also *Malone* v. *United Kingdom*, § 64; *Kruslin* v. *France*, § 26; *Huvig* v. *France*, § 25; *Halford* v. *United Kingdom*, § 46; *Kopp* v. *Switzerland*, § 53; *Lambert* v. *France*, § 21; and *KD* v. *Netherlands* Application 21307793.   [39] See also Wildhaber and Breitenmoser N 509, 510.
[40] For an analysis of this case-law, see e.g. Kaufmann in Starmer (2001) N 16.60–16.71. For a critical view of the early case-law of the Commission, see van Dijk and van Hoof (1998) 528.
[41] *JRT and the WG Party* v. *Canada*, at 25, § 8(c).

It is therefore legitimate to conclude that so far the right to respect for correspondence has not given rise to serious disputes in the area of criminal proceedings.

2. Principles Concerning Prisoners' Correspondence

Most of the issues arising in connection with the restrictions imposed on the correspondence of prisoners were dealt with in the first case decided by the Court. It came before the Court following the conclusion of relatively time-consuming proceedings before the Commission, which had led to the adoption of a friendly settlement with regard to part of the complaints. The case involved seven separate applications which were joined together. The basic principle underlying the judgment, which had also been followed by the Commission, was that it was generally justified for prison authorities to open and read the correspondence of inmates for the purpose of safeguarding security in prison and preventing further delinquency or escape.[42] Besides these grounds, the interception of letters was held to be only acceptable for the purpose of protecting the rights of other prisoners[43] but this justification does not extend to protecting the reputation of prison wardens; similarly letters which contain complaints about prison conditions may not be stopped.[44] The Court has not always kept its promise to interpret the exceptions narrowly. In one case the fact that the applicant Mr Noe had been convicted of fraud was sufficient to justify the stopping of a letter mentioning business matters.[45]

However, there are some exceptions to the entitlement of the authorities to open letters. One of them has already been discussed in connection with the right to counsel.[46] Another one concerns correspondence with the Strasbourg Commission and Court.[47] Here, special provisions apply as set out in the European Agreement Relating to Persons Participating in Proceedings of the European Commission and Court of Human Rights of 6 May 1969. Article 3 § 2(a) says that 'if their [*scil.* persons in detention exercising the right to present an individual application] correspondence is examined by the competent authorities, its despatch and delivery shall nevertheless take place without undue delay and without alteration'. This clearly implies that the authorities may legitimately control the contents of the correspondence. On the other hand, sub-paragraph (c) of the same paragraph grants 'the right to correspond, and consult

---

[42] *Silver and others* v. *United Kingdom.* This can justify stopping a letter which contains threats (ibid., § 103).

[43] See e.g. *Silver and others* v. *United Kingdom,* § 102. This is also the view of the HRC; see *Miguel Angel Estrella* v. *Uruguay,* at 150, § 9.2.

[44] *Silver and others* v. *United Kingdom,* §§ 64, 99(c); *Pfeifer and Plankel* v. *Austria,* § 47.

[45] *Silver and others* v. *United Kingdom,* § 101.

[46] See e.g. *Campbell* v. *United Kingdom,* §§ 46 et seq. An exception is only justified when there exists a reasonable suspicion of abuse. See also p. 278 et seq. above.

[47] *Campbell* v. *United Kingdom,* § 62; *Sałapa* v. *Poland,* § 94.

out of hearing of other persons, with a lawyer'. There seems to be a certain contradiction—the Explanatory Report suggests that the competent authorities did have the right to examine such correspondence. The Court, however, pointed out that the Agreement cannot prejudice the Convention rights. It rightly stressed that the 'right to respect for correspondence is of special importance in a prison context where it may be more difficult for a legal adviser to visit his client in person'.

While the Court still followed a rather cautious approach in _Campbell_, its subsequent experience with numerous cases against Turkey, and in particular the intimidation of applicants which led to findings of a violation of the second sentence of Article 25 (now Article 34),[48] have led to a much more radical approach. In _Sałapa_ the Court stated 'that it is of prime importance for the effective exercise of the right of individual petition under the Convention that the correspondence of prisoners with the Court not be subject to any form of control, which might hinder them in bringing their cases to the Court'.[49]

There are different types of interference including opening, scrutinizing, monitoring, inspecting, perusing, or reading the letter, and withholding or delaying it. The mere possibility of inspecting and scrutinizing the letter constitutes an interference[50] because the correspondents may have to adapt their writing accordingly; _a fortiori_ the opening of a letter is enough to constitute an interference. It is not necessary (and will rarely be possible to establish) that the letter has also been read.[51] It is sometimes difficult to see exactly where the Court draws the line between the finding of a violation and no violation. It decided that there had been no violation in a case where a letter was delayed for three weeks[52]—prisoners are expected to be patient and the matter was 'not really urgent'. Another possibility is to censor the document (in French '_caviardage_') by making certain parts illegible.[53]

As to the lawfulness of the interference, the Court found the vague rules for mental patients in Austria quite insufficient. Section 51(1) of the Hospital Law stipulated that patients compulsorily detained 'may be subjected to restrictions with respect to . . . contact with the outside world'. Specifications of the scope and conditions of the exercise of the discretionary power, according to the Court, 'appear all the more necessary in the field of detention in psychiatric institutions in that the persons concerned are frequently at the mercy of the medical authorities, so that their correspondence is their only contact with the outside world'.[54] However, the Court did not specify the elements which ought to be set out in the law. In two cases against Italy, the relevant law was held not to indicate with sufficient precision the 'scope and manner' in which the authorities were to exercise their discretion, such as the length and the reasons for the interference,

---

[48] See e.g. the judgments in _Akdivar and others_ v. _Turkey_ and _Kurt_ v. _Turkey_.
[49] _Sałapa_ v. _Poland_, § 94. [50] _Campbell_ v. _United Kingdom_, § 33. [51] Ibid., § 57.
[52] _Silver and others_ v. _United Kingdom_, § 104.
[53] This was applied in _Pfeifer and Plankl_ v. _Austria_, § 43. [54] _Herczegfalvy_ v. _Austria_, § 91.

as it only identified the category of persons whose correspondence could be censored.[55]

Later on, the case-law became more specific. The law is expected to distinguish between categories of persons with whom correspondence is permitted, to require reasoned decisions setting out why a letter could be intercepted. Moreover, there must be rules on the manner and timeframe for the control and governing of the way in which the prisoner is informed of the interference. Finally, a remedy against the interference must be at the detainee's disposal.[56]

The law must, of course, be followed. In *Matwiejczuk* the Court found that according to the Code of Execution of Criminal Sentences of 1997, letters had to be opened in the presence of the detainee. In this case the Government had not presented any evidence to rebut the applicant's allegation that he had in fact not been present when they had been opened.[57]

The Commission accepted as legitimate the refusal of the authorities to deliver a letter from two German nationals suspected of belonging to a terrorist organization and detained in Zurich, as the letter referred approvingly to a terrorist act.[58]

IV. TECHNICAL SURVEILLANCE

I shall now turn to surveillance through means such as wire-tapping, covert videotaping, the use of listening devices and the like. As we shall see, the main problems involve the lack of an adequate legal basis to regulate such measures.

A. The Scope of Private Life in this Context

Private life is a broad term not susceptible to exhaustive definition. Aspects such as gender identification, name, sexual orientation and sexual life are important elements of the personal sphere protected by Article 8. The Article also protects a right to identity and personal development, and the right to establish and develop relationships with other human beings and the outside world and it may include activities of a professional or business nature. There is, therefore, a zone of interaction of a person with others, even in a public context, which may fall within the scope of 'private life'.[59]

---

[55] *Calogero Dana* v. *Italy*, §§ 32, 33; *Domenichini* v. *Italy*, §§ 32, 33. A similar list was established in *Klass and others* v. *Germany*, § 50 for secret surveillance as a preventive measure of security.

[56] *Sałapa* v. *Poland*, § 97; the need for a remedy is recognized in ECHR, Art. 13. See also *Niedbała* v. *Poland*.

[57] *Matwiejczuk* v. *Poland*, § 101; see also *Mianowski* v. *Poland*, § 66. For another case of clear disregard of the domestic law, see *GK* v. *Poland*, § 110.

[58] *X* v. *Switzerland* Application 7736/76.

[59] *Perry* v. *United Kingdom*, § 36; see also *PG and UH* v. *United Kingdom*, § 56.

The areas protected in the context of criminal proceedings are, in the first place, conversations by any technical means, telephone, radio, communication assisted by a pager,[60] any verbal or other interaction with other people as long as the person does not have reason to expect to be observed or recorded, even outside homes, for example, in a police station, a prison cell or in public.[61] Unless there has been a formal warning, a person may also trust that the telephone line at his office will offer privacy.[62]

B. The Interference

The case-law reveals a surprising variety of types of interference with private life. The classical case involves the interception of a conversation which is then listened to or watched, stored, and then made use of, for example, as evidence in criminal proceedings. However, there is definitely no need for all these elements to be present. For instance, it is no defence for the government that information has not been recorded or used.[63] The bugging of a telephone line will constitute an interference not just with the rights of the person whose line is being tapped, but also with the rights of any other parties to the conversation.[64]

Furthermore, the mere gathering and storing of information that indicates that there has in fact been some communication will constitute an interference, irrespective of the fact that the content has not been monitored. This is called 'metering': each telephone connection is registered and information as to its time, duration, and the number dialled is noted. Such a process can legitimately be carried out for the purpose of billing the subscriber. Yet, there is an interference with the right to respect for private life if the telephone company releases such information to the police without the consent of the subscriber.[65]

The protection goes even further. The nature of electronic surveillance is such that, in order to be effective, it must be undertaken covertly. Who would use his telephone for conversations for criminal purposes if he had been warned in advance that the conversation would be monitored? Secrecy poses particularly difficult problems with regard to control. In *Klass*, the applicants, including a public prosecutor ('*Staatsanwalt*'), did not claim that they were actually the victims of surveillance. However, they asserted that they could not exclude the possibility that they had been under surveillance because there was no way they could find out whether they had been or not. Both the Commission and the Court accepted this argument: 'The Court finds it unacceptable that the assurance of the enjoyment of a right guaranteed by the Convention could be

---

[60] *Taylor-Sabori* v. *United Kingdom.*
[61] *PG and JH* v. *United Kingdom*, § 52; *Allan* v. *United Kingdom*, §§ 34 et seq.
[62] *Halford* v. *United Kingdom*, §§ 42 et seq.; *Kopp* v. *Switzerland.*
[63] *Kopp* v. *Switzerland*, § 53.   [64] *Kruslin* v. *France*, § 26.
[65] *Malone* v. *United Kingdom*, §§ 1, 83, 84; *Valenzuela Contreras* v. *Spain*, § 47; *PG and JH* v. *United Kingdom*, § 42.

thus removed by the simple fact that the person concerned is kept unaware of its violation'.[66] It follows, that an interference can exist directly by virtue of legislation which allows for secret surveillance to be undertaken.

In later decisions, the principle was softened somewhat. The Commission did 'not consider that this case-law can be interpreted so broadly as to encompass every person in the United Kingdom who fears that the security service may have compiled information about them'; it called for 'a reasonable likelihood that the security service has compiled and retained information concerning private life'.[67] This approach was discussed but not followed by the Court. In *Halford* it repeated the conclusions which it had reached in *Malone*: '[T]he existence in England and Wales of laws and practices which permit and establish a system for effecting secret surveillance of communications amounted in itself to an "interference".[68] The test of "reasonable likelihood" was only required because Ms Halford did not complain of the general situation under the laws of England and Wales but of an alleged interference against herself personally which was not in accordance with the domestic law'.[69] In other words, legislation which allows for secret surveillance can amount in itself to an interference with the right to privacy of all persons covered by that legislation simply by virtue of the chilling effect which it will have.[70]

Finally, recordings of a person's voice and appearance may be needed for identification. The applicant in *Perry* was suspected of robbery and despite agreeing to attend an identity parade, he failed to appear. Subsequently he was covertly filmed by the custody-suite camera at a police station. The Court did not distinguish this situation from other forms of interference. It stressed that the normal use of security cameras (for example, in supermarkets, railway stations, entrances to public and other buildings, etc.) which people were aware of, did not constitute an interference with the guarantees of Article 8. Here, however, using the tape for the purposes of identification and showing it at the hearing did constitute an interference.[71]

With some slight hesitations, it seems that the Court also regards the taking of a voice sample as an interference. In one case the applicants were taped when answering formal questions in the presence of police officers, and a permanent record had been made which could then be used for identification purposes.[72]

---

[66] *Klass and others* v. *Germany*, §§ 30–8, 36; see also *Malone* v. *United Kingdom*, § 64; *Halford* v. *United Kingdom*, § 56.

[67] *Hewitt and Harman* v. *United Kingdom* Application 12175/86, § 33 (Report).

[68] *Malone* v. *United Kingdom*, § 64.   [69] *Halford* v. *United Kingdom*, §§ 57, 58.

[70] The HRC even accepted a complaint concerning correspondence although it was not established that letters of or to the applicant had been intercepted or stopped; *Larry James Pinkney* v. *Canada*, at 95, § 34. See also Reed and Murdoch (2001) N 6.18.

[71] *Perry* v. *United Kingdom*, §§ 40 et seq. The Court distinguished this case from a case decided by the Commission, *Lupker* v. *Netherlands* Application 18395/95, unreported, where pictures of the applicant were shown in an album, and the Commission had denied the existence of an interference, in that the pictures had been handed over to the police voluntarily.

[72] *PG and JH* v. *United Kingdom*, § 59.

On the other hand, photographing somebody who is participating in a public event does not constitute an interference, providing that it is not entered into a data-processing system and not stored together with the name of the person.[73] The taking of fingerprints and photographing a suspect constitutes an interference which, however, will normally be justified as being necessary for the prevention of crime.[74] The same must, in my view, apply to the storing of DNA evidence after a trial, at least with regard to serious crimes such as murder or rape. In *Williams* the applicant's DNA had only been stored for nine months which the Commission did not find excessive—the applicant had not established that he was a 'victim'.[75]

Paragraph 2 of Article 8 of the ECHR uses a surprising expression when it formulates the conditions for the exception by referring to an 'interference *by a public authority*'. It is strange because the Convention is generally only binding on the authorities and not directly on individuals. On the other hand, there is no reason to assume that there was any intention to exclude from the Convention the duty of the state to protect individuals against invasions into their private lives by third parties. In fact, the case-law goes rather in the opposite direction. There are many examples of judgments which affirm that the state is under a positive obligation to protect private and family life.[76]

The matter was raised by the French Government in a case where a private individual, Mr Gehrling, informed the police of the applicant's plans to murder another man. A higher-ranking police officer then asked him to call the applicant from his office and organized for the conversation to be recorded. This use of police premises and facilities and the consent of a high-ranking officer was the reason for the Court's conclusion that there had been an interference within the meaning of Article 8 § 2, but it added: 'In any event the recording represented an interference in respect of which the applicant was entitled to the protection of the French legal system'.[77] In *Verliere* the applicant complained of the fact that she had been under the surveillance of private detectives retained by an insurance company. The Court did not address this aspect but declared the application inadmissible because it found that the economic interests of the company overrode those of the applicant.[78] It seems therefore justified to conclude that the reference to a 'public authority' can be regarded as superfluous.[79]

---

[73] *Friedl* v. *Austria* Application 15225/89, report of 19 May 1994, annexed to the judgment of the same case, §§ 49–51.
[74] *X* v. *United Kingdom* Application 5877/72; *X* v. *Austria* Application 8170/78; *Mc Veigh, O'Neill and Evans* v. *United Kingdom* Applications 8022/77, 8025/77, and 8027/77.
[75] *Williams* v. *United Kingdom* Application 19404/92.
[76] See Wildhaber and Breitenmoser (2001) N 52 et seq. with the examples in nn. 11 and 12; Haefliger and Schürmann (1999) 248 et seq.; Frowein and Peukert (1996) Art. 8 N 9 et seq.; Harris, O'Boyle, and Warbrick (1995) 320 et seq.; Nowak (1993) Art. 17 N 6, 7; Ovey and White (2002) 218 et seq.; Reed and Murdoch (2001) N 6.19; Sudre (2003) 370.
[77] *A* v. *France*, § 36.   [78] *Verliere* v. *Switzerland* Application 41953/98.
[79] See also Esser (2002) 149.

C. Special Requirements for the Legal Basis

A surprising feature of the case-law on private life in the area of electronic surveillance is the fact that the respondent government's justification failed in the vast majority of cases because of the lack of an adequate legal basis for the interference.[80] In one case there was a sufficient basis in law but it was not respected.[81]

The most obvious cases are those where the interference is not regulated by any legal rules. This was the case with the surveillance of a house in the United Kingdom in *Chalkley*. The facts of the case were particularly puzzling. The police arrested the applicant under false pretences so as to ensure that he was out of the house and that they were free to install the devices. They compounded their actions by later recalling him to the police station so that they could send someone to his house to change the batteries. In such cases the violation appears flagrant.[82] In another case, the French Government admitted that there had been no legal basis for 'entrapping' a suspect by having an informer call him from a police office and recording the conversation in the hope of obtaining evidence.[83]

The principle of lawfulness as adapted to the surveillance of communications has been summed up by the Court in the following way:

[W]here a power of the executive is exercised in secret the risks of arbitrariness are evident. In the context of secret measures of surveillance or interception by public authorities, the requirement of foreseeability implies that the domestic law must be sufficiently clear in its terms to give citizens an adequate indication as to the circumstances in and conditions on which public authorities are empowered to take any such secret measures... It is essential to have clear, detailed rules on the subject, especially as the technology available for use is constantly becoming more sophisticated...

(iv) The Kruslin and Huvig judgments mention the following minimum safeguards that should be set out in the statute in order to avoid abuses of power: a definition of the categories of people liable to have their telephones tapped by judicial order, the nature of the offences which may give rise to such an order, a limit on the duration of telephone tapping, the procedure for drawing up the summary reports containing intercepted conversations, the precautions to be taken in order to communicate the recordings intact and in their entirety for possible inspection by the judge and by the defence and the circumstances in which recordings may or must be erased or the tapes destroyed, in particular where an accused has been discharged by an investigating judge or acquitted by a court.[84]

---

[80] A violation of ECHR, Art. 8, was found for this reason in e.g. *Malone* v. *United Kingdom; Kruslin* v. *France; Huvig* v. *France; A* v. *France; Halford* v. *United Kingdom; Kopp* v. *Switzerland; Valenzuela Contreras* v. *Spain; Khan* v. *United Kingdom; PG and JH* v. *United Kingdom; Armstrong* v. *United Kingdom; Taylor-Sabori* v. *United Kingdom; Allan* v. *United Kingdom; Lewis* v. *United Kingdom;* and *Chalkley* v. *United Kingdom*.

[81] *Perry* v. *United Kingdom*; the applicant had not been asked for his consent to the video, he had not been informed of the operation, and had not been given an opportunity to view the material.

[82] *Chalkley* v. *United Kingdom*, § 25; this deficiency was first brought to light in the Commission's Report in *Govell* v. *United Kingdom* Application 27237/95. The Court's first case was *Khan* v. *United Kingdom*, § 25; see also *PG and JH* v. *United Kingdom*, § 38; *Armstrong* v. *United Kingdom*, § 20; *Allan* v. *United Kingdom*, § 36; *Lewis* v. *United Kingdom*, § 19.   [83] *A* v. *France*, § 38.

[84] *Valenzuela Contreras* v. *Spain*, § 46 (quotations omitted).

Closer scrutiny reveals that the Court has added a number of additional requirements. Thus, the requirement of 'foreseeability' 'cannot mean that an individual should be enabled to foresee when the authorities are likely to intercept his communications so that he can adapt his conduct accordingly. Nevertheless, the law must be sufficiently clear in its terms to give citizens an adequate indication as to the circumstances in which and the conditions on which public authorities are empowered to resort to this secret and potentially dangerous interference with the right to respect for private life and correspondence'.[85] The requirement is not fulfilled when the law is 'somewhat obscure and open to differing interpretation'.[86]

There are also shortcomings where there seems to be a discrepancy between the theory according to which legal professional privilege is respected and the practice applied in the case at issue. In *Kopp* the telephone lines of the applicant, who was a lawyer, were under surveillance because he was suspected of using them for purposes other than client–attorney communications. The Court, however, criticized the fact that 'the law does not clearly state how, under what conditions and by whom the distinction is to be drawn between matters specifically connected with a lawyer's work under instructions from a party to proceedings and those relating to activity other than that of counsel'.[87]

On the other hand, the Court has been less strict with regard to rules governing the storage or destruction of evidence obtained by way of surveillance—the absence of detailed rules was not considered to create a risk of arbitrariness.[88]

D. The Scope of the Interference

As already indicated, there has not yet been a judgment where the scope of the interference was discussed. It is accepted that the prosecution of offences serves also 'public safety' and 'the prevention of disorder and crime'.[89] There is no reason to criticize this approach.

E. 'Necessary in a Democratic Society'

As in most decided cases the violation of Article 8 of the ECHR was based on the lack of a sufficient legal basis, the Court has had little opportunity to discuss the aspect of 'necessity'. The question becomes obsolete when a violation has already been found.[90]

---

[85] *Malone* v. *United Kingdom*, § 67. See also *Kruslin* v. *France*, § 30; *Huvig* v. *France*, § 29; *Halford* v. *United Kingdom*, § 49; *Kopp* v. *Switzerland*, § 64.
[86] *Malone* v. *United Kingdom*, § 79.   [87] *Kopp* v. *Switzerland*, § 73.
[88] *PG and JH* v. *United Kingdom*, § 47.   [89] See e.g. *Lambert* v. *France*, § 29.
[90] See e.g. *Malone* v. *United Kingdom*, §§ 82, 88; *Kruslin* v. *France*, § 37; *Huvig* v. *France*, § 36; *Kopp* v. *Switzerland*, § 76; *Valenzuela Contreras* v. *Spain*, § 62. In *Halford* v. *United Kingdom* the issue was not even mentioned.

The issue *was*, however, discussed at length in *Klass*[91] and again in *Lambert*.[92] The dominant question was not whether the means had been proportionate to the aim pursued or whether less invasive methods would have been at the disposal of the authorities, but whether there were sufficient safeguards so as to avoid any arbitrariness. In other words, whether there existed 'adequate and effective guarantees against abuse'.[93] As *Klass* turned on the specific facts of the case and was not related to criminal proceedings, I shall concentrate on *Lambert*.

The *Lambert* case involved surveillance. The applicant had complained that his telephone conversations had been tapped over a prolonged period of time. He complained first to the Indictment Division ('*chambre d'accusation*'), a section of the court responsible *inter alia* for determining the legitimacy of any coercive measures which had been enforced; his complaint was admissible but it came to the conclusion that it was not well founded. He then appealed to the Court of Cassation which ruled that the application was inadmissible because Mr Lambert had no *locus standi*. In fact, it was not his telephone line, but that of a third person which had been put under surveillance. The Court observed that this approach could lead to 'a very large number of people' being deprived of a remedy and would 'in practice render the protective machinery largely devoid of substance'.[94]

This is a very typical example of how international human rights work. While on the domestic level and in the application of constitutional law the judiciary tends to approach the issues from their substantive side, balancing the interests at stake or at least controlling whether the balancing was done in a correct or non-arbitrary way, the international court will shy away from putting its own appreciation of the case in place of that of the domestic authorities[95] and, instead, stresses the need for effective mechanisms of control, including effective remedies and appeals.

F. Subsequent Notification

In view of the above, there is an obvious dilemma. As long as the surveillance is conducted covertly, it will be virtually impossible to ensure that there are effective remedies against it. As the person concerned cannot establish the very fact that he or she wants to complain about, any appeal at his or her disposal will hardly be effective. The Court dealt with this issue in *Klass* and came to the conclusion that, as a general rule, any person who is affected by a measure of covert surveillance is entitled to be informed of the measure once it has ceased. However, there must be room for some exceptions. The Court has argued as follows:

The activity or danger against which a particular series of surveillance measures is directed may continue for years, even decades, after the suspension of those measures. Subsequent

---

[91] *Klass and others* v. *Germany*, §§ 50 et seq.   [92] *Lambert* v. *France*, §§ 30 et seq.
[93] *Klass and others* v. *Germany*, § 50.   [94] *Lambert* v. *France*, § 38.
[95] See e.g. *Klass and others* v. *Germany*, § 49. See also *MS and PS* v. *Switzerland* Application 10628/83; *Spillmann* v. *Switzerland* Application 11811/85; *X* v. *Switzerland* Application 13563/88.

notification to each individual affected by a suspended measure might well jeopardise the long-term purpose that originally prompted the surveillance. Furthermore, as the Federal Constitutional Court rightly observed, such notification might serve to reveal the working methods and fields of operation of the intelligence services and even possibly to identify their agents ... in so far as the 'interference' resulting from the contested legislation is in principle justified under Article 8 para. 2 ..., the fact of not informing the individual once surveillance has ceased cannot itself be incompatible with this provision since it is this very fact which ensures the efficacy of the 'interference'.[96]

It must be admitted that from a 'liberal' perspective, this is not very satisfactory. In fact, it is nothing less than a capitulation before certain threats to democracy and the rule of law.

However, the tragic fact is that in order to preserve liberty, it is necessary to tolerate certain restrictions of liberty. The three human-rights instruments examined here take this reality into account when they exclude the use of fundamental rights for the purpose of destroying or curtailing those rights.[97] Here, we are not exactly in the situation envisaged by those Articles, but the basic idea is the same. Unfortunately, there will always be persons who do not adhere to the values which form the basis of human rights. Those people believe in some absolute truth, for example, of a religious or political nature, which they value higher than the life of individual human beings or entire groups of human beings, let alone the classical liberties such as freedom of expression, of opinion, of religion, etc. As they have adopted deviant value systems, it is necessary to suspend certain fundamental rights for the purpose of maintaining a social order in which such rights can find protection. Fortunately, it can be assumed that there will hardly ever be room for the operation of the exception in criminal proceedings.[98] At any rate, fairness of the proceedings may not be abandoned just because an accused appears to be particularly dangerous, for example, when he or she is a suspected terrorist.

On the other hand, this is not to say that the individual remains unprotected. As the Court demonstrated in detail in *Klass*, the legislation at issue must provide for an elaborate system of checks and balances which serve to reduce to a minimum the dangers of misuse.

V. STORAGE OF DATA

In a few cases the Court has had to deal with the allegation that the right to respect for private life had been violated by the storage of personal data

---

[96] *Klass and others* v. *Germany*, § 58.   [97] ICCPR, Art. 5 § 1; ECHR, Art. 17; ACHR, Art. 29(a).

[98] Esser (2002) 156 suggests that the exception was not meant to apply other than to the interference for the protection of state security, as was the case in *Klass and others* v. *Germany*. In my opinion, however, it may also operate in the context of criminal inquiries into organized crime and similar phenomena.

concerning the applicant.[99] This is more a matter of security and policing than of criminal proceedings, but it is so closely related to the latter that a short discussion is justified. Three questions must be answered in this context. Does Article 8 of the ECHR extend to such situations? Is there an interference with the right to privacy? And is the interference justified under paragraph 2?

A. Applicability of the Right to Respect for Private Life

The ability to store data on persons is by no means a new phenomenon, but the development of electronic data processing has made it easy to assemble huge and easily accessible amounts of information which can be connected in a way which permits a rather accurate picture of the person concerned to be obtained. Information about a person which is normally limited to that same person thus becomes open to outsiders, and the person risks appearing as if made of glass, largely transparent. Autonomy, however, an aspect of privacy, calls for self-determination in the area of information. The individual basically ought to be able to decide what information to disclose and to whom.

It is obvious that such an absolute view of personal autonomy has become quite illusionary. Just imagine what conclusions could be drawn about your customs and preferences from the analysis of data held by your credit-card company—they probably know more about us that we do ourselves.[100] The fact that data are stored, does not deprive the individual of all protection. During the second half of the twentieth century a number of legal instruments for data protection were created.[101]

The data-protection movement has also had an influence on the international stage. In 1981 the Council of Europe adopted a Convention for the Protection of Individuals with Regard to the Automatic Processing of Personal Data.[102] The preamble establishes a link to Article 8 of the ECHR when it stresses 'that it is desirable to extend the safeguards for everyone's rights and fundamental freedoms, and in particular the right to the respect for privacy'.[103]

The Court referred to this instrument when it concluded that the storage of personal data concerns the right to respect for private life.[104] The protection is not limited to strictly personal or even intimate matters such as sexual preferences, but also to business and political activities and relations, and even 'public information' 'where it is systematically collected and stored in files held by the authorities'.[105]

---

[99] *Leander* v. *Sweden; Amann* v. *Switzerland; Rotaru* v. *Romania.*
[100] Renucci (2002) N 87, 159, rightly recalls George Orwell's *Nineteen Eighty-Four.* See also Soyer (2000) 9. [101] This issue cannot be addressed in depth here.
[102] CETS 108; the Convention was adopted on 28 Jan. 1981 and came into force on 1 Oct. 1985. [103] The scope is then confirmed in Art. 1.
[104] *Amann* v. *Switzerland,* § 65; see also *Rotaru* v. *Romania,* § 43. In *Leander* v. *Sweden,* § 48, the issue had not been contested.
[105] *Rotaru* v. *Romania,* § 43; see also *AS* v. *Austria* Application 15220/89, report pursuant to the friendly settlement of 15 Oct. 1993.

B. The Interference

The Court distinguishes the issues of applicability of the guarantee and the existence of an interference, but in fact this separation is rather artificial. Information on a person only becomes the object of protection once it is fixed in words or pictures and stored. In other words, the collection and storage as such constitutes an interference with the right to respect for privacy. It is not necessary that the person concerned was ever inconvenienced by the collection of the data or that anyone ever consulted it.[106]

In *Rotaru* the Court introduced a further aspect of 'interference', the fact that there is no possibility for the person concerned to refute entries in databases which contain information about him.[107] This is definitely a serious aspect, but I do not agree that it is an element of 'interference'. Such an interference is already constituted by the mere existence of the database. The refusal of access and/or the possibility to correct errors and comment on doubtful evaluations is an element which ought to be taken into account in connection with the issue of proportionality as an aggravating factor.

C. The Justification of the Interference

In determining whether the interference can be justified, the usual aspects are examined: it must be in accordance with the law, it must pursue a legitimate aim, and it must fulfil the proportionality requirement of being necessary in a democratic society.

1. The Legal Basis

The requirement that there be a sufficient legal basis for this type of interference corresponds to that which applies in the context of wire-tapping. In *Leander* the Court referred expressly to *Malone*.[108] In *Leander*, the storage of the information was held not to constitute a violation of the provision; the applicant, having been classified as a 'security risk', had been excluded from employment as a carpenter at a naval museum. In both *Amann* and *Rotaru* the Court held that the legal regulations governing the storage and use of the information lacked the necessary precision.

In *Amann* the violation was rather obvious—the law only stated that the public prosecutor's office would be allocated money 'to run a uniform investigation and information service'.[109]

In *Rotaru*, however, the Court gave more indication as to what such legislation ought to cover: the law ought to 'define the kind of information that may be recorded, the categories of people against whom surveillance measures such as gathering and keeping information may be taken, the circumstances in which

---

[106] *Amann* v. *Switzerland*, §§ 68–70. [107] *Rotaru* v. *Romania*, § 46.
[108] *Leander* v. *Sweden*, § 50; see also *Rotaru* v. *Romania*, § 55.
[109] Art. 17 of the Swiss Federal Criminal Procedure Act as quoted in *Amann* v. *Switzerland*, § 33; for the discussion, see §§ 72–80.

such measures may be taken or the procedure to be followed [and the] ... limits on the age of information held or the length of time for which it may be kept'. Furthermore, the Court called for 'explicit, detailed provision concerning the persons authorised to consult the files, the nature of the files, the procedure to be followed or the use that may be made of the information thus obtained'.[110] Finally, an effective mechanism of supervision was required.

2. *The Aim of the Interference*

As with the other types of interference within the framework of criminal proceedings, the legitimate aim does not pose any problem—the prevention of disorder and crime will always be held to constitute a legitimate aim.

3. *Necessary in a Democratic Society*

In deciding whether there is a 'pressing social need' for the interference, 'the national authorities enjoy a margin of appreciation, the scope of which will depend not only on the nature of the legitimate aim pursued but also on the particular nature of the interference involved'. In particular, '[t]here can be no doubt as to the necessity, for the purpose of protecting national security, for the Contracting States to have laws granting the competent domestic authorities power ... to collect and store in registers not accessible to the public information on persons'.[111] This discretion is indeed very broad, as matters of security are highly political and the Court is extremely reluctant to say that in a particular case certain measures could not have been regarded as 'necessary'.

However, the Court again finds protection for the individual in safeguards against abuse and therefore insists on procedural guarantees of all kinds. In *Leander* the Government had listed no less than twelve such instances of control. Although the Court found some of them to be irrelevant in the context of the case, it was satisfied that the safeguards were adequate.[112]

The problem is similar to the case of secret surveillance. There is no entirely satisfactory solution, no convincing answer to the question '*quis custodiet custodes?*'. Yet, it is possible to attain an optimal standard which permits adequate security at a reasonable price of interference with the rights of individuals. The political attitude of the observer will in each case lead to the conclusion that the balance was maintained or tipped.

VI. UNDERCOVER AGENTS

In the case-law of the Court, the issue of undercover agents comes up under two different aspects. We have already discussed the issue of entrapment, as an aspect of the fairness of criminal proceedings. In the first case of this kind, however,

---

[110] *Rotaru* v. *Romania*, § 57.   [111] *Leander* v. *Sweden*, § 59.   [112] Ibid., §§ 63–7.

the applicant also claimed that the very fact that he had been approached and closely observed by a policeman disguised as someone interested in drug dealing, constituted an unlawful interference with his right to respect for private life.

The Commission had earlier declared inadmissible an application where it was alleged that the activity of an undercover agent violated the right to respect for private life—it concluded that there had been no interference.[113] In *Lüdi*, it ruled that the facts differed from that first case.[114] The essential distinguishing feature was that here the task of the agent was not to spy on a criminal organization but to approach a single individual, an activity which was combined with the monitoring of telephone conversations.

The Court, following the Government, came to a different conclusion. It assumed, although the facts do not mention this, that the Swiss authorities thought that they were investigating a network of traffickers of drugs. According to information passed to them from the German police, the applicant had asked for a considerable sum of money in order to purchase five kilos of cocaine. Thus the Court rather abruptly concluded: 'Mr Lüdi must therefore have been aware . . . that he was engaged in a criminal act punishable under Article 19 of the Drugs Law and that consequently he was running the risk of encountering an undercover police officer whose task would in fact be to expose him'.[115]

With due respect, the Court's reasoning in this case is far from convincing.[116] Could the very same reasoning not be used with regard to wire-tapping, search, or even arrest? Why should anybody (or even everybody) engaged in criminal activities have forfeited his or her right to privacy? Is there no interference with the right to correspondence if somebody is aware of the risk that it might be intercepted by the authorities?

In my view, the opinion of the Commission is by far the more convincing one. In fact, this also seems to be the view of the Swiss Government which has since, following the German example, introduced legislation on the matter which was adopted by parliament.[117]

VII. SEARCH AND SEIZURE: INTERFERENCE WITH THE HOME

One of the most typical interferences with the fundamental rights of an individual in criminal proceedings involves search and seizure whereby the authorities enter his or her home, in order to search and seize evidence or to find a suspect. The home is primarily the physical sphere in which the individual

---

[113] *B* v. *Germany* Application 10747/84.
[114] *Lüdi* v. *Switzerland*, Report of the Commission, § 56.   [115] *Lüdi* v. *Switzerland*, § 40.
[116] See also the critical view of Esser (2002) 170.
[117] Bundesgesetz über die verdeckte Ermittlung ('Federal Statute on masked investigation') of 20 June 2003, to enter into force on 1 Jan. 2005, BBl 2003 4465; cf. Schmid (2004) N 772.

develops his private life, the place of his family and other relationships. Unauthorized entry is a criminal offence. As the term 'home' is embedded within the broader notion of 'private life', there is no need for a precise limitation. Ironic as it may sound the prison cell is, of course, a 'home'.[118] The Commission did not hesitate, for example, to regard the search of a car as an interference.[119]

As far as criminal procedure is concerned, the case-law is not particularly inspiring.[120] The issues are again whether Article 8 applies and whether the interference is lawful, pursues a legitimate aim, and is proportionate. The element 'necessary in a democratic society' has been discussed more thoroughly here than in the context of the interference with communications.[121]

A. The Interference with the Right to Respect for the 'Home'

A 'home' is primarily the dwelling place of a person. The protection of privacy extends, however, beyond that. The extensive interpretation is justified by a general principle that fundamental rights must not be construed narrowly and with reference to the French word, '*domicile*', which the Court considers to have a broader meaning than the English term. Therefore the Court has rightly applied Article 8 in cases where lawyers' offices were searched.[122]

The reasons given for the extensive interpretation are varied and credible. In the leading case *Niemietz*, it was held that the working place is an important centre of human relations, sometimes individual and professional activities can hardly be distinguished, particularly in the liberal professions, and often professional activity is also exercised 'at home' in the narrow sense of the word.

In *Camenzind* the question arose whether there was an interference when rooms which the applicant had let to other persons were searched. The Court left this question open as it was of no relevance in that case.[123] In my view, the question ought not to be answered *in abstracto*. What must be protected is the space actually used by a person, where this person has a legitimate expectation of not being disturbed by the authorities or other intruders. In general this will mean that rooms and apartments let by the owner or sublet by the tenant are excluded from the protection offered to the 'home' as far as the owner is concerned.

B. The Legal Basis

The Court has confirmed with regard to 'home' the same principles which it has developed in the context of telephone-tapping.[124] The lawfulness of the search

---

[118] *McFeeley and others* v. *United Kingdom* Application 8317/78.

[119] *X* v. *Belgium* Application 5488/72.

[120] One rather peculiar case, *Chappell* v. *United Kingdom*, concerns the search by a private plaintiff pursuant to an *Anton Piller* order.   [121] See also Esser (2002) 116.

[122] *Niemietz* v. *Germany*, §§ 29, 30. See also *Roemen and Schmit* v. *Luxembourg*, § 65; *Elci and others* v. *Turkey*, § 696.   [123] *Camenzind* v. *Switzerland*, § 35.

[124] Ibid., § 37; referring to *Kruslin* v. *France*.

was not seriously contested in any of the cases.[125] This is not surprising, because search and seizure are old, almost archaic elements of criminal investigation. The problems arise where new technical possibilities are used before the law, which is always and rightly some steps behind the technological advances, has developed the necessary safeguards.

C. The Aim of the Interference

Again the aim of the interference has not given rise to much discussion. In the three French cases the aim was not primarily the prevention of disorder and crime but the economic well-being of the country.[126]

D. Necessary in a Democratic Society

The most difficult issue in search and seizure is the proportionality requirement, and here the Court has applied relatively strict standards.

The first case where a violation was found concerned the search of a lawyer's office, a particularly delicate matter, because of the threat to the lawyer's professional duty of confidentiality. Similar difficulties would arise in relation to a search of a doctor's surgery. The lawyer's office is, however, almost a sanctuary in a democracy based on the rule of law: 'where a lawyer is involved, an encroachment on professional secrecy may have repercussions on the proper administration of justice and hence on the rights guaranteed by Article 6 of the Convention'.[127]

Besides this element, the relevant criteria include the seriousness of the offence and the precision with which the warrant is drawn up, particularly important is the identification of the document or other object to be seized. It is preferable to have additional safeguards such as those applied in Luxembourg where the warrant was executed 'in the presence of an investigating judge, a representative of the public prosecutor and the President of the Bar Council. In addition, the President of the Bar Council's presence and the observations he considered it necessary to make on the question of the protection of professional confidence were recorded in the police department's report'.[128] Even in this case, however, there was a violation because the warrant was deemed to have been drafted in too imprecise terms. Furthermore, the search was aimed at finding a journalist's source and thus conflicted with the right to freedom of expression as guaranteed by Article 10.[129]

The third case involving a lawyer's office was characterized by the gross neglect of elementary safeguards. The Turkish police's search of the offices of lawyers close to ERNK—the political wing of the PKK—resembled a raid rather than a lawful intervention.[130]

---

[125] In *Murray v. United Kingdom*, § 88, the Court convincingly rejected the allegation of the applicant that certain aspects of the entry into her home, the temporary confinement of the members of the family in one room, and the questioning, had not been lawful.

[126] *Crémieux v. France*, § 35; *Funke v. France*, § 52; *Miailhe v. France*, 33.

[127] *Niemietz v. Germany*, § 37.   [128] *Roemen and Schmit v. Luxembourg*, § 69.

[129] cf. *Goodwin v. United Kingdom*.   [130] *Elci and others v. Turkey*, §§ 697–9.

Three cases against France all concerned applicants suspected of involvement in financial crimes involving tax evasion and the transfer of capital to foreign countries. Customs officers carried out searches and seized huge amounts of documents, many of which were not needed. The Court recognized that attempts to prevent capital outflows and tax evasion were legitimate and difficult 'owing to the scale and complexity of banking systems and financial channels and to the immense scope for international investment, made all the easier by the relative porousness of national borders'.[131] Therefore the Court accepted that search and seizure could prove indispensable. Again, however, the requisite safeguards against abuse were missing. The Court criticized in particular the fact that the customs authorities enjoyed very wide discretionary powers. The legal rules were 'too lax and full of loopholes' 'in the absence of any requirement of a judicial warrant'.[132] This comes close to requiring a judicial warrant as the basis for the search, but for the time being, one will have to accept Starmer's rather vague formulation: 'Judicial authorisation is a highly relevant factor, but not determinative'.[133] Velu and Ergec are more affirmative—even before the judgment in *Funke* they stated that the need for a '*mandat de perquisition*' was implicit in the guarantee—they do not, however, expressly say that it must be a *judicial* warrant.[134]

In *Camenzind* the applicant had broken the law by using an unauthorized type of cordless telephone. Although he had admitted the offence, the Court nevertheless found the carrying out of a search in order to get hold of the *corpus delicti* to be acceptable. It listed carefully all the safeguards set out in the relevant law and came to the conclusion that the search did not constitute a disproportionate interference with the applicant's right.[135]

There was also found to be no violation in *Murray* where the Court accepted the necessity of the search and the way it was carried out, on the basis of the need to fight against terrorism.[136]

VIII. THE PROTECTION OF PROPERTY

A. The Texts

No corresponding right.

ICCPR

Every natural or legal person is entitled to the peaceful enjoyment of his possessions. No one shall be deprived of his possessions except in the public interest and subject to the conditions provided for by law and by the general principles of international law.

---

[131] *Crémieux* v. *France*, § 39; *Funke* v. *France*, § 56; *Miailhe* v. *France*, 37.
[132] *Crémieux* v. *France*, § 40; *Funke* v. *France*, § 57; *Miailhe* v. *France*, 38.
[133] Starmer (2001) N 15.38.   [134] Velu and Ergec (1990) N 678.
[135] *Camenzind* v. *Switzerland*, §§ 45, 46.   [136] *Murray* v. *United Kingdom*, §§ 92, 93.

The preceding provisions shall not, however, in any way impair the right of a State to enforce such laws as it deems necessary to control the use of property in accordance with the general interest or to secure the payment of taxes or other contributions or penalties.

ECHR, Protocol No. 1, Art. 1

1. Everyone has the right to the use and enjoyment of his property. The law may subordinate such use and enjoyment to the interest of society.

2. No one shall be deprived of his property except upon payment of just compensation, for reasons of public utility or social interest, and in the cases and according to the forms established by law.

3. Usury and any other form of exploitation of man by man shall be prohibited by law.

ACHR, Art. 21

One particularly striking aspect of the right to property is its absence from the text of the Covenant. While it was included in the Universal Declaration,[137] the communist block successfully opposed what was considered to be a capitalist guarantee.[138] As this section will be very brief, there is no need to conduct a comparative discussion of the respective texts.[139]

B. Introduction

The authorities may interfere with the right to property in various respects. It is necessary to make a distinction between interferences of a procedural nature and those imposed as a sanction. The latter can take the form of a fine, or can involve the confiscation either of dangerous objects such as weapons or drugs, or of other assets in order to prevent a convict from benefiting from the proceeds of his or her crime.

Only procedural interferences fall within the scope of the present study.

C. Confiscation

Confiscation occurs when the authorities take possession of things. There are a number of possible reasons for such a course of action such as securing pieces of evidence, preventing dangers inherent in the thing, securing the restitution of stolen goods to the lawful owner, or to prevent a criminal from benefiting from the proceeds of his or her crime. It is always a provisional measure—the ultimate fate of seized goods will be decided either as part of the judgment determining the charge, the decision not to prosecute, or any other final decision.

---

[137] UDHR Art. 17: '1. Everyone has the right to own property alone as well as in association with others. 2. No one shall be arbitrarily deprived of his property'.

[138] On the ideological controversy, see Partsch (1966) 217 et seq.

[139] On Art. 1 of the Protocol, see e.g. Padelletti (2001) 801–27.

Under the Protocol to the Convention seizure or confiscation is regarded as falling under the terms of the second paragraph of Article 1 which refers to the right of the state to 'control the use' of property as it sees fit.[140] As this leaves the determination of whether the intervention is necessary to the states, their discretion is almost unlimited. Still, the Court requires a certain proportionality.

As seizure is a measure imposed to serve the proceedings, it must end when the proceedings themselves end. This will occur, at the latest, with the final decision. Some time is allowed for the organization of the practicalities associated with returning the property, but it may not last for months. Two cases against Italy involved such unjustified delays and the Court, accordingly, found a violation.[141]

The seizure of documents may also fall to be examined under aspects other than property. It will often be difficult to identify any pecuniary value. Where, however, documents, such as medical records, contain sensitive information about a person, their seizure and in particular their disclosure, will raise issues under Article 8.[142]

[140] *Handyside* v. *United Kingdom*, § 62; *Raimondo* v. *Italy*, § 27.
[141] *Raimondo* v. *Italy*, § 36; *Venditelli* v. *Italy*, §§ 39 et seq.   [142] See *Z* v. *Finland*.

Select Bibliography

Abraham, R., 'Article 25', in Pettiti, L., Decaux, E., and Imbert, P. (eds.), *La Convention Européenne des Droits de l'Homme: Commentaire article par article* (Paris: Economica, 1995).

Achermann, A., Caroni, M., and Kälin, W., 'Die Bedeutung des UNO-Paktes über wirtschaftliche, soziale und kulturelle Rechte für das schweizerische Recht', in Kälin, W., Malinverni, G., and Nowak, M. (eds.), *Die Schweiz und die UNO-Menschenrechtspakte/La Suisse et les Pactes des Nations Unies relatifs aux droits de l'homme*, 2nd edn. (Basel: Helbing und Lichtenhahn, 1997).

Ackerman, J.B. and Ebensperger, S., 'Der EMRK-Grundsatz, ne bis in idem'—Identität der Tat oder Identität Strafnorm? *AJP* (1999) 823.

Addo, M.K., 'Are Judges Beyond Criticism under Article 10 of the European Convention on Human Rights?', *ICLQ* 47/2 (1998) 425.

Albrecht, P., 'Die Funktion und Rechtstellung des Verteidigers im Strafverfahren', in Niggli, M., and Weissenberger, P., (eds.), *Strafverteidigung* (Basel: Helbing and Lichtenhahn, 2002).

Alkema, E.A., 'Note', in *Netherlands Jurisprudentie*, 267 (1991) 2630.

Alkema, E.A., 'The 3rd-party Applicability or "Drittwirkung" of the EMRK', in Matscher, F., and Petzold, H. (eds.), *Protecting Human Rights: The European Dimension, Studies in Honour of G.J. Wiarda* (Cologne: C. Heymanns, 1988).

Alkema, E.A., *Studies over europese grondrechten* (Deventer: Kluwer, 1978).

Ambos, K., 'Der Europäische Gerichtshof für Menschenrechte und die Verfahrensrechte', *ZStW*, 115/3 (2003) 583.

Ancel, M., *La défence sociale nouvelle: un mouvement de politique criminelle humaniste*, 3rd edn. (Paris: Cujas, 1981).

Andersen, R., 'L'arrêt Vermeulen et le rôle de l'auditeur au Conseil de l'Etat', in de Fontbressin, P., et al. (eds.), *Les droits de l'homme au seuil du troisième millénaire, Mélanges en hommage à Pierre Lambert* (Brussels: Bruylant, 2000).

Andreu-Guzmàn, F. (ed.), *Terrorism and Human Rights* (Geneva 2002).

Andrews, J.A., *Human Rights in Criminal Procedure: A Comparative Study* (The Hague: Nijhoff, 1982).

Antonopoulos, N., *La jurisprudence des organes de la Convention européenne des droits de l'homme* (Leiden: Sijthoff, 1967).

Arquint, S., 'Anwalt der ersten Stunde? Ein Positionspapier', in Schindler, B., and Schlauri, R. (eds.), *Auf dem Weg zu einem einheitlichen Verfahren* (Zurich: Schulthess, 2001).

Arzt, G., 'Moderner Zeugenbeweis und Verhältnismässigkeitsprinzig', in Donatsch, A., Forster, M., and Schwarzenegger, C. (eds.), *Strafrecht, Strafprozessrecht und Menschenrechte, Festschrift für Stefan Trechsel* (Zurich: Schulthess 2002).

Ashworth, A., 'Case Comment on *Magee* v. *United Kingdom*', *Crim LR* (2000) 681.

Auvret, P., 'Le droit à la présomption d'innocence', *JCP* I (1994) 3892.

Baauw, P., 'Reasonable Time and Successive Proceedings: A Case-study', in Bulterman, M., Hendriks, A., and Smith, J. (eds.), *To Baehr in Our Minds: Essays on Human Rights from the Heart of the Netherlands* (Utrecht: Netherlands Institute of Human Rights, 1998).

Badinter, R., 'La présomption d'innocence, Histoire et modernité', in *Mélanges Catla* (Paris: Litec, 2001).

Baker, L., *Miranda: Crime, Law and Politics* (New York: Antheneum, 1982).

Barreto, I. Cabral, *A Convenção Europeia dos Direitos do Homem*, 2nd edn. (Coimbra: Coimbra Editora, 1999).

Bassiouni, M. C., 'Human Rights in the Administration of Justice: Identifying International Procedural Protection and Equivalent Protections in National Constitutions', *Duke J. Comp. & Int'l L.* 3 (1993) 235.

Beernaert, M.-A., 'Mafia, maltraitance, en prison et repentis', *Rev. trim. dr. h.* 45 (2001) 124.

Bernhardt, R., *Die Auslegung völkerrechtlicher Verträge, insbesondere in der neueren Rechtsprechung internationaler Gerichte* (Cologne: Heymann, 1963).

Bernhardt, R., Trechsel, S., Weitzel, A., and Ermacora, F., 'Report on the Conformity of the Legal Order of the Russian Federation with Council of Europe Standards', *HRLJ* 14 (1994) 249.

Berz, U., 'Möglichkeiten und Grenzen einer Beschleunigung des Strafverfahrens', *NJW* (1982) 729.

Bommer, F., 'Öffentlichkeit der Hauptverhandlung zwischen Individualgrundrecht und rechtsstaatlich-demokratischem Strukturprinzip', in Donatsch, A., Forster, M., and Schwarzenegger, C. (eds.), *Strafrecht, Strafprozessrecht und Menschenrechte: Festschrift für Stefan Trechsel* (Zurich: Schulthess, 2002).

Bonichot, J.-C., 'L'indépendance et l'impartialité des juridictions disciplinaires au regard de la Convention européenne des droits de l'homme: Les conclusions du Commissaire du gouvernement, Conseil d'Etat, 14 janvier 1998', *Les Petites Affiches/La Loi* 387 (91) (1998) 27.

Bribosia, E., and Weyembergh, A. (eds.), *Lutte contre le terrorisme et droits fondamentaux* (Brussels: Bruylant 2002).

Bouissou, A., *Le droit à ne pas s'auto-incriminer en droit européen des droits de l'homme, Mémoire de DEA, Université Robert Schumann—Strasbourg III, Année universitaire 2002–2003* (not yet published).

Buergenthal, Th., 'Vergleich der Rechtsprechung der nationalen Gerichte mit der Rechtsprechung der Konventionsorgane bezüglich der verfahrensrechtlichen Garantien der europäischen Menschenrechtskonvention (Artikel 5, 6 und 13)', in Vasak, K. (ed.), *Menschenrechte im Staatsrecht und im Völkerrecht* (Karlsruhe: C.F. Müller, 1967).

Burgstaller, M., 'Geldwäscherei durch Annahme eines Rechtsanwaltshonorars?', *Anwaltsblatt* (2001) 574.

Butler, A.S., '*Funke v France* and the Right Against Self-Incrimination: A Critical Analysis', *CLF* 11 (2000) 461.

Cahen, N., 'Le droit à la assistance d'un défenseur', *Rev. trim. dr. h.* 7 (1991) 371.

Callewaert, J., 'L'article 3 de la Convention européenne: une norme relativement absolue ou absolument relative?', in *Liber amicorum Marc-André Eissen* (Brussels: Bruylant—L.G.D.J., 1995).

Callewaert, J., 'L'affaire Herczegfalvy ou le traitement psychiatrique à l'épreuve de l'article 3 . . . et vice versa', *Rev. trim. dr. h.* 15 (1993) 433.

Callewaert, J., 'Au-delà des apparences . . . d'un revirement', *Rev. trim. dr. h.* 10 (1992) 204.

Callewaert, J., 'Témoignages anonymes et droits de la défense, Observations sur l'arrêt *Kostovski c. Pays-Bas'*, *Rev. trim. d. h.* 12 (1990) 270.

Cambi, A., 'Le droit à l'examen des moyen de défense', *Rev. trim. dr. h.* 18 (1994) 223.

Cançado Trindade, A., 'The Right to a Fair Trial under the American Convention on Human Rights', in Barnes, A. (ed.), *The Right to a Fair Trial in International and Comparative Perspective* (Hong Kong: Centre for Comparative and Public Law, 1997).

Carlier, J-Y., 'La détention et l'expulsion collective des étrangers', *Rev. trim. dr. h.* 53 (2003) 198.

Caspar, J.D., Tyler, T., and Fisher, B., 'Procedural Justice in Felony Cases', *LSR* 22 (1988) 483.

Caspar, J.D., 'Having their Day in Court: Defendant Evaluation of the Fairness of their Treatment', *LSR* 12 (1978) 237.

Cassin, R., 'Les dimensions internationales de l'attitude de la France devant la Convention', *RDH* 3/4 (1970) 628.

Castberg, F., Ouchterlony, T., and Opsahl, T., *The European Convention on Human Rights* (Leiden: Sijthoff, 1984).

Charrier, J., *Code de la Convention Européenne des Droits de l'Homme*, 2nd edn. (Paris: Litec, 2002).

Chiavario, M., 'Droit aux témoins, droits de la défense et équité du procès', *Recueil Dalloz 1er cahier (rouge)*, 179e année, 9 (2003) 594.

Chiavario, M., 'Art. 6', in Bartole, S., Conforti, B., and Raimondi, G. (eds.), *Commentario alla Convenzione Europea per la tutela dei diritti dell'uomo e delle libertà fondamentali* (Milan: Cedam, 2001).

Chiavario, M., 'La presunzione d'innocenza nella giurisprudenza della Corte europea dei diritti dell'uomo', *Giurisprudenza italiana* (2000) 1089.

Chiavario, M., 'Le procès pénal en Italie', in Delmas-Marty, M. (ed.), *Procès pénal et droits de l'homme* (Paris: Presses universitaires de France, 1992).

Chiavario, M., 'Cultura italiana del processo penale e Convenzione europea dei diritti dell'uomo: Frammenti di appunti e spunti per una "microstoria" ', *RIDU* 3 (1990) 433.

Clements, L., *European Human Rights: Taking a Case under the Convention* (London: Sweet & Maxwell, 1994).

Closset-Marchal, G., 'Le droit à la comparution personnelle, et son applicabilité en cas de pluralité de degrés de juridictions', *Rev. trim. dr. h.* 11 (1992) 394.

Codt, J., de, 'La preuve par témoignage anonyme et les droits de la défense', *Rev. trim. dr. h.* 33 (1998) 57.

Cofee, J. C., 'Corporate Criminal Liability: An Introduction and Comparative Survey', in Eser, A., et al. (eds.), *Criminal Responsibility of Legal and Collective Entities, International Colloquium* Berlin 1998 (Freiburg i. Br.: Edition Iuscrim, 1999).

Cohen-Jonathan, G., *La Convention européenne des droits de l'homme* (Paris: Economica, 1989).

Cohen-Jonathan, G., 'Cour européenne des droits de l'homme: chronique de jurisprudence, 1979', *CDE* 16/4 (1980) 463.

Conso, G., 'Diritti Umani e Procedura Penale', *L'Italia e l'Anno Internazionale dei Diritti dell'Uomo* (Padua: Cedam, 1969).

Cook, A., 'Preventive Detention—International Standards and the Protection of the Individual', in Frankowski, S., and Shelton, D. (eds), *Preventive Detention* (Dordrecht: Martinus Nijhoff, 1992).

Corstens, G., and Pradel, J., *European Criminal Law* (The Hague: Kluwer Law International, 2002).

Costa, J.-P., 'Il diritto ad un giudice indipendente ed imparziale in materia amministrativa: brevi considerazioni', *RIDU* 14 (3) (2001) 709.

Costa, J.-P., *Le juge indépendant et impartial en droit comparé, selon la Cour européenne des droits de l'homme* (Strasbourg: Conseil de l'Europe, 2002).

Council of Europe, *Problems Arising from the Co-existence of the United Nations Covenants on Human Rights and the European Convention on Human Rights*, Doc. H (70) 7 (Strasbourg: Council of Europe, 1970).

Coussirat-Coustère, V., 'Article 8–2', in Pettiti, L., Decaux, E., and Imbert, P. (eds.), *La Convention Européenne des Droits de l'Homme: Commentaire Article par Article* (Paris: Economica, 1995).

Crawshaw, R., and Holmström, L. (eds.), *Essential Texts on Human Rights for the Police: A Compilation of International Instruments* (The Hague: Kluwer Law, 2001).

Dahs, H., *Die Revision im Strafprozess* (Munich: C.H. Beck, 2001).

Danelius, H., *Mänskliga rättigheter i europeisk praxis, En kommentar till Europakonventionen om de mänskliga rättigheterna* (Stockholm: Norstedts Juridik AB, 1997).

Danelius, H., 'L'indipendenza e l'imparzialità della giustizia alla luce della giurisprudenza della Corte europea dei diritti dell'uomo', *RIDU* 5(2) (1992) 443.

Danovi, R., 'Le délai raisonnable de la procédure et le droit au respect des biens, en Italie', *Rev. trim. dr. h.* 23 (1995) 447.

Danovi, R., 'De la responsabilité professionnelle de l'avocat à l'obligation de statuer à "bref délai" sur la légalité d'une détention', *Rev. trim. dr. h.* 2 (1990) 168.

de Figueiredo Dias, J., *Direito processual penal*, vol. 1 (Coimbra: Coimbra Editora, 1974).

de Salvia, M., *Compendium de la CEDH: les principes directeurs de la jurisprudence relative à la Convention européenne des droits de l'homme* (Kehl: Engel, 1998).

de Salvia, M., 'Principes Directeurs d'une Procédure Pénale Européenne: la Contribution des Organes de la Convention Européenne des Droits de l'Homme', *Collected Courses of the Academy of European Law*, vol. V/2 (The Hague: Kluwer Law 1997).

de Salvia, M., and Villiger, M.E. (eds.), *The Birth of European Human Rights Law L'éclosion du droit européen des droits de l'homme: Liber Amicorum: Studies in Honour of mélanges en l'honneur de Carl Aage Nørgaard* (Baden-Baden: Nomos-Verlagsgesellschaft, 1998).

de Schutter, O., 'L'interprétation de la Convention européenne des droits de l'homme: un essai en démolition', *Revue de Droit International de Sciences Diplomatiques et Politiques* (1992) 83.

de Zayas, A., 'The United Nations and the Guarantees of a Fair Trial in the International Covenant on Civil and Political Rights and the Convention Against torture and Other Cruel, Inhuman or Degrading treatment or Punishment', in Weissbrodt, D., and Wolfrum, R. (eds.), *The Right to a Fair Trial* (Berlin: Springer, 1998).

Delmas-Marty, M. (ed.), *Procès pénal et droits de l'homme* (Paris: PUF, 1992).

Delmas-Marty, M., and Vervaele, J.A.E. (eds.), *La mise en oeuvre du corpus juris dans les Etats Membres* (Antwerpen: Intersentia, 2000–1).

Dennis, I., 'Rethinking Double Jeopardy: Justice and Finality in Criminal Process', *Crim LR* (2000) 933.

Dennis, I., 'Instrumental Protection, Human Right or Functional Necessity? Reassessing the Privilege against Self-incrimination', *CLJ* 54(2) (1995) 342.

Dickson, W.G., *Evidence*, 3rd edn. (Edinburgh: T & T Clark, 1887).

Donatsch, A., 'Art. 271 Abs. 1 StGB und das Recht auf Befragung von Entlastungszeugen', in Donatsch, A., Forster, M., and Schwarzenegger, C. (eds.), *Strafrecht, Strafprozessrecht und Menschenrechte, Festschrift für Stefan Trechsel* (Zurich: Schulthess, 2002).

Doswald-Beck, L., and Kolb, R. (eds.), *Judicial Process and Human Rights. United Nations, European, American and African systems. Text and Summaries of International Case-law* (Kehl: N.P. Engel, 2004).

Douraki, T., *La convention européenne des droits de l'homme et le droit à la liberté de certains malades et marginaux* (Paris: Librairie générale de droit et de jurisprudence, 1986).

Dourneau-Josette, P., 'Le cadre juridique: l'article 6 de la Convention', in Vallens, J.-L., and Storck, M. (eds.), *Impartialité et justice économique en Europe* (Strasbourg: Presses universitaires de Strasbourg, 2003).

Driendl, J., 'Verfahrensdauer und Strafprozessform in Österreich aus deutscher Sicht', *Juristische Blätter*, 103/5–6 (1981) 125.

Drzemczewski, A.Z., *European Human Rights Convention in Domestic Law: A Comparative Study* (Oxford: Clarendon Press, 1983).

Duffy, P.J., '*Luedicke, Belkacem and Koç*: A Discussion of the Case and of Certain Questions Raised by It', *HRR* (1979) 98.

Dumont, M., 'Le Conseil d'Etat, tribunal indépendant et impartial', in de Fontbressin, P., et al. (eds.), *Les droits de l'homme au seuil du troisième millénaire. Mélanges en hommage à Pierre Lambert* (Brussels: Bruylant, 2000).

Earley, P., and Schur, G., *Witsec:, Inside the Federal Witness Protection Program* (New York: Bantam Books, 2003).

Egli, P., *Drittwirkung von Grundrechten* (Zurich: Schulthess 2002).

Emmerson, B., 'The Human Rights Act: Its Effect on Criminal Proceedings', in Butler, F. (ed.), *Human Rights for the New Millenium* (The Hague: Kluver, 2000).

Emmerson, B., and Ashworth, A., *Human Rights and Criminal Justice* (London: Sweet & Maxwell, 2001).

Eryilmaz, M.B., *Arrest and Detention Powers in English and Turkish Law and Practice in the Light of the European Convention on Human Rights* (The Hague: Martinus Nijhoff Publishers, 1999).

Esposito, A., 'Protocol No. 7, Art. 3', in Bartole, S., Conforti, B., and Raimondi, G. (eds.), *Commentario alla Convenzione Europea per la tutela dei diritti dell'uomo e delle libertà fondamentali* (Milan: Cedam, 2001).

Esser, R., *Auf dem Weg zu einem europäischen Strafverfahrensrecht: Die Grundlagen im Spiegel der Rechtsprechung des Europäischen Gerichtshofs für Menschenrechte (EGMR) in Strassburg* (Berlin: De Gruyter Recht, 2002).

Fahrenhorst, I., 'Art. 6 EMRK und die Verhandlung gegen Abwesende: zugleich eine Besprechung der Entscheidungen Colozza und Rubinat des EGMR vom 12. 02. 1985', *EuGRZ* 10 (1985) 629.

Farthouat, J.R., 'La présomption d'innocence', *Justices*, 10 (1998).

Fawcett, J.E.S., *The Application of the European Convention on Human Rights*, 1st edn. (Oxford: Oxford University Press, 1969).

Fawcett, J.E.S., *The Application of the European Convention on Human Rights*, 2nd edn. (Oxford: Claredon Press, 1987).

Feteris, M.W.C., *Fiscale administratieve sancties en het recht op een behoorlijk process* (Deventer: Kluwer, 1993).

Field, S., and Young, J., 'Disclosure, Appeals and Procedural Traditions, *Edwards v United Kingdom*', *CrimLR* (1994) 264.

Fitzpatrick, B., 'Tinkering or Transformation? Proposals and Principles in the White Paper, "Justice for All" ', *Web JCLI* 5 (2002).

Fitzpatrick, B., and Walker, C., 'Holding Centres in Northern Ireland, the Independent Commissioner and the Rights of Detainees', *EHRLR* (1999) 27.

Flauss, J.-F., 'Le droit à un recours effectif au secours de la règle du délai raisonnable: un revirement de jurisprudence historique', *Rev. trim. dr. h.* 49 (2002) 179.

Flauss, J.-F., 'La banalisation du contentieux indemnitaire devant la Cour européenne des droits de l'homme', *Rev. trim. dr. h.* 25 (1996) 93.

Flauss, J.-F., 'Convention européenne des droits de l'homme et exécution des condamnations pénales prononcées à l'étranger', *Rev. trim. dr. h.* 17 (1994) 98.

Fleiner-Gerster, T., 'Verpflichten die Grundrechte den Staat zu positiven Leistungen?', in Aubert, J., and Bois, P. (eds.), *Mélanges André Grisel* (Neuchâtel: Editions Ides et Calendes, 1983).

Fletcher, G., *Re-Thinking Criminal Law* (New York: Oxford University Press, 2000).

Fontbressin, P. de, 'Liberté d'expression, vie privée et impartialité du juge', *Rev. trim. dr. h.* 35 (1998) 581.

Fornito, R., *Beweisverbote im schweizerischen Strafprozessrecht* (St Gallen: University of St Gallen, 2000).

Framer, I., 'Interpreters and their Impact on the Criminal Justice Systems: The Alejandro Ramírez Case', *Newsletter of the National Association of Judiciary Interpreters and Translators*, 9 (2000).

Frei-Siponen, S., *Einfluss der EMRK auf das Strafprozessrecht Finnlands und der Schweiz— eine vergleichende Studie* (Bamberg: Difo-Druck GmbH 2003).

Fribergh, E., 'La décision', in Cour de Cassation (ed.), *Les principes communs d'une justice des Etats de l'Union Européenne, Actes du Colloque des 4 et 5 décembre 2000* (Paris: La documentation Française, 2001) 187.

Friedmann, R.D., 'Confrontation and the Definition of Chutzpah', *IsLR*, 31/1–3 (1997) 506.

Frowein, J.A., 'Conclusions', in Cour de Cassation (ed.), *Les principes communs d'une justice des Etats de l'Union Européenne, Actes du Colloque des 4 et 5 décembre 2000* (Paris: La documentation Française 2001) 215.

Frowein, J.A., 'Die Europäische und die Amerikanische Menschenrechtskonvention— Ein Vergleich', *EuGRZ* 7 (1980) 442.

Frowein, J.A., and Peukert, W., *Europäische MenschenRechtsKonvention: EMRK Kommentar*, 2nd edn. (Kehl: Engel, 1996).

Fyfe, N.R., *Protecting Intimidated Witnesses* (Aldershot: Ashgate, 2001).

Gaede, K., 'Das Recht auf Verfahrensbeschleunigung gemäss Art. 6 I 1 EMRK in Steuer- und Wirtschaftsstrafverfahren', *wistra* 23 (2004) 166.

Geppert, K., *Der Grundsatz der Unmittelbarkeit im deutschen Strafverfahren* (Berlin: Walter de Gruyter, 1979).

Gilliadin, J., 'Une étape nouvelle dans la protection des droits fondamentaux des aliénés', *Rev. trim. dr. h.* 4 (1990) 407.

Gollwitzer, W., 'Europäische Menschenrechtskonvention, Internationaler Pakt über bürgerliche und politische Rechte', in Rieß, P. (ed.), *Löwe-Rosenberg StPO, Grosskommentar*, 24th edn. (Berlin: de Gruyter, 1992).

Golsong, H., *La Convention Européenne des Droits de l'Homme et les Personnes morales*, in *Premier colloque du département des droits de l'homme* (Brussels: Université Catholique de Louvain, 1970).

Gomien, D., 'The Future of Fair Trial in Europe: The Contribution of International Human Rights Legal and Political Instruments' (1991) *NQHR* 9 263.

Gomien, D., Harris, D., and Zwaak, L., *Convention européenne des Droits de l'Homme et Charte sociale européenne* (Strasbourg: Council of Europe, 1997).

Gonzales, G., 'Chaud et froid sur la compatibilité du cumul des fonctions consultatives et contentieuses avec l'exigence d'impartialité (en marge de l'arrêt Cour eur. dr. h., Gde ch., 6 mai 2003, Kleyn c. les Pays-Bas)', *Rev. trim. dr. h.* 18 (2004) 365.

Grabenwarter, C., *Europäische Menschenrechtskonvention: ein Studienbuch* (Munich: Beck, 2003).

Grabenwarter, C., *Verfahrensgarantien in der Verwaltungsgerichtsbarkeit: eine Studie zu Artikel 6 EMRK auf der Grundlage einer rechtsvergleichenden Untersuchung der Verwaltungsgerichtsbarkeit Frankreichs, Deutschlands und Österreichs* (Vienna: Springer, 1997).

Grigori, G., *La tutela europea dei diritti dell'uomo* (Milan: Suger Co, 1979).

Grote, R., 'Protection of Individuals in Pre-Trial Procedure', in Weissbrodt, D., and Wolfrum, R. (eds.), *The Right to a Fair Trial* (Berlin: Springer, 1998).

Guerrin, M., 'Le témoignage anonyme au regard de la jurisprudence de la Cour européenne des droits de l'homme', *Rev. trim. dr. h.* 16 (2002) 45.

Haefliger, A., and Schürmann, F., *Die Europäische Menschenrechtskonvention und die Schweiz: Die Bedeutung der Konvention für die schweizerische Rechtspraxis* (Bern: Stämpfli & Cie AG, 1999).

Hamm, R., 'Wie man in richterlicher Unabhängigkeit vor unklaren Gesetzeslagen kapituliert', *NJW* (2001) 1694.

Harris, D., 'The Right to a Fair Trial in Criminal Proceedings as a Human Right', 16 *ICLQ* (1964) 352.

Harris, D., O'Boyle, M., and Warbrick, C., *Law of the European Convention on Human Rights* (London: Butterworths, 1995).

Hartmann, A.R., and van Russen Groen, P.M., ''Criminal charge' uitgekleed: Bendenoun gerelativeerd', *NJB* 69 (1994) 1520.

Hauser, R., *Der Zeugenbeweis im Strafprozess mit Berücksichtigung des Zivilprozesses* (Zurich: Schulthess, 1974).

Hauser, R., and Schweri, E., *Schweizerisches Strafprozessrecht*, 5th edn. (Basel: Helbing und Lichtenhahn, 2002).

Heine, G., 'Sanctions in the Field of Corporate Criminal Liability', paper presented at the International Colloquium on Criminal Responsibility of Legal and Collective Entities, 4–6 May 1998, Berlin, Germany.

Heine, G., Ronzani, M., and Spaniol, M., 'Verteidiger und Strafverfahren: eine rechtsvergleichende Skizze zu Funktion und Stellung des Strafverteidigers in den Bundesrepubliken Deutschland und Österreich sowie der Schweiz', *Strafverteidiger* (1987) 74.

Heinz, A.M., 'Procedure versus Consequences: Experimental Evidence of Preferences for Procedural and Distributive Justice', in Talarico, S. (ed.), *Courts and Criminal Justice* (Beverly Hills: Sage, 1985).

Helmholz, H.R., Gray, Ch. M., Langbein, J.H., Moglen, E., Smitz, H.E., and Alschuler, A.W., *The Privilege against Self-Incrimination: Its Origins and Development* (Chicago: University of Chicago Press, 1997).

Herzog, F., 'Wider den "kurzen Prozess": Plädoyer für die Abschaffung des beschleunigten Verfahrens nach 212, 212a, 212b StPO', *ZRP* (1991) 125.

Holdgaard, M., 'The Right to Cross-Examine Witnesses: Case Law under the European Convention on Human Rights', *NJIL* (2003) 83.

Hume, D., *Commentaries on the Law of Scotland Respecting Crimes*, vol. II, 4th edn. (Edinburgh: Bell and Bradfute, 1844).

Jacobs, F.G., 'The Right to a Fair Trial in European Law', *EHRLR* (1999) 141.

Jacobs, F.G., *The European Convention on Human Rights* (Oxford: Clarendon Press, 1975).

Jacot-Guillarmod, O., 'Rights Related to Good Administration of Justice', in Macdonald, R. St. J., Matscher, F., and Petzold, H. (eds.), *The European System for the Protection of Human Rights* (Dordrecht: Martinus Nijhoff, 1993).

James, A., Taylor, N., and Walker, C., 'The Reform of Double Jeopardy', *Web JCLI*, 5 (2000).

Jennings, A., 'Fair Trial', in Starmer, K., Strange, M., and Whitaker, Q. (eds.), *Criminal Justice, Police Powers and Human Rights* (London: Blackstone, 2001).

Joseph, S., Schultz, J., and Castan, M., *The International Covenant on Civil and Political Rights: Cases, Materials, and Commentary* (Oxford: Oxford University Press, 2000).

Kaiser, G., *Kriminologie*, 3rd edn. (Heidelberg: CF Müller Verlag, 1996).

Kälin, W., Malinverni, G., and Nowak, M., *La Suisse et les Pactes des Nations Unies relatifs aux droits de l'homme*, 2nd edn. (Basel: Helbing & Lichtenhahn, 1997).

Kastanas, E., *Unité et diversité: Notions autonomes et marge d'appréciation des Etats dans la jurisprudence de la Cour européenne des droits de l'homme* (Brussels: Bruylant, 1996).

Kempf, E., 'Anmerkung zu den Urteilen Lietzow, Schöps und Garcia Alva', *Strafverteidiger* 21 (2001) 207.

Khol, A., 'Implications de l'article 5 de la Convention européenne des droits de l'homme en procedure pénale', *JT* 108 (1989) 468.

Kiener, R., *Richterliche Unabhängigkeit, Verfassungsrechtliche Anforderungen an Richter und Gerichte* (Bern: Stämpfli, 2001).

Killias, M., *Grundriss der Kriminologie* (Bern: Stämpfli & Cie AG, 2002).

Killias, M., *Précis de droit pénal général*, 2nd edn. (Bern: Stämpfli & Cie AG, 2001).

Kinzig, J., 'Als Bundesrecht gescheitert—als Landesrecht zulässig?', *NJW* (2001) 1455.

Klees, O., 'De l'obligation de témoigner au droit au silence (Observations sur l'arrêt K. c. Autriche)', *Rev. trim. dr. h.* 8 (1994) 243.

Kley, A., 'Zeugenschutz im internationalen Recht—Erfahrungen im Hinblick auf das künftige eidgenössische Strafprozessrecht', *AJP* (2000) 177.

Kley-Struller, A., 'Der Anspruch auf unentgeltliche Rechtspflege: die aktuelle Rechtsprechung des Bundesgerichts zu Art. 4 Abs. 1 BV und der Organe der Europäischen Menschenrechtskonvention zu Art. 6 EMRK', *AJP* (1995) 179.

Koering-Joulin, R., 'Le juge impartial', *RGDP*, 10 (1998) 1.

Koering-Joulin, R., '(Protocole additionnel No 7) Article 4', in Pettiti, L., Decaux, E., and Imbert, P., *La Convention Européenne des Droits de l'Homme: Commentaire article par article* (Paris: Economica, 1995).

Koering-Joulin, R., '(Protocole additionnel No 7) Article 3', in Pettiti, L., Decaux, E., and Imbert, P.-H., *La Convention Européenne des Droits de l'Homme: Commentaire article par article* (Paris: Economica, 1995).

Kohlbacher, U., *Verteidigung und Verteidigungsrechte unter dem Aspekt der Waffengleichheit* (Zurich: Zurich Diss., 1978).

Koschwitz, J., *Die kurzfristige polizeiliche Freiheitsentziehung* (Berlin: Duncker and Humblot, 1970).

Kramer, B., *Die europäische Menschenrechtskonvention und die angemessene Dauer von Strafverfahren und Untersuchungshaft* (Diss. Recht Tübingen, 1973).

Krauss, D., 'Die Unmittelbarkeit der Hauptverhandlung im schweizerischen Strafverfahren', *recht*, 5 (1987) 42.

Krauss, D., 'Der Umfang der Strafakte', *BJM* (1983) 49.

Krüger, H.C., 'Die Auswahl der Richter für den neuen Europäischen Gerichtshof für Menschenrechte', *EuGRZ* 24 (1997) 397.

Kühl, K., 'Der Einfluss der EMRK auf das Strafrecht und das Strafverfahrensrecht in der BRD', *ZStW* (1988) 406.

Kühl, K., 'Unschuldsvermutung, Freispruch und Einstellung' (Köln: Carl Heymanns Verlag KG, 1983).

Kühne, H.H., and Esser, R., 'Die Rechtsprechung des Europäischen Gerichtshofs für Menschenrechte (EGMR) zur Untersuchungshaft', *Strafverteidiger* (2002) 383.

Kuijer, M., *The Blindfold of Lady Justice: Judicial Independence and Impartiality in Light of the Requirements of Article 6 ECHR* (Leiden: University of Leiden, 2004).

Küng-Hofer, R., *Die Beschleunigung des Strafverfahrens unter Wahrung der Rechtsstaatlichkeit* (Bern: Diss. Jur., 1984).

Kunz, K.-L., *Kriminologie*, 3rd edn. (Bern: Verlag Paul Haupt, 2001).

Kuty, F., 'Observations: L'obligation de motivation des décisions judiciaires au regard de la jurisprudence de la Cour européenne des droits de l'homme', *Rev. trim. dr. h.* 36 (1998) 843.

Labayle, H., 'L'éloignement des étrangers', *RUDH* 3 (1991) 296.

Lambert, P., 'Vers la restitution au juge de son rôle d'arbitre', *Rev. trim. dr. h.* 28 (1996) 621.

Lambert, P., 'Perquisition au cabinet d'un avocat et droit au respect de la vie privée, de la correspondance et du domicile', *Rev. trim. dr. h.* 15 (1993) 470.

Landis, J.M., and Goodstein, L.,'When is Justice Fair? An Integrated Approach to the Outcome versus Procedure Debate', *Am. Bar Found. Res. J.* (1986) 675.

Larralde, J.-M., 'La Cour européenne des droits de l'homme face aux traitements contraires à l'intégrité physique et morale des individus', *Rev. trim. dr. h.* 38 (1999) 283.

Leach, P., 'Automatic Denial of Bail and the European Convention', *Crim LR* (1999) 300.

Levi, R., 'Zum Einfluss der Europäischen Menschenrechtskonvention auf das kantonale Prozessrecht: Erwartungen und Ergebnisse', *ZStrR* 106 (1989) 225.

Linke, R., 'The Influence of the European Convention of Human Rights on National European Criminal Proceedings', *DePaul L.R.* XXI (1971) 397.

Liszt von, F., 'Die Zukunft des Strafrechts', in *Strafrechtliche Aufsätze und Vorträge*, vol. 2 (Berlin: J. Guttentag, 1905).

Lombardini, C., and Cambi, A., 'Le droit du détenu de communiquer librement avec son conseil' (1993) 14 *Rev. trim. dr. h.* 14 (1993) 297.

Lombois, Cl., 'La présomption d'innocence', *Pouvoirs*, 55 (1950) 81.

Loucaides, L., 'Questions of Fair Trial Under the European Convention of Human Rights', *HRLR* 3 (2003) 27.

Luhmann, N., *Legitimation durch Verfahren* (Darmstadt: Luchterhand, 1975).

Malinverni, G., 'Variations sur un thème encore méconnu: l'article 13 de la Convention européenne des droits de l'homme', *Rev. trim. dr. h.* 35 (1998) 647.

Mann, F.A., 'Reflections on the Prosecution of Persons Abducted in Breach of International Law', in Dinstein, Y. (ed.), *International Law at a Time of Perplexity* (Doordrecht: Nijhoff, 1989).

Marauhn, T., 'The Right of the Accused to be Tried in his or her Presence', in Weissbrodt, D., and Wolfrum, R. (eds.), *The Right to a Fair Trial* (Berlin: Springer, 1998).

Marcus-Helmons, S., 'La durée de la détention provisoire et la nécessité d'une procédure contradictoire lors des demandes d'élargissement', *Rev. trim. dr. h.* 16 (1993) 544.

Marguénaud, J.-P., 'Le droit de se défendre soi-même contre les conclusions du parquet de cassation', *Rev. trim. dr. h.* 47 (2001) 829.

Martens, P., 'La tyrannie de l'apparence. Observations. Cour européenne des droits de l'homme. Affait Bulut c. l'Autriche, 22.2.1996', *Rev. trim. dr. h.* 28 (1996) 627.

Massias, F., 'Peine perpétuelle obligatoire et maintien de la détention', *Rev. trim. dr. h.* 55 (2003) 945.

Massias, F., 'Les seuils d'âge de la responsabilité pénale et la peine', *Rev. trim. dr. h.* 49 (2001) 129.

Massias, F., 'L'atteinte au bon ordre de procédures judiciaires', *Rev. trim. dr. h.* 31 (1997) 503.

Matsopoulou, H., 'La présence du rapporteur du conseil de la concurrence au délibéré, au regard de la Convention européenne des droits de l'homme', *Les Petites Affiches. La loi*. 385/114 (1996) 4.

McBarnet, D., *Conviction: Law, the State and the Construction of Justice* (Oxford: Macmillan 1981).

McBride, J., 'The Continuing Refinement of Criminal Due Process', *ELRevHR* (1977) 1.

McConville, M., Sanders, A., and Leng, R., *The Case for the Prosecution: Police Suspects and the Construction of Criminality* (London: Routledge, 1991).

McGoldrick, D., *The Human Rights Committee, Its Role in the Development of the International Covenant on Civil and Political Rights* (Oxford: Oxford University Press, 1994).

Melchior, M., 'Le procès équitable dans la jurisprudence de la Cour et de la Commission européennes des droits de l'homme', in *Les droits de la défense en matière pénale, Actes du colloque des 30 et 31 mai et 1ᵉʳ juin 1985* (Liège, 1985).

Mella, E., 'Les validations législatives au regard du droit à un procès équitable', *Rev. trim. dr. h.* 44 (2000) 796.

Merrills, J., and Robertson, A., *Human Rights in Europe: A Study of the European Convention on Human Rights*, 4th edn. (Manchester: Manchester University Press, 2001).

Merryman, J.H., *The Civil Law Tradition*, 2nd edn. (Stanford: Stanford University Press, 1985).

Meyer-Ladewig, J., *EMRK—Handkommentar* (Baden-Baden: Nomos 2003).

Mock, H., 'Une clarification bienvenue de la portée du principe "Ne bis in idem" au sens de l'article 4 du Protocole no. 7' (1999) 39 *Rev. trim. dr. h.* 39 (1999) 623.

Moglen, E., 'Taking the Fifth: Reconsidering the Origins of the Constitutional Privilege against Self-incrimination', *Mich. L.R.* 92 (1994) 1086.

Mole, N., and Harby, C., *A Guide to the Implementation of Article 6 of the European Convention on Human Rights* (Strasbourg: Council of Europe, 2001).

Morrisson, C., *The Developing European Law of Human Rights* (Leiden: Sijthoff, 1967).

Müller, E., 'Der Grundsatz der Waffengleichheit im Strafverfahren', *NJW* (1976) 1063.

Müller, J.P., 'Die Garantie des verfassungsmässigen Richters in der Bundesverfassung', *ZBJV* 106 (1970) 249.

Murdoch, J., 'A Survey of Recent Case Law under Article 5 ECHR', *ELRevHR* 23 (1998) 31.

Murdoch, J., 'Safeguarding the Liberty of Person: Recent Strasbourg Jurisprudence', *ICLQ* 42 (1993) 494.

Myjer, E., 'Equality of arms in het Nederlandse strafproces', *Delikt en Delinkwent*, 6/1 (1976) 17.

Myjer, E., Hancock, B., and Cowdery, N. (eds.), *Human Rights Manual for Prosecutors* (The Hague: International Association of Prosecutors, 2003).

Naismith, S.H., 'Self-Incrimination: Fairness or Freedom?' *EHRLR* (1997) 229.

Nançoz, M.-A., 'La durée du procès pénal', *Rev. dr. pénal crim.* 100/4 (1983) 384.

Nijboer, J.F., and Sprangers, W.I.J.M. (eds.), *Harmonisation in Forensic Expertise: An Inquiry into the Desirability and Opportunities for International Standards* (Amsterdam: Thela Thesis, 2000).

Nowak, M., *U.N. Covenant on Civil and Political Rights: CCPR Commentary* (Kehl: N.P. Engel, 1993).

Nowak, M., 'Überprüfung der Schubhaft durch die unabhängigen Verwaltungssenate', *ZfV* 4 (1991) 288.

Nowak, M., 'Neuere Entwicklungen im Menschenrechtsschutz des Europarats', *EuGRZ* (1985) 240.

O'Boyle, M., 'Freedom from Self-incrimination and the Right to Silence: A Pandora's Box?', in Mahoney, P., Matscher, F., Petzold, H., and Wildhaber, L. (eds.), *Protecting Human Rights: The European Perspective, Studies in Memory of Rolv Ryssdal* (Cologne: Carl Heymanns Verlag, 2000).

Omerod, D., 'ECHR and the Exclusion of Evidence: Trial Remedies for Article 8 Breaches', *Crim LR* (2003) 61.

O'Neill, A., 'The European Convention and the Independence of the Judiciary: The Scottish Experience', *MLR* 63 (2000) 429.

Osborne, C., 'Hearsay and the European Court of Human Rights', *Crim LR* (1993) 265.

Ost, F., 'Originalité des méthodes d'interprétation de la Cour européenne des droits de l'homme', in Delmas-Marty, M. (ed.), *Raisonner la raison d'état* (Paris: Presses Universitaires de France, 1989).

Ovey, C., and White, R., *Jacobs & White: The European Convention on Human Rights*, 3rd edn. (Oxford: Oxford University Press, 2002).

Owen, T., 'Disclosure', in Starmer, K., Strange, M., and Whitaker, Q. (eds.), *Criminal Justice, Police Powers and Human Rights* (London: Blackstone, 2001).

Packer, H., *The Limits of the Criminal Sanction* (Stanford, Calif.: Stanford University Press, 1968).

Padelletti, M.L., 'Art. 1, Prot. 1', in Bartole, S., Conforti, B., and Raimondi, G., *Commentario alla Convenzione Europea per la tutela dei diritti dell'uomo e delle libertà fondamentali* (Milan: Cedam, 2001).

Papaux, A., 'La jurisprudence de la Cour européenne des droits de l'homme et du Tribunal fédéral en matière de témoignage anonyme', *SJZ* 89 (1993) 274.

Papier, H.-J., Die richterliche Unabhängigkeit und ihre Schranken', *Neue Juristische Wochenschrift*, 54/15 (2001) 1089–94.

Partsch, K.J., *Hoffen auf Menschenrechte: Rückbesinnung auf eine internationale Entwicklung* (Zurich: Ed. Interform, 1994).

Partsch, K.J., *Die Rechte und Freiheiten der europäischen Menschenrechtskonvention* (Berlin: Duncker und Humblot, 1966).

Peters, A., *Einführung in die Europäische Menschenrechtskonvention* (Munich: Verlag C.H. Beck, 2003).

Pettiti, L.-E., 'L'évolution de la défense et des droits de la défense à partir de la Déclaration universelle des droits de l'homme', *Rev. trim. dr. h.* (2000) 5.

Pettiti, L.-E., 'Les droits de l'inculpé et de la défense selon la jurisprudence de la Cour européenne des droits de l'homme', in Carbonnier, J. (ed.), *Mélanges Georges Levasseur* (Paris: Litec, 1992).

Peukert, W., 'Die Garantie des "fair trial" in der Strassburger Rechtsprechung', *EuGRZ* (1980) 267.

Picard, E., 'Art. 26', in Pettiti, L., Decaux, E., and Imbert, P. (eds.), *La Convention européeenne des droits de l'homme: commentaire article par article* (Paris: Economica, 1995).

Picard, M., and Titiun, P., 'Article 5-3', in Pettiti, L., Decaux, E., and Imbert, P. (eds.), *La Convention Européenne des Droits de l'Homme: Commentaire article par article* (Paris: Economica, 1995).

Pieth, M., *Strafverteidigung—wozu?* (Basel: Helbing und Lichtenhahn, 1986).

Pieth, M., *Der Beweisantrag des Beschuldigten im Schweizer Strafprozessrecht* (Basel: Helbing und Lichtenhahn, 1984).

Pieth, M., 'Anmerkung', *EuGRZ* 7 (1980) 210.

Piquerez, G., *Procédure pénale suisse: Traité théorique et pratique* (Zurich: Schulthess, 2000).

Pisani, M., 'Art 5', in Bartole, S., Conforti, B., and Raimondi, G., *Commentario alla Convenzione Europea per la tutela dei diritti dell'uomo e delle libertà fondamentali* (Milan: Cedam, 2001).

Poncet, D., 'Un arbitre indépendant et impartial aux termes de l'article 6, 1 de la Convention européenne des droits de l'homme: un point de vue de la Suisse', in de Fontbressin, P. et al. (eds.), *Les droits de l'homme au seuil du troisième millénaire, Mélanges en hommage à Pierre Lambert* (Brussels: Bruylant, 2000).

Poncet, D., *La protection de l'accusé par la Convention européenne des droits de l'homme* (Geneva: Georg, 1977).

Poncet, D., 'Le droit à l'assistance de l'avocat durant la procédure', in Bridel, M., and Clerc, F. (eds.), *Recueil des travaux suisses présentés au VIIIe Congrès international de droit comparé* (Basel: Helbing und Lichtenhahn 1970).

Pouget, P., 'Les délais en matière de rétention, garde à vue et détention provisoire au regard de la Convention européenne de sauvegarde des droits de 1'homme', *Rev. Sc. Crim.* 1 (1989) 78.

Pradel, J., *Droit pénal comparé*, 2nd edn. (Paris: Dalloz, 2002).

Pradel, J., 'Criminal Liability of Legal Persons in Legislation of European Countries', *Juridica*, VIII (1999) 370.

Pradel, J., 'La notion de procès équitable en droit pénal européen', *RGD* (1996) 505.

Pradel, J., and Corstens, G., *Droit pénal européen* (Paris: Dalloz, 2000).

Préfontaine, D. C., 'Effective Criminal Sanctions Against Corporate Entities— Commentary: Canada', paper presented at the International Colloquium on Criminal Responsibility of Legal and Collective Entities, 4–6 May 1998 Berlin, Germany.

Priebe, R., 'Die Dauer von Gerichtsverfahren im Lichte der EMRK und des Grundgesetzes', in Schwarze, J., and Graf, W. (eds.), *Grundrechtsschutz im nationalen und internationalen Recht* (Baden-Baden: Nomos-Verlag, 1983).

Quigley, J., 'Criminal Law and Human Rights: Implications of the United States Ratification of the International Covenant on Civil and Political Rights', *Harv. Hum. Rts. J.* 6 (1993) 58.

Quillere-Majzoub, F., *La défense du droit à un procès équitable* (Brussels: Bruylant, 1999).

Ravaud, C., 'Article 36', in Pettiti, L., Decaux, E., and Imbert, P., *La Convention Européenne des Droits de l'Homme: Commentaire article par article* (Paris: Economica, 1995).

Raymond, J., 'L'article 6 de la Convention européenne des droits de l'homme et la loi pénale nationale', in *Droit pénal européen* (Brussels: Presses universitaires de Bruxelles, 1970) 81.

Reed, R., and Murdoch, J., *A Guide to Human Rights Law in Scotland* (Edinburgh: Butterworths, 2001).

Reid, K., *A Practitioner's Guide to the European Convention of Human Rights* (London: Sweet & Maxwell, 1998).

Reindl, S., 'Probleme der Untersuchungshaft in der jüngeren Rechtsprechung der Strassburger Organe', in Grabenwarter, C., and Thienel, R. (eds.), *Kontinuität und Wandel der EMRK: Studien zur Europäischen Menschenrechtskonvention* (Kehl: N.P. Engel Verlag, 1998).

Renucci, J., *Droit Européen des Droits de l'Homme*, 3rd edn. (Paris: Librairie Générale de Droit et de Jurisprudence, 2002).

Robert, C.N., *La détention préventive en Suisse Romande et notamment à Genève* (Geneva: Georg-Librairie de l'Université, 1972).

Roberts, P., 'Double Jeopardy Law Reform: A Criminal Justice Commentary', *MLR* 65/ 3 (2002) 393.

Rodley, N., *The Treatment of Prisoners under International Law*, 2nd edn. (Oxford: Clarendon Press, 1999).

Rogall, K., *Der Beschuldigte als Beweismittel gegen sich selbst* (Berlin: Duncker und Humblot 1977).

Roggen, F., 'L'application de l'article 421 du code d'instruction criminelle (belge) face à l'arrêt *Poitrimol*', *Rev. trim. dr. h.* 24 (1995) 623.

Rosenberg, D., 'L'arrêt Assenov: un premier pas vers une reconnaissance juridictionnelle des droits des Tsiganes en Europe?', *Rev. trim. dr. h.* 38 (1999) 388.

Rosenmayr, S., 'Das Recht auf persönliche Freiheit und Freizügigkeit bei der Einreise von Ausländern', *EuGRZ* 15 (1988) 153.

Rothenfluh, W., 'Die Dauer des Strafprozesses', *ZStrR* 100 (1983) 366.

Rouiller, C., 'L'effet dynamique de la Convention européenne des droits de l'homme. Réflexions éparses sur le jugement par défaut, la défense d'office et le droit à un interprète', *ZStrR* 116 (1998) 233.

Roxin, C., *Strafverfahrensrecht*, 25th edn. (Munich: Beck, 1998).

Rudloff, S., *Droits et libertés de l'avocat dans la Convention européenne des droits de l'homme* (Brussels: Bruylant, 1995).

Russo, C., 'Article 8-1', in Pettiti, L., Decaux, E., and Imbert, P., *La Convention Européenne des Droits de l'Homme: Commentaire article par article* (Paris: Economica, 1995).

Rzepka, D., *Zur Fairness im deutschen Strafverfahren* (Frankfurt am Main: Vittorio Klostermann, 2000).

Sace, J., 'L'audition contradictoire des témoins', *Rev. trim. dr. h.* 9 (1992) 51.

Sanders, A., and Young, R., *Criminal Justice* (London: Butterworths, 1994).

Schäfer, K., *Strafprozessrecht: Eine Einführung* (Berlin: Walter de Gruyter, 1976).

Schefer, M., *Die Kerngehalte von Grundrechten* (Bern: Stämpfli & Cie AG, 2001).

Schlauri, R., *Das Verbot des Selbstbelastungszwangs im Strafverfahren: Konkretisierung eines Grundrechts durch Rechtsvergleichung* (Zurich: Schulthess, 2003).

Schleiminger, D., *Konfrontation im Strafprozess—Art. 6 Ziff. 3 lit. d EMRK mit besonderer Berücksichtigung des Verhältnisses zum Opferschutz im Bereich von Sexualdelikten gegen Minderjährige* (Basel: Helbing & Lichtenhahn 2001).

Schlothauer, R., and Wieder, H., *Untersuchungshaft*, 3rd edn. (Heidelberg: Müller, 2001).

Schmid, N., *Strafprozessrecht: Eine Einführung auf der Grundlage des Strafprozessrechtes des Kantons Zürich und des Bundes*, 4th edn. (Zurich: Schulthess, 2004).

Schmid, N., 'Anwalt der ersten Stunde', in Donatsch, A., Forster, M., and Schwarzenegger, C. (eds.), *Strafrecht, Strafprozessrecht und Menschenrechte, Festschrift für Stefan Trechsel* (Zurich: Schulthess, 2002).

Schmid, N., *Das amerikanische Strafverfahren, Eine Einführung* (Heidelberg: C.F. Müller, 1986).

Schmidt, E., *Deutsches Strafprozessrecht: Ein Kolleg* (Göttingen: Vandenhoeck und Ruprecht, 1967).

Schokkenbroek, J.G.C., *Toetsing aan de Vrijheitsrechten van het europees verdrag tot bescherming van de rechten van de mens* (Leiden: s.n., 1996).

Schomburg, W., 'Die Europäisierung des Verbots doppelter Strafverfolgung—ein Zwischenbericht', *NJW* (2000) 1833.

Schomburg, W., *Internationale Rechtshilfe in Strafsachen* (Munich: Beck, 1998).

Schroeder, F.-C., 'Die Gesamtprüfung der Verfahrensfairness durch den EGMR', *GA* 150 (2003) 293.

Schroth, U., 'Strafrechtliche und strafprozessuale Konsequenzen aus der Überlänge von Strafverfahren', *NJW* (1990) 29.

Schubarth, M., *Kommentar zum schweizerischen Strafrecht*, vol. 3 (Bern: Stämpfli & Cie AG, 1984).

Schubarth, M., 'Die Artikel 5 und 6 der Konvention, insbesondere im Hinblick auf das Schweizerische Strafprozessrecht', 94 *ZSR* (1975) 465.

Schubarth, M., *Die Rechte des Beschuldigten im Untersuchungsverfahren, besonders bei Untersuchungshaft: eine Analyse der schweizerischen Strafprozessgesetze unter rechtsstaatlichen Gesichtspunkten* (Berne: Stämpfli, 1973).

Schünemann, B., 'Placing the Enterprise Under Supervision ("Guardianship") as a Model Sanction Against Legal and Collective Entities', paper presented at the International Colloquium on Criminal Responsibility of Legal and Collective Entities, 4–6 May 1998, Berlin, Germany.

Schürmann, F., 'Prinzipien und Prinzipienlosigkeit in der Strassburger Rechsprechung zum Strafverfahren', *ZStrR* 119 (2001) 352.

Schürmann, F., 'Der Anspruch auf amtliche Verteidigung', *AJP* (1992) 661.

Schutter, O., de, 'Vie privée et protection de l'individu vis-à-vis des traitements de données à caractère personnel', *Rev. trim. dr. h.* 45 (2001) 148.

Schwarzenegger, C., 'Art. 117' in Niggli, M.A., and Wiprächtiger, H. (eds.), *Basler Kommentar, Strafgesetzbuch* (Basel: Helbing und Lichtenhahn, 2003).

Scouflaire, I., 'Le délai raisonnable de la détention provisoire', *Rev. trim. dr. h.* 12 (1992) 517.

Seiler, S., *Strafprozessrecht* (Vienna: WUV Universitätsverlag, 2003).

Sendler, H., 'Politikermeinung und richterliche Unabhängigkeit' *NJW* (2001) 1909.

Senese, S., 'L'autogoverno delle magistrature italiane', *CIMA/CIJL Yearbook 1992 Garanties constitutionnelles pour l'indépendance du pouvoir judiciaire*, 1 (1992) 57.

Sermet, L., 'L'incidence de la Convention européenne des droits de l'homme sur le contentieux administratif français' (Marseille, 1994).

Sermet, L., 'L'arrêt *Kress c. la France*: avancée, statu quo ou régression des droits fondamentaux du justiciable?', *Rev. trim. dr. h.* 49 (2002) 237.

Sloss, D. L., 'International Decisions—*United States* v. *Duarte'*, *AJIL* 97 (2003) 410.

Soyer, J. -C., 'L'avenir de la vie privée face aux effets pervers du progrès et de la vertu', in Tabatoni, P. (ed.), *La protection de la vie privée dans la société d'information* (PUF: Cahiers des sciences sociales et politiques, vol. I, 2000, 9).

Soyer, J., and de Salvia, M., 'Article 6', in Pettiti, L., Decaux, E., and Imbert, P.-H. (eds.), *La Convention européenne des droits de l'homme: commentaire article par article* (Paris: Economica, 1995).

Spagniol, M., *Das Recht auf Verteidigerbeistand im Grundgesetz und in der Europäischen Menschenrechtskonvention* (Berlin: Dunker and Humblot, 1990).

Spangher, G., '(Protocol No 7) Art. 4', in Bartole, S., Conforti, B., and Raimondi, G., *Commentario alla Convenzione Europea per la tutela dei diritti dell'uomo e delle libertà fondamentali* (Milan: Cedam, 2001).

Spencer, J., 'La décision Système anglo-saxon', in Cour de Cassation (ed.), *Les principes communs d'une justice des Etats de l'Union Européenne, Actes du Colloque des 4 et 5 décembre 2000* (Paris: La documentation Française 2001).

Spielmann, D., 'La notion de l'impartialité: une application de la théorie de l'apparence', *Feuille de liaison de la Conférence Saint-Yves, Luxembourg*, 88 (1996) 21.

Spielmann, D., 'Procès équitable et présomption d'innocence', *Rev. trim. dr. h.* 24 (1995) 661.

Spronken, T.N.B.M., *Verdediging: Een onderzoek naar de normering van het optreden van advocaten in strafzaken* (Deventer: Gouda, 2001).

Spühler, K., 'Die Europäische Menschenrechtskonvention in der bundesgerichtlichen Rechtsprechung zum Straf- und Strafprozessrecht', *ZStrR* 107 (1990) 313.

Stanfield, P., 'Right to Free Assistance of an Interpreter in Judicial Proceedings, Concerning a "Regulatory Offence", *Öztürk* case', *HRLJ* 5 (1984) 293.

Starmer, K., *European Human Rights Law* (London: Legal Action Group, 1999).

Starmer, K. with Byre, I., *Blackstone's Human Rights Digest* (London: Blackstone Press, 2000).

Starmer, K., Strange, M., and Whitaker, Q. (eds.), *Criminal Justice, Police Powers and Human Rights* (London: Blackstone, 2001).

Stavros, S., *The Guarantees for Accused Persons under Article 6 of the European Convention on Human Rights* (Dordrecht: Martinus Nijhoff, 1993).

Stavros, S., 'The Right to a Fair Trial in Emergency Situations', *ICLQ* 41 (1992) 343.

Steinmann, G., 'Sanktionen im Fall übermässiger Dauer von Strafverfahren', *EuGRZ* 18/20 (1991) 427.

Stessens, G., 'The Obligation to Produce Documents Versus the Privilege against Self-incrimination: Human Rights Protection Extended Too Far?', *EL Rev* 22 (1997) 50.

Strange, M., 'Evidence', in Starmer, K., Strange, M., and Whitaker, Q. (eds.), *Criminal Justice, Police Powers and Human Rights* (London: Blackstone, 2001).

Stratenwerth, G., *Schweizerisches Strafgesetzbuch, Allgemeiner Teil I: Die Straftat*, 2nd edn. (Bern: Stämpfli & Cie AG, 1996).

Sudre, F., *Droit européen et international des droits de l'homme*, 6th edn. (Paris: PUF, 2003).

Sudre, F., 'Chronique de la jurisprudence de la Cour européenne des droits de l'homme', *RUDH* 6 (1994) 254.

Swart, A.H.J., *De toelating en uitzetting van vreemdelingen* (Deventer: Kluwer, 1978).

Tanca, A., 'Human Rights, Terrorism and Police Custody: The *Brogan* Case', *EJIL* 1 (1990) 269.

Tavernier, P., 'Le droit à un procès équitable dans la jurisprudence du Comité des droits de l'homme des Nations Unies', *Rev. trim. dr. h.* 7 (1996) 3.

Thibaut, J.W., and Walker, L., 'A Theory of Procedure', *Cal. L.R.* 66 (1978) 541.

Thibaut, J.W., and Walker, L., *Procedural Justice: A Psychological Analysis* (New York: Hillsdale, N.J., 1975).

Tierney, S., 'Human Rights and Temporary Sheriffs', *ELRev* (2000) 223.

Tophinke, E., *Das Grundrecht der Unschuldsvermutung* (Bern: Stämpfli & Cie AG, 2000).

Trechsel, S., 'Akteneinsicht', in Schweizer, R., Burkert, H., and Gasser, U. (eds.), *Festschrift für Jean Nicolas Druey zum 65. Geburtstag* (Zurich: Schulthess, 2002).

Trechsel, S., 'La décision—système continental', in Cour de Cassation (ed.), *Les principes communs d'une justice des Etats de l'Union Européenne, Actes du Colloque des 4 et 5 décembre 2000* (Paris: La documentation Française, 2001).

Trechsel, S., 'Unmittelbarkeit und Konfrontation als Ausfluss von Art. 6 EMRK', *AJP* 9 (2000) 1366.

Trechsel, S., *Inflation in the Field of Human Rights?* (Nijmegen: Nijmegen University Press, 2000).

Trechsel, S., 'Why Must Trials be Fair?' *IsLR*, 31(1–3) (1997) 94.

Trechsel, S., 'Liberty and Security of Person', in Macdonald, R. St. J., Matscher, F., and Petzold, H. (eds.), *The European System for the Protection of Human Rights* (Dordrecht: Martinus Nijhoff, 1993).

Trechsel, S., 'The Role of International Organs Controlling Human Rights in the Field of International Cooperation', in Eser, A., and Lagodny, O. (eds), *Principles and Procedures for a New Transnational Criminal Law* (Freiburg i. Br.: MPI-Eigenverlag, 1992).

Trechsel, S., 'Das verflixte Siebente? Bemerkungen zum 7. Zusatzprotokoll zur EMRK', in Nowak, M., Steure, D., and Tretter, H. (eds.), *Progress in the Spirit of Human Rights, Festschrift für Felix Ermacora* (Kehl am Rhein: N.P. Engel Verlag, 1988).

Trechsel, S., 'Grundrechtsschutz bei der internationalen Zusammenarbeit in Strafsachen', *EuGRZ* 14 (1987) 69.

Trechsel, S., 'Gericht und Richter nach der EMRK', in Hauser, R., Rehberg, J., and Stratenwerth, G. (eds.), *Gedächtnisschrift für Peter Noll* (Zurich: Schulthess, 1984).

Trechsel, S., 'Strassburger Rechtsprechung zum Strafverfahren: Die Urteile Schiesser, Deweer, Artico und Luedicke, Belkacem und Koc', *JR* 10(4) (1981) 133.

Trechsel, S., 'Quelques observations au sujet de la "mise au secret" ', *ZStrR* 98 (1981) 235.

Trechsel, S., 'Struktur und Funktion der Vermutung der Schuldlosigkeit, Ein Beitrag zur Auslegung von Art. 6 Ziff. 2 EMRK', *SJZ* 77 (1981) 317.

Trechsel, S., 'The Right to Liberty and Security of the Person: Article 5 of the European Convention on Human Rights in the Strasbourg Case-law', *HRLJ* 1 (1980) 88.

Trechsel, S., 'Die Verteidigungsrechte in der Praxis zur Europäischen Menschenrechtskonvention', *ZStrR* 96 (1979) 337.

Trechsel, S., 'The Protection of Human Rights in Criminal Proceedings', *RIDP* 49(3) (1978) 541.

Trechsel, S., *Die Europäische Menschenrechtskonvention, ihr Schutz der persönlichen Freiheit und die schweizerischen Strafprozessrechte* (Bern: Stämpfli & Cie AG, 1974).

Trechsel, S., 'La durée raisonnable de la détention préventive (Art. 5 par. 3 de la Convention européenne des Droits de l'Homme)', *RDH* 4(1) (1971) 119.

Trechsel, S., and Noll, P., *Schweizerisches Strafrecht Allgemeiner Teil I :Voraussetzungen der Strafbarkeit*, 6th edn. (Zurich: Schulthess, 2004).

Triffterer, O., and Binner, H., 'Zur Einschränkbarkeit der Menschenrechte und zur Anwendbarkeit strafprozessualer Verfahrensgarantien, Anmerkungen zum *Engel*-Urteil', *EuGRZ* 4 (1977) 136.

Trüg, G., *Lösungskonvergenzen trotz Systemdivergenzen im deutschen und US-amerikanischen Strafverfahren: ein strukturanalytischer Vergleich am Beispiel der Wahrheitserforschung* (Tübingen: Mohr Siebeck, 2003).

Tulkens, F., 'Les droits de l'homme en détention', *Rev. Sc. Crim.* (2001) 881.

Tulkens, F., 'La procédure pénale: grandes lignes de comparaison entre systèmes nationaux', in Delmas-Marty, M. (ed.), *Procès pénal et droits de l'homme* (Paris: Presses universitaires de France, 1992).

Tyler, T.R., *Why People Obey the Law* (New Haven, CT: Yale University Press, 1990).

Utz, H., *Die Kommunikation zwischen inhaftiertem Beschuldigten und Verteidiger* (Basel: Helbing and Lichtenhahn, 1984).

Valkeneer, C., de, 'L'infiltration et la Convention européenne des droits de l'homme', *Rev. trim. dr. h.* 14 (1993) 313.

Vallens, J.-L., 'Faillite personnelle et impartialite du juge', (CA Metz, 9 septembre 1997), *Petites Affiches: La loi.* 386 (150) (1997) 21.

Van Bemmelen, L.J.M., 'De methode koppejan en de Lawless-case', *NJB* (1966) 701.

Van Compernolle, J., 'Impartialité du juge et cumul de fonctions au fond et au provisoire: réflexions sur des arrêts récents', in de Fontbressin, P. et al. (eds.), *Les droits de l'homme au seuil du troisième millénaire, Mélanges en hommage à Pierre Lambert* (Brussels: Bruylant, 2000).

Van Compernolle, J., 'Le droit à un tribunal impartial en droit belge au regard de la jurisprudence de la Cour européenne des droits de l'homme' in Mahoney, P., Matscher, F., Petzold, H., and Wildhaber, L. (eds.), *Protection des droits de l'homme: la perspective européenne, Mélanges à la mémoire de Rolv Ryssdal/Protecting Human Rights: The European Perspective, Studies in Memory of Rolv Ryssdal* (Cologne: Carl Heymanns Verlag, 2000).

Van Compernolle, J., 'Evolution et assouplissement de la notion d'impartialité objective', *Rev. trim. dr. h.* 19 (1994) 437.

Van de Kerchove, M., 'La preuve en matière pénale dans la jurisprudence de la Cour et de la Commission européennes des droits de l'homme', *Rev. Sc. Crim.* (1992) 1.

Van den Wyngaert, C., *Strafrecht en het strafprocesrecht in hoofdlijnen* (Antwerpen: Maklu, 1991).

Van Dijk, P., 'Article 6'1 of the Convention and the concept of "objective impartiality" ', in Mahoney, P., Matscher, F., Petzold, H., and Wildhaber, L. (eds.), *Protection des droits de l'homme: la perspective européenne. Mélanges à la mémoire de Rolv Ryssdal/ Protecting Human Rights: The European Perspective, Studies in Memory of Rolv Ryssdal* (Cologne: Carl Heymanns Verlag, 2000).

Van Dijk, P., *The Right of the Accused to a Fair Trial under International Law* (Utrecht: SIM Special, 1983).

Van Dijk, P., and van Hoof, G.J.H., *Theory and Practice of the European Convention on Human Rights*, 3rd edn. (The Hague: Kluwer Law International, 1998).

Van Drooghenbroeck, S., 'Interprétation jurisprudentielle et non-rétroactivité de la loi pénale', *Rev. trim. dr. h.* 27 (1996) 463.

Veldt, M., *Het EVRM en de onpartijdige strafrechter* (Deventer: Kluwer, 1997).

Velu, J., and Ergec, R., *La Convention européenne des droits de l'homme* (Brussels: Bruylant, 1990).

Verniory, J.-M., *Les droits de la défense dans les phases préliminaires du procès pénal* (2005, forthcoming).

Villiger, M.E., *Handbuch der Europäischen Menschenrechtskonvention (EMRK): unter besonderer Berücksichtigung der schweizerischen Rechtslage*, 2nd edn. (Zurich: Schulthess, 1999).

Villiger, M.E., 'Geltungsbereich der Garantien der Emrk', *ZBI* 18 (1991) 81.

Vogler, T., 'Artikel 6', in Golsong, H., Karl, W., Miehsler, H., Petzold, H., Rogge, K., Vogler, T., and Wildhaber, L. (eds.), *Internationaler Kommentar zur Europäischen Menschenrechtskonvention* (Cologne: Carl Heymann, 1986).

Vogler, T., 'Das Recht auf unentgeltliche Beziehung eines Dolmetschers (Art. 6 Abs. 3 Buchst.e EMRK) Anmerkung zum Dolmetscherkosten-Urteil des EGMR', *EuGRZ* 6 (1979) 640.

Vogler, T., 'Straf- und Strafverfahrensrechtliche Fragen in der Spruchenpraxis der Europäischen Kommission und des Europäischen Gerichtshofs für Menschenrechte', *ZstW* 89 (1977) 761.

Wagner, B., and Wildhaber, L., 'Der Fall Temeltasch und die auslegenden Erklärungen der Schweiz', *EuGRZ* (1983) 145.

Wagner, C., 'L'indemnisation d'une détention provisoire suivie d'un acquittement', *Rev. trim. dr. h.* 20 (1994) 563.

Walischewski, L., *Probleme des Akteneinsichtsrechts der Verteidigung im Ermitt-lungsverfahren im Lichte der Rechtsprechung des Bundesverfassungsgerichts und des Europäischen Gerichtshofes für Menschenrechte* (Frankfurt: Peter Lang, 1999).

Walker and Walker, *Law of Evidence in Scotland* (Edinburgh: Hodge, 1964).

Walsh, B., 'Article 6 of the European Convention on Human Rights: The Right to Fair Trial Within a Reasonable Time of any Criminal Charge', in *The Domestic Application of International Human Rights Norms*, Interights, Judicial Colloquy, Ankara, 3–14 Sept. 1990 (Ankara: Ankara University Press, 1990).

Wąsek-Wiaderek, M., *The Principle of 'Equality of Arms' in Criminal procedure under Article 6 of the European Convention on Human Rights and its Function in Criminal Justice of Selected European Countries: A Comparative View* (Leuven: Leuven University Press, 2000).

Weissbrodt, D., *The Right to a Fair Trial: Articles 8, 10 and 11 of the Universal Declaration of Human Rights* (The Hague: Kluwer Law, 2001).

Whitaker, Q., 'Stop and Search, Arrest and Detention', in Starmer, K., Strange, M., and Whitaker, Q. (eds.), *Criminal Justice, Police Powers and Human Rights* (London: Blackstone, 2001).

Wildhaber, L., 'Erfahrungen mit der EMRK', *ZSR* 98 II (1979) 365.

Wildhaber, L., and Breitenmoser, S., *Internationaler Kommentar zur Europäischen Menschenrechtskonvention, Kommentierung des Artikels 8* (Cologne: Heymann, 1992).

Wils, W.P.J., 'The Principle of Ne Bis in Idem in EC Antitrust Enforcement: A Legal and Economic Analysis', *World Competition* 26(2) (2003) 131.

Wimmer, A., 'Unschuldsvermutung—Verdacht—Freispruch', *ZStW* 80 (1968) 369.

Wohlers, W., 'Geldwäscherei durch die Annahme von Verteidigerhonoraren—Art. 305bis StGB als Gefahr für das Institut der Wahlverteidigung', *ZStrR* 120 (2002) 197.

Wohlers, W., 'Art. 6 Abs. 3 lit.d) EMRK als Grenze der Einführung des Wissens anonym bleibender Zeugen', in Donatsch, A., Forster, M., and Schwarzenegger, C. (eds.), *Strafrecht, Strafprozessrecht und Menschenrechte, Festschrift für Stefan Trechsel* (Zurich: Schulthess, 2002).

Wolffers, B., 'Der Schuldinterlokut in der Schweiz, insbesondere im Kanton Bern', *ZStrR* 117 (1999) 215.

Wyss, P.M., ' "Miranda warning" im schweizerischen Verfassungsrecht?', *recht* 2001 132.

Yernault, D., 'Le fisc, ses amendes et la matière pénale', *Rev. trim. dr. h.* 23 (1995) 427.

Yernault, D., 'Les pouvoirs d'investigation de l'administration face à la délinquance économique: les locaux professionnels et l'article 8 de la Convention européenne', *Rev. trim. dr. h.* 17 (1994) 121.

Yourow, H. C., *The Margin of Appreciation Doctrine in the Dynamics of European Human Rights Jurisprudence* (The Hague: Kluwer Law International, 1996).

Zanghí, C., 'La nouvelle Cour unique prévue dans le Protocole n. 11 à la Convention Européenne des Droits de l'Homme: réexamen des arrêts et impartialité des Juges', in Busuttil, S. (ed.), *Mainly Human Rights, Studies in Honour of J. J. Cremona* (Valletta: Fondation Internationale Malte 2000).

Zweifel, M., 'Das rechtliche Gehör im Steuerhinterziehungsverfahren', *ASA* 60 (1992/93) 453.

Index*

* This Index is the work of Kim Harris, on behalf of Oxford University Press.